INTRODUCTION TO TRANSACTIONAL LAWYERING PRACTICE

■ ■ ■

By

Alicia Alvarez
Clinical Professor of Law
University of Michigan Law School

Paul R. Tremblay
Clinical Professor and Faculty Director of Experiential Learning
Boston College Law School

AMERICAN CASEBOOK SERIES®

WEST®

Mat #40919678

American Casebook Series is a trademark registered in the U.S. Patent and Trademark Office.

© 2013 LEG, Inc. d/b/a West Academic Publishing
    610 Opperman Drive
    St. Paul, MN 55123
    1-800-313-9378

West, West Academic Publishing, and West Academic are trademarks of West Publishing Corporation, used under license.

Printed in the United States of America

ISBN: 978–0–314–25450–4

DEDICATION

This book is dedicated to:

Josefina Meiriño and the memory of Alfredo Álvarez, Hilda M. Meiriño and Donina Pérez. With much love and appreciation.

A.A.

Barbara J. Tremblay and the memory of Raymond J. Tremblay. With much love and gratitude.

P.R.T.

PREFACE

For the past ten or fifteen years, law schools have experimented with a new form of clinical offering for law students—clinics engaged in transactional work. A few law schools had offered transactional clinical opportunities to students in the past, but these opportunities have grown dramatically recently. The typical or traditional law school clinic offers students rich experiences and training in the context of litigation and dispute resolution—in civil legal services practice or criminal defense or prosecution, as well as in specialty clinics such as those focusing on domestic violence, employment, housing, immigration or juvenile justice. Those courses offer excellent education and a meaningful introduction to the lawyer's role, and the education students receive and the insights and identities they develop in those programs are quite transferable to just about any other form of law practice. But still, none of those traditional clinics invites students to work directly on corporate matters, deals, compliance counseling, real estate closings, or other forms of transactional practice—what many consider to be the "happier" side of the law industry.

The law school world has now changed for the better. Now, in 2013, just about every law school in the nation offers some form of transactional clinic, and any school that does not offer such a program is actively exploring adding such a course to its experiential learning agenda. Known as community economic development, nonprofit, small business, microenterprise, entrepreneurship, or intellectual property clinics, these programs do not engage in litigation, send their students to courts or hearings, or help disputing parties resolve their conflicts by litigation or mediation. Instead, these clinics offer students the opportunity to assist community groups, nonprofit organizations, social enterprises, entrepreneurs, and small businesses in a wide range of corporate, economic development, tax (or tax exemption), community organizing, and regulatory compliance matters. Students who hope to use their legal education to embark on a career as corporate, or economic development, or tax lawyers, or students who don't know what it is like to be that kind of lawyer but want to try it out, now have the opportunity to do so as part of their law school education.

With the emergence of transactional clinics, a critical need arises for teaching materials dedicated to this form of practice. Clinics inevitably teach students about some essential, fundamental lawyering competencies, including interviewing, counseling, negotiation, strategic planning, writing and advocacy. Many helpful textbooks and other teaching materials exist on these topics. But virtually all of those resources emerged from the world of litigation. And, while we noted just above that much work in a litigation clinic is useful in and transferable to non-litigation settings, we have realized that the existing teaching materials are not the most elegant fit for students in a transactional clinic. There is a need for materials that address transactional practice directly. Hence the idea for this book.

Each of us had taught in litigation settings for many years, and each of us then changed our practice and our teaching to the transactional side. We have paid attention to the ways in which the litigator's orientations are different from those of the deals lawyer. Sometimes the differences are subtle; sometimes the differences are quite obvious. But the differences are there.

In this book, we offer instruction in three kinds of contexts. The first part of the book covers the fundamental skills that students and new practitioners need to master in order to serve their clients well. You will find chapters on interviewing, strategic planning, counseling, negotiation, and drafting. The middle part of the book addresses some critical topics emerging from transactional practice which we might call "role" questions, as a complement to the earlier skills topics. We believe that transactional lawyers will grapple with questions of multicultural lawyering, ethics, working with groups, and community economic development, so we address those topics here. And the latter part of the book includes three chapters serving as primers on typical substantive law topics transactional lawyers will likely encounter in their work. You will find a chapter each on for-profit business entities, nonprofit organizations, and intellectual property. As we emphasize in those chapters, these primers can be little more than overviews, given the depth of complexity of each of those areas. But students and new lawyers need orientation, and we hope these chapters assist in that aim.

We have learned from so many dear colleagues in our developing the ideas we include here. While we surely will inadvertently omit some of them, we offer our deep gratitude to our colleagues who have educated, challenged, and inspired us in this work. We thank Susan Bennett, Kendra Chencus, Michael Diamond, Robin Golden, Jim Jacobs, Susan Jones, Praveen Kosuri, Gowri Krishna, Brian Price, Emily Satterthwaite, Sandy Tarrant, Dana Thompson and Paula Williams.

At Boston College, we thank Michael Richman and Deans Vincent Rougeau, George Brown and John Garvey for their ongoing support of this project and of the Community Enterprise Clinic, Alexis Anderson, Lynn Barenberg, Alan Minuskin and Fred Yen for their relentless and unflagging encouragement, David Bartholomew, Christine Coletta, Julie Dahlstrom, Jamie Eldridge and Dara Newman for leading the charge to create the transactional clinic here, and Mo Siedor, Diana Chang, Josh Minty, Laura Mehalko, Brendan Boyle, Allison Diop-Frimpong and Nick Mills for helpful research assistance. And Linda, Chris and Jen, for everlasting patience and support.

At Michigan, we thank Deans Evan Caminker, Bridget McCormack and Paul Reingold and the William J. and Claire W. Bogaard Fund for Clinical Education for their ongoing support of this project and the Community and Economic Development Clinic, Nicole Appleberry, Priya Baskaran, Gowri Krishna and Dana Thompson for their support and encouragement, and Elizabeth Lamoste, David Fautsch, Haley Waller and Christina Lee for helpful research assistance. And family and friends for all their support, students and colleagues who have taught us so much, especially Helen Cropper, Julie A. Nice, Paul R. Tremblay and Mark Spiegel, and colleagues at the University of Valencia for support and hospitality.

And, finally, we are forever in the debt of Gary Bellow, Bea Moulton, David Binder, Susan Price and Paul Bergman, whose pioneering ideas fill this book.

A.A.
P.R.T.

March, 2013

SUMMARY OF CONTENTS

TABLE OF CONTENTS

TABLE OF CASES

Introduction to Transactional Lawyering Skills

CHAPTER 1

AN INTRODUCTION TO TRANSACTIONAL PRACTICE

■ ■ ■

Welcome to the world of transactional practice. If you are reading this text, the odds are good that you are involved in some form of transactional clinic in your law school. We are confident that you will find the work you encounter in this clinic to be engaging, educational, challenging and, perhaps most importantly, a lot of fun.

In this introductory chapter we aspire to capture for you what we mean by *transactional* practice, and to offer you some orienting ideas about what you might expect in this kind of work. This chapter will first describe the idea of transactional practice, and will then catalogue the kinds of lawyering projects that transactional lawyers tend to do, including the types of activities that you should expect to engage in. Some of those activities, as you will see, are not necessarily limited to what lawyers are uniquely trained to perform, so we explore why clients in these settings should (and do) rely on lawyers for help. We then ask some central questions about whether a law school clinic, or a law school simulation course, can offer to students who will later engage in transactional lawyering any real benefit given the demands and the work experiences of firm practice. (Want to guess what our answer to those questions will be?)

I. WHAT DO WE MEAN BY *TRANSACTIONAL* PRACTICE?

The concept of transactional practice is a bit more elusive than you might initially think, but it has a relatively identifiable core which has some meaning for your ongoing work. That core involves value creation. To us, transactional work represents lawyering activity in which parties come together voluntarily to create something that will generate value—usually economic, but also social or relational.

To appreciate more clearly what this means, we might first compare transactional practice to what it is not. (This may feel a little bit like cheating, but it seems like it might be useful to approach the topic in this way.) Transactional legal practice is *not litigation*. Everyone understands lawyers as litigators—the defenders of those who have been wrongly accused, the advocates for those who have suffered injustices, or perhaps the greedy lawyers who exploit juries to gain unfair windfalls. All of the iconic lawyers in popular culture and history—think Perry Mason, Atticus Finch, John Adams, Thurgood Marshall, David Boies, Johnnie Cochran, Jan Schlichtmann, Ally McBeal, Victor Sifuentes, Abbie Carmichael, Jack McCoy, Michael Clayton, the list goes on and on—were courtroom lawyers, that is to say, litigators. Can you think of *any* iconic lawyers in American history or culture who were transactional lawyers? We didn't think so.[1]

Legal education tends to follow that penchant to privilege litigation. Most of your law school experience is imbued with litigation stories.[2] In your first year courses, as well as in most upper-level doctrinal courses (including, interestingly, courses about business law, like Corporations or Business Organizations), you read appellate cases in order to understand the substantive law and policies governing that area. Appellate cases, of course, emerge from lawsuits, from disputes between or among parties after something bad had happened.[3] The litigators created the world about which you read so carefully. Most likely, your research and writing courses focus on litigation as well, with exercises involving pre-lawsuit "objective" memos followed by complaints, motions, and briefs, applying the "advocacy" concepts.

Even state bars fall into this litigation-privileged trap. Most state bars provide law students with the right to represent low-income clients in clinical courses or in public interest settings through student practice rules.[4] Those rules almost without exception refer to students' practice in courts, and tend to be silent about students' practice in non-litigation settings.[5]

---

[1] OK, here's one possibility: In the 2010 film *The Social Network*, the story about the founding of Facebook, a business lawyer dominates a famous scene when the lawyer, played by Darin Cooper and called in the credits only "Facebook Lawyer 2," explains to Eduardo Saverin that the lawyer was not Saverin's lawyer, but the company's lawyer, when Saverin signed documents which permitted Mark Zuckerburg to dilute Saverin's shares in the Facebook corporation. *See* THE SOCIAL NETWORK (Paramount 2010). Hardly iconic, though.

[2] For a commentary on the marginalization of transactional topics in the law school curriculum, see Rachel Arnow–Richman, *Employment as Transaction*, 39 SETON HALL L. REV. 447, 449–50 (2009).

[3] Few law school classes consider the inevitable stories of pain and distress that preceded the original filing of the lawsuits which eventually became the leading cases in a classroom textbook. Lawsuits almost never arise without some considerable wrangling among the litigants before a plaintiff takes the dramatic step of filing suit. Even in those few instances where the parties file suit collaboratively, such as in a class action where the plaintiffs and the defendant have agreed to terms before the plaintiff formally files the action, the dispute negotiations preceding the collaborative filing are always very contentious. For a discussion of the collaboratively-filed class action model, see, e.g., Susan P. Koniak, *How Like A Winter? The Plight of Absent Class Members Denied Adequate Representation,* 79 NOTRE DAME L. REV. 1787, 1797 (2004); William B. Rubenstein, *A Transactional Model of Adjudication*, 89 GEO. L.J. 371 (2001).

[4] *See, e.g.*, MASS. R. SUP. JUD. CT. 3:03.

[5] *See* Sara B. Lewis, Comment, *Rite of Professional Passage: A Case for the Liberalization of Student Practice Rules*, 82 MARQ. L. REV. 205, 207–09 (1998) (addressing inadequacies in cur-

We can describe pretty easily what litigators do, and we can use that description as a baseline for a comparison to what transactional lawyers do. Litigation, of course, arises as a result of a dispute, something that has occurred or arisen in which the parties disagree about how to allocate certain goods, usually money, but also property or relationships (as in child custody and visitation matters). Good lawyers will assist clients to resolve those disputes in ways that are meaningful, effective, efficient, and least costly. And, while many thoughtful observers have criticized this quality of litigation, the process tends to seek the maximum return for the lawyer's client at the expense of the "adversary," the person or entity with whom the lawyer's client has the dispute.[6] Litigation practice can be aggressive and committed to short-term gain at the expense of long-term benefit.[7] But it can also, at times, be a very efficient avenue for justice.[8]

That ubiquitous litigation world, however, is not the world of the transactional lawyer. Litigators resolve disputes; transactional lawyers, by contrast, make deals, or create arrangements for the participants' future use. Your orientation in transactional practice is different from that of a litigator. Litigators are trained to view the world retrospectively, looking backward to understand the nature of the dispute, and to resolve factual uncertainties in favor of the lawyer's client. It is usually very important to know what happened back then in order to develop an effective "theory of the case" in dispute resolution, and equally important to marshal evidence to prove the factual assertions that help the lawyer's client. The lawyers and clients who present the most coherent and most believable factual stories have the better chance of "winning" the dispute, and obtaining a favorable judgment, verdict, or settlement.

That backwards-looking perspective is not usually the stance of a transactional lawyer. In transactional practice, the clients and the lawyers look to the future, to arrange affairs in order to accomplish desired objectives later on. The previous facts and histories matter, of course, but in different, and often less critical, ways than they do in litigation.

---

rent student practice rules and proposing a better mode of regulation for students in clinical settings).

   [6]   In recent years especially, litigation has developed a more collaborative quality, as participants understand the benefits of identifying shared goals and of "expanding the pie," especially in dispute negotiation. *See, e.g.,* Alex J. Hurder, *The Lawyer's Dilemma: To Be or Not to Be a Problem–Solving Negotiator,* 14 CLINICAL L. REV. 253, 266 (2007); Carrie Menkel–Meadow, *Whose Dispute Is It Anyway?: A Philosophical and Democratic Defense of Settlement (in Some Cases),* 83 GEO. L.J. 2663, 2691 (1995). But that softer approach still remains the less prominent character of litigation. *See* John Lande, *Failing Faith in Litigation? A Survey of Business Lawyers' and Executives' Opinions,* 3 HARV. NEGOT. L. REV. 1, 18–22 (1998) (describing business executives' opinions that litigators' aggressive nature and zero-sum orientation inhibit future relationships).

   [7]   *See, e.g.,* Hurder, *supra* note 6.

   [8]   *See, e.g.,* Goodridge v. Dept. of Pub. Health, 798 N.E.2d 941 (Mass. 2003) (overturning a ban on same-sex couples marrying in Massachusetts).

Having explored what transactional lawyering is not, it is now time to describe affirmatively what transactional lawyering is. Transactional lawyers assist clients to produce effective and workable plans for the future. Your work in this realm will guide clients who have ideas about creating something that does not yet exist, or making something that does exist function better. Your legal skills will both assist with the creation of the new or revised idea or product, and ensure that the end product will work as hoped, and have the best chances to withstand any future challenges. In this way your work is collaborative, forward-looking, and imaginative.

Many observers point out that transactional lawyering is at its essence *value creation*. In a classic early article describing the role of the business lawyer (that is to say, the transactional lawyer), Professor Ronald Gilson articulated the importance of creating value through the lawyer's work.[9] Gilson, writing about *deals* (that is, contracts for the sale of some product, like a business), noted the obvious reality that parties engage in a deals transaction when the value of doing the deal exceeds the benefit of not doing the deal, for both parties. He then observed, "If what a business lawyer does has value, a transaction must be worth more, net of legal fees, as a result of the lawyer's participation."[10] The participants do not just create value, but the lawyer's services add value to the transaction. We return to Gilson's thesis below, but we see here how his insight applies to all of the work you will be doing. Not everything that a transactional lawyer does qualifies as a deal as just described, but everything that lawyer contributes must offer some value to the client. Business owners are known to complain about the complicating role that their lawyers play in their business developments,[11] but yet they pay (and sometimes pay a lot) for the lawyers' work just the same. Keep that apparent puzzle in mind as you read the rest of this chapter, and as you perform your work for your clients (who, we note, may *not* be paying for your services[12]).

---

[9]   *See* Ronald Gilson, *Value Creation by Business Lawyers: Legal Skills and Pricing*, 94 YALE L. J. 239 (1984).

[10]   *Id.* at 243.

[11]   *See, e.g.,* Tina L. Stark, *Thinking Like a Deal Lawyer*, 54 J. LEGAL EDUC. 223, 229 (2004) (noting that young lawyers fail to exercise judgment and perceive complications unnecessarily).

[12]   If you are reading this as a student in a clinical course, chances are that you are offering your services for free. Most, but not all, transactional clinics do not charge their clients for the services the students provide. *See* Client Information, Northwestern Law Bluhm Legal Clinic, http://www.law.northwestern.edu/legalclinic/elc/clientinfo/; Entrepreneurial Law Clinic Fact Sheet, University of Washington School of Law, http://www.law.washington.edu/clinics/entrepreneurial/ELCfactsheet.pdf; Transactional Law Clinics, Harvard Law School, http://www.law.harvard.edu/academics/clinical/tlc/other/documents/tlc_brochure.pdf.

II. THE KINDS OF PROJECTS TRANSACTIONAL LAWYERS OVERSEE

Another way to understand transactional practice is to list the typical kinds of work these lawyers tend to do. Imagine a larger law firm with several practice areas. The firm likely will have a litigation department, of course. But the firm will also have corporate or business, tax, real estate, intellectual property, mergers and acquisitions, and other similar practice specialties. Most of the latter work will be considered transactional. The lawyers in those departments will be creating entities, organizing business arrangements, buying and selling property, and planning for the future. When the work in these departments starts to get contentious, or when a deal falls apart and the participants seek some resolution of the dispute, then the lawyers might bring in the members of the litigation team. Otherwise, the litigation department will leave the transactional lawyers alone.[13]

We can describe the projects that are typical of transactional practice in the following way, and connect the list to the work you may experience in a law school clinical program. We start with *deals*. A transaction is essentially a deal, so transactional lawyers do deals.[14] As we saw above, Ronald Gilson used the sale of a business as a paradigmatic project for a business lawyer in his discussion of that kind of lawyer's work.[15] In your clinic experience, you might oversee a deal, say, one small business purchasing another small business, or a nonprofit buying the rights to some intellectual property. Perhaps more commonly, you might serve as the student lawyer on a lease negotiation for an organization or sole proprietor, or a real estate transaction involving a first-time home buyer.[16]

But transactional practice involves a lot more than simply doing deals.[17] Perhaps most of the projects on which you will work will involve creating products or devices to be used by businesses or business people, or guiding those entities and people through regulatory thickets. In this way you will be engaged in *preventative law*. Perhaps because of your training in the court-based doctrine, your work will assist businesses to

---

[13] One of our former students, working as an associate in the litigation department of a national law firm, when hearing about the new clinic his former teacher had instituted at the law school, commented, "In our firm, we describe the corporate department as the place where the clients actually *like* their lawyers."

[14] *See* BLACK'S LAW DICTIONARY 712 (9th ed. 2009) (defining "transaction" as "the act or an instance of conducting business or other dealings; esp., the formation performance, or discharge of a contract").

[15] Gilson, *supra* note 9, *passim.*

[16] *See* Praveen Kosuri, *'Impact' in 3D—Maximizing Impact through Transactional Clinics,* 18 CLINICAL L. REV. 1, 9 (2011); Susan R. Jones, *Small Business and Community Economic Development: Transactional Lawyering for Social Change and Economic Justice,* 4 CLINICAL L. REV. 195, 212–213 (1997). *See also Transactional Law Clinics: What We Do – Real Estate,* HARVARD LAW SCHOOL (Aug. 13, 2010), http://www.law.harvard.edu/academics/clinical/tlc/other/documents/tlc_brochure.pdf (describing Harvard Law School's Real Estate Clinic).

[17] George Dent, *Business Lawyers as Enterprise Architects,* 65 BUS. L. 279, 297 (2009).

understand what might go wrong, and advise them about ways to minimize risks as they conduct their affairs.

The following is a no doubt incomplete list of the types of legal projects that transactional lawyers will do for their clients. Think of how many of these activities you might encounter in your practice setting. Think also, as you review this catalogue, why the participants might benefit from having a lawyer as a participant in the activity. (And here's a quick note about terminology as you read our list: We refer sometimes to the "business" or "enterprise" as your client, and in doing so we intend those terms to include nonprofit organizations, community groups, sole proprietors, and other similar actors whom you will be helping. Much important transactional work involves enterprises which may not be conventional for-profit industries, and your clinical work especially is likely to expose you to those kinds of enterprises.[18])

- *Purchase or sale of a business*: This prototypical "deal" served as the basis for Gilson's analysis of what business lawyers add to the otherwise nonlegal transaction.

- *Purchase or sale of real property*: This item reminds us that transactional lawyering is not just business law. Real estate lawyers are transactional lawyers. You may serve as the lawyer for a first-time home buyer as she purchases her house or condominium.

- *Negotiate a real property or equipment lease for an enterprise*: A lease is a "deal." Lawyers often assist businesses and community organizations to understand the terms of a lease and to negotiate better terms.

- *Advising an enterprise or group about regulatory requirements and compliance*: A significant part of a client's activity will be subject to some federal, state, or local government oversight. A common role for the business lawyer is to ensure that her client understands the regulatory environment and complies with it.

- *Advising a client about tax consequences of certain actions*: This item is a subset, but a discrete and extremely important subset, of the previous item. Business operators will be acutely aware of the need to understand the tax consequences of the actions they take. Lawyers may assist in achieving that goal.

- *Drafting or reviewing contracts*: Most businesses use contracts in their operation. Contracts must work efficiently and effectively.

---

[18] Roger Clay and Susan Jones have captured nicely the nature of the work that many transactional clinics engage in. *See* Roger A. Clay & Susan R. Jones, *What Is Community Economic Development?, in* BUILDING HEALTHY COMMUNITIES: A GUIDE TO COMMUNITY ECONOMIC DEVELOPMENT FOR ADVOCATES, LAWYERS AND POLICYMAKERS 3 (Roger A. Clay & Susan R. Jones eds., 2009); SUSAN R. JONES, LEGAL GUIDE TO MICROENTERPRISE DEVELOPMENT (2004).

Lawyers frequently help clients by reviewing and drafting contracts.

- *Advising about employment law*: Businesses often use other people, aside from the owners or founders, to perform the business's function. The business typically pays those people, but at times would prefer to ask the helpers to volunteer. The laws governing how to treat those who perform services for the business are very complicated and potentially very critical.

- *Creating entities, both for-profit and nonprofit*: Many for-profit businesses operate through an entity rather that as default sole proprietorships. (A partnership may be considered as an entity, even if it can arise just by default through the mere operation of a business.) Most nonprofit ventures choose to operate as some type of formal entity. Lawyers can assist the business owners, founders and group leaders to decide whether to create an entity, to choose which entity if one will be used, and to create that entity.

- *Advising an organization about corporate governance*: Some organizations operate through a set of procedures set down in writing. Often, the organization has more than one individual responsible to manage the operations. Lawyers may assist the manager or managers to understand, and to comply with, the written procedures governing the organization's functioning.

- *Creating documents to transfer or allocate corporate stock*: Many business owners possess the interests in the business through shares of stock or comparable devices. As the business develops the owners at times wish to add new owners, shift some shares, or otherwise change the allocation of interests. Lawyers advise the business about the procedure to accomplish those ends, and review or draft the documents needed to effect any changes.

- *For nonprofit organizations, preparing applications to the Internal Revenue Service for tax-exempt status*: Transactional lawyers often represent nonprofit entities, and very often those nonprofits wish to obtain tax-exempt status from the IRS in order to raise funds for their good work. Lawyers assist nonprofits with the application to the IRS for that status, including advocating before the IRS if some questions arise after the entity files its application.

- *Assisting a group or an entity with obtaining permits or licenses*: Recall the item above regarding the regulatory regimes governing businesses. In this example of a regulatory reality, for-profit businesses, nonprofit organizations, and community groups often need to obtain some permit or license in order to conduct some activity at a certain location. Lawyers may assist with that process, including advocating before the agency or board responsible for issuing the permit or license.

- *Advising an organization about financing opportunities*: Private businesses need money to operate, which they obtain from investors and from customers. Nonprofit organizations similarly need money to operate, which they obtain from donors, foundations, and customers. Businesses also seek financing from lenders, either in a purely private capacity or through some economic-development program, like those overseen by the Small Business Administration, an economic development or tax credit program, or a state's enterprise zone scheme. Lawyers assist clients in their strategic plan, and applications for, these kinds of funding arrangements.

- *Predicting and preventing liability exposure*: A critical aim for any enterprise, whether nonprofit or for-profit, is to minimize, or plan for, the risks it faces in its operations. Things will go wrong, participants will be unhappy, lawsuits may occur. Lawyers will predict the likelihood of those bad occurrences, and develop schemes and advice intended to limit the business's exposure to risk.

- *Protecting a client's intellectual property*: All enterprises produce some intellectual property, and often the enterprise has an interest in securing the best protection of its interests and rights in the IP, or an important need to use others' IP in order to operate effectively. Lawyers may play an important role in achieving the best protection of those rights and interests, and in navigating the use of others' material.

- *Assisting to resolve disagreements among organizational constituents*: When we refer to a transactional lawyer representing an organization business, we understand the *organization* to be the client, not the individual owners or managers.[19] In her role as counsel to the entity, the lawyer sometimes needs to advise management about how best to resolve internal disputes within the management team or among other constituents. While the lawyer may not take sides, she may, and will, offer advice useful to the enterprise about whose rights appear to have priority.

- *Advising unincorporated associations*: Transactional lawyers sometimes represent groups, including neighborhood community

---

[19] We discuss the role tensions involved in this topic later in this book. *See* the chapter on Ethical Issues in Transactional Practice. Of course, it is possible that the lawyer does represent a constituent and not the business, or does represent both the business and a constituent. That arrangement, though, is the exception, and for our purposes we will presume that the transactional lawyer's client is the business.

groups and multiple individuals conducting a grass-roots business together. Most everything we have listed thus far could apply to this kind of client, but community groups present unique challenges as well, such as negotiating community benefits agreements affecting varying constituencies,[20] or organizing nascent grass-roots collectives.[21] Also, with unincorporated associations the lawyer faces some extra challenges, especially in identifying the proper lines of authority.[22]

• *Achieving justice and inculcating fairness in the clients' work*: We end our list with an item which is less discrete and not really a "project" in the way the previous items might be described. But good lawyers will serve their clients more than as merely technicians and experts about complex legal machinations. Good lawyers will influence the transactions they encounter in ways that achieve some measure of justice, and that are fair to all of the participants. We do not pretend that this quality of your transactional work is not controversial, and we concede that not all teachers or writers would agree that lawyers have this responsibility. We do believe it, and we can easily invite you to consider seriously this mission as you represent your clients.

This list, as we noted above, is not at all comprehensive, but it offers you a glimpse of the varied nature of transactional work. For each of the items on the list, ask yourself the following questions:

(1) *What do lawyers add to this activity?* Lawyer time is expensive, and many business advisors offer their services at rates far less than what lawyers tend to charge. Should clients use lawyers for these tasks? *Must* they use lawyers for these tasks? (The unauthorized practice of law rules and doctrines play a role here.[23])

(2) *What can you as a law student or new lawyer offer to this activity?* Even if we end up understanding how lawyers can be either essential or valuable to the business clients, we still face the ever-present question for beginning lawyers and students practicing in a clinical program: Can *you* offer much of value to the processes? As you will learn, much of the assistance business lawyers offer to their clients represents a meld of pure, technical legal analysis and some experience-based practical wisdom

---

[20] For a discussion of community benefits agreements, see Scott Cummings, *The Emergence of Community Benefits Agreements*, 17 J. AFFORDABLE HOUSING & COMMUNITY DEV. L. 5 (2008); Richard C. Schragger, *Mobile Capital, Local Economic Regulation, and the Democratic City*, 123 HARV. L. REV. 482, 508–12 (2009).

[21] *See* Michael Diamond & Aaron O'Toole, *Leaders, Followers, and Free Riders: The Community Lawyer's Dilemma When Representing Non–Democratic Client Organizations*, 31 FORDHAM URB. L.J. 481, 486–87 (2004).

[22] We discuss the question of representing unincorporated associations in the chapter on Working with Groups, at Part IV.C.

[23] We encounter the unauthorized practice of law topic in the chapter on Ethical Issues in Transactional Practice, at Parts IV and V.

about how the world actually operates. As a beginning lawyer or an upper-level law student, you can be terrific at the former but (perhaps) a bit less confident about the latter. Consider this question regularly as you work with your clients, and, as you do so, attend to how your lawyering experience enhances your skill level in both of these arenas.

(3) *Does the transactional/litigation distinction really hold up?* We began this chapter by asserting that transactional lawyers can most easily be identified by what they are not—that is, litigators, who engage in dispute resolution. Note, though, the slipperiness of that temptingly clear dividing line. Transactional lawyers negotiate on behalf of their clients "against" other parties (see the deal categories and the leases, for instance), and they advocate actively on behalf of the clients (see the IRS application and the advocacy for permits, licenses and financing). That's pretty much exactly what the litigators do each day. As you engage in this work, think about whether the differences between the litigator's job and your job are real ones. We believe they are, but we suspect you will discover that the line is more fuzzy than we initially implied.

III. THE NATURE OF YOUR WORK

You now have a reasonably good sense of the kinds of tasks and projects that you might encounter as a transactional lawyer. In this Section we describe the nature of the work you will perform as you participate in those projects. We asked you earlier to consider the "Why lawyers?" question as you conduct your practice. This discussion should help us understand more fully the answer to that question.

So what will you *actually be doing* in your role as a transactional lawyer? You probably already know what is coming, but making the list explicit ought to help you prepare for this work. Here's our best stab at capturing what your life will look like as you practice this kind of law:

a) Legal Research: We start at the beginning, with the most obvious activity law students and lawyers engage in—although it may not be the most *common* activity you perform in this role. In order to assist your clients most productively, you will need to understand what the law says *now*, today, and how the law works in practice. Your training in parsing statutes and regulations, and in understanding common law doctrine and interpretation will permit you to know something that your clients will find useful.

b) Non-legal Research: Knowing the law—and even knowing it extremely well—will not be enough for you to serve as a productive participant in your client's endeavors. Understanding how your state supreme court interprets the scope and enforceability of liability waivers is important as you work with your clients to minimize their exposure to risk, but so is knowing how insurance companies protect businesses and how much they charge for that protection. Your expertise regarding the city's community development ordinances may play a far less important role as far as your client's success is concerned than being familiar with who enforces those ordinances and how they do so. You tended to learn about the legal world in a law library (or wherever students study the law these days), but your client's business exists on the streets and in the marketplace. You will need to know that terrain, and become the same expert there as you are with the books or with Lexis or Westlaw.

c) *Interviewing*: Another way of saying "non-legal research" is to say "fact investigation" or "gathering information." Your aim will be to understand the facts of your client's project, and the way you start is to conduct an initial interview. You then follow up with later interviews, with your client and with other actors who affect your client's business. Interviewing is an art, and may be done well or not so well. Our aim in this book is to help you do it well.

d) *Counseling*: It is not fair to rank order the many activities you engage in, but if you pushed us we would likely rank counseling as one of the most critical activities you will engage in as a transactional lawyer. Clients retain transactional lawyers for guidance and advice. Your primary mission will be to help your clients make choices and achieve goals by educating them about the options available to them, and the consequences of those options. (By contrast, litigators, who also counsel clients a lot, have a separate major aim of getting benefits from courts or from the other side in a dispute.) Effective counseling will require not just your mastery of the law and the facts, but a compassionate method of relating to your clients and understanding their needs in a genuine way.

e) *Writing*: Transactional lawyers write.[24] They write a lot. And the best transactional lawyers write with precision and clarity. So prepare to do a lot of drafting in your practice. You do not conduct jury trials in this line of work; instead, you type. You create important documents. You will find that often the end product of your various work components will be one document that serves to achieve a client goal. The best transactional lawyers are very good writers.

f) *Negotiation*: This skill may be less apparent in your work than in other types of lawyering, but it is still a very central part of the transactional lawyer's toolkit. Especially (but not only) if you are engaged in any form of a deal, you will negotiate with other participants whose interests are not identical to—and may be precisely opposite to—those of your client. It is likely (but not surely the case) that your negotiations will be

---

[24] Some observers distinguish "writing" from "drafting," using the former to refer to the production of persuasive documents such as motions and briefs, and the latter to refer to "the preparation of binding legal texts." *See* WAYNE SCHEISS, PREPARING LEGAL DOCUMENTS NONLAWYERS CAN READ AND UNDERSTAND 25 (2008); Robert Statchen, *Clinicians, Practitioners, and Scribes*, 56 N.Y.L. SCH. L. REV. 233, 235 n.7 (2011/2012).

more collaborative and amicable than those of your litigation department colleagues, but the adjectives "collaborative" and "amicable" do not imply "unimportant" or "less than zealous."

g) Organizing Your Work: This one may surprise you. The work activities listed so far make sense to you, as they capture what you'd expect to be doing when you stroll into the office on any given day. But, as we describe in a later chapter,[25] you cannot accomplish the functional activities you have to get done unless you can make sense of a bigger picture, one that helps you coordinate your work in a coherent, elegant and productive way. Therefore, some discrete, identifiable segment of your work life will involve the "meta" practice of organizing the flow of your work. And, because you will likely have more than one active client project at any given time, your organizational efforts will include developing priorities and tickler systems to permit a fair amount of attention to each ongoing project.

IV. WHAT YOU ADD TO YOUR CLIENTS' ENDEAVORS

The questions raised by Ronald Gilson, noted earlier,[26] are important ones for you to consider as you enter this area of practice. To return once again to our comparison to the litigation world, we can understand pretty easily why an individual who has suffered a legal wrong or a harsh injustice, or who is owed money, will want to hire a lawyer. The most common route for resolving disputes and achieving enforceable remedies is through the court system. That court system is technical, arcane, and possesses its own language and culture. The only agent a person may hire to assist him or her in court is a lawyer, because of the unauthorized practice of law statutes. In the dispute resolution world, then, the market for lawyers is pretty solid.[27] In the transactional world, by contrast, the need for retaining a lawyer is far less imperative. Hence Gilson's im-

---

[25] *See* the chapter on Organizing Your Transactional Work.

[26] *See supra* text accompanying notes 9–10.

[27] We admit that we are simplifying and exaggerating this point here. Many persons do not hire lawyers because of the cost, and attempt to navigate the court system as unrepresented litigants. Indeed, the wave of *pro se* participants in the state court systems, especially in what we might call the "people's" courts such as family, housing, and state community courts, has created what many consider a crisis. *See, e.g.,* JONA GOLDSCHMIDT ET AL., MANAGING THE CHALLENGE OF PRO SE LITIGATION (1998); Russell Engler, *And Justice for All—Including the Unrepresented Poor: Revisiting the Role of Judges, Mediators, and Clerks,* 67 FORDHAM L. REV. 1987 (1999). And creative court systems are exploring relaxing the unauthorized practice bans on lay advocacy to permit some assistance by nonlawyers to litigants in some court settings. *See* Derek A. Denckla, *Nonlawyers and the Unauthorized Practice of Law: An Overview of the Legal and Ethical Parameters,* 67 FORDHAM L. REV. 2581, 2588 (1999); *see also* Quintin Johnstone, *Law and Policy Issues Concerning the Provision of Adequate Legal Services for the Poor,* 20 CORNELL J.L. & PUB. POL'Y 571, 637 (2011); Soha F. Turfler, *A Model Definition of the Practice of Law: If Not Now, When? An Alternative Approach to Defining the Practice of Law,* 61 WASH. & LEE L. REV. 1903, 1944 (2004). But the thrust of what we describe in the text is true. The role and the need for lawyers in litigation are much clearer than in the transactional world.

portant questions: Why do business clients use lawyers? What value do we add?

Let us separate out the "deals" from the rest of the work that transactional lawyers do.[28] We will describe the value lawyers might add to deals in a moment. But first, consider the list of projects we offered in Section III above, and apply the Gilson questions to those projects. The value lawyers may add should be relatively apparent. We see three primary sources of value.

The first, of course, is the direct legal guidance lawyers offer to business clients. Aside from the unauthorized practice limitations, which probably preclude nonlawyers from engaging in many of the projects on our list,[29] lawyers will simply be the best source available to advise businesses about what the law requires of them and what will happen when things go wrong. Advice about regulatory compliance, the risks and likely results of lawsuits, the meaning of a contract's provisions, and so forth can best come from a lawyer, and perhaps may only come from a lawyer. For some observers, the transactional lawyer's role as a "compliance counselor" triggers some important gatekeeping responsibilities, encouraging business to respect social norms.[30]

The second reason why clients do, and should, hire lawyers for the transactional activities we are discussing is a little less powerful than the first, but powerful nonetheless. While this statement may strike some as surprising,[31] lawyers will often serve as better drafters, or document creators, for the client's purposes than nonlawyers. Our list of projects included creating contracts, and creating entities along with the entities' governing documents. Notwithstanding the legal profession's reputation for producing terrible prose, a lawyer has the training and expertise to create contracts, corporate articles, bylaws, and similar constitutive documents in a way that will most likely *work*. Understanding contract doctrine assists a lawyer to craft terms which courts will enforce. Understanding corporate law and fiduciary duties, and having experience with how cor-

---

[28] *See* Dent, *supra* note 17, at 288 (noting Gilson's focus on just one aspect of a business lawyer's work).

[29] That statement in the text might lead you to wonder, if you are not yet a lawyer, "How may *I* do this work?" If the state statutes uniformly limit most of the work we have just described to lawyers, and if you are not a lawyer, you will question why you are not acting unlawfully (which we agree is not a great way to start your legal career). This question is not a silly one, and the law one looks to is not the clearest. But we (along with your supervisors) conclude that you may function in the lawyer role as long as your are properly supervised by a licensed lawyer. We discuss this in our chapter on Ethical Issues in Transactional Practice.

[30] *See, e.g.,* Robert Gordon, *Corporate Law as a Public Calling*, 49 MD. L. REV. 255 (1990); Christine E. Parker, Robert Eli Rosen & Vibeke Lehmann Nielsen, *The Two Faces of Lawyers: Professional Ethics and Business Compliance with Regulation*, 22 GEO. J. LEGAL ETHICS 201 (2009).

[31] *See* David Foster Wallace, *Authority and American Usage*, in CONSIDER THE LOBSTER AND OTHER ESSAYS 73 (2006). In reviewing BRYAN A. GARNER, A DICTIONARY OF MODERN AMERICAN USAGE (2d ed. 2003), Wallace writes, "[Garner is] both a lawyer and a usage expert (which seems a bit like being a narcotics wholesaler and a DEA agent)."

porations actually operate, permits a lawyer to write articles and bylaws that capture the founders' wishes and withstand later challenges. While entrepreneurs may use popular online document production services such as LegalZoom,[32] lawyers will produce a better and more reliable product for the entrepreneurs (at a higher price, of course).

The third reason we offer why business owners choose to hire lawyers instead of nonlawyers is quite likely the least powerful or persuasive, but it has some weight. Even when considering those tasks where nonlawyers lawfully may compete with lawyers, and where the nonlawyers may have comparable expertise (consider, say, advising about financing or assisting with obtaining permits or licenses), lawyers add value because of their exercise of professional judgment. Many observers of the legal profession have commented that lawyers by virtue of their work with clients develop a form of wisdom, of reflective judgment, that serves them as advisors to clients in ways that nonlawyers do not.[33] This assertion might be distorted by the legal academy's self-interest,[34] but we do not dismiss it out of hand. There seems to be a distinct qualitative judgment that the best lawyers develop which permits them to perceive themes and synergies, and to meld the interpersonal aspects of a business with the hard, technical legal aspects of the endeavor. Experts from other professions may not be as perceptive as lawyers in making the kinds of wise choices that business owners or community group leaders wish to make.

These three reasons, then, help us to appreciate why clients engaged in transactional activity will look to lawyers for assistance. But you will recall that we deferred one important aspect of the transactional universe—that of the deal. When we consider the deal, we encounter a topic where the role of lawyers is the least clear (businesses engage in purchases and sales of products all the time without legal assistance), but where we have the most thoughtful exploration, given the treatment offered by Ronald Gilson and the many writers who have commented on his work. Before we end this section, we will describe briefly Gilson's thesis, and some scholarly reaction to his ideas.

---

[32] LegalZoom's offer to create corporate documents for customers for a fee may constitute the unauthorized practice of law. *See* Janson v. LegalZoom.com, Inc., 802 F. Supp. 2d 1053 (W.D. Mo. 2011) (concluding that certain of LegalZoom's activities constitute the unauthorized practice of law); John Levin, *Yes, Virginia. Computers Can Practice Law. Sort Of*, 25–OCT. CBA REC. 50 (2011); Margaret Hensler Nicholls, *A Quagmire of Internet Ethics Law and the ABA Guidelines for Legal Website Providers*, 18 GEO. J. LEGAL ETHICS 1021, 1037 (2005). Notwithstanding that concern, LegalZoom continues to operate openly. *See* LegalZoom, www.legalzoom.com.

[33] *See, e.g.,* DAVID MCGOWAN, DEVELOPING JUDGMENT ABOUT PRACTICING LAW (2011); ANTHONY KRONMAN, THE LOST LAWYER (1993); RICHARD A. ZITRIN, MORAL COMPASS OF THE AMERICAN LAWYER (1999).

[34] *See* Peter Margulies, *Progressive Lawyering and Lost Traditions*, 73 TEX. L. REV. 1139 (1995) (review essay, reviewing KRONMAN, *supra* note 33); Tanina Rostain, *The Company We Keep: Kronman's The Lost Lawyer and the Development of Moral Imagination in the Practice of Law*, 21 LAW & SOC. INQUIRY 1017 (1996).

Gilson wondered why deal participants hired lawyers at all given the cost of that service. Any deal will make economic sense only if it generates some gains which the participants will divide. If the role of lawyers were to assist the respective parties in the *distributive* bargaining about dividing those gains (that is, if the lawyers assist their respective clients simply to gain a better share of a fixed pie), Gilson reasons that "there is little doubt that . . . the clients' joint decision would be to hire *no* lawyers at all because, net of lawyers' fees, the surplus from the transaction to be divided between the clients would be *smaller* as a result of the participation of lawyers, rather than larger."[35] He therefore concludes that parties will only hire lawyers if the lawyers add some value to the deal as a whole. That addition "must be in the overall value of the transaction, not merely in the distributive share of one of the parties."[36]

But how might expensive lawyers add value to a deal the parties could accomplish on their own? Gilson suggests that lawyers serve as "transaction cost engineers."[37] Without any transaction costs, and with perfect information flow, the parties to deals would not need lawyers. But outside of economists' thought experiments, in the real world of economic activity, the parties encounter transaction costs and the parties operate with imperfect information. Lawyers may decrease the transaction costs and increase the flow of reliable information, thereby adding enough value to justify their costs.[38] Gilson supposes that lawyers accomplish those savings in several ways, most of which involve complicated explanations which would not serve our overview purposes here. Described generally, Gilson sees lawyers as having the skill to create transactional structures that protect parties against information distortion or disparity (he includes covenants, conditions, representations and warranties, and legal opinions in his discussion[39]), and in that way limit the opportunism of any of the deal participants.[40] Those devices also make the production, and the verification, of reliable information substantially less costly.[41] Gilson also recognizes that lawyers possess valuable reputational capital, and may use that asset to serve as a "reputational intermediary: someone paid to verify another party's information."[42] The lawyers' reputation for integrity permits parties to decrease their efforts to determine the trustworthiness of the other participants' proffered information.

---

[35] Gilson, *supra* note 9, at 245–46.

[36] *Id.* at 246.

[37] *Id.* at 253.

[38] *Id.* at 253–56.

[39] *Id.* at 262–87.

[40] *Id.* at 288–89.

[41] *Id.* at 269–71, 280.

[42] *Id.* at 289.

Gilson adds one other component to his hypothesis. Actors other than lawyers (consider, say, investment bankers[43]) may accomplish some of the benefits just described, so in some ways the discussion thus far begs some parts of the "Why lawyers?" question. Gilson's response is to identify the "economies of scope" that lawyers bring to deals.[44] It is more efficient for parties to use lawyers even for the activities that nonlawyers might perform comparably well, because the lawyers need to be present because of the regulatory influences which only lawyers may address. The economy of scope suggests that it makes economic sense to the parties for the lawyers to perform some of the not-necessarily-legal parts of the transaction while they are in place monitoring and influencing the purely-legal elements of the deal. Gilson describes it this way:

> Because the lawyer must play an important role in designing the structure of the transaction in order to assure the desired regulatory treatment, economies of scope should cause the nonregulatory aspects of transactional structuring to gravitate to the lawyer as well.[45]

Gilson's insights have had a far-reaching influence on the thinking about the role that transactional lawyers play in the business world.[46] While later writers have refined[47] and critiqued[48] his thesis, his insights are fundamentally sound observations about the role for transactional lawyers in business and economic development contexts. You may evaluate your ongoing work for your clients by constant reference to the benchmark Gilson identifies—that is, how is your work adding value to the clients' projects?[49]

---

[43] *Id.* at 297. Although, as some have noted, investment bankers are no less expensive to retain than are law firms. *See* Dent, *supra* note 17, at 313.

[44] *Id.* at 298.

[45] *Id.*

[46] Gilson's article has garnered considerable attention in the scholarly literature about business lawyers. *See, e.g.,* Edward A. Bernstein, *Law & Economics and the Structure of Value Adding Contracts: A Contract Lawyer's View of the Law & Economics Literature,* 74 OR. L. REV. 189 (1995); Nestor M. Davidson, *Values and Value Creation in Public–Private Transactions,* 94 IOWA L. REV. 937 (2009); Karl S. Okamoto, *Reputation and the Value of Lawyers,* 74 OR. L. REV. 15 (1995); Statchen, *supra* note 24.

[47] *See, e.g.,* Larry A. DiMatteo, *Strategic Contracting: Contract Law as a Source of Competitive Advantage,* 47 AM. BUS. L.J. 727 (2010).

[48] *See, e.g.,* Frank B. Cross, *The First Thing We Do, Let's Kill All the Economists: An Empirical Evaluation of the Effect of Lawyers on the United States Economy and Political System,* 70 TEX. L. REV. 645 (1992) (lawyers have a positive effect on the American economy, extracting the most money possible out of every deal, and limiting waste from transactions).

[49] For an example of the application of that standard within a small business clinic, see Statchen, *supra* note 24, at 251–59.

V. THE BENEFITS OF TRANSACTIONAL EXPERIENTIAL LEARNING IN LAW SCHOOL

Our last section of this introductory chapter visits a question relevant to those of you who are representing clients in transactional matters in a law school setting—most likely through a clinical course (either in-house or a formal externship), but perhaps in a co-op or summer employment experience. Will the kind of practice you encounter in law school assist you to develop the habits, skills, and judgments needed for you to develop into a successful transactional lawyer after graduation?

Of course, we need not rehearse in any depth here the incessant refrain of recent times that law schools have failed to prepare students adequately for the practice of law. Any sentient observer of the legal academy in the past ten years understands the critique. The confluence of a very prestigious and well-received evaluation of the legal education industry in 2007, known colloquially as the Carnegie Report,[50] followed by the economic recession which began soon after the report's publication and which dramatically affected law firm employment and client service practices, has led to a wave of calls for law schools to revisit their curriculum and their mission to enable their graduates to enter the profession more "practice ready."[51] The Carnegie Report emphasized the importance of law schools developing practice skills in their students, including the capacity to exercise judgment, to counsel clients, and to respond effectively to the factual and ethical ambiguities of real world practice.[52]

It is easy to conclude, then, that a law school experience that permits you to interact with actual clients facing real business and enterprise development challenges, to create documents and vehicles for those clients to use in a fundamentally genuine way, and to live with a deal's unfolding or a company's beginning cannot help but aid you in developing the practice skills and the reflective judgment that the emerging consensus of opinion agrees you ought to have. Several commentators in recent years have urged law schools to take this aspect of legal education about transactional practice far more seriously, and have described their own models for doing so.[53]

---

[50] WILLIAM M. SULLIVAN ET AL., EDUCATING LAWYERS: PREPARATION FOR THE PROFESSION OF LAW (2007). The *Carnegie Report* appeared at the same time as another similar critique of the academy, known as the Best Practices report. *See* ROY STUCKEY ET AL., BEST PRACTICES FOR LEGAL EDUCATION: A VISION AND A ROADMAP (2007).

[51] *See Symposium: The Way to Carnegie: Practice, Practice, Practice—Pedagogy, Social Justice, and Cost in Experiential Legal Education*, 32 B.C. J.L. & SOC. JUST. 215 (2012); Margaret Martin Barry, *Practice Ready: Are We There Yet?*, 32 B.C. J.L. & SOC. JUST. 247 (2012). The critiques have made headlines in the popular press as well. *See, e.g.,* Jonathan D. Glater, *Training Law Students for Real–Life Careers*, N.Y. TIMES, Oct. 31, 2007, at B9; David Segal, *What They Don't Teach Law Students: Lawyering*, N.Y. TIMES, Nov. 20, 2011, at A1.

[52] SULLIVAN, ET AL., *supra* note 50, at 115–20, 128–32.

[53] *See, e.g.,* Eric J. Gouvin, *Teaching Business Lawyering in Law Schools: A Candid Assessment of the Challenges and Some Suggestions for Moving Ahead*, 78 UMKC L. REV. 429

But some observers have questioned the apparent logic of the above syllogism, which holds that law students need to learn effective practice, transactional clinics offer business and entrepreneurship practice opportunities, so therefore the law school experiences are useful avenues through which students will develop high quality transactional skills. Ronald Gilson, for instance, expressed skepticism that law schools are capable of effective teaching of the skills and habits needed by good business lawyers.[54] Gilson identified "a number of problems" with the prospect of law schools teaching business practice skills, including the lack of competence and experience in the field of most business law professors, the considerable advantages available to learning by apprenticeship in actual practice, and the high cost of the kind of supervision needed to provide law students sufficient immersion in transactional competencies.[55] Other commentators have expressed similar worries.[56]

There is merit to this critique, but at the same time the critique elides some important realities about the rewards of clinical and simulation experiences during your law school years. Of course you will learn the most, and the best, about complex deals and transactions through your immersion in their developments as a practicing lawyer for one of the participants. The question for you is whether you will join that practice setting with only an exposure to the intellectual or cognitive qualities of the practice of law, or whether you will start practice with some reflective exposure to the interpersonal, factual, and ethical components of the work. The answer seems obvious to us.

The Carnegie Report identified three "apprenticeships of professional education," all of which are essential to the development of effective and reflective practitioners, and all of which law schools ought to address as part of the professional training of their students.[57] The first apprenticeship is the intellectual or cognitive, and it is the talent taught most directly in traditional law school curriculum—the abilities to perform rigor-

---

(2009); Celeste M. Hammond, *Borrowing from the B Schools: The Legal Case Study as Course Materials for Transaction Oriented Elective Courses: A Response to the Challenges of the Mac-Crate Report and the Carnegie Foundation for Advancement of Teaching Report on Legal Education,* 11 TRANSACTIONS: TENN. J. BUS. L. 9 (2009); Kosuri, *supra* note 16; Karl S. Okamoto, *Teaching Transactional Lawyering,* 1 DREXEL L. REV. 69 (2009); Statchen, *supra* note 24.

[54] Gilson, *supra* note 9, at 304. While Gilson, in 1984, wrote for and about a different generation of law students and lawyers, his worries are not insignificant ones.

[55] *Id.* at 304–05.

[56] *See* Michael A. Woronoff, *What Law Schools Should Teach Future Transactional Lawyers: Perspectives from Practice* 12, 17, *available at* http://ssrn.com/abstracts=1430087 (2010) (edited version of remarks at the 2009 mid-year meeting of the AALS Conference of Business Associations). Woronoff, a self-described "sophisticated" transactional partner at the Los Angeles office of a national law firm and an adjunct professor at UCLA School of Law, argued that "transactional legal clinics . . . have only limited value," and law schools ought to do what he perceives law schools can do best, which is "transmitting a complex body of substantive knowledge."

[57] SULLIVAN, ET AL., *supra* note 50, at 27–29.

ous analysis, to comprehend deep theories, and to "think like a lawyer."[58] The second apprenticeship the Carnegie Report calls "the forms of expert practice shared by competent practitioners,"[59] and the third is "the apprenticeship of identity and purpose."[60] Law school classroom teaching has tended to neglect the latter two components of legal education, but through simulations, problems, and especially clinics and externships law schools may begin to address those critical competencies.

Your work with clients will begin the process of your assimilating the habits necessary to serve clients well.[61] Even if you are working on less complex matters than you might later encounter in a law firm setting, and even if your understanding of the substantive law will be rudimentary at first, you will discover that a clinical experience permits you to begin to develop the judgment and the comfort necessary for you to respond to ambiguity of facts, to understand the interpersonal aspects of legal work, and to solve problems in creative ways.

---

[58] *Id.* at 28.

[59] *Id.*

[60] *Id.*

[61] In the introduction to his popular book on contract drafting, Charles Fox describes a first-year associate in a law firm assigned to assist with a business acquisition, and compares her with a colleague of similar experience whose assignment is to prepare a memo of law applicable to a lawsuit for breach of contract. The latter associate understands well the context of his assignment, while the former is rather lost, because law school has not exposed her to the machinations of a deal. CHARLES M. FOX, WORKING WITH CONTRACTS: WHAT LAW SCHOOL DOESN'T TEACH YOU 1–2 (2d ed. 2008).

CHAPTER 2

INTERVIEWING: THE BEGINNING OF THE ATTORNEY–CLIENT RELATIONSHIP

■ ■ ■

I. INTRODUCTION

Most lawyering skills texts that discuss interviewing skills do so in the context of litigation. This chapter provides an outline for conducting an initial interview in a transactional context by giving the novice lawyer guidelines for structuring the interview while at the same time providing flexibility for the wide range of matters you may encounter as an attorney in a transactional setting, especially in a community setting.

In this chapter, we will address the many considerations you will face in achieving an effective interview through the lens of two clinic projects:

Dolores Robinson has called the clinic asking for assistance in creating a nonprofit organization to work on ecology issues with children.

Amanda Estrada, the Executive Director of the Domestic Workers Center (DWC), a domestic workers organization, would like the clinic to negotiate a lease for DWC's office space.

A. WHAT IS SO IMPORTANT ABOUT INTERVIEWING, ANYWAY?

All of the major texts on lawyering skills devote substantial amounts of time and space to interviewing. Many lawyers and law students, however, approach interviewing as innate, a skill that we do not necessarily need to learn and develop but one with which we all (or most of us, at least) are born. We do not agree. This chapter begins from the position that interviewing is a skill that can be learned and improved as you gain experience and spend time thinking about, planning for and reflecting on your interviews.

Clients expect lawyers to have solid legal skills. These skills include more than the analytical skills that all lawyers should possess and which law school tends to emphasize. Communication skills, including listening, and business relationship skills are among the most important factors to being an effective lawyer.[1] According to a recent report, corporate clients identify "the absolute best client service" as "client focus," which is when the client perceives the lawyer as committed and proactively responsive to the client.[2] "Client focus" includes putting yourself in the client's shoes and understanding the client fully.[3] The second most important factor, per the report of these clients, is understanding the client's business. Studies of individual clients have found that effective two-way communication, including attentive listening, clear explanations, empathy and respect, were important lawyer qualities to clients.[4] Clients often value "client relationship skills" as much as or more than pure technical skills.[5] The most important of these "relationship skills" are caring about the client, keeping the client informed and effective listening. The lawyer begins to demonstrate these important attributes to the client in the initial interview.

In medicine, empirical research has found that strong relationship skills correspond to overall physician effectiveness per patients' reports about satisfaction.[6] These strong interpersonal skills are just as important for the lawyer.

For clients new to the clinic, the interview is the place where first impressions are created, both for you as the lawyer as well as for the client. For clients who have already worked with the lawyer, as is the case in many transactional settings, the initial interview on a new matter is still the time when the client assesses whether she can trust you as the lawyer on this matter and the place for you as the lawyer to assure the client that you are competent to handle the matter.

B. GOALS OF INTERVIEWING

Lawyers and clients have multiple goals for the initial interview. These goals are often in tension with each other. Both parties want to decide if they want to enter into a relationship. As the lawyer, you are using the interview to ascertain if this is the type of matter you can handle and if the client is the type of person or organization you would like to have as a client. At the same time, you are trying to get the client to retain you as

---

[1] MARJORIE M. SCHULTZ & SHELDON ZEDECK, IDENTIFICATION, DEVELOPMENT AND VALIDATION OF PREDICTORS FOR SUCCESSFUL LAWYERING 26–27 (2008).

[2] Neil Hamilton & Verna Monson, *The Positive Empirical Relationship of Professionalism to Effectiveness in the Practice of Law*, 24 GEO. J. LEGAL ETHICS 137, 164 (2011) (citing BTI CONSULTING GROUP, *Executive Summary, in* THE BTI CLIENT SERVICE ALL–STAR TEAM FOR LAW FIRMS 6–7 (2008)).

[3] *Id.*

[4] *Id.* at 165 (citing CLARK CUNNINGHAM, WHAT CLIENTS WANT FROM THEIR LAWYERS 2–3 (2006), *available at* http://law.gsu.edu/Communication/WhatClientsWant.pdf).

[5] *Id.* at 162.

[6] *Id.* at 176–77 (citing Mark A. Hall et al., *Measuring Patients' Trust in Their Primary Care Providers*, 59 MED. CARE RES. & REV. 293, 314 (2002) and Barbara L. Leighton, *Why Obstetric Anesthesiologists Get Sued*, 110 ANESTHESIOLOGY 8, 8–9 (2009)).

the lawyer. The client wants to know whether you are a lawyer who will competently handle her matter, whether you will do so in a way consistent with the client's view of how the matter should be handled and whether you will treat the client as she would like to be treated. As the lawyer, you want to gather the information necessary for the representation. As we will see below, in tension during the initial interview, and to some extent throughout the relationship, are the goals of getting information and developing an effective relationship. Both you and the client balance these goals during the initial meeting. If you and the client have worked together before, the relationship might already have been established in a satisfactory way. If that is so, the primary goal for both parties during the interview will be getting (and giving) information. For you as the lawyer, that means gathering information in an organized way to help you formulate a plan for proceeding with the matter; for the client that means communicating accurately her aims and preferences and learning information from you about the status of the matter.

C. WHY ORGANIZING AN INTERVIEW IS IMPORTANT

One of the ways that you can communicate competence is by being organized in the initial interview. Organization communicates to the client that you are knowledgeable about and interested in the client since you have thought about the client's issues ahead of time. In addition, a well-organized interview allows you to be more efficient by saving your time and that of the client since you will not need to go back and fill in the information that you did not ask during the initial meeting. Finally, preparation assists you with gathering information. By thinking through the information you need to gather, you are less likely to forget key issues that are relevant to resolving the client's concerns. A well-structured interview should also help the client recall information that is important to handling the matter.

In this chapter, we suggest some considerations you might use in structuring your interview in an organized, but still flexible, manner.

D. PREPARING FOR THE INTERVIEW

Preparation for an interview is essential to its success, especially for a newer lawyer like you. Because an interview by its very nature involves your not knowing in advance what the client will say or want, the idea of preparation for this "unknown" experience might seem a bit challenging (if not counterintuitive). We agree that it is challenging, but it is a skill you will learn in the clinic. Your preparation will include learning something about your client (especially if your client is an ongoing enterprise), learning something about the law involved in the client's matter, and creating a tentative plan for the order of your inquiries.

fact research

Your preparation will often include **researching your client**. If the client is not a new client to the clinic, you might review what other matters the clinic has handled for that client. For new organizational clients, you might look at the organization's web page or corporate or organizational filings available from the state or other electronic resources. As with much of our recommendations in this book, this advance work will require a balance between finding more out about the client in order to be prepared for the interview and to demonstrate genuine interest in the client and its work on the one hand, and on the other, presuming that you already know the client's story before the interview begins. Also, in preparing for your interview with an organizational client, you might want to know which client representatives will be at the initial meeting and in what capacities they serve the organization.

legal research

Your second preparatory task will involve **legal research**. Most lawyers interviewing new clients have some sense of the issue for which the client is seeking legal assistance. In order to be able to ask relevant questions, a lawyer needs to know something about the areas of law that the client's matter might raise. For new lawyers that will mean you will need to spend some time researching those areas of law. Remember, the point here is to know enough to be able to ask questions. You do not necessarily need to know so much as to be able to counsel the client. The goal of research is to help you ask relevant questions. As above, the risk here is that your advance research will lead you to prejudge the issues that the client brings to you. Remember, throughout the interview you will need to keep an open mind.

Let us consider your initial meeting with Ms. Robinson, who will come to the clinic wanting help with creating a nonprofit organization. In most states, this project will involve two separate state statutes, the nonprofit corporation act and the solicitation act, as well as the federal tax exemption regime.[7] In preparation for your meeting with Ms. Robinson, you will likely review your state's nonprofit act; the requirements for charitable exemption under the federal tax act, and especially the regulations (including researching the definitions of "charitable," "educational" and the other categories for exempt organizations[8]) and the general requirements of your state's solicitation statute. If good secondary sources exist for your state, you might want to begin your preparation by reading these resources.[9] It is important, though, for you not to assume that creating a new nonprofit corporation is the only option in this project just because that is what the client told you or told the clinic's staff. Throughout this research, keep an open mind to other possible goals for the client and other possible ways to achieve the client's goals.

---

[7]   26 U.S.C. § 501(c)(3) (2006).

[8]   26 C.F.R. § 1.501(c)(3)–1 (2008).

[9]   Most states have continuing education materials.

In preparation for your meeting with Ms. Estrada, who will come to the clinic wanting assistance with negotiating and drafting a lease, you will want to start by reviewing some secondary sources on commercial leases, especially sources covering the specific requirements of your state or locality.

In addition to your research about the client and the laws most likely to apply to your client's situation, your preparation will include an outline of your plan for the meeting. As you read through this chapter, think about how you might prepare for each of the stages of the interview we discuss. Some segments of the interview, like learning the client's goals or the background narrative, are resistant to anything but the most general planning (e.g., "Ask the client about her goals"); other segments, such as the space for the narrower questions you expect to ask in the latter part of the meeting, or the suggestions about how you will proceed after the meeting, will benefit from careful planning. You will most likely find that planning for the very beginning parts of the interview, including any "housekeeping" discussions, will be quite useful to you.

Finally, preparing for the interview will require you to decide the appropriate place for the meeting, whether in the client's office or in the clinic. Where you choose to meet might depend on whether the client has an office, the number of people attending the meeting and the convenience of the various parties. Holding the meeting in the clinic will be more convenient for you as well as minimize the possibility of distractions for the client.[10] Holding the meeting in the client's office may allow you to learn more about the client and, for community-based organizations, the community in which the client works.

If the meeting is to take place in the clinic, you will have to decide whether to hold the meeting in a conference room or some other office. The size of the group might control that as well as the facilities available to you in the clinic. Regardless, you will have to decide how to arrange the furniture in the room to create the best working atmosphere. Sitting behind a desk may create more of a barrier between you and the client. Here are some questions to consider. Do you want everyone to sit around a table? Should you and your clinic partner (if you have one) sit next to each other? Do you want to sit across from the client so you can have eye contact or next to each other so the table is not between you? How should you arrange the seating if your client has multiple representatives attending? If your supervisor is going to be in the room, where will she sit?

---

[10] Some clinic offices have facilities for recording the meeting on videotape or digital camera, offering one advantage to holding the meeting in your office. (Assuming, that is, that you find it to be an advantage to have the meeting recorded for you and your supervisor to watch together.)

E. INTERVIEWING WITH A CLINIC PARTNER

If two or more student lawyers are conducting the interview, you will need to decide how you will plan the interview. Will you work together to plan the entire interview, divide responsibility for sections of the interview or work separately on sections of the interview but get feedback from your clinic partner? If you decide to work together, what decisions will you make together? Are there certain tasks that are better suited for collaborative work or separate work with feedback from the other? How will you share the interview? Will one of you take the lead for certain parts of the interview and will those parts be divided by length of time or topic? Will your co-counsel be able to ask questions during the parts you lead? Your decisions in the planning phase will determine whether your clinic partner is prepared to participate in the parts of the interview you lead.

You will also have to decide how you will handle note-taking during an interview conducted with a partner. One option might be for one person to take the lead with questions while the other takes notes. The "first" chair for a particular section might turn to the other lawyer before proceeding to another section of the interview. The second "chair" might then fill in with questions that might not have occurred to the lead lawyer for that section or topic. Should you decide to proceed this way, your co-counsel will need to be as familiar as you are with a certain topic or line of questions.

Finally, you should think about and discuss how you will communicate with each other during the interview. How will you tell your partner that you are done with your section and are ready to proceed to the next section? In arranging the seating for the meeting consider the communication between members of the team as well as with the client representatives. Are we making client interviewing more complicated than you think it needs to be?

II. CLIENT–CENTERED REPRESENTATION

This book approaches representation of clients from the perspective of the client. The concept of "client-centered" representation was pioneered by David A. Binder and Susan C. Price in their ground-breaking book on legal interviewing and counseling.[11] Client-centered lawyering begins from the premises that first, legal problems raise both legal and non-legal concerns for clients; second, collaboration between lawyers and clients is "likely to enhance the effectiveness of problem-solving";[12] and

---

[11] DAVID A. BINDER & SUSAN C. PRICE, LEGAL INTERVIEWING AND COUNSELING: A CLIENT–CENTERED APPROACH (1977).

[12] DAVID A. BINDER, PAUL BERGMAN, PAUL R. TREMBLAY & IAN WEINSTEIN, LAWYERS AS COUNSELORS: A CLIENT–CENTERED APPROACH 3 (3d ed. 2012).

third, clients are normally in the "best position to make important decisions."[13]

Client-centeredness offers a critique of traditional lawyering practice by focusing particularly on the location and role of power in the relationship between the lawyer and the client.[14] The critique recognizes the tendency of lawyers to undervalue or disregard the decision-making abilities of clients, to substitute their judgment for that of the client and to see a client matter in overly narrow legal terms without considering the non-legal issues these matters raise.[15] Client-centeredness critiques the traditional notion that lawyers as the experts control the decisions clients make by convincing clients about what is in their best interest. Client-centeredness also requires careful consideration of the differences in race, ethnicity, gender, class, age, sexual orientation and gender identity, immigration status, educational background, professional privilege and language that inform this power dynamic.[16]

Though regarded as the "traditional" (and therefore older) view, many new lawyers feel more comfortable with the authoritarian role for the lawyer. This traditional view of lawyering presupposes that there is a "best" solution to legal problems and that the lawyer's training, experience and judgment place her in a better position to make those decisions. By contrast, the client-centered model views the community of clients as owners of their problems and thus in a better position to identify and weigh the non-legal (political, financial, social, psychological, moral and other) ramifications of the legal issues since they (and their communities) will have to live with the consequences of their decisions.[17] The approach also recognizes that clients are the ones who should determine the risk they are willing to take with respect to possible outcomes.[18] The client-centered approach is characterized by:

1. Recognizing non-legal ramifications to legal problems;

2. Having clients identify potential solutions;

3. Having clients make important decisions;

4. Providing advice based on the client's values (as opposed to based on the consequences the lawyer personally thinks are important); and

5. Acknowledging the client's feelings and recognizing their importance.

---

[13] *Id.*

[14] Muneer I. Ahmad, *Interpreting Communities: Lawyering Across Language Difference*, 54 UCLA L. REV. 999, 1047 (2007).

[15] *Id.*

[16] *Id.* at 1049.

[17] BINDER ET AL., *supra* note 12, at 4–6.

[18] *Id.* at 7.

As we shall see, your interviewing techniques will reflect your commitments to client-centeredness. Lawyer domination of the interactions between themselves and clients may be evident in interviewing by lawyer control of conversational time and the topic of the conversation.[19]

We discuss some of the critiques of client-centered lawyering in the Counseling chapter. Though these critiques raise important points, we remain committed to the notion of client-centered lawyering. The critiques, we believe, are important cautions for lawyers engaging in client representation. They do not, however, lead us to counsel against undertaking representation from the perspective of the client. As a result, the remainder of this book continues from the premise of client-centered lawyering.

III. AN OUTLINE FOR THE INITIAL TRANSACTIONAL INTERVIEW

A. GENERALLY

This section looks to provide the novice lawyer with a possible structure for the initial client interview. This structure will help new lawyers plan for gathering information for a new client matter. Our hope is to provide you with enough flexibility to make adjustments based on the particular facts of the matter, and the client's and your personalities. At the same time, it is important to provide you with some guidelines in structuring the initial client interview in order to help make your initial interview well-organized. As we emphasized in the previous section, well-organized interviews help build client trust and help you gather information.

Our proposed outline for the initial client interview is as follows:

Introduction

Issue Identification

Gathering General Information

Gathering Detailed Information

Concluding the Initial Interview

---

[19] Carl J. Hosticka, *We Don't Care About What Happened, We Only Care About What Is Going to Happen: Lawyer–Client Negotiations of Reality*, 26 SOC. PROBLEMS 599, 605–06 (1976). This study found that "individual lawyers exercised topic control 91.4%–97.4% of the time." *Id.* at 605. In this study, more than one-fourth of the lawyers' questions were leading questions. *Id.* Lawyers also controlled the timing by interrupting clients. *Id.* The study also found lawyers interrupting clients over ten times per interview at approximately every three minutes. *Id.* Lawyers interrupted a client to ask questions 7.8 times per interview. *Id.* at 606. The general picture that emerged from the study is one of lawyer control over the process of the interaction including the evaluation of what ought to happen.

B. INTRODUCTION: THE BEGINNING OF THE INITIAL CLIENT INTERVIEW

In the beginning of the interview, you will have several goals, including:

1. Putting the client at ease;

2. Giving the client a sense of what is going to happen during the meeting;

3. Explaining that you are a law student;

4. Explaining confidentiality;

5. Explaining fees for the initial consultation (including whether the clinic charges for the initial consultation); and

6. Discussing how the decision to accept the client and retain the clinic's services will be made.

When you first meet the client, you will introduce yourself to the client and explain who you are. You and the client may have spoken on the telephone or may have been in contact by email in order to schedule the meeting, so the client may already know your name.

Whether you want to do so or not, you will inevitably engage in some small talk with your client at the beginning of the interview. This "ice-breaking" (as some interviewing texts refer to it) is an important part of the interview, and it really does help you and the client establish a warm relationship. Preparing for small talk, though, may seem awkward to you, and the resulting "chit-chat" may seem contrived. Practice makes perfect in this area. Here's one suggestion: Try not to think of what you might say to a new client as a new lawyer. Instead, approach the situation as if you had just met someone new in a relatively formal setting. Imagine you just met one of your partner's colleagues for the first time, or you just met the new minister in your church. What would you say to that person?

Whatever small talk you engage in might happen when you greet the client in the law office waiting room and escort the client back to the interview space or when the client sits down in the meeting room. This conversation can be as simple as talking about someone you know in common, offering to take the client's coat, or offering the client something to drink. Having a natural, comfortable conversation in this setting is especially important if the meeting is taking place in the clinic. Your goal is to try to put the person at ease before you proceed to talk about business.

As you begin to move to discuss the issue that brings the client to the clinic, you should give the client a sense of how you envision the meeting proceeding. You might tell the client how you would like to structure the interview. You should ask the client if the proposed agenda is acceptable and make any adjustments accordingly.[20] If you have any time constraints for the meeting, you should communicate that to the client, as well as get a sense of whether the client has time constraints of her own. This map should give the client a sense of how you envision the meeting proceeding and what will happen at the end of the meeting. Though you were the one who established the outline, sharing it gives the client some control over your meeting.

At some point early in the meeting, you will need to tell the client that you are a law student and that you are allowed to represent her because a licensed attorney is supervising you.[21]

You should also discuss with the client how decisions regarding representation will be made. In some situations the clinic has already decided to accept the client's matter for representation. In other situations, that decision will be made after the initial consultation. You should clarify the expectations in the early stages of the meeting. Remember that whether you work with this client is not just your decision; the client also needs to decide whether to retain the clinic. The conversation about forming an attorney-client relationship will likely happen toward the end of the meeting, after you have gathered information and the client has gotten a better sense of your thoughts about the project, but you cannot assume that the client will retain the clinic.

An important question at this beginning stage of the meeting is whether to explain confidentiality and, if so, how detailed any such explanation should be.[22] Rule 1.6 of the American Bar Association's Model Rules of Professional Conduct, which covers confidentiality, provides that a lawyer "shall not reveal information relating to the representation of a client unless the client gives informed consent, the disclosure is impliedly authorized in order to carry out the representation or the disclosure is permitted"[23] by one of the rule's exceptions. According to that rule, the lawyer may reveal information the lawyer "reasonably believes necessary" either to prevent death, substantial bodily injury or the client from committing a crime or fraud, to secure legal advice, to defend herself in a controversy with the client, and to comply with other law or court order.[24]

---

[20] Alex Hurder suggests that a lawyer should be prepared to modify a proposed process for information gathering, such as the agenda for a meeting. Alex J. Hurder, *Negotiating the Lawyer–Client Relationship: A Search for Equality and Collaboration*, 44 BUFF. L. REV. 71, 92 (1996).

[21] You will need to review your state's student practice rule. If the rule covers your practice, you can explain that you are practicing under the state's student practice rule. If your state's rule does not cover your practice, you should tell the client you are a student attorney supervised by a practicing attorney. In either case, you should discuss this with your supervisor before the interview. *See* Paul R. Tremblay, *Shadow Lawyering: Nonlawyer Practice Within Law Firms*, 85 IND. L. J. 653 (2010).

[22] Clark D. Cunningham, *How to Explain Confidentiality*, 9 CLINICAL L. REV. 579 (2003).

[23] MODEL RULES OF PROF'L CONDUCT R. 1.6 (2012).

[24] The rules afford the same protections for former clients, providing that lawyers shall not "reveal information relating to the representation except as these Rules would permit or require

Your state will have its own rule which will most likely substantially track the Model Rule.

Confidentiality issues are as important in transactional matters as in litigation settings.[25] The duty of confidentiality exists to inspire client trust and candor, but it only may do so if the client knows about it. You therefore will want to tell your client about the confidentiality protection. A broad statement that everything a client says to the lawyer will remain confidential would seem to encourage the most trust and openness from the client. While encouraging the widest revelations from the client, that statement unfortunately misstates the Rule. On the other hand, if you cover all the instances when a lawyer may reveal client confidences, you may discourage your client from being fully open, and your explanation would have to be long and overly legalistic. A client's eyes might glaze over as the lawyer explains all the details of the Rule. The challenge for you, then, is to balance the desire and need to encourage trust and honest disclosure by the client with honesty about the parameters of the confidentiality rule.[26] You therefore need to be able to explain the rule of confidentiality in a succinct and understandable way. We will see an example of one explanation in the dialogue below.

A final topic for the beginning of the interview is that of the fees a client might need to pay to your program. During the opening section of the interview, you should explain to the client any fees that apply for the initial consultation. If the office does not charge fees for the initial consultation, you may wish to say that at the beginning of the meeting even if you intend to discuss fees at the end of the meeting.[27]

You see that the list of "housekeeping" topics is a long one. You might assume from the previous discussion that this part of the meeting will consist of a monologue by the lawyer as she explains each item to the cli-

---

with respect to a client." MODEL RULES OF PROF'L CONDUCT R. 1.9 (2012). The rules also afford the same protections for prospective clients, providing that "[e]ven when no client-lawyer relationship ensues, a lawyer who has had discussions with a prospective client shall not use or reveal information learned in a consultation" except as the Rules would permit or require with respect to a client. MODEL RULES OF PROF'L CONDUCT R. 1.18(b) (2012). A prospective client is someone who has a reasonable expectation that the lawyer is willing to discuss the possibility of forming a client-lawyer relationship. MODEL RULES OF PROF'L CONDUCT R. 1.18 cmt. (2012).

[25] *See* Fred C. Zacharias, *Rethinking Confidentiality*, 74 IOWA L. REV. 351, 409–11 (1989) (containing hypotheticals regarding confidentiality in tax, corporate, real estate and charitable solicitation settings).

[26] Several authors have written about the lawyer's duty to discuss confidentiality and its exceptions. *See* Cunningham, *supra* note 22; Lee A. Pizzimenti, *The Lawyer's Duty to Warn Clients About Limits of Confidentiality*, 39 CATH. U. L. REV. 441 (1990) (arguing that lawyers should assume that clients consider the limits of confidentiality material in deciding what to disclose to the lawyer); Roy M. Sobelson, *Lawyers, Clients and Assurances of Confidentiality: Lawyers Talking Without Speaking, Clients Hearing Without Listening*, 1 GEO. J. LEGAL ETHICS 703 (1988) (proposing that the lawyer send a written form to the client prior to the interview).

[27] Most law school clinics do not charge any fees for their legal services, so for many of you this topic will not appear on your agenda, except perhaps to remind the client of that fact.

ent. That, of course, would not be a good practice. Your planning will include thoughts about how to engage the client in a conversation about each of the matters on your list. And, on some of the items, including whether you will end up forming a long-term relationship, you will surely have a mutual conversation, as both parties will need to agree to that relationship.

Let us now observe what this beginning stage might look like in practice. Imagine that Susan Cho, a student in the clinic, is meeting with Dolores Robinson, the prospective client who wishes to form a nonprofit organization. The interview begins:

Susan: Hello Ms. Robinson, I am Susan Cho, one of the student attorneys in the clinic. It is good to finally meet you. You found our office easily enough, I hope?

Ms. Robinson: Well, funny you should ask. I knew where the law school campus was, of course, but finding your building was not all that easy. Sorry that I'm a little late after my wandering around.

Susan: No, no, not a problem at all. I'm sorry that you got a bit lost. You're not the first person who has told us how hard it is to find the clinic's office. Those maps on the campus are not nearly as clear as we wish they were. Can I offer you some water or coffee?

Ms. Robinson: Thanks, but I'm fine.

Susan: Well, I am glad we were able to finally connect and find a time that works for both of us. I am looking forward to hearing about your work and seeing how the clinic might be able to help.

Ms. Robinson: Yes, I am glad we were able to come up with a time that works. This time of the year is difficult for me since I am busy working with the children in the morning, weeding, feeding the ducks and geese and harvesting as many vegetables as I can. During the week I work with the kids by myself.

Susan: I know nothing about gardening. What kinds of vegetables are you growing?

Ms. Robinson: This year, we planted tomatoes, squash, a variety of greens and a few other things. We thought we should start small since it's our first growing season. I've been gardening in my back yard for many years but this is much bigger.

Susan: Sounds great. Should we start since I know you have to get home in time to pick up your grandchildren from school?

Ms. Robinson: Sure. Yes, as I told you on the telephone I have to pick them up by 2:30 so I need to leave here by 1:45.

Susan: I would like to start by giving you a sense of what I'd like to do today. I'll start by discussing a bit about how the clinic works; then, I'd like to hear about the work you are doing and what you want to accomplish. I think that will raise some questions for me so I would like to ask follow-up questions that your work raises for me. I'd like to end by talking about the next steps, such as whether you would like the clinic to help and what we think the clinic can do for you. Does that seem like a good plan?

(handwritten margin note: lay out meeting agenda →)

Ms. Robinson: Definitely.

Susan: As you know, I am a third-year student at the law school. The state Supreme Court rules allow students who have completed their first year of law school to practice law in a clinic as long as a licensed attorney supervises them and the client agrees to be represented by a student. I am being supervised by Donna Fink, a licensed attorney who is also a professor in the law school. I meet with her on a weekly basis to discuss my work, and she reviews all my work. The goals of the clinic are both to provide a service to the community and an opportunity for students to develop as lawyers.

Ms. Robinson: Okay. Will I ever meet Ms. Fink?

Susan: Definitely. I am not sure when. Did you want to meet her today or were you thinking of a later date?

Ms. Robinson: No, it does not have to be today. I was just wondering if all my dealings will be with you.

Susan: Professor Fink is not in the clinic right now. She is attending another meeting. I am sure she will accompany me to some other meeting though. We can make a point of seeing if she is around the next time you come in. Was there something in particular you wanted to discuss with her?

Ms. Robinson: No. I talked to her initially when I called the clinic, that's all.

Susan: I also wanted to talk about confidentiality with you. With a few exceptions, everything you tell me today is confidential. I cannot tell anyone else what you tell me unless you give me permission. I may discuss what you tell us here today in order to comply with a court order or other law, to prevent death or bodily harm to someone else or to prevent a crime or fraud, or to defend against a claim that we are not following the rules of lawyer conduct. Would you like to talk about that more?

Ms. Robinson: No, I trust you. But you'll tell your supervisor what I say, no?

Susan: Yes, I'll talk to my supervisor about what you discuss. Actually, when I said what you tell us, I meant the "us" as more than just my supervisor and me. We also sometimes talk to the other student attorneys in the clinic about our cases. But we are all bound by confidentiality. So no one can talk about what you tell us beyond that. Is that clearer now?

Ms. Robinson: Yes, I understand.

Susan: As I mentioned earlier, I'll talk at the end of the meeting about next steps. After today's meeting I will talk to my supervisor about what you told me. Assuming you want the clinic to help you, we'll send you a letter of engagement that will set out what we think the clinic can do for you. It's basically the contract that spells out what we can do, what our responsibilities are and what the group's responsibilities will be. If you agree with that, you'll sign the letter and return it to us. We will start work once we have the signed letter back.

Ms. Robinson: What if I don't agree with what you want to do?

Susan: We can talk about it more at that point. For example, we might feel we can only commit to research an issue and advise you about it before deciding whether we can do more. We may think about the work in steps and be able to commit to one step at a time. But we can talk about that when the time comes. Does that seem fair?

Ms. Robinson: Okay.

Susan: The clinic does not charge fees for its services. But you will need to pay any costs related to our work. For example, if we were to incorporate the organization and file an application for tax exemption with the Internal Revenue Service, the organization would have to pay those filing fees.

Ms. Robinson: What if we don't have the money?

Susan: We would discuss that with you in order to time it when the organization has the money. But the government will not waive those fees.

Ms. Robinson: Okay.

Susan: Any questions before we begin talking about your work?

Ms. Robinson: No, not yet.

In this segment, Susan addressed the issues she needed to cover at the beginning of the interview with this new prospective client. Susan began the meeting by telling Ms. Robinson how she planned to conduct the interview; explained that she is a law student and what that meant; told Ms. Robinson about confidentiality; explained that she would discuss next steps at the end of the meeting and how decisions about the representation would take place, and informed this prospective client about possible fees and costs. Susan also engaged in a short "ice-breaker" regarding the difficulty people have finding the clinic's offices on campus and chatted a little bit about gardening. In addition, her manner was conversational and she took the time to make sure Ms. Robinson understood things and gave her space to ask questions.

Assess for yourself how well this segment worked. Did Susan address Ms. Robinson's questions about the role of the supervisor well enough? Did she explain confidentiality in a way that made sense to a new prospective client? Is there anything you might have done differently?

C. ISSUE IDENTIFICATION

In order to better prepare for gathering detailed information during the rest of the interview, you will need to understand what brings the client to the lawyer's office, the client's goals and the way the client sees those goals being achieved. Asking the client to identify the issues that bring her to your office allows the client to frame the question from her perspective and gives you some sense of the client's concerns. Though you might think you know what prompts the client to consult a lawyer at this particular time, you should not assume that what the client initially told someone in the office is the same as what really motivates her to consult an attorney.[28] It is important that you give the client the opportunity to frame the question in her words at the time she knows she can begin to discuss possible resolutions. In addition, the client's thinking about the situation might have changed since she first called the office to schedule an appointment.

Beginning with the client's concerns is likely to give you more complete and accurate information. It will give you a fuller picture of the issues faced by the client and may lead you to see solutions that may not be readily apparent otherwise. Research in the medical field confirms this premise.[29] Medical training emphasizes that solicitation and development

---

[28] You should also not assume that what the client told your office is necessarily the same as what appears on your intake form. As we all know, things can get lost in the translation.

[29] Gay Gellhorn, *Law and Language: An Empirically–Based Model for the Opening Moments of Client Interviews*, 4 CLINICAL L. REV. 321, 335–336 (1998) (citing Howard B. Beckman &

of the patient's concern at the outset of the meeting is of critical importance to diagnosis and treatment; doing so helps to prevent forming premature hypotheses. It is also more cost-effective in the long run since it captures both content (the factual information the lawyer is trying to gather) and context (additional information relevant and related to the legal issues).[30] Clients often reveal key contextual material in the early stages of the interview, information that will be helpful as you proceed in the meeting. Unless you ask the client to define what she sees as the issue you may not get this information.

Two risks arise from your asking for the client's identification of the concern this early in the meeting. One risk is that you will begin to put legal labels on the client's issues based on these early cues, which may lead to your prejudging the client's situation and closing off other possibilities. Your goal throughout the interview will be to suspend your judgment as much as possible and not to apply your finely-honed legal analysis skills until you have a full and reliable picture of the client's goals and needs.

The second risk of asking for the client's take on the matter is that the client will go into an elaborate and detailed explanation of the issues involved. This risk, it seems to us, is well worth taking. The benefits of the client giving you a sense of how she sees the situation far outweigh the negative aspects of the client taking the conversation on a bit of a tangent. You can try to prevent the elaborate response by asking the client to give you the *short* version of her goals, promising that you will ask for more detail later. At the same time, it is important for the client to begin framing the issue from her perspective. More often than not, you will be the one who allows the interview to go off in a different direction by asking follow-up questions that take it there.

As you inquire broadly about the client's goals and needs, keep in mind that, if the person with whom you are meeting is a constituent of an organizational client, the vision you hear will be that as understood by that constituent, and may not necessarily represent the views of the group as a whole. This insight cannot change how you conduct this part of the interview, as you will only have the constituent available to learn what you need to know. But you will constantly be aware that any particular agent of an organization may not reflect perfectly the views of the larger entity.

Let us see what the issue identification might look like in the meeting Susan Cho has been having with Ms. Robinson:

Richard M. Frankel, *The Effect of Physician Behavior on the Collection of Data*, 101 ANNALS INTERNAL MED. 692 (1984)) (discussing an empirical study of medical interviews).

[30] *Id.* at 340.

Issue ID

Susan: Before I begin hearing about your work in more detail, I would like to have a brief sense of what brings you to get legal assistance—in other words, what your goals are and what do you see as possible ways of accomplishing those goals?

Ms. Robinson: Well, I would like to incorporate a new organization and be tax-exempt so I can continue doing the gardening work that I am doing with the kids in the neighborhood. I am trying to raise some funds to buy some supplies since right now I am doing it with my own money. We just received some money from the Heifer Foundation that gives me a little bit of a salary for the work I am doing. I would like to raise more money but everyone tells me that I will not get any more money unless I am a 501(c)(3).

Susan: Oh, I see. This is very helpful. It helps me understand a lot.

Many preliminary issue identification phases will take longer than the one above. You may need to ask more follow-up questions to get a fuller sense of what brings the client to the office. The risk in the preliminary issue identification phase is that you will go directly into asking detailed questions or that the client will go into more detail than you would like at this point in the meeting. You can see that Susan prompts Ms. Robinson not to go into too much detail at this point by saying she would like a "brief" sense of what brings her to seek legal assistance.

Did you notice that Susan's question to Ms. Robinson was actually two, or even three, questions rolled into one? Susan asked a "compound question." Compound questions present some problems. When you ask a compound question, you cannot be sure which of the questions the client is answering (and the client may not know which question you want answered first). As you can see from this example, it is not clear from Ms. Robinson's answer whether incorporating a new organization and getting recognition as a tax-exempt organization is Ms. Robinson's goal or what brings her to the lawyer's office. It is possible that the tax exemption issue is what brings her to the lawyer's office (say, because she has external pressure, such as from a foundation giving her financial support or from a board member), but that it is not her goal. She could have other goals. For instance, it is possible that if Susan asked Ms. Robinson about her goals directly she would talk about doing gardening work with children. When you ask a compound question (and you surely will, even if you try to avoid them), you will need to go back to make sure that you ask each question separately so that you will have all the information you want and need.

What do Ms. Robinson's answers reveal? Ms. Robinson confirms that she wants the clinic to help her incorporate a nonprofit organization and obtain tax-exempt status and that she is working with children. In addition, she tells us that she is already doing some work on the project (she also told Susan that during the introductory part of the meeting). She also tells Susan that she has received some funding already and that she sees the lack of tax exemption as keeping her from obtaining more funding. Susan also finds that Ms. Robinson is using some of her own money to finance her work. We begin to see that funds for the work, including a salary for herself, might be goals of Ms. Robinson, even if they are unarticulated at this point in the meeting. Also, although Ms. Robinson does not identify this issue explicitly, Susan should begin to have some concerns about potential liability issues since Ms. Robinson is working with children. With a clearer understanding of Ms. Robinson's goals, do you believe that incorporating a new organization and getting tax exemption are the only ways to achieve some of her goals? What might be other ways to achieve those goals?

Once Susan has explored her prospective client's goals, either in the fashion she did here (knowing that she will have the opportunity to explore them in greater depth as the interview proceeds) or with more follow-up questions, she will move to a more substantive, information-gathering segment of the interview. The next part of her plan, then, would be to gather general information about the client's story.

D. GATHERING GENERAL INFORMATION

The leading texts on interviewing in litigation matters suggest beginning fact gathering by having the client narrate a "chronology" of the events.[31] Some of the texts then recommend moving into a "theory development" phase where the lawyer takes a more active part in the meeting, as she begins to connect possible legal principles with the client's facts.[32] More often than not, transactional matters do not have a "chronology." While some do—say, a contract matter when the parties have already had extensive dealings and negotiations with each other before meeting with their attorneys or prior dealings with each other—most lack the narrative quality that litigation disputes have. Transactional cases encompass a wide range of legal subjects in different contexts. The client could be consulting you to create a new corporation or other business entity, or to draft a contract, such as a lease, real estate contract or a community benefits agreement. The client could be seeking advice regarding an employment relationship, or the client may consult a lawyer to protect some in-

---

[31] BINDER ET AL., *supra* note 12, at 111–12; STEFAN H. KRIEGER & RICHARD K. NEUMANN, JR., ESSENTIAL LAWYERING SKILLS: INTERVIEWING, COUNSELING, NEGOTIATION, AND PERSUASIVE FACT ANALYSIS 73–77 (4th ed. 2011) (suggesting that chronology is a good approach); ROBERT M. BASTRESS & JOSEPH D. HARBAUGH, INTERVIEWING, COUNSELING AND NEGOTIATION: SKILLS FOR EFFECTIVE REPRESENTATION 99–100 (1990) (suggesting that usually "the most efficient sequence for topics is chronological").

[32] BINDER ET AL., *supra* note 12, at 149–51.

tellectual property. These matters tend not to have a preexisting chronology or timeline available for the lawyer to explore.

Even if the client's matter does not lend itself to a timeline, you might think of the main fact-gathering part of the interview in transactional matters in two phases: one where you gather general information about the client and the matter and a second part where you gather more detailed information about the issues that the matter raises. In this section, we will discuss the first, general, part of the information gathering.

Eliciting a narrative from your client serves a couple of important purposes. Consistent with the aim we outlined earlier of resisting premature diagnosis, the narrative invites your client to describe in an open and undirected fashion what has led to her asking you for some help. In contrast with the following segment, where you inquire about more specific facts emerging from your legal analysis, the narrative overview limits any distortions your interpretive lens might create. The narrative, by its reliance on more open questions and greater client control, serves the further goal of affirming the centrality of the client's position in this interview. The interview is hers, not yours. The narrative gives her the floor.

Therefore, in this part of the interview, the client should be doing most of the talking. Your role should be to encourage the client to give you as full a picture as possible of its workings and planned activity. You accomplish this objective by using open-ended questions,[33] especially at the beginning of each sub-section. You will have the chance later on in the interview to fill in any gaps you think need filling.

In the absence of an apparent timeline by which to organize a narrative, you will need to consider other typical aspects of a transactional matter that lend themselves to a client's offering the broad overview that this segment hopes to achieve. Some ideas for the context of the narrative follow.

1. Information about the client and its work or business

In this part of the interview, you have the chance to gather information about the client. You will want to understand how your client operates, or hopes to operate, if the client is a start-up organization or business. You will inevitably want to understand the client's business or activities and its mission or vision for its work, whether nonprofit or for-profit. You may never be able to fully understand your client's goals without understanding its business or mission. This understanding in turn will be indispensable to counseling your clients. For example, in the Do-

---

[33] We discuss question types *infra* in Section IV.C.

mestic Workers Center project, you will need to understand workers centers generally and this particular workers center.[34]

2. General information about the matter

You will also want the client to begin to flesh out the details of her vision for the project or matter that brought her to look for a lawyer. In the issue identification part, the client will have given you a general sense of her reasons for consulting you and her goals for the project. You now want a fuller picture of the matter from the client's perspective. This inquiry includes significant non-legal information. What are the political, business, financial, social and other issues involved? Again, you should use open-ended questions to gather this information. You will have time to ask for details later.

3. Relationships and history

Every transactional client seeking the assistance of a lawyer has some "story" about why it is doing what it is doing at that moment. That story involves other persons, agencies and enterprises. The narrative phase of the interview is your opportunity to explore systematically what led the client to the point where it is today and which actors have influenced that development.

Let us observe what this narrative section of the interview might look like in the meeting with Ms. Robinson:

Susan: Ms. Robinson, I want to understand better the work you are doing. Why don't you tell me about it?

Ms. Robinson: Well, as I mentioned, I have been gardening in my backyard for a long time. I enjoy it. With so few healthy food options in the neighborhood I started growing more and more for my family. As my grandkids grew older I saw there were few options for healthy things to keep them occupied after school and during the summer when they are out of school. There just are not enough summer camp possibilities and those that are available do not keep the kids busy all day. Lots of parents and grandparents have to work so no one is watching the children when they get home from school. So I thought of combining my interest in gardening and the knowledge I've gotten over the years with my interest in doing something positive for the kids in the neighborhood.

Susan: That is wonderful. And so good that you have this expertise. When did you begin doing this work?

---

[34] For one description of workers centers, see Julie Yates Rivchin, *Building Power Among Low–Wage Immigrant Workers: Some Legal Considerations for Organizing Structures and Strategies,* 28 N.Y.U. REV. L. & SOC. CHANGE 397 (2004).

Ms. Robinson: Well, it kind of has grown over the last few years. Last summer, I had some kids help me with the community garden that I tend to in the neighborhood. Several families have plots but since I'm retired I am kind of the manager of the garden. I look after it. Then last fall the pastor at a local church started talking to me to see if I was interested in doing some work in the land that the church owns. One thing led to the other. The church paid to do an environmental study on the land to make sure it was not contaminated. In the early part of the winter I talked to some of the teachers at the local elementary school and found one interested in working with me through his science class. This spring, we got a grant to buy some tools and other supplies. Through the university's extension program I got some seeds. I got the students and the teacher from the science class to work with me to clear the land in March. We started some seeds in the school. The kids watered them. It was a challenge to get into the school during spring break but we managed to keep the seeds alive. We planted some things in the soil in the spring; later on we planted the seedlings. So as I said things have evolved over time.

Susan: Did you work with the kids over the summer?

Ms. Robinson: Some of the kids in the science class have stayed with me over the summer. Others from the neighborhood tagged along.

Susan: What did they do over the summer?

Ms. Robinson: We weeded the garden, harvested whatever was ready, planted new things and distributed the food we harvested. Some of the seeds you can keep planting throughout the growing season, so we did that. We got some geese and ducks as well so we fed them.

Susan: And now in the fall, are you working with kids still?

Ms. Robinson: Yes, I am back to working with the science teacher but he has a new group of students. Some of the ones from last year are working with me again as are the other neighborhood children who were not in the science class last year but found me over the summer. We have to build a shelter for the geese and ducks though the pastor is a bit concerned about that.

Susan: It sounds like you are doing great work. And that a number of different things fell into place together. What do you want to do? Do you want to keep doing what you have been doing? Do you want to do some different things?

Ms. Robinson: Well, a combination of things. . . .

In this part of the interview, Susan learns more about Ms. Robinson's work. She began by asking a broad open-ended question, asking Ms. Robinson to tell her about her work. Even though Ms. Robinson wants to create a new organization, she has already begun the work of that organization. Learning about the work Ms. Robinson has been doing allows Susan to learn about the work Ms. Robinson proposes for the new organization. You can see that Ms. Robinson is doing most of the talking in this segment. Susan prompts Ms. Robinson to continue by narrowing the scope of her questions, yet still asks open-ended questions, such as "When did you begin doing this work?" Susan does ask some narrow questions, including a "yes-no" question, "Did you work with kids over the summer?" Susan transitions to the next phase of the interview by asking what Ms. Robinson wants to do in the future.

Note how this narrative from Ms. Robinson includes some sense of a timeline or chronology, especially when Susan learns about the collaborating between Ms. Robinson and the local church and the local school. ("One thing led to the other.") Think about how Susan might explore this time line more systematically. Could Susan learn more about this "story" with more texture without succumbing to a host of detailed, closed questions?

We have seen how the general information-gathering part of the interview might proceed for a start-up organization. Let us now see how that phase might proceed with an organization that has been in existence for some time. Let us switch focus to the initial information gathering part of the meeting with Amanda Estrada, the Executive Director of the DWC, who wants the clinic to negotiate a lease for its office space. Alex Taylor and Laura Gonzalez are the clinic students working with DWC. Let us assume that during the issue identification stage, the students learned from Ms. Estrada that DWC is looking for new space since its lease is expiring and the organization is outgrowing its current office. DWC's five-year lease ends in six months. Ms. Estrada knows Scott Jones, the Executive Director of Eastlake Family Services (Eastlake), and she knew that Eastlake was in the process of buying a building to consolidate its operations. Eastlake rents space for its administrative staff in various buildings throughout the city. It has decided that it wants everyone together in one space and it has an opportunity to buy a building. Let us now go to the beginning of the information-gathering phase of this initial interview:

Alex: Ms. Estrada, we would like to hear from you about the work of DWC and the lease situation. It would be very helpful to

us to hear about the work of DWC first. We are a bit familiar with what DWC does but it would be good to have you
tell us about that work.

Ms. Estrada: Well, we are a workers center for domestic workers,
nannies, caregivers to the elderly and housekeepers. In that
sense we take a sectoral approach to our work. We are a
membership organization. We provide training for our
members, leadership training, computer classes and nanny
training courses. We also provide legal services to members
with the aim of enforcing labor laws. We also conduct research about workers in the sector, which is a challenge
since most of them work in isolation. We organize those
workers and do policy work to improve the working conditions of the workers and promote fair labor standards and
an end to exploitation and oppression. That's a combination
of our mission and work on a day-to-day basis.

Alex: When you say a sectoral approach, what do you mean?

Ms. Estrada: That instead of organizing all workers in the city, we
take a sector of workers, domestic workers in our case, and
work with them. Some workers centers work with all workers. We have decided to work with a subset of workers
thinking that it's a more effective way to organize and do
policy work.

We have seen Laura and Alex get more information about the organization, the client's business and work in this first part of the information
gathering phase of the interview. Ms. Estrada gave a very detailed explanation of the work of the organization so Alex asks very few questions,
many fewer than Susan in the previous example. Let us now see how the
students move to gathering information about the matter:

Laura: Understanding the work of DWC is very helpful to us as we
try to understand the project more. I think that explanation
was very helpful as we move forward. We had looked at the
organization's web page but having you explain the individual projects that you take on is very useful. We'd also like to
get more details of the lease situation. Why don't you tell us
about your dealings with Eastlake Family Services so far. If
you can, it would be helpful if you could tell us in chronological order.

Ms. Estrada: One day about three weeks ago I saw Scott Jones at a
breakfast event, we were talking about ED stuff, we got to
talking about space and I think the light bulb went off in
both of our heads. The building they are buying is larger
than they need; they would not mind having some income to

help with their mortgage. So we started talking about the possibility of DWC renting space from them. I know the building they are looking to buy and he told me they plan to do some build-out of the space. He tells me the building is solid but the offices need cosmetic work. The next day, I looked at our current space and figured our space needs and after talking to the President of our Board, I emailed Scott about our interest and needs. He responded that he was interested in the idea and told me he would try to schedule a meeting with me, him, and their Chief Operating Officer who is also a lawyer.

Laura: Has that meeting taken place yet?

Ms. Estrada: No. I have not pushed to schedule it. The President of our Board did not think we should go to the meeting without having legal help especially since their COO is a lawyer. So I called the clinic to schedule an appointment. I've worked with the clinic before. But time is ticking for us because if this does not work out then we have to look at other space.

Laura: Have you had any other conversations with Mr. Jones since that breakfast meeting and the email message?

Ms. Estrada: I have seen him in passing and we both say we need to follow up but no, other than that vague mention we have not discussed any details with him or his COO.

Laura began this part of the questioning by asking an open-ended question—"tell us about your dealings with Eastlake Family Services." Laura focuses the question on the lease matter but gives Ms. Estrada broad discretion in what to discuss. Laura then prompts Ms. Estrada for additional information by asking, "Has that meeting taken place?" At the end, she tries to get a full chronology by asking "Have you had any other conversations with Mr. Jones?" For the most part, Laura allows Ms. Estrada do the talking without interrupting to get more details. Laura and Alex decide to ask for the telling of the story in a chronological order.

The students have not—yet, at least—explored the history of DWC's operations and its experiences during its current five-year lease. Would understanding that background and narrative be useful to the students as they contemplate representing DWC on a new lease negotiation? If so, would you have asked about the topic before the Eastlake lease discussion? And if you wished to cover the topic at some time during this segment, how would you do so?

As you can see from these two examples, the initial information gathering will differ depending on the client and the matter. The goal in this section is for the client to describe in her words the issues that bring her to seek legal assistance and provide you with enough information to understand how the client operates. In certain matters, it might help to ask for the information in chronological order. In the case of DWC, a series of events took place before Ms. Estrada came to the clinic. Asking for the chronology of events may help Ms. Estrada recall the dealings between the parties up to this point and give you a better sense of the state of negotiations. The information you gather about the client and the matter should give you a good background to move on to the next level of the interview, which is gathering detailed information specific to the matter.

E. GATHERING DETAILED INFORMATION SPECIFIC TO THE MATTER

Once you have heard the overall narrative from your client, the goal for the next part of the interview is to gather enough information that will allow you to begin to assess the client's situation and goals, and plan some possible avenues for reaching those goals. Ultimately, at the end of the interview you want to have sufficient information to create a plan for proceeding, begin to take actions, or continue to research avenues. It is in this part of the interview that you will fill in the blanks from the other parts of the interview. You will play a more active role in this segment. In many ways this part can be the most challenging one of the interview. It is the section of the interview that requires the most planning and at the same time the one that requires the greatest flexibility on your part. It is the section of the interview that is more likely to be unorganized if you have not thought it through, yet it is the part of the interview that will require you to do the most thinking in the moment.

The primary activity in this part of the interview will be your asking questions regarding the various topics that you identify as relevant to the issues the client's matter presents. The specific topics will differ depending on the matter, of course. Your questions will be informed by your research and your knowledge of the law. As the client was telling you her goals and how she envisioned reaching those goals in the previous part of the meeting, you were beginning to think of the issues presented by the project. It is important, regardless of how you approach the topics, that your question format be organized. In structuring this part of the interview you need to determine the important elements of the project that the client has brought to your office. In cases where there are statutes and regulations covering a particular matter, what do the statutes and regulations require? What are best practices in these types of transactions? What are the possible ways the client might be able to achieve her goals?

Your interview will be more effective if you can complete one topic before moving on to the next. Covering topics fully before moving on to the next will ensure that you do not get sidetracked and forget to go back to the original topic. Staying on one topic until you exhaust it also helps the client recall information. If new topics come up as you explore one, "park" that new topic until you complete the current topic.[35] You can "park" it by writing it down so you can remember to go back to that topic.

In the litigation context, the *Lawyers as Counselors* text refers to this phase of the interview as "theory development," the phase where you look for evidence that bolsters your client's case and look to counter your adversary's legal contentions.[36] The lawyer begins identifying the legal theories that apply to the client's case and breaking them into their constituent elements. The process involves restating the legal elements of a theory as factual propositions and then looking for those facts during the theory development phase of the interview.

In transactional matters, the lawyer often goes through a similar process. Transactional projects that are grounded in statutes, regulations and case law are based on particular legal principles. The lawyer's role in those projects is to determine if the client's facts are consistent with those legal principles. The transactional lawyer's role in these projects, however, is much more forward-looking, compared to the litigator's act of looking back at something that has already happened. In your transactional work, some of the "facts" already exist, but others are yet to be created by the parties in the transaction. The transactional lawyer's "discovery" of the information may be based on the client's wishes and aspirations instead of on historical information.

The transactional lawyer, then, is not filling in the blanks of what happened, but instead learning what may happen. The process of questioning is similar, though. Instead of asking the client "Did *X* happen?" the transactional lawyer asks the client how she would feel about *Y* and *Z* happening. This process requires that the lawyer obtain a complete understanding of the client's goals and begin thinking about all the possible ways to achieve those goals. You do not have to think of all the possibilities in the interview, but the more you cover, the more successful the meeting will be. Preparation is key.

Your exploration of each topic should proceed in an organized way by exploring one topic before moving on to the next. You should begin the questioning under each topic with open-ended questions and move to closed questions if those are necessary to explore greater detail that you did not obtain with the open-ended questions. The authors of *Lawyers as Counselors* refer to this technique as the "T-funnel" questioning pattern.[37] The information gathering on a particular topic is done by a combination of open and closed questions, beginning with open-ended questions and

---

[35] The "parking" metaphor comes from the Binder & Price models. *See* BINDER ET AL., *supra* note 12, at 176–78.

[36] *Id.* at 151. For a detailed discussion of "theory development questioning," see *id.* at 151–96.

[37] *Id.* at 169–84.

then followed by closed questions to fill in details and eliminate other options. Open-ended questions invite the client to share whatever comes to her mind related to a topic. Closed questions allow you to identify information based on your legal knowledge that might not occur to the client.[38] Closed questions also try to elicit the details that might not come out in the answers to the open questions.

Let us return to the meeting with Ms. Robinson. Your initial "legal theories," the topics you will cover in the meeting, are taken from your state's nonprofit act and the requirements for charitable organizations of the Internal Revenue Code. Before your meeting with her, in addition to reading the Internal Revenue Service (IRS) regulations, you will have reviewed IRS Form 1023, the form you will have to complete to request tax exemption. We will let you determine what your state's nonprofit act requires.

Given what we know about Ms. Robinson's desires and the basics of nonprofit formation, your topics for this part of the interview might include:

1. What the group wants to be able to do (its mission);

2. The day-to-day work the group will do (its programs);

3. The people involved (including possible board members and staff);

4. Financial issues—how they plan on funding and carrying out their work, including budget and fundraising;

5. Why they want to incorporate and get tax exemption;

6. Timelines and any deadlines;

7. The geographic area where the group wants to work; and

8. Possible collaboration with other groups (including the church or the school).

What other topics might you explore?

Because these topics are interesting to you and to Ms. Robinson, and because some of them relate to each other, you might have a tendency to skip around and ask questions as they occur to you. That will make the interview less focused, however. Take the time to think whether you have exhausted a topic before moving on to the next. This is the time where preparation will pay off. If you have thought through the interview, you will have prepared most of the areas you want to delve into. But some silence is fine in the meeting, as you decide whether it is time to move to a new topic.

---

[38] *Id.* at 70–71.

Let us review how the questions for Ms. Robinson regarding its mission (topic 1 above) might proceed:

Susan: Ms. Robinson, I'd like to hear a bit more about the mission of the group, what you want to be able to accomplish as a result of your work?

Ms. Robinson: Oh, I think a number of things. I want to teach kids about eating right. With the obesity epidemic in this country and the lack of healthy food options in our communities, I want them to see that there are other ways. In that sense I want to teach them about taking care of their bodies, themselves. Maybe that teaches them some self-esteem.

Susan: I see.

Ms. Robinson: And by getting at the kids I am trying to impact the families, hoping that the kids will move the family to consider healthier food.

Susan: That is very nice. You've covered a number of things. Are there other things you want the organization to be able to do?

Ms. Robinson: I also want to teach kids about taking care of our earth in addition to taking care of their bodies.

Susan: Go on.

Ms. Robinson: Understanding the choices each of us can make. How to compost. How so much of the land is contaminated. How they might be able to do their part but also to create some awareness so they can push their school to compost or recycle more.

Susan: So, teaching them about taking care of themselves, their bodies, by the food they put into it. And teaching them about taking care of the earth. Any other things you are trying to accomplish?

Ms. Robinson: I also want to teach the kids by doing, so they'll learn about science and expose them to different jobs and careers. We work with plants and animals. I want them to understand how the worms turn waste into compost. We have the geese and ducks. I want to have fish tanks as well where we can grow tilapia. I want them to see fish grow and reproduce and understand that.

Susan: Will you be doing that work as part of the organization or with the schools?

Ms. Robinson: A little bit of both. I don't know the science but I am learning some of it. But finding that schoolteacher who was interested gave me the idea to try to do more. So I have not totally thought through how that might work. Whether that will be a permanent thing depends on the school.

Susan: Anything else?

Ms. Robinson: Well, down the line I'd like for us to be able to sell what we grow at a farmer's market in the neighborhood so we expand the people who have access to healthy food. So it's not just the kids I'm working with. But we are not there yet. That's all.

Susan: So you want to provide fresh and healthy food to the broader community as well, beyond the children that will work with you.

Ms. Robinson: Yes.

Susan: Any other things you'd like the organization to be able to accomplish?

Ms. Robinson: No that's it. That's enough don't you think?

Susan: I think these are great things you are trying to do. Will you work only with children or do you see your environmental and healthy food work trying to reach the community generally, beyond making some of what you grow available more generally to the community down the road?

Ms. Robinson: I want to work with kids only. They can be the way we reach the parents and grandparents. I think it's much harder to change the parents and grandparents.

Susan: Where do you see yourself doing this work, only in your neighborhood, in the entire city, in the region? *Scope*

Ms. Robinson: I am only thinking about the neighborhood now. That's all I can manage. Plus there are others doing this type of work in other parts of the city.

Susan: I hear in what you are saying that much of what you want to do is teach children about different things. Do you think teaching is the main way you will do this work?

This conversation can go on a bit longer as Susan explores the mission of the organization. It might end with Susan asking Ms. Robinson if she has a mission or purpose statement in mind for the organization. Susan's organization of topics was driven by the requirements of the state nonprofit organization statute and the IRS regulations. Susan has chosen to start with the mission of the organization since she will need a purpose statement in order to file the Articles of Incorporation with the state corporate office. Ms. Robinson's description of what she hopes to achieve with her work will help Susan draft that purpose statement. Susan also wants to know if the mission of the organization satisfies the IRS standard for tax exemption. Some of her questions about the purpose of the organization were framed by trying to determine if the IRS would classify the nonprofit organization as a charitable or educational organization.[39] Susan would then continue her questions by topic and try to get enough information to determine if the organization would meet the IRS definition of charitable and help her begin to draft the Articles of Incorporation.

As Susan completes one topic and prepares to move to the next one on her outline, she could do two additional things. She could summarize for Ms. Robinson what she has learned about the just-completed topic. That summary not only helps Susan confirm that she understood her client, but it also permits Ms. Robinson to add anything new or different. It also helps the client understand that she has been heard. The second thing Susan might do is to label the fact that she is ending one topic and moving on to a new topic. Doing so helps Susan and Ms. Robinson to follow explicitly the structure of the meeting.

Let us now move to the meeting with Ms. Estrada, who has come to the clinic with a desire to achieve a lease. Compared to the last example, the questions in this interview will not be informed by a particular statute or regulations, although most likely there will be some case law in your state regarding interpretations of lease provisions.[40] Here, your structure will be informed by what could be characterized as "best practices" or "business practices." Your outline of the topics you will want to explore in this part of the interview might be as follows:

1. Premises to be leased (the building layout, any common areas included, parking);

2. Rent (including how increases over time will be calculated, taxes, late payments);

3. Services included in the rent (such as cleaning, trash removal, any snow removal or landscaping, extermination);

4. Term of lease (start and duration of lease, renewal and termination provisions);

5. Utilities (who provides and pays for heat, air conditioning, water, hot water, telephone and other communication equipment; if provided by the landlord, times when they are provided);

---

[39] 26 C.F.R. § 1.501(c)(3) (2008) (specifically subsections 1(d)(2) and 1(d)(3)).

[40] There might be case law surrounding evictions in commercial lease situations as well.

6. Maintenance and repairs (which party will maintain and repair what—plumbing, electrical, HVAC, structural and non-structural repairs);

7. Signs;

8. Time issues, including:

    a. Closing date for Eastlake;
    b. Firmness of that date (is financing in place?);
    c. Lease term for current space for DWC;
    d. Build-out for new space;
    e. Proposed move-in date; and

9. DWC's insurance policy (the extent of coverage).

Because of the length of this list of topics, Alex and Laura will have to decide if they can be ready to discuss all the provisions DWC will like included in the lease at the initial meeting. But note that some of these items do not capture "facts" the students would learn from Ms. Estrada, but instead possible *future* terms she and DWC may want to adopt. As an interviewing matter (as opposed to the students' *counseling* meeting with DWC at a later date), the students will need to develop a plan about how to question the client about these items in an early meeting. A more experienced attorney may be able to combine both into one meeting. A less experienced lawyer may not be able to do both in one meeting. It is also possible that Ms. Estrada will not have time to do both in one meeting or she may want DWC's board of directors involved in those decisions.

Let us observe Alex and Laura gather more detailed information for the lease, using the T-funneling technique described earlier:

Alex: Ms. Estrada, now we'd like to get more details about the lease. We'd like to discuss the space, rent, length of the lease, what would be included in the rent, such as services, utilities, maintenance and repairs, signs, timing issues and insurance. Are there any other topics you think we should discuss today?

Ms. Estrada: No, I'm looking to you to give me the ideas. I can't think of any others right now. You've just listed more than I came up with.

Alex: Okay. What we'd like to do is go through each topic and explore it fully before moving to the next. Which topic would you like to discuss first?

Ms. Estrada: Let's talk about rent. It's what my Board is most concerned about.

Alex: Okay, let's start there.

. . . . .

Alex: Okay, I think that's all I need to cover today for the issues of repairs and maintenance. I think the last topic we wanted to cover was timing questions, so let's move to that topic.

Ms. Estrada: Okay.

Alex: Tell us what you know about the timing involved in this project.

Ms. Estrada: Well, I can only tell you from our end since I don't know much about Eastlake. We have six more months left on our lease but we have to notify the landlord in the next two months if we are going to renew.

Alex: I'd like to see a copy of your current lease to give me a better sense of the language. How easy do you think it will be for your landlord to lease out your space?

Ms. Estrada: I don't think it will be that easy so we may have some time past that four month time. But I don't want to get too close to the end date in case we have to find another space. It takes a lot of planning to move an office. If the lease with Eastlake falls apart and our landlord finds another tenant, then we are really in trouble.

Alex: Have you thought about the possibility of trying to stay at your current location for a few more months until things can be worked out or until you have a better sense of where things are going?

Ms. Estrada: I had not thought about that. Everything is happening so quickly that all my energy has gone to thinking about making this happen.

Alex: Well, what do you think about that idea?

Ms. Estrada: I think it's a good idea if we can make it work.

Alex: Do you think your landlord might be receptive to letting DWC extend its lease on a month-to-month basis if you could not be out by the end of the lease, but, let's say a month or two after that?

Ms. Estrada: I think so. They have been great. It's a question of whether they would have the space rented. I just would not want to wait too much longer to ask them that. Or whether they think that waiting will make it more difficult to lease the space because of the time of year.

Alex: Do you know when Eastlake is going to close on its building?

Ms. Estrada: They were supposed to have closed at the end of last month but I am not sure they did. I'm not sure when it's supposed to happen or if it has happened. I don't think it has happened. I think Mr. Jones would have called me but it might be that he is just too busy. I have not wanted to follow up once my board suggested I get legal help.

Alex: Do you think they know?

Ms. Estrada: I don't know.

Alex: Do you think they'd tell you if they knew?

Ms. Estrada: I am not sure.

Alex: Do you know what their financing situation is like?

Ms. Estrada: Not totally. I know they have some conventional financing in place but I've also heard a rumor that they have been doing a capital campaign for some time in order to buy a building. I just don't know if they raised all they needed to raise to buy and rehab the building.

Alex: Do you know anything about the contingencies in their purchase contract?

Ms. Estrada: I am not sure. I think they are applying for some loans but they have been doing a capital campaign for a while. I just don't know if they have raised the money they needed to.

Alex: Do you know if they need to do structural things to the building before they move in?

Ms. Estrada: No, I don't know those details.

Alex: What would you need in terms of build-out to move in?

. . . .

In this section of the interview Alex seeks to gather more detailed information about the matter. Alex starts each topic by signaling to Ms. Estrada that he is moving to the next topic and asking an open-ended question. He then fills in details by asking closed questions and, in some instances, "yes-no" questions. Look back at Alex's choice of questions on the timeline topic above. Do you think he asked enough open-ended questions before he moved to his narrower questions? What feedback would you give him about his questioning patterns?

This segment of the interview completes your information gathering. Before you end it, you will want to be as confident as you can that you have not missed anything critical. You will ask your client a question or two—perhaps in combination with a summary of what you have learned thus far—to confirm that it is appropriate to move on to the final part of the interview. Let us see how Susan does this:

Susan: Ms. Robinson, I think our conversation has given me a pretty good idea of what you would like to do. If I might summarize briefly, [and here Susan describes what Ms. Robinson has told her so far]. Is there anything else you think might be helpful for me to know?

Ms. Robinson: No, I think we've talked about everything I was thinking and more.

F. CONCLUDING INITIAL CLIENT INTERVIEWS

At the beginning of the meeting, you told the client what you wanted to discuss in this initial meeting. Did you do what you promised? At the conclusion of the meeting you should:

1. Discuss establishing an attorney-client relationship;

2. Establish a fee arrangement;

3. Outline for the client what you see as the next steps (for you and for her); and

4. Ask for any documents or other information you need.

Depending on the arrangements in the clinic, you might need to discuss whether there will be an ongoing attorney-client relationship.[41] In that case, you will need to discuss the process for deciding whether to take on representation. If the clinic has already decided to take on representation, you should inform the client about that, even if you think she already knows it. If not, you will need to tell the client what needs to happen before you can make that decision. If you do not have the authority to make that decision, you will need to explain to the client how the clinic will reach its decision and how and when you will communicate that decision to the client. Of course, the formation of a relationship requires that the client hire you as the lawyer as well. You should not assume that the client will hire you just because you would accept representation. It is your responsibility to initiate this conversation. Just as you may need some time before deciding whether to have the clinic agree to represent the client, the client may need some time to decide whether to accept an offer of representation.

Assuming the client will retain your services, you should discuss the scope of that relationship. What has the client authorized you to do? What are you willing to do for the client? Do not assume that either will be

---

[41] Of course, in your role as an interviewer with a prospective client, you are acting as a lawyer and most of the attorney-client responsibilities are in place for that limited interaction. *See* MODEL RULES OF PROF'L CONDUCT R. 1.18 (2012).

clear. You should have a clear conversation with the client regarding what you are willing or able to do. Finally, you should discuss any letter of engagement or retainer agreement that your office uses.[42]

At the beginning of the meeting, you may have discussed fees with the client. If you only discussed the fees for the initial consultation, you will need to have a more detailed conversation regarding fees at this point. Raising the topic during the initial meeting will allow the client to ask questions and clear up any confusion. Even if your office does not charge fees, you should discuss the issue of costs. Though your retainer agreement will discuss fees and costs, raising it at the initial meeting will allow you to give the client a cost estimate.

You will also need to discuss what you see as the next steps. Assuming a relationship is established, you should tell the client the steps you intend to take in the immediate future and when you will take those steps. At the conclusion of the meeting, the client should be clear regarding your expectations for what she will do as well. Do you need some documents or information from the client? You will want to have a sense of when you can expect that information as well. Even if you asked for the information during the meeting, it is a good idea to summarize your requests at the end of the meeting.

Depending on the situation, you may need to explain to the client something about the area of law. At the conclusion of your interview with Ms. Robinson, you might explain the process for incorporating a nonprofit organization and obtaining tax-exempt status. You may want to explain some of the requirements for a new organization. If you have raised certain concerns during the meeting, you might want to highlight those for her. Even if the organization has not yet established a purpose statement, do you want to give Ms. Robinson a sense of whether the new organization's goals satisfy the IRS's definition of "charitable" or "educational"?

Finally, you should give the client an opportunity to ask any questions she may not have asked during the rest of the meeting. Let us see how Susan concludes the meeting with Ms. Robinson:

Susan: Ms. Robinson, before we finish, there are a few things I'd like to discuss with you. I told you at the beginning of the interview that we would discuss whether you would want to retain the clinic to help you with this project and whether the clinic can help you. I spoke with my supervising attorney before the meeting, and based on what you've told me today we would be happy to work with you on this project. I think

---

[42] Some clinics send the client an "engagement letter." Other offices will employ a formal retainer agreement, signed by the client and a representative of the clinic (perhaps you). In the latter setting, you might bring a template agreement with you to the initial meeting to complete at the end of the meeting.

you are doing great work and would like to support it. We would like to help you to decide the best way to proceed. So we can commit at this point to help you make some decisions about what you think is best. I would like to help you think about doing your work by starting a new organization or exploring options for doing your work without incorporating a new organization. If this would be agreeable to you, the clinic can put this in writing in a letter of engagement. Do you think you would like to hire the clinic to work with you?

Ms. Robinson: Yes, I'd love the help. I just don't have time to figure these things out. But what if I decide I want to start a new organization?

Susan: If that's what you decide we can do that. I think we can write the letter of engagement that way.

Ms. Robinson: Okay.

Susan: I'd also like to discuss the issue of costs with you. As I mentioned at the beginning of our meeting today, the clinic does not charge fees for its services. But if there are any costs associated with our work we would expect you or the organization to pay those. For example, if you decide you want to incorporate and apply for tax-exempt status from the IRS, the organization would be responsible for the costs of filing the incorporation documents with the state and the IRS fees for filing the tax exemption application.

Ms. Robinson: What would those be?

Susan: Incorporation costs $40 in our state[43] and the cost of the tax exemption application depends of the organization's budget; if the organization's budget in the first few years is below $10,000 a year it costs $400, and if the budget is over $10,000 it's $850.[44]

Ms. Robinson: Do I need to have that money now?

Susan: No, you don't need to have it now. But if you decided you wanted to go that route then we would need to know you had it or could get it soon before we filled out the paperwork.

Ms. Robinson: Okay.

Susan: But, as I said, I think we would like to explore other options with you first so you can make a decision based on all the

---

[43] Obviously, this number will differ depending on your jurisdiction.

[44] *Exempt Organizations User Fees - 2012*, Internal Rev. Serv., http://www.irs.gov/ Charities-&-Nonprofits/Exempt-Organizations-User-Fees-2012. You will perform your own research before advising any of your clients, of course.

options. What I think makes sense is for me to do more research and some thinking about what might be good ways to
proceed and then meet with you again. At that point I think
I could present some options for you and then we can take it
from there.

Ms. Robinson: When would that be?

Susan: That's a great question. I think I can be ready in two to
three weeks. I'll call you next week or the week after that to
schedule another meeting with you.

Ms. Robinson: Okay.

Susan: At that time I can be ready to discuss what I see as the various options you have and hopefully you can make a decision
then. Before then, I'll send you the letter of engagement. We
will need to get it back from you before we can start working
on this though.

Ms. Robinson: Okay. When will you send it?

Susan: I think I can send it tomorrow or the day after. Let's say the
day after to be safe. When you receive it, let me know if you
have any questions. Otherwise, sign it and send it back to
us. Oh, I forgot to ask, have you come up with a name for
what you'd like to call the new organization?

Ms. Robinson: No, not yet.

Susan: That's fine. Before we end today, do you have any questions?
Is there anything else you would like to discuss?

Ms. Robinson: No, I think we've covered the main questions I had.

Susan: Okay. I'll be in touch soon. It was a pleasure to meet you
and I am looking forward to working with you.

Ms. Robinson: Thank you for your time. It was good to meet you as
well. I'll wait to hear from you.

In this dialogue, Susan covers the issues she must address before the
meeting ends. She clarifies the relationship status, plans for a letter of
engagement, advises Ms. Robinson about costs, and establishes a timeline
for the next steps (with a helpful nudge from her client). What Susan did
not have to do here, but you very well may, is to answer some questions
about the fine points of the law as applied to the client's project. A client
might ask you, "So, is this a strong case for tax exemption?" Or, perhaps,
"Do you think it's safer for me to establish a nonprofit corporation?" Most
of the times you will not want to answer these questions, because you will
not be *able* to answer these questions. You should prepare some explana-

tion in advance to use when your client asks you for your legal advice at the end of an interview. You might say something like this:

> That's exactly the question I'd expect you to ask, and I'd love to tell you my opinion. But I can't tell you whether you have a strong case because I'll need to spend more time with your papers and with the law. I'll need to continue my research and to learn more about your business. We will surely discuss that question in one of our later meetings. Is it okay with you if I don't answer that right now?

After the meeting, while the conversation is still fresh in her mind, Susan will write a memorandum to the file summarizing her meeting with Ms. Robinson. She will draft the letter of engagement for her supervisor's approval. You will learn more about how a student like Susan might proceed in planning this project in the chapter on Organizing Your Transactional Work.

How might you end the meeting with Ms. Estrada?

IV. SOME ADDITIONAL ISSUES FOR THE INITIAL CLIENT INTERVIEW

Up to now, we have offered a semblance of a structure or model for how you might organize your client interviews. This section of the chapter will cover a number of issues that will arise during the interview process but not covered above, such as listening skills, inhibitors and facilitators to communication, the types of questions you should use at different times in the interview, note-taking and the need for flexibility throughout the interview process.

A. LISTENING

Listening is one of the most important lawyering skills. In the interviewing context, listening is key to building an effective relationship with the prospective client and gathering information. You might ask yourself, "How can I listen when I have to keep track of so much during the interview?" Being present in the moment is key to being able to listen. Even experienced interviewers can be distracted by what is going on in their professional or personal lives, by the client, or by other performance distractors. You might be thinking of the deadlines you have in other matters or in other classes. You might be thinking about the argument you had with your partner yesterday or your sick child. You might want to make an especially good impression on this client, perhaps because you want his business or the referrals he might be able to make through his connections. This client might have a very interesting and intellectually challenging project. Or you might want to prove to yourself, the client, your supervisor or your clinic partner that you are competent. Regardless of whether you are a student conducting your first attorney-client interview or an experienced attorney, it takes effort to concentrate on what the client is saying during an interview.

Genuine listening requires concentration and discipline.[45] True listening requires us to "bracket," to temporarily give up or set aside our prejudices and frames of reference so as to experience as much as possible the speaker's world from the inside, "stepping inside his or her shoes."[46] True listening requires that we suspend judgment and assumptions, and refrain from evaluating, disagreeing, giving advice, or preparing a response. You might say, "Is the purpose of the initial interview not to gather the relevant information and identify the legal issues?" It is, but listening requires that we listen to the client's story first, explore and understand it fully, before beginning the work of legal strategy. Without listening to and understanding the client's goals, motivation and perspective, your legal representation will likely suffer. As lawyers we are trained to separate the relevant from the irrelevant, to spot legal issues, to measure the client's story against legal paradigms and to slot client information into certain legal boxes or categories. Listening requires that we pay attention to the client's feelings, motivations, relationships and priorities.[47]

Though we discuss some listening techniques below, effective listening is more than a technique. Listening is "an attitude, a motivation, a disposition."[48] Lawyers need the ability to listen and judge accurately what a client is saying. A lawyer can learn more from the client when the client feels she is being heard and understood. As a result, listening helps build rapport. The lawyer's first step in listening is to hear and understand the content and the feeling of a client's statement. The second step is communicating to the client what the lawyer has heard from the client.[49] You can communicate to the client that you are listening using a number of techniques. *Passive listening* techniques encourage the client to talk without much prompting from you. *Active listening* techniques reflect an understanding of the client's message to you with you using other words, and it lets the client know that you understand what she is trying to say.

One important *passive listening* technique is silence. Silence gives space for the client to collect her thoughts and to continue talking or to respond when she feels comfortable or is ready to continue. You will have

---

[45] Timothy W. Floyd, *Spirituality and Practicing Law as a Healing Profession: The Importance of Listening, in* THE AFFECTIVE ASSISTANCE OF COUNSEL: PRACTICING LAW AS A HEALING PROFESSION 473, 487 (Marjorie A. Silver ed., 2007).

[46] *Id.* (citing M. SCOTT PECK, THE ROAD LESS TRAVELED 127–28 (1978)).

[47] *Id.*

[48] *Id.* at 489.

[49] John L. Barkai, *How to Develop the Skill of Active Listening*, 30 THE PRACTICAL LAWYER 73, 75 (1984).

to make a judgment as to whether and how long to allow the silence to go on, and you can gauge the appropriate amount of time by looking for non-verbal cues. Other passive listening techniques include facilitators, continuers, or minimal prompts. Each is another way to communicate that you are listening without any content. These prompts include "Mm-hmm," "Uh-huh," "Interesting," "Really," "You did, eh?," "Oh," "I see," "Hmm," "I understand," "Sure, sure," "Yes," or "Go on."[50] Non-verbal facilitators, such as hand gestures and facial expressions including nodding, leaning forward and eye contact, are other techniques for communicating to the client that you are listening and that she should continue. Open-ended questions or statements allow you to communicate to the client that she should continue without your interrupting her. These include "Please continue," "Can you tell me more about that?," "What else happened?," or "What other concerns do you have?" These techniques, with little interruption, communicate to the client that you want her to continue talking.

Contrast the passive listening techniques with a more active approach. *Active listening* reflects the client's statements back to him in a form that mirrors what you have heard. These responses are not a mere repetition of what the client said. Instead, they demonstrate to the client that you heard and understood what he is saying. Active listening responses may mirror both content and feeling. Since the client feels understood, the response encourages the client to continue talking. Through active listening you can respond to feelings that are expressed vaguely as well as unstated feelings in addition to feelings that are clearly articulated. Active listening requires that we discern whether we are accurately identifying the content or the feeling expressed by the client and the intensity, strength, or level of feeling expressed.[51] Active listening is not easy; it requires hearing the client accurately and then "immediately verbalizing, in different words, the content of the speaker's feeling."[52] The emotional dimension of the client's words can be expressed directly or can be implied from the words the client may use. We engage in empathy when we use active listening to respond exclusively to the client's feelings.[53] Talking about feelings may get the client to disclose more information, and as a result may give the lawyer more information about the underlying facts that may be of "legal significance" to the matter.[54]

Let us observe what an active listening response might look like for a client interested in creating a limited liability company, to be owned by three sisters, to run a bakery:

---

[50] Gellhorn, *supra* note 29, at 346–47; BINDER ET AL., *supra* note 12, at 45; Barkai, *supra* note 49, at 75.

[51] Barkai, *supra* note 49, at 78–79.

[52] *Id.* at 74.

[53] *Id.* at 75.

[54] *Id.* at 77.

Client: I want to make sure that the operating agreement is drafted so it's the three of us who control the business decisions and no one else. I think we can work it out. We've been working through disagreements all our lives.

Lawyer: I'm quite sure we can accomplish that goal. But do I hear from you some concerns about this arrangement?

Client: For some crazy reason that I do not get, my youngest sister has given a power of attorney to her husband. I want to make sure he does not have power over the bakery though. He is a know-it-all and thinks he knows better than anyone else. It's one thing to have to deal with him in family matters but to have to deal with him in the bakery. I could not handle that!

Lawyer: So you are puzzled by your sister's giving of that decision-making power to your brother-in-law and you want to make sure that he cannot meddle in the business directly.

In this short interchange we see a client expressing strong feelings in a business matter. Whether it is business matters between family members, total strangers, people with previous dealings or disagreements between community members, feelings are almost always involved in our work. We enhance our communication with our clients if we understand those feelings and are able to acknowledge how they affect the client. It is important to understand that active listening does not mean that the lawyer agrees with the client's view. It only means that the lawyer understands the feeling and communicates that understanding to the client. If the lawyer continues with questions and does not acknowledge client feelings, especially when expressed explicitly, the client may feel ignored or that she has not been heard.

How often you use each technique discussed here will depend on the situation and your own comfort level with them as you gain experience. The most important point here is that you need to be engaged in the interview, understand what your client is communicating and know that your client needs to feel you are listening and understanding.

B. INHIBITORS AND FACILITATORS TO COMMUNICATION

A person's various needs may affect his ability to communicate and form productive attorney-client relationships. Several factors may inhibit or interfere with someone's ability to fully participate in an interview or counseling meeting. Other factors facilitate full participation. These factors may play a role in both how the client and the lawyer communicate.[55]

Several factors can encourage clients to fully participate in information gathering and counseling conversations. Empathic understanding makes clients trust and have confidence in you as a lawyer and may motivate them to contribute to the relationship in a more meaningful way. *Empathy* involves understanding the experiences and feelings of someone else. Feeling listened to and understood makes us more willing to engage in a conversation. The passive or active listening techniques we discuss above are some ways to communicate empathy toward a client. You can motivate clients to participate fully by communicating to them that you expect them to do so; when they do so, they are fulfilling your expectations. Human beings usually seek attention and recognition from others. You encourage clients to participate by *praising* their help or cooperation.[56] You may also be able to motivate clients with *altruistic appeals*, appealing to a cause that is beyond their immediate self-interest.[57] You can also encourage clients to participate more fully by pointing out that it is likely to help them achieve a more *satisfactory result*.[58] *Cross-cultural openness* on the part of the lawyer may also enable the client to participate more fully in the conversation.[59]

In contrast, several factors may interfere with a client's full participation in an interview. One such factor is *ego threat*,[60] which leads clients not to disclose information that they perceive as threatening to their self-esteem. Ms. Robinson, for example, may not be willing to admit that she does not feel she is capable of fundraising for the environmental project. *Case threat*[61] may lead clients not to reveal information they feel could be detrimental to their case. For example, Ms. Estrada may be reluctant to disclose her bottom line in negotiations over the lease because she thinks if you know it you will not try to get DWC better terms. Some clients may have *expectations* about various roles, including that of lawyer and client. They may act a certain way or say certain things in keeping with what they perceive as the proper client role, not how they actually feel or think. These expectations also may differ depending on someone's cultural values. The lawyer's inability to see beyond her culture may also inhibit full client participation.[62]

---

[55] Most of the factors discussed in this section appear in other interviewing and counseling texts. *See, e.g.*, BINDER ET AL., *supra* note 12, at 16–40.

[56] *Id.* at 30.

[57] *Id.*

[58] *Id.* at 30–31.

[59] Ascanio Piomelli, *Cross-Cultural Lawyering by the Book: The Latest Clinical Texts and a Sketch of a Future Agenda*, 4 HASTINGS RACE & POVERTY L.J. 131, 139 (2006).

[60] BINDER ET AL., *supra* note 12, at 19.

[61] *Id.* at 20.

[62] Piomelli, *supra* note 59, at 139.

Another inhibitor may be *etiquette barrier*.[63] Some clients may not be willing to disclose certain things to "outsiders." A board may be willing to discuss something among itself but may not be willing to discuss it in front of the lawyer who is not a member of its community. Clients may not discuss something with you because they do not see it as *important or relevant* to their matter. Clients may not want to discuss a topic that is of interest to you or that you perceive as the most relevant because they want to discuss something else. You will need to discuss that topic before moving on to the other ones that you feel you need to discuss. For example, a client may want to understand the parameters of just cause for firing an employee, the issue he came to discuss with you, even though you feel you need to discuss the employment contract that the senior staff drafted without board approval. Finally, certain events may be *unpleasant* to the client so she may be reluctant to discuss them because they bring up feelings of anger, humiliation, or fear.

Your own personality needs may affect positively and negatively your relationships with clients. The psychologist Abraham Maslow developed a "hierarchy of needs" to describe human motivation.[64] The hierarchy includes five general categories of needs—physiological (food, shelter, clothes and sex), safety (freedom from of bodily harm, predictability and financial security), belonging and love (close and meaningful human relationships), esteem and self-actualization. The esteem needs include the desire for strength, achievement, adequacy, mastery and competence, independence and freedom, and confidence in the face of the world. The esteem needs also include the desire for reputation or prestige, status, dominance, recognition, attention, importance or appreciation. In lawyers, the higher needs manifest themselves through the needs for power (safety and esteem), achievement (esteem and autonomy), association (love and esteem) and order (safety).[65]

The need for power can move individuals to assume positions of leadership. It can also have negative consequences in client relationships since it leads to conflicts with client priorities and can lead to a domineering approach to lawyering. The achievement need manifests itself through competitiveness, aggressiveness, independence and persistence. Clients benefit when lawyers fight hard to get favorable outcomes. But "super-competitors" can let their drive to win overpower their clients' feelings. These lawyers may not have the patience and tolerance necessary for effective counseling and negotiation.

The need for association leads one to look for meaningful involvement with others. The need expresses itself though empathic communication

---

[63] *Id.* at 23.

[64] BASTRESS & HARBAUGH, *supra* note 31, at 285 (citing ABRAHAM MASLOW, MOTIVATION AND PERSONALITY 80–106 (1954)).

[65] *Id.* at 287–95.

with others and through conciliatory and cooperative attitudes.[66] This need can express itself in relationships with clients and other lawyers, but the need to avoid conflict can diminish a lawyer's effectiveness in negotiations and in counseling clients (if the lawyer avoids confronting clients or telling them bad news). Law attracts people who seek order in their lives and in the world. Organization skills are important for lawyers (e.g., drafting, managing time). People with a high need for order may feel frustrated by the uncertainty in law and may tend to oversimplify legal issues for clients. Understanding your strengths and those aspects of lawyering you most enjoy will help you better understand your interactions with your clients.

Many other factors, some of which we discuss below as well as in the Multicultural Lawyering chapter, may influence your communication with clients. Psychological type theory describes ways people differ in their preferred approaches to acquiring information, using that information to make decisions and interacting with their external environment.[67] The Myers Briggs Type Indicator (MBTI) addresses difference in four contexts: sensing versus intuition, extroversion versus introversion, thinking versus feeling, and judging versus perceiving.[68] The first of these looks to how a person prefers to gather information (differentiating between those of us who prefer sensing and those who prefer to rely on intuition). Some of us prefer to rely on observable facts or happenings (through one of our five senses) and others prefer abstract, symbolic and theoretical use of data (looking to patterns, possibilities and meanings to gather information).[69] When making decisions, some people analyze situations, weigh facts and outcomes, and pursue logical, objective and impersonal results consequences (thinking). Others base their judgments on personal or social values, looking to what matters to others and the human aspects of problems (feeling).[70] Extroverts focus attention externally to objects and people in the environment, think before talking, and tend to be action-oriented. Introverts do most of their thinking before acting and focus inward on their thoughts and ideas.[71] In making decisions, people oriented toward judging seek structure and choose closure over keeping things open; they make decisions quickly and firmly. Persons oriented

---

[66] *Id.* at 291.

[67] Don Peters & Martha M. Peters, *Maybe That's Why I Do That: Psychological Type Theory, the Myers–Briggs Type Indicator, and Learning Legal Interviewing*, 35 N.Y.L. SCH. L. REV. 169, 173 (1990). *See also,* ROBERT F. COCHRAN, JR., JOHN M.A. DIPIPPA & MARTHA M. PETERS, THE COUNSELOR–AT–LAW: A COLLABORATIVE APPROACH TO CLIENT INTERVIEWING AND COUNSELING 225–47 (2d ed. 2006).

[68] Peters & Peters, *supra* note 67, at 173 n.17 .

[69] *Id.* at 175–76. Most of the population of the U.S. prefers sensing though intuition grows as the level of education increases. *Id.* at 176.

[70] *Id.* at 176–77. A majority of women report a feeling preference and a majority of men prefer thinking. *Id.*

[71] *Id.* at 177.

toward perceiving prefer to keep things open, unstructured, fluid and spontaneous.[72]

This section has tried to give you insights into some factors that may affect your relationships with clients. The better you know yourself, your own needs and preferences, and your personality, the better able you will be to establish meaningful relationships with your clients.

C. QUESTION TYPES

This section will discuss the various types of questions and when you might want to use a particular form of question. The way you phrase a question may send a message to the client about how much information you want her to provide. It may influence the client's ability to recall and provide information. It may also affect your ability to create a productive working relationship with your client. In and of itself, no one form of question is better than another; oney might be better at a particular time or for a particular purpose. During the interview you should also consider the form of the question in addition to its content. Most questions can take one of four different forms: open, closed, yes-no and leading.

Open questions[73] give clients the greatest freedom to choose the information they provide in response and its phrasing. They may even allow the client to choose the subject matter of the answer (see question 1 below). You may narrow the question by providing the subject matter (question 2 below). You may also limit it by focusing the client on a particular time (question 3 below). Some examples of open questions are:

1. Tell me what brings you here.

2. Tell me about your business.

3. What happened during your conversation with Scott Jones?

4. How will the other directors react if the organization does not have employment contracts?

5. Before we end, is there anything else you would like to discuss?

6. What are you hoping to get out of the lease?

Closed questions[74] normally ask for specific information. They select the subject matter (which some open questions above did) but also limit the scope of the reply. Some examples are:

1. What is a sectoral approach to organizing?

2. How would you like to work with the school?

---

[72] *Id.*

[73] BINDER ET AL., *supra* note 12, at 65.

[74] *Id.* at 66.

3. How many square feet of space do you think DWC needs?

4. How many square feet of space does DWC have in its current space?

5. What effect will the lease negotiations have on your relationship with Mr. Jones?

Yes-no questions[75] are a form of closed questions that further limit the scope of the response by including in the question all the information that you want to find. With these questions, you are asking the client to confirm or deny a proposition. Some examples are:

1. Did you work with the kids over the summer?

2. Do you want to continue to work with the science teacher?

3. Are you looking for more space for DWC?

4. Do you see yourself working only with children from your neighborhood?

5. Would you like the organization to have its own space?

Leading questions[76] are yes-no questions that provide not only the information you are looking for but also suggest the answer. They are assertions accompanied either by a tone of voice or language that communicates that you want a particular answer.

1. So you worked with kids over the summer?

2. I take it you want to continue working with the school's science teacher.

3. You want to be able to keep using the church's space until you find better space?

4. So you want to maintain a good working relationship with Mr. Jones?

Each question type has advantages and disadvantages and may be more appropriate at certain times in the interview. Open questions allow you to get information that may not occur to you and also encourage client recall of information. These questions allow the client to describe matters in her own words and maintain her paths of association. Open questions also promote the accuracy of information.[77] Open questions are also efficient because they allow you to pursue details with fewer questions and capture both context and content.[78] Open questions motivate the client to participate since they communicate that you trust her judg-

---

[75] *Id.*

[76] *Id.*

[77] BINDER ET AL., *supra* note 12, at 69.

[78] Gellhorn, *supra* note 29, at 339–40.

ment in deciding what is relevant. They also allow you to ask clients about sensitive topics in their own way and when they are ready, such as for example family conflicts in a business. Open questions do have disadvantages. They do not explore the client's full memory, and they encourage the client to provide irrelevant material. Open questions may be inefficient for some clients, especially those who cannot focus.

The greatest advantage of closed questions is that they elicit details. Closed questions may motivate clients who did not understand or were confused by your open question. Closed questions may allow you to pursue difficult topics slowly and a little bit at a time. Too many closed questions, however, may damage rapport. For example, a client may feel that he never got a chance to tell you his goals if you only asked closed questions. The more limited the scope of the question, the less likely you are to elicit what is on the client's mind. Closed questions also may keep you from learning important information, and may keep you from getting correct information. The closed question may signal particular expectations to the client.[79] In certain moments, moving to closed questions too quickly may discourage (and even prevent) clients from completing their thoughts and disclosing additional relevant information.[80]

Leading questions can be advantageous as they may help a client overcome certain inhibitors that make a client reluctant to disclose certain information, such as sensitive or embarrassing information.[81] On the downside, these questions may also enhance the possibility of gathering incorrect information as the client may feel pressure to affirm it even if the question's words or characterizations are not completely accurate. Leading questions may be ethically improper if they suggest the "correct" answer to the client. This problem does not only arise in the context of litigation but can also be a problem, for example, when applying for tax exemption.

An effective interview, then, will involve a mix of open and closed questions and even some leading questions. Premature diagnosis may lead you toward closed questions as opposed to open questions. Premature diagnosis occurs when you put client narratives into legal categories before hearing about the situation from the client's perspective. You may begin to think "the best solution for this client is an LLC" and begin to ask the questions that will help you structure one. In the interview with Ms. Robinson, you may only ask questions about incorporating a nonprofit organization and may not ask her about other possible collaborations short of incorporating a new organization. As we mention below, you will need to remain flexible during the interview. At the same time that you

---

[79] BINDER ET AL., *supra* note 12, at 72.

[80] Gellhorn, *supra* note 29, at 337.

[81] BINDER ET AL., *supra* note 12, at 73.

are exploring questions regarding the legal categories you researched and know, for example in the interview with Ms. Robinson, the requirements for incorporating a nonprofit organization in your state, you will need to think of and ask open questions that explore other possibilities.

The tendency to "fill in" stories may also lead you to think that stories are more complete than they actually are. We tend to "fill in" stories with information drawn from our experiences, details that are logical to us given certain information. We all approach interviews with a view of what the world is or should be like. We need to resist this tendency in the lawyering process since we do not all approach decisions or see the world in the same light, and resisting this tendency is difficult because much of the "filling in" we do is subconscious. We thus need to be more intentional about working to avoid this tendency.

D. TAKING NOTES

One of the challenges for a new lawyer is how to integrate all the things in this chapter—how to listen to what the client is saying, think about the substantive law, the organization of the interview and the form of questions, and formulate the next question, all simultaneously. At the same time, you want to take notes to be able to remember what the client has said. You see the challenge. You cannot establish rapport with a client and keep your head down looking into a legal pad or laptop computer. You will need to engage the client in the conversation.

How, then, do you take notes in order to remember what the client said and create some record of the initial meeting? One method is to write a memorandum describing the conversation to the file soon after the meeting while the conversation is fresh in your mind. Also, you do not have to write down every word the client utters and you do not have to write full sentences. Think about taking notes by writing words or phrases that will aid your recall of the fuller details. If you are interviewing with another lawyer, think about taking turns taking notes, so that your partner takes notes while you take the lead asking questions and vice versa. For important matters, you can take the time to write something down and then continue with the conversation after. Some silence is appropriate; someone does not have to be talking during the entire meeting.

E. FLEXIBILITY

This chapter has offered an outline that we hope is helpful as you think about planning and structuring a client interview. While we offer a proposed structure for your meetings, we stress that the initial interview with your client, like much of lawyering, will require flexibility.

Imagine this scene: You have prepared for an initial interview with the Directors of the Southeast Association of Neighborhoods (SAN) about drafting an employment manual for the entity. You researched the law and thought about the topics you will need to explore in the meeting. At the meeting, something unexpected happens. One of the Directors tells you that the Director Collaborative has employment contracts that they drafted but the Board of Directors did not approve those contracts. SAN now wants you to draft employment contracts for the Directors. You did not research employment contracts and know nothing about employment contracts. What do you do?

Does client-centered representation mean that you have to go where the client takes you? As you might have guessed, the answer to that depends. You will have to make a judgment about whether getting off course to answer the question is worth the risk of distracting you and your client from your interview plan. Another option might be to tell the client that you will go back to that question at a later point in the meeting. You will have to make the judgment based on where you are in the interview, your sense of how the client feels about it, and how you feel about getting off course or responding to the question at a later point. If it really makes more sense to cover that question later, you could point it out to the client. If your sense is the client will not be able to concentrate on the rest of the interview until you answer the question, it might be worth it to go off course.

We hope this chapter gives you a useful structure and technique for planning and conducting initial client meetings. We also hope it has also given you some sense that a plan is just that, as plans often need to be adjusted mid-stream and client meetings are no different.

V. CROSS–CULTURAL ISSUES IN THE INITIAL CLIENT INTERVIEW

The issue of culture in your practice is a very significant one. We will discuss cultural issues further in the Multicultural Lawyering chapter, but the remainder of this chapter will provide an introduction to cultural differences in the interview setting.

A. GENERALLY

You and your clients may not necessarily share ways of communicating, interacting with and understanding the world. These differences may at times be due to cultural differences as "much of what we understand about our interpersonal effectiveness is connected to cultural understandings, learned practices, and traditional customs."[82] Your family

---

[82] Paul R. Tremblay, *Interviewing and Counseling Across Cultures: Heuristics and Biases*, 9 CLINICAL L. REV. 373, 376 (2002).

background, race, ethnicity, religion, gender, country of origin, dominant language, education, income, occupation, disability and sexual orientation, and those characteristics of your clients will influence the interviewing process. The challenge is to recognize and respect those differences without reducing people to stereotypes.

Culture can be defined as "the socially transmitted values, beliefs and symbols that are more or less shared by members of a social group."[83] These values, beliefs, and symbols make up the framework through which members of the group "interpret and attribute meaning to their own and others' experiences and behavior."[84] Culture provides individuals with the frameworks for interpreting their own behavior and motives and that of others.[85] Susan Bryant has said that culture is like the air we breathe, largely invisible, yet it is "the logic by which we give order to the world."[86] Culture is not only a property of racial, ethnic, religious or national groups, the "containers" for culture that most people think of in defining culture.[87] Indeed, "organizations, institutions, professions and occupations are also containers for culture and sites of cultural differences."[88]

Since each of us belongs to multiple groups, every interaction between individuals is likely to be multicultural. At the same time, there is intra-cultural variation as culture is rarely perfectly shared by all members of the group or community. We lawyers have our own culture as we have discovered in talking to friends and family members. All lawyering, then, is likely to be cross-cultural. The greater the differentiation between two individuals, however, the more likely we are to experience it as multicultural and the more likely that we will have difficulty in communication.

The first step in working across cultural difference is recognizing that each of us has a cultural identity (or, in reality, identities) and that we have learned certain beliefs, customs, habits, ways of thinking and values. Those attributes define who we are and our lawyering activities cannot but reflect them.[89] Our learned preferences for dealing with the world may, however, interfere with our understanding of our clients.

A good starting point for cross-cultural communication is the acceptance that not everyone thinks about the world in the way you may.

---

[83] Kevin Avruch, *Culture as Context, Culture as Communication: Considerations for Humanitarian Negotiators*, 9 HARV. NEGOT. L. REV. 391, 393 (2004) (discussing culture in the negotiation context).

[84] *Id.*

[85] *Id.* at 396.

[86] Susan Bryant, *The Five Habits: Building Cross Cultural Competence in Lawyers*, 8 CLINICAL L. REV. 33, 40 (2001).

[87] Avruch, *supra* note 83, at 398.

[88] *Id.*

[89] Paul R. Tremblay & Carwina Weng, *Multicultural Lawyering: Heuristics and Biases, in* THE AFFECTIVE ASSISTANCE OF COUNSEL, *supra* note 45, at 143.

Essential in cross-cultural settings are a critical awareness of our own ethnocentrism, a tolerance for differences and a capacity to suspend judgment.[90] Important in this initial interview is for you not to attribute differences that you may find puzzling or disturbing to the personality or character of the individual with whom you are meeting since they may be due to "external" factors such as cultural differences, the larger environment or the situation.[91]

B. WORKING WITH CLIENTS WHO SPEAK OTHER LANGUAGES

One of the most obvious ways we encounter cultural differences is when we interview a client who does not speak English. Communication with a client is complicated by use of interpreters. Our relationship with clients is mediated by a third party when we work with interpreters. Even when we are representing groups of individuals, the interpreter disrupts the lawyer-client relationship on which the client-centered model is premised.[92] The goal and challenge of any communication is attributing to particular communication the meaning intended by the speaker.[93] Any given utterance by someone is made up of both the literal, semantic meaning of the words used, and the force or intention that the speaker intends for the words. The process of making meaning from language requires that the listener know the semantic meaning of the speaker's utterance as well as figure its intended meaning in context. The use of two different languages and two cultural contexts complicates the semantic and cultural dimensions of communications.[94] The interpreter must now understand vocabulary, diction and grammar in both languages as well as differences in dialect, colloquial expressions and technical terminology. Interpreting the intended meaning of the speaker's utterance is even more difficult when using an interpreter. The use of an interpreter magnifies the possibility of communication errors since another person now mediates the speaker's intentions. Nonlinguistic cues, such as intonation, volume, speech rate and nonverbal communication, such as physical gestures, are fundamental to the process of making meaning. Inferring intended meaning requires that the interpreter actually interpret these cues. Muneer Ahmad suggests thinking of interpreters as experts, and screening, evaluating and working with them as team members in the process of lawyering across language difference.[95] This might require the lawyer to examine both the linguistic qualifications of the interpreter as well as the factual bases of the cultural knowledge he purports to possess.

---

[90] Avruch, *supra* note 83, at 406.

[91] *Id.*

[92] Ahmad, *supra* note 14, at 1002.

[93] *Id.* at 1033 (citing Bryant, *supra* note 86, at 43).

[94] *Id.* at 1034.

[95] *Id.* at 1072.

In working with clients across cultural differences, one of the first decisions you will have to make is whether the client needs an interpreter. Partial English speakers may need an interpreter in complicated, sensitive interviewing and counseling situations. A client may be able to schedule an appointment and carry on a conversation in work settings but may not be able to understand technical language in English. You should consider the client's wishes but will need to make an independent assessment of whether you and the client will need an interpreter to communicate effectively.

If you decide that the client needs an interpreter, you will need to find an interpreter and determine if he is competent. In finding an interpreter, you will need to find someone with excellent command of both languages. The interpreter should be a neutral person, someone without an interest in the matter. In certain situations, a family member may not be appropriate. Imagine a client consulting you about establishing an LLC where a number of family members are to be members. Even those family members who are not involved in the LLC may not be appropriate interpreters. Friends and neighbors may not be appropriate in certain settings since the client may not wish to discuss certain financial or family matters in front of persons known to them or the other parties. In other situations, friends and family members may be appropriate. The client may be the one who brings the interpreter because she trusts that he will interpret accurately. In making this decision, you will have to consider the resources of the clinic, the availability of speakers of the client's language, the language skills of the potential interpreter and the client's feelings.

You should prepare the interpreter for his role. You should clarify your expectations of him. This is especially important if the interpreter has not worked in legal settings. The expectations include the need to provide accurate interpretation of what each person says. You should explain to the interpreter some of the information you will be asking of and giving to the client. You should talk to the interpreter before the meeting and provide her any technical words or concepts. You may want to provide those words or concepts in writing to the interpreter, and take some time to explain them to the interpreter. In many instances the clients may not be familiar with U.S. legal, administrative and regulatory processes, so you will have to use the interpreter to explain the meaning of those words as well as the actual words. You will need to make sure that the interpreter understands that he is to abide by confidentiality.[96]

---

[96] It is a good practice to have an interpreter sign a confidentiality agreement. *See* Angela McCaffrey, *Don't Get Lost in Translation: Teaching Law Students to Work with Language Interpreters*, 6 CLINICAL L. REV. 347 (2000). You might want to give the interpreter the code of professional responsibility of interpreters and explain the obligations contained in it even if he is not a professional interpreter. *See also* Susan J. Bryant & Jean Koh Peters, *Six Practices with Clients Across Culture: Habit Four, Working with Interpreters and Other Mindful Approaches, in* THE AFFECTIVE ASSISTANCE OF COUNSEL, *supra* note 45, at 228 (providing a sample Interpreter Con-

At the beginning of the interview, you will need to explain the role of the interpreter to the client. During the interview, you will want to have a conversation with the client and not the interpreter. Direct your questions to the client and use the first and second person as opposed to the third person. For example, you will ask "How can I help you?" or "What brings you to our office?" as opposed to directing your question to the interpreter and saying "What brings her to our office?" This technique will minimize the possibility that the interpreter will summarize the conversation as opposed to interpreting the exact words the client uses. You should avoid words or concepts that are difficult to interpret, such as idiomatic expressions or metaphors. You may not have that option with legal concepts. With those, make sure you are explaining the concepts, not just using the words. When you are dealing with a client who does not speak English you are most likely dealing with a client who is less familiar with legal concepts in this country. You should also use plain language and divide long and complicated sentences into several short ones. Pause to allow for interpretation. The pause will ensure that the interpreter is translating the exact words and meaning in your question as opposed to paraphrasing your words since he cannot remember the words you used. When planning a meeting using an interpreter consider that the meeting will take longer since everything will be said in both languages. Working with clients across language differences can help you pay closer attention to communication issues. These meetings can improve your communication skills. They also require planning and careful consideration of communication errors that can take place in any lawyering relationship.

VI. CONCLUSION

In this chapter, we have sought to introduce you to some important elements to consider during your initial client meeting and to provide you with a framework for how to structure that meeting. The particular matter and client will require you to remain flexible, of course, as we have described above. But, a well-planned and structured interview will assist you in gathering information and strengthening the trust between you and your client.

---

fidentiality Agreement developed by Susan Bennett and Muneer Ahmad at American University).

CHAPTER 3

ORGANIZING YOUR TRANSACTIONAL WORK: DECISION-MAKING, STRATEGIC PLANNING, AND A "THEORY OF THE PROJECT"

■ ■ ■

I. INTRODUCTION

Imagine this scene: It's the second week of your semester in the Entrepreneurship Clinic, in which you were lucky enough to land a spot. Your clinical supervisor has assigned you to meet with Filippa Sands and Bill Sherman, who have come to the clinic for its help in establishing a limited liability company (LLC) for their new business in town. You are thrilled with this assignment. You know something about LLCs from your Business Organizations course last semester, and you have noticed that the clinic has form templates for LLCs readily available. At your meeting with them you confidently tell Filippa and Bill that you can have the LLC papers drafted by the end of the week, which makes them happy. After the two entrepreneurs leave, you find some of the clinic's LLC template forms on its server and start plugging in the correct information for Filippa and Bill. You really like this experience as a corporate lawyer, and you sure feel like you know what you are doing.

So, have you done well? Is this the way that good transactional lawyers work?

This chapter addresses the organization of your work on your clients' projects. To be successful in the work in your clinic, you will need to begin to achieve some mastery of many discrete (and challenging) lawyering skills—including interviewing, counseling, drafting and negotiation. This book addresses each of those skills in those respective chapters. But separate from those skills are the questions of how you decide *what to do* for your clients when you work on their projects, and how to make your work coherent and structured. Those questions are what we will explore here. Learning how to engage in comprehensive and organized strategic planning is as important a skill as, if not more important than, the other skills you will learn in your clinical experience.

There are at least three kinds of planning approaches you will learn about here. When Filippa and Bill leave your office (or, perhaps, even before you first meet them, as you prepare for that meeting), you will think about an overarching *blueprint* for the project you will work on. The blueprint device permits you to envision where you should start, what the end product might look like, and, most critically, how you plan to get to that end product. That blueprint, though, will not tell you enough about the content of the project unless you craft what we will refer to as your "theory of the project." All of the work you will perform for your clients will reflect some theory or conception of what you want to create. That theory could be implicit, but you will want it to be as explicit as possible. The art of developing a coherent, masterful theory is the second approach to good strategic planning we will address. The distinction between a blueprint and a theory is sometimes elusive, but we believe that you will find the terms to describe different, separable elements of your work.

The third approach to project organization and planning focuses on more concrete, day-to-day work. Virtually all of your lawyering work involves making *decisions*. You might decide how to organize the seating in your interview room when you first meet your clients. You might decide on a certain model of interviewing to use during that meeting. You might decide what kind of LLC clauses to include, and which to exclude, when you draft organizational documents. Because so much of your work involves decision-making, you should understand a bit about what goes into making sound, reliable decisions. We will introduce you to some ideas about that later in this chapter.

II. A BEGINNING EXAMPLE

Our exploration of strategic planning themes will work better if we have an example or two to use as we move along. Just above we introduced the clients Filippa Sands and Bill Sherman. Let us add a little texture to their story:

> Your supervisor assigns you a new intake. The prospective clients are named Filippa Sands and Bill Sherman. Filippa and Bill are entrepreneurs who live in the local neighborhood. They have plans to open a bakery café on Prospect Street, about a mile from the clinic's office. The intake sheet states that Bill is an unemployed chain grocery store manager, and Filippa works full time as an assistant financing clerk at a GM dealership in town. They heard from the local Small Business Development Center (SBDC)[1] that they should consult a lawyer before embarking on this endeavor. The SBDC gave Filippa and Bill the names of the county bar association as well as that of your law school clinic.

---

[1] The federal Small Business Administration establishes regional Small Business Development Centers throughout the country to support emerging enterprises. *See* Small Business Development Center Act, 15 U.S.C. § 648 (2010); Susan R. Jones, *Promoting Social and Economic Justice Through Interdisciplinary Work in Transactional Law*, 14 WASH. U. J.L. & POL'Y 249, 268 (2004) (describing SBDCs).

They decided to try the clinic instead of a private lawyer (the price made a difference), and the clinic agreed to interview them. The two prospective clients would like to meet a lawyer or student as soon as possible to get things rolling.

This somewhat typical transactional clinic story will help us examine the planning ideas we intend to address. One advantage of this story, we shall see, is that it is relatively *well-structured*. Later in this chapter we will offer two different stories as examples of fuzzier, less well-defined client projects.[2] As you will likely experience in your clinic work, the fuzzy stories are not at all uncommon in community-based transactional work.[3]

III. DEVELOPING A BLUEPRINT FOR YOUR WORK

Here's a dilemma inherent in good planning within lawyering practice: The best planners will think long term about what they want to do, but of course no one—not even the really good planners—know for sure what will happen as the project moves ahead. Therefore, the challenge is to organize a client project without knowing for sure that your organization will work. You might start with what we will call the "blueprint"— the broad overview of how you might envision the progress and development of the work you will be doing. The blueprint idea will not tell you enough about what specific work you will be doing; that will await your theory development, which we will discuss in Section IV. But it should offer you a road map (to mix metaphors a bit) with whose help you might structure your legal tasks.

[handwritten: Broad plan]

In the following subsections we will describe a crude linear model of strategic planning. We follow that with ideas for making the crude approach work better.

A. A LINEAR BLUEPRINT

Let us introduce the blueprint concept by starting with a simple, linear plan. This kind of organizational stance is, we have found, a rather common approach by earnest students to organize the work on matters like Filippa and Bill's. Such a plan might look something like this:

1.   You arrange a convenient time for an interview.

2.   You then prepare a checklist of questions needed in order to cover the basics in an interview with an emerging for-profit business.

3.   You next meet with Filippa and Bill, and using your interview plan learn more details about their wishes and the expected op-

---

²   *See* Section V below.

³   *See* Susan D. Bennett, *Embracing the Ill–Structured Problem in a Community Economic Development Clinic*, 9 CLINICAL L. REV. 45 (2002).

eration of their business. You inquire in this meeting about whether they would prefer an S–Corporation or an LLC. For ease of illustration, let us assume that Filippa and Bill choose to form an LLC.

4. Knowing what your clients want, you will then perform the necessary legal research about creating an LLC in your state. Using whatever research materials you have available, you become a bit of an expert in LLC formation.

5. You then prepare some generic template documents for the LLC, and arrange a second meeting with Filippa and Bill.

6. At this second meeting, which works more like a counseling meeting than your first interview session, you review the draft template papers with Filippa and Bill to tweak the details and to have them decide among the choices of language that will inevitably arise.

7. After the counseling session, you finalize the documents based on your clients' preferences. You then file all of the proper papers to create the LLC with the Secretary of State (or whichever agency in your state oversees entity formation). The LLC now exists.

8. You are now done with what you were hired to do. If Filippa and Bill want you to do anything further, like negotiate the Prospect Street lease for example, you will start this planning process over again for that task.

The planning arrangement we have just described evidences a skillfulness in planning which is independent of the skills required to complete each of the steps within the plan. You can now see how your talents of interviewing or drafting are separate from the skill of crafting the organizing template for your work for these clients. The arrangement also does not address, yet, many of the specific choices you will face about how you will craft the LLC so that it serves as a comprehensive and sufficient vehicle for the clients' needs. That level of planning is what we understand to be the "theory" development, which we will address soon.

There are benefits to a simple blueprint such as this. By creating the plan before you have taken any single step in your actual work (except, of course, the step of making the blueprint), you have organized the first part of your semester's work in an intentional and explicit way. You have established visible and reliable benchmarks against which you may compare your actual progress. (Indeed, you could have, and perhaps would have, included an estimated timeline for each task, allowing you to predict when the project would be finished.) The linear chart builds in the necessary progression of events and tasks, limiting the risk that you will perform an action before you have taken care of its needed preconditions.

In an elegant way, this plan tells you how to start and when you have finished your work.

The linear plan also permits you to include within it your own professional personality and your ethical commitments. The plan sketched out here implies a commitment to client-centeredness, as it assumes a meeting with Filippa and Bill where they choose the details of the LLC project. It also permits you a fair degree of independence and autonomy as a lawyer, as you do all of the creation of the first draft of the LLC documents, and you therefore get to choose which places warrant Filippa and Bill's input and which you will describe as essentially boilerplate.

In our clinics, students who create plans like the one just described have done good work (subject, of course, to the skillfulness of the actual lawyering work that they produce along the way). We would be pleased to see students organizing their work in this kind of explicit way, and their client representation would be stronger as a result of having a plan like this as a guide. But you should be able to do better than this. You will learn that this kind of blueprint will not serve you well enough to provide your clients with the most effective transactional lawyering services.

The major worry about the linear blueprint is that its implied rigor does not comport very well with the reality of your work with your clients. Your client interactions, and the work you do outside of those meetings, most likely will be messier, less crisp, and much more contingent than the above plan allows. The crude linear plan also includes several assumptions and premature diagnoses about the goals of your clients. Good lawyers will try to avoid those traps. What we are hoping for, then, is a blueprint scheme which includes the qualities of a planning device, but which accepts the inevitable contingencies and uncertainties that characterize the world of practice. That may seem like a contradiction or oxymoron, but we think good lawyers can strive to achieve it. Let us now turn to how you might make your blueprint less linear and more effective.

B. A MORE TEXTURED BLUEPRINT

1. The Qualities of a More Textured Blueprint

A more effective blueprint will acknowledge better the realities of lawyering work, including these qualities:

The Circular and Iterative Nature of Project Planning: The linear plan assumed that your Filippa and Bill project would start at Step 1 and end at Step 8. But it won't, and you probably realized that. Consider, for instance, the decision of your clients to go the LLC route rather than the S–Corporation route (Step 3 in your plan, if you're counting). That decision is itself enormously complicated, and could easily shift two or three times in the course of your work with the entrepreneurs. And if we assume that some decision will emerge after several conversations, and if we continue to assume that the LLC will be the way to go, creation of the documents is more fluid and circular than the plan describes. The plan assumes a process of interview (get facts and learn goals), research (understand the legal options and constraints), draft (use facts), then counsel (elicit from the clients the best way to apply the facts to the legal alternatives). In fact, the four tasks just listed are typically all jumbled up, with emails and telephone calls and meetings where you test out iterations and draft clauses, get some input from the clients, try a revision, call the clients again for clarification about facts, use those clarified facts in the next version of the document, and so on and so on. Your planning, then, must acknowledge, somehow, the complex nature of lawyer and client collaboration leading up to a final product.

The Contingent Quality of Project Planning: Separate from the circularity of this process is its inevitable contingent quality. By "contingent" we mean that none of the linear steps on which you construct your planning scheme is fixed; each may change mid-process, and your work somehow has to anticipate that. Two examples among many will serve us here. First, consider the nature of your relationships with Filippa and Bill. Your linear plan assumed (pretty wisely) that the two entrepreneurs would be your clients. Your plan elided (for now) the complications of representing two persons together on a business deal,[4] but otherwise treated the two persons as equal clients. A more sophisticated plan would flag from the very beginning the uncertainty of the client relationship status, acknowledging that the planning structure would develop based upon a tentative assumption of two co-equal clients.

Next, perhaps more realistically, consider the plans for proceeding after your interview, even with the assumption of two cooperative co-clients. Your plan understandably moves from the place where you learn your clients' goals and objectives (that's the interview) to the stage where you start to explore how to achieve those goals and objectives (that's the research and drafting stages). The linear model works from the fixture of the first premise ("I know my clients' objectives") to the inevitability of the corollary ("I will conduct legal research to learn about how to accomplish those goals"). But the clients' goals are not fixed at all. They might change with time and circumstances, and may change as the direct result of what you tell them about their legal alternatives. Indeed, in many ways clients need the help of their lawyers to understand the true nature

---

[4] Recall that in the Filippa and Bill example, Bill does not have a "day job," while Filippa does. This implies a strong possibility that the two partners will contribute unequally to the endeavor, perhaps with Bill offering labor and Filippa offering financing. For discussion of this kind of arrangement and the ethical implications of the lawyer's role, see, e.g., Jesse v. Danforth, 485 N.W.2d 63 (Wis. 1992); Darian M. Ibrahim, *Solving the Everyday Problem of Client Identity in the Context of Closely Held Businesses*, 56 ALA. L. REV. 181 (2004); Carl A. Pierce, *Representing One Client at a Time in Connection with the Formation and Organization of a Corporation*, 38 TENN. J. BUS. L. 327 (2007); Paul R. Tremblay, *Counseling Community Groups*, 17 CLINICAL L. REV. 389, 407 (2010). *See also* the chapter on Ethical Issues in Transactional Practice.

of their goals and to unpack their meaning.[5] Treating the goals as fixed landmarks, as the linear plan did, fails to account for that reality.

The Critical Role of Judgment: The crude linear model does not exclude the exercise of reflective judgment on your part, but it seemingly downplays that deliberation. Effective lawyering inevitably involves the exercise of judgment,[6] and judgment consists of something qualitatively different from the analytic exercise of listing and organizing topics. The listing and the organizing are typically essential, but not sufficient, for effective client service. By "judgment," we refer to that reflective capacity Karl Llewellyn called "situation-sense,"[7] that ability to read and respond to ambiguity in a way that has effective pragmatic use. Judgment is sometimes known as "practical wisdom," an Aristotelian concept that most observers appreciate as the essence of professional service.[8] People with practical judgment can discern from a situation some truths that are more than the mere collection of the parts. You will continue to develop your practical judgment skills in your client work, and your focus on the linear organization scheme might lead you to downplay the importance of the bigger picture.

An effective blueprint will account for these factors. You can see how much more challenging developing a textured blueprint will be than crafting a linear one, whose simplicity is seductive but not as reliable or productive for your clients' legal needs. The textured blueprint must, at the same time, work as a planning and organizing device, but incorporate into the blueprint notions of contingency, uncertainty and reflective judgment. Gary Bellow and Bea Moulton, pioneer chroniclers of the planning process in the litigation clinic setting, noted the daunting quality of this endeavor, especially for novices, such as clinic students.[9] As Bellow and Moulton wrote more than 25 years ago, the challenge here is steep, but this is what good lawyers do.

2. Creating a Textured Blueprint for Filippa and Bill

At this point our central message seems to be that strategic blueprints for transactional lawyering are not static and reliable, as an architect's blueprint might be, but that you should create one just the same.

---

[5] *See* STEPHEN ELLMANN, ROBERT D. DINERSTEIN, ISABELLE R. GUNNING, KATHERINE R. KRUSE & ANN C. SHALLECK, LAWYERS AND CLIENTS: CRITICAL ISSUES IN INTERVIEWING AND COUNSELING 139–214 (2010).

[6] Mark Neal Aaronson, *We Ask You to Consider: Learning About Practical Judgment in Lawyering*, 4 CLINICAL L. REV. 247 (1998).

[7] KARL N. LLEWELLYN, THE COMMON LAW TRADITION: DECIDING APPEALS 123 (1960).

[8] Aaronson, *supra* note 6, at 256 (quoting ARISTOTLE, THE ETHICS OF ARISTOTLE: THE NICOMACHEAN ETHICS, BOOK VI, chs. 5–13, at 176–92 (J.A.K. Thomson trans., 1953)).

[9] *See* GARY BELLOW & BEA MOULTON, THE LAWYERING PROCESS: MATERIALS FOR CLINICAL INSTRUCTION IN ADVOCACY 299–301 (1978) (describing a dialogue between a junior counsel and a senior counsel about the flexible judgments involved in strategic decision-making in litigation). Here, as in many places in this book, we are deeply indebted to the insights of Gary Bellow and Bea Moulton.

That's pretty much right. It is a useful exercise to imagine a static world, where stages proceed seamlessly, if only to get yourself oriented for the complexity about to come. What you will do, then, is to take a linear blueprint and make it messy—but explicitly and intentionally messy.

Here's what your more useful blueprint for the Filippa and Bill project might look like:

First, you need not conceive of the blueprint until after your initial interview, except in the broadest of ways. It can't hurt to envisage what a project like theirs might entail when deciding whether it fits with your other commitments, but beyond that you will know too little to be useful until you meet the clients. Of course, planning for the interview is still critically important.

Next, you cannot assume that you will end your first meeting with Filippa and Bill with the clients having made an affirmative choice about what type of entity they would like, or even that they want to create an entity at all. Your blueprint, then, will resemble less a chart and more of a *decision tree*. You will foresee that Filippa and Bill will likely need a second (or third) meeting at which you will help them decide two related questions: (a) do they want an entity at all?; and (b) if so, would their needs be met better by an LLC, an S Corp., or some other entity?

Using the decision tree as a model, one possible planning blueprint after the initial meeting with Filippa and Bill might look something like this (and we will start but not finish the blueprint):

I have formally accepted Filippa and Bill as clients of the clinic, as two individuals each of whom has retained our firm for representation. Before we proceed to do any substantive work, however, we will need to ensure that we have dealt adequately with any potential conflicts of interest between these two clients. Or, perhaps our jurisdiction will treat the two individuals by some default rule as constituents of the forthcoming, or nascent, or embryonic organization. I will need to develop a separate research plan to ensure that I know the law on that conflict of interest topic, and then create a plan to make sure I can explain it well enough to the two individuals, whatever their status ends up being. (I will also need to ascertain whether I must have any of this conversation with each individual separately.)

Assuming, though, that we can represent the two persons in some capacity, I next need to ensure that I have understood their goals well enough. After reviewing my notes, I will arrange to communicate with Filippa and Bill to confirm the goals as I understand them and, most likely, refine them as my thinking and my conversation with them progress.

Once I am reasonably confident about the entrepreneurs' goals, I will articulate the business operation choices available to them as they proceed with establishing the café. That means first discerning whether they want an entity of some sort—a formal structure recognized by our state offering some separation between the individuals and the business. To accomplish that goal, I will need to understand all of the relevant implications of proceeding without an entity but (presumably) with some insurance in place. My blueprint needs to include some consideration of how I will learn what I need to know about this. I must then counsel the entrepreneurs about that first choice.

If the answer to the entity question is no, then I will proceed to advise Filippa and Bill about what steps they might take to operate as a partnership (or, perhaps, as a sole proprietorship, should one of the two individuals emerge as the sole owner of the business). My plan for now will be to understand these implications well enough to counsel the two, but not in such great depth as I will need to understand later and to implement the selection, were they to choose this avenue.

But if the answer to the entity question is yes, that the couple would likely prefer an entity, I must then be prepared to counsel the two owners about the differences between an LLC and a corporation, and the differences between a C corporation and an S corporation.

And so forth . . . .

You can see how your planning has become more tentative and contingent. If Filippa and Bill want an entity, you proceed down one path, which has its own branches (LLC? S Corp.?); if they do not want an entity, you will have to advise them about whatever it means to do business without the structure and protections of an entity.[10] Each "branch" suggests further questions and lines of inquiry. For instance, if the clients choose an entity and then opt for an LLC, you may have dozens of potential operating agreement templates available, so your plan will note that you will have to find a sensible way to choose among them to meet your clients' particular needs. Of course, you will not develop a blueprint that investigates and plans for each respective branch and its inevitable ripple effects, except in the most tentative and broad way. You understand now how your blueprint is always morphing and adjusting to the latest information from, or choice made by, your clients.

planning contingent on client action/ choices

---

[10] Without an entity, the entrepreneurs will likely qualify as general partners, and much law exists for you to use to advise them of the implications of that. The owners also would not obtain the limited liability protections of the entity options, so you would need to offer advice about that consequence as well. We describe this in more depth in the Introduction to Business Entities chapter.

You see that this is a complicated enterprise. You are probably by now asking the most reasonable question under the circumstances: Given that the best so-called "blueprint" we can offer to you is amorphous, tentative, uncertain, and hardly ever reliable, why create one at all? Why not, you may ask, just approach each lawyer task independently, with no larger vision beyond the immediate task before you at any given time?

Our answer to your question is simple, and two-fold: Proceeding without a blueprint is bad lawyering, and it is impossible. It is bad lawyering *because* it is impossible. Even if you think you could accomplish each step of your lawyering work as an independent action, you would, whether you recognized it or not, always be making choices based on some assumed long-term goal and plan. You cannot accomplish any of your interviewing, counseling, drafting or negotiating without having some sense of where you want to get by doing so. Our suggestion is to make that longer-term strategy as explicit as possible, so you may recognize whether any given step seems like it has accomplished what you hoped.

It will help you appreciate the non-linear blueprint idea if we now introduce the concept of the "theory of the project," and see how the two concepts interact.

IV. DEVELOPING A "THEORY OF THE PROJECT"

A. "THEORY OF THE PROJECT" EXPLAINED

Your project blueprint will, if successful, offer you a reasonably structured approach to the work you will do for your clients. What it does not do, though, is to offer you enough *content* for that work. While closely related, the idea of theory development differs from the organizational blueprint by providing the basis for the actual work you will perform.

We borrow the "theory" concept from the world of litigation, where good planners rely on what they call a "theory of the case."[11] In litigation and similar dispute resolution contexts, the challenge for lawyers is to marshal arguments which will persuade others (a judge, a jury, the other party's lawyer) that their clients' version of the facts is true, or that the best legal interpretation favors their clients. They aim for a coherent theory of the case in which the law, the facts, the inferences from the facts, and the equities favor their side. When bad facts or unfavorable law appear, those lawyers adjust the theory to account for the news.

---

[11] *See, e.g.* BELLOW & MOULTON, *supra* note 9, at 305 ("a theory of the case [is] a view of how fact, law and circumstance can be put together to produce the outcome you and your client seek"); John B. Mitchell, *Narrative and Client–Centered Representation: What Is a True Believer to Do When His Two Favorite Theories Collide?*, 6 CLINICAL L. REV. 85, 99 (1999) ("[t]heories of the case are stories").

Your work involves transactions, and not disputes. Most of the time, your clients will not be engaged in proving that their version of the facts is more plausible than some other person's version. So you will not be using the conventional idea of a theory of the case in your clinic work as often as lawyers in the litigation sphere would do.[12]

But we still see significant benefits from the theory concept as applied to transactional work. For our purposes, the "theory of the project" is your effort to identify what you are hoping to accomplish, and how you believe you will be able to accomplish it. For each step of the blueprint, your plan must generate some work product, and the theory evaluates the quality of the work product. The concept of the theory of the project is substantive while the blueprint is procedural. It also encourages you to think creatively, to clarify your clients' goals, and to resist premature diagnosis of what your client needs.

Let us explore these qualities in the context of Filippa and Bill. We will then return to the blueprint and theory concepts in the context of a less well-structured legal issue, using a messier story involving community economic development.

Substantive theory of the case

B. A THEORY FOR FILIPPA AND BILL

There are many parts of the Filippa and Bill project which invite your thinking about a coherent theory. Using the textured blueprint from just above, let us identify two of those junctures.

You will recall that the blueprint identified as an early, and necessarily pre-conditional, step of your work the clarification of the status of Filippa and Bill as clients. For blueprint purposes, noting that task as an essential element of the larger scheme is precisely what a good lawyer needed to do. But noting it (the blueprint work) does not help at all to resolve it, or make sense of it (that is the theory work). The theory consideration arises when you start your work on that piece of the plan. You can easily imagine better or worse attempts to make sense of the client status. The best substantive legal work on that discrete topic will be *comprehensive* and *coherent*, accommodating the founders' wishes, the relevant ethical rules of your jurisdiction, the common law in your state about the responsibilities of organizational constituents, the psychology and interpersonal skill components of effective communication with laypersons, especially those with non-aligned interests but who hope to work togeth-

---

[12] The text likely overstates the case for the inapplicability of litigation-based "theory of the case" strategies in transactional work. Imagine, say, a commercial lease negotiation, where you represent the prospective tenant-merchant. The landlord wants high rent and a lot of protections; your client wants lower rent and fewer obligations. Your bargaining will often include competing versions of the "facts"—such as the prevailing commercial rental rates, the likelihood of default, the likely income of the business, the availability of alternative sites, and so forth. As you prepare a negotiation strategy, you will need a coherent theory of the case on which to base that strategy. For more about how that works in the negotiation context, see the chapter on Transactional Negotiations.

er, and the strategic implications of the role of any documents you might create as part of this task.

Imagine now a broader "theory of the project" emerging from the Filippa and Bill assignment. Recall that when you first encountered this couple you understood from their request to the clinic for legal services that they wanted to form an LLC. One might think that an adequate "theory of the project" for this assignment would include a vision of a smart LLC that complies nicely with state statutes and federal tax law, has no grammatical or typographical errors, and satisfies requirements of the Secretary of State (or whatever governmental agency oversees LLC initiation in your state) for effective and prompt filing.

We can use the "theory of the project" concept to unpack that obviously simplistic notion of what your mission should be with Filippa and Bill. The problem with the above description is that at the same time it assumes too much and views your clients' world too narrowly. Filippa and Bill do not "want" an LLC. Filippa and Bill (most likely) want to operate the café on Prospect Street, profitably and equitably, with the fewest distractions and the greatest protection of their personal assets, and at the least cost, financial and transactional. Or maybe not. Maybe they have some other goals in running this business together. Clients like Filippa and Bill come to a transactional lawyer like you not to purchase an LLC, but to take care of whatever they have to take care of to get the business going in the way they hope to run it. Your role in this transaction is to identify and explore those interests and needs, and to prepare the best package of legal rights and benefits available—or, more likely, an array of differing packages—which will accomplish their goals. Your theory of the project will capture the goals of your clients and your best vision of how to accomplish those goals.

Your textured blueprint recognized this strategy as well. The blueprint promoted a scheme to ensure that you have the opportunities to craft the most comprehensive and coherent package of legal products to accomplish the goals of your client, and recognized your need to think creatively about the nature of those goals. The theory stage is where you use those opportunities to design the package, or an assortment of packages, that can meet the goals.

C. QUALITIES OF EFFECTIVE STRATEGIC THEORY DEVELOPMENT

Strategic planning writers have identified a number of useful heuristics to assist you to develop a coherent theory. Their advice includes the following:

- *Avoid premature diagnosis*: This advice appeared in our thinking about the blueprint idea above and in the Interviewing chapter.

Well-trained lawyers and law students like yourselves learn to recognize useful schemes and patterns amid a lot of ambiguous data.[13] That is what law school trains you to do well, and it is a talent for which people will pay you (sometimes handsomely) to share with them. But that most essential attribute of legal training comes with a cost—you begin to see the world as a lawyer. When Filippa and Bill come to your office looking to organize their business, you quickly categorize the couple as "an LLC matter."[14] You might be completely right, and, indeed, you probably *are* completely right, in that characterization. But your planning has to suspend that otherwise well-grounded judgment, and avoid what several writers refer to as premature diagnosis.[15] Your work with Filippa and Bill needs to involve careful, nonjudgmental listening to their needs, aspirations and goals. You will then need to think creatively about all of the ways, legal and otherwise, that Filippa and Bill might run their business without running into the problems they worry about. From there, you will begin to craft your coherent theory.

- *Use Backward Mapping*: Strategic planning is goal-driven. You might think that the most effective approach to achieving your client's goal would be forward-looking—from where you are toward the goal you want to reach. In fact, in many respects the opposite will be true. In litigation circles, the most elementary advice to a lawyer preparing for a courtroom trial is to start with her closing argument.[16] Once you know what you want to be able to say to a jury at the end of the trial, you may then work backwards to investigate how you could possibly get there. The same principle applies to transactional work, if perhaps in a more subtle way. A first task for you at the beginning of a new project might be to write a draft of your closing memo, with some detail. (Do not just write, "Solved all of clients' problems. They are happy. Closed the file.") Describe how you achieved your clients' goals, and how you solved any problems they brought to the lawyer. This exercise also triggers your recognizing possible obsta-

---

[13] *See* Gary L. Blasi, *What Lawyers Know: Lawyering Expertise, Cognitive Science, and the Functions of Theory*, 45 J. LEGAL EDUC. 313 (1995).

[14] Indeed, within the clinic office you'll find yourself referring to the Sands and Sherman project as an "LLC matter."

[15] *See, e.g.* BELLOW & MOULTON, *supra* note 9, at 323–34; STEFAN H. KRIEGER & RICHARD K. NEUMANN, JR., ESSENTIAL LAWYERING SKILLS: INTERVIEWING, COUNSELING, NEGOTIATION, AND PERSUASIVE FACT ANALYSIS 37 (4th ed. 2011). Because of the risks involved in too quickly categorizing a client's matter, the established interviewing texts craft their models to try to counteract this tendency. *See, e.g.*, DAVID A. BINDER, PAUL BERGMAN, PAUL R. TREMBLAY & IAN WEINSTEIN, LAWYERS AS COUNSELORS 765–76, 258 (3d ed. 2012).

[16] *See, e.g.*, MARILYN J. BERGER, JOHN B. MITCHELL & RONALD H. CLARK, TRIAL ADVOCACY: PLANNING, ANALYSIS AND STRATEGY 68 (2d ed. 2008); ROGER HAYDOCK & JOHN SONGSTEN, TRIAL: ADVOCACY BEFORE JUDGES, JURORS AND ARBITRATORS 32 (4th ed. 2011).

cles along the way, obstacles which you might not have anticipated until your strategy was far down one branch of your decision tree scheme.

Think about how you might use backward mapping for Filippa and Bill. There will be no closing argument to be given in this transactional matter, but instead there will be a functioning business for you to envision. Your plan for Filippa and Bill will imagine that business with their help, and think of the issues that your plan will need to have covered. Here are a few of the questions their project evokes: What do the couple want their business to do? What financing do they envision? How large do they want to get? Do they envision inviting other people into the business? Do they want this to be their livelihood forever? Do they want to be able to sell if they get successful? You can continue this process to add more considerations. A good theory of the project will account for and anticipate as many of those questions as possible, and its design will incorporate their responses in as comprehensive and coherent a fashion as possible.

- *Beware of Labels*: Once a concept has a name, we tend to visualize it as fitting within the category of things with that name. Kenney Hegland tells this story:

  > Given a metal ball, a string and a nail, test subjects were asked to construct a pendulum. No problem. They used the metal ball as a hammer. The experiment was then repeated, this time with the metal ball labeled "Pendulum Ball." This stumped many. Looking at the ball, they saw "pendulum ball," not "potential hammer."[17]

  Labeling your work can have a similar limiting or distorting effect. Sometimes you slap on the label ("my new intake is going to be an LLC matter"); sometimes your clients perform that task ("we came here because we want to incorporate our business in Nevada"). Either way, once in place the label might affect how you envision solutions to the problems the label represents. Your theory development, therefore, should provisionally resist labeling. *Why* might the clients want to incorporate the business, and why in Nevada? What goals would that accomplish? What might be the best way to achieve those goals? If a corporation or an LLC will do the trick, that's great. But don't necessarily assume so.

- *Resist the First "Good" Idea and Favoring Your Comfort Zones*: We introduced this chapter with a quick story of your meeting

---

[17] KENNEY F. HEGLAND, TRIAL AND PRACTICE SKILLS IN A NUTSHELL 20 (3d ed. 2001)

Filippa and Bill and quickly pulling together an LLC package. Lawyers (even more so than law students) have a tendency to act first, and fit the results of that action into their strategies later. A lawyer might pick up the phone and make a quick call to try to resolve an issue, before fitting that tactic into a larger strategy and plan.[18] Stefan Krieger and Richard Neumann describe this "weak" strategic habit as follows: "The lawyer seems to 'slide' into strategies. . . . Tactics are chosen by acting on the first 'good' idea that appears."[19]

A related habit that interferes with thoughtful project planning is to succumb to your own preferences and comfort zones. Most of us find comfort in certain kinds of lawyering activities, and experience stress in others, given our individual personalities and talents. Some of you might relish the idea of a risky, high-stakes event; others will admit that they went into transactional work for exactly the opposite reason. The point for theory development purposes is that you should be as aware as possible of your inclinations, strengths, and weaknesses, and you should do your best to resist having your lawyering strategies driven by those motivators rather than your theory.[20]

- *Brainstorm*: "Brainstorming" is a term of art in the world of strategic planning.[21] It describes an explicit and intentional practice in which you generate ideas without judging them. Our creativity is hampered by our worry about looking foolish or stupid. Brainstorming permits us the freedom to identify a wide swath of ideas without regard to their elegance. A rigorous brainstorming exercise will generate many silly ideas, but perhaps some unexpectedly brilliant idea will appear as well. And, if not, at least you've had some fun.[22]

- *Your Theories Must Be Coherent and Comprehensive*: We have been noting this all along, but it warrants this explicit mention. Your clients will bring with them many goals, aspiration, needs, and constraints. An effective and elegant theory of the project will accommodate all of those factors, at least as well as it can. If no single measure or package of measures will satisfy all of your client's wishes (and that's quite likely, as you might imagine),

---

[18] *Id.* at 13–14.

[19] KRIEGER & NEUMANN, *supra* note 15, at 39.

[20] *Id.* at 42–43.

[21] *Id.*; HEGLAND, *supra* note 17, at 22.

[22] The research on the effectiveness of brainstorming is not entirely uniform about its usefulness. *See, e.g.,* Paul B. Paulus & Vincent R. Brown, *Enhancing Ideational Creativity in Groups: Lessons from Research on Brainstorming, in* GROUP CREATIVITY 110 (Paul B. Paulus & Bernard A. Nijstad eds., 2003).

you will most often create multiple theories leading to alternative packages, and your guidance will help your clients choose among a collection of imperfect alternatives.[23]

- *Using Checklists*: Checklists are terrific organizational devices. Checklists are dangerous crutches which interfere with creative lawyering. We agree with both of these statements. For years, thoughtful observers have warned about the dangers of relying upon checklists in strategic planning.[24] Given all we have said above about avoiding premature diagnosis and ineffective labeling, your dependence on a predetermined checklist as a central part of your plan seems to serve as a hindrance to effective lawyering. At the same time, recent research, especially that popularized by the elegant writer Atul Gawande,[25] demonstrates the effectiveness—and, indeed, the critical necessity—of checklists in medicine, airline safety, and other fields. The trick, we believe, lies in how you use your checklists. Use them later, not earlier. Do not rely exclusively on others' checklists to drive your planning, but find or create them for the work you do that has important component parts.[26]

You can apply these heuristics to your work for Filippa and Bill. Instead of immediately applying a label to their project ("an LLC matter"), you would suspend judgment, explore their interests and goals, and identify as many possible solutions to the challenges they face. Let us assume that you learn that Filippa and Bill want to operate the business for creative satisfaction, want to make some money doing so, want to minimize outlandish risk but not all risk, and prefer not to face the prospect of personal bankruptcy if the business were to fail.[27] Your list of alternatives for your "theory of the project" would of course include an S Corporation and an LLC, but might you be more creative? The couple could operate as a general partnership or a limited partnership. The two could work for an outside owner given the right arrangements and guarantees of autonomy. Filippa could own the business and Bill could be her employee. Or Filippa

---

[23] We discuss this responsibility in our chapter on Counseling.

[24] For some examples, see Philip G. Schrag, *Constructing a Clinic*, 3 CLINICAL L. REV. 175, 220–21 (1996) (critiquing practice manuals); Alexander Scherr, *Lawyers and Decisions: A Model of Practical Judgment*, 47 VILL. L. REV. 161, 182 (2002) (noting the "thin" value of checklists).

[25] *See* ATUL GAWANDE, THE CHECKLIST MANIFESTO: HOW TO GET THINGS RIGHT (2009); Atul Gawande, *A Surgical Safety Checklist to Reduce Morbidity and Mortality in a Global Population*, 360 NEW ENG. J. MED. 491 (2009).

[26] Checklists are essential tools for transactional lawyers, especially those who must engage in due diligence efforts as part of a sale or merger. *See, e.g.*, Andrea M. Mattei, *A Due Diligence Checklist Based on Expansive Representations and Warranties*, in COMMERCIAL REAL ESTATE FINANCING: STRATEGIES FOR CHANGING MARKETS AND UNCERTAIN TIMES, ST053 ALI–ABA 209 (2012).

[27] Your exploration of their goals would likely uncover more personal aspirations regarding, say, the relationship between the two and the number of hours each hopes to dedicate to the enterprise.

could own the business at first, with Bill slowly earning equity over time, perhaps with voting rights, or perhaps not. See how many other alternatives you might generate.

Working closely with Filippa and Bill, you would then refine your theory as you sort through your intentionally-broad set of alternatives. Some you will reject quite easily (no general partnership, as it leaves too great an exposure); others, a bit more gradually; and others will stay as possibilities. You might opt *tentatively* for Option 4, while keeping Options 2 and 5 on the table, in case you discern later as the work progresses that Option 4 presents an unacceptable risk or hurdle. In that way your theory of the project need not be perfectly comprehensive, and it cannot be so. The best theory will permit some hedging, with alternative avenues on hold in case the primary plan does not work as well as you may have hoped.

V. WORKING WITH ILL–STRUCTURED PROJECTS

We noted above that the Filippa and Bill project was a relatively straightforward transactional matter, and as such it serves as a useful example for our considering both the blueprint organizational ideas and the development of a coherent theory of the project. But how do these ideas work when clients bring to the clinic a less tidy venture? Much of your transactional clinic work will qualify as, at a minimum, somewhat "ill-structured."[28] While we do not have the space here (nor you the readers the patience) to explore in great depth a robust plan for a more complex and ambiguous client matter, we will offer two brief examples of less well-structured projects and share some thoughts about how you apply the planning ideas to that kind of lawyering work. Our message is that not only ought you use the strategic planning ideas outlined above in more complex and ambiguous cases, but in many ways it is *more imperative* to apply them when the matters are more confusing and harder to make sense of.

In this Section we will describe two stories with increasing degrees of fuzziness. The first of the two is more complex and messier than the Filippa and Bill story; the next one is more complicated still. In each instance we will offer some preliminary ideas about how you might begin to create useful blueprints and theories to assist you to add structure to these projects.

---

[28] *See* Bennett, *supra* note 3, at 48 ("It is in the very nature of community development projects to be 'complex' or 'ill-structured.'"); Ian Weinstein, *Lawyering in the State of Nature: Instinct and Automaticity in Legal Problem Solving*, 23 VT. L. REV. 1, 14 (1998) ("Cognitive scientists call hard problems, like lawyering problems, 'ill-structured' problems.").

A. A SECOND STORY: A LESS–WELL–STRUCTURED CLINIC PROJECT

1. The Story of MAHC

This second example, a story from one of our own clinics but adequately sanitized,[29] might work with for our purposes here. Consider this tale:[30]

> Your supervisor has assigned you to work with a group calling itself the Montrose Affordable Housing Coalition, or MAHC. MAHC has worked with community institutions on affordable housing issues, engaged in community organizing, and advocated for low-income tenants for 30 years in Essex County, where your clinic operates. MAHC has not been a client of the clinic before now. One of its officers, the president Suzanne Dubus, asked for the clinic's help about organizing the group as a 501(c)(3) tax-exempt nonprofit.
>
> In your initial interview with Suzanne, you learned that MAHC is not a corporation, and has never been a corporation. It has been functioning for many years as an unincorporated association. It has named some officers, but until recently it did not have any formal bylaws. Last year a group of its constituents approved a set of bylaws, which provided for a board of directors with 15 members. The bylaws by their terms give to "members" of the organization the power to elect all board members and to have ultimate control over the organization's operations, including approval of its budget and any amendments to the bylaws. The bylaws define a "member" as a person who supports the mission of MAHC and pays dues. The bylaws do not specify how a member, having qualified as such by paying dues, might lose or forfeit membership status.
>
> MAHC has been using a local tax-exempt nonprofit group to serve as a fiscal sponsor when it applied for some grant funding. (A fiscal sponsor can accept donations intended for a non-tax-

---

[29] Two quick side notes about our use of an example from our clinic. First, as you know and will see in greater depth in the chapter on Ethical Issues in Transactional Practice, you owe a duty of confidentiality to your client, a duty you breach if you use the client's story, without consent, in a way that identifies the client. *See* MODEL RULES OF PROF'L CONDUCT R. 1.6 cmt. 4. Second, the use of your client's stories for educational and publication purposes, even if sufficiently disguised to satisfy the duties inherent in Rule 1.6, may still raise some questions about fairness and respect for your client's dignity. Some commentators have addressed that question. *See, e.g.,* David F. Chavkin, *Why Doesn't Anyone Care About Confidentiality? (and, What Message Does That Send to New Lawyers?),* 25 GEO. J. LEGAL ETHICS 239 (2012); Abbe Smith, *Telling Stories and Keeping Secrets,* 8 U. D.C. L. REV. 255 (2004). We believe that the story we use here does not affect our client's interests in any appreciable way.

[30] For a more elaborately told, and frankly more "ill-structured," community group story, see Bennett, *supra* note 3.

exempt organization, and give the donations to that organization, if the recipient shares the nonprofit's mission.) Suzanne,
the MAHC president, contacted your clinic because the organization has been exploring the option of becoming its own 501(c)(3)
organization. She and others on the board have heard that there
are some important advantages to becoming an independent
501(c)(3) entity, and there has been some subtle but distracting
tension recently between MAHC and the nonprofit organization
which has been serving as its fiscal sponsor.

At the present, MAHC has more than $25,000 in a bank account,
funds accumulated from its grant writing and from dues paid by
members. MAHC also has a "project" within its larger operations
known as the Tenant Advocacy Project (TAP). TAP offers lay advocacy services to public housing tenants in Montrose. The steering committee in charge of TAP has disagreed with the MAHC
board about how much of the organization's funds should be
spent on TAP instead of the other MAHC activities. In your
meeting, Suzanne described the TAP steering committee members as a bit rigid and dogmatic, and a little difficult to deal
with.

Suzanne's goal is quite clear and simple—she wants the clinic to
assist MAHC to become a separate tax-exempt organization.
Your clinic has represented many clients in that kind of process
before the IRS, and MAHC's mission is very attractive to the
clinic's community economic development and social justice
commitments.

*   *   *

Let us conclude the description at this point. As you might imagine,
in your clinic work you would have developed layers and layers of more
detailed facts about this basic story, but we know enough now to consider
developing a blueprint and a theory for this project—or, at least, for puzzling through the process of doing so.

At one level, this new client project is pretty straightforward—
interesting, and perhaps challenging, but straightforward all the same.
You may use the clinic's resources to research creating a nonprofit corporation in your state, and preparing the Form 1023 for the IRS.[31] Your instinct is that supporting low-income tenants and affordable housing is
likely to be a qualifying mission under the IRS regulations, but you also
know you can research that question in a pretty manageable way. You're
ready to proceed, and you conclude that you can work on a pretty effective
description of your theory of the project, which you can refine through
your ongoing conversations with Suzanne.

---

[31] *See* the chapter on nonprofit organizations below for an overview of these processes.

But, as you surely have realized, you *cannot* proceed right now, at least not in that somewhat comfortable and cabined fashion just described. The story you just learned has a host of complexity, and your first responsibility will be to make some principled sense of the various elements and decide how you will make sense of them to craft a meaningful narrative.

We will not use this part of this chapter to perform that task in any detail, but here are the more untidy elements that you must factor into your plan:

First, who is your client? MAHC is an unincorporated association (UA), and most authorities agree that a lawyer may represent a UA.[32] But Suzanne wants you to create a corporation rather than to maintain the UA, a strategic choice which in your legal judgment is quite sound (for reasons we will not delve into here) given the IRS's scrutiny of the governance of the organization when it reviews the application for tax exemption. You will learn that you may not be able to simply "convert" a UA into a corporation in your state; you may need to create a separate corporation and then transfer the assets of the UA to the new corporate entity. But that might require the consent, not just of a majority the UA board, or even a majority of the UA membership, but of *every* member of the UA.[33] And that presents a problem because you do not know, with any certainty, who qualifies as a member for purposes of that vote, given the ambiguity of the bylaw language.

Even if you can resolve the client question in some sensible fashion, you have discerned some tension on the board about how the organization should operate. The TAP faction seems to have some ideas about the use of the UA's funds which Suzanne, for one, does not share. This issue might lend itself to a plausible answer based on coherent legal analysis (for instance, you might, after a careful review of the bylaws, poll the board and count the votes to see whether the TAP faction has more support than the position espoused by Suzanne). Yet, that response might be terrible in practice. Counting votes to resolve an intramural dispute within a UA might not be a very effective solution for this organization. Your strategic theory about how to obtain sound direction from your "client" must include your practical judgment about how this group most effectively will function.[34]

---

[32] We address that question in the chapters on Ethical Issues in Transactional Practice and Working with Groups.

[33] That may be true. *See* 7 C.J.S. *Association* 111 (2012) ("if the members of an association unanimously vote to incorporate it, the creation of the corporation pursuant thereto ipso facto dissolves the association and transfers its property and rights to the corporation. . . . [T]o have this effect, all members must consent to the incorporation, since the act of a mere majority in securing a corporate charter is insufficient"); McFadden v. Murphy, 149 Mass. 342, 346 (1889).

[34] For a fuller discussion of the group process, particularly with community groups, see Chapter 9.

In addition to those two challenges, your theory development would also surely include the ultimate question—the governance and faction questions aside—whether MAHC ought to proceed with its independent 501(c)(3) pursuit or whether it might work out its issues with its current fiscal sponsor, or perhaps search for a new fiscal sponsor. And there is yet another somewhat-concealed issue lurking in this story—that of possible unauthorized practice of law. TAP seems to be offering legal advice to tenants, and TAP is not a law firm. Your assistance of unauthorized practice may itself be a violation of the Model Rules.[35]

You now see how this short narrative invites levels of complexity and possible confusion. At first, you should experience some disorientation and hesitance about how to proceed. You will then begin to construct both a beginning blueprint, and then a series of substantive theories, to assist you to proceed.

2. Working With the Less–Well–Structured Project

A moment's reflection will show that an organizational blueprint can assist you to make sense of this cluttered and interwoven collection of issues. In the end, you *might* prepare corporation papers and assist your client with a Form 1023 application to the IRS, but to reach that goal (or perhaps an alternative end-state, where your client, whoever ends up serving in that capacity, instructs you to negotiate a better or a new fiscal sponsorship arrangement), you have to resolve some of the uncertainties in some recognizable order. Discerning that order will require the exercise of some judgment on your part, but the best you can do is to start with a tentative outline. That beginning outline might look something like this:

> The client identity question requires some research (e.g., how does your state treat UAs?; how does it respond to bylaws adopted by a loosely assembled group of individuals?) along with some further factual development (who voted for the bylaws?; who maintains lists of the plausible or purported members of the UA?).

> Your research and factual development will generate a series of options, each of which will incorporate a dose of risk and uncertainty, for which you will generate some predictions and gauge the costs and benefits. For instance, perhaps the control group will arrange a vote to revise the bylaws to provide a simpler operating process in the future; or perhaps the research will show that the fiscal sponsor has some ownership of the funds in the bank account, and you can rely on that entity to transfer the funds to a new corporation; or perhaps you hold a general mem-

---

[35] MODEL RULES OF PROF'L CONDUCT R. 5.5.

bership meeting and seek unanimous consent from existing members to the transfer of the funds.

The question of the control of the UA (and then of the resulting corporate structure) *probably* should precede resolution of the intramural dispute about funding the TAP. The reasoning would be that you need to understand the organizational authority structures in order to put the board's internal dispute into some context. Recall that you hope you will not need to use the organizational authority structure to resolve the TAP funding disagreements, but understanding them seems necessary as context for whatever intervention or mediation you might engage in with the board members.

And so forth. . . .

You can see how your orienting plan for the progress of the project throughout your semester lends itself to some tentative and provisional ideas which you may sketch out as we have just done, and you also see how none of the steps—almost quite literally none—is fixed or certain. At each juncture you are assessing risk, inputting research results, and having ongoing conversations with some constituents.

That process serves as, to use our language, the blueprint of this ill-structured project. But the blueprint also hints at the qualitative theories that you will develop for each of the steps you will consider. Your research and your ongoing fact development will permit you to refine a theory of management and control over a member-managed UA. That theory will itself cohere with a theory of corporate management for the new organization. You will devise a separate theory for the lawyer's role in mediating among constituents of a community group. Those theories will inform your actual work, while the blueprint oriented you about how the various tasks and steps come together to form a workable and sensible whole.

We tend to believe that you may begin to understand and organize any clinic project, no matter how fuzzy, complicated, and poorly-structured, by its blueprint and its applicable theories. For some projects, the uncertainties will be less, and the ensemble will come together more easily. For others, you will find the ambiguities nearly intolerable, and the efforts required of you will be much greater. And you might fail in your effort to make sense of a project, for instance if you simply cannot identify the facts that you need to know, or if the imprecision of the relevant law makes any responsible prediction implausible. But you will reach those conclusions by your having made the efforts to articulate the strands of your inquiry, documenting your plans, and refining your theories.

B. A THIRD STORY: AN ILL–STRUCTURED CLINIC PROJECT

For our next example of a project which is messier and more slippery than the previous two projects we have described, we offer an example of a client hoping to effect change in a community in a creative way.

1. The Story

A local community-based nonprofit organization, Faces of Hope in Our Neighborhood (FHON), has developed a transitional housing program for women who have been victims of domestic violence. FHON recently added to its programming a job training program for the women living in the transitional housing units. The staff and board of FOHN are now considering, as part of the employment and career training program, the prospect of establishing a social venture, one where the women would manufacture and sell soaps and other bath products. (By "social venture," the nonprofit's constituents conceive of a money-making enterprise that has elements of good and responsible practices that typically characterize nonprofit organizations.[36]) They want to know how they should structure the social venture. Can they do it as part of the job training program of the organization? Should they perhaps create a subsidiary? Or an entirely separate organization? Or maybe a cooperative with the women as part owners? The executive director and the board president arranged a meeting with you to seek your advice and direction, and during that meeting you learned of these ambitions and plans.

* * *

Note how this brief story differs from the original Filippa and Bill story, and from the less-well-structured MAHC story above. The Filippa and Bill project was relatively manageable. It lent itself to careful, progressive analysis and the use of decision-tree reasoning to imagine the various alternatives that might fit the needs of the two entrepreneurs. The MAHC project, by contrast, was more complicated, with some inherent ambiguities about the identity of your client and some strategic tensions about how best to work with the group writ large, as well as with the factions within the group's leadership. But MHAC was not really *ill-structured*; it was complicated, but it could respond to mapping, backwards reasoning, and its own set of decision-tree projections.

Here, the FOHN project is pretty close to ill-structured. It has more moving parts, more uncertainties, and more contingencies than the previ-

---

[36] For a useful discussion of social ventures, see MARC J. LANE, SOCIAL ENTERPRISE: EMPOWERING MISSION–DRIVEN ENTREPRENEURS (2011); Thomas Kelley, *Law and Choice of Entity on the Social Enterprise Frontier*, 84 TUL. L. REV. 337 (2009).

ous two examples. But a good lawyer will have to make sense of this project, using both the blueprint concept and the effort to create useful theories to provide substantive content to the lawyering work. Let us explore preliminarily how that might occur.

2.   Working With the Ill–Structured Project

Imagine that you are the lawyer whose responsibility it will be to assist FOHN in this enterprise, and to advise its staff and board about how the enterprise ought to look. How might you start to make sense of this project?

Let us begin with the blueprint. Where will the lawyering work start? You do have a discrete and identifiable client here, one with (presumably) clear organizational chains of command and divisions of labor, given that it is an established nonprofit agency. But the proposed project seemingly invites community input and perhaps even direction, especially if the new enterprise might be a cooperative owned by the women who receive the housing and job training. So one aspect of your blueprint will include consideration of who will provide direction, and whose voice counts, as you evaluate alternatives and make decisions about ways to proceed.

The blueprint also generates consideration of the many substantive law questions the enterprise evokes. Your plan will include a mechanism by which you can identify and then address the specific legal topics you will need to understand. May a nonprofit job-training program sell soap and bath products? If so, are there limits to that component of the nonprofit's mission, or other implications about which the nonprofit should be aware? May a nonprofit "own" a nonprofit affiliate? May it own a for-profit business? If the new enterprise is a cooperative, what is the connection of that entity (and is a cooperative an entity?) to FOHN? And will the women participants in the cooperative remain owners once they have left the transitional housing and the job training program? May they ever sell their interests to others? The list goes on. Think of what other legal research questions you can generate.[37]

Your blueprint, then, will include a plan for discerning a decision-making scheme among the constituents and your client, and a plan by which you will understand the nature of the several available options. It will then proceed to sketch out a plan for assessing the implications of the several alternatives (including identifying which criteria will matter for that task), and some ideas, including perhaps a timeline, for your imple-

---

[37] It should be apparent that each question you generate, such as those offered in the text as examples, will have some achievable answer discernible from some authority somewhere. The answer to any given question may not necessarily be clear ("It depends on these factors and circumstances . . . ."), but a good lawyer should be able to arrive at a sensible resolution of any question evoked by the project.

menting the alternative that the decision-makers ultimately select. What other elements would you include in the blueprint for this project?

As for your developing the theory of the project, the considerations we have just introduced for the blueprint should have evoked for you some beginning conceptions of this project's coherent and comprehensive mission. You will need to craft a strategic theory by which to evaluate the decision-making process, especially who decides things in the end. (Just FOHN? FOHN and those residents who participate in the job training? Other community members or organizations?) You will need a strategic theory to rely upon to evaluate the several options you will investigate and then describe. And, once you have a tentative direction for your work ("We are very attracted by the worker cooperative idea," say), you will devise a strategy that incorporates the available substantive law, the local regulatory constraints and opportunities, the ethical and political commitments of the participants, and the practical realities of the workaday lives of the residents and trainees, to arrive at a final product that, as best as you can accomplish, *works*.

What other kinds of strategic theories do you foresee as being necessary or likely in this project?

VI. DECISION-MAKING WITHIN STRATEGIC PLANNING

A. THE IMPORTANCE OF DECISION-MAKING TO STRATEGIC PLANNING

In this part of our chapter we highlight some insights from decision-making theory to assist you with your strategic planning. If the blueprint idea represents the broad view of the process of working on a client matter, and if theory development represents the organizing themes and content of the project, decision-making refers to your choices at any given moment along the way. We have to be careful here, of course, because "decision-making" encompasses everything you do for a client, including your choices in devising your blueprint or in crafting your theory of the project. To be useful to you, we hope to consider decision-making as the process of making the strategic choices necessary as you move through your blueprint and implement your theory.

Many of the ideas generated by writers about decision-making will reappear in our chapter on counseling.[38] When you counsel your clients, you assist the clients to make important decisions in a reliable way, and so the deliberative process involved in making critical choices has great relevance to your work in that area. In the strategic work on your pro-

---

[38] *See* the chapter on Counseling Transactional Clients.

jects, by contrast, *you* are making the vital decisions. So it makes sense to introduce the topic here.

B. DECISION-MAKING AS AN ART

In your role as a lawyer you will make decisions all the time—that is, essentially, your job. Some decisions will be relatively innocuous (Do you leave yet *another* voice mail for the agency bureaucrat after having left two previous ones, or should you hang up and call later?; or, Which of your clients' cases should you work on during your three hours in the clinic today?); others will have much more significant implications (Should you call the executive director of the nonprofit to inform her of the actions of the department head you have been dealing with?; or, Should you file the Form 1023 today to meet the 27–month deadline,[39] or work to improve it some more and seek a waiver or extension of that deadline?[40]). In either context, you can and will evaluate the quality of your decisions. Some resourceful people have offered useful ways to think about the process of making quality, reliable decisions. Here are some of their ideas:

- *Maximizing Information*: A decision means alternatives. Without options, there is nothing to decide. Your decision is your choice among the available alternatives based on your judgment about which of them meets your goals most effectively, using whatever criteria you apply (efficiency, cost, return on investment, and so forth). While quite obvious, writers remind us that access to information most often aids in the success of your choices.[41] In thinking about decision-making as an art, you will want to favor those choices which increase your store of information.

- *Simplification and Elegance*: Too much information overwhelms us. Information overload leads to unwise decisions, as researchers have shown.[42] Your decision-making therefore wants to maximize your available information as we noted above, but while at the same time not missing, as you've heard the saying, the forest for the trees. Recall Occam's Razor, the principle that stresses simplicity in our efforts to understand the world.[43] Your decision-making will favor choices which offer needed information without overwhelming you.

---

[39] 26 C.F.R. 1.508–1(a)(2)(i) (as amended by Rev. Proc. 92–85, 1992–2 C.B. 490). *See* I.R.S., U.S. DEP'T OF THE TREASURY, INSTRUCTIONS FOR FORM 1023: APPLICATION FOR RECOGNITION OF EXEMPTION UNDER SECTION 501(C)(3) OF THE INTERNAL REVENUE CODE 4 (June 2006), *available at* http://www.irs.gov/pub/irs-pdf/i1023.pdf.

[40] Treas. Reg. 1.508–1(a)(2)(i); Treas. Reg. 1.508–1(a)(3)(i).

[41] *See, e.g.,* BELLOW & MOULTON, *supra* note 9, at 298.

[42] *See* JONAH LEHRER, HOW WE DECIDE (2009).

[43] *See* Marjorie Anne McDiarmid, *Lawyer Decision Making: The Problem of Prediction*, 1992 WIS. L. REV. 1847, 1918–1919 (describing the theory of William of Occam, an English philosopher in the 1200s).

- *Minimizing Risk*: Your clients are entitled to take as many risks as they wish, consistent with your duty to honor your legal and moral obligations. But in your decision-making, even if you are a risk-taker by nature, you will want to minimize the unnecessary risks of any given decision, lest you find yourself having made a commitment which you cannot back away from. This sentiment leads to the following insight.

- *Reversibility*: Gary Bellow and Bea Moulton describe "the value of alternatives that offer some chance of benefit and no loss if the hoped-for gains do not materialize."[44] Your decision-making will prefer those choices which do not foreclose options irrevocably, in order to preserve as much flexibility as possible in the future. When you choose an option-foreclosing alternative, do so with a clear understanding of what choices you are abandoning.

- *Intuition versus Deliberation*: Most of what we have described here so far favors deliberate, intentional, and carefully reasoned choices. Our very first vignette opening this chapter depicted a student acting impulsively and viscerally, and (as you suspected then and know now) we intended that vignette as an example of not the best strategic planning. A central message of this entire chapter has been that the most successful strategic planning is calculated, purposeful, and thoughtful.

  But we have to be careful here, because that message is correct but misleading. The roles of emotion and intuition in decision-making are critical. Purely analytic thinking about choices, research now shows quite powerfully, is distorting and often ineffective. Jonah Lehrer describes New England Patriots quarterback Tom Brady's talent to "read" a terrifically complex terrain in a split second and make extremely wise choices about where and how to throw a football, all based on his experienced but visceral judgments.[45] Brady's talent, while exceptional, is typical of the best expert thinking, and Lehrer offers other examples of airline pilots,[46] firefighters,[47] professional poker players[48] and others who rely as much upon emotion and instinct as upon reasoned, analytical deliberation. The emotional component is essential to good decision-making. In Lehrer's words, "The process of thinking requires feeling, for feelings are what let us under-

---

[44] BELLOW & MOULTON, *supra* note 9, at 298.

[45] LEHRER, *supra* note 42, at 1–8.

[46] *Id.* at 120–32; 256–59.

[47] *Id.* at 92–100.

[48] *Id.* at 219–32.

stand all of the information that we can't directly comprehend. Reason without emotion is impotent."[49]

So why is our initial vignette an example of bad planning?[50]
Why should that clinic student not have relied on his instincts about how to proceed to address his client's legal
needs? The answer lies in the concepts of judgment and wisdom. Until you are an expert, your "read" of the complex ter-
rains in front of you will be imperfect. Until you have a lot of
experience, your only reliable method of understanding ambiguous, complex and changing landscapes will have to be by
breaking them down into component parts. Think of the difference between a novice and an expert chess player.[51] The
former—like you in the clinic, most likely—will make his individual chess moves by thinking about each successive possible reaction and counter-reaction. He will be deliberate
and, likely, slow (and, likely, less successful). The latter—
like the experienced lawyers you observe and work with—
will "see" patterns, openings and moves immediately; she
will make choices more reliably and more quickly because of
that judgment. At the beginning of your clinic experience you
will most likely be a novice;[52] by the end of your tenure in the
clinic, you will have grown substantially in your capacity to
read the complex world within which you practice.

The other reason why that student's initial planning ideas
were not reliable is that in the vignette the student had insufficient information on which to make his strategic judgments about the trajectory of the client project. His planning
assumed many facts and client goals which he did not yet
know. His reliance on intuition and instincts was risky both
because he did not yet have enough expertise, and because,
even if he had that level of skill, he did not have enough textured information on which to base his judgments.

- *Cognitive Illusions*: Our last topic related to your decision-
  making processes is an important one—the role that what some

---

[49] *Id.* at 26.

[50] *See* the first page of this Chapter, *supra.*

[51] Other writers have noted this analogy as well. *See* BELLOW & MOULTON, *supra* note 9, at
303–04; Brook K. Baker, *Learning to Fish, Fishing to Learn: Guided Participation in the Interpersonal Ecology of Practice*, 6 CLINICAL L. REV. 1, 45 (1999); Blasi, *supra* note 13, at 335–36.

[52] The experiences that increase your judgment come only partly from the direct practice of
law. The relevant experiences also emerge from other interpersonal, business or work environ-
ments. Even if the clinic experience is your first effort at the practice of law, you may still have
developed the capacity for good judgments through other life experiences before or during law
school.

writers call "cognitive illusions"[53] will play on your "reasoned" deliberations. We address the cognitive illusion frameworks in more detail in our chapters on counseling[54] and negotiation,[55] but we will highlight a few of them here. Behavioral psychologists and economists show us that we all rely upon short cuts in our thinking (sometimes called "heuristics and biases"[56]) to organize the massive amounts of information we encounter each day. Those short cuts are enormously valuable; without them we would be overwhelmed and unable to make even the simplest of daily choices. But the short cuts, which reflect some deeply-imbedded workings of the human brain, can lead to decisions which are not fully "rational," as we tend to understand rationality. Your being aware of these common cognitive tendencies can only make your decision-making more intentional and, we hope, more successful.

Consider the following common heuristics and biases:

—*The Anchoring Effect*: Our assessment of the value of some object or claim might be distorted irrationally by our encountering a reference to some random number. Researchers at MIT asked students to bid on a series of common everyday objects, indicating how much they would pay for each. Before the bidding began, the researchers asked the students to write down the last two digits of their Social Security numbers, and then to indicate whether the bid for any item was higher or lower than that number. Students with higher Social Security number digits bid substantially more than students with lower digits for the items for sale—even though the digits had no relationship at all to the value of the items or the bidding process.[57] That "anchoring" phenomenon is well-known among behavioral economists, and may have a serious effect on buyers, sellers, and negotiators.[58]

—*The Availability Heuristic*: We all tend to overestimate the likelihood of events that have happened recently or vividly. "The availability heuristic posits that the probability assessments that people make are frequently based upon how

---

[53] *See* Chris Guthrie, *Inside the Judicial Mind*, 86 CORNELL L. REV. 777, 780 (2001); Robert E. Scott, *Error and Rationality in Individual Decision-making: An Essay on the Relationship Between Cognitive Illusions and the Management of Choices*, 59 S. CAL. L. REV. 329, 340 (1986).

[54] *See* the chapter on Counseling Transactional Clients below.

[55] *See* the chapter on Transactional Negotiations below.

[56] *See* Amos Tversky & Daniel Kahneman, *Judgment Under Uncertainty: Heuristics and Biases, in* JUDGMENT UNDER UNCERTAINTY: HEURISTICS AND BIASES 14 (Daniel Kahneman, Paul Slovic & Amos Tversky eds. 1982). For a popular discussion of cognitive illusions, see DAN ARIELY, PREDICTABLY IRRATIONAL: THE HIDDEN FORCES THAT SHAPE OUR DECISIONS (2008).

[57] ARIELY, *supra* note 56, at 26–28.

[58] *See* Russell Korobkin & Thomas S. Ulen, *Law and Behavioral Science: Removing the Rationality Assumption from Law and Economics*, 88 CAL. L. REV. 1051, 1100 (2000).

easily we can think of examples."[59] We all tend to believe that events that are recent or vivid in our mind are more likely to occur, even when the statistics readily show that they are not.[60] This is a very entrenched and powerful cognitive illusion. "[A]ll heuristics are equal, but availability is more equal than the others," as one source describes it.[61] While it is very hard to resist this innate tendency, your awareness of it can aid in your assessment of risks.

—*Prospect Theory, Framing and Loss Aversion*: "In human decision making, losses loom larger than gains."[62] The "prospect theory" tells us that people are risk-avoiding in the face of gains, and risk-seeking in the face of losses.[63] The theory also tells us that any choice may be "framed" as a gain or a loss, depending on the point of reference chosen. Here is a simple but telling example:

We give you $50 and ask you to play a game with that money. The game has a choice of two options: keep $20, or take a 40% chance of keeping the entire $50, but a 60% chance of losing everything. Most of you will keep the $20. It's a free $20.

Now let's change the language of the game, using the same $50. The two choices are now these, after we give you the $50: Lose $30, or take a 40% chance of keeping the entire $50. Studies show that most of you will take the gamble of keeping the $50.[64] Of course, the two games are *exactly identical* in effect—you will have either $20 or a 40% chance of $50 in both games. The only thing that changed is the frame, from a gain to a loss. This tendency is widespread and quite innate.[65]

---

[59] Michael J. Kaufman, *Summary Pre–Judgment: The Supreme Court's Profound, Pervasive, and Problematic Presumption About Human Behavior*, 43 LOY. U. CHI. L.J. 593, 614 n.112 (2012); *see also* Fred Schauer, *Do Cases Make Bad Law?*, 73 U. CHI. L. REV. 883, 895 (2006). Schauer notes that this phenomenon also goes by the names "salience heuristic" or "vividness heuristic." *Id.*

[60] DANIEL KAHNEMAN, THINKING, FAST AND SLOW 129–36 (2011).

[61] Timur Kuran & Cass R. Sunstein, *Controlling Availability Cascades*, in BEHAVIORAL LAW & ECONOMICS 374 (Cass R. Sunstein ed., 2000), *quoted in* KAHNEMAN, *supra* note 60, at 142.

[62] Daniel Kahneman & Amos Tversky, *Prospect Theory: An Analysis of Decision Under Risk*, 47 ECONOMETRICA 263, 279 (1979) (quoted in LEHRER, *supra* note 42, at 77).

[63] MAX BAZERMAN, JUDGMENT IN MANAGERIAL DECISION MAKING 49–52 (5th ed. 2002)

[64] LEHRER, *supra* note 42, at 105–06 (42 percent of players gambled in the first version, but 62 percent gambled in the second).

[65] Daniel Kahneman reports the same experiment. *See* KAHNEMAN, *supra* note 60, at 365–66. Here is another famous example of loss framing and prospect theory's application:

[S]ubjects in one experiment were told to assume that a disease outbreak in the United States was expected to kill 600 people. They were then asked to choose between two programs:

—*The Endowment Effect*: This heuristic is an offshoot of the loss aversion tendency. Research shows that we all tend to value things we own more than if we do not own them. The mere fact of ownership adds a premium to its value for which we expect another to pay.[66]

—*The Sunk Cost Phenomenon*: This cognitive illusion affects decision-making in a palpable way. "Sunk costs are those that, once expended, cannot be retrieved."[67] In making choices, we frequently overvalue moneys already spent and not recoverable. We evaluate the wisdom of an option not from the present moment, but with reference to resources already invested. The reaction is entirely understandable but, most of the time, not economically rational.

—*The Self–Serving Bias*: A psychologist once made this now-famous slip of the tongue: "I'll see it when I believe it."[68] That inadvertent line captures the self-serving bias—our tendency to perceive and observe what fits comfortably within our belief system. Since well-reasoned decisions call for our assessing facts and making predictions, the distortions created by a self-serving bias can serve as a hindrance to reliable decision-making. While this bias is widely-shared and embedded within our cognitive processes, your awareness of it can assist you to resist some of its most dangerous implications.

—*The Planning Fallacy*: Closely connected to the self-serving bias is what Daniel Kahneman has dubbed the "planning fallacy."[69] This cognitive bias has special relevance to your transactional work. Kahneman's research showed that individuals persistently and sometimes irresponsibly make plans

---

If Program A is adopted, 200 people will be saved. If Program B is adopted, there is a one-third probability that 600 people will be saved, and a two-thirds probability that no people will be saved.

In the experiment, subjects preferred Program A by almost a three-to-one margin. With the same introductory facts, the choices were then presented slightly differently:

If Program C is adopted, 400 people will die. If Program D is adopted, there is a one-third probability that nobody will die, and a two-thirds probability that 600 people will die.

In this case, subjects preferred Program D by more than a three-to-one margin. Jeffrey L. Harrison, *Egoism, Altruism, and Market Illusions: The Limits of Law and Economics*, 33 UCLA L. REV. 1309, 1354–55 (1986).

[66] *See* Russell Korobkin, *The Endowment Effect and Legal Analysis*, 97 NW. U. L. REV. 1227 (2003).

[67] Robert S. Adler, *Flawed Thinking: Addressing Decision Biases in Negotiation*, 20 OHIO ST. J. ON DISP. RESOL. 683, 738 (2005)

[68] The story is reported by Thomas Gilovich. THOMAS GILOVICH, HOW WE KNOW WHAT ISN'T SO 49 (1991).

[69] KAHNEMAN, *supra* note 60, at 249–51.

using predictions that are "unrealistically close to best-case scenarios."[70] As a rule we tend to be overconfident in our assessments and inattentive to the many ways in which things might go wrong. Recognizing this fallacy might help you in a couple of ways. First, it will affect your own planning for the work you will perform with and for your clients. Second, you will likely observe this phenomenon operating powerfully with your clients as they begin their businesses. Most businesses fail, but most entrepreneurs believe, genuinely and in good faith, that their businesses will succeed.[71] Indeed, as Kahneman notes, our world may be better off because of this fallacy.[72]

VII. SOME FINAL THOUGHTS

Here is a prediction: Of all of the lawyering skills you will be learning as you perform your transactional work—interviewing, counseling, negotiation, drafting, and so forth—this organizational challenge will feel the most slippery and ephemeral to you. While the exercise of reflective judgment is a central component of any of the lawyering skills you will be discovering, in this arena it is most central and pervasive. And judgment, by its very nature, is hard to grasp and to assess. It is neither formulaic nor does it lend itself to objective benchmarks for accuracy. Consider the following description of the ideas of John Dewey, the famed American pragmatist, about this skill:

> According to Dewey, a person makes a judgment, what he called a reflective judgment, to bring closure to situations that are uncertain. In such uncertain or problematic situations, there is no way to apply a formula to derive a correct solution and no way to prove definitively that a proposed solution is correct. . . . [T]he problem solver engaged in reflective thinking must evaluate the potential solutions to the problem in light of existing information, information that may be incomplete and unverifiable. . . . Reflective thinking requires the continual evaluation of beliefs, assumptions, and hypotheses against existing data and against other plausible interpretations of the data. The resulting

---

[70] *Id.* at 250.

[71] *Id.* at 256–27 (referring to "entrepreneurial delusions"). Kahneman writes, "The chances that a small business will survive for five years in the United States is 35%. But the individuals who open such businesses do not believe that such statistics apply to them." *Id.* (citing Manju Puri & David T. Robinson, *Optimism and Economic Choice*, 86 J. FIN. ECONOMICS 71 (2007)).

[72] KAHNEMAN, *supra* note 60, at 256.

judgments are offered as reasonable integrations or syntheses of opposing points of view.[73]

In her account of ill-structured projects in community economic development clinics, Susan Bennett describes how daunting it can be for students to begin to develop the comfort and what she terms the "equanimity" of the seasoned expert in managing ambiguity and complexity, especially given the short span of any law school clinic.[74]

But you will only gain the desired confidence, equanimity and wisdom by practice, practice accompanied by a lot of reflection and critique. We expect you will engage in much rich and productive discussion with your colleagues and your supervisors about these challenges, and through that engagement you will develop, slowly but surely, into reflective practitioners.[75]

---

[73] PATRICIA M. KING & KAREN STROHM KITCHENER, DEVELOPING REFLECTIVE JUDGMENT: UNDERSTANDING AND PROMOTING INTELLECTUAL GROWTH AND CRITICAL THINKING IN ADOLESCENTS AND ADULTS 6–7 (1994), *quoted in* Aaronson, *supra* note 6, at 297.

[74] Bennett, *supra* note 3, at 61 (referring to "the equanimity of the long-distance problem solver").

[75] *See* DONALD A. SCHÖN, THE REFLECTIVE PRACTITIONER: HOW PROFESSIONALS THINK IN ACTION (1983).

CHAPTER 4

COUNSELING TRANSACTIONAL CLIENTS

■ ■ ■

I. INTRODUCTION

One of your most important responsibilities as a transactional lawyer is serve as a *counselor*: to advise your clients about the law, to help them understand complex documents and deal terms, and to assist them to make important decisions regarding their matters. Indeed, as a transactional lawyer, your counseling responsibilities are perhaps the most central component of your professional role. Compared to your colleagues who are litigators, who must play the role of advocate in dispute resolution contexts as well as serve as counselor, your primary connection to your client is as an advisor.

This chapter introduces you to the role of counselor. It will help you understand the different components of the counseling process, and it will offer you a couple of models—but not recipes—for organizing your counseling meetings with your clients. The chapter will also revisit the fundamental notion of *client-centeredness*, a philosophy we encountered in the Interviewing chapter, and which will influence in some way or another all of your advising interactions with your clients.

II. COUNSELING CONTEXTS

There are many ways in which you will serve as an advisor to your clients, and it should help you to recognize the distinctions among them. Because each type of counseling calls for a distinct interaction with your client, your method for organizing a meeting or a telephone call with a client will differ depending upon the context. Also, as we shall see below, your commitment to the client-centered approach may also vary depending upon which context applies.

A taxonomy of counseling contexts will account for two kinds of variations. First, it obviously matters what your goal is—are you simply explaining something relatively static, like the state of the law or the meaning of a clause in a document, or are you assisting your client to arrive at a decision among several alternatives, such as whether to proceed as a 501(c)(3) or a 501(c)(6) nonprofit organization?[1] Second, the role of the

---

[1] For a review of how tax-exempt organizations work, see the Introduction to Creating and Operating Nonprofit Organizations chapter.

person or persons with whom you are working affects your approach. Are you counseling an individual about her or his personal stake in a transaction? Or, perhaps more common in transactional matters, are you working with an officer or board member of an organization who possesses a fiduciary responsibility for (and perhaps, but perhaps not, a personal stake in) the outcome? That distinction can be critical in the role you play in arriving at an ultimate course of action.

With those two factors in mind, we might divide the counseling world into the following classifications:

1. *Advice About the Law*: This type of counseling is actually rarer than you might think, when you compare it to what will follow. Sometimes, your goal in a meeting will be simply to communicate to a client what the law *is* or what the law *means*. Usually, if you are doing this, you are in the process of helping a client make a decision, which we encounter as a different category below.

2. *Advice About Business*: You might think that this isn't your role— you're a lawyer, not an MBA (well, for most of you that's true). And you're probably right that it should not be your role, at least some of the time. But you fool yourself if you deny that transactional lawyers can perceive business and practical implications of a client's actions. For present purposes, it is important that you recognize providing business advice as a form of counseling, which you may or may not want to engage in depending on the circumstances.

3. *Assisting an Individual (or Constituent) to Choose Among Discrete Choices*: Note the qualifiers here—they are important. A transactional lawyer will commonly work with an individual to assist him or her to choose among a finite set of alternatives. Imagine a sole proprietor who wishes to create a business organization, and may choose among a Limited Liability Company (LLC), a Subchapter S corporation, or a Subchapter C corporation. You will quickly see that a lawyer has an important role to play in assisting the client with such a decision (but, usually, not suggesting to the client which option to choose). If the person with whom you work is serving as a constituent for an entity client, your counseling role *might* be different as a result of that factor.

4. *Assisting an Individual (or Constituent) to Establish a "Bottom Line" Authority for a Sale or Negotiation*: This category of counseling might not be very self-evident to you, like the preceding three examples will have been. But it makes sense when you think about it. Helping a person choose between Option A and Option B, in a world of finite choices, is a quite different activity from assisting the person to decide how much authority to delegate to a lawyer in a negotiation, or what limit to establish on a payment for a desired object or service. One observer has labeled this kind of counseling as "pre-negotiation

counseling."[2] As above, your participation in this form of counseling may end up different if the person you work with is a constituent and not a direct client.

This chapter will discuss some basic ideas underlying client counseling, and will suggest two working models—again, not recipes—for the latter two types of professional activity. Before we reach the models, though, we must review the basic premise of client-centeredness, because that ethical and strategic stance affects our understanding of your role in any of these contexts.

III. A CLIENT–CENTERED APPROACH TO LAWYERING

A. THE UNDERLYING PREMISES OF CLIENT–CENTEREDNESS

This book adopts a client-centered approach for lawyering work generally. It accepts the insights first developed by David Binder and Susan Price in their pioneering work on legal interviewing and counseling,[3] insights which several critical commentators have refined and reappraised over the years.[4] It is a very elegant and compelling commitment, although when you begin to work with your clients you quickly learn that its elegance can become complicated by the messiness of real world practice.

A client-centered approach to lawyering respects an individual's autonomy, and warns against a lawyer's interference, either willingly or otherwise, with a client's full ownership of her legal matter. Its basic premise is this: A lawyer must aim to assist a client to make choices and to proceed with her legal work in ways which reflect *the client's* preferences, values, goals, and commitments. It is profoundly anti-paternalist in its philosophy. It also makes a good deal of sense. A lawyer is an agent of a client, who is the principal in the relationship. Each lawyer brings to

---

[2] Paul R. Tremblay, *Pre–Negotiation Counseling: An Alternative Model*, 13 CLINICAL L. REV 541 (2006).

[3] DAVID BINDER & SUSAN PRICE, LEGAL INTERVIEWING AND COUNSELING: A CLIENT CENTERED APPROACH (1977). The authors of this classic text refined their thinking in later variations of the book. See DAVID A. BINDER, PAUL BERGMAN & SUSAN PRICE, LAWYERS AS COUNSELORS: A CLIENT CENTERED APPROACH (1990); DAVID A. BINDER, PAUL BERGMAN, SUSAN PRICE & PAUL R. TREMBLAY, LAWYERS AS COUNSELORS: A CLIENT CENTERED APPROACH (2d ed. 2004); DAVID A. BINDER, PAUL BERGMAN, PAUL R. TREMBLAY & IAN WEINSTEIN, LAWYERS AS COUNSELORS: A CLIENT CENTERED APPROACH (3d ed. 2012).

[4] See, e.g., THOMAS L. SHAFFER & ROBERT F. COCHRAN, LAWYERS, CLIENTS AND MORAL RESPONSIBILITY (2d ed. 2009); Robert D. Dinerstein, *Client–Centered Counseling: Reappraisal and Refinement*, 32 ARIZ. L. REV. 501 (1990); Stephen Ellmann, *Lawyers and Clients*, 34 UCLA L. REV. 717 (1987); Michelle S. Jacobs, *People from the Footnotes: The Missing Element in Client–Centered Counseling*, 27 GOLDEN GATE U. L. REV. 345 (1997); Katherine R. Kruse, *Fortress in the Sand: The Plural Values of Client–Centered Representation*, 12 CLINICAL L. REV. 369 (2006); Mark Spiegel, *Lawyering and Client Decisionmaking: Informed Consent and the Legal Profession*, 128 U. PA. L. REV. 41 (1979).

the interaction her or his own peculiar set of values, fears, likes and dislikes, and it is wrong, as a moral measure, for the lawyer, the professional with power and status, to suggest choices based upon the lawyer's preferences instead of the client's.

A commitment to client-centeredness leads us to craft counseling models imbued with *neutrality*. By "neutrality" we refer to the quality of the lawyer's preferences and values, and not the lawyer's opinion about, say, the likelihood of some strategy working or not. To understand why neutrality is so important (and to appreciate the challenges of this stance), we should consider for a moment the expectation of a client seeking help from a lawyer on a complicated and serious legal matter. Imagine that the client has agreed to pay the lawyer a lot of money for the lawyer's services (which won't be the case in your clinic work, but may be the case after you graduate). The client might expect that for the high prices she charges, the lawyer will offer direct and definitive advice: "My expert, considered opinion is that you should do the following. . . . " The client-centeredness approach suggests that the lawyer will seldom provide that kind of direction to her clients. Why not?

The reason why not is grounded in what lawyers assist clients to do. Suppose that a client wants to know from his lawyer what legal device will accomplish Goal X, and that only one plausible legal maneuver, Device Z, will accomplish Goal X. In that case, the lawyer should and will offer her expert advice: "We'll use Device Z." But few legal matters have such straightforward and definitive solutions. Most legal matters—and virtually all of the legal matters that are interesting and challenging—involve multiple alternative actions, uncertainties about each, assessments of levels of risk, trade-offs in results, and imperfect predictions about what some other people are likely to do in the future, and about how the participants will feel about the choices in the future. A smart and wise lawyer will recognize the relevant alternatives, describe the inherent uncertainties, offer reliable predictions about other participants' likely behaviors and feelings, and assess the risk levels. But then, once the lawyer has performed her role and communicated all of that critical information to her client, only the client can choose among the available alternatives based on factors peculiarly within the client's competence.

Perhaps like you, many clients will want the lawyer to go further, and to make the ultimate choices for them, or at least to recommend a decision. But, while a lawyer is well equipped to perform the role just described, she is ill-equipped to understand *what choice meets the client's preferences most fully*. The lawyer may know her client really well, but the odds are that she does not know the client as well as the client knows himself. Because of the risks and uncertainties involved, the "best" decision is the one which accommodates the client's preferences, values, and position on the risk-taking versus risk-avoiding scale. It is also becoming more well-accepted that good decision-making is far more dependent on emotion than on reason.[5] A choice will be "right" not because of some reasoned, objective calculus, but because it meets the personal (and often unconscious[6]) needs of the person who will live with the results.

Clients, not surprisingly, often wish it were different—that the lawyer will discern and communicate the important decisions to them.[7] Lawyers are not the only profession facing this kind of angst. Interior designers and financial planners are two professions which quickly come to mind, where customers tend to find the available choices overwhelming and hope—usually in vain—that the expert paid by the customers will make the hard choices for them.

For these reasons, counseling models revolve around processes intended to inhibit a lawyer's tendency to decide issues for clients—or even to imply a favored choice and therefore distort the client's thinking about options. As you will see when you work with your clients, true neutrality is really hard—and maybe even impossible. It is an ideal to seek to attain, even if you never quite reach it. But some factors and settings might call for more direction and less neutrality by the lawyer. Consider the examples in the following section.

B. CLIENT–CENTEREDNESS IN PRACTICE— EXCEPTIONS AND COMPLICATIONS

The neutral, client-centered approach just defended is a perfectly sensible account of the human interaction between the expert lawyer and the client who relies on the lawyer's expertise. It accounts for the reality of lawyering practice by recognizing that legal solutions are not math problems, and that only clients can appreciate in any meaningful way how to respond best to the levels of risk and uncertainty inherent in legal decision-making.

Years of practice have led observers to suggest a more pragmatic view of the client-centeredness agenda, however. In this section we describe a few settings where, notwithstanding the elegance of the justifications described above, you might find yourself diverging from the neutrality principle, and feeling reasonably okay about doing so.

The Legal Technician Exception: This is the most pragmatic and the most easily defended of the exceptions to a neutral stance. You might understand it in its strong and its weak sense. The strong sense is this: Many of your lawyering "decisions" are not for the client to make at all, so

---

[5] *See* JONAH LEHRER, HOW WE DECIDE (2008).

[6] *Id.* at 35–42.

[7] One observer has characterized a follower of this approach as a "two handed lawyer, . . . one who can analyze a problem on one hand and on the other hand, but tosses the actual decision back to the client." Jeffrey M. Lipshaw, *On the Two–Handed Lawyer: Thinking Versus Action in Business Lawyering*, at http://ssrn.com/abstract=2095357 (2012).

you will make them without any attempt to counsel your client with a neutral stance. Here's an exaggerated example to make the point: Your "decision" to send to the lawyer representing the seller in a real estate deal a version of the draft purchase and sale agreement by a scanned PDF rather than by a first class letter is not one about which you will seek your client's consent.[8] As many observers have pointed out, though, be careful of reading too much into this otherwise obvious exception. While the Model Rules of Professional Conduct state that "objectives" are for the client to decide and "means" are left to the lawyer's discretion (subject to a "consultation" with the client),[9] most thoughtful commentators reject that distinction as unworkable, and suggest that many "means" choices are as crucial to the client as the "objectives" would be.[10]

The weak version of this exception hearkens back to the simple example above of a legal device which is the right answer to the client's questions.[11] You will see in your transactional practice that some choices will be pretty sensible and pretty inevitable even if they are not the *only* right choice, and even if they have an important effect on your client's business. You may do your client a significant favor by simply suggesting those choices rather than by "counseling" your client in a neutral way about all available options.[12] Especially when a client is paying a handsome hourly fee to your firm for its work, simplifying choices in this way serves the client well.[13]

You should be keenly aware, however, that *this exception is a very seductive one*, and you will be tempted to overuse it. If you accept this pragmatic exception to the client-centeredness stance—as you must, and will—you should exercise exquisite care to limit its use to settings where the choices before you do not implicate the client's personal values and preferences in any meaningful way. Because client-centeredness and neutrality are hard to implement, and because clients also find the stance to be uncomfortable (for the reasons described above), the temptation to jettison neutrality will be great. So try to resist it.

---

[8]   Lest you think of the example in the text as an entirely silly way to make the intended point, note that *sometimes* the PDF-versus-letter question might be an important decision, if either safety of email or timing of transmission is an important strategic consideration in your particular circumstances.

[9]   MODEL RULES OF PROF'L CONDUCT R.1.2(a) (2012).

[10]   *See, e.g.,* BINDER, BERGMAN, TREMBLAY & WEINSTEIN, *supra* note 3, at 321–27; Spiegel, *supra* note 4, at 65–67.

[11]   *See* page 110 *supra.*

[12]   For example, imagine that your client has approached you about forming a nonprofit organization and obtaining tax-exempt status under Section 501(c)(3) of the Internal Revenue Code. Most lawyers would begin that process by creating for the client a corporation, even though the IRS rules permit an unincorporated association to seek tax exempt status. You need not be *neutral* about the choice to form a corporation, although you may be *agnostic* about a client's choice to proceed as an unincorporated association.

[13]   *See* BINDER, BERGMAN, TREMBLAY & WEINSTEIN, *supra* note 3, at 379–81.

The "Architecture" Exception: In some settings, and seemingly more often in transactional than in litigation contexts, a lawyer must sacrifice some neutrality in order to be an effective counselor because the choices available are too multifaceted and interdependent to lend themselves to the kind of careful counseling we describe below. Where the choices available to a client represent ensemble-like blends of different elements, the usual client-directed choice models simply may not work. In those instances, a lawyer will suggest, if tentatively, the packages that seem to the lawyer to fit the client's needs best, as the client has communicated those needs to the lawyer.

In the paradigmatic counseling opportunity, your client must make a choice among a finite series of discrete alternatives, none of which is perfect and each of which presents its own combination of costs and benefits. (If one of the choices is indeed "perfect," that happenstance is what we labeled the "technician" exception above.) In this paradigmatic setting, the client-centered ethical commitment urges the lawyer to withhold recommendations or opinions lest her preferences overtake those of the client, perhaps without the lawyer even realizing that she has done so.[14]

In many transactional contexts, though, the alternatives available to a client are not well cabined, are not finite and not discrete, but represent an almost unlimited variation of factors, imagined in countless different packages or ensembles. Imagine, for instance, your counseling the founders of an incipient nonprofit corporation about the bylaw provisions that would work best for the new organization. Each distinct bylaw provision in isolation presents many possible variations. Perhaps you could, with enough time and patience, articulate each possible permutation of each separate provision, and seek the undistorted and unmanipulated clean choice of the founders about that provision, moving then to the next provision, and so forth, until you have successfully "counseled" your client[15] about this matter. Not only would that process take much more time than either you or the founders wish to dedicate to this single element of the nonprofit establishment process, but it would also not be terribly effective in the end. The bylaw provisions are not easily isolated, but affect one another. A change in thinking at Article XIII of the bylaws might require rethinking decisions you elicited about provisions of Article IV.

What your client would expect, and what you would do in practice, is to begin the counseling engagement by exploring the client's preferences, goals, leanings, and history, to understand generally what seems most important to the founders. You then would *propose* a package of provi-

---

[14] We describe below the operations of cognitive biases within the counseling process. *See* Part IV *infra*.

[15] Note that we use the singular to refer to the "client," while using the plural to refer to the "founders." Would you think that the founders themselves are the clients, in which case the plural would be more apt here? Think of that issue as you work with your own clients and constituents.

sions that *might* fit the needs of the group. In this way you may be less neutral, but equally client-centered. We describe this variation as the "architecture exception," because it seems to mimic the interaction between architects and those who hire them to design living or work space.[16] We return to this idea later in this chapter.[17]

The Entity Constituent Exception: As we have seen, the client-centeredness approach emerges from a respect for the individual autonomy as well as the personal values and preferences of the lawyer's client, and the concomitant recognition that the lawyer has her own preferences and values which the client may not share. When you counsel an individual about *his* business or *his* real estate closing, all of the justifications for a neutral stance outlined above fit nicely, and make good sense. But what if the person you are working with is a constituent of an organization? At a minimum, the justifications for a client-centeredness stance are more complicated in this setting.

Imagine, for instance, that you are advising the executive director (ED) of a small nonprofit about whether to pay for the services of a web designer as an employee or as an independent contractor. The choice before the ED is one with competing considerations, and there is no one correct legal answer.[18] Hiring the web designer as an employee adds costs and responsibilities to the nonprofit,[19] but provides the nonprofit with greater control and oversight of the designer's work.[20] By and large, the lawyer will be neutral about whichever alternative the ED chooses. How-

---

[16] The American Institute of Architecture has established "Best Practices" for architects to honor, some of which emphasize the importance of attending to the client's wishes and goals. *See* American Institute of Architecture, Best Practices: Defining the Architect's Basic Services, available at http://www.aia.org/aiaucmp/groups/ek_members/documents/pdf/aiap026834.pdf (the architect "produces a final schematic design, to which the owner agrees after consultation and discussions with the architect"). The Institute's National Ethics Council has issued ethics opinions addressing Institute members' obligation to respect client wishes. *See, e.g.,* American Institute of Architecture, National Ethics Council, Code of Ethics and Professional Conduct Decision 2006–20 (designing a home that did not meet the client's objectives, and engaging in a conflict of interest); Decision 2002–16 (finding no violation given evidence of regular consultation with client about plans and progress).

[17] *See* Part IV *infra.*

[18] Whether a person paid for services rendered qualifies as an employee or as an independent contractor is an important one under the Internal Revenue Service rules and state employment laws, although sometimes the dividing line between the two can be fuzzy. *See, e.g.,* Richard R. Carlson, *Why the Law Still Can't Tell an Employee When It Sees One and How It Ought to Stop Trying*, 22 BERKELEY J. EMP. & LAB. L. 295 (2001); Susan Schwochau, *Identifying an Independent Contractor for Tax Purposes: Can Clarity and Fairness Be Achieved?*, 84 IOWA L. REV. 163 (1999). A business may choose to pay for services under either arrangement, assuming that the nature of the work performed and the circumstances of its supervision comply ultimately with the option selected.

[19] If the worker is an employee, the employer will pay a share of the employee's Social Security and Medicare taxes, and may pay into the state's workers compensation and unemployment insurance programs. *See* 26 U.S.C. § 3101 (employee share of payroll taxes); § 3111 (employer share).

[20] If the web designer is an employee, the employer may terminate him at will, and may impose the conditions of the day-to-day work experience. *See* Schwochau, *supra* note 18, at 175–76.

ever, because the ED is not the lawyer's client, but is instead a constituent or representative of the lawyer's client, the rationales developed above for the neutral approach to counseling and for respecting the preferences of the counselee have considerably less weight. Indeed, the ED's *personal* preferences and values should be largely irrelevant, except insofar as the nonprofit has chosen the ED for precisely those qualities.

While you might think that this uncertainty can be resolved by working not with the ED but instead with the nonprofit's board of directors, that answer is unsatisfactory on two counts. First, as a practical matter, the board may not wish to be a party to every such decision made for the organization, and organizational theory would suggest it ought not.[21] Second, even if you were able to move from counseling the ED to counseling the board, the same constituent issues would remain, only they would be multiplied by your having several individual board members to work with, none of whom is "the entity."

This example begins to demonstrate why the usual client-centeredness stance may apply differently in organizational settings. You will likely conclude in your work that most of the same justifications apply in this setting as in the individual setting, and that you will assume the neutral stance rather than a directive stance. You will realize that, imperfections notwithstanding, the constituent still knows the organization better than you do.

The Immoral Choice Exception: When you think about it, client-centeredness is a fancy way of saying "hired gun." By respecting your client's autonomy and his wishes and preferences, you end up serving his will and suppressing your own views and opinions. The entire client-centeredness enterprise is crafted on that premise. As we saw above, that makes good sense. But what if your client isn't such a nice guy? What about your own moral conscience? Does client-centeredness require lawyers to be moral ciphers?

This is a central question that you will confront often in your practice. Many critics have tried to connect the client-centeredness model with the justifications for immoral lawyering activity.[22] The apparent criticism is sound, but only if client-centeredness is understood in a crude sense. In fact, a faithful client-centered lawyer would reject the connection, and resist a pure "hired gun" philosophy. And so, likely, will you. A sophisticated understanding of the client-centered approach respects the lawyer's moral autonomy while it embraces the client's legal autonomy.

---

[21] *See* GUIDEBOOK FOR DIRECTORS OF NONPROFIT CORPORATIONS (George W. Overton & Jeannie C. Frey eds., 2d ed. 2002).

[22] *See, e.g.*, SHAFFER & COCHRAN, *supra* note 4; Ellmann, *supra* note 4; Ann Shalleck, *Constructions of the Client Within Legal Education*, 45 STAN. L. REV. 1731, 1742–48 (1993).

Many insightful commentators have written about this tension, and if you are interested you should explore the rich literature.[23] For our present purposes, consider the following basic distinctions: Sometimes your client will consider choices which are lawful and not morally troublesome; in those instances, your role is to assist him to choose the alternatives which best suit his needs, values and preferences, as he understands them. Sometimes, though, your client will consider choices which are simply illegal as you understand the law. Your role in that setting is of course to inform your client about the status of the law, but you will not assist him to pursue one of the unlawful choices. The law of lawyering prohibits you from doing so,[24] as does your moral sensibility (we hope). At other times, though (and here's the hardest iteration, and perhaps the most interesting one), your client will consider choices which are perfectly lawful but morally unconscionable. (You will agree that sometimes an act can be both "legal" and "immoral," right?) In that setting, you will not necessarily be client-centered or neutral in your discussion with your client. You may engage your client in what some have termed a "moral dialogue"[25] with your client, and in that conversation you will not be agnostic about the choices before the client.[26]

This is a complicated topic which warrants a far more extensive discussion than this chapter can offer. You will certainly encounter it in your practice as a lawyer, and you will likely encounter it in your experience as a clinical student. You will struggle with questions about how you distinguish between a serious moral disagreement and a respectful difference of personal opinion. In the end, you will recognize the difference, but you will benefit from a lot of input from your colleagues in arriving at that judgment.

The Disabled Client Exception: The final exception to the client-centered commitment we will consider here concerns clients who suffer from a disability which impairs the client's capacity to exercise autonomy responsibly. The premises of client-centeredness invite this exception. If the purpose of a neutral and non-directive approach to counseling is to respect the autonomy and independence of your client, then it makes lit-

---

[23] *See, e.g.,* DAVID LUBAN, LAWYERS AND JUSTICE: AN ETHICAL STUDY (1988); WILLIAM H. SIMON, THE PRACTICE OF JUSTICE: A THEORY OF LAWYERS' ETHICS (1998).

[24] *See* MODEL RULES OF PROF'L CONDUCT R. 1.2(d); Stephen L. Pepper, *Counseling at the Limits of the Law: An Exercise in the Jurisprudence and Ethics of Lawyering*, 104 YALE L.J. 1545 (1995). As Stephen Pepper explains, the distinction between explaining the consequences of unlawful conduct ("there is a small penalty, and from my experience you will not get caught") and encouraging the unlawful conduct is a fine one.

[25] *See* Eleanor W. Myers, *"Simple Truths" About Moral Education*, 45 AM. U.L. REV. 823, 853 (1996) ("Engaging in moral dialogue is an essential ingredient of moral growth.").

[26] If you want to know more about how the moral dialogue might work, you could read one of the legal counseling texts which address this issue in more depth than this text. *See, e.g.,* BINDER, BERGMAN, TREMBLAY & WEINSTEIN, *supra* note 3, at 339–41; ROBERT F. COCHRAN, JR., JOHN M.A. DiPIPPA & MARTHA M. PETERS, THE COUNSELOR-AT-LAW: A COLLABORATIVE APPROACH TO CLIENT INTERVIEWING AND COUNSELING 169–90 (2d ed. 2006).

tle sense to remain faithful to that approach if your client, because of a serious mental illness or disease, cannot make reasoned choices or appreciate the consequences of his actions.

Model Rule 1.14 recognizes that lawyers sometimes must act in a paternalistic fashion with a disabled client; otherwise, the lawyers would find themselves bound to assist in causing harm to clients who never *really* chose to experience that harm. Note the implication of that last sentence. If your client is not disabled, if the client fully appreciates the consequences of his choices (and assume for now that he is not acting as a constituent of an entity, and not acting unconscionably to hurt another), then your role is to assist him in carrying out his lawful choices, even if you believe that the choices are foolish. Even ridiculously foolish. Your clients have every right to make lousy and imprudent choices, and it is not your role to interfere with a knowing decision to do so.[27] (Of course, it is entirely your role to make sure the client *understands* the implications and consequences of his unwise choices. If he does not learn from you about the risks he is facing, you have not done your job as a lawyer.)

You will agree with the distinction just outlined—you must respect the foolish choices your client knowingly makes; but foolish choices made because of some defect in the client's thinking deserve your intervention. You will discover, though, that in practice that theoretical distinction is frustratingly difficult to discern. You might think it is impossible to discern in practice. "Mental illness" does not appear in your office with clear, 16–point font labels. You are not (most likely; though some of you will be) a trained mental health professional, so even the premise of the distinction will be elusive. In those settings where you confidently accept that Rule 1.14 applies, you will find it challenging to know how to proceed, assuming you opt to act in a more directive fashion. May you unilaterally overrule your client and make choices for him? Should you intervene by seeking a lawful surrogate (like a guardian or conservator) who can serve as your substitute client and make decisions for your disabled client? Like the topics above, this subject deserves more attention that this primer can offer. A helpful literature is available if you are interested in understanding this topic better.[28]

---

[27] The medical world operates on the same principle. *See, e.g.,* Lane v. Candura, 376 N.E.2d 1232 (Mass. App. 1978) (patient who refuses life-saving amputation procedure not incompetent by virtue of having made that choice, and medical providers must honor her choice even if it hastens her death). For an early discussion of this tension, see Paul R. Tremblay, *On Persuasion and Paternalism: Lawyer Decisionmaking and the Questionably Competent Client,* 1987 UTAH L. REV. 515.

[28] *See, e.g., Conference on Ethical Issues in Representing Older Clients,* 62 FORDHAM L. REV. 989 (1994); Carol M. Suzuki, *When Something Is Not Quite Right: Considerations for Advising a Client to Seek Mental Health Treatment,* 6 HASTINGS RACE & POVERTY L.J. 209 (2009). At the risk of engaging in dangerous overgeneralization, here is an observation you might appreciate: In the transactional clinic world, the incidence of major mental illness among your clinic's clients will likely be less than in the poverty-focused litigation clinical environment. The prevalence of mental illness in poverty law practice (and therefore in many litigation clinics) is substantial.

IV. HEURISTICS, BIASES, AND COGNITIVE ILLUSIONS

Before you learn about a couple of models (not recipes!) to help guide your meetings with clients, there is an important topic for you to begin to understand—the world of behavioral economics. Nothing has called traditional counseling conceptions into question more than the emerging insights from behavioral economists, and you will have a hard time serving as an effective advisor if you do not have at least a little bit of familiarity with heuristics, biases and cognitive illusions.[29]

Most traditional counseling literature is grounded in classical economic theory, which understands persons first and foremost as maximizers of utility, as rational agents who make decisions based upon a reasoned process of assessing costs and benefits. (We hear the subject of these ideas referred to as *homo economicus.*[30]) The role of a counselor, according to this economic theory, is to assist a client to understand and appreciate, in as organized and careful a way as possible, all of the positive and negative implications of the various alternatives, so that the client may then engage in a careful cost/benefit analysis and arrive at the choice which maximizes utility.

Classical economic theory is not wrong, of course. People, including your clients, do want to make choices in a way that maximizes the good things and minimizes the bad things. A counselor needs to nurture practices that encourage that result, and to incorporate structures to assist in careful deliberation. But classical economic theory is also *not right*. It misunderstands, and at times profoundly so, the way that people think and the way they make decisions. The behavioral economists have shown us many important ways in which we need to rethink our understanding of how people decide, and therefore how professionals help their clients decide. One such economist compares the classical *homo economicus* with

---

Poor persons suffer from mental illness at a higher rate than the overall population; you can debate what is cause and what is effect. *See* National Center for Health Statistics, Health, United States 2011: With Special Feature on Socioeconomic Status and Health, 38 (2012), http://www.cdc.gov/nchs/data/hus/hus11.pdf; Carey Goldberg, *Mental illness and poverty: Does one cause the other?*, BOSTON GLOBE, March 8, 2005, http://www.boston.com/yourlife/health/mental/articles/2005/03/08/mental_illness_and_poverty_does_one_cause_the_other. Clients of transactional clinics tend to be less poor, tend to have more education, and tend to be functioning better within the business environment than clients of litigation clinics. As a result, you will likely encounter the Rule 1.14–triggering contexts more rarely than your litigation clinic colleagues.

[29] You will recall that we introduced this topic, and covered it briefly, in the chapter on Organizing Your Transactional Work, at Section VI B. We also revisit this topic in the chapter on Transactional Negotiations, at Section IV.

[30] *See, e.g.*, Richard H. Thaler, *From Homo Economicus to Homo Sapiens*, 14 J. ECON. PERSPECTIVES 133 (2000).

a more accurate subject he refers to as "Homer economicus," after the character from the television comedy show *The Simpsons*.[31]

Behavioral economics has been around for decades, but it has enjoyed a fascinating popularity in the recent years in the semi-popular literature. Books like *Predictably Irrational*,[32] *Thinking, Fast and Slow*,[33] *How We Decide*,[34] *Nudge*,[35] *Sway*,[36] and *The Drunkard's Walk*[37] each try to explain some of the cognitive illusions which influence how individuals actually make decisions. Since counseling is, at bottom, assisting your clients to make decisions which will be the "best" for them (however one defines that qualifier), you should know a little bit about what factors affect and distort the thinking and decision-making of most of us.

In processing information and acting upon it, we all rely upon *heuristics*, and we all are subject to *biases*. Heuristics are shorthand processing devices which allow us to make quick judgments amid uncertainty. Biases are, well, our biases—the unthinking preferences and leanings which we each own as a result of how we have learned things in the past. A few of these heuristics and biases have special relevance to the kinds of decisions your client will make with your help. We will address those few here, as an introduction for you to this intriguing topic. The factors we will identify here are the following three: (1) prospect theory and the framing effect; (2) anchoring; and (3) the self-serving bias.

A. PROSPECT THEORY AND THE FRAMING EFFECT

Prospect theory, developed by the famed cognitive psychologists Daniel Kahneman (who later won a Nobel Prize for his work on this topic) along with Amos Tversky, predicts a subject's risk attitudes based upon whether the event to be evaluated is understood as a gain or as a loss. Here is how one commentator describes the theory:

> The "most distinctive implication of prospect theory," according to Kahneman and Tversky, is that individuals tend to exhibit a "fourfold pattern of risk attitudes" when making risky decisions: (1) risk aversion for moderate-to-high-probability gains, (2) risk seeking for moderate-to-high-probability losses, (3) risk seeking

---

[31] Richard H. Thaler, *Economic View: Mortgages Made Simpler*, N.Y. TIMES, Sunday, July 4, 2009, available at http://www.nytimes.com/2009/07/05/business/economy/05view.html.

[32] DAN ARIELY, PREDICTABLY IRRATIONAL: THE HIDDEN FORCES THAT SHAPE OUR DECISIONS (2008).

[33] DANIEL KAHNEMAN, THINKING, FAST AND SLOW (2011).

[34] LEHRER, *supra* note 5.

[35] RICHARD H. THALER & CASS R. SUNSTEIN, NUDGE: IMPROVING DECISIONS ABOUT HEALTH, WEALTH, AND HAPPINESS (2008).

[36] ORI BRAFMAN & ROM BRAFMAN, SWAY: THE IRRESISTIBLE PULL OF IRRATIONAL BEHAVIOR (2009).

[37] LEONARD MLODINOW, THE DRUNKARD'S WALK: HOW RANDOMNESS RULES OUR LIVES (2008).

for low-probability gains, and (4) risk aversion for low-probability losses.[38]

Prospect theory correctly predicts that in most civil litigation, plaintiffs (who stand to gain) will exhibit risk-aversive behaviors, while defendants (who face a potential loss) will tend to be risk-takers.[39] In nuisance suits, where the odds of winning are low, the pattern is reversed.[40]

The "framing effect" is a natural corollary of prospect theory. "Framing" refers to the characterization of a situation of uncertainty as representing a risk of gain or a risk of loss. In many conditions of uncertainty, the same consequence may be described as a loss (from a chosen starting point X) or a gain (from a different chosen starting point Y). If the prospect theory holds, a decision maker will behave differently depending upon that choice of reference point.[41] You can quickly see how prospect theory and the framing effect inform the role of a lawyer counseling her client. The lawyer's choice of how to present a collection of alternatives to her client can, inadvertently or otherwise, influence the client's choice among the alternatives.[42] A lawyer may also understand better a client's perspective by listening carefully to the client's framing of the choices.

B. THE ANCHORING BIAS

The cognitive bias known as "anchoring" is yet another insight of the behavioral psychologists Kahneman and Tversky.[43] It is a simple but surprisingly powerful cognitive illusion. In evaluating an uncertain quantity, we will unknowingly (or sometimes knowingly) make our assessments with reference to an anchor point. Sometimes that anchor point is explicit and has some rational basis. If you are counseling your client about the

---

[38] Chris Guthrie, *Framing Frivolous Litigation: A Psychological Theory*, 67 U. CHI. L. REV. 163, 166–67 (2000) (quoting Amos Tversky & Daniel Kahneman, *Advances in Prospect Theory: Cumulative Representation of Uncertainty*, 5 J. RISK & UNCERTAINTY 297, 298 (1992)).

[39] Chris Guthrie, *Prospect Theory, Risk and the Law*, 97 NW. U. L. REV. 1115, 1117–19 (2003); Jeffrey J. Rachlinski, *The "New" Law and Psychology: A Reply to Critics, Skeptics, and Cautious Supporters*, 85 CORNELL L. REV. 739, 750–52 (2000).

[40] Guthrie, *Framing Frivolous Litigation*, *supra* note 38.

[41] In a well-known experiment conducted to test the framing effect in litigation, two sets of auto accident plaintiffs faced identical risks of winning at trial and identical settlement offers. One set of plaintiffs had been reimbursed by insurance for most of their losses, so the settlement represented a gain; the other set of plaintiffs had been reimbursed far less, so the settlement offer represented a loss. While the dollar value of the economic choices available to the two sets of plaintiffs was precisely the same, the plaintiffs facing a loss turned down the settlement offer significantly more often than those realizing a gain. *See* Russell Korobkin & Chris Guthrie, *Psychological Barriers to Litigation Settlement: An Experimental Approach*, 93 MICH. L. REV. 107, 131–33 (1994).

[42] Dozens of scholarly articles have examined the influence of prospect theory and framing on lawyering practice. Most focus on litigation, perhaps not surprisingly. While none has applied prospect theory to transactional decision-making explicitly, the theory's lessons to transactional counseling are plainly evident.

[43] Amos Tversky & Daniel Kahneman, *Judgment Under Uncertainty: Heuristics and Biases*, *in* JUDGMENT UNDER UNCERTAINTY: HEURISTICS AND BIASES 14 (Daniel Kahneman, Paul Slovic & Amos Tversky, eds. 1982).

purchase of a small business, figures showing the assessed value of the real property or the inventory, or the cash flow from the previous quarter, will serve as obvious anchors. But just as often the anchors are not rational and may not even be conscious, but they still can have a powerful effect on decision-making.

Dan Ariely and his colleagues conducted a clever experiment to prove this point.[44] They arranged a number of MIT undergraduates to declare how much they would pay for a number of items, including bottle of fine wine, a cordless trackball, a cordless mouse, and a box of Belgian chocolates. Before the bidding for the items began, they asked each participant to write the last two digits of his or her Social Security number on the page listing the items, and to place that two-digit number next to each item, as a hypothetical price. Then, the participants listed the prices they would pay for each item. The result was exactly as the anchoring effect would have predicted: those participants with low digits at the end of their Social Security number bid significantly smaller amounts than those with high digits. The entirely random, and entirely irrelevant, Social Security number digits had anchored the perceptions of the participants, and influenced directly their decision-making.

Because the anchoring effect is so powerful and so arbitrary, its influence on counseling (and, when you think about it, negotiation[45]) can be profound. Imagine that you are assisting a business owner about a possible lease on some attractive storefront space. You and your client must decide whether to accept an offer suggested by the storefront's landlord, and your role, as her lawyer, is to assist in that process, so that the business owner makes the "right" choice. Once you recognize that her understanding of a fair price may be influenced by certain anchors, some legitimate but some purely irrelevant, you can account for that in your counseling of her. If you are perceptive, you can identify the anchors and their effect, and (if you believe it would assist your client to make a "better" decision) you can introduce a more reliable anchor to offset any irrelevant anchors to which your client might unknowingly be responding. (And, of course, the landlord will be subject to the same anchoring distortions, which your actions might influence.)

---

[44] ARIELY, *supra* note 32, at 26–31 (describing an experiment conducted by Ariely, Drazen Prelec, a professor at MIT's Sloan School of Management, and George Loewenstein, a professor at Carnegie Mellon University). You will recognize this story from the Organizing Your Transactional Work chapter of this book.

[45] In a negotiation, a first offer can serve as an anchor. *See* Adam D. Galinsky & Thomas Mussweiler, *First Offers as Anchors: The Role of Perspective–Taking and Negotiator Focus*, 81 J. PERSONALITY & SOC. PSYCHOL. 657, 657 (2001) ("[W]hichever party . . . made the first offer obtained a better outcome. In addition, first offers were a strong predictor of final settlement prices."); Russell Korobkin & Chris Guthrie, *Opening Offers and Out-of-Court Settlement: A Little Moderation May Not Go a Long Way*, 10 OHIO ST. J. ON DISP. RESOL. 1, 18–19 (1994) (discussing the anchoring effect of the first offer in settlement negotiation). *See also* the chapter on Transactional Negotiations.

C. THE SELF–SERVING BIAS

People tend to believe strongly in themselves, often more strongly than the facts would warrant. The Garrison Keillor line from "A Prairie Home Companion" about all of the Lake Wobegon children being "above average" captures a central truth about how our brains operate.[46] We tend to think of ourselves as better than average on most scales, and we usually perceive justice on our side. This "self-serving" bias affects how we make choices, and its distortions are further influenced by two related cognitive processes—the "representativeness" heuristic and the "availability" heuristic, each of which we will learn about in a moment.

Researchers have demonstrated the self-serving bias in a pithy way with a simple experiment. In two separate negotiation simulations, participants were randomly assigned to represent either the plaintiff or the defendant in a litigated personal injury dispute. Both sides were provided identical information about the victim's losses and injuries. The researchers then asked the participants to estimate a fair trial award to the injured plaintiff. In both experiments, the plaintiffs evaluated the case as worth substantially—and significantly—more money than the defendants, despite the purely random and temporary role assignments.[47] The participants' rational, analytical judgments about the value of certain data was influenced directly by the point of view they were asked to adopt. Their judgments were different based upon their temporarily assigned point of view.

The self-serving bias is well-known to lawyers (who, of course, exhibit it themselves whether they will admit it or not). Lawyers often report their clients' overly rosy predictions about future consequences and likelihood of success. The lawyers wonder whether their role is to overcome those misperceptions. The self-serving bias is augmented by the related heuristics of representativeness and availability. The representativeness heuristic is familiar to us all—it refers to our tendency to magnify the importance of small numbers of examples or anecdotes. As one writer puts it, "a small number of anecdotes might be idiosyncratic and their lessons not broadly generalizable," but we rely on them in a stubborn way.[48] It closely resembles the "availability" bias. "People use the availability

---

[46] In his weekly radio program A Prairie Home Companion, Garrison Keillor describes his fictional home town of Lake Wobegon with the following phrase: "Where all the women are strong, all the men are good-looking and all the children are above average." Am. Pub. Media, A Prairie Home Companion with Garrison Keillor, http://prairiehome.publicradio.org/. *See* Nan L. Maxwell & Jane S. Lopus, *The Lake Wobegon Effect in Student Self–Reported Data*, 84 AM. ECON. REV. 201, 201 (1994) (discussing this bias).

[47] Linda Babcock & Greg Pogarsky, *Damage Caps and Settlement: A Behavioral Approach*, 28 J. LEGAL STUD. 341, 352–54 (1999); George Loewenstein, Samuel Issacharoff, Colin Camerer & Linda Babcock, *Self–Serving Assessments of Fairness and Pretrial Bargaining*, 22 J. LEGAL STUD. 135, 141 (1993).

[48] Russell Korobkin, *Psychological Impediments to Mediation Success: Theory and Practice*, 21 OHIO ST. J. ON DISP. RESOL. 281, 281 (2006).

heuristic whenever they take action or reach conclusions about the world based on how easily they can recall or imagine instances of what they are thinking about. This heuristic guarantees that events that are more vividly and emotionally implanted in our minds will leap to our consciousness when we face a decision."[49] So, people tend to fear airplane accidents or shark attacks even when, empirically, their statistical likelihood is much more scarce than, say, an auto accident.

The availability and representativeness heuristics contribute to another common if puzzling fallacy, sometimes known as "the myth of the hot hand." Most of us succumb to this cognitive illusion, and, indeed, many of us resist any suggestions that it is a fallacy at all. The illusion is this—we tend to see *streaks* in athletic performances (and elsewhere— notably mutual fund performances) when what we in fact observe is simply the result of random distributions of good and bad results. Professional sports managers make their living by adjusting to the "hot" or "cold" spells of their teams' players, as though some players in fact were in a groove or in a funk. Careful analysis of the actual performances has proven that the streaks most of us believe we see are nothing more than expected, random patterns explainable by chance.[50]

Recognizing the self-serving, representativeness and availability biases will make you a more effective counselor, if by "more effective" we mean better able to assist your clients to make important decisions based upon a reliable and sound factual basis.

V. STRUCTURING YOUR COUNSELING SESSION

Counseling clients effectively is a difficult responsibility, particularly if your goals include non-directive guidance and a commitment to client-centeredness. One way to make the process more manageable is to develop schemas for your counseling meetings.[51] Your organization of your meetings can influence the interactions between you and your client. In this part we suggest three separate schemas for your counseling sessions, each applicable to a different kind of project or activity in which you and your client may be engaged. We start with what we describe as the "conventional" counseling undertaking, that is, assisting a client to make a choice among several discrete options. We then describe a similar but modified schema to account for what we have called the "architecture exception," where the client's alternatives are more ensembles than discrete choices. Finally, we suggest a model for counseling a client about arriving

---

[49] Robert S. Adler, *Flawed Thinking: Addressing Decision Biases in Negotiation*, 20 OHIO ST. J. ON DISP. RESOL. 683, 700 (2005).

[50] *See* LEHRER, *supra* note 5, at 62–67; MLODINOW, *supra* note 37.

[51] Note that a telephone call, or perhaps even an elaborate email correspondence, might serve as a counseling meeting.

at some negotiation authority, the activity we call "pre-negotiation counseling."

The schemas we suggest are orienting templates. We believe that their structure makes sense given the goals of your meetings and some baseline understanding about how people process information and make choices. But of course the templates are intended to be fluid and flexible, as you exercise your reflective judgment about your work with your clients.

A. A PRIMER ON THE STRUCTURE OF A CONVENTIONAL COUNSELING SESSION

This part of this chapter introduces you in a simplified way to a model for organizing what you might think of as a "conventional" counseling meeting—a meeting where your role is to assist a client (or a constituent of a client) to make a sound choice among a finite set of alternatives. We think of this kind of counseling as conventional because it is quite common, and because the rich literature about counseling tends to focus on this kind of meeting.[52]

The model described here emerges primarily from the pioneering work of David Binder and Susan Price, and their later co-authors.[53] Because this is an orienting primer and overview, you may wish to review the latest version of *Lawyers as Counselors* for a much more elaborate discussion of a model similar to the one described here. The model assumes a client who wishes to engage in careful and rational deliberation about alternatives, and proceeds with the goals of clarity, structure, and neutrality on the part of the lawyer, who will not try to influence her client's decision except in an exceptional circumstance.

Let us use the following typical example to introduce the model: Imagine that you are representing Sandy Litmanovich, an entrepreneur who has begun a catering business as a sole proprietor. As her business grows, Sandy wonders whether she ought to establish a more formal business structure, like an S Corp or an LLC. She visits you to serve as her lawyer as she decides whether to proceed with a business entity and, if so, which entity to adopt. Let's assume that she is honestly perplexed about what avenue would serve her interests most effectively, and really does need some smart and compassionate assistance to make this decision. That assumption seems a perfectly fair one, given the clients you will encounter in your clinical work.

---

[52] The textbooks listed in footnotes 3 and 26, *supra*, and 55 *infra* assume that this kind of counseling is the paradigm of legal advising.

[53] *See* note 3, *supra*.

1.   A Model Structure

A model for structuring your meeting with Sandy could look something like this, with the following separable stages developing in this order:

1) Welcome and small talk;

2) Review and confirmation of goals and interests, including a preparatory explanation;

3) A *brief* description of the discrete options to be discussed;

4) A choice by Sandy about which order to review the options;

5) A *descriptive* (not normative) review of each option in order;

6) A *normative* comparison of the options, with pros and cons identified;

7) A refinement of the alternatives and a tentative choice; and finally,

8) A choice by Sandy of one option (or a string of options).

Some of these steps are entirely intuitive; some, though, may warrant some further explanation. Let us review the model and defend it using the goals of clarity, structure, and neutrality.

2.   An Explanation of the Model's Stages

You will recall that above we recognized than an orienting model is not a recipe, and not a script to be followed rotely. That caveat deserves this reminder here. But there is a wisdom in generally organizing your meeting along the lines just discussed. Let us review some of the insights that led to this model.

Steps 1) and 2): One benefit of this early introductory part of the meeting is to agree upon the meeting's agenda and to discuss with Sandy your intentions for the meeting. Sandy may believe that the question she brings to you is a technical one, to which you can provide an answer for her by the end of the meeting ("You should create a Subchapter C corporation."). Since Sandy would likely be wrong in that assumption, the beginning part of the meeting permits you to help her understand what you can accomplish today (or, by the end of the counseling process, which may take more than this one meeting). You can remind her of your goal of neutrality—to emerge with the solution that *Sandy* prefers.

You can also resist the tendency to assume that you know what your client's goals and interests are, by explicitly reviewing them. This part of the counseling session follows up on your interview, where you would have inquired about the client's goals and aspirations, but obviously does not simply repeat that line of inquiry. Instead, you will check back with the client to make sure you understood her during the interview, and to learn whether anything has changed since the previous conversation. Your check-in might look something like this:

> Before we start reviewing the choices available to you, Sandy, I want to make sure I understand what is important to you as we consider the options. I recall from our last meeting that your short-term plans are to operate the catering business alone, without any partners or co-owners. But down the road, especially if the business thrives (as we expect it will, right?), you would like to have the flexibility to share the business with a partner or two, and maybe to look for investors if that would help the business grow. I also understand that cash flow is really tight for you right now, and that you are especially concerned about protecting your home and your savings in case something were to go wrong with the business. And finally, I remember you saying that you prefer the least complicated arrangement possible. You told me about your tendency to focus more on the baking and marketing and less on the administrative drudgeries that come with owning a business. Do I have this right?

Steps 3) and 4): These steps represent an effort to avoid any hint of favoritism by you for any of the choices on the table. The model asks that you look to Sandy to decide which option she wants to discuss first, second, and so forth. To permit her to make that choice, you of course have to list the options serially for her, with the briefest of "headline" descriptions, but with little else for now. So, for example, you might explain the choices for discussion to Sandy in this way:

> It makes a lot of sense for you to be thinking about whether you should create some kind of formal business for the good work you've been doing. I don't know whether you should do so or not, of course, but we can review the choices you have and see what you decide in the end. My sense is that you have four realistic options available here. You could continue as a sole proprietor as you've been doing. Or, you could create what's called an "S Corp.," which is a corporation usually intended to stay rather small. You could start what's known as an LLC, which is like an S Corp. but with some important flexibilities built in but also some possible disadvantages. Or you might start a C Corp., which usually gets chosen when there are plans for the business to get large or to seek outside investors. I can and will tell you a lot more about each of these four choices, but that's a basic headline about each. I'll let you decide which we discuss first. I am completely agnostic about the array, so I'll happily talk about them in whatever order you wish.

Sandy might not care about the order and express that sentiment to you, in which case you can easily choose an order. The primary insight here is that you do not come into the meeting having chosen one option above the others to consider first. As you discuss this part of the model in class or with your supervisor, you will consider whether there might be some meetings where your selecting the order makes very good sense, because there might be very good legal reasons to prefer one over the others, or where the necessary sequence of the legal activity determines the order. Again, this model represents a suggestion, and invites your reflective critique.

Steps 5) and 6): These two steps represent the integral philosophy of the model, but they are also the most likely areas where the model will completely fall apart in practice. They capture the model most elegantly because they recognize that before a client can compare options the client needs to understand what the options entail. The structure aims to discourage premature diagnosis by providing description before analysis and comparison.[54] The companion steps also recognize that advantages and disadvantages are inherently *relative* to a compared object; so, if Sandy wants to understand the advantages of a sole proprietorship, she needs to know, "compared to what?"

Therefore, Step 5 proposes a non-comparative, purely descriptive review of each choice before consideration of its attractiveness. You will describe what a sole proprietorship gives Sandy, without evaluating *yet* whether those attributes are good or bad. You do the same for the other three options.

Once Sandy understands the four options, the next task is to compare them, analytically and in a structured, organized way. This seldom happens smoothly in practice, by the way, but it will be your fervent goal. In Sandy's case, you will likely first compare "entity versus no entity," to see whether creating some formal business is where Sandy wants to go. If not, there is little reason to compare the three entity options. If the answer to that question is "yes" (or, if Sandy is not sure of "no" yet), then you proceed to compare the S Corp., the LLC, and the C Corp. Many writers suggest using a chart or some visual aid to help Sandy compare the differences between the options.[55]

The fundamental insight here is this: There are differences among the options, those differences will be advantages or disadvantages depending upon Sandy's needs and interests, and she must in the end decide how to weigh those advantages and disadvantages. Your job is to as-

---

[54] *See* BINDER, BERGMAN, TREMBLAY & WEINSTEIN, *supra* note 3, at 350–52.

[55] *Id.* at 367–68; STEFAN H. KRIEGER & RICHARD K. NEUMANN, JR., ESSENTIAL LAWYERING SKILLS: INTERVIEWING, COUNSELING, NEGOTIATION, AND PERSUASIVE FACT ANALYSIS 276 (4th ed. 2011).

sist her to make a systematic assessment of the options' relative strengths and weaknesses.

Let us observe one small part of your comparative discussion with Sandy Litmanovich. As we join the meeting, you are wrapping up your discussion of the baseline question of whether Sandy would choose not to create any entity at all. If she were to choose that route, the meeting is essentially over. In your meeting, Sandy is not convinced that no entity is preferable to some entity, so the conversation moves ahead:

> Lawyer: I hear you, Sandy, that you are not ready to decide yet that you should stay as a sole proprietor. Perhaps you will end up there, but perhaps not. So let's now move to a comparison of the entity choices. If you did decide to create a formal business, let's see which one would make the most sense for you. Once we have some read on that, we can circle back and see whether your preferred entity is better than staying a sole proprietor. Does that make sense?

> Sandy: Sure. That's fine. I think I'd prefer the LLC given how you've described it, although I'm still a little confused about how that will protect me compared to the corporations.

> Lawyer: That's great that you're seeing some things you like about one of the choices, and that you're leaning toward the LLC. But if it's OK with you, let's not make any choices yet until we have compared the good and the bad, the pros and the cons, about all three choices. Once we've done that, we'll see how things look to you. As you know, I am happy to create whatever structure you wish, but I want to make sure you choose the one that fits your needs best.

> Sandy: Makes sense to me.

> Lawyer: And why not start with the LLC since you mentioned it. Let's see what advantages you see with the LLC, given how we've discussed it. And as we talk, I'll use this chart here that I've created, and note the pros and cons for each of the three choices. At the end of our discussion we'll look at the chart to see how things compare.

> Sandy: Well, one good thing that my friends have told me about and you confirmed is that there's no double taxation for the LLC, like there is with the—was it the C Corp.? But isn't it more expensive to set up an LLC than a C Corp.? And didn't you say some investors prefer the C Corp.?

> Lawyer: You have just identified a number of pros and cons for two of the options, so let me both clarify and label them so our

discussion can stay as organized as we can make it. As I mentioned at the beginning, there are a lot of factors to consider here. As I hear you, a pro of the LLC is the pass-through taxation, without your business having to pay income taxes separately. We discussed earlier how that factor might play out for your particular business, so I will jot that down as a pro for the LLC but as a con for the C Corp.

You also noted the start-up cost factor. Money is always an important issue for a beginning business owner. A disadvantage you see with the LLC is that it is more expensive in our state to register an LLC than a corporation, so I will list that as a con for the LLC and a pro for both the C Corp. and the S Corp. But remember that after the initial set-up fees, the LLC actually has a slightly cheaper annual fee than the corporations for each year in the future, so should I list that as a plus for the LLC and a con for the others?

Sandy: Thanks for reminding me of that. So can we note the short-term cost as a very slight disadvantage of the LLC? Cash flow is very tight right now.

Lawyer: Got it. Now, what else do you like about the LLC?

Sandy: You mentioned its flexibility, and that sounded good. But isn't that also a problem? I find I need structure in my business life, as I get so busy and distracted running the operations.

Lawyer: You like flexibility but you want structure. Let's spend a little more time comparing the three choices based on those factors to flesh out how they might work for you, or not work for you. First, with the LLC . . . .

In this segment, you have already described for Sandy what her business would get with the S Corp., the C Corp., and the LLC. Your goal now is to help Sandy compare them, and none of the choices is unambiguously better in all respects than the others. This dialogue shows you first gently nudging Sandy not to decide too soon. It may surprise you to see the client-centered model, with its commitment to antipaternalism, urging you to act in this decidedly directive way, but it makes good sense.[56] Your goal as Sandy's advisor is to assist her to make the most appropriate choice, and your meeting structure should encourage a fair deliberation among all options.

---

[56] This seeming tautological aspect of the client-centered approach has not escaped commentary. *See, e.g.,* Ellmann, *supra* note 4.

You then attend explicitly to identify each of Sandy's reactions and observations as an advantage or a disadvantage of a given option. You try to maintain some organized consideration of the choices, lest the process become a jumbled maze of factors. (Do you think you did well enough to organize her consideration of the choices?) And you use the chart to serve as a visual aid which can capture her preferences and dislikes in a retrievable way.

Steps 7) and 8): At some point Sandy will decide whether to create an entity or not. (If she remains completely unable to make any choice, she will have decided just the same—to opt for the sole proprietorship, for the status quo, the default option.) In these final two steps you will listen to her reactions to the evaluative processes you've just engaged in, and help her make sense of the conflicting considerations. Some choices will, in the end, be easy—and your role will be pretty minimal. Often, though, the choice will be very difficult, and she will want the most help from you. Conceptually, what you do at this stage of your interaction is to reflect back to Sandy what you are hearing and learning from her, to help her match her inclinations and needs with the substance of the available choices. You will work with her to assemble, analyze, and grapple with the information you have provided to her.

This is the most important place for you to think hard about the limits of your neutral stance. Recall our discussion earlier about client-centeredness. Whether Sandy chooses to start an S Corp. or an LLC *cannot* be based on your preferences—you will not run her business, and, to boot, you might have all sorts of conflicts of interest about that choice. That fundamental reality does not mean, however, that you cannot express your opinions about the choices at this end of the process. Having heard Sandy's concerns and understood her goals and opportunities, and having listened to her struggles with how to choose, you certainly may— and perhaps must—suggest ways that the options can meet, or not meet, her particular needs.

It is very common for a client to ask you what option she should choose at this stage, and you might think you have to resist answering her question, even if she pleads for your advice. It is a good thing if you sense that resistance, because the best instinct is to avoid taking control, rather than the more common lawyer reaction of stepping in and serving as the authority. But done well, and with ample respect for Sandy's circumstances, you can suggest, tentatively, an option that seems to meet what she has told you are her concerns. Consider this:

> You're right, Sandy. This is a really hard choice to make. I hear you enticed by the traditional recognition that the S Corp. receives, but worried about some of its limitations. Meanwhile, the LLC attracts you because of its flexibility, but it is more expensive to establish and cash flow is a short-term worry. As you

know, I'm happy to draft either one, and it makes no difference to my life as a lawyer which one you choose. I do sense, though, that the LLC might serve your purposes better given what you've said this afternoon. You are attracted to the LLC's options of having flexible ownership arrangements, compared to the S Corp.'s one class of stock rule. Also, as I hear you, you like the fact that the LLC permits the option, at least, of having a member which is not an individual person, unlike the S Corp. All of those seem to favor the LLC.

You worry about the greater cost of establishing the LLC, and that's a serious consideration. But down the road, the LLC's annual costs may actually be slightly less in our state than the annual filings due from an S Corp. I raise this to help you compare some short-term costs with some long-term savings.

So, let's think some more about what worries you would have if we opted for the LLC. . . .

That dialogue shows a lawyer who is offering an opinion, but not based on the lawyer's preferences, values, or interests. (Or, at least, that's how the dialogue is intended. One never knows whether one's principled considerations are really masking some underlying self-interest or bias. But this is the best one can do.) If you were working with Sandy on this problem, you could use this kind of reflective expertise to test one of the options, while—and this is critical—always welcoming her to disagree with you.

3. What If Sandy Were a Constituent of an Entity?

Our last consideration for this conventional counseling model is to address briefly what, if anything, would look different in this meeting if Sandy were not a sole proprietor operating the catering business, but one of four partners running the same business. It is perhaps unusual, but certainly not unheard of, to find four individuals participating in a business without any formal structure, especially, for instance, in a family business. As a matter of substantive law, the unincorporated business would be a general partnership, but without any limited liability or similar protections.[57] Imagine that Sandy visited you as the lawyer for the partnership, intending to use your legal services to help her and her partners decide whether to change the form of the business. Essentially, it is exactly the same situation as that we have just explored. The eight stages and their respective justifications would apply to this meeting just as they did to Sandy as a solo owner of the business.

There is one potentially critical difference, though. In assisting Sandy to make the hard choices—especially the interactions at Steps 7

---

[57] *See* SCOTT B. EHRLICH & DOUGLAS C. MICHAEL, BUSINESS PLANNING 42–43 (2009).

and 8—you may find yourself *less deferential* to Sandy when she is a constituent compared to when she owned the business outright. As a partner, Sandy is *not the client*. (This true statement would have far more obvious meaning if the business were a formal corporation instead of an unincorporated partnership, but it still remains a true statement of professional ethics and substantive law.[58]) If the fundamental premise of client-centeredness is the lawyer's fidelity to the preferences, values, and predilections of her client, you must avoid conflating Sandy's preferences, values, and predilections for those of the partnership. It would make sense that you would treat Sandy's voice as *presumptively* reflecting that of the partnership. Absent some information that you know from your work with the four partners in the past, you are in no better position than Sandy to speak for this entity, and likely are in a far worse position.

But that assertion is rebuttable. As a result, your interplay with a constituent might be—and ethically, may be—less neutral and less deferential than in the solo context. This is a topic which deserves much more careful consideration; with hope, you will encounter it in your clinical work and can explore it more with your supervisor and your classmates.

B. MODIFYING THE CONVENTIONAL PRIMER FOR "ARCHITECTURE" SETTINGS

In the conventional counseling schema, we saw how you strived for as much neutrality as possible, even in the lower-level decision about which option to discuss first. Your aim was not to communicate, even implicitly, to your client that you favored one of the choices over the other. The structure aimed to discern your client's undistorted preferences, to the extent that is possible.

As we suggested above, in transactional work the notion of finite, discrete choices is less common than it might be in litigation settings. In counseling your clients about deals, about business arrangements, or about corporate governance, your clients surely will make decisions, but in less isolated fashion. Instead of your asking a client, "Would you prefer X or Z?," you will find yourself asking the client something like, "Does package W or package Y better meet your needs, or some combination of the two?" Or, perhaps more commonly, you will say something like this: "Here's a package of terms that I believe might potentially meet your needs. Let's review the proposal and see if it works. If it doesn't, we'll see if we can adjust the provisions that do not seem right."

---

[58] While a lawyer for a general partnership owes her professional allegiance to the partnership which is her client, she might, in some jurisdictions and under some fact scenarios, owe some fiduciary duties to each partner. This is a complicated subject beyond the scope of this chapter or, indeed, this book. *See, e.g.,* Pucci v. Santi, 711 F. Supp. 916, 927 (N.D. Ill. 1989) (noting that a lawyer for partnership represented all the partners, general and limited); James M. Fischer, *Representing Partnerships: Who Is/Are the Client(s)?*, 26 PAC. L.J. 961 (1995).

This kind of interaction calls for a different schema. Unlike the conventional counseling meeting above, or the pre-negotiation meeting we will discuss below, this kind of collaborative work typically will not be accomplished in one meeting. If we were to suggest an adjustment to the model above, that altered model would look like this:

First Meeting

1) Welcome and small talk;

2) A preparatory explanation; and

3) A review of the goals, preferences, and values which the lawyer's work will honor, with specific reference to the lawyering task at hand.

Second Meeting

4) Welcome and small talk;

5) Presentation of a proposed package/ensemble that the lawyer believes could work for the client;

6) A collaborative review of the critical aspects of the package;

7) Discussion of alternatives for each place where Sandy might prefer a different term; and

8) A final package that Sandy accepts.

This schema varies the first model in a few important ways. To see these differences in some practical context, imagine the following development in Sandy Litmanovich's business planning: After some conventional counseling as we described above, Sandy has decided to create a Subchapter S corporation. Your next step is to develop her basic corporate documents—the articles, the bylaws, and the stock share arrangements. As you likely know, those documents will not be entirely lock-step and boilerplate. Sandy has choices about how the S Corp. will get structured and how its governance procedures will look. In order to create the kind of corporate operation that meets Sandy's needs, you will have to work with her to decide which provisions she will prefer—in other words, you will *counsel* her. You could treat each separable choice within the documents as a conventional counseling task, and follow the model described above, but doing so would be time-consuming, patience-draining, and not terribly effective. Instead, you will work with Sandy on this project similar to the way an architect would treat her client. What you will do is first to explore Sandy's goals, leanings, preferences, and uncertainties about the future. You will then craft a proposal that seems to address those considerations as best you can, and present the proposal to Sandy. Those two interactions will typically not occur in one meeting, for apparent reasons.

The First Meeting: Before you can make a presentation to Sandy, you need to know how she hopes to operate her business. If the articles, bylaws and stock arrangements for any given S Corp. are subject to some variations, you will need to learn from Sandy what plans she has for the business's operations, what preferences she has for managing and financing the company, and who will join her in the future. You also need to learn from Sandy about her areas of deep uncertainty—where she needs to maintain greatest flexibility for possible future changes in direction.

Your counseling of Sandy about what kind of company structure she will have requires that you explore these factors, and it makes much more sense that you do so before you begin to craft a package for her. Note that you may have accomplished everything you need by the process of your conventional counseling regarding whether she wants an entity at all, and if so what entity she prefers. The important insight is that you need to know a lot about this entrepreneur's plans and preferences before you make your own provisional choices for her.

The Second Meeting: Here is where we encounter the most noticeable adjustment of the conventional counseling model. For the reasons we described above, your counseling of this client about how to organize this business will not consist of separable, isolated choices for which you will profess your neutrality and about which you will discern Sandy's undistorted preferences, item by item. Instead, based on what you have learned in your previous work with her, you will come to the second meeting with a proposal which you have concluded will likely work for Sandy, and which respects the implications triggered by the substantive law as you have researched it.[59] You will explain to Sandy the assumptions you have relied upon in crafting your proposal. Your aim in the second meeting is to remain just as client-centered as you were in your conventional counseling meeting about the choice of entity. There is no reason here why you should have any greater influence about what Sandy chooses than you permitted yourself in the previous setting. Your structure of this second meeting will seek to ensure as much neutrality and deference as possible, even though you will have offered a proposal as the subject of the discussion.

In order to achieve as much deference to Sandy as possible notwithstanding your having staked out a position among the various choices, your preparatory explanation for the second meeting is critical. Sandy must understand that she will decide whether these terms work, and her values and preferences will control. Even though you wrote the proposal, you do not recommend it in any strong fashion, if at all. Here is how you might introduce this second meeting:

> Sandy, in today's meeting we will review the package I have put together as a first take on how you might operate your S Corp. I sent you the documents a few days ago, and today we can discuss

---

[59] In practice, you will more likely have provided Sandy with your proposal before the meeting for her review. You would most likely spend some time at the beginning of this meeting asking Sandy whether she had had an opportunity to review the materials.

them and see whether they work for you. There are many different ways that one might organize a business like yours, and this is obviously just one variation, so feel free to let me know if you want to change or adjust anything here.

Let me stress that last point, because it is especially important. I created this package by considering the things we've spoken about in our earlier meetings, knowing what your current plans are and where you would like to retain some flexibility in the future. While I created it, I am not at all committed to it, and I will happily revise, add or remove provisions given our discussion today, in light of what you wish and given the requirements of the law. I will show you as we go along where I made some choices that I *think* fit with what you've told me, but all of those choices are just my tentative judgments.

Does that make sense? Do you have any questions about how we'll proceed today?

This preparatory explanation should minimize the risk that your client will read into your proposal an inference that this is "the answer" to the puzzles she is facing, or that it is the answer that you recommend as the best one available.

In an effective second meeting, your client will question whether some of your proposed terms work to meet the business's needs. It would be either a serendipitous happenstance, or a flaw in the process, if the client agreed with everything you have included in your package. For any given item where your client is uncertain about whether that term will work effectively, and for which there happens to be one or more alternative provisions available, you will then counsel the client about the alternatives, essentially in the same fashion as we described in the conventional counseling schema.

Let us suggest an example of this last point. Imagine that your draft bylaws for Sandy's S Corp. includes a provision permitting the board of directors to oust a member of the board "with or without cause," upon a proper quorum of the board at a properly called meeting and a sufficient number of board members voting to oust the member. If Sandy wonders whether she might be better off with a "for cause" provision instead of the version you proposed (and assuming that such an alternative is lawful), you and she must decide which of the two alternatives to include. You should include one or the other, and you cannot include both.[60] You now

---

[60] For the sake of the counseling point we hope to make here, assume that these two options are the only two plausible alternatives. In fact, a creative drafter might insert a provision where some factual circumstances would permit a "cause" ouster while other settings would permit a "not for cause" removal. Or, perhaps a drafter could omit any mention of removal of existing board members, but that option may trigger some state law remedies. We ignore those complexities in our simple example.

encounter precisely the type of counseling opportunity we labeled above as "conventional," where you and your client face a discrete choice with finite alternatives, one of which will have to occur. Your role would then be to counsel Sandy about the choices in such a way that she may choose, without distortion from you, the alternative that best meets her goals, just as she did when choosing her form of entity.[61]

C. A PRIMER ON THE STRUCTURE OF A "PRE–NEGOTIATION" COUNSELING SESSION

As we saw above, not all counseling consists of aiding a client to choose among a finite set of discrete options, even though most counseling textbooks address only that kind of interaction. Another common alternative version of counseling addresses the activity a lawyer engages in when preparing a client to make a purchase or sale offer, or to develop some bottom line authority for the lawyer to rely upon when negotiating the terms of some transaction. If we consider any such purchase or sale as a form of negotiation, we can refer to this kind of counseling as "pre-negotiation" counseling.[62]

Pre-negotiation counseling differs from conventional counseling in a couple of important ways. To highlight those differences, let us start with an example.

Imagine that you are representing Alan Minuskin, the owner and chef of an innovative little café in Center City. Alan has had great success with his café since he opened it two years ago, so much so that he now seriously considers moving to a better and larger location. He has located a storefront which would be quite fitting for his restaurant, considering the location, the kinds of people who walk by, and the size and layout of the space. The storefront is occupied, but by a business which seems like it is not thriving, and Alan believes that the owner might be willing to rent the space to a new business like his. Alan retains your legal clinic to represent him in the possible negotiation of a lease with the owner of the space, a woman named Kerianne Byrne. Before you approach Ms. Byrne to begin discussions, you invite Alan in for a meeting in order to counsel him about what authority he will give you for a monthly rent for the premises, and what his bottom line would be on that price item. (Assume, for simplicity's sake, that you will try to negotiate a flat monthly rent for the space, rather than the more likely complicated multi-term price structure of a commercial lease.)

Notice how your meeting with Alan in this case is quite different in its goal from your conventional counseling meeting with Sandy. Sandy's meeting was actually more elegant and straightforward—she needed to

---

[61] *See* Section V.A *supra.*

[62] As one of us has in an earlier publication. *See* note 2 *supra.*

choose between options A, B, C, or D, and in the end she could choose but one of them. If the owner of the desired space, Ms. Byrne, had offered to you a take-it-or-leave-it price of $2500/month, your meeting with Alan would parallel your meeting with Sandy, except that Alan would have only two options—take the deal, or leave the deal. But you haven't met yet with Byrne, and Alan has no finite, discrete choices to make yet. Your purpose in this meeting is to *test* Alan for how high he would go before he walks away from the deal (or you do so as his agent). To discern that authority from Alan calls for a counseling meeting, but it is a fundamentally different kind of counseling meeting. This is what we mean by pre-negotiation counseling.

Because your goals are different in this setting, and because your discussions will vary in important ways from the conventional kind of decision-making you assist your clients with, the schema for a pre-negotiation counseling session will look different as well.

1.   A Model Structure

A model for structuring your meeting with Alan could look something like this, with the following discrete stages developing in this order:

1) Welcome and small talk;

2) Review and confirmation of his goals and interests, including a preparatory explanation;

3) A description of the status quo, "default" scenarios, assuming no deal is made;

4) Identification of some hypothetical rental price for discussion's sake;

5) Full consideration of that price when compared to the status quo;

6) If the hypothetical price is not acceptable, explore successively lower alternatives until an acceptable price emerges;

7) If the hypothetical price is acceptable, explore a higher price, and continue until finding a limit;

8) Determine the highest price Alan would pay; and

9) Discuss a plausible opening offer in light of the identified "bottom line."

Compared to the conventional counseling session described above, few of these steps are intuitive, so this process as a whole warrants some further explanation. As we did above, let us review the model and defend it using the same goals of clarity, structure, and neutrality on which we have relied in the previous schemas.

2. An Explanation of the Model's Stages

Let us review the model's successive steps, so we can best understand some of the complexities and challenges in this kind of client meeting.

Steps 1) and 2): This introductory and preparatory part of the meeting needs little discussion, except for the following caveat: We will see in a few moments that a meeting like this can leave a client believing that you are in favor of his paying a higher price, a result of your testing to see whether your client would in fact pay a higher price. This will become more evident as we progress, but for now accept this reminder that you might use the preparatory explanation in Step 2 to ensure Alan that you have no interest in his paying any particular price, and that you will be happy with whatever authority he ends up providing to you after the counseling is finished.

Step 3): This step deserves some explanation, because it is not self-evident in its purpose but it is critical to the success of your meeting with Alan. When you begin to discuss hypothetical rent figures with Alan, you and he need a *benchmark* in order to evaluate whether Alan should agree to rent the new space for that price, or should decline to do so. His decision on that score will *always* refer, implicitly or explicitly, to the only alternative—*not* renting at that price. Therefore, you and Alan need to explore and understand the status quo, which could include alternative sites which Alan could rent if he cannot obtain a fair lease on this new space.

Note how this part of your meeting with Alan is different from the early stages of the conventional counseling model. In the prior model, you asked Sandy to choose what topic to discuss in depth first, lest you inadvertently skew the later evaluation by seeming to favor one choice over others. Here, you cannot offer Alan any such choice. Indeed, no such array of alternatives exists. You may act in a directive fashion here, and recommend to Alan that you start with a discussion of the status quo.

Step 4): In order to determine, in the end, what Alan's authority is, you must start somewhere. It doesn't matter where you start, as we shall see, but you have to begin your work with your client by imagining some hypothetical rent. The next two stages represent the interesting part of this meeting, where you test for better or worse deals. For now, you have to arrive at some number to start with.

Conceptually, it might be better for Alan to choose a beginning rent figure for discussion, to minimize the implication that you believe that a rent figure you choose is reasonable and that Alan should agree to it. But it does not matter that much, because you will press Alan regardless of how he responds to the first number. Conceptually it also makes some sense that you start with a "reasonable" figure, to save time, but again it does not make a difference to your process.

Let's imagine that Alan is paying $2000 per month at his current location. And let's imagine further that, in this step of your meeting, where you ask Alan what rent would make him willing to move to the new space, he says, "If Byrne would rent the space to me for $1500 a month, I'd be there in a flash." You would have thus accomplished your purpose for Step 4.

Steps 5), 6) and 7): Here's where the fun begins. Your first responsibility as Alan's counselor is to make sure he has chosen the first figure wisely. In this part of the counseling meeting, you are pretending that Alan had before him two binary choices—status quo, or move to the new space at $1500/month. Before you irrevocably accept Alan's decision about that choice, you need to replicate the conventional counseling process above, and compare the two to make sure he is happy with the selection he has made. In our example, it is easy to perform this step, because Alan has chosen a seemingly very favorable rent figure. If Alan really could obtain better and larger space at less money, it would be a simple decision for him and for you. You now have authority to accept that deal from Kerianne Byrne were she to offer it.

But you know that Byrne is really unlikely to rent the bigger and better space to Alan for less than his current rent. And even if you had no idea whether that were the case or not, you still have a responsibility as Alan's lawyer and counselor to determine *whether you should reject* a proposal from Byrne that demands a higher figure. You therefore have to press Alan about a higher rent. That development looks something like this:

> I understand, Alan, that if Byrne will rent you the space for $1500 a month, I have your blessings to accept a deal on those terms. That's helpful—and why I wanted to meet with you today. What I need to know next, though, is whether you would accept a deal from her with a higher rent figure than that. For instance, what if she offered to rent it to you for, say, $2100 per month, slightly higher than your current rent? Would $2100 be acceptable to you?

You *have to know* the answer to this question. If you ended your meeting after hearing Alan's target of $1500/month, proceeded to negotiate with Byrne, and then rejected an offer for a lease at $2100/month (thinking that $1500/month was the limit of your authority), you could have committed malpractice.[63]

---

[63] Readers with any passing familiarity with negotiation will be quick to point out that your meeting with Byrne is not necessarily the final opportunity to close a deal. You could try for $1500, get turned down, and return later with authority for $2100 if Alan would indeed accept such a lease. That objection is true, but it misses the point. Your meeting today with Alan ought to elicit, as best as you can, Alan's "price" for the space. You have much to gain and little to lose by learning his final price in your meeting. For a more elaborate discussion of this point (including some further arguments supporting the objection just described), see Tremblay, *supra* note 2.

You can see how the meeting progresses. Alan may well agree, after careful review with you, that $2100/month is a fair price for the new space. If he does so, you need to inquire further, for the very same reasons that you pursued the $2100 question:

> So, I now understand your thinking about the $2100 rent figure—if that's the best I can do, I will accept it rather than walking away. But I'm afraid that I can't leave you alone yet. In order for me to know what I need to know before I meet with Byrne, I have to ask you this: What if she insists on, say, $2500/month? Should I say no? Or say yes? And before we discuss that rent price, let me remind you—if you end up thinking that $2500 is acceptable, that does not mean that I will tell that to Byrne, or make that offer to her unless I am against the wall, and it's the best I could do. I also need to remind you of what I said at the beginning about my role here. It matters not at all to me whether you give me authority for $2500, or $1500, or $4500. It simply doesn't matter. My job will be the same. I just need to make sure I don't walk away from a deal that you would, in fact, prefer to have.
>
> So, my question: What if Byrne insisted on $2500? Do I agree? Or do I walk?

This is the part of pre-negotiation counseling where your client might feel like you are wearing him down. (Indeed, the interaction above could be repeated several times if Alan's true "price" is much higher than $2500.) You can minimize the client's feelings through the explicit discussion included in the dialogue above. You could also minimize that reaction by engaging in a different tactic from the one shown here. That tactic would look like this: After Alan has suggested, and then accepted, a figure of $1500, you could reframe the discussion by moving him to the far end of the spectrum. You could suggest a figure of, say, $4500, just to test his spending limits. If Alan says no to $4500, you know that his "price" is somewhere between $1500 and $4500. You can test for numbers in between those endpoints to learn what the ultimate authority actually is. (It could be $1500; or it could be $4450.)

One last note about this process, which is very rich in its implications and deserves much critique and discussion in your seminar and supervision meetings. The model described here implies that Alan somehow "has" a price, and that your job is to find it through the inquiries and comparisons described here. Of course, Alan's "price" is likely not known to him, and will be influenced by your discussions. The best you could expect to do is to discern a ballpark figure which seems like the limits of Alan's authority, and then, if you cannot negotiate a lease with Byrne within those limits, you will return to Alan for further counseling (informed by what you have learned from Byrne) before breaking off negotiations for good.

Steps 8) and 9): At some point, you will end your counseling with a sense that Alan would pay, say, $3000/month but not more for the new space. As you have promised Alan, your having learned this authority does not mean that your first offer to Byrne would be for a lease at $3000/month. You would be a quite inept negotiator if you led with your authority limit. Indeed, you might even walk away from your talks with Byrne at $2700, if you sensed that such a tactic could influence Byrne to accept that figure. All you know from your counseling meeting is that Alan, all things considered, would prefer a $3000/month lease over no lease and the status quo. That is critical information for you, but it does not tell you how to use it.

All of this invites the question, then, of what you would suggest as your opening offer. Many wise lawyers believe that this tactic deserves some input from your client. An offer of $1000 would seemingly insult Byrne, and might irrevocably affect your credibility for the rest of the interactions with her. A proposal of $2850 seems to be far too generous given your authority. However you choose to exercise your judgment as a skilled negotiator, you can benefit a lot by including your client in that thinking. For this reason, the final step of this process covers your having a careful, thoughtful discussion with Alan about your upcoming strategy in the negotiation.

To understand better how you might craft such a strategy, please refer to Chapter 5 of this text, covering transactional negotiation.

VI. CONCLUDING THOUGHTS

You will find the counseling process to be very interesting and quite challenging in practice. Your clients will need your advice and guidance, sometimes desperately so, and they will rely on what you tell them. You will find yourself exercising complex judgments about how effectively you can answer the questions they pose to you, especially if you hope to respect the client-centered commitment we describe here. The models we suggest here should help, but even more important will be your reflective approach to the inevitable tensions that arise in this part of the lawyering experience.

CHAPTER 5

NEGOTIATIONS IN TRANSACTIONAL SETTINGS

■ ■ ■

I. INTRODUCTION

We negotiate every time we try to influence someone into doing something we want. We begin to negotiate in our childhood and do so continuously throughout our lives. We negotiate with our family (including parents, siblings, children, spouses and partners), friends, school mates, teachers, co-workers and others with whom we come into contact in our daily lives.

In the professional setting, negotiation involves both interpersonal skills and legal analytical skills. Like interviewing, negotiation involves human interaction. In negotiating, we interact with both the lawyer representing the counterpart[1] and our client. Negotiation also involves the analytical consideration of the issues involved and the solutions that are legally and creatively possible.[2]

Transactional lawyers regularly engage in negotiations, acting as advocates for their clients. While transactional lawyers may deal with conflicts or disagreements between parties, the parties in many transactions have relationships they hope will continue beyond that particular negotiation. In many transactional settings, neither party has a pre-existing legal claim against the other. The alternative to reaching agreement is often to go elsewhere in the market.

More often than not, transactional lawyers are working to add value to the transaction. Many transactions are in fact completed without lawyers. Even when lawyers are involved, the clients often interact with each other and may have already negotiated some of the key terms of the agreement. Lawyers may become involved when clients have already

---

[1] We use "counterpart" instead of "opponent," the term used by many respected negotiation authorities, because our theory of negotiation treats the other participants as sharing in value-creation instead of acting as opponents. *See, e.g.,* Charles Craver, *What Makes a Great Legal Negotiator?*, 56 LOY. L. REV. 337, 352 (2010); Reed Elizabeth Loder, *Moral Truthseeking and the Virtuous Negotiator*, 8 GEO. J. LEGAL ETHICS 45, 90 (1995).

[2] CARRIE J. MENKEL-MEADOW, ANDREA KUPFER SCHNEIDER & LELA PORTER LOVE, NEGOTIATION: PROCESSES FOR PROBLEM SOLVING 3 (2006).

drafted a letter of intent (LOI)[3] outlining the broad parameters of the agreement. Lawyers are often involved in transactions when the assets to be transferred are difficult to define or idiosyncratic, when the parties make promises that extend over time, when the value of the agreement hinges on external contingencies, such as regulatory approval, and when the risks associated with the transaction are not well known.[4]

This chapter introduces you to negotiation theory and the application of those concepts to the transactional setting. We begin by examining the preparation for negotiating, focusing primarily on the lease negotiations between the Domestic Workers Center (DWC) and Eastlake Family Services (Eastlake), the organizations we introduce you to in the Interviewing chapter. We then discuss two different negotiation models and proceed to look deeper at the idea of creating value in problem-solving negotiations. We then turn our focus to the actual process of negotiation, discussing the activities that take place at the negotiation table including information gathering and persuasion. We also discuss fairness in the negotiation process as well as questions of difference (a topic we introduce you to in the Interviewing chapter and discuss further in the Multicultural Lawyering chapter). We introduce several psychological considerations in negotiation relating to both persuasion and decision-making. We conclude the chapter by exploring issues of negotiation ethics.

II. PREPARING TO NEGOTIATE

Throughout the chapter, we will use the example of the lease negotiation between the DWC and Eastlake. In the Interviewing chapter, we met Amanda Estrada, the Executive Director of the DWC, a workers rights organization. DWC is looking to move to new office space because its five-year lease is expiring in six months and the organization is outgrowing its current space. Eastlake, another organization in the neighborhood, is in the process of purchasing a building with more space than it needs. The two organizations have discussed the possibility of DWC renting office space from Eastlake. DWC has engaged the Clinic to negotiate its lease with Eastlake.

In preparation for negotiating DWC's lease, you will have to engage in both internal and external preparation. Your counseling meetings with DWC[5] comprise the beginning of your internal preparation. An important

---

[3]   For a more detailed discussion of letters of intent, see, e.g., Gregory G. Gosfield, *The Structure and Use of Letters of Intent as Prenegotiation Contracts for Prospective Real Estate Transactions*, 38 REAL PROP. PROB. & TR. J. 99 (2004); Thomas C. Homburger & James R. Schueller, *Letters of Intent—A Trap for the Unwary*, 37 REAL PROP. PROB. & TR. J. 509 (2003).

[4]   ROBERT H. MNOOKIN, SCOTT R. PEPPET & ANDREW S. TULUMELLO, BEYOND WINNING: NEGOTIATING TO CREATE VALUE IN DEALS AND DISPUTES 129 (2000).

[5]   We will assume for the sake of our discussion that Amanda Estrada has been given authority by DWC's Board of Directors. Otherwise, your conversation might happen with the entire Board of Directors or a subset of the Board, for example the Executive Committee, should the organization have one.

starting point is to think about the key issues, your client's interests and *comparative* your counterpart's interests. Your preparation will include determining *interests* what your client wants to get out of the negotiation, your client's options if it is not able to reach an agreement and what your client is willing to accept. We explore those concepts further below.

If you have reviewed any commercial leases, you have noticed that they are fairly long and complex in comparison to residential leases. While the state in which you practice may have statutes governing residential leases and case law interpreting those statutory provisions, you will most likely find few parallels in the commercial setting. As a result, more is open to the parties to negotiate. Entire books and articles (including most likely in your state's continuing legal education materials) are devoted to commercial lease terms and those sources may contain sample *Samples* lease terms. We will not discuss all the possible lease terms, but we will cover some of the clauses that may be most important to DWC and Eastlake.

We can imagine that for both DWC and Eastlake there are going to be some crucial terms for the lease. For both parties, the amount of rent is going to be an important clause. Other important clauses may be the lease term (the length of the lease), the occupancy date (or move-in date), how rent is going to be paid (some lump-sum payments up front or in equal installments), taxes and other assessments (such as utilities), services (such as electricity, gas, heat and air conditioning, if necessary, water, cleaning, snow removal, if applicable, and garbage collection), build-out (in order to make the space suitable to DWC's use), condition of the premises (most likely more important to DWC), repairs and alterations, and insurance. The parties may also care about signage, subletting, breach and termination of the tenancy and holding over. DWC may care about parking, access to the building and security. Eastlake may be concerned about the activities DWC will carry on in the space. You may remember that these are some of the issues we discussed with Ms. Estrada during the initial interview and of course you would have discussed them further in the counseling meetings leading up to the start of negotiations.

The occupancy date is going to be a significant provision for the parties as they discuss the lease terms. DWC has a lease in its current space. Unless it can reach agreement with its current landlord to stay longer at the current rental amount, DWC most likely needs to move out of its current space by the end of its lease term. DWC does not want to move out too much earlier than the end of its current lease since it will then be paying double rent. Whether the Eastlake space can be available by that time is an important consideration for DWC. Can Eastlake assure DWC that it will have closed on its purchase of the building by then? Even if Eastlake owns the building by then, will renovations to the building, and more importantly perhaps to the DWC space, be completed by then? Eastlake may want DWC to commit to moving into the space as soon as it closes or as soon as it completes renovations on the space. What if that happens before DWC's lease ends?

Rent + other financial concerns

As DWC begins to plan for its conversation with Eastlake about the possibility of leasing space, it needs to consider several factors. DWC cannot consider the rent term in isolation; it must also consider other financial issues. DWC will have to think through what it may have to pay in taxes, utilities and other services in addition to the monthly rental amount. Eastlake may want DWC to pay more of the first year's rent early in the term since it may have higher expenses early in the lease term. If Eastlake is concerned about DWC's ability to pay, this arrangement might also serve as a form of security deposit (though the amount of a formal security deposit is another term to be negotiated). DWC might be able to agree to pay a larger proportion of the rent up front if it has received a large grant that can cover its rent. On the other hand, this might be impossible for DWC if it has not yet secured its budget for the year. We might even imagine that the same foundation is providing funds to both organizations and that foundation may be willing to be flexible to help its grantees. For Eastlake, it might be more important to have a signed lease than to get top dollar for the space. If Eastlake is applying for a mortgage, the signed lease may take on greater significance. Eastlake may be interested in a long lease term so it can guarantee (well, almost) cash flow for a certain period of time. DWC may be less willing to do that if it is concerned about its finances or if it anticipates one of its programs ending during the lease term (and therefore losing funding for that activity or not needing as much space). DWC might be willing to risk the rent increasing in return for a shorter lease term.

Counter-party's considerations

We are just beginning to scratch the surface of all the factors involved in the parties reaching agreement. Let us look more closely at the considerations for these negotiations.

A. RESERVATION POINT AND BARGAINING ZONE

In preparation for the negotiations, DWC is going to have to make certain key decisions. Let us first examine what DWC is willing to pay for rent (even if DWC cannot make this decision in isolation). The maximum amount of rent DWC will pay (and the minimum amount Eastlake will accept) is referred to as the parties' *reservation points* or *reservation values*.[6] The distance between DWC's and Eastlake's reservation points is the *bargaining zone* or *zone of possible agreement*.[7] If the bargaining zone for DWC and Eastlake overlap, agreement is possible (but not guaranteed

---

[6] Russell Korobkin, *A Positive Theory of Legal Negotiation*, 88 GEO. L.J. 1789, 1792 (2000); MNOOKIN, PEPPET & TULUMELLO, *supra* note 4, at 19–20.

[7] Korobkin, *supra* note 6, at 1792; MNOOKIN, PEPPET & TULUMELLO, *supra* note 4, at 20–21.

even assuming rent is the only issue to be negotiated). Let us assume *Zone of possible agreement* DWC is willing to pay up to $3,000 per month in rent and that Eastlake would not accept (and perhaps cannot accept if it is to be able to afford the mortgage) anything lower than $2,500 per month. The bargaining zone then is $500, or the amount that the parties' reservation points overlap. If, on the other hand, DWC cannot afford (or is not willing) to pay more than $2,000 per month and Eastlake would not accept less than $2,500, there is no bargaining zone and the parties will not be able to reach an agreement. Knowledge of the parameters of the bargaining zone is the "most critical information" for the negotiator to have because it tells the negotiator whether agreement is possible.[8]

B. BEST ALTERNATIVE TO NEGOTIATED AGREEMENT

Before DWC can determine its reservation point (the highest rent it will pay), it needs to determine its alternatives to reaching an agreement. It is important to recognize that "alternatives to reaching an agreement can be nearly limitless in some transactional negotiations, and creativity in generating the list is a critical skill of the negotiator."[9] For DWC, some of these alternatives might be staying at its current location (renewing its lease or going month-to-month if its current landlord will allow it) or moving to another location. *Can we walk away?* DWC will need to explore these options further before it can determine which alternative is most desirable—the *best alternative to a negotiated agreement* (BATNA).[10] In setting the BATNA, you will first need to help DWC brainstorm all of its alternatives to an agreement. The second step is choosing the best alternative—the one that leaves DWC in the best situation. Finally, you have to translate the BATNA into a reservation value, the point where DWC would be better off with its BATNA.[11]

A party's reservation point has two components—the market value of its BATNA and the difference between the value of its BATNA and the value of the subject of the negotiation.[12] To set its reservation point, DWC would add to its BATNA (let us assume that is renewing its current lease) if the Eastlake space is more valuable; or, DWC would subtract from its BATNA if staying in its current space is more valuable than moving into the Eastlake space.[13]

---

[8]   Korobkin, *supra* note 6, at 1793.

[9]   *Id.* at 1795.

[10]   ROGER FISHER, WILLIAM URY & BRUCE PATTON, GETTING TO YES: NEGOTIATING AGREEMENT WITHOUT GIVING IN 101–08 (3d ed. 2011).

[11]   MENKEL–MEADOW, SCHNEIDER & LOVE, *supra* note 2, at 53–54.

[12]   Korobkin, *supra* note 6, at 1796.

[13]   Eastlake would do the opposite to reach its reservation point—subtract if reaching agreement with DWC is more valuable than its BATNA and add if its BATNA is more valuable than reaching agreement with DWC. We can imagine Eastlake might have other parties interested in the space or it might have to hire (and therefore pay) someone to market its space.

Let us consider the additional factors that might affect the reservation point. We mentioned above that in setting its reservation point, DWC will first have to consider the *alternatives*[14] it has to reaching agreement. DWC could choose to stay at its current location or find other space. DWC will need to talk to its landlord to discuss the possibility of renewing the lease (and the rental price). DWC will also need to explore other suitable space.[15] What other alternatives might be available to DWC?

DWC's *preference*[16] is another factor to consider in determining its reservation point. DWC might like the Eastlake space more because the building is in better condition, is more centrally located, or is in the neighborhood the organization serves. The new space might also allow for expansion of DWC's operations as the organization grows. In addition, DWC's current space might also have parking for the employees (something the Eastlake space may not have). DWC might not want to commit to a longer lease, something that Eastlake would like (or the other way around). A third factor is the *probability of future events*. Reaching agreement gives DWC some certainty. Pursuing its BATNA could result in two or more different state of affairs, each with some probability of occurring that is less than 100 percent.[17] A fourth factor is DWC's *risk preference*.[18] The organization might be risk-averse, feeling it cannot take chances with donor and foundation money. It might not want to risk that it can find better space or negotiate better terms in another space. A fifth consideration is the relative *transaction costs*[19] of reaching agreement and of pursuing the BATNA. Moving from its current space, for example, brings certain transaction costs as does not reaching agreement. A sixth consideration is the *value of time*.[20] Because time has opportunity costs, two alternatives that take place at different times have different values.[21] Time is an important consideration for DWC since its lease is up in six months and it needs to find space that is available by then if it will not renew the lease at its current location. DWC's current lease may have holdover provisions that greatly increase the cost of overstaying its tenancy period. In addition, DWC has to consider the time it will take to try to reach an agreement. A seventh consideration is the *effect of future op-*

---

[14]   MNOOKIN, PEPPET & TULUMELLO, *supra* note 4, at 19–20.

[15]   To determine its BATNA, DWC might consider ascertaining the fair market value of similar space. By working with a real estate specialist, DWC might be able to classify the different spaces it is considering and the going price per square foot for that type of space.

[16]   RUSSELL KOROBKIN, NEGOTIATION THEORY AND STRATEGY 33–34 (2d ed. 2009).

[17]   DWC will need to do an "expected value" calculation, which "converts a range of probabilistic possibilities to a single weighted average of those possibilities" so DWC can compare a probabilistic alternative to certain alternative. DWC would do this by multiplying the possible future state of the world (the rental price) by its best estimate of the probability that it will come to pass and add all the products. *Id.* at 32.

[18]   *Id.* at 34–35.

[19]   *Id.* at 35–36.

[20]   *Id.* at 36–37.

[21]   *Id.* at 36.

portunities, the possibility that the parties might be able to interact in the future.[22] While DWC may not be looking to lease space from Eastlake in the future, it needs to consider how failure to reach agreement may affect the relationship of the organizations generally, especially if they collaborate on certain projects. There may also be other considerations for DWC. For example, a foundation that is a major funder of both DWC and Eastlake might want Eastlake to lease space to DWC and for DWC to move into the Eastlake space.

In preparation for the negotiation, you will need to decide which lease terms will need to be evaluated in the same way. Not every term may require the same type of evaluation. Additionally, you should consider the other terms the lease is likely to contain, which will allow you to determine the legal and factual investigation that you need to conduct. What are some legal issues you might need to research? One example might be the allocation of real estate taxes. How does the state in which you practice tax commercial real estate (whether owned or leased by a nonprofit organization)?[23]

C. ASPIRATIONS AND GOALS

Your client's BATNA and reservation points are not the only considerations you need to take into account as you prepare for the negotiation. While it is important to know the least your client will accept and its alternatives to reaching agreement, you also will need to explore your client's hopes for the negotiation, its *aspirations* or goals. This analysis encompasses the result that leaves your client better off than a minimally acceptable agreement. By determining DWC's aspirations before meeting with Eastlake, you go into the negotiations with a goal to aspire to reach. Determining your client's aspirations is an important activity. Research shows that negotiators with high aspirations generally do better.[24] If DWC were to set its aspirations too high, however, it risks not reaching agreement. Alternatively, if DWC sets its aspirations too low, it may end up not feeling satisfied. Some individuals may set modest goals to protect their self-esteem,[25] to avoid conflict, or because they have insufficient information about the other party.[26] If your client's aspirations are justifiable, you are more likely to convince your counterpart that the outcome is fair and objective.[27] When setting one's bottom line is difficult, aggressive

---

[22] *Id.* at 37.

[23] For example, you may need to consider a leasehold interest tax. *See, e.g.,* WASH. REV. CODE. § 458–29A–100 (2010).

[24] Andrea Kupfer Schneider, *Aspirations in Negotiations,* 87 MARQ. L. REV. 675, 676 (2004) (citing SIDNEY SIEGEL & LAWRENCE E. FOURAKER, BARGAINING AND GROUP DECISION MAKING: EXPERIMENTS IN BILATERAL MONOPOLY 64 (1960)).

[25] MENDEL–MEADOW, SCHNEIDER & LOVE, *supra* note 2, at 44 (citing G. RICHARD SHELL, BARGAINING FOR ADVANTAGE: NEGOTIATION STRATEGIES FOR REASONABLE PEOPLE 31–34 (1999)).

[26] Schneider, *supra* note 24, at 679–80.

[27] *Id.* at 678.

aspirations are likely to lead the negotiator to set her bottom line higher than might be appropriate and thus make reaching impasse more likely.[28] One commentator recommends setting "optimistic but justifiable" aspirations.[29]

Now that we have considered your client's reservation point, BATNA and aspirations, let us turn our attention to your external preparation. Part of your external preparation consists of doing the same analysis but from the point of view of your counterpart—estimating your counterpart's reservation point, BATNA and aspirations. As DWC's lawyer, you will need to try to determine if there is a likelihood of reaching agreement. The bargaining zone is fixed by both parties' reservation points. Trying to predict your counterpart's reservation point helps determine the likelihood of agreement. Trying to anticipate your counterpart's BATNA helps you determine the strength of your positions. Determining your counterpart's goals in the negotiation will also help you ascertain the possibilities for reaching agreement. One of the values a lawyer can add in negotiations is helping her client think of the alternatives to a negotiated agreement and weigh those alternatives against the possibility of reaching an agreement.

Let us now look at some models that inform our planning for the negotiation and interaction with our counterpart.

III. PROBLEM-SOLVING NEGOTIATION

A. NEGOTIATION MODELS

We introduce negotiation models in order to provide a theoretical framework for the rest of our discussion and your negotiation work. We differentiate between "integrative," "problem-solving" or "value-creating" negotiations and "distributive," "positional" or "adversarial" negotiations. Traditionally, negotiation has been seen as adversarial, a zero-sum game focusing on one side maximizing its take at the expense of the other party. This approach assumes that both parties want the same "scarce" items and that any solution is predicated on a division of those goods.[30] The "winner" in distributive bargaining is the party that gets more of the thing that is the subject of the negotiation.

In their seminal book *Getting to Yes*, Roger Fisher, William Ury and Bruce Patton introduce the concept of principled bargaining.[31] The authors recommend judging every negotiation method by three criteria—1) whether it produces a wise agreement (if agreement is possible); 2)

---

[28] *Id.* at 679.

[29] *Id.*

[30] Carrie Menkel–Meadow, *Toward Another View of Legal Negotiation: The Structure of Problem Solving,* 31 UCLA L. REV. 754, 764–65 (1984).

[31] FISHER, URY & PATTON, *supra* note 10, at xxviii.

whether it improves (or at least does not damage) the relationship between the parties; and 3) whether it is efficient.[32] Fisher, Ury and Patton define a "wise agreement" as one that meets the legitimate interests of all sides to the extent possible, resolves conflicting interests fairly, is durable and takes community interests into account.[33] They suggest that positional bargaining produces unwise agreements because the parties lock themselves into positions to save face.[34] Arguing over positions creates incentives that stall settlement since the parties start with extreme positions, hold on to their positions, make small concessions when necessary, and use other tactics to stall. These arguments take time and are unlikely to yield positive results, making positional bargaining inefficient. Finally, positional bargaining risks jeopardizing the relationship between the parties because it is a contest of wills.[35] "Principled negotiation" separates the *people* from the problem; focuses on *interests*, not positions; generates *options* before deciding what to do; and bases the result on objective *criteria*.[36]

Much of adversarial negotiation proceeds in a linear fashion, starting with the setting of a target point (what the parties would like to achieve and we called goals or aspirations above), resistance or reservation points (the point below which the party seeks not to go and what some refer to as the "bottom line") and a "ritual of offer and demand with patterns of 'reciprocal concessions.'"[37] Carrie Menkel–Meadow, a leading scholar in the negotiation field, sees several limits to the adversarial approach.[38] A linear negotiation structure may work in those cases where there is only one issue but it is unlikely to work in cases where there are multiple issues,[39] such as the lease negotiations between DWC and Eastlake. In these instances, trade-offs between issues are possible. For example, this might happen if DWC were willing to pay several months of rent up front (perhaps even a year) because it receives a large grant all at once. Eastlake may be willing to accept a lower monthly rent in order to be able to cover some of the building renovation costs. By assuming that a negotiation only concerns a single issue, negotiators fail to consider the parties' other needs or issues that may go unresolved.

A second problem with the zero-sum orientation is the assumption that the parties value the fixed resource (such as money) equally.[40] By "focusing on maximizing immediate individual gain, negotiators fail to

---

[32] *Id.* at 4.

[33] *Id.*

[34] *Id.* at 4–5.

[35] *Id.* at 7.

[36] *Id.* at 11.

[37] Menkel–Meadow, *supra* note 30, at 768–69.

[38] *Id.* at 757.

[39] *Id.* at 771.

[40] *Id.* at 787.

appreciate the long-term consequences of a particular solution."[41] Zero-sum negotiations often fail to consider transaction costs, in terms of both the process costs and the costs of a less than ideal solution. Third, by assuming that there is only one issue, the amount of rent for example, other issues or concerns of the parties may be masked and remain unsolved.[42] Fourth, by assuming that the resources are limited, fixed and valued equally by all parties, the negotiators might miss opportunities to find solutions that might be more satisfactory to the parties.[43] The adversarial model fails to exploit the differences in values that could broaden the range of possible solutions, missing opportunities to expand what the parties may divide or trade.[44]

Distributive negotiation assumes that a gain to one party necessarily means a loss to the other party.[45] In reality, few negotiations involve only one issue with the parties' interests in direct opposition. Most human interactions are more complex and thus allow for multiple ways of structuring the transaction. When an agreement benefits both parties, without burdening either, the parties have "shared" or "common" interests.[46] In these situations, the parties not only enjoy a net benefit but neither gives up anything of value.[47]

Negotiations in dispute resolution cases take place "in the shadow of the law,"[48] with the parties assuming that what can be achieved is limited by what the court would award. Transactional negotiations have a parallel risk. The "common business practice" or "form provision" often serves this same limiting function.[49] The "shadow of the form contract" may encourage a habit of mind in the negotiators to rely on common solutions and not seek solutions that may be more appropriate for their particular needs.[50] This could certainly be the case in the Eastlake–DWC lease negotiation. Eastlake, as the landlord, is likely to have a form lease that it uses. If that were the case, it might be difficult to be creative in problem-solving. One advantage DWC has is that Eastlake is probably a new landlord. As such, it might be more likely that it does not have a form lease it has been using for a long time. On the other hand, Eastlake's attorney may use such a form.

---

[41] *Id.* at 793.

[42] *Id.* at 788.

[43] *Id.* at 788–89.

[44] *Id.* at 789.

[45] *Id.* at 765.

[46] DAVID A. LAX & JAMES K. SEBENIUS, THE MANAGER AS NEGOTIATOR: BARGAINING FOR COOPERATION AND COMPETITIVE GAIN 106–07 (1986).

[47] *Id.* at 107.

[48] Robert H. Mnookin & Lewis Kornhauser, *Bargaining in the Shadow of the Law: The Case of Divorce*, 88 YALE L. J. 950 (1979).

[49] Menkel–Meadow, *supra* note 30, at 766.

[50] *Id.*

Problem-solving is an "orientation to negotiation which focuses on finding solutions to the parties' . . . underlying needs and objectives."[51] This model of negotiation suggests that the parties in a negotiation have underlying needs or objectives that they hope to achieve. Because not all parties are likely to value the same things in the same way, the different needs can be exploited to produce a wider range of options. Even in negotiations when money is involved, we may be able to explore a variety of solutions that will satisfy the parties more fully and directly by looking at why the parties desire money (or how they intend to use that money). In our example, Eastlake may want a higher rent in order to do the build-out that DWC wants. Eastlake may have limits on how the construction can take place, such as whom it must hire, based on the source of its funding. DWC, however, may be able to get volunteer labor to do some of the build-out of its office.

Because many parties want to interact with each other in the future and since resources are often not fixed, we believe you will find that most transactional negotiations best fit the problem-solving or integrative model. As a result, let us now look a bit deeper at the idea of creating value in the negotiation process.

B. CREATING VALUE IN THE NEGOTIATION PROCESS

The process of creating value begins with understanding your client's interests. This process starts at the initial interview and continues through all client meetings including the counseling meeting in preparation for beginning negotiations. We might think of the process as a spiral, going back and forth between counseling and negotiation. Carrie Menkel–Meadow suggests thinking ahead to the negotiation that might occur during the initial interview and asking the client "How would you like to see this turn out?" or "What would you like to accomplish here?"[52] Your negotiation plan begins by considering the economic needs and objectives of the client. You can ask your client, "What are the financial requirements now and in the future?"[53] Your plan will go further than considering economic needs and the social needs of the parties—the client's relationship to others.[54] In addition, your planning will require taking into account the psychological needs of the parties—the personal needs generated by the

---

[51] *Id.* at 794.

[52] *Id.* at 801. These are good open-ended questions for the part of the interview where you are asking questions related to the matter. Of course even if you forget to ask these questions at the initial interview, you will most likely have other opportunities to ask these questions.

[53] *Id.* These include compensation, return on investment and liquidity of payment. Are there cash substitutes available and acceptable? What are the transaction costs? What are the tax consequences of the economic solutions?

[54] *Id.* at 802. Will business associates, community members, employers, employees, family members or friends be affected by the actions taken by the parties?

transaction.[55] You should also consider exploring the ethical concerns of the parties. How fair do they want to be with each other? In order to fully engage in problem-solving negotiation, you should explore the client's underlying needs and objectives as well.[56]

Value-creating trades make both parties better off or make one party better off without making the other party worse off.[57] Integrative agreements seek to expand the zone of agreement.[58] This expansion is possible both when the parties may appear to want the same thing (but may have different interests) and when it is clear the parties have opposing interests.[59] When the parties appear to want the same thing (in our example, lower rent for DWC and higher rent for Eastlake), resources can be expanded by exploring what can be distributed, when it can be distributed, by whom it can be distributed, how it can be distributed and how much of it can be distributed.[60] Since the parties have different preference structures, they place a differential value on the items that are the subject of the negotiation even if they want the same things.[61]

Integrative bargaining is also possible even when the parties have opposing interests.[62] The parties can then realize joint gains by exploiting the differences between them. This might seem counter-intuitive since you might think that people reach agreement by finding common ground.[63] Differences, however, provide opportunities for exchanges.[64] In order to see the opportunity for exchange, you need to explore how the parties are different from each other. You can then begin to match what one side finds or expects to be relatively costless with what the other finds or expects to be most valuable.[65]

Differences of interest give rise to opportunities for exchanges. The parties can create value by trading on their differences. These include differences in *resources* (for example, if one of the parties had a construction company that could do some of the repairs or renovations to the building); *relative valuation* (if for example DWC did not care if the offices were cleaned by the landlord); *probability* (when the parties differ on the forecast for the likelihood that something may occur); *risk aversion* (if for example DWC were willing to assume liability for taxes thinking it could

---

    [55] *Id.* Even if you are representing entities, the constituents are individuals. Does someone desire power? What are their motivations for pursuing their aims?

    [56] *Id.* at 804.

    [57] MNOOKIN, PEPPET & TULUMELLO, *supra* note 4, at 12.

    [58] KOROBKIN, *supra* note 16, at 109–12 (discussing how to use integrative bargaining to expand the bargaining zone by adding issues, subtracting issues, swapping issues and logrolling).

    [59] *Id.*

    [60] Menkel–Meadow, *supra* note 30, at 810.

    [61] KOROBKIN, *supra* note 16, at 92.

    [62] *Id.*

    [63] MNOOKIN, PEPPET & TULUMELLO, *supra* note 4, at 14.

    [64] *Id.* at 15.

    [65] LAX & SEBENIUS, *supra* note 46, at 100–02.

get them waived after you counseled the organization of the likelihood of that happening)*; and *time preferences* (when something would occur).[66]

Fisher, Ury and Patton suggest that the skill of inventing options is an important one for negotiators. They see four major obstacles to thinking of multiple ways to accomplish something—1) when we reach premature judgment; 2) when we search for a single answer; 3) when we assume that the pie is fixed; and 4) when we think that solving the problem is our counterpart's responsibility.[67] Premature judgment may hinder imagination. Seeing their assignment as narrowing the gap between the parties can lead to barriers for negotiators since they risk not considering broadening the available options.

Obstacles to Add-Value negotiation

Fisher, Ury and Patton outline a process for inventing options that starts by generating multiple options without judging them. In order to reach agreement, you need to come up with a solution that appeals to the self-interest of the other party. A starting point is to separate the act of generating solutions from the act of judging them, broaden the options on the table, search for mutual gain and look for ways to make the decision easy.[68] This process requires that you begin brainstorming solutions to the problem. In brainstorming, negotiators should approach the question from every conceivable angle.[69] Another commentator recommends that you begin the brainstorming process by first articulating the problem or issue and then engaging in wordplay with the resulting sentence by shifting the emphasis, changing a word, deleting a word and adding a new word.[70] Changing a word might help reformulate the problem in a way that suggests new solutions. Broadening the statement by deleting a word might capture its essence more accurately. Random word association and thinking of ways to associate a new word to the problem might also spur creative thinking. Another technique, called "six thinking hats," has the problem solver focus on six different aspects of the problem—emotions, facts, positive aspects, future implications, critique and process.[71]

generating multiple options

After brainstorming, Fisher, Ury and Patton recommend beginning the process of narrowing ideas by starring the ones that are most promising.[72] They suggest inventing improvements for the most promising idea—looking for ways to make it better and more realistic so as to make the idea as attractive as possible.[73] Fisher, Ury and Patton suggest mov-

---

[66] MNOOKIN, PEPPET & TULUMELLO, *supra* note 4, at 14–15, 31; LAX & SEBENIUS, *supra* note 46, at 100–02.

[67] FISHER, URY & PATTON, *supra* note 10, at 59.

[68] *Id.* at 62.

[69] *Id.*

[70] Jennifer Gerarda Brown, *Creativity and Problem–Solving*, 87 MARQ. L. REV. 697, 699–702 (2004).

[71] *Id.* at 702–03 (citing EDWARD DE BONO, SIX THINKING HATS (rev. ed. 1999)).

[72] *Id.* at 64.

[73] FISHER, URY & PATTON, *supra* note 10, at 64. Fisher, Ury and Patton suggest saying, "What I like best about that idea is . . . . Might it be even better if . . .?" *Id.*

ing from the specific and general in what they call the "circle chart."[74] The task of inventing options involves four types of thinking. First, think about the particular *problem*, the factual situation you dislike. You look to what is wrong in the real world, what you dislike. The second step requires generating a descriptive *analysis*—diagnosing the situation in general terms, sorting the problems into categories and tentatively suggesting causes. This step is a theoretical one, looking to what is wrong. The third step involves thinking, in general terms, of *approaches*, what ought to be done. You develop prescriptions the theory may suggest. As with the previous one, this step happens in the theoretical realm, looking to what might be done. The fourth and final step goes back to the real world, and requires coming up with specific and realistic suggestions for *action*.[75] The circle chart serves the purpose of using one good idea to generate others. Diagram 5–1 shows you what the circle chart[76] looks like:

Diagram 5–1

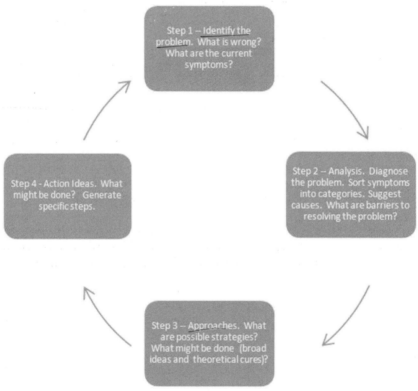

---

[74] *Id.* at 68. This analysis is also called the four-quadrant analysis. *See* ROGER FISHER, ELIZABETH KOPELMAN & ANDREA KUPFER SCHNEIDER, BEYOND MACHIAVELLI: TOOLS FOR COPING WITH CONFLICT 68–71 (1994).

[75] FISHER, URY & PATTON, *supra* note 10, at 68–69.

[76] *Id.* at 69.

Fisher, Ury and Patton also suggest looking at the problem through the eyes of different experts.[77] In addition, they recommend thinking of agreements of different levels of strength and changing the scope of the possible agreement—partial agreements; agreements involving fewer parties, covering only certain subject matter, remaining in effect for a limited period of time, applying only to a particular geographic region; or even enlarging the scope of the agreement.[78] In looking for mutual gain, you need to realize that shared interests do not appear obvious.

With some theoretical context, we now turn our attention to what the process of negotiation might look like.

IV. THE NEGOTIATION PROCESS

A. AT THE NEGOTIATION TABLE

Let us now consider what is likely to happen at the negotiation table. Though our description of the negotiation process might appear as linear, in reality it is quite circular, alternating between discussions with your client and your counterpart. Over the course of your representation, you have developed a relationship in which you have begun to uncover your client's goals for the transaction through a series of interviewing and counseling meetings. In the Counseling chapter, we set out a model for counseling a client in preparation for a negotiation. At that counseling meeting (or meetings), you will explore the client's goals and interests and thus the counseling conversation will be part of your preparation for the negotiation process.

Our goal in this section is not to give you a prescription for what you should do—where to meet, whether to make the first offer, how and when to make concessions. Instead we hope this section and the ones that follow inform those decisions. We will outline three phases in a negotiation meeting or meetings—a beginning phase, a middle stage where the bulk of the actual negotiating happens and, assuming the parties reach agreement, a conclusion phase.

In the first stage, the parties begin to discuss how they are going to engage in the negotiation. Some of these preliminary conversations may happen at the beginning of the negotiation meeting or they may also happen during a telephone call prior to the meeting when the parties schedule the negotiation meeting. At the beginning of the meeting the parties may engage in some ice-breaking, either to get to know each other or to re-connect if they already know each other. Let us go back to the meeting between DWC and Eastlake. One of the important decisions the parties will make is how to discuss the lease. Will Eastlake's lawyer send a draft

---

[77] *Id.* at 70.
[78] *Id.* at 71–72.

Stage 1

*How to discuss.-
Who will draft?*

lease?[79] Will the parties meet first to discuss the major terms of the lease, such the rent amount, the occupancy date and the other provisions that each views as important? Even if Eastlake's counsel sends DWC a draft lease, will the parties discuss the lease in the order in which the terms appear on that lease or in the order of importance of the terms to the parties? Should they begin with the terms on which they cannot agree? Or the terms on which they are of the same mind? All this will be part of this initial phase of the negotiation. In some sense, it is a mini-negotiation within the larger negotiation.

Stage 2

*- present proposals
- persuade*

In the middle phase, the parties exchange proposals and determine if they can reach agreement. Three principal activities take place in this phase—information gathering, presenting proposals and persuasion. The heart of any negotiation session is making proposals and the counterpart responding to them, by accepting them, rejecting them outright or responding to the proposal with a counter-proposal. In the process of making proposals, the parties try to gather information from and give information to the other side in order to understand why the party making the proposal wants that or why the counterpart cannot accept that proposal. The parties also try to persuade the counterpart of why the proposal is a fair one and the counterpart should accept it. We discuss information gathering and persuasion in greater depth below.

We previously discussed your preparation for the negotiation by determining your reservation point, BATNA and goals. With that information, you will have to decide what opening offer to make and how you will communicate (and support) your proposals to the counterpart. You also need to anticipate the offers your counterpart is likely to make. You also need to prepare for the concessions you are willing to make, how you will make them and how you will justify them. You need reasons for the positions you take and for the concessions you make in response to the positions of your counterpart.

Let us go back to the DWC and Eastlake negotiations. Alex and Laura, the students we met in the Interviewing chapter, are representing DWC. Robert Johnson, a lawyer in a small law firm in the community, is representing Eastlake. Let us listen to their conversation:

Robert: We think the annual base rent of $42,000 for the first year of the five-year lease is a fair one given what comparable space is going for in this part of the city. We also think that paying $10,000 of that amount at the time that DWC is going to move in is fair. We are asking very little in security deposit (only two months of rent or $7,000) so we think that this assures us of rent while at the same time not being overly onerous on DWC.

---

[79] See our discussion of competitive negotiation tactics *infra* for a discussion about the order of discussing terms and the possibility of beginning with a complete draft of Eastlake's lease.

Laura: We would like to talk about the three points you just raised—the yearly rent, the term of the lease (five years) and the upfront payment. I'll talk about the monthly rent first and then about the large prepayment. We appreciate that Eastlake will be taking over the building and will have some big expenses early on, but we do not agree that your rent proposal is a fair one. First, the rent per square foot in our current space is much lower than what you are proposing. Eastlake's proposal is a substantial jump in our rent per square foot. We think that $2,000 per month is a fair rent given the fair market value of the space. Second, asking us to pay $10,000 up front is not fair and is not normally done in this type of lease. While we understand that Eastlake will have large expenses when it first moves into the building, DWC is a small organization and while we are expanding we cannot commit that much of our yearly budget that far ahead of time. What is Eastlake's concern in asking for that amount of money upfront?

Robert: We think $3,500 is a fair price for the space. That's the going rate for comparable space in the neighborhood. Once we close on the building we plan to install new mechanicals. We also plan on doing renovations to the office space your client is interested in. Those investments warrant that rental amount. What are you using as your comparables to determine that $2,000 is a fair price?

Alex: We have analyzed the office buildings in the area. Plus, Eastlake will not have to pay real estate taxes since it is renting the space to another nonprofit organization. That will bring in additional savings we think it can pass on to us. Certainly if it leased to a for-profit business it would have to pay real estate taxes. But not with DWC as the tenant.

. . .

In this conversation, we see Eastlake make the initial proposal. Robert Johnson spends some time substantiating his proposal. Laura counters with $2,000 monthly rent and resists the up-front payment of $10,000. Both parties use persuasion to convince the other that their valuation is a fair one. Alex points out the savings in real estate taxes and suggests that Eastlake should pass on those savings to DWC. Finally, we see both parties seeking and providing information. Eastlake asks the basis for DWC's determination that its offer is fair. Laura asks why Eastlake wants such a large lump-sum payment up front. The parties will continue this exchange for the most important lease terms until they can reach agreement. DWC is likely to see many of the financial terms as related—rent, taxes, utilities. As such, DWC will want to discuss those terms together or in proximity to the related ones. Each party will have to decide what initial offer to make, what concessions it can make and what counteroffers to make. As they go through the agreement, the parties might agree to leave one term and come back to it after they have discussed others.

Assuming they are able to reach agreement, the parties will spend the latter part of the meeting confirming the exact terms of the agreement and spelling out the specifics of that agreement. This process may take some time as the parties exchange draft language for the terms of agreement and may in turn involve more negotiations. We refer you to the Drafting chapter for assistance in setting out that agreement in writing.

We hope that some of the concepts we discuss in the next few sections will inform some of the decisions you make as well as provide you with insight into the ramifications of the actions you or your counterpart take.

Russell Korobkin, a leading scholar in the negotiation field, categorizes every action taken by negotiators in preparation for negotiation or at the bargaining as either zone definition or zone allocation.[80] Negotiators attempt to define the bargaining zone—the distance between the reservation points of the parties—in the manner that is most favorable to their respective client.[81] Strategies used in zone definition include exploring alternatives to agreement, questioning, persuading, misleading, committing to positions and redefining the negotiation's subject matter.[82] Negotiators engage in zone allocation when they try to convince their counterpart to agree to a single "deal point" within the bargaining zone.[83] Reaching agreement at any point in the bargaining zone is more advantageous to the parties than not reaching agreement. If the offers and counteroffers are in the zone of possible agreement, the parties appeal to "community norms of either procedural or substantive fairness" in order to convince their counterpart to accept their proposal.[84]

B. THE ROLE OF PERSUASION

Persuasion is an essential part of the negotiation process, with each lawyer attempting to persuade the counterpart's attorney that "her client's positions, interests, and perspectives should be honored."[85] When you justify your proposal to your counterpart, you use persuasion. You also use persuasion when you explain why your client cannot accept your

---

[80] Korobkin, *supra* note 6, at 1791–92.

[81] *Id.*

[82] *Id.* at 1792.

[83] *Id.*

[84] *Id.*

[85] Chris Guthrie, *Principles of Influence in Negotiation*, 87 MARQ. L. REV. 829 (2004).

counterpart's proposal. Transactional lawyers serve as advocates for their clients in negotiations much as litigators advocate for their clients in court. In attempting to persuade, you need to tell a coherent story about what your client wants. Legal arguments may play a role in the telling of your story. You can also base your argument on policy, a principle to be upheld, the advantages in agreeing to your proposal or the general custom in that business or industry.[86] You can use framing and analogy to bolster your argument.[87] You can make your arguments more persuasive by using metaphors and labels. You can also organize and simplify a complex reality into a structure by using frames. You can also accomplish that by using details, specifics, statistics or expert authority.[88]

C. PRINCIPLES OF INFLUENCE

Let us look at some of the components of persuasion that you can use (and your counterpart is likely to use) during the negotiation process. Psychologists have identified six persuasive devices or "weapons of influence" that a lawyer can use to persuade her counterpart to the terms she proposes—*liking, social proof, commitment and consistency, reciprocity, authority* and *scarcity*.[89] Research shows that individuals prefer to comply with requests made by those they know and *like*.[90] Our counterpart is more likely to agree to our request if he likes us. As a result, building a relationship with the opposing counsel can be helpful during the negotiation process. We tend to like those who are physically attractive, those with whom we share something in common and those with whom we are familiar.[91] Even if Laura and Alex do not have an existing professional relationship with Mr. Johnson, they can build rapport with him as members of the same profession (almost), perhaps as graduates of the same law school, or as sharing something else in common. Under the related principle of *social proof*, individuals view behavior as correct in a given situation to the extent that we see others engaging in it.[92] We are most persuaded by social proof when we see similarities between us and the person we are observing.[93] Psychologists believe we are most influenced by social proof in unclear or ambiguous situations.

Another principle of influence, *commitment and consistency*, tells us that once we make a decision or take a stand, we feel personal and interpersonal pressures to behave consistently with that commitment.[94] This

---

[86] MENKEL–MEADOW, SCHNEIDER & LOVE, *supra* note 2, at 78.

[87] *Id.*

[88] *Id.* at 79.

[89] Guthrie, *supra* note 85, at 830 (citing ROBERT B. CIALDINI, INFLUENCE, SCIENCE AND PRACTICE (4th ed. 2001)).

[90] *Id.* at 831.

[91] *Id.*

[92] *Id.* at 831–32.

[93] *Id.* at 832. Social proof can work hand in hand with the liking principle. *Id.*

[94] *Id.* at 832–33.

concept plays out in the negotiation process such that when a lawyer induces her counterpart to make a small commitment early in the negotiation process, the lawyer may be able to obtain a much more substantial agreement later in the process.[95] According to the *reciprocity* norm, one "should try to repay, in kind, what another person has provided us."[96] We see it play out in the negotiation process when by making a concession a lawyer can create in her counterpart a sense of obligation to respond similarly. This norm is something you can expect to happen in the negotiation dynamic. In addition, a lawyer can request a substantial concession, get turned down, and then make a more modest request.[97] The *authority* principle finds that individuals feel an obligation to comply with a person who is in a real or perceived authority position and thus defer to leaders and officials.[98] Appeals to legal precedent also fall under this principle, as might appeals to industry standards. Laura and Alex need to be careful about Mr. Johnson's trying to appeal to the authority principle as a more experienced and senior member of the profession. Under the sixth principle, *scarcity,* opportunities seem more valuable when they are less available. Scarcity induces compliance because it threatens our freedom of choice—e.g., if I don't act now I will lose this opportunity.[99]

These principles will influence how the parties will act during the negotiation process. You should be aware of them so you can recognize if your counterpart is attempting to use them with you or your client. Some lawyers may feel ethical concerns about using them with their counterparts. How do you feel about using them with your counterpart?

D. DISCLOSING AND GATHERING INFORMATION

As we mentioned earlier, information exchange is a key activity within the negotiation process. If the parties in negotiation are going to try to address each other's interests they will have to gather and disclose information. In preparing for negotiation you will need to determine what information you need before you are able to reach agreement. The information you receive from your counterpart will help you determine how well the actual situation fits the assumptions you made. Each party will need to seek information in order to assess whether its estimate of its own and the counterpart's reservation point is accurate. Asking your counterpart for information is likely to lead to private information that you could not discover during your preparation. In addition, information seeking is crucial to knowing your counterpart's subjective evaluation of even public information.[100]

---

[95] *Id.* at 833.

[96] *Id.* at 834 (citing CIALDINI, *supra* note 89, at 65).

[97] *Id.* at 834. Cialdini calls this tactic "rejection-then-retreat." *Id.*

[98] *Id.* at 835.

[99] *Id.*

[100] Korobkin, *supra* note 6, at 1804.

Questions asked by your counterpart have an added advantage. In answering questions you have the opportunity to persuade.[101] Your strategy and plan for the negotiation will include decisions regarding what information you will want to disclose. You will need to decide what you want to answer directly and what you might want to answer less directly or not at all. Some beginning negotiators may feel they have to withhold as much as possible. You need to consider the risk that obfuscation may imply that there is no bargaining zone and may lead to impasse.[102] Deciding what information you want to make sure you disclose and what information you want to conceal is as much a part of your preparation as determining what information you want from your counterpart.

E. FAIRNESS IN THE NEGOTIATION PROCESS

Korobkin believes one of the goals of each lawyer during the negotiation is to establish a fair way of reaching agreement.[103] Negotiations raise four principal questions of fairness—structural, process, procedural and outcome.[104] Structural fairness concerns the overall structure of the negotiation process that encompasses the parties to the negotiation, the issues to be negotiated, the rules, the physical features of the negotiation (including the location and access to information) and codes of conduct (such as agenda setting, communication procedures and use of deadlines and other time limits).[105] Process fairness concerns whether the parties treat and relate to each other fairly and how the parties' notions of fairness influence the dynamics of the negotiation process, including whether the parties have a chance to be heard and have input into the process.[106]

Outcome fairness refers to the principles underlying the allocation (whether exchange or division) of the benefits or burdens inherent in the agreement.[107] Three such principles are equity, equality and need. The equity principle holds that "resources (rewards) should be distributed proportionally to relevant contributions (inputs)."[108] Under the equality principle parties divide the same or comparable rewards regardless of their contributions or needs. Examples are when each party receives equal shares or compromises in the middle. Compensatory or distributive justice principles underlie the need principle. The parties in a negotiation, however, may not agree on how to define fairness—equity, equality or

---

[101] *Id.* at 1806. Research suggests that negotiators' perceptions of their opponents' interests become more accurate during the course of the negotiation. *Id.* (citing Leigh Thompson & Reid Hastie, *Social Perception in Negotiation*, 47 ORGANIZATIONAL BEHAV. & HUM. DECISION PROCESSES 98, 107–08 (1990)).

[102] *Id.*

[103] *Id.* 1819.

[104] Cecilia Albin, *The Role of Fairness in Negotiation*, 9 NEGOT. J. 223, 225 (1993).

[105] *Id.* at 226–28.

[106] *Id.* at 228.

[107] *Id.* at 237.

[108] *Id.* at 238.

need. Part of the persuasion that may take place during the meetings is how to define "fairness."

In searching what is perceived as fair to the parties, negotiators often seek some "objective" criteria. These may include market price, reached by averaging the sale price of recent transactions or by an independent appraiser's determination. If the negotiators believe that the market price is a neutral decision criterion, they will feel the outcome is fair.[109] In order to achieve substantive fairness, much of the discussion during negotiation between the parties can center on what is an appropriate reference point under the circumstances.[110] We saw this earlier in the discussions between Alex, Laura and Mr. Johnson. Justifying the reference point you are proposing is a key component of persuasion during negotiation. Fisher, Ury and Patton advocate the use of objective criteria.[111] They suggest looking to market value, precedent, scientific judgment, professional standards, reciprocity, costs, efficiency, equal treatment, tradition and moral standards, among others, as the basis for agreements.[112] We can imagine, however, instances when these criteria may not appear "fair" to one party in negotiations.

Procedural fairness encompasses the mechanisms used for arriving at an agreement.[113] Many common negotiating tactics are best understood as attempts to establish a procedure that the other party will feel is fair.[114] The reciprocity norm, which we discuss above, suggests that parties feel an agreement point is fair if both parties have made concessions to reach that point. This plays out in calls for splitting the difference, making equal concessions or equal sacrifices, and "tit-for-tat."[115] Negotiators can perceive focal points, or deal points that may some special significance to the parties, as neutral and fair.[116]

F. NEGOTIATION STYLES AND STRATEGIES

Scholars have analyzed different negotiation styles, strategies and tactics. Style (as opposed to strategy) looks to the interpersonal behavior of the negotiator and identifies "how that behavior affects the negotiation process."[117] In a study of lawyers, negotiation scholar Gerald R. Williams

---

[109] Korobkin, *supra* note 6, at 1827.

[110] *Id.* A seller's cost plus a certain amount of profit can be a reference point. Trade custom is another reference point. *Id.*

[111] FISHER, URY & PATTON, *supra* note 10, at 83. Fisher, Ury and Patton see the alternative as a contest of "will." *Id.*

[112] *Id.* at 86.

[113] Albin, *supra* note 104, at 234.

[114] Korobkin, *supra* note 6, at 1821.

[115] Albin, *supra* note 104, at 234–35.

[116] Korobkin, *supra* note 6, at 1824–25. Round numbers tend to be natural focal points when the subject of the negotiation is in currency. *Id.* at 1825.

[117] ROBERT M. BASTRESS & JOSEPH D. HARBAUGH, INTERVIEWING, COUNSELING AND NEGOTIATING: SKILLS FOR EFFECTIVE REPRESENTATION 390 (1990).

identified two bargaining styles, competitive and cooperative, and two bargaining strategies, adversarial and problem-solving.[118] Competitive negotiators want to experience "winning" as they enjoy feeling in control and being partisans.[119]

Andrea Kupfer Schneider recently updated the Williams study on negotiation styles and strategies.[120] She acknowledges confusion about the terminology used by different scholars and commentators and how that terminology has also changed over the years.[121] Schneider concludes that styles of negotiation have clearly diverged in the twenty-five years since Williams conducted his study, and that an increase in adversarial bargainers has resulted in an increase of ineffective lawyers.[122] The adversarial or competitive group seems to be growing more extreme and negative.[123] Despite those findings, Schneider reports that both effective problem-solving and effective adversarial bargainers shared similar qualities. They were dedicated to the best interests of their client, to representing their client zealously and within the bounds of the law, to maximizing the agreement for their client and meeting their client's needs, and were assertive, smart and prepared.[124] Those qualities, more than the label style or strategy, distinguished the most effective negotiators.

We want to highlight some competitive negotiation strategies so you may recognize them and plan responses to them. Competitive bargainers tend to see negotiation as an information game ("the party with the most accurate information wins"), take either a high or low opening position, hold firm and do not make a concession in return for a concession, make small, infrequent or declining concessions, select an opening position by reference to the mid-point, and link positions and concessions to convincing justifications.[125] Competitive bargainers might set a *precondition* to begin bargaining, which is a way to get a concession before bargaining even begins.[126] One way to counter attempts by competitive bargainers to get as much information as possible (and disclose as little as possible) is

limits of
competitive
bargaining

---

[118] GERALD R. WILLIAMS, LEGAL NEGOTIATION AND SETTLEMENT 48–54 (1983).

[119] Robert H. Mnookin, Scott R. Peppet & Andrew S. Tulumello, *The Tension Between Empathy and Assertiveness*, 12 NEGOT. J. 217, 223 (1996).

[120] *See* Andrea Kupfer Schneider, *Shattering Negotiation Myths: Empirical Evidence on the Effectiveness of Negotiation Style*, 7 HARV. NEGOT. L. REV. 145 (2002).

[121] *Id.* at 150–52. She points to the use of the terms problem solver/adversarial; hard bargainer/soft bargainer/principled bargainer; accommodating/avoiding/competing/problem solving; accommodating/avoiding/concerned with fairness/concerned with relationships/competitive. *Id.*

[122] *Id.* at 189.

[123] *Id.* at 190.

[124] *Id.* at 188–89.

[125] Gary Goodpaster, *A Primer on Competitive Bargaining*, 1996 J. DISP. RESOL. 325, 346–49 (1996).

[126] *Id.* at 350.

to ask that they make the first offer.[127] *Extreme first offers* are an indication that a negotiator is going to use competitive tactics.[128]

Competitive bargainers sometimes use the tactic of *false demands* and *false concessions*.[129] This tactic gives the counterpart the sense that the negotiator feels strongly about something when in reality she does not. When the negotiator purports to offer a compromise, she gives the impression she has made a concession when in reality she has not. In a related ploy, the negotiator may *inflate* the significance of an issue the other side cares about.[130] When she gives in, the negotiator demands a large concession on an issue she truly finds important. Yet another tactic that a competitive negotiator might use is to *escalate* a demand. *Nibbling* is an attempt to escalate at the end of the negotiation when it seems the parties have reached agreement.[131] The nibbler raises a small item not previously discussed and insists that it is a "must have" item.[132] *Lowballing* involves reaching agreement and then changing the original terms that induced the agreement.[133] Another tactic is called *salami*, where a negotiator makes a series of small demands, which are easier to tolerate and concede but which add up to something considerable.[134]

A competitive negotiator using the *deadlock and concede* tactic starts by discussing her least important issue first and her most important issue second.[135] She deadlocks on the first issue and then concedes. When the parties appear to deadlock on the second issue, she demands that the counterpart concede since she conceded on the first issue.[136] Remaining issues are handled in the same manner, alternating less important and more important issues. Another ploy is the *"take-it-or-leave-it"* attitude, with the initial offer being the final offer.[137] Using a related tactic, a negotiator might state that an offer is the *"final offer"* and will concede no further.[138] Negotiators may also call something a deadlock and call an end to negotiations in order to communicate that the negotiations have reached the party's bottom line and induce major concessions.[139] In an effort to try to exercise power over their counterparts some lawyers engage in tactics aimed at intimidating and belittling their counterparts. One such tactic is creating an intimidating atmosphere by insisting that meetings be held in

---

[127] *Id.* at 351.

[128] *Id.* at 342.

[129] *Id.* at 352.

[130] *Id.*

[131] *Id.* at 353.

[132] *Id.*

[133] *Id.*

[134] *Id.* at 354.

[135] *Id.* at 359.

[136] *Id.*

[137] *Id.* at 355.

[138] *Id.* at 356.

[139] *Id.*

their office, scheduling meetings for inconvenient times, making the other party wait and claiming that certain issues are non-negotiable. Other lawyers may use anger, aggression and threats as a tactic. Another ploy sometimes used by lawyers is setting artificial deadlines.

Some of these tactics are difficult to counter. You need to be firm and let your counterpart know that you recognize he is using certain tactics. One way to respond to the precondition tactic is to make it clear that the precondition is part of bargaining.[140] You may choose to ignore an extreme first offer by naming it as extreme or state that you will not use it as a basis of bargaining.[141] The false demands/false concessions tactic is a difficult tactic to counter since much of the information about needs comes from the counterpart. You may counter this tactic by gaining outside information, assessing probabilities and asking probing questions to try to get at the justifications for the other party's claims.[142] You may counter escalation by calling attention to it, by refusing to agree or by indicating that you may escalate as well.[143] One way to counter low-balling and nibbling is to communicate a willingness to accept that the deal may fail. Competitive bargainers may use other strategies as well. When your counterpart is engaging in competitive or bullying tactics, the most important thing you can do is recognize it so you can think through how to respond.

G. DIFFERENCE IN NEGOTIATIONS AND CONVERSATIONS ABOUT THEM

In every negotiation, differences exist between the negotiators—religion, sexual orientation, politics, interests, affiliations, region (where you practice or grew up)—any of which could have a greater influence on the negotiation process than race or ethnicity, gender and culture.[144] These are differences, however, that negotiators perceive most easily. Studies indicate differences in negotiating styles between rural and urban lawyers and among lawyers in different practice areas.[145] In reality, the differences between individuals within groups may be greater than the difference between groups. Nevertheless, we discuss these issues because in some instances those differences will matter, and because some negotiators may have certain stereotypes about how some people act and will act on them. Those generalizations could affect the way some negotiators bargain with members of certain groups.

---

[140] *Id.* at 350–51.

[141] *Id.* at 351.

[142] *Id.* at 352.

[143] *Id.* at 352–53.

[144] MENKEL–MEADOW, SCHNEIDER & LOVE, *supra* note 2, at 377.

[145] Donald G. Gifford, *A Context–Based Theory of Strategy in Legal Negotiation,* 46 OHIO ST. L.J. 41, 68 (1985); WILLIAMS, *supra* note 118, at 81–82.

We introduced you to some concepts of culture in the Interviewing chapter and will discuss culture further in the Multicultural Lawyering chapter. Here we briefly touch on how differences can affect the negotiation. Some of the most important effects of culture are felt even before negotiators sit down across from one another and begin to exchange information.[146] Culture may be a "powerful organizing prism, through which we tend to view and integrate all kinds of disparate interpersonal information."[147] The label of culture may be "a 'hook' that makes it easy for one negotiator (the perceiver) to organize what he or she sees emanating from the 'different person' seated at the other side of the table."[148] Some of the research indicates a powerful effect of culture, pointing us to hold a set of expectations of our counterpart that guide and inform our judgments even before we have the chance to gather information.[149] Once these beliefs are in place it may be impossible to disprove them. As we will see below, we tend to gather interpersonal information in such a way that we pay attention to the "facts" that support our hypotheses, ignoring or dismissing evidence that might disprove it or contradict it.[150]

Research indicates evidence of discrimination in negotiations. Studies have shown that buyers of cars get different prices depending on their race and gender.[151] White males were offered lower prices than anyone else. African–American men were charged higher prices than African–American women. We feel it is important for us to understand these shortcuts we might take so we can be aware and work against some of the effects of those judgments. Why do you think that is? What implications do these findings have for negotiations between attorneys? A number of studies also suggest that negotiators bargain with members of their own race more cooperatively than they do with those of another race.[152] In addition, studies have shown difference in negotiating behavior based on race.[153] At the same time, researchers have found no statistically significant race-based difference in negotiation results.[154]

---

[146] Jeffrey Z. Rubin & Frank E. A. Sander, *Culture, Negotiation and the Eye of the Beholder*, 7 NEGOT. J. 249 (1991).

[147] *Id.*

[148] *Id.* at 251. The authors describe an experiment in which students with the same measured aptitude as others were labeled "intellectual bloomers" and scored significantly higher than the others at the end of the academic year and hypothesize that teachers gave the students labeled as intellectually superior more attention. *Id.*

[149] *Id.* at 252.

[150] *Id.*

[151] *See* Ian Ayres, *Further Evidence of Discrimination in New Car Negotiations and Estimates of its Cause*, 94 MICH. L. REV. 109 (1996); Ian Ayres, *Fair Driving: Gender and Race Discrimination in Retail Car Negotiations*, 104 HARV. L. REV. 817 (1991).

[152] JEFFREY Z. RUBIN & BERT R. BROWN, THE SOCIAL PSYCHOLOGY OF BARGAINING AND NEGOTIATION 163 (1975).

[153] One study suggested that African–Americans tend to speak with greater verbal aggressiveness than Whites during negotiations, perhaps reflecting a tendency to adopt an adversarial style. Martin N. Davidson & Leonard Greenhalgh, *The Role of Emotion in Negotiation: The Impact of Anger and Race*, 7 RESEARCH ON NEGOTIATION IN ORGANIZATIONS 22 (Robert J. Bies et al.

Empirical evidence indicates differences between men and women in behaviors that may influence negotiation processes. Women are not as effective at employing deceptive tactics as men, are more inclined to be trusting and tend to be less forgiving of deceitful behavior.[155] Men, on the other hand, find it easier to behave in a Machiavellian manner.[156] Studies involving encounters, however, do not consistently substantiate the proposition that more competitive male negotiators should achieve more beneficial results than female negotiators.[157] What may be relevant is that people believe certain characteristics, for example that women are more cooperative than men, and do not think about whether those characteristics hold true.[158] One commentator notes that it is not gender but power that makes a difference in negotiations. Power leads to "greater dominance, competitiveness, and success for both genders."[159] This finding would imply that women are no more fair-minded or nicer than men and that they are no less effective negotiators than men.

The wisest thing we can do to prepare for negotiations is to be aware of our biases and predispositions and gather as much information as possible about our counterpart as an individual.[160]

If you encounter comments or behavior that you perceive as sexist, racist or otherwise inappropriate during negotiation or otherwise, you will have to decide how to respond. One negotiation scholar suggests checking our assumptions before deciding how and whether to respond to perceived insults, biased comments or questionable personal statements.[161] Checking our assumptions involves a four-step process—1) what assumptions are we making about the other side's biases; 2) on what data do we base our assumptions; 3) what additional non-conforming data we have not considered; and 4) what new conclusion might we reach given this new data.[162] We can take one of four approaches in response to these comments—ignoring, confronting, deflecting (acknowledging and moving

---

eds., 1999) (citing THOMAS KOCHMAN, BLACK AND WHITE STYLES IN CONFLICT (1981); William Labov, *Rules for Ritual Insults, in* RAPPIN' AND STYLIN' OUT: COMMUNICATION IN BLACK URBAN AMERICA 265 (Thomas Kochman ed., 1972)).

[154] Charles B. Craver, *Race and Negotiation Performance,* 8 DISP. RESOL. MAG. 22 (2001).

[155] Charles B. Craver & David W. Barnes, *Gender, Risk Taking and Negotiation Performance,* 5 MICH. J. GENDER & L. 299, 317 (1999) (citing RUBIN & BROWN, *supra* note 152, at 172–73).

[156] *Id.* (citing Alan A. Benton et al., *Reactions to Various Degrees of Deceit in a Mixed–Motive Relationship,* 12 J. PERSONALITY & SOC. PSYCHOL. 170, 179 (1969)).

[157] *Id.* at 317–318 (citing ELEANOR EMMONS MACCOBY & CAROL NAGY JACKLIN, THE PSYCHOLOGY OF SEX DIFFERENCES 249–51 (1974); RUBIN & BROWN, *supra* note 152, at 169–74)).

[158] Carol M. Rose, *Bargaining and Gender,* 18 HARV. J.L. & PUB. POL'Y. 547, 549–50 (1995).

[159] Carol Watson, *Gender Versus Power as a Predictor of Negotiation Behavior and Outcomes,* 10 NEGOT. J. 117 (1994).

[160] Rubin & Sander, *supra* note 146, at 252.

[161] Andrea Kupfer Schneider, *Effective Responses to Offensive Comments,* 10 NEGOT. J. 107 (1994).

[162] *Id.* at 109.

on) or engaging in a conversation by asking questions.[163] In deciding whether to respond you should consider whether the other party's behavior is repeated, how much the comment offends you, your purpose in responding and what you hope to achieve. The other party may be thrown off by your questions. Engaging also lets you take control of the conversation.[164]

Other commentators suggest that winning over or persuading your opponent is not the way to approach difficult conversations.[165] They recommend beginning such conversation with what matters. For example, you might begin by saying "For me, what this is really about is . . . ."[166] In these situations, it is important not to present your conclusions as truth, but as your opinion, conclusion, perception, point of view.[167] Second, you should share the basis of your conclusions. Finally, you should avoid words such as "always" and "never."[168]

V. PSYCHOLOGICAL CONSIDERATIONS IN NEGOTIATIONS

As we mentioned in the introductory paragraphs, negotiation is an inherently interpersonal activity that requires each party to make individual judgments and decisions. Each party must evaluate the agreement and weigh the various possible courses of actions. The field of "decision theory" provides both a normative account (how people *should* act) and descriptive account (how people *do* act) in making decisions during the negotiation process.[169] Scholars posit that negotiators should compare the subjective expected value of an agreement to the value of not reaching an agreement, considering risks, transaction costs, and reputational and relational consequences.[170] The party should then select the choice that promises the greatest return. There is less agreement about how individuals involved in negotiations actually make decisions.

"Rational choice" theorists assume that individuals will make decisions based on the model just outlined—they will select the option that maximizes their expected utility after gathering all the necessary information and drawing accurate inferences.[171] Skeptics of rational choice believe that individuals normally employ more intuitive approaches to

---

[163] *Id.* at 111.

[164] *Id.* at 113.

[165] DOUGLAS STONE, BRUCE PATTON & SHEILA HEEN, DIFFICULT CONVERSATIONS: HOW TO DISCUSS WHAT MATTERS MOST 196 (1999).

[166] *Id.* at 190.

[167] *Id.* at 196.

[168] *Id.* at 198–99.

[169] Russell Korobkin & Chris Guthrie, *Heuristics and Biases at the Bargaining Table*, 87 MARQ. L. REV. 795 (2004).

[170] *Id.* at 795–96.

[171] *Id.* at 796.

choice and rely on mental shortcuts to reduce the complexity and effort needed in the process. Some commentators believe this process is conscious while others believe it is less so.[172] In deciding whether to accept or reject an agreement, a party must first evaluate the various options. This search for facts about the world, such as evaluating the market value of a product, involves the exercise of "judgment." Second, the party must choose whether she would rather agree to the terms or reject the agreement in favor of continuing her search.[173] To estimate values and probabilities, individuals are likely to rely on heuristics, or mental shortcuts, allowing them to make judgments in an efficient manner.[174] We want to discuss these heuristics and introduce how they might affect the decision-making processes in negotiations both for your client (and you) and your counterpart. We introduced you to some of these heuristics[175] in the Organizing Your Transactional Work and Counseling chapters—anchoring, availability, self-serving bias, prospect theory and the framing effect. Here we discuss status quo bias and reactive devaluation contrast effect as well.

Individuals are risk-averse and loss-averse. We are more likely to take a sure thing over a gamble, even when the gamble may have a somewhat higher expected payoff—this behavioral trait is called "risk aversion."[176] Cognitive psychologists Daniel Kahneman and Amos Tversky have found that individuals also have loss aversion—in order to avoid what would be a sure loss, many people will gamble, even if the expected loss from the gamble is larger.[177] Decision-makers choosing between a certain gain and a probabilistic gain most often prefer the alternative that has the same expected value but promises a probabilistic gain—these decision makers are thus risk averse.[178] Decision-makers also usually prefer a probabilistic loss to a certain loss when they have the same expected value, again, a form of loss aversion.[179] The notion that individuals will prefer certain alternatives to risky ones when gains are at

Risk aversion

---

[172] *Id.* at 796–97.

[173] *Id.* at 798.

[174] *Id.*

[175] For a fuller definition and discussion of the meaning of the term "heuristic," see *id.* at 796. *See also* Paul R. Tremblay, *Interviewing and Counseling Across Cultures: Heuristics and Biases*, 9 CLINICAL L. REV. 373, 384–85 (2002).

[176] Robert H. Mnookin, *Why Negotiations Fail: An Exploration of Barriers to the Resolution of Conflict*, 8 OHIO ST. J. ON DISP. RESOL. 235, 243–44 (1993). Mnookin uses the example of a lecture hall where if you choose the north exit you will be given an envelope with $20; if you choose the south exit, one-quarter of the envelopes contain $100 and three-quarters of the envelopes are empty. In experiments, the majority of the people choose a sure gain of $20 instead of gamble on the possibility for $100. *Id.*

[177] *Id.* at 244. Mnookin uses the example of the same lecture hall, where most people would go out the south door where they have a one in four chance of having to pay $100 and a three in four chance of leaving without paying, as opposed to going out the north door where they will have to pay $20 as an exit fee.

[178] KOROBKIN, *supra* note 16, at 34.

[179] *Id.* at 75.

stake but will prefer risky alternatives to certain ones when losses are at stake is known as the *framing effect*.[180] Risk aversion suggests we would not gamble for a gain, and loss aversion suggests we would gamble to avoid a sure loss.[181] Risk aversion and loss aversion suggest that in the negotiation context, parties may not agree in order to avoid a loss even when there is a chance that the loss may end up being far higher than the proposed settlement. In addition, whether something is viewed as a gain or loss depends on a reference point.[182] This is important to know in the negotiation context because your client's and counterpart's decision to accept a particular term or offer may be affected by whether they view the term as a gain or loss.[183] Whether the negotiator or party views the term as a gain or loss depends on the reference point the party or negotiator relies on when evaluating the alternatives.[184] Characterizing a decision as a "loss" or "gain" is the decision's "frame."[185]

Additionally, under the concept of loss aversion, individuals prefer to keep an item they already have (avoiding a loss) than trading it for an item of objectively identical value (and thus achieve a "gain"). This *status quo bias* or *endowment effect* suggests that the negotiator who possesses property (or other legal entitlement), such as the seller, is likely to have a higher reservation price than the negotiator who does not possess the property (or entitlement), such as the buyer.[186] In our example, Eastlake is likely to value the rental price as higher than DWC. Thus, all things being equal, an individual is likely to have a higher reservation price for an item if she owns it than if she does not own it. The result is smaller bargaining zones and fewer successful transactions than we might expect to be the case.[187] Thus, "the endowment effect results from a difference between the relative preferences for the good and the money."[188]

The power of inertia has parties agreeing to contract terms that operate without the party having to take any affirmative action. This *status quo bias* has special application in the transactional context because negotiators will prefer a term if it is a law-supplied default or if it is a term

---

[180] *Id.* at 81.

[181] Mnookin, *supra* note 176, at 244.

[182] *Id.* at 245.

[183] Do we as lawyers advise our clients to accept or reject an offer based on these same biases?

[184] Mnookin, *supra* note 176, at 245.

[185] *Id.* at 246.

[186] KOROBKIN, *supra* note 16, at 75. This concept implies holding constant differences in preferences between the two negotiators.

[187] *Id. See also* Daniel Kahneman, Jack L. Knetsch & Richard H. Thaler, *Experimental Tests of the Endowment Effect and the Coase Theorem*, 98 J. POL. ECON. 1325 (1990) (discussing findings from an experiment where consumption objects were distributed to one-half of test subjects and when markets were conducted, significantly less than half of the mugs were traded even though the Coase Theorem predicts that one-half of the mugs should have been traded).

[188] Kahneman, Knetsch & Thaler, *supra* note 187, at 1339.

prescribed by a commonly used form contract.[189] The party benefitted by the default term is akin to the "seller" of the term since she will demand compensation in return for contracting around the default term that benefits the "buyer" of the term. The "buyer" will therefore have to offer compensation for her agreement to add a term that avoids the default or form language.[190] Also, "negotiators will prefer an advantageous term more strongly (or oppose a disadvantageous term less strongly) if the term is perceived to result from inaction rather than from action."[191] One commentator suggests this behavior might be because individuals want to minimize the likelihood of experiencing future regret as a result of their decision.[192] This is likely to affect DWC's negotiation with Eastlake because many of the terms are likely to be "commonly used" ones, for example the repair and alterations clauses, the hold-over clause, and the insurance clauses.

When individuals are required to put a value on something, they often determine that value by starting with the value of a known option (an "anchor") and adjusting to compensate for the differences between the known and unknown value.[193] Research shows that people often fail to adjust sufficiently away from the initial "anchor" position and as a result undervalue the differences between the known and unknown values.[194] Evidence indicates that opening offers may anchor the counterpart's expectations in negotiation.[195] The *anchoring* effect, considered in isolation, suggests that an extreme opening offer can benefit the negotiator by favorably shifting the counterpart's reservation point, thus enlarging the bargaining zone so long as the offer is not so extreme that the opponent will not even consider it as a starting point for negotiations.[196] Of course, you will need to consider other factors in deciding what your initial offer should be.

When a negotiator has an option with multiple consequences, each probabilistic, rather than a single outcome, the negotiator will often evaluate the likelihood of the various possible outcomes based on the ease with which the options come to mind.[197] The negotiator thus makes judgments on the mental *availability* of the possible results.[198] This shortcut

---

[189] KOROBKIN, *supra* note 16, at 77.

[190] *Id.* at 81.

[191] Russell Korobkin, *Inertia and Preference in Contract Negotiation: The Psychological Power of Default Rules and Form Terms*, 51 VAND. L. REV. 1583, 1609 (1998).

[192] *Id.* at 1610–11.

[193] Korobkin & Guthrie, *supra* note 169, at 799.

[194] *Id.*

[195] Russell Korobkin & Chris Guthrie, *Psychological Barriers to Litigation Settlement: An Experimental Approach*, 93 MICH. L. REV. 107, 138–42 (1994).

[196] *See* MAX H. BAZERMAN & MARGARET A. NEALE, NEGOTIATING RATIONALITY 29 (1992); Russell Korobkin & Chris Guthrie, *Opening Offers and Out-of-Court Settlement: A Little Moderation May Not Go a Long Way*, 10 OHIO ST. J. DISP. RES. 1, 21 (1994).

[197] Korobkin & Guthrie, *supra* note 169, at 800.

[198] *Id.*

can lead to flawed predictions if the available outcomes are not typical or if there are important differences between past and future circumstances.[199]

Individuals are more likely to select an option in the presence of a similar inferior option than in the absence of an inferior option.[200] Choice can thus depend on the full range of options available to the decision maker even when that would seem to be irrelevant. *Contrast effect* implies that a negotiator's preference for one agreement possibility over another might depend on whether other options which make the proposed agreement desirable in contrast are also considered as part of the equation.[201]

In order for negotiators to establish reservation points that will help them reach desirable agreements and avoid undesirable agreements, they need to be able to accurately measure the value to them of reaching a negotiated agreement and accurately measure the value of their BATNA. Studies demonstrate, however, that negotiators' estimates of value can be biased because of a psychological tendency to view uncertain evidence in the best possible light. *Self-serving bias* can result in buyers setting relatively low and sellers setting relatively high reservation points, thus reducing the size of the bargaining zone or eliminating the bargaining zone that might have existed.[202] One explanation for this phenomenon is that individuals are selective in the attention they pay to various facts, focusing more on the facts that support their position than those that undermine their position.[203] Another possible explanation is overconfidence on the part of the negotiators. First, this might happen because individuals act as though they can control situations over which they have no control. Second, this might happen because individuals show more confidence in their ability than is warranted when ability matters.[204] If negotiators are overconfident in their abilities this might lead them to overvalue alternatives with probabilistic outcomes relative to those with certain outcomes, on the theory that they can exercise more control over the probabilistic outcome than is realistically practical.[205] Some evidence suggests the effect of self-serving bias may depend on how confident negotiators are in their evaluation of their position.[206]

---

[199] *Id.*

[200] *Id.* at 803.

[201] *Id.* at 804.

[202] KOROBKIN, *supra* note 16, at 53. *See also* George Lowenstein et al., *Self–Serving Assessment of Fairness and Pretrial Bargaining,* 22 J. LEGAL STUD. 135 (1993).

[203] KOROBKIN, *supra* note 16, at 66.

[204] *Id.* at 66–67.

[205] *Id.*

[206] *Id.* at 67 (citing Cynthia S. Fobia & Jay J. Christensen–Szalanski, *Ambiguity and Liability Negotiations: The Effects of the Negotiators' Role and the Sensitivity Zone,* 54 ORG. BEHAV. & HUM. DECISION PROCESSES 277 (1993)).

Another important frame is the concept of *reactive devaluation* of compromises and concessions.[207] Psychologists have found that parties will rate a compromise proposal less favorably when proposed by someone they view as an adversary or opponent as opposed to when proposed by a neutral or ally.[208] You need to be aware of this possibility as you counsel clients regarding whether to accept a proposal. This barrier might require that lawyers more fully explore a range of options with clients before beginning the negotiation process. As we have discussed, exploring a wide range of options is in keeping with problem-solving negotiation.

As the representative of a party in negotiation, you will have to think how to counter the effects of these psychological processes to increase the likelihood of reaching agreement, assuming the parties in fact want to reach agreement. It is important to be aware of these psychological effects as you begin preparing your negotiation strategy as well as when you anticipate your counterpart's strategy. As we mentioned when we discussed preparation, anticipating your counterpart's strategy is an important part of your preparation. These considerations alone, however, cannot guide your decision-making since some of these psychological processes cut one way and others cut the other way.

VI. NEGOTIATING THROUGH AGENTS

One important consideration that distinguishes legal negotiation from other settings is that lawyers act as agents for clients, the principals. Clients hire lawyers because we have expertise. We have substantive expertise (we know the law), skills (we may have the experience, training or natural ability to negotiate) and we might have resources that the principal does not (for example, we might provide access and opportunities that the principal does not have).[209] Another reason clients use lawyers to negotiate is because we are detached from the situation. This detachment can be good and bad. In settings when emotions run high, agents can defuse the conflict. In other settings, you may want the personal stake that the agent cannot provide. Finally, clients may use lawyers because the agent can bring tactical flexibility.[210] The lawyer, for example, can claim lack of authority in order to gain time to more fully con-

---

[207] Mnookin, *supra* note 176, at 246.

[208] *Id.* When the opponent proposes something that the party might have been willing to accept, the party is suspicious, thinking the opponent is likely to know something she doesn't know. *Id.*

[209] Jeffrey Z. Rubin & Frank E. A. Sander, *When Should We Use Agents? Direct vs. Representative Negotiation*, 4 NEGOT. J. 395, 396–98 (1988). MNOOKIN, PEPPET & TULUMELLO, *supra* note 4, at 71, 93–96.

[210] Rubin & Sander, *supra* note 209, at 397–98. Mnookin, Peppet & Tulumello refer to this concept as "strategic advantage." MNOOKIN, PEPPET & TULUMELLO, *supra* note 4, at 71.

sider the situation.[211] Agents may be able to settle disputes even if the principals are in conflict.[212]

Bringing an agent into negotiations introduces the possibility of tension between the agent and principal. In addition to the client having to pay the lawyer's fees, the attorney and client may differ in interests, preferences, incentives and information.[213] The ethical rules impose certain ethical requirements on lawyers but you need to be aware of the tension these differences will create in your relationship with your client and engage the client in honest conversation about them. Of course, as with many of your clients, the principal-agent questions are further complicated by another layer—your client may also be an agent for an organization.[214]

For lawyers negotiating on behalf of clients, the incentives may induce behavior that fails to serve the interests of the principal. Generally, principals and agents may have different incentives. The agent's fee structure may create incentives for the agent to act contrary to the principal's interests. If you are the lawyer representing Eastlake, you will want the fee structure that will give you the highest return for your time spent. If Eastlake were paying you by the hour, you have little incentive to cooperate with the counterpart. If, on the other hand, you are on retainer and not paid an hourly fee, you will have an incentive to complete the agreement as quickly as possible. The differences in interest go beyond financial—the lawyer may have an interest in gaining a certain type of experience or developing a certain type of reputation.[215] The principal and agent also have different information. Ethical agents, however, act in the best interest of the principal when their interests are in conflict.[216]

Negotiating through agents has several advantages. Lawyer-agents may be more objective than clients and thus have a more realistic assessment of the client's opportunities and attributes.[217] One commentator argues that lawyers as agents can create value in the design of transactions (as "transaction cost engineers") particularly in order to assure the desired regulatory treatment.[218]

---

[211] That might be a reason why the lawyer may not want a client present during negotiations.

[212] MNOOKIN, PEPPET & TULUMELLO, *supra* note 4, at 71.

[213] *Id.* at 75.

[214] For an interesting discussion of differences in a corporation between shareholders and management involving a dispute between Texaco and Pennzoil, see Mnookin, *supra* note 176, at 242–43; Robert H. Mnookin & Robert B. Wilson, *Rational Bargaining and Market Efficiency: Understanding* Pennzoil v. Texaco, 75 VA. L. REV. 295 (1989).

[215] KOROBKIN, *supra* note 16, at 290–91.

[216] MODEL RULES OF PROF'L CONDUCT R. 1.7 (2012). *See also* cmts. 10, 11, 12.

[217] *See* Lowenstein et al., *supra* note 202, at 156–57.

[218] Ronald J. Gilson, *Value Creation by Business Lawyers: Legal Skills and Asset Pricing*, 94 YALE L.J. 239, 297–98 (1984).

VII. ETHICS IN NEGOTIATION

We conclude with a discussion of ethics not because we intend for these issues to be after-thoughts, but because we believe they are all-encompassing and are better discussed after we have examined various negotiation issues. We believe you have a better sense of the ethical issues that may arise in negotiations now that we have explored a number of aspects of the negotiation process. What and how much information to disclose is a question that arises in virtually all negotiations. Is non-disclosure of information ethically permissible? How about partial disclosure? Is there a difference between puffing and lying? A discussion of the ethics of negotiations must include substantive areas of law as well as professional responsibility rules. In addition, you will have to consider questions of your own personal moral and ethical values.

Let us go back to our discussion of the tactics of a competitive bargainer to discuss some of the ethical issues that arise. A negotiator may conceal her goals in negotiating and minimize the giving of clues regarding her real intentions; for example, she may pretend she has other alternatives in order to persuade her counterpart that she has bargaining power.[219] A negotiator may bluff, trying either to show strength in order to hide a weakness or to convince her counterpart that there is no weakness.[220] A negotiator may make claims or assertions of fact, such as "We can't do X."[221] A negotiator may make exaggerated claims of value or worth.[222] A negotiator may also make untrue statements in order to deceive or mislead or make technically true statements that raise false impressions.[223] Negotiators misrepresent their bargaining positions on issues. They may also withhold information, fail to disclose specific information when requested or provide false factual information.[224]

Let us begin analyzing this behavior by looking at the Model Rules of Professional Conduct. You will need to review the rules of the state in which you practice. Under Model Rule 4.1, a "lawyer shall not knowingly . . . make a false statement of material fact . . . to a third person . . . or fail to disclose a material fact to a third person when disclosure is necessary to avoid assisting a . . . fraudulent act by a client . . . ."[225] The Comments explain that misrepresentation can also occur by failure to act.[226] The Rule's apparent high standard for honesty is modified by the Comments, however. The Comments explain that the Rule only applies to

MRPC

---

[219] Goodpaster, *supra* note 125, at 364.

[220] *Id.*

[221] *Id.* at 365.

[222] *Id.*

[223] *Id.* Goodpaster calls these statements "misinformation." *Id.*

[224] *Id.* at 366–67.

[225] MODEL RULES OF PROF'L CONDUCT R. 4.1 (2012).

[226] "Misrepresentations can also occur by partially true but misleading statements or omissions that are the equivalent of affirmative false statements." *Id.* at cmt. 1.

facts and that what may be regarded as "fact" depends on the circumstances.[227] The Comments further qualify that a lawyer "generally has no affirmative duty to inform an opposing party of relevant facts."[228] By referring to "generally accepted conventions in negotiation," the Comments provide that statements as to the party's reservation point ("an acceptable settlement of a claim"), estimates of value or price placed on the subject of the transaction and the existence of an undisclosed principal are normally not taken as statements of fact.[229] The Comments thus define away as not material several notions of how negotiations are conducted including inflated offers and demands, known as "exaggeration" or "puffing." With the exception of providing false factual information, much of the behavior we outlined above, therefore, does not seem prohibited by the Model Rules.

Carrie Menkel–Meadow is critical of Rule 4.1, arguing that there are no such things as "generally accepted conventions" because different lawyers will act differently in situations that raise ethical questions.[230] The Ethics 2000 Commission of the American Bar Association amended some of the comments to Rule 4.1 but did not substantially modify it.

Other rules also have implications in the negotiation setting. Rule 1.2 provides that a lawyer shall not counsel a client to engage in conduct that the lawyer knows is fraudulent,[231] implicating the substantive law of fraud. Most importantly, the Rules require lawyers to communicate negotiation offers to clients.[232] Additionally, the Rules allocate decision-making authority responsibility between lawyers and clients in the course of representation.[233] Clients make decisions about the objectives of representation and lawyers, in consultation with clients, may make decisions about the means of representation.[234] Should the discussion of "means" include different models of negotiation or different strategies?[235] Finally, Rule 8.4 provides that it is professional misconduct for a lawyer to engage in conduct involving "dishonesty, fraud, deceit, or misrepresentation."[236]

One scholar notes that in negotiation, more than in other contexts, ethical norms can probably be violated with greater confidence that there will be no discovery and punishment.[237] Does a lawyer forfeit a significant

---

[227] *Id.* at cmt. 2.

[228] *Id.* at cmt. 1.

[229] *Id.* at cmt. 2.

[230] Carrie Menkel–Meadow, *Ethics, Morality and Professional Responsibility, in* DISPUTE RESOLUTION ETHICS 135 (Phyllis Bernard & Bryant Garth eds., 2002). She refers to how legal and ethics experts would resolve important disclosure dilemmas differently. *Id.* at 132.

[231] MODEL RULES OF PROF'L CONDUCT R. 1.2(d) (2012).

[232] MODEL RULES OF PROF'L CONDUCT R. 1.4(a)(1) (2012).

[233] MODEL RULES OF PROF'L CONDUCT R. 1.2(a) (2012).

[234] *Id.*

[235] Menkel–Meadow, *supra* note 230, at 132.

[236] MODEL RULES OF PROF'L CONDUCT R. 8.4(c) (2012).

[237] James J. White, *Machiavelli and the Bar: Ethical Limitations on Lying in Negotiation*, 1980 AM. B. FOUND. RES. J. 926, 926–27 (1980).

advantage for his client to others who do not follow the rules because there is a low probability of punishment? Do you believe that is a justification for not following the rules?

Legal obligations also exist outside the ethical rules for the lawyers and the parties. The common law requires truthfulness in many elements of negotiation. Some negotiation behavior may be actionable as misrepresentation or fraud and may make the contract voidable. You will need to examine how cases in your jurisdiction define elements of misrepresentation, material fact and omission. The Restatement (Second) of Torts recognizes liability for fraudulent misrepresentation when one fraudulently makes a misrepresentation of fact, opinion, intention or law for the purpose of inducing another to act or refrain from acting in reliance upon it.[238] The Restatement (Second) of Contracts recognizes instances when the non-disclosure is equivalent to an assertion of a fact.[239] A contract is voidable if one party's assent is induced by fraud or material misrepresentation by the other party and the party assenting is justified in relying.[240]

Carrie Menkel–Meadow raises some important considerations in the area of ethics and negotiation. What do we owe other human beings with whom we negotiate over something that we or our clients want?[241] Are the other people with whom we interact in negotiations just means to our ends or people like us deserving of respect? How do we conceive our goals when we approach others to help us accomplish together what we cannot alone? As you engage in negotiations you will have to ask yourself: What should you do? What may you do?

Menkel–Meadow suggests looking at the limits of your goals and behavior using the mirror test (from within), the videotape test (what your mother, teacher, child or clergy person would think of you if they watch this) and formally (the rules, laws, ethical standards and religious or moral principles to which you must or choose to adhere).[242] As lawyers who negotiate as agents, our duty to the client complicates matters more. How do we reconcile our goals if they are different from those of our client? When do legal rules such as that of fiduciary relationships define the obligations? Do we merely use them as an excuse? There is also the question of duty, responsibility and relationship to our counterpart. Do we live by the rule of "treat others as we would like to be treated"? Finally, there are the social effects of the negotiation. Has it done more good than harm to those inside the negotiation? To those who are not parties but are af-

---

[238] RESTATEMENT (SECOND) OF TORTS § 525 (1977).

[239] RESTATEMENT (SECOND) OF CONTRACTS § 161 (1981).

[240] *Id.* at § 164.

[241] Carrie Menkel–Meadow, *What's Fair in Negotiation? What Is Ethics in Negotiation?, in* WHAT'S FAIR: ETHICS FOR NEGOTIATORS xiii, xiii-xxxv (Carrie Menkel–Meadow & Michael Wheeler eds., 2004).

[242] *Id.* at xv.

fected by the negotiation, such as employees, shareholders, vendors, clients, consumers and the public? Are we as the negotiators morally accountable for impacts on third parties and those in the future?[243]

---

[243] *Id.* at xvi-xvii.

CHAPTER 6

DRAFTING TRANSACTIONAL DOCUMENTS

■ ■ ■

I. INTRODUCTION

As students in a transactional clinic, a substantial segment of your work experience will involve creating documents. To be successful in your role—both as a student and then as a lawyer—you will need to practice writing and think hard about what distinguishes good drafting from poor drafting. In this chapter we offer some introductory ideas about the processes you will face. Before we jump into our discussion, we offer you one overarching insight we have heard from others: To be a good writer, you first must be a good *reader*.[1] And we don't mean reading emails or tweets (although good writers craft much better emails than sloppy ones, as you've no doubt noticed). We mean solitary, extended, luxurious (perhaps) time with books and journals.

In this chapter we proceed as follows. We first highlight some of the goals of good writing in the transactional arena. We then offer a (somewhat artificial, but we hope helpful) taxonomy of five different categories of documents you might encounter in this kind of work. We proceed to review each of the categories in light of the goals we first articulated. We then end with a section where we share some of the stylistic conventions we understand to be quite well-accepted in the writing world and therefore very useful for you to understand and, usually, to honor.

One important caveat for you to understand: There are many excellent book-length explorations of what goes into effective writing, and we will cite several of them here. This one chapter does not pretend to be, and cannot be, a replacement for those more elaborate and thorough treatments of the topics we address here. As with most of this book, we offer here some highlights that we hope you will find instructive as you begin your transactional work.

II. THE GOALS OF EFFECTIVE WRITING

Now that we all have Spell–Check on our computers, we can produce error-free documents with just a little bit of judgment and care. We might ask what else we need to think about when we evaluate the documents

---

[1] Jon Michaud, *Finding The Writer's Voice*, THE NEW YORKER (May 30, 2011), http://www.newyorker.com/online/blogs/backissues/2011/05/louis-menand-writers-voice.html.

we produce. What other goals might we have for our written product? Here are some apparent benchmarks.

Accuracy: Your document must communicate accurately what you wish its readers to understand. If your client wants new board members to be elected only at an annual or a special meeting, and you write that board members may be replaced at "any meeting," you have not communicated what you set out to do.

Clarity: Clarity is different from accuracy. The language quoted just above is clear, but wrong. Obtaining clarity, though, can be a real challenge in transactional writing. Many of your documents (like bylaws, or contracts, or waivers) will be read most carefully many months after you create them, at a time of some uncertainty or crisis, by persons you never have met, and without you being around to assist them to follow what you meant. Your writing must anticipate those realities, and strive to be as clear as possible when read by an utter stranger.

Clear

Organization: A document could be quite clear and quite accurate, but very disorganized. Usually, though, organization assists in clarity. You will generate the documents you create in order to change or influence someone's behavior in the future, and the more organized your ideas are, the better the chances that your intentions will be met.

Brevity: Often, being as clear, accurate and organized as possible means writing a lot of words to cover everything that you set out to cover. This goal, then, is in tension with the goals just above. The best writing will communicate what you need to say, in the fewest words possible.

Sufficiency: Your documents must satisfy whatever legal standards or norms govern the transaction you are aiming to accomplish. Your research and planning must ensure that you address adequately every legal element necessary for your client's project.

Persuasion: In many documents you produce, the writing will serve to influence the reader to accept its propositions. In this way some of your documents serve the same purpose as advocacy writing in the litigation setting. Sometimes the advocacy will be apparent—say, a Form 1023 submitted to the IRS as an application for tax-exempt status. In other instances the advocacy will be more subtle—for instance, when you create the first draft of a proposed contract, and you hope to persuade the contracting party to accept your characterization of the terms. In either instance you will, in your drafting process, expressly anticipate the persuasive effect of your language and organizational choices.

Respect: This goal is separate and different from each of the preceding goals. Whether or not you have achieved the above goals, your writing's craft will create in your reader some impression about your skill and character as a writer. Writing that understands the accepted conventions of style, grammar and punctuation engenders respect, and that respect is valuable capital to your lawyering career.

III. A TAXONOMY OF TRANSACTIONAL WRITING TASKS

Law school tends to teach effectively the craft of creating litigation documents—think of pleadings, research and planning memos, and persuasive correspondence. Transactional lawyers write different kinds of documents, and the law school curriculum traditionally has paid them less attention. In this Section we identify five categories of transactional writing,[2] and we then review each in light of the goals identified in the previous section. It seems that any substantial drafting you accomplish in a transactional clinic will fit into one of the following five categories:

1. Guidance and governance documents (e.g., bylaws or articles);

2. Agreements (e.g., contracts or waivers);

3. Persuasive projects (e.g., Form 1023 or permit applications);

4. Information gathering forms (e.g., application or enrollment devices); or

5. Correspondence or opinions (e.g., opinion letters, explanatory letters or emails).

[handwritten margin note: Types of transactional docs]

Each of these categories calls for somewhat different strategic thinking, although, as you might imagine, many of the same goals and techniques will apply to each type of document. What follows is a brief consideration of ways you might approach each separate variety of writing project.

A. GUIDANCE AND GOVERNANCE DOCUMENTS

A common task for a transactional lawyer is creating rules, standards and procedures to govern the operation of an organization. In your clinical work you may produce articles of organization,[3] corporate bylaws, employment manuals, conflict of interest or document retention policies, and similar documents that serve essentially as "private lawmaking." Once adopted by the governing body of the organization, the processes and standards you generate will bind those who work for and within your

---

[2] Note that each of the categories here, while prominent in transactional work, also covers some important parts of litigation practice. Litigators sometimes create guidance documents (e.g., a discovery schedule); contracts (e.g., any written settlement agreement); persuasive projects (most of litigation writing, such as a brief); information gathering forms (e.g., most interrogatories), and correspondence or opinions (e.g., objective advice memos to a client before negotiation).

[3] The operating agreement you create for an LLC is a mix between a governing document and a contract between or among the LLC members.

client's entity.[4] Your drafting today, therefore, has critical implications for your clients in the future.

Indeed, the most likely use of these governing and guidance documents will occur some time in the future, at a time of some uncertainty or perhaps crisis within the entity, when the entity's management or constituents—individuals who quite likely will have had no previous contact with you at all—will retrieve the relevant document to guide or constrain their actions. Your drafting process, and especially your attention to the goals of accuracy, clarity, organization, and brevity, will anticipate this common use of governing documents, as you strive to make the product as useful and reliable as it possibly can be.

You will find, though, that achieving those goals is not at all an easy process. We will consider the challenges involved in this kind of writing by using a simple example: creating a set of bylaws for a nonprofit corporation.[5] Your work on such a project will likely involve the following steps and considerations:

The Content of the Bylaws: Planning and Counseling: The process of understanding what will go into the bylaws is separate from how you communicate that content in a formal document to be adopted by the entity's board. The latter is the writing challenge, but the former task must precede, at least in part, the latter. Your mission is to understand from the organizational constituents with whom you are working what choices they wish to make about how the organization will run.[6] The client must

---

[4]　DEL. CORP. LAW tit. 8 § 141(a) (1953) ("If any such provision is made in the certificate of incorporation, the powers and duties conferred or imposed upon the board of directors by this chapter shall be exercised or performed to such extent and by such person or persons as shall be provided in the certificate of incorporation"); Carr v. Acacia Country Club Co., 970 N.E.2d 1075, 1086 (Ohio 2012) ("A corporation's code of regulations establishes the procedural rules that govern the relationships among the corporate shareholders, directors and officers. . . . The regulations have the force of contracts between the corporation and its shareholders."); Abraham v. Diamond Dealers Club, Inc., 896 N.Y.S.2d 848, 851 (Sup. Ct. 2010) *aff'd*, 914 N.Y.S.2d 152 (2011); Kansas Heart Hosp. LLC v. Idbeis, 184 P.3d 866, 882 (Kan. 2008) ("It is a well-settled rule that the bylaws of a corporation are self-imposed rules, resulting from an agreement or contract between the corporation and its members to conduct the corporate business in a similar particular way"); Isaacs v. American Iron & Steel Co., 690 N.W.2d 373, 376 (Minn. Ct. App. 2004) ("Bylaws establish rules for a corporation's internal governance and may contain any provision relating to management of the business that is not inconsistent with state law. . . . [They] must be obeyed by the corporation and its directors, officers, and shareholders."); Harrah's Entm't, Inc. v. JCC Holding Co., 802 A.2d 294, 309 (Del. Ch. 2002) ("In general terms, corporate instruments such as charters and bylaws are interpreted in the same manner as other contracts"); Cummings v. Webster, 43 Me. 192, 197 (1857) ("So here the by-laws of the company, made in pursuance of their charter, are equally binding on all their members . . . as any public law in the State.").

[5]　This example has general applicability to other governing or guidance documents, such as bylaws for a for-profit organization or articles of organization.

[6]　That decision-making process is itself a delicate one which we address in the Counseling chapter, where we encounter the questions about your role in counseling an entity client. As that chapter notes, you likely will not make decisions through the entity's full board or even its highest management figures, but instead through other constituents or agents, whose reliability and representativeness you will need to confirm in some fashion. Indeed, in the context of creating the original set of bylaws, you might be operating *before* any formal organization exists, as some

decide the size of the board, the meeting structures and processes, notice protocols, election of board members and officers, proxy voting, and so forth. For any one of those items you must develop a strategic plan to educate your client about the choices available and counsel the client about which avenues it prefers.

Using Templates: A quite common strategic device by which you will introduce your client to the issues to be covered and decided is to share with your client a generic template or form of bylaws, off of which you may then work together. The template will then, of course, influence your writing, since the form will no doubt serve as a first draft of the ultimate document. From a lawyering perspective, is it problematic to work with forms?

You will readily see the risks and disadvantages of working from forms, but we agree with virtually all commentators that you will, and ought to, use reliable templates as a starting point for your governance and guidance documents.[7] The problem is using the template reflexively and uncritically. The challenge, and what distinguishes the most talented lawyers in this area (and could distinguish *you* in your clinical work), is how to adapt creatively and responsibly any given form for your client's particular purposes. Using a form uncritically is quite dangerous. You will likely end up with language that is not accurate, not clear, and not internally consistent. You will also encounter one of the most serious worries in using forms—that is, including in the final document some terms or clauses whose significance or relevance you simply do not understand.[8]

But despite those risks and dangers, you simply cannot operate as a transactional lawyer without using forms. Templates have significant and critical advantages. If they are good ones produced by smart and thoughtful lawyers, they will have refined the language necessary to accomplish some repeated, expected goals of the document. It is more efficient and, frankly, better service to your client if you discover through the template language which works, and which you might never have come up with yourself. Templates also serve the critical (and malpractice-discouraging) "checklist" function.[9] A good and comprehensive checklist provides a law-

---

state's law may require that you have bylaws in place before you create the corporation. Your constituent contact will most likely be through the "founders" of the organization.

  7   Ronald Gilson, *Value Creation By Business Lawyers: Legal Skills and Asset Pricing*, 94 YALE L.J. 239, 257 (1984) ("Without having become boilerplate—enormous amounts of time still are spent on their negotiation—the general contents of the agreement have by now become pretty much standardized.").

  8   Of course, responding to that worry by simply *eliminating* the clauses or terms whose significance or relevance you do not understand is equally dangerous and short-sighted.

  9   ATUL GAWANDE, THE CHECKLIST MANIFESTO: HOW TO GET THINGS RIGHT (2008); Gilson, *supra* note 7, at 258 ("Because the overall approach and coverage of typical acquisition agreements, and the types of contractual relationships they contain, are largely the same, they can be taken fairly to reflect not merely an individual lawyer's inspired response in a particular situation, but the collective wisdom of business lawyers as a group."); Laura Fitzpatrick, *Atul*

yer with a reminder of most issues that the lawyer must cover or address. A reliable template will accomplish that goal.

Therefore, a common starting scheme for your planning for developing corporate bylaws might look something like this: You will meet with your client[10] to discuss generally the goals and aspirations for the organization's functioning. You then prepare a first, preliminary draft of the bylaws using a reliable template, editing provisionally for your starting purposes based on what your client has told you so far. You share that tentative draft with the client, and together review each relevant topic so you can understand what content the client chooses. Note the difference between deciding the content of the bylaw document (for instance, "we'd prefer a board with no more than seven directors, with staggered board terms of two or three years per term, and with some term limits") and the crafting of the actual words on paper that capture the commitments the client has chosen. Those processes are related, of course, but they call for different skills.

Drafting the Bylaws: Consistency, Clarity, Organization, Brevity: Recall that your mission in drafting bylaws is to produce a set of private, internal "laws" which will in a clear fashion guide future readers. You will therefore need to make sure that the various provisions of the bylaws harmonize with one another, that the lay readers can understand what the provisions mean without retaining a lawyer to translate the language for them, and that the result is organized in a way that the reader/users can locate what they need to find, all while also remaining concise. We see now how challenging it can be to craft effective bylaws.

For example, imagine that your client has decided that it wants a board of no more than seven directors with staggered terms of two (or perhaps three) years, representing a commitment not to require all of the directors to leave the board at the same time. Let us look at the following language, which you draft with your "brevity" goal in mind:

Example 1

Article III - Board Members

The board of directors shall have no more than seven members, who shall have staggered terms of two or three years.

Does this work? We would critique this effort by noting its substantive weaknesses, as well as a couple of stylistic missteps. Substantively, this

---

Gawande: How to Make Doctors Better, TIME.COM (Jan. 4, 2010), http://www.time.com/time/health/article/0,8599,1950892,00.html.

[10] Again, by "client" we refer to the founder or the appropriate constituent directing you on behalf of the organizational client.

simple provision is just too ambiguous. It fails to guide the users about how the terms will apply to any given director. While it is probably inadvisable to leave open the question of two- or three-year terms, if the client wants to include that option this bylaw provision does not help the directors understand how to implement the choice. So, as a substantive matter, the first draft is not precise nor accurate enough. The draft language also includes two stylistic problems. First, the title does not match the substance of this provision. You should aim to craft titles that are accurate and reliable. Second, and far more picky, the drafter included a *hyphen* in the title when an *em-dash* would be the appropriate connector (assuming you want such a connector). We note this latter critique not because it is an important one (indeed, most reviewers would ignore it, and some would never even notice it), but because we believe that small editing details matter to some readers, and it is cost-free to attend to those details.[11]

accuracy + substance

Your second draft, then, will respond to these critiques. You will search for language that more accurately communicates what you want the future board members to follow. With that in mind, you might try something like the following:

Example 2

Article III—Composition of Board; Terms of Board Members

The board of directors shall consist of an odd number of directors, either three, or five, or seven in number, but never more than seven members. The terms of the board members should be staggered so that all of the board members do not leave the board at the same time. Each board member shall serve a two year term. If the board has three members, two of the members shall start out with three year terms, and the successors of those board members shall have two year terms. If the board has five members, three of the members shall start out with three year terms, and the successors of those board members shall have two year terms. If the board has seven members, four of the members shall start out with three year terms, and the successors of those board members shall have two year terms.

Example 2 is better than Example 1. It communicates more accurately and more clearly the intentions of the founders, and a careful reader may follow its instructions. Its heading is also improved compared to Example 1. But can you see any writing problems with Example 2?

Our worry is that Example 2 is too messy and a little too prolix. It would be better to communicate the content of the provision in a more

---

[11] See Section IV below, where we describe this philosophy in more depth.

organized or structured way. Your revision might look something like Example 3:

[handwritten margin note: organize/structure]

Example 3

Article III—Composition of Board; Terms of Board Members

(a)   The board of directors shall consist of an odd number of directors, no fewer than three and no more than seven in number.

(b)   There shall be an initial board, the majority of whose members shall serve an initial term of three years, and the remainder of whom shall serve two year terms.

(c)   After the expiration of the terms of the initial board members, each successor director shall serve a two year term.

Example 3 seems to work better than Example 2, even if each communicates precisely the same substantive ideas. It is shorter, more organized, and easier for the readers to follow. Can you improve it even more?

With this simple and brief example we intend to demonstrate the kinds of refinement that you will engage in when creating governing documents. We next turn to the drafting of contracts and agreements. You will see in the next section some further writing suggestions which will have direct applicability to drafting governing documents, as the two categories are very similar.

B. AGREEMENTS

Here is what some contract terms might look like to a layperson:

[ ] By checking the box below, but not this box, I indicate my denial of these terms and conditions.

[ ] By checking the box above, but not this box, I indicate the acceptance of these terms and conditions, unless I have also checked the box below, in which case I indicate my denial, unless I have checked a total of three or more boxes, in which case I have passed beyond denial, cycled through anger, bargaining, and depression, and am now back at acceptance.

[ ] I agree that, for purposes of box-checking, "above" shall be defined as "below" and "below" shall be defined as "above," unless the box below is checked.

[ ] *Ceci n'est pas un box.*[12]

---

[12] Jacob Sager Weinstein, *Shouts and Murmurs: Before the Movie Begins*, THE NEW YORKER, Feb. 6, 2012, at 35, *available at* http://www.newyorker.com/humor/2012/02/06/120206sh_shouts_weinstein.

A second significant type of document you will create in your practice is the agreement, or contract. While you will find several useful book-length treatments of the finer points of creating contracts,[13] we will highlight here some general ideas which should help you in your work.

While the governing documents discussed above are, in some respects, "agreements,"[14] we distinguish them from the basic form of contract you studied during your first year of law school—the result of an offer, acceptance, and consideration. With agreements, you are developing terms to capture the accord among two or more parties, who frequently have some differing interests. Your client may be offering goods or services to customers, or may be purchasing materials from a supplier. The contract may be a lease for a storefront or the purchase of an office condominium. While substance of agreements will vary considerably, the underlying principles of effective contract drafting are subject to some broad generalizations.

For the purposes of our overview, we will review the *process* of arriving at a contract, describe some typical contract terms, and suggest some writing conventions to help you achieve your goal.

1) *The Process*: The kinds of contracts you draft in a transactional clinic will tend to fall into two categories—(1) negotiated contracts between two (or among more than two) parties, and (2) contracts of adhesion, offered by a merchant or other enterprise to an employee or a consumer.[15] The process of creating each will differ, but your drafting goals may not be very different.

    a) <u>Negotiated Contracts</u>: Imagine that your client, The Prospect Street Café LLC, locates an office that seems to meet its needs, and asks you to draft a lease agreement between The Prospect Street Café and the landlord. (Suspend temporarily, just for our instructional purposes, your reliable understanding that the tenant is very unlikely to be the party to offer the first draft of a commercial lease agreement.) The drafting of a contract in this setting is a bit of a *dialectical* process. You need to know the terms you will include in the agreement, but those terms will be the

---

[13] *See, e.g.*, KENNETH A. ADAMS, A MANUAL OF STYLE FOR CONTRACT DRAFTING (2d ed. 2008); CHARLES M. FOX, WORKING WITH CONTRACTS: WHAT LAW SCHOOL DOESN'T TEACH YOU (2002); LOUIS KAPLOW & STEVEN SHAVELL, CONTRACTING (2004); TINA L. STARK, DRAFTING CONTRACTS: HOW AND WHY LAWYERS DO WHAT THEY DO (2007).

[14] *See, e.g.*, Renee Jones, *Law, Norms and the Breakdown of the Board: Promoting Accountability in Corporate Governance*, 92 IOWA L. REV. 105 (2006) (discussing bylaws as agreements among the organizational control group members).

[15] We use the term "adhesion contract" loosely here, to represent an agreement you will create without any active engagement with the other contracting party or parties. Some of these documents might qualify as adhesion contracts as understood by contract doctrine, and others may not. But for present purposes, we lump all of those kinds of deals under that one term. For an understanding of adhesion contracts generally, see, e.g., Todd D. Rakoff, *Contracts of Adhesion: An Essay in Reconstruction*, 96 HARV. L. REV. 1173, 1177–80 (1983).

subject of some, or even a lot of, bargaining between you and the land-lord's attorney. A common time line might resemble something like this:[16]

    i.)   You and the landlord's lawyer, or your client and the land-lord, meet to discuss the basic terms of the agreement—the length of time, the rent due, any security deposits, who pays for utilities, and so forth.;

    ii.) You then meet with your client to review the potential additional terms or conditions beyond those basics, whether terms your client hopes to have or terms your client hopes never to see—for instance, who will cover repairs, subletting terms, renovation details, etc.;

    iii.) You then develop a *first draft* of a contract whose goal is to capture the parties' agreement in a reliable and accurate way, but to present them and any other terms in a light as favorable to your client as you conclude is reasonably fair to the landlord;[17]

    iv.) You share that first draft with your client to ensure that you have accurately captured your client's wishes and have not over-committed to any position on any issue likely to be the subject of some negotiation;

    v.)   You send the resulting draft to the landlord's lawyer;[18]

    vi.) The landlord's lawyer reviews your draft and returns it to you, suggesting—or insisting upon—some changes; and

    vii.) The above steps iii-vi repeat until either the deal falls apart or the parties agree to a final set of terms, at which time the principals sign the document and the transaction proceeds.

        b) <u>Adhesion Contracts</u>: Imagine that your client, PRT Web Design, LLC, sells software packages to businesses. Each sale includes a "click-through" licensing agreement specifying the terms of the purchase and sale. Each time a business clicks "Accept" and consummates the purchase, a binding contract comes into existence. Your drafting of the licensing agreement is surely a form of contract drafting, but, because you are not negotiating the terms with any of the individual purchasers of the

---

    [16] This process would apply to any kind of negotiated agreement—say, for supplies or to provide some technical services to a business.

    [17] This moment presents for you something of an ethical decision point, as well as a strategic one as well. The more benefits you gain for your client by your careful and subtle drafting of terms, the greater the gain for your client at the landlord's expense. Of course, too aggressive a posture will likely backfire. For considerations of these points, see the chapters on Negotiation and Ethics.

    [18] If you have typed your document in Microsoft Word, you ought to "scrub" the document of any "metadata" before sending it to the other party, who otherwise might be able to read earlier comments on or versions of the document. *See generally* David Hricik & Chase Edward Scott, *Metadata: The Ghosts Haunting e-Documents*, 13 GA. B. J. 16 (Feb. 2008), *available at* http://www.gabar.org/newsandpublications/georgiabarjournal/loader.cfm?csModule=security/getfile&pageID=4602.

software, the process is not the same as that just described above. The strategies for your drafting differ as a result. Here is a typical adhesion contract process:

i.) Your client asks you for language to include in its licensing agreement, and you interview your client to understand its desired terms; *adhesion*

ii.) You create a first draft of a contract covering the issues your client wants as well as those other terms (some of which may be considered "boilerplate") which you, with your legal training, perceive as necessary to address in the transaction (for instance, limitation on liability, limits on use, choice of law, warranties, etc.);

iii.) Your client reviews the agreement and you discuss any concerns the client has; and

iv.) You revise the draft to address and such concerns or suggestions, and arrive at a final product, which your client inserts into the purchasing scheme.

You will note immediately the more delicate *ethical issues* that are implicated in this process. Not only are you not negotiating the terms of this agreement with the ultimate purchasers of the software, but you know that some purchasers (indeed, perhaps most purchasers, depending on the context) will click "Accept" without ever reading through the licensing agreement. The purchasers who do read the agreement will likely not be lawyers. Your client may desire that you insert the most stringently protective language in the least apparent fashion. While whether to take such a stance has important business judgment implications for your client (is it a wise business policy to try to hoodwink one's customers?), you will still need to grapple with your proper role as a lawyer if your client opts for a more aggressive stance in this kind of setting.[19]

2) *Typical Terms*: Let us consider some typical terms involved in a *negotiated* agreement. You may then decide which of these also have relevance to a contract of adhesion.

Consider a simple agreement for the sale of goods, say, special whole wheat flour for the café. A contract between the buyer and the seller will typically include language addressing the following: The goods, described clearly enough to be identified; the price to be paid; the form and timing of the payment; the terms for the delivery of the goods; any warranties about the goods and their fitness or usefulness (or the express absence of *terms in sales agreement*

---

[19] *See* Michael J. Madison, *Rights of Access and the Shape of the Internet*, 44 B.C. L. REV. 433 (2003) (arguing "that shrinkwrap and click-through caselaw, the original line of argument regulating 'access' to electronic places, has outlived the contract-as-assent metaphor on which it relies"); *see also* William J. Condon, Jr., *Electronic Assent to Online Contracts: Do Courts Consistently Enforce Clickwrap Agreements?*, 16 REGENT UNIV. L. REV. 433 (2003) (discussing the validity of clickwrap agreements, including challenges in court).

any such warranties, if permitted by governing law); and a process for resolving any disputes about the purchase and sale (which could include an alternative dispute resolution forum).

In some settings, with more complex transactions, you will consider terms such as the following: representations and warranties about the seller, the purchaser, the goods, or the performance; a financing scheme; and conditions precedent.

The basic principle guiding you in any contract drafting will be your anticipation of developments in the future, and the agreement's addressing the parties' mutual understanding about what should happen, how and when. Your role is to identify the contingencies and future consequences. Whether you include terms about those matters in the agreement is a tactical question considered by you and your client, as well, of course, by the other party and its lawyer.

3) *Drafting Suggestions*: Think back to the original list of goals of effective transactional writing, and see how aptly most of them fit here. One central goal of contract drafting is *accuracy*—your draft should represent to a neutral, objective reader the true intentions of the parties. Your draft also needs to be unambiguous and precise, so that the parties (and reviewers, like a judge, jury, or arbitrator) will understand clearly the meaning of your terms, and so that the document's various terms harmonize with one another. If possible, the agreement should also be concise, which may (but not always will) aid in the goals of precision and clarity.

Some common techniques in your drafting to achieve these goals include the following:

a)   Use of Definitions: By defining terms, and then using the shorthand placeholder throughout the document, you may increase the accuracy and the clarity of your terms. Drafters often capitalize the defined terms throughout the agreement, alerting the reader that the word or phrase has a specified definition within the agreement.

b)   Anticipate Complications: The parties at the beginning of a contractual relationship may have every confidence that the transaction will proceed smoothly and amicably. The parties may be entirely correct in that assumption. Your role, however, is to anticipate and consider all of the various ways that the deal might falter. To say this is not to recommend that you become what some term a "deal-killer."[20] To anticipate problems is not to trigger them. To discuss them with your client does not neces-

---

[20]   Gilson, *supra* note 7, at 242 ("At worst, lawyers are seen as deal killers whose continual raising of obstacles, without commensurate effort at finding solutions, ultimately causes transactions to collapse under their own weight.").

sarily mean that the contingencies get covered in the agreement expressly. And to include the contingency and dispute resolution language in the agreement does not mean that the deal is threatened. Besides serving as a careful and comprehensive *drafter* about these worries, you will also be a thoughtful *counselor* and *negotiator* about them.

c)   Rely on Others' Work: It will be an unusual agreement whose terms and contingencies have not occurred to others in the past. Like with governance documents discussed above, templates will serve as a useful device for your consideration of how to describe complicated or subtle concepts.

As we noted at the outset of this chapter, contract drafting is the subject of several excellent books, which break down the elements of a contract in fine detail, and review several drafting techniques and principles to guide lawyers through the process. We recommend those books to you.[21]

C. PERSUASIVE DOCUMENTS

Transactional clinic students create documents whose primary purpose is to persuade a reader, or a decisionmaker, to grant some benefit, status or similar valued good to the student's client. A common example of this kind of document in transactional clinics is the Form 1023, the application to the IRS for tax-exempt status.[22] Other examples include permit applications, property or excise tax exemption applications, financing proposals, or grant applications. The writing required for persuasive documents such as these is different in important ways from the writing you will employ in drafting governing documents and contracts.

As many observers have noted, law schools train their students much more thoroughly and comprehensively for persuasive writing, compared to the kind of writing we address elsewhere in this chapter.[23] We therefore may address this topic more briefly. But the persuasive writing you will accomplish in your transactional settings is different in some important respects from the kinds of litigation-oriented projects you likely encountered in your first year legal wring courses in law school. Consider the following topics:

---

[21] *See supra* sources cited at note 13.

[22] *See* I.R.S., U.S. DEP'T OF THE TREASURY, FORM 1023, APPLICATION FOR RECOGNITION OF EXEMPTION UNDER SECTION 501(C)(3) OF THE INTERNAL REVENUE CODE, CAT. NO. 17133K (June 2006) [hereinafter I.R.S. FORM 1023], *available at* http://www.irs.gov/pub/irs-access/f1023_accessible.pdf. We know anecdotally that many law school transactional clinics represent organizations to achieve tax-exempt status.

[23] *See* FOX, *supra* note 13, at 1–2. *See also* Lisa Penland, *What a Transactional Lawyer Needs to Know: Identifying and Implementing Competencies for Transactional Lawyers*, 5 J. ASS'N. LEGAL WRITING DIRECTORS 118, 120 (2008); Louis N. Schulze, Jr., *Transactional Law in the Required Legal Writing Curriculum: An Empirical Study of the Forgotten Future Business Lawyer*, 55 CLEV. ST. L. REV. 59, 95–96 (2007).

Audience: The audience for litigation-driven advocacy writing tends to be courts, judges, clerks, or the other lawyers involved in the disputes. By contrast, the audience for your persuasive writing in transactional settings will include those actors less often. Your understanding of your audience, then, might call for more creative thought and investigation than in the former settings.

Conventions: Litigation-oriented writing, most notably pleadings, have a well-established set of conventions, perhaps unwritten or uncompiled, but known comfortably to repeat players in the court systems. Good legal writing professors will introduce students to those conventions. But those conventions do not necessarily apply to your transactional work, so you will need to suspend some learned judgments as you create documents for your entrepreneur or nonprofit clients.

In light of our aim in this book to offer you general, broad overviews of topics which warrant much more in-depth inquiry through your own particular work for your clients, we will suggest here some drafting ideas using one sample persuasive writing project, the Form 1023. You may use this example as one from which you might glean insights applicable to other transactional settings which you will encounter.

As noted above (and described in more depth in the chapter on nonprofit organizations), Form 1023 serves as the formal application to the IRS for 501(c)(3) status for a nonprofit.[24] While the completion of the form itself mostly involves checking the correct boxes (a process which, while not really "drafting," calls for important and sophisticated legal judgments in many instances), the most *persuasive* parts of the form are the "narrative" elements called for, or sometimes implied by, the template. One section, Item IV, explicitly requires the applicant to present a narrative explanation of the entity's nonprofit activities and its eligibility for 501(c)(3) status. Other sections require written explanations of certain checked boxes or similar answers on the form.[25] The words you write in these narrative sections offer you the opportunity to persuade the reader of the soundness of your client's application—or, if mishandled, the

---

[24] A similar form applies to 501(c)(4) organizations, which are social welfare organizations. Organizations applying for 501(c) status other than 501(c)(3) generally use Form 1024. *See* I.R.S., U.S. DEP'T OF THE TREASURY, FORM 1024, APPLICATION FOR RECOGNITION OF EXEMPTION UNDER 501(A), CAT. NO. 12343K (Sept. 1998), *available at* http://www.irs.gov/pub/irs-access/f1024_accessible.pdf.

[25] For instance, Part VIII, Item 10 of the Form 1023 asks for an explanation of the organization's intellectual property ownership and other arrangements. *See* I.R.S. FORM 1023, *supra* note 23. Part VIII, Item 12 asks for an explanation of the entity's activities in a foreign country. *Id.* at 7. Schedules A–G include the opportunity for examples and explanations of answers chosen for questions on Form 1023. For example, in Schedule B, Question 7 is as follows: "Do you or will you contract with another organization to develop, build, market, or finance your facilities? If 'Yes,' explain how that entity is selected, explain how the terms of any contracts or other agreements are negotiated at arm's length, and explain how you determine that you will pay no more than fair market value for services." *Id.*

chance to convince the reader that your entity does not meet the IRS's standards for tax-exemption.

Your role, then, in drafting the Form 1023 is as an *advocate*. Your aim is to leave the reader with no other principled choice but to conclude that the charity satisfies the IRS's requirements. As you write the narrative (and make other judgments about how to complete the form), keep these drafting principles in mind:

- *Understand Your Audience*: More experienced IRS practitioners will assist you to understand the practices of the IRS office where the Form 1023 gets reviewed at the time you are drafting the form's contents. But you may also use your imagination—and your powers of empathy—to consider the setting and the context of the reviewer who will read your words. He (we'll call the reviewer "he" for convenience) reads many applications each week. He may wish to be generous, but his superiors will have legitimate worries if he grants 100% of all of the applications he reviews, and he will know that. He may have also developed a learned and healthy skepticism about this process—tax exempt status is a valuable public benefit, and only those charities who fit perfectly Congress's and the IRS's requirements should obtain his approval. His working routine will include separating out the "clear" applications from those which, while perhaps meritorious, trigger some questions needing further answers, or some uncertainty needing further consideration within the agency.[26]

  Imagining the setting of your reader should help you to offer a written product most likely to qualify as one of the "clear" applications.

- *Tell a Story*: Many observers have noted the benefit of "narrative" and storytelling to effective advocacy.[27] To persuade an audience, you must communicate a world which makes sense, has coherence, and fits a shared understanding of how people in fact behave. While most storytelling ideas fit best in the context of dispute resolution (where each side presents a differing conception

---

[26] When it receives a completed Form 1023, the IRS mails the applicant a letter explaining this division of the applications upon its review of them. The letter describes the IRS's division of applications into three groups: "1. Those that can be processed immediately based on the information submitted; 2. Those that need minor additional information to be resolved; and 3. Those that require additional development." While referral to the category of "needs further review" does not necessarily mean than an application's success is in jeopardy, practitioners agree that such a result is a serious setback for the applicant, if only because the referral makes the process considerably longer.

[27] *See, e.g.*, Binny Miller, *Telling Stories About Cases and Clients: The Ethics of Narrative*, 14 GEO. J. LEGAL ETHICS 1 (2000); Jo A. Tyler & Faith Mullen, *Telling Tales in School: Storytelling for Self–Reflection and Pedagogical Improvement in Clinical Legal Education*, 18 CLINICAL L. REV. 283 (2011).

of facts), readers of the mission and history of a charity also look for the same components of coherence and fit.

- *Address the Legal Standards*: Substantial IRS "law" exists in the world; your client will obtain its 501(c)(3) status only if its work meets the standards within that law. Your role in creating an advocacy document is to recognize the specific nuances of the standards and address them in an explicit, methodical way. But note the next suggestion.

- *Do Not Be Too Lawyerly*: The IRS reviewers likely know far more about the law and procedure than you will (well, most of you), but they are usually not lawyers. They are surely not appellate justices nor trial judges.[28] Given the context of the IRS review process, your writing will benefit from a nimble, plain-spoken clarity, as opposed to a more blustery, pointed "argument." (Of course, *all* advocacy, in court and out, benefits from that advice.)

- *Address Weaknesses*: Like most effective litigation advocacy, your writing will possess more power and credibility if it acknowledges and confronts the likely problems the reader will encounter. Especially given the disadvantage to your client of the reviewer slotting your application into the "needs further follow-up" basket,[29] your anticipating and resolving uncertainties in advance can serve your client well. But this suggestion does call for some careful lawyering judgment on your part. A poor use of this technique might identify problems for the reviewer that the reviewer may never have perceived on his own. You will therefore be prudent in your consideration of this tactic.

- *Be Concise*: This item may be your biggest challenge. Your first draft of your narrative, like the first draft of most documents, will be longer than it could be, and longer than it should be. Given the suggestions above, the demands of the IRS legal standards, and your particular insights about your client's project, you will have a lot to say. Your mission is to say everything you need to say, in half the space you started out saying it. Revise, edit, streamline. Have a colleague read it, and then revise, edit, and streamline again. Repeat.

D. INFORMATION–GATHERING FORMS

We now come to a topic which plays a limited, but sometimes important, role in transactional practice. It warrants some brief consideration in our taxonomy of the writing projects you may encounter. As a law-

---

[28] This consideration also affects what authorities you cite. For example, you will need to consider whether citation to a Revenue Ruling or even a Private Letter Ruling might be more persuasive to an examiner than an opinion from the Seventh Circuit Court of Appeals.

[29] *See supra* discussion at note 26.

yer for enterprises, you may be asked to create a document for the enterprise to employ to collect and assemble information it needs to perform some function. An employer may need an application for prospective employment; a nonprofit might have a protocol through which it chooses the beneficiaries of its publicly-supported programming, and it needs to screen applicants through some process. Think of scholarship applications, or screening for medical issues before a community organization's field trip for children. In these settings, your client will need from you *info gathering form* some template which will serve to solicit complete, reliable, consistent and useful information from those who complete the form.

You will now start to appreciate the challenges of creating such templates or forms. Brevity is essential, both for those who will complete the form and for those who will assemble and use the resulting information. Consistency is critical, because in most instances the form will serve *comparative* and *exclusionary* functions, through which some applicants will be chosen and others rejected. And the form needs to be reliable for users who come from different cultures and backgrounds. Unlike users of the IRS forms such as the Form 1023 discussed in the previous section, the users of the forms you create will not have the opportunity (nor the desire) to wade through some elaborate separate instructions to understand the meaning of the questions and terms. The form needs to be clear on its face.

Thinking of those goals, consider the following pointers for creating forms:

- You might start by creating, in narrative fashion, a collection of all of the information your client needs the form to elicit.

- You could then organize the collection of items by sensible headings or topics.

- You then create a first draft of the form itself, longer than it will be when you are done, but serving as a rough sketch for the form's organization.

- Perhaps using a colleague (and perhaps a colleague who knows very little about your project), review the form critically to discern ways to refine it, narrow it, make it clearer and more comprehensive. This process may lead you to *add* items as well, if you realize (as you often will) that your first draft did not elicit some important data your client needs to obtain.

- Once you have the form in reasonable satisfactory shape, search for some comparable form from some other organization or context to which to compare your product. We suggest you perform this step *after* you have done the hard work above. Otherwise, the temptation simply to borrow language from another's template may be too strong. Our sense—and we are relying purely on hunch here—is that your product will be better suited to your client's particular needs if you proceed in the order we suggest here.

- You will often have questions which fit underneath, and follow from, broader and more introductory questions. When you encounter that phenomenon, be sure that your narrowing process follows a clear, logical path. You may also find that some of your branching question formats might work better as broader narrative questions. Consider the following three examples. Note how Example 5 flows more logically than Example 4. And note also how Example 6 seeks similar information in a more narrative fashion.

Example 4

5.   Did you attend college?

     (a)   What college did you attend?

     (b)   What year did you graduate?

Example 5

5.   Did you attend college? Yes ___ No ___ If you answered "yes," please provide the following information:

     (a)   The name of each college you attended, with your years of attendance and course of study.

     (b)   If you graduated, please indicate for each school the degree you obtained.

Example 6

5.   In the space below, please describe your educational history. If you attended school beyond high school, please include (a) the name of each school you attended, (b) the subject matter of your studies at each, (c) any degrees you received, and (d) any honors you received.

Alternatively, you may produce a résumé conveying the above information.

E. CORRESPONDENCE AND OPINIONS

Thus far, each of the document types we have addressed has called for some special rhetorical or organizational quality beyond simple, expositional writing. We conclude this part of the chapter with examples of some writing you will produce in your practice which is more straightforward and, for lack of a better term, "objective." While much writing will fit this description, we think in particular of two related drafting tasks you will encounter in your work—correspondence and opinions. The two categories will often be combined. You will quite likely find yourself preparing a document—whether a formal memo, a letter, or an email—to your client where you simply aim to explain some state of affairs which you understand and which your client (as yet) does not.[30]

[handwritten: explanatory docs]

All of the goals identified in the beginning of this chapter apply to this rather straightforward task. Your note or memo to your client must be organized, clear, accurate, complete and concise. Perhaps even more so here than in the other topics we have covered, your language must be as plain and jargon-free as possible.

We offer you two additional stylistic considerations for this kind of drafting:

- In many instances, you will write to your client in such a way that a stranger will be able to understand your points from the four corners of your document. In fact, in many instances you will *presume*, while writing, that a stranger at some point in the future will read the letter, email or memo. You may find yourself including introductory clauses such as, "As you know, we have been researching whether a company might . . . ." You will include that language even if you have just hung up the telephone with your client after having discussed the very issue you write about.

[handwritten: audience]

- Related in some respects to the above, you will also attend to the following perspective in your expositional writing to your clients: If something by chance happened to go wrong in your client's transaction, and some opposing lawyer or judge were to read your communication to your client after that happenstance, how would it look? We do not intend to appear overly gloomy in this sugges-

---

[30] Of course, some important opinion writing is expressly intended for third party non-clients, especially in the transactional context. Consider, for instance, an opinion letter prepared by the seller's lawyer for the buyer in a complex transaction, confirming for the buyer certain assurances necessary for the transaction to proceed. As a matter of drafting, the writing process for that type of opinion-giving is not terribly different from that discussed in the text. Opinion letters are meant to be relatively *objective*, as opposed to slanted in an advocate's voice. The actual strategic implications of how you might prepare such a letter for a third-party's reliance is beyond the scope of our coverage here. For a treatise-length treatment of the legal opinion phenomenon, see DONALD W. GLAZER, SCOTT T. FITZGIBBON & STEVEN O. WEISE, GLAZER AND FITZGIBBON ON LEGAL OPINIONS: DRAFTING, INTERPRETING AND SUPPORTING CLOSING OPINIONS IN BUSINESS TRANSACTIONS (3d ed. 2008).

tion, but we encourage you to keep that long view in mind as you communicate legal advice and ideas in writing.[31]

IV. USEFUL WRITING CONVENTIONS

You may draft the most persuasive, precise, elegant prose for your client's project, but if the end product is sloppy or has errors, you will have undercut much of your effort. Using wrong grammar, leaving misspellings or other typographical errors, applying inconsistent formatting, misunderstanding accepted language conventions—any of these can have a visceral and sometimes powerful effect on the readers of your work. Because you may easily prevent these errors, your mission should be to present a product with no such distractions. Some of the errors are easily caught if you review your work in the proper way. Other errors may result from your misunderstanding accepted customs in English language prose. (Our experience is that many newer professionals do not know as many of the rules and conventions as they could know.) We offer some suggestions about each here.[32]

What follows is a list, no doubt an incomplete list, of the kinds of errors we most often catch, or suggestions we make, when reviewing our students' (or, occasionally, our colleagues' and our own) work.[33] Our descriptions will be brief, but a good, reliable usage guide will provide you with more specific instruction and elaboration of our points.[34]

- *Proofread your work.* This is the easiest suggestion with which to start. You should proofread carefully even informal email messages to your clients. Sloppiness, including misspellings, missed

---

[31] In our chapter on Organizing Your Transactional Work, we describe the power of "hindsight bias," which would be operative in the happenstance we describe here. See the chapter on Organizing Your Transactional Work.

[32] There is some healthy risk in attending to writing conventions, and especially in pointing out in others' work some deviations from accepted conventions. Individuals who engage in the latter activity are often referred to as "language police," "pedants," and far worse. *See* Oliver Burkeman, *This Column Will Change Your Life: The Language Police*, THE GUARDIAN (Dec. 16, 2011), http://www.guardian.co.uk/lifeandstyle/2011/dec/16/language-police-error-hunters-oliver-burkeman. In a brilliant article about this topic, the late novelist David Foster Wallace defends his being what he calls a "SNOOT." David Foster Wallace, *Authority and American Usage*, in CONSIDER THE LOBSTER AND OTHER ESSAYS 69 (2006) (reviewing BRYAN A. GARNER, A DICTIONARY OF MODERN AMERICAN USAGE (2nd ed. 2003)). As Wallace explains, SNOOT "is this reviewer's nuclear family's nickname à clef for a really extreme usage fanatic. . . . [The] term itself derives from an acronym, with the big historical family joke being that whether S.N.O.O.T. stood for 'Sprachgefühl Necessitates Our Ongoing Tendance' or 'Syntax Nudniks Of Our Time' depended on whether or not you were one." *Id.*

[33] We noted just above that our students sometimes do not know enough of the accepted rules and customs of proper writing. Of course, our understanding of those conventions is also imperfect, and we may not appreciate the places where we also have misunderstood a rule or custom. As a reader of this work, do not hesitate to tell us about any such errors you see in our writing. We expect to have future editions of this text, and we can always learn more about this topic. For very apparent reasons, we need to know if we are overlooking some rule or custom.

[34] A few usage guides tend to have the broadest loyalty. *See, e.g.,* THE CHICAGO MANUAL OF STYLE (16th ed. 2010); BRYAN A. GARNER, DICTIONARY OF MODERN LEGAL USAGE (2d ed. 2003); DIANA HACKER, RULES FOR WRITERS (5th ed. 2004).

words, mistaken words, etc., leave such a powerful impression on readers.[35] Of course, as you know, simply relying on Spell Check is not sufficient, both because Spell Check might leave a correctly spelled but unintended word in place, but also because the function on occasion suggests the wrong word when fixing a misspelled word.

The other challenge with proofreading is that we all find it difficult to review our own work objectively. We fill in what we intended to write when reviewing what we did write. For important documents, ask a colleague to read your draft, and/or read each line separately, using a ruler, and out loud.

- *Use the active voice.* Observers readily note the crispness and clarity that accompanies the active voice. Experienced readers instinctively recognize passive voice, and that recognition will be distracting. On occasion you will have some strategic reason to use passive voice, for instance to soften a chain of responsibility, but most of the time you will benefit from changing your sentences to the active voice. *[handwritten: Active voice]*

- *Watch for subject-verb correspondence.* We confidently predict that this is the distraction you will struggle most frequently, and with the greatest puzzlement. Your drafts will include sentences like, "Each officer will complete their full term until their successor has been appointed." "Each officer" is singular; "their" is plural. The sentence therefore contains what many understand to be a grammatical error. You may correct this very common habit in one of four ways: (1) you may use "his or her" throughout, which is more accurate but, admittedly, inelegant; (2) you may use a plural noun ("all officers") to start, if the context permits; (3) you may use one gender (say, "her") and include a boilerplate definition in your document confirming that "her" means "his or her" throughout (that option only works with certain kinds of guidance or contract documents, but not with persuasive documents); or (4) you may rewrite the sentence to avoid having any such correspondence. Our students (and we) grapple with this challenge repeatedly. And, while much of the world may use "their" as a singular modifier,[36] it still is the wrong convention. Or, at least, many readers will think so.[37]

---

[35] We have heard often from law firm partners who have emphasized this point regarding the work of the firm's newer associates. That fact may be very important for you to know.

[36] Here is one favorite example: On the popular and entertaining weekly National Public Radio show "Wait, Wait, Don't Tell Me," the host invites callers to play a game on the radio. Each week he tells the audience, "The lucky contestant will get Carl Kassel's voice on their home voice mail or answering machine." (Kassel is a venerable NPR newscaster.)

[37] The use of "they" or "their" as a singular modifier is in fact the subject of considerable, and quite interesting and sometimes heated, debate among the language mavens. *See, e.g.,* Bry-

- *Keep your formatting consistent.* Your document will likely include headings, subheadings, sub-subheadings, and so forth. It is common for drafts to fail to keep the formats consistent across the various levels of the document. If you are using italics, or bold, or capitals, or large and small capitals, or various indentations, check to ensure that you apply the formats the same way in equivalent sections of your document.

- *Watch for common grammar, custom, and punctuation errors.* Small misunderstandings of conventions and of the rules of grammar and punctuation can serve as distractions to your readers. Understanding the most common mistakes can serve as a subtle but real indication that you know how to write. We list here ten of the most common errors we see in others' writing, so you may avoid them in yours.

  1) *Quotation marks* go outside commas and periods, always, without exception, unless you write in Great Britain. They go inside semicolons, however.

  2) A *closing parenthesis* ends outside the period if the opening parenthesis started at the beginning of the sentence; it ends inside the period if its corresponding item appears in the middle of the sentence. Consider the following two examples. (In this setting the parentheses will end after the period.) If we included the opening parenthesis in the middle of the sentence, the result would look like this (as you well know).

  3) *Skip a line* between single-spaced paragraphs when typing in Microsoft Word or the Mac equivalent.

  4) *Use em-dashes*, and not hyphens, to separate clauses in sentences. An em-dash—which you will see on either end of this inserted clause here—is the proper device for this purpose. A hyphen distracts the reader, as its intended use is to combine two words into one term.[38]

  5) *Beware of noun-verbs*, and especially beware of using "impact" as a verb. Most style authorities frown on the use of "impact" as a verb, and for readers familiar with

"Text."

---

an A. Garner, *Garner's Usage Tip of the Day: Sexism (4),* LAW PROSE (Aug. 2, 2012), http://www.lawprose.org/blog/?p=502.

[38] You may use an *en-dash* instead of an em-dash if you prefer. An en-dash is shorter than an em-dash but longer than a hyphen. So, the choices you have available include the often-misused hyphen (see what just passed by in the middle of that adjectival phrase), the sometimes-used en-dash – showing up on either end of this phrase – or the more common em-dash—as we have now just typed so you may see what it looks like and compare it to the en-dash.

that well-accepted rule, its appearance can be quite annoying. No harm in avoiding it just to be safe.

6) *Be careful with split infinitives.* The old "rule" was never to split infinitives. (A split infinitive would insert a modifier between "to" and the verb—as in, "The old 'rule' was to never split infinitives.") Most authorities now recognize that in some contexts a split infinitive is much smoother than following the old rule. But readers still note this phenomenon, so avoid splitting your infinitives in any situation where you may comfortably follow the old rule.

7) *Do not separate independent clauses with a comma when using "however."* Many writers use "however" as a link between two independent thoughts within one sentence. If you happen to do that, separate the two parts of the sentence with a semicolon, not a comma, or use two sentences. It is common to encounter sentences like the following: "Nonprofit organizations often choose to be governed by a board of directors, however some prefer to authorize members to make the important decisions for the organization." The two independent clauses of that sentence should be separated by a semicolon, not a comma.

8) *Watch for common misused words and phrases.* Among the most common mistaken words or phrases we see or hear are these (in each instance the second is the correct one): "hone in" instead of "home in"; "different than" for "different from"; "jive" instead of "jibe"; and "hopefully" instead of "with hope" or something communicating that message.[39]

9) *Use "that" and "which" correctly.* Actually, we have never been able to figure this one out satisfactorily ourselves, but some readers understand the rule and are distracted by its misapplication. The rule is simple to state: "that" introduces a restrictive clause, and "which" introduces a nonrestrictive clause. It is often difficult to apply, however. Consider these two examples: "The president may reschedule a board meeting that ad-

---

[39] The use of "hopefully" is the subject of the same kind of debate, in the same circles, as the use of "they" and "their" as singular words. *See, e.g.,* GARNER, *supra* note 34, at 407 ("So much has been written of this word that little can be added here except to suggest striking this word from your vocabulary"); Lynn Gaertner–Johnson, *"Hopefully" Gets Upgrade at AP*, BUSINESS WRITING (Apr. 18, 2012), http://www.businesswritingblog.com/business_writing/2012/04/hopefully-gets-upgrade-at-ap-.html (reporting that the Associated Press Stylebook has upgraded the use of the term to "acceptable").

journs without a quorum." "The June, 2012 board meeting, which took place in the morning, adjourned without a quorum." The former sentence restricts the board meetings described in the sentence; the latter does not.

10) *Attend to your commas*.[40] Misplaced commas can and will be a distraction to your readers. We do not presume to cover the many rules about commas in this primer, but we do offer two small suggestions, based on many edits we have made over the years. First, when using commas surrounding an internal clause in a sentence, consider this: What would the sentence look like if the whole phrase were removed from the sentence? The resulting remaining sentence should be a complete, coherent sentence. Your commas should serve in effect as a set of parentheses.[41]

Second, do not assume that you need a comma merely because the subject of your sentence covers many words. (You may prefer to rewrite the subject's description to avoid this issue, but that is a separate matter.) We often see writers offering something like the following: "The fact that an entrepreneur operates her business without insurance while using employees and independent operators to perform essential functions, is an important consideration in her consideration of purchasing an insurance policy." Putting aside the inelegance of the sentence, our point is that the comma does not fit where you just saw it.

---

[40] With this suggestion we respectfully disagree with the band Vampire Weekend, who sing, "Who gives a fuck about an Oxford comma?" VAMPIRE WEEKEND, *Oxford Comma, on* VAMPIRE WEEKEND (XL Recordings 2008). Actually (as you may have noticed in this book), we do not necessarily adhere to the Oxford comma convention itself, but we do care a lot about using commas in a way that ensures clarity. The Oxford comma, sometimes known as the "serial comma," is the convention which includes a comma immediately before the "and" or "or" in a list of nouns. So if we write "Boston College, Michigan, and Yale are among the top law schools in the country," we have used the Oxford comma. If we were to write, "The Red Sox, White Sox and Cubs had disappointing endings to the 2012 baseball season," we would not be using the Oxford comma. Both conventions are acceptable, it seems. *See* Linda Holms, *Monkey See: Going, Going, And Gone?: No, The Oxford Comma Is Safe . . . For Now*, NATIONAL PUBLIC RADIO (June 30, 2011), http://www.npr.org/blogs/monkeysee/2011/06/30/137525211/going-going-and-gone-no-the-oxford-comma-is-safe-for-now.

[41] Here's an example. In an earlier part of this chapter we originally wrote the following sentence: "You need to know the terms you will include in the agreement, but those terms will be the subject of some, or even a lot, of bargaining between you and the landlord's attorney." See what happens when you remove the parenthetical clause marked by the last two commas.

CHAPTER 7

MULTICULTURAL LAWYERING AND CULTURAL COMPETENCE

■ ■ ■

In this chapter we discuss the importance of paying attention to differences between you and your clients. We believe it is important to acknowledge these differences, recognize how they influence the lawyer-client relationship and work toward bridging some of these differences. We believe awareness is an important component of working with clients who are different from us, but that we cannot stop at awareness. This chapter will provide some concepts to help you approach your cross-cultural work; however, we will not provide a recipe for how to bridge those differences. There are no easy recipes in this work, which is what makes it challenging yet interesting. We hope to raise your awareness of some of the issues that affect our relationships with other human beings. We believe understanding the communities our clients work in and come from is an important part of this work. In that sense, cross-cultural lawyering will involve work on your part that we cannot introduce to you in this chapter. *You* will have to get to know the particular client and specific community and context in which you and your clients work. As a result, you will need to continue some of the concepts we introduced to you in the Interviewing chapter, such as getting to know and understand the work of your clients, their business and industries. That work will include their point of view about creating change in their communities.

In this chapter, we will introduce you to some of the concepts of culture and cultural competence. We will define culture from multiple perspectives, drawing on work from other disciplines, especially sociology and anthropology. We take an expansive view of culture, not limiting ourselves to individuals from other countries. We will discuss research from social psychology (which we have discussed in the Organizing Your Work, Counseling and Negotiation chapters) to understand why all lawyers have work to do when it comes to cultural competence. We then move to discuss sociopolitical aspects of culture, including questions of power and privilege. We end the chapter by discussing some techniques for becoming more conscious of differences and similarities between us and our clients, understanding how those similarities and differences affect the lawyer-client relationship and your work on behalf of your clients, and better understanding and bridging the differences. This discussion will draw from the rich literature on multi-cultural counseling in psychology and social work.

In her seminal article on cross-cultural lawyering, Michelle Jacobs is critical of lawyer training in working across difference.[1] While the client-centered model of lawyering recognizes the importance of lawyer-client interaction in decision-making, it fails to address "the effects of race, class and . . . gender on the interactions between lawyer and client."[2] Clients come to lawyers with their own narrative and different sets of expectations based on their cultural experiences and personal values.[3] Jacobs argues against a "race neutral" training of lawyers because it fails to recognize that the lawyer and the client each bring a context to the relationship.[4] True client-centered lawyering requires that we look at clients (and ourselves) "culturally, politically and economically."[5] We otherwise risk disregarding who the client really is.[6] Michelle Jacobs calls on each of us as lawyers to examine 1) our unconscious racism and cultural bias and how they may affect our relationship with our client and 2) how our client's cultural experience and internalization of microaggressions affect the client's view of the relationship not just with the lawyer but with law itself (including the legal system and legal institutions).[7]

In working across difference, the challenge is remaining open to difference (and explaining some of our reactions or our clients' reactions as relating to our differences) without stereotyping our clients. In these instances we have to proceed from the perspective of *informed not-knowing*.[8] Our hope is that this chapter will both inform you and make you more comfortable with not knowing.

I. WHAT DO WE MEAN BY CULTURE?

The word "culture" is often conceived in terms of geography. In this chapter we define the concept of culture in broader terms. Culture is the unique character of social groups, "the values and norms shared by its members that set it apart 'from other social groups."[9] Culture refers to

---

[1] Michelle S. Jacobs, *People from the Footnotes: The Missing Element in Client-Centered Counseling*, 27 GOLDEN GATE U. L. REV. 345 (1997).

[2] *Id.* at 346.

[3] *Id.* at 348.

[4] *Id.* at 348–49.

[5] *Id.* at 352.

[6] *Id.* at 361.

[7] *Id.* at 377. For a discussion of microaggressions, see *infra* Section II.D.

[8] Paul R. Tremblay, *Interviewing and Counseling Across Cultures: Heuristics and Biases*, 9 CLINICAL L. REV. 373, 382 (2002); Paul R. Tremblay & Carwina Weng, *Multicultural Lawyering: Heuristics and Biases, in* THE AFFECTIVE ASSISTANCE OF COUNSEL 150, 153 (Marjorie A. Silver ed., 2007).

[9] LEIGH L. THOMPSON, THE MIND AND HEART OF THE NEGOTIATOR 253 (5th ed. 2012) (citing Anne L. Lytle, Jeanne M. Brett, & Debra L. Shapiro, *The Strategic Use of Interests, Rights and Power to Resolve Disputes*, 15 NEGOT. J. 31 (1999)).

the "knowledge, values and beliefs shared in a society or community."[10] It is the sum of inter-generationally transmitted lifestyle ways, behavior patterns and products of a people that includes language, music, art, artifacts, interpersonal styles, habits, history, eating preferences, customs and social rules.[11] Cultures exist in a specific time in history; they are not static but fluid and in flux.[12] Cultures are "neither timeless nor changeless."[13] But culture is situated in and defined by a particular society.

Culture "organizes and is constituted by beliefs, norms, behaviors and institutional practices."[14] These values, beliefs and symbols make up "the framework through which members interpret and attribute meaning to both their own and others' experiences and behavior."[15] Culture is a quality of social groups and communities. Culture is made up of several dimensions and in that sense is a "complex whole."[16] Since each of us belongs to multiple groups and thereby several cultures, "culture always comes 'in the plural.'"[17] As a result, "interaction . . . between individuals is likely to be multicultural on several levels."[18] In addition, culture is "rarely, if ever, perfectly shared by all members of a group or community."[19] Thus, we cannot assume that because we share some characteristics with another person (even several characteristics for that matter) she is likely to share the same values, attitudes and beliefs as we may have. Psychologists ascertain that each of us has three levels of identity—1) individual (uniqueness); 2) group (shared cultural values and beliefs); and 3) universal (those common features of being human).[20] Even within a group, individuals vary greatly in their levels of cultural identity, acculturation and enculturation.[21]

---

[10] Michael Wylie, *Enhancing Legal Counseling in Cross-Cultural Settings*, 15 WINDSOR Y. B. ACCESS JUST. 47, 48 (1996). Others define culture as "shared meanings, beliefs, values, and symbols that accounts for patterns of interpersonal/intergroup behaviour within a specific community." *Id.* (citing AUGIE FLERAS & JEAN LEONARD ELLIOTT, MULTICULTURALISM IN CANADA 314 (1992)). Still others define it as a "'system of knowledge' that is shared by a large group of people." Id. (citing WILLIAM GUDYKUNST, BRIDGING DIFFERENCES 44 (1991)).

[11] Frederick D. Harper, *Background: Concepts and History, in* CULTURE AND COUNSELING: NEW APPROACHES 1 (Frederick D. Harper & John McFadden eds., 2003).

[12] *Id.*

[13] Kevin Avruch, *Culture as Context, Culture as Communication: Considerations for Humanitarian Negotiators*, 9 HARV. NEGOT. L. REV. 391, 400 (2004).

[14] Howard Gadlin, *Conflict Resolution, Cultural Differences and the Culture of Racism*, 10 NEGOT. J. 33, 35 (1994).

[15] Avruch, *supra* note 13, at 393.

[16] THOMPSON, *supra* note 9, at 254.

[17] Avruch, *supra* note 13, at 393.

[18] *Id.*

[19] *Id.*

[20] DERALD WING SUE & DAVID SUE, COUNSELING THE CULTURALLY DIVERSE: THEORY & PRACTICE 45, 41–44 (6th ed. 2013).

[21] GARRETT MCAULIFFE & ASSOCIATES, CULTURALLY ALERT COUNSELING: A COMPREHENSIVE INTRODUCTION 574 (2008) (citing DAVID MATSUMOTO & LINDA JUANG, CULTURE AND PSYCHOLOGY (2004)).

Culture has also been equated with an "iceberg" in the shape of a pyramid or triangle.[22] The part of the iceberg that is visible to us (one of the points in the triangle) constitutes traditions, customs, habits, behavior, artifacts and institutions of that culture.[23] The part just below the surface is comprised of norms, beliefs, values and attitudes and is "fairly easily accessible to sensitive observers."[24] Invisible even to members of the group are "the fundamental assumptions and presuppositions, the sense-and-meaning-making schemas and symbols . . . about the world and the individuals' experience with it."[25] These "fundamental assumptions about the world and humanity" are the drivers behind the values and norms.[26] Culture gives us a context through which we understand how the world works; it gives us the cognitive and affective frameworks for interpreting our own behavior and motives and those of others.[27]

Culture is thus not merely the property of national, ethnic, racial or religious groups, the "usual 'containers' for culture."[28] Organizations, institutions, and professions or occupations, including our own legal profession, are also containers for culture and sites for cultural differences.[29] In that sense, all lawyering is in some ways cross-cultural. The law itself is a "culture with strong professional norms that give meaning and reinforce behaviors."[30] Being a lawyer involves similar tasks, comparable experiences (during three years of law school and in practice) and comparable organizational views.[31] Some of the attributes of this culture include a communication style in which argument predominates, a high value on competition,[32] a particular way of organizing ideas, conversation and describing events, and the predominance of a particular form of linear, analytical thinking which involves rules and categories.[33]

Profession and many other things (groups) can shape culture

---

[22] Avruch, *supra* note 13, at 394; THOMPSON, *supra* note 9, at 254 (citing WENDELL L. FRENCH & CECIL H. BELL, ORGANIZATION DEVELOPMENT: BEHAVIORAL SCIENCE IN INTERVENTIONS FOR ORGANIZATION IMPROVEMENT 18 (1923)).

[23] Avruch, *supra* note 13, at 394.

[24] *Id.*

[25] *Id.*

[26] THOMPSON, *supra* note 9, at 254.

[27] Avruch, *supra* note 13, at 395–96.

[28] *Id.* at 398.

[29] THOMPSON, *supra* note 9, at 254.

[30] Sue Bryant & Jean Koh Peters, *Five Habits for Cross-Cultural Lawyering, in* RACE, CULTURE, PSYCHOLOGY, & LAW 47 (Kimberly Holt Barrett & William H. George eds., 2005). *See also* Russell G. Pearce, *White Lawyering: Rethinking Race, Lawyer Identity, and the Rule of Law*, 73 FORDHAM L. REV. 2081, 2084 (2005) (calling professional socialization as a lawyer an "organizational group identification").

[31] Pearce, *supra* note 30, at 2084 (citing Russell G. Pearce, *Jewish Lawyering in a Multicultural Society: A Midrash on Levinson*, 14 CARDOZO L. REV. 1613, 1632 (1993)).

[32] Bryant & Koh Peters, *supra* note 30, at 47.

[33] *See* Susan Bryant, *The Five Habits: Building Cross-Cultural Competence in Lawyers*, 8 CLINICAL L. REV. 33, 84–85 (2002). *See also* Carla Boutin-Foster, Jordan Foster & Lyuba Konopasek, *Physician, Know Thyself: The Professional Culture of Medicine as a Framework for Teaching Cultural Competence*, 83 ACAD. MED. 106 (2008) (discussing elements of medical cul-

While we may be socialized in the lawyering culture, our membership in some groups, such as educational, socioeconomic, institutional, is more fluid and changeable. No one identity is likely to define a person. But though we belong to more than one cultural group, for each person some group identities may be more salient than others.[34]

II. WHAT IS CULTURAL COMPETENCE AND WHY IS IT IMPORTANT?

In this section, we will discuss why cultural competence is important, what cultural competence might look like and barriers to cultural competence. We begin by talking about why we think this work is important for lawyers.

A. WHY IS CULTURAL COMPETENCE IMPORTANT?

As we wrote in the Interviewing chapter, client-relations skills are an important component of the work of the lawyer. Certainly, a lawyer needs legal knowledge. But a lawyer needs to be able to deal with clients if he is going to be retained and if the clients are going to be satisfied with his work.[35] Studies have found that clients whose case managers were more sensitive to cross-cultural issues have more positive experiences with the services they received and the persons working with them.[36] Trust is an important component of the attorney-client relationship. Cross-cultural communication affects client trust of the lawyer and the ability of the client to fully participate in the lawyer-client relationship.[37]

Cultural competence is an important client-relations skill for three principal reasons. First, you are likely to encounter difference in your lawyering relationships constantly, including your clients, other lawyers with whom you come into contact, and decision-makers with whom you will interact. Second, lawyers need to be able to deal with an increasingly diverse and connected world. As the U.S. is becoming increasingly diverse, lawyers must confront this increasing complexity even considering only diversity in the context of race and ethnicity. By the middle of the

---

ture such as the white coat, physician's explanatory model and doctor talk, including use of acronyms, depersonalizing the patient by referring to him as baby boy, not mentioning the provider of care and using the technology as the agent).

[34] SUE & SUE, *supra* note 20, at 43.

[35] *See* Carolyn Copps Hartley & Carrie J. Petrucci, *Practicing Culturally Competent Therapeutic Jurisprudence: A Collaboration Between Social Work and Law*, 14 WASH. U. J. L. & POL'Y 133, 160-61 (2004) (citing to studies where clients ranked lawyers who had received client-relations skills training higher than those who had not).

[36] *Id.* at 169 (citing Sharron M. Singleton-Bowie, *The Effect of Mental Health Practitioners' Racial Sensitivity on African Americans' Perspective of Services*, 19 SOC. WORK RES. 238, 242 (1995)). *See also* Jacobs, *supra* note 1, at 390.

[37] Jacobs, *supra* note 1, at 388–89 (discussing studies of African-American clients in counseling relationships where counselors were not able to develop rapport with the client).

21st century, the U.S. is projected to become a plurality nation, with no one racial or ethnic group in the majority.[38] The U.S. will become the first major post-industrial society in the world where "minorities will be the majority."[39] Depending on where you live, practice or intend to practice, you may already live in a state or metropolitan area that is majority minority.[40] In addition to the diversity in our own country, we are likely to come into contact with people from other countries. Globalization has meant that our economies are becoming more inter-connected, with businesses operating on a global basis.[41] We *will* encounter others who are different from us. Third, by becoming better at dealing with difference and working across difference, we become better communicators. The skills involving in developing our cross-cultural capacities are the skills of better communicators. By becoming better communicators we become better lawyers and better human beings, benefiting our clients and the rest of society.

B. WHAT IS A CULTURALLY COMPETENT LAWYER?

A culturally competent lawyer is one who is able and willing to acknowledge how race, ethnicity, gender and other group dimensions may influence identity, values, behaviors and the perception of reality for himself and his client. While we define culture broadly (including socioeconomic status, sexual orientation and gender identity, and ability/disability), we acknowledge that race, prejudice, racial discrimination and systemic racial oppression play an important role in U.S. history and society.

A culturally competent lawyer is one who 1) is actively in the process of becoming aware of his assumptions about human behavior, values, biases, and preconceived notions and how those affect his relationship with clients and others in his work; 2) actively tries to understand the worldview of his client, including her beliefs, values, biases, assumptions about human behavior and how those affect the lawyer-client relationship and the nature of the work that the lawyer and client are involved in to-

---

[38] Press Release, United States Census Bureau, U.S. Census Bureau Projections Show A Slower Growing, Older, More Diverse Nation a Half Century from Now (Dec. 12, 2012), *available at* http://www.census.gov/newsroom/releases/archives/population/cb12-243.html. By 2060, Whites are projected to be 43% of the U.S. population; Latinos are projected to make up 31% of the population; African Americans are projected to make up 14.7% of the population; and Asians are projected to make up 8% of the population. *Id.*

[39] *Id.*

[40] As of early 2013, when we write this, four states (Hawai'i, California, New Mexico and Texas) and the District of Columbia have minority populations that exceed 50% of the total population. Press Release, U.S. Census Bureau, Most Children Younger than Age 1 are Minorities (May 17, 2012), *available at* http://www.census.gov/newsroom/releases/archives/population/cb12-90.html.

[41] Marina Primorac, *The Global Village: Connected World Drives Economic Shift*, INT'L MONETARY FUND (Aug. 30, 2012), *available at* http://www.imf.org/external/pubs/ft/survey/so/2012/new083012a.htm.

gether; and 3) is in the process of actively developing strategies and skills for working with culturally diverse clients.[42]   Understanding our client's worldview may mean understanding the communities in which she lives and works.

We can try to understand the experience of our clients even when they differ from us.   Empathy, which we discussed in the Interviewing chapter, helps us understand others.[43]   Psychologists Derald Sue and David Sue differentiate between cognitive and affective empathy so that while we may not have lived a lifetime as a person of color, a woman, a lesbian, gay, bisexual or transgender person, or a person with a disability, we may acquire "practical knowledge concerning the scope and nature of the client's cultural background, daily living experience, hopes, fears, and aspirations."[44]   This cognitive empathy includes understanding the "wider sociopolitical system with which minorities contend every day of their lives."[45]   We think of cultural competence in lawyering as "the awareness, knowledge and skills needed to function effectively in a pluralistic democratic society."[46]

Empathy

Cultural competence entails awareness, attitude, knowledge and skills.[47]   At the level of awareness, cultural competence requires that we be aware of our own cultural heritage, be aware of our values and biases, be comfortable with the differences that exist between us and our clients, and value and respect those differences.[48]   As one anthropologist recognizes, there is "a great distance between knowing that my gaze transforms and becoming aware of the ways that my gaze transforms."[49]   Awareness is the beginning but we must go further.   At the level of knowledge, cultural competence requires that we be knowledgeable and informed about culturally diverse groups and the historical treatment of those groups; and that we understand concepts of bias and prejudice at both the individual and societal level.   Finally, at the skills level, cultural competence requires that we be able to communicate accurately, effectively and appropriately with diverse clients.

awareness,

openness

knowledge

Communication

---

[42] SUE & SUE, *supra* note 20, at 48.

[43] Psychologist Lillian Comas-Díaz refers to "cultural empathy" as the ability to connect with the client's cultural orientations while being able to acknowledge similarities and differences. LILLIAN COMAS-DÍAZ, MULTICULTURAL CARE: A CLINICIAN'S GUIDE TO CULTURAL COMPETENCE 4, 140 (2012).

[44] *Id.* at 48–49.

[45] *Id.* at 49.

[46] SUE & SUE, *supra* note 20, at 49 (citing Derald Wing Sue & Gina C. Torino, *Racial Cultural Competence: Awareness, Knowledge and Skills, in* HANDBOOK OF MULTICULTURAL PSYCHOLOGY AND COUNSELING 3–18 (Robert T. Carter ed., 2005)).

[47] COMAS-DÍAZ, *supra* note 43, at 23.   *See also* SUE & SUE, *supra* note 19, at 49–50; Jacobs, *supra* note 1, at 409–10.

[48] SUE & SUE, *supra* note 20, at 50.

[49] Bryant & Koh Peters, *supra* note 30, at 47 (quoting RAYMONDE CARROLL, CULTURAL MISUNDERSTANDINGS: THE FRENCH-AMERICAN EXPERIENCE 3 (1988)).

While we like others to see us as unique and complex, we sometimes view others as one dimensional, defining them by reference to their most visible characteristic. The more we recognize the complexity of human experience and identity, the more we are able to understand those individuals we perceive as different.[50] Psychologist Pamela Hays has created a mnemonic ADDRESSING to understand the complexity of identity and "multiple memberships":[51]

A=Age. What are the age-related issues and generational influences on this person? Children, adolescents and elders are minority in our culture.

D=Development Disability. What is this person's experience with developmental disability?

D=Disabilities acquired later in life. For both Ds, might she have a disability that is not immediately apparent? Might she have experienced the impact of disability as a caregiver for a child, parent or partner?

R=Religion. What is her religious upbringing and what are her current religious or spiritual beliefs and practices? How might those beliefs and practices influence the work you are to do together? The client might come from a religious minority culture.

E=Ethnic or racial identity. Does this person identify with a racial or ethnic minority? What might it mean to be a member of a racial/ethnic minority where she lives or works? We include skin color here as well.

S=Socioeconomic status. What is her current socioeconomic status defined by her occupation, income, education, marital status, gender, ethnicity, community and family income? Might this status be different from that of her parents? If she is an immigrant is her current status different from that before immigration?

S=Sexual orientation. What is her sexual orientation?

I=Indigenous heritage. Is she from an indigenous community in the U.S. or elsewhere? If she is an immigrant, is that part of her national identity?

---

[50] PAMELA A. HAYS, ADDRESSING CULTURAL COMPLEXITIES IN PRACTICE 6 (2d ed. 2008) (citing Gary W. Harper, Nadine Jernewall & Maria C. Zea, *Giving Voice to Emerging Science and Theory for Lesbian, Gay and Bisexual People of Color*, 10 CULTURAL DIVERSITY & ETHNIC MINORITY PSYCHOL. 187 (2004); Gregory A. Hinrichsen, *Why Multicultural Issues Matter for Practitioners Working with Older Adults*, 37 PROFESSIONAL PSYCHOLOGY: RES. & PRAC. 29 (2006); Pamela T. Reid, *Multicultural Psychology: Bringing Together Gender and Ethnicity*, 8 CULTURAL DIVERSITY AND ETHNIC MINORITY PSYCHOL. 103 (2002)).

[51] HAYS, *supra* note 50, at 7, 18.

N=National identity. Is she an immigrant, refugee, international student? What is her national identity and primary language? Does she have an accent?

G=Gender identity. What is her gender identity?

This framework can help us become aware of those aspects of our own and a client's multiple identities that might influence our relationship and life experiences. Not all these identities might be relevant for us or our client. In addition, we or our clients may have other identities.[52]

Several commentators identify three important characteristics of cultural competence—humility, charity and veracity.[53] Humility helps us to avoid judging others as less than or inferior to us.[54] Humble lawyers are realistic about what they have to offer, aware of their own limitations (and the limitations of legal solutions) and are accepting of the contributions of others.[55] Charity, defined as having compassion toward others, allows us to work with and appreciate people who challenge our beliefs and values. Veracity is the ability to see things as they are.[56] Critical thinking, which can guide us toward truths, helps us to continually challenge our assumptions and helps us look for explanations that go beyond the obvious.[57] Critical thinking allows us to identify and challenge assumptions, "examine contextual influences . . . and imagine and explore alternatives."[58]

Before discussing practices for becoming better cross-cultural lawyers, we believe it is essential that we consider some barriers to understanding differences between us and our clients and the social implications of those differences. First, we explore social psychology ideas of how we categorize others whom we see as different from us. Second, and related to those categories we form, we discuss the social manifestations of that categorization. We begin discussing cognitive psychology concepts of prejudice and stereotyping and then discus concepts of privilege.

---

[52] These might include marital status, physical characteristics, role in family, birth order, or other characteristics. Bryant & Koh Peters, *supra* note 30, at 48.

[53] HAYS, *supra* note 50, at 21. Pamela Hays points out that these are virtues shared by the major religions as well as spiritual traditions. *Id.*

[54] *See* Marci Seville, *Chinese Soup, Good Horses, and Other Narratives, in* VULNERABLE POPULATIONS AND TRANSFORMATIVE LAW TEACHING: A CRITICAL READER 284 (Society of American Law Teachers and Golden Gate University School of Law eds., 2011) (referring to Shauna Marshall's reflection that she needed to find humility by listening, observing and reading in order to gain cultural competence). *See also* Tremblay & Weng, *supra* note 8, at 149; COMAS-DÍAZ, *supra* note 43, at 5 (defining cultural humility as the "lifelong commitment to develop empowering relationships through self-evaluation and self-critique" (citations omitted)).

[55] HAYS, *supra* note 50, at 29.

[56] *Id.* at 21.

[57] *Id.* at 21, 29.

[58] *Id.* at 29 (citing STEPHEN D. BROOKFIELD, DEVELOPING CRITICAL THINKERS: CHALLENGING ADULTS TO EXPLORE ALTERNATIVE WAYS OF THINKING AND ACTING (1987)).

C. SOME BARRIERS TO BECOMING A CULTURALLY COMPETENT LAWYER

As with the process of becoming a better lawyer, we believe becoming a culturally competent lawyer is a lifetime process. Becoming a culturally competent lawyer is a developmental process of becoming a better communicator. It requires respect and curiosity, interest in learning about other people, their perspective and their life experiences, being open to learning (including from other disciplines) and effort. Becoming a culturally competent lawyer is an aspirational process rather than one that is achieved.[59] This process requires more than having an open mind or genuinely believing we harbor no prejudice. Psychology teaches us that we all have work to do in this area.

Barriers

Social psychologists have found that "the behavior of human beings is often guided by racial and other stereotypes of which they are completely unaware."[60] Those stereotypes begin with the individual's tendency to create categories but are given meaning by the society's construction of meaning, for example that of race. Those of us living in the U.S. "share a common historical and cultural heritage in which racism has played and still plays a dominant role."[61] In that sense, racial differences are "as much a reflection of our common culture as they are of the cultural differences among the various racial and ethnic" groups.[62] We therefore share many ideas, attitudes and beliefs that attach significance to an individual's race, which induce negative feelings and opinions about non-Whites, and about which we are unaware.[63] A large part of our behavior is "influenced by unconscious racial motivation."[64] The human mind defends against this guilt by denying or refusing to recognize those ideas. As a result, the mind excludes this racism from our consciousness.[65] The individual, therefore, is unaware of the "ubiquitous presence of a cultural stereotype."[66]

Stereotypes

We introduced you to some cognitive psychology research in the Organizing Your Work, Counseling and Negotiation chapters. We will introduce you to other concepts of social psychology in the chapter on Working with Groups. We introduce you to other cognitive psychology concepts

---

[59] SUE & SUE, *supra* note 20, at 48.

[60] Gary Blasi, *Advocacy Against the Stereotype: Lessons from Cognitive Social Psychology*, 49 UCLA L. REV. 1241, 1243 (2002).

[61] Charles Lawrence, *The Id, the Ego and Equal Protection: Reckoning with Unconscious Racism*, 39 STAN. L. REV. 317, 322 (1987).

[62] Gadlin, *supra* note 14, at 38.

[63] Lawrence, *supra* note 61, at 322. We discuss racism *infra* in Section II.D.

[64] *Id.*

[65] *Id.* at 323.

[66] *Id.*

in this chapter as a starting point to talking about issues of prejudice.[67] Social cognition theory informs our discussion by providing three important points. First, cognitive theory demonstrates that all people use categories "to simplify the task of perceiving, processing, and retaining information about people in memory."[68] Categorizing objects and people is essential to normal cognitive functioning. Second, stereotypes bias our intergroup judgment and decision-making.[69] Third, stereotypes are beyond the reach of the individual's self-awareness so that we do not have access to our own cognitive processes.[70] Cognitive bias may be both unconscious and unintentional.[71] These implicit biases are not reflected in explicit self-reported measures.[72]

Categorization as natural instinct

As we discuss in the Negotiation chapter, the human brain creates categories in order to allow us to simplify the information we receive and act on that less-than-perfect information.[73] We create these categories or schemas[74] out of necessity, as a way to simplify the stimuli and data stream of information we have to process.[75] In that sense categories are "guardians against complexity."[76] In order to categorize we must decide that a stimulus object is "both equivalent to other stimuli in the same category and different from stimulus objects not in that category."[77] It appears that we create a mental prototype of the "typical" category member.[78] We seem to match the object that we perceive with the prototype for that category and determine the distance between the two.[79] When we need to make a decision, a "salient aspect of that event or situation will activate a relevant schema."[80] Once activated, the "schema

---

[67] A number of law review articles that focus on constitutional equal protection, employment discrimination, and jury deliberation jurisprudence summarize the social psychology literature on implicit bias. For a listing of some of them, see Seville, *supra* note 54, at 295, n. 25. *See also* Kim Taylor-Thompson, *Empty Votes in Jury Deliberations*, 113 HARV. L. REV. 1261, 1290–95 (2000).

[68] Linda Hamilton Krieger, *The Content of Our Categories: A Cognitive Bias Approach to Discrimination and Equal Employment Opportunity*, 47 STAN. L. REV. 1161, 1188 (1995).

[69] *Id.*

[70] *Id.*

[71] *Id.*

[72] Jerry Kang, *Trojan Horses of Race*, 118 HARV. L. REV. 1489, 1494 (2005).

[73] Krieger, *supra* note 68, at 1188.

[74] A schema is a "cognitive structure that represents knowledge about a concept or type of stimulus, including the attributes and the relations among those attributes." Kang, *supra* note 72, at 1498 (citing SUSAN T. FISKE & SHELLEY E. TAYLOR, SOCIAL COGNITION 98 (2d ed. 1991)).

[75] *Id.* at 1498–99.

[76] Krieger, *supra* note 68, at 1189.

[77] *Id.*

[78] *Id.* at 1189 (citing Eleanor Rosch, *Principles of Categorization, in* COGNITION AND CATEGORIZATION 1, 35–38 (Eleanor Rosch & Barbara B. Floyd eds., 1978); Nancy Cantor & Walter Mischel, *Prototypes in Person Perception, in* 12 ADVANCES IN EXPERIMENTAL SOCIAL PSYCHOLOGY 2, 28–31 (Leonard Berkowitz ed., 1979)).

[79] *Id.*

[80] *Id.* at 1190.

influences the interpretation, encoding, and organizing of incoming information."[81] These schemas allow us to identify stimuli quickly, to fill in missing information and decide on a strategy for filling in information, solving a problem or reaching a goal.[82] The structures of these categories, however, "bias what we see, how we interpret it, how we encode and store it in memory, and what we remember about it later."[83]

Social psychologists have also shown that individuals react to the concept of "groupness."[84] When individuals are made to think that objects belong to different groups, they systematically exaggerate the variation between the objects from different groups.[85] This behavior has been called the "bias of enhancement of contrast."[86] Once people are divided into groups, "strong biases in their differences, evaluation, and reward allocation result."[87] When the concept of "groupness" is introduced, we perceive members of our group as more similar to us and members of other groups as more different from us.[88] We also perceive members of other groups as more like each other (an "undifferentiated mass") and the members of our group as less homogeneous.[89] We are better able to remember undesirable behavior of members of the other group as opposed to similar behavior of members of our group.[90] We also tend to attribute the failure of our group members to situational factors and the failures of members of the other group to dispositional factors.[91] Social psychologists theorize that we tend to pay more attention to salient or distinctive stimulus objects than to those that are not salient or distinctive.[92] Additionally, we recall visually encoded information more readily than verbally encoded infor-

---

[81] *Id.*

[82] *Id.* (citing Shelley E. Taylor & Jennifer Crocker, *Schematic Bases of Social Information Processing, in* SOCIAL COGNITION: THE ONTARIO SYMPOSIUM 93–94 (Edward Tory Higgins, C. Peter Herman & Mark P. Zanna eds., 1981)).

[83] *Id.*

[84] *Id.* at 1186.

[85] *Id.* at 1186.

[86] *Id.* at 1187.

[87] *Id.* at 1191. This happens even when the division into groups is done on a random or trivial basis.

[88] *Id.*

[89] *Id.* at 1192.

[90] *Id.*

[91] *Id.*

[92] *Id.* at 1194. This explains why salient individuals are judged more harshly than non-salient individuals. In an experiment, Whites judged a solo Black participant in an otherwise all-White group in more extreme ways and perceived him more prominently in group discussions than when the group was more fully integrated. *Id.* at 1193. Black applicants to law school with strong credentials were judged more favorably than identical White applicants; while Black applicants with weak credentials were judged less favorably than identical White applicants. *Id.* at 1194.

mation.[93] Since physical characteristics such as skin color, gender and age are readily perceived, they are more likely to be salient features.[94]

Society, however, provides us with a set of racial categories into which we map individuals according to the racial mapping.[95] Once we assign a particular racial category to someone, that category has particular racial meanings.[96] These racial meanings include thoughts or beliefs (such as generalizations about the person's particular attributes) as well as emotions, feelings and evaluations (positive or negative; good or bad).[97] While categories may happen in the individual mind, the way we categorize is not in our brain. It is the society that gives us the categories into which to put people. In that sense, prejudice and racism are societal diseases.[98]

Cognitive psychology has shown that racial schemas regularly influence social interactions. These stereotypes are, however, "more easily activated in people who display more conscious prejudice."[99] These racial schemas can be primed sometimes even by subliminal stimuli.[100] One observer notes that the existence of such an automatic process "disturbs us because it questions our self-understanding as entirely rational, free choosing, self-legislating actors."[101] We have no conscious awareness of these stereotypes.[102] We may lack "introspective access to the racial meanings embedded within our racial schemas."[103] These stereotypes are easy to maintain and overcoming them requires effort.[104]

Using the Implicit Association Test, where participants make judgments rapidly about subjects of different races (and other categories),

---

[93] *Id.* at 1194. We are particularly sensitive to physical and visual cues. Kang, *supra* note 72, at 1503. We tend to "understand and process information about most categories not with reference to features, but by means of prototypes . . . or 'idealized cognitive models.'" Blasi, *supra* note 60, at 1255. Blasi uses the example of imagining a carpenter and when you have that image settled in your mind, describing the color of *her* hair. *Id.*

[94] Tremblay & Weng, *supra* note 8, at 170.

[95] Kang, *supra* note 72, at 1499.

[96] *Id.*

[97] *Id.* at 1500.

[98] Charles Lawrence, *Unconscious Racism Revisited: Reflections on the Impact and Origins of "The Id, the Ego, and Equal Protection,"* 40 CONN. L. REV. 931, 942 (2008).

[99] Blasi, *supra* note 60, at 1249 (citing ZIVA KUNDA, SOCIAL CONDITION 334 (1999)). "Words associated with the negative features of a stereotype will activate the stereotype in persons of both low and high prejudice," yet positive or neutral words will activate the stereotype only in more prejudiced people. *Id.* at 1249–50.

[100] *Id.*

[101] *Id.* This stereotype activation takes place at the preconscious or subconscious level. *Id.* at 1252.

[102] *Id.* at 1249. This process is totally opaque to the individual. Kang, *supra* note 72, at 1506–07.

[103] Kang, *supra* note 72, at 1508. Psychologists found this by conducting tests involving speed. *Id.* at 1508–09. The Implicit Association Test (IAT) has become the "state-of-the-art measurement tool." *Id.* at 1509. You can take the IAT yourself at the Project Implicit website.

[104] Blasi, *supra* note 60, at 1253.

psychologists have "documented the implicit bias against numerous social categories."[105] There is also "overwhelming evidence that implicit bias is disassociated from explicit bias measures" so that there is "a discrepancy between our explicit and implicit meanings."[106] We may report positive attitudes toward Latinos in a survey, but the implicit bias study may show that we have negative attitudes toward Latinos. There is, however, a correlation between our explicit and implicit bias. Those who self-report (explicit) bias also show the highest implicit bias and vice versa.[107] There is also evidence that implicit bias toward a category predicts discriminatory behavior.[108] In some of these experiments the race of the person engaged in the behavior did not matter.[109] The data reveal that racial minorities show both impulses—to favor their own group ("in-group") but also those on top of the racial hierarchy (Whites).[110]

You might think that because biased behavior is automatic it cannot be altered. But the evidence supports the contrary conclusion. In order to counter the effects of this automatic behavior we must first accept the existence of the problem.[111] Some studies find that exposure to "positive" or "counterstereotypic" exemplars" of subordinated groups can decrease implicit bias.[112] Studies also show that we can behave in substantially non-prejudiced ways if we are so motivated.[113] If in fact our values include self-awareness and treating people as individuals, then increasing self-awareness should decrease our application of stereotypes.[114]

What does all this social psychology research tell us? First, that there is unlikely to be such a thing as a non-racialized setting in the United States.[115] Second, race matters, especially in settings where significant issues, problems, concepts, or categories are connected to race.[116]

Overcoming bias

---

[105] Kang, *supra* note 72, at 1512.

[106] *Id.* at 1512–13.

[107] *Id.* at 1514.

[108] *Id. See id.* at 1514–28 for a discussion of an experiment using employment interviews and shooting. Nonverbal behaviors thus "leak out from our implicit bias." *Id.* at 1524. The "unfriendly nonverbal behavior" can cause retaliatory responses as well from target group members thus creating a vicious cycle.

[109] *Id.* at 1527.

[110] *Id.* at 1534. African-Americans on average exhibited no implicit in-group favoritism. Latinos in the U.S. showed no in-group favoritism regardless of whether the person primed was light or dark skinned. Both light-skinned and dark-skinned Latinos favored light-skinned Latinos, though none of this bias manifested itself in explicit surveys. *Id.* at 1534 n. 230. Whites show substantial implicit in-group favoritism. *Id.*

[111] *Id.* at 1529.

[112] *Id.* at 1557, 1561.

[113] Blasi, *supra* note 60, at 1276 (citing Samuel R. Sommers & Phoebe C. Ellsworth, *White Juror Bias: An Investigation of Prejudice Against Black Defendants in the American Courtroom*, 7 PSYCHOL. PUB. POL'Y & L. 201, 220 (2001)).

[114] *Id.* at 1277.

[115] *Id.*

[116] *Id.*

Racial minorities and others whom we tend to stereotype "suffer silent consequences even when, and sometimes . . . *especially* when, group identity is unmentioned or unmentionable."[117] Third, we need to accept that there are differences in what stereotypes mean in our society. We need to recognize, as Gary Blasi points out, that the consequences are far different for being subjected to a "While male law professor" stereotype and a "young Black male" stereotype.[118] Fourth, we need to accept that stereotyping happens. Denying it "can lead us to continue acting in ways that perpetuate division and oppression."[119] We can start by accepting and learning more about prejudice in our society, how it is that society gives us the categories into which we place people.

D. THE SOCIETAL ASPECTS OF PREJUDICE— UNDERSTANDING POWER AND OPPRESSION

We move from talking about individual bias to discussing how this bias plays out in society. For some of you this will be the most difficult section of the chapter. For others of you the absence of this section would be difficult. We may not see some of the points in this section because of our perspective, because of where we stand in our own culture. We may not want to acknowledge how a society with such laudable ideals and that has accomplished much good can fall short of those ideas. It may be too painful to discuss these issues or to recognize that each of us plays a part in the subordination and mistreatment of others.[120] Or we may feel a sense of helplessness and inability to change what seems inevitable. Regardless, we think racism and other forms of subordination is the reality for many people living in the U.S., including some of your clients. We focus on racism because it plays such a central role in the history of the U.S.[121] It also provides an explanation for the issues facing the communities in which some of your clients may work.[122]

Implicit bias research demonstrates the "prevalence of forms of bias that motivate and justify behavior that creates and perpetuates racial hierarchy and other conditions of dominance and subordination."[123] While it is important to understand individual bias, it is also important to understand how our society ("culture") transmits prejudice to all those living within it and how that prejudice affects each of us but especially those

---

[117] *Id.* at 1274.

[118] *Id.* at 1276.

[119] *Id.*

[120] Copps Hartley & Petrucci, *supra* note 35, at 164. *See also* HAYS, *supra* note 50, at 32–33.

[121] *See supra* Section II.C.

[122] *See* Barbara J. Flagg, *"Was Blind, But Now I See": White Race Consciousness and the Requirement of Discriminatory Intent*, 91 MICH. L. REV. 953 (1993) (discussing disproportionate rates of poverty, unemployment, mortality rates, inferior schools, poor health care and environmental conditions in African-American communities).

[123] Lawrence, *supra* note 98, at 965.

who are the subject of that prejudice. As we discuss above, it is through socialization that we receive the sets of categories (racial and otherwise, for example, religious) into which we map individuals. Society also provides us with the particular meaning to assign to that category—for example, how to recognize and label the groupings based on dress, skin color, mannerism, language used, accent and other factors. Those meanings include thoughts or beliefs (such as generalizations about the person's particular attributes) as well as emotions, feelings and evaluations (positive or negative; good or bad).

The process of categorization has content.[124] The content is what defines the categories and gives meaning to them. Charles Lawrence's concern with the emphasis on social psychology's attention on the working of the individual mind is that it may cause us to think of racism as a private concern.[125] Our private implicit biases "implicate collective responsibility for racial subordination."[126] Racism, sexism, homophobia and other systems of oppression are societal diseases.[127] The fact that implicit bias predicts policy preferences suggests that implicit bias is more than personal preference.[128] In fact, the prejudice in implicit bias is learned prejudice.[129]

Race is a social construct with biological justifications. Social psychologists have described race as a way of valuing one's own group over others, a handy way to encapsulate and rationalize social conflict, a useful means of talking about group differences, values, social hierarchy and competition, and a system that accords privilege and dominance to those in power.[130] Racism is institutionalized discrimination and includes the ability to maintain a social structure that endorses those in power, those controlling legal, cultural, religious, educational, economic, political and military institutions.[131]

Racism is a system of power. As a result, "the most central concept to an understanding of the influence of sociocultural biases on individuals is that of power."[132] Since high status groups in our society "hold more power, they can exert more control over their own situations and the situ-

---

[124] *Id.* at 942.

[125] *Id.*

[126] *Id.*

[127] *Id.*

[128] *Id.* at 958.

[129] *Id.* at 961.

[130] JAMES JONES, PREJUDICE AND RACISM 352, 373 (2d ed. 1997).

[131] Dietra Hawkins, Terri Johnson & Josefina Alvarez, *The Chicago Dinners: A Model for Community Engagement and Social Change, in* 4 THE PSYCHOLOGY OF PREJUDICE AND DISCRIMINATION: DISABILITY, RELIGION, PHYSIQUE AND OTHER TRAITS 236 (Jean Lau Chin ed., 2004) (citing Joe R. Feagin & Melvin P. Sikes, LIVING WITH RACISM: THE BLACK MIDDLE-CLASS EXPERIENCE (1994); JONES, *supra* note 131).

[132] HAYS, *supra* note 50, at 26 (citing PAUL KIVEL, UPROOTING RACISM (2002)).

ations of lower status groups."[133] Examining racism means exploring how systemic racial inequalities function to assign roles of racial advantage and how some benefit from those advantages.[134] Stereotypes are one way that power groups exert control.[135] Descriptive stereotypes, which define how people in a group behave, what they prefer, where their competence lies, create expectations on the person being stereotyped.[136] The expectation places a burden on the individual because she must either choose to stay within the boundaries or go outside.[137] Prescriptive stereotypes define how a group "should think, feel, and behave."[138]

Because of oppression, unprivileged groups need to pay more attention to differences and rules since "the outcome of their lives are more dependent on those who hold power."[139] People who belong to powerful groups, however, are not socialized to perceive the rules and barriers separating the unprivileged because they do not need to.[140] This is because "oppressed groups have little impact on their daily lives."[141] Members of dominant groups often find it difficult to recognize the existence of systems of privilege.[142] The idea of privilege seems antithetical to our concepts of democracy and meritocracy ("you can succeed if you work hard").[143] Systems of privilege, however, harm both those with the privilege as well as those without.[144] Privilege keeps information, knowledge and skills from dominant groups. Privilege prevents personal growth on the part of the dominant group by internalizing feelings of superiority and elitism, and inhibiting individuals from developing coping mechanisms that less privileged persons develop to survive.[145]

In our society, overt racism, sexism and other forms of oppression have become more subtle and ambiguous, perhaps reflecting people's be-

[133] *Id.* at 26–27 (citing Bernice Lott, *Cognitive and Behavioral Distancing from the Poor*, 57 AM. PSYCHOL. 100 (2002)). *See also* ANTONIA DARDER, CULTURE AND POWER IN THE CLASSROOM 41 (1991) (defining institutional racism as "a form of racial discrimination woven into the fabric of power relationships, social arrangements, and practices through which collective actions result in the use of race as a criterion to determine who is rewarded in society" (citation omitted)).

[134] Copps Hartley & Petrucci, *supra* note 35, at 179.

[135] HAYS, *supra* note 50, at 27.

[136] *Id.*

[137] *Id.* (citing Susan T. Fiske, *Controlling Other People: The Impact of Power on Stereotyping*, 48 AMER. PSYCHOL. 621 (1993)).

[138] *Id.* (citing Fiske, *supra* note 138, at 623). Pamela Hays gives the example of the dominant culture's expectations that disabled people are expected to cheerfully make daily adjustments to the nondisabled world and overcome or transcend despite physical and social barriers caused by the fears and hostilities of others. *Id.*

[139] *Id.* (citing Fiske, *supra* note 138).

[140] *Id.*

[141] *Id.*

[142] *Id.* at 28.

[143] *Id.*

[144] *Id.* (citing Don C. Locke & Mark S. Kiselica, *Pedagogy of Possibilities: Teaching About Racism in Multicultural Counseling Courses*, 77 J. OF COUNSELING & DEV. 77 (1999)).

[145] *Id.*

liefs that blatant acts of prejudice are not acceptable.[146] These more subtle forms of prejudice play out in the form of microaggressions, brief and
commonplace daily verbal or behavioral indignities, sometimes intentional and at other times not, that communicate hostile, derogatory or negative slights and insults that potentially have a harmful or unpleasant
psychological impact on the person who is the target.[147] Microaggressions
can be delivered environmentally through the physical surroundings,
making people feel "unwelcome, isolated, unsafe, and alienated."[148] They
tend to be subtle, indirect and unintentional; often occurring in situations
where there are alternative explanations and are more likely to occur
when people pretend not to notice differences, thereby denying that race,
gender, sexual orientation, religion or other characteristics had anything
to do with these actions or comments.[149] Racism, sexism, and stigmatiza-
tion based on sexual orientation have been found to cause significant psychological distress and negative health outcomes.[150]

With that understanding of both individual bias and societal oppression, let us move to discussing our work with our clients.

III. BECOMING A MORE CULTURALLY COMPETENT LAWYER

In our lawyering, we use our cultural lens to judge people as serious,
honest, intelligent, hard-working, committed or rude. Because culture is
the lens through which we gather meaning from behavior and words, we
are "constantly attaching culturally based meaning to what we see and
hear, often without being aware that we are doing so."[151] Part of becoming
more culturally competent involves becoming more conscious of that
meaning-making. In this section, we provide some frameworks for that
developmental process of becoming more culturally competent. Earlier in
the chapter we discussed that cultural competence requires awareness,
knowledge and skills.[152] We now turn to these factors of cultural competence.

A. AWARENESS, ATTITUDE AND KNOWLEDGE

Growing as a culturally competent lawyer begins with an open attitude—seeing how cultural differences can affect the lawyering process. A

---

[146] SUE & SUE, *supra* note 20, at 150.

[147] *Id.* at 151. Microaggressions include microassault, microinsult and microinvalidation.
Id. at 154–56. For a list of sample microaggressions, see *id.* at 156–60. *See also* Peggy C. Davis,
Law as Microaggression, 98 YALE L.J. 1559 (1989).

[148] SUE & SUE, *supra* note 20, at 153.

[149] *Id.* at 154.

[150] *Id.* at 163–64.

[151] Bryant & Koh Peters, *supra* note 30, at 48.

[152] *See supra* Section II.B.

starting point is appreciating that differences can affect the relationships
we build with our clients, for example, by understanding that differences
can affect rapport[153] and communication. Our own class, race and ethnicity, gender and sexual background influence what we hear, what we say
and how we say it.[154] Our definition of challenges, difficulties and solutions are influenced by our cultural identities.

The first step in the process of becoming more culturally competent is
to understand our own cultural influences—to become aware or raise our
awareness of them. You may find the ADDRESSING framework we outlined above[155] useful in doing so or approach your self-assessment another
way. What are your identities? How do they influence you? What are
the influences you consider most salient? Think about both your upbringing and your current identities.[156] The categories are not mutually exclusive so you may find some overlap between several of the categories. You
can do this alone or in a group, for example with your classmates in the
clinic (or your clinic partner if you work in teams).

After recognizing your cultural influences, take some time to recognize your privilege and opportunities.[157] For example, while your religion
may be a minority religion, your gender may be a source of privilege and
your education may be a source of opportunity (and privilege). Review
your ADDRESSING assessment and identify in which areas you hold a
dominant cultural identity.[158] Privilege can change over time. You may
have grown up in poverty but now live a middle-class lifestyle. Privilege
can also change with context—what is privilege in the U.S. may not be
privilege in another country. Next, think about how your cultural influences affect your lawyering. For example, how might your religious or
spiritual beliefs influence your lawyering? How do your cultural influences affect your values? Which of those values influence your lawyering
and how? Understanding our cultural influence and how they affect us is
difficult. It requires us to step back and reflect. We are trained to engage
in this detached analysis about our client's matter but it is more challenging to do it to ourselves.

You can also use the ADDRESSING framework to recognize the cultural influences on your client. Of course, you cannot be aware of all of

---

[153] Bill Ong Hing, *Raising Personal Identification Issues of Class, Race, Ethnicity, Gender
Sexual Orientation, Physical Disability and Age in Lawyering Courses*, 45 STAN. L. REV. 1807,
1809 (1993).

[154] *Id.* at 1810.

[155] *See supra* Section II.B.

[156] HAYS, *supra* note 50, at 42.

[157] *Id.* at 45.

[158] *Id.* You hold a dominant cultural identity if you are between 30–60 years of age; do not
have a disability; grew up in a secular or Christian home; are of European American heritage;
were brought up in a family that was middle class or higher, or are currently of middle class or
higher; are heterosexual and are male. *Id.*

the influences on your client. You and your client may have discussed some identities. You may be guessing about others based on physical characteristics, such as gender. This analysis is tentative lest you stereotype your client. Other influences may come up in the context of conversation.[159] Still others you may never learn. What do you *think* are your client's salient cultural influences? What is your basis for thinking that? Sue Bryant and Jean Koh Peters suggest analyzing the similarities and differences between you and your client and then exploring the significance of those similarities and differences.[160] Where do you think the cultural challenges might occur? Why? Think about the assumptions you may be making regarding the client's goals or decisions. If you perceive the client to be making choices you do not understand, what can you do to try to understand? How might similarities and differences affect the client's ability to build a relationship with you?

It is important that we think about two caveats as we begin mapping out our identities. First is the risk that we "essentialize." Early in the chapter, we discussed that while members of groups share some characteristics, not everyone experiences them the same way.[161] Essentialism is the notion that a unitary, "essential" experience can be isolated and described for any one category separate from all other aspects of someone's identity.[162] It is not possible, then, to isolate the "essential" women's experience and describe it independently of race, class, sexual orientation, and other realities of experience.[163] Our categories need to be "explicitly tentative, relational and unstable."[164] Second, as we think about our own identity (and that of our clients) it is also important to remember as we discussed earlier in this chapter that culture comes in the plural since we hold multiple identities.[165] In that sense, "our identities are constructed through the intersection of multiple dimensions."[166]

When examining our (as well as our client's) racial and ethnic identity, it is important to recognize that all of us have a racial identity even if we are not always conscious of it. Some Whites do not "think about

---

[159] For example, one of us works with a client who begins every meeting with the students in the clinic by telling them about himself. He discloses many of his values to the students in this conversation. He then invites students to tell him about themselves.

[160] Bryant, *supra* note 33, at 64–67; Bryant & Koh Peters, *supra* note 30, at 51–53.

[161] *See supra* Section I.

[162] Angela P. Harris, *Race and Essentialism in Feminist Legal Theory,* 42 STAN. L. REV. 581, 585 (1990). *See also* Melissa Harrison & Margaret E. Montoya, *Voices/Voces in the Borderlands: A Colloquy on Re/Constructing Identities in Re/Constructed Legal Spaces,* 6 COLUM. J. GENDER & L. 387 (1996).

[163] Harris, *supra* note 162, at 585.

[164] *Id.* at 586.

[165] *See supra* Section I.

[166] Kimberlé Crenshaw, *Mapping the Margins: Intersectionality, Identity Politics, and Violence Against Women of Color,* 43 STAN. L. REV. 1241, 1299 (1991). To say all categories are socially constructed is not to say that the category has no significance in our world. *Id.* at 1296.

whiteness, or about norms, behaviors, experiences, or perspectives that are white-specific."[167] One commentator calls this the "transparency phenomenon" because to be White is to have an everyday option not to think about oneself in racial terms.[168] Whites often do not think of race as belonging to them.[169] The "tendency to treat whiteness as a neutral norm or baseline, and not a racial identity," tends to view racial issues as belonging to people of color.[170] We think this tendency is problematic on many fronts. This perspective often views race as an issue for people of color to deal with and not all of us. There is also evidence that more mature racial identity correlates with higher levels of cultural competence.[171]

Lastly, we need to acquire knowledge of our clients and their communities. You can read about the client community or watch films (including documentaries). You can read literature written by members of the client community or about the client community. You can attend client events, for example, if you represent an organization and that organization holds events in its community. Even if the client group does not invite you, consider telling them you would be interested in attending their events. The organization may not invite you because the group representatives think you are not interested in going (and do not want to put you in the awkward position of saying no) and not because they do not want you to attend. The client may see it as saving you the embarrassment of declining an invitation. You can also attend cultural events in the client's community.[172] Finally, and most importantly, you can gain information from your client. You client is your best source of information about her world view, understanding, priorities, goals, and aspirations.

B. SKILLS IN MULTICULTURAL LAWYERING

The skills of the culturally competent lawyer are no different from those of client-centered lawyering, the concept we discussed in the Interviewing and Counseling chapters. The culturally competent lawyer listens with a multicultural ear[173] and sees with multicultural eyes.[174] The

---

[167] Flagg, *supra* note 122, at 957. "The most striking characteristic of whites' consciousness of whiteness is that most of the time we don't have any." *Id.*

[168] *Id.* at 957, 969. *See also* SUE & SUE, *supra* note 20, at 317.

[169] SUE & SUE, *supra* note 20, at 319. Whites too need to see themselves as racial beings. Flagg, *supra* note 122, at 957 n. 20.

[170] *See* Pearce, *supra* note 30, at 2083, 2090.

[171] Copps Hartley & Petrucci, *supra* note 35, at 169 (citing Thomas M. Ottavi, Donald B. Pope-Davis & Jonathan G. Dings, *Relationship Between White Racial Identity Attitudes and Self-Reported Multicultural Counseling Competencies*, 41 J. COUNSELING PSYCHOL. 149 (1994)).

[172] Tremblay & Weng, *supra* note 8, at 154.

[173] COMAS-DÍAZ, *supra* note 43, at 9.

[174] Paul Tremblay notes that the lawyer needs to be "cross-eyed," with one eye focused on the differences and the other focused on the similarities between the client and the lawyer. Tremblay, *supra* note 8, at 378 (citation omitted).

culturally competent lawyer works with curiosity and humility.[175]   He pays attention to differences when counseling and interviewing clients because ignoring the differences is tantamount to malpractice.[176]   The culturally competent lawyer listens mindfully, without letting thoughts of strategy interfere with listening.[177]   Mindfulness, which we discussed in the Interviewing chapter, requires that we pay attention and be aware.[178] Mindfulness also requires that we be open to the client's experience and attentive and ready for the possibly complex and messy aspects of the client's matter.[179]   Mindfulness requires that we not begin to think about ways to accomplish the client's goals until we have heard the client's story and probed further for full understanding.   Mindful listening also requires that we not judge.[180]   We need to step back to make sure we are not making assumptions and make sure we fully understand the issues from the client's perspective.   The multicultural lawyer does not make assumptions about *why* a client may want to do something a certain way or at all. The culturally competent lawyer makes sure he understands the *why*.

What might be some ways that the differences between you and your client play out in the lawyer-client relationship?   Differences may require that you modify your style of interviewing or counseling or adjust the substance of your presentations.   One way differences in communication may play out is in differences between direct and indirect communication (high and low context).   Low context communication is more direct and explicit so meaning is conveyed without nuance.   In high context communication, little information is in the message itself so meaning is inferred as opposed to directly interpreted.[181]   There may be differences in narrative preferences.[182]   You may need to adjust your plan to gather information or present information in a particular way (in chronological order, in a written format).   You will need to be able to read both verbal and non-verbal behavior, including bodily movements, preferences for physical space, silence, eye contact (or lack thereof), time and facial expressions.[183]   You may need to adjust your lawyering in other ways.

In the U.S., the dominant culture values individualism, independence and autonomy, is action-oriented and competitive, has a written tra-

---

[175] Tremblay, *supra* note 8, at 382.

[176] *Id.* at 378.   We believe this is the case because without awareness of the differences you are likely to make assumptions and substitute your judgment.

[177] Susan J. Bryant & Jean Koh Peters, *Six Practices for Connecting with Clients Across Culture: Habit Four, Working with Interpreters and Other Mindful Approaches, in* THE AFFECTIVE ASSISTANCE OF COUNSEL, *supra* note 8, at 196–97.

[178] *Id.* at 198.

[179] *Id.*

[180] *Id.* at 199.

[181] SUE & SUE, *supra* note 20, at 219–21.

[182] Tremblay, *supra* note 8, at 396–99.

[183] HAYS, *supra* note 50, at 97–100; Tremblay, *supra* note 8, at 389–96.

dition, plans for the future, views time as a commodity, has a pragmatic and utilitarian view of life, believes hard work brings success, emphasizes objective, rational and linear thinking and values economic power including owning goods and property.[184] Of course, there are many more attributes, but these have some relationship to lawyering in the transactional settings. You can imagine how some of these might influence your representation of a family-owned business that may value the extended family and common ownership of property or in the representation of a nonprofit organization that places a high value on community process, consensus decision-making or community control of resources.

understand client values

We need to ask our clients questions in order not to make judgments and assumptions. At times, that will mean we are indirectly asking the client to inform us about their cultural influences. Many clients will not mind; others will tell you when they do. Cultural competence requires that you include the client in discussions about strategy about their matter, including whether to raise issues of prejudice or oppression in the representation.[185]

When you do not understand a client's decision, Sue Bryant and Jean Koh Peters suggest using a technique they call "parallel universe" to explore multiple alternative interpretations of a client's behavior.[186] Take the time to think of all the possible explanations for the client's actions or the possible reasons she may have for making a particular decision. This technique helps us not judge the decisions the client makes or attribute the worst explanation for it without knowing more.

explore client's reasoning

As with all other lawyering, becoming a more culturally competent lawyer will require practice and reflection. As one commentator notes, "practice doesn't make perfect, but it sure does help."[187] You will no doubt make mistakes along the way to becoming a more culturally competent lawyer, as you will make mistakes in other parts of your journey to becoming a better lawyer. You will get some things wrong, attributing certain behavior to culture and thus stereotype your client. As with other mistakes, you will need to forgive yourself, have a sense of humor, and look for ways to learn from the mistakes. You will be puzzled by some behavior that is explained by difference. You will get some things right, becoming a better communicator and developing better and richer relationships with clients along the way. We think the risks of being wrong are well worth taking. We encourage you to try (and sometimes fail) as

---

[184] SUE & SUE, *supra* note 20, at 182 (citing Judith Katz, *The Sociopolitical Nature of Counseling*, 13 COUNSELING PSYCHOLOGIST 615, 618 (1985)).

[185] *See* Clark Cunningham, *The Lawyer as Translator, Representation as Text: Towards an Ethnography of Legal Discourse*, 77 CORNELL L. REV. 1298 (1992). *See also* Pearce, *supra* note 30, at 2092.

[186] Bryant & Koh Peters, *supra* note 30, at 56.

[187] HAYS, *supra* note 50, at 203.

you take this journey through the various neighborhoods, communities and cultures in this country and the rest of the world.

CHAPTER 8

ETHICAL ISSUES IN TRANSACTIONAL PRACTICE

■ ■ ■

This chapter reviews some common ethical issues you are apt to confront in your transactional clinic work. The ethics issues that arise in representing entrepreneurs, small businesses, nonprofits and those involved in real estate deals are particularly interesting. They differ in important ways from the common (and equally interesting) tensions that arise in litigation practice, such as the demands of zealous advocacy, the worry about possible fraud on a tribunal, and the harm to one's case engendered by playing fair with an adverse party. In transactional practice, your ethical worries might include some of the tensions experienced by litigators (for example, your temptation to mislead a person with whom you are negotiating, or omitting some relevant facts in an application for a permit). Generally, though, the ethical conundra you will face will connect to the fact that your clients are organizations but your work will always be with individuals who are, legally and practically, distinct from the organization.

Our aim in this chapter is to highlight some of those common issues and to suggest some frameworks for you to use to puzzle through the tensions. This chapter will, at best, orient you to issues whose complexity will exceed what we can cover here. You will surely take, or have taken already, a full course in professional responsibility, and that course will complement what you learn about here.

The topics we choose to explore here are the following:

- Identifying your client when you create a new business entity;
- Identifying your client when you represent an ongoing business entity;
- Confidentiality obligations in the entity context, including the attorney-client privilege;
- Students' right to practice law in transactional clinics;
- Students' (and lawyers') right to advise clients about the law of a different jurisdiction; and

- The level of responsibility you may have for the effects your clients' business activities impose on others.

I. WHO IS THE LAWYER'S CLIENT (OR WHO ARE THE LAWYER'S CLIENTS) AT ENTITY FORMATION?

The first two topics here represent the central ethical challenge for lawyers whose clients are businesses or groups. While litigators frequently represent organizations, and therefore face a similar tension, there is a distinct quality to this puzzle for transactional lawyers counseling entity clients. In this section we address the question at the very beginning—at the formation stage. The next section addresses the question as its appears in ongoing representation of entity clients.

A. AN EXAMPLE

Let us begin with a familiar example, one we have seen in other chapters:

> The prospective clients are named Filippa Sands and Bill Sherman. Filippa and Bill are entrepreneurs who live in the local neighborhood. They have plans to open a bakery café on Prospect Street, about a mile from the clinic's office. Their plan is to call the store "The Prospect Street Café." The intake sheet states that Bill is an unemployed chain grocery store manager, and Filippa works full time as an assistant financing clerk at a GM dealership in town. They heard from the local Small Business Development Center that they should consult a lawyer before embarking on this endeavor. The SBDC gave Filippa and Bill the names of the county bar association as well as your law school clinic. They decided to try the clinic instead of a private lawyer (the price made a difference), and the clinic agreed to interview them. The two prospective clients would like to meet a lawyer or student as soon as possible to get things rolling.

B. A TAXONOMY OF REPRESENTATION OPTIONS

Let us assume that the clinic wants to represent Filippa and Bill to advise the founders about the options of creating a business structure, and that the two entrepreneurs, initially at least, desire to retain the clinic. Once you are ready to begin work on the matter, you will now officially, and for all relevant substantive law purposes, have a *client*. What you need to be clear about is the identity of that client, or perhaps those clients. You may notice that there are three distinct, and seemingly mutually exclusive, possibilities here:

1) You represent Filippa and Bill as two individuals—so you have two clients.

2) You represent Filippa and Bill together, as a nascent and unincorporated "group," or association, or entity—so you have one client.

3) You may only represent Bill *or* Filippa if you are to do any work, because their interests are materially different—so you have only one client if you have any client at all.

Before you begin any work at all on this project—and, indeed, before you can even create an engagement letter or retainer agreement—you need to resolve the question of which of those categories fits your situation. To answer that question, you must confront two separable inquiries: Does the substantive law of your jurisdiction compel an answer for you? And, if not—that is, if you and the prospective clients have a choice about which of the three scenarios will apply—how do you determine which to choose?

C. WHY THE CLIENT IDENTITY QUESTION MATTERS

Before we explore the factors you will use to sort out your representational status with Filippa and Bill, we should pause to reflect on why it matters who gets the technical title of "client" in this clinic project. It seems like it should not really matter, because in any of the three scenarios you will perform the same good, smart work, advising whoever your client happens to be about the law and the strategies involved in entity formation and getting a business off the ground.

But, as you know, it does matter. Once a person or an association qualifies as your *client*, you incur important duties which you will not owe to those who are not your clients. You have important fiduciary responsibilities to care for the client, more than you care for others. You owe your clients important confidentiality commitments, limiting what you might say or write to others about what you have learned during the representation.[1] The federal and state evidence laws offer you and your clients a privilege against testimony about your conversations, a privilege which does not apply to your communications with non-clients.[2] You must scrupulously avoid conflicts of interest, ensuring that your work, and your non-work, activities do not interfere with your clients' interests.[3] And, importantly, if you do not comply with your various duties owed to clients,

---

[1] *See* MODEL RULES OF PROF'L CONDUCT R. 1.6 (2011). Our discussion of the ethical responsibilities of transactional lawyers will rely upon the American Bar Association's Model Rules, even though in any particular jurisdiction the treatment of a particular issue may differ in some minor, or perhaps significant, way. In general, though, most states follow the guidance of the Model Rules in their regulation of lawyer activity.

[2] *See* RESTATEMENT (THIRD) OF THE LAW GOVERNING LAWYERS § 68 cmt. d (2002) [hereinafter "RESTATEMENT"] (describing the scope of the attorney-client privilege).

[3] MODEL RULES OF PROF'L CONDUCT R. 1.7, 1.8, 1.9.

the clients may sue you for malpractice, a right that non-clients do not have.[4]

It is therefore critical for you to know whether Bill is your client, whether Filippa is your client, whether both are clients, or whether some other configuration serves as your client at this beginning stage.

D. REPRESENTING FILIPPA AND BILL AS TWO INDIVIDUAL, JOINT CLIENTS

Two persons have walked into your office and have spoken to you about providing them with legal advice. The ordinary presumption would be that, if you agree to take their matter, you should represent them both. Let us explore that possibility.

Whether you *may* represent Filippa and Bill together as two individual joint clients depends on the law of your jurisdiction, as discussed in the next Subsection E, as well as the ordinary conflict of interest laws as applied to the particular circumstances of their case. Some jurisdictions treat founders of businesses not as individual clients but instead as inchoate organizations, subject to the entity representation rules; other jurisdictions permit treatment of the founders as individual clients. In this subsection we will assume your jurisdiction permits the possibility of treating Filippa and Bill as two individual clients whom you will represent together as joint clients.

It is entirely possible under conventional legal ethics doctrine for a lawyer to represent two clients in the same matter, so long as there are no conflicts of interest between the two, or, if there are such conflicts of interest, they are manageable and the clients consent to the joint representation.[5] Therefore, if you opt to accept joint representation of Filippa and Bill, you need to be sure, first, that any conflicts are not so serious as to disqualify you from accepting the matter, and, second, that you have obtained their informed consent in writing.[6]

Do Filippa and Bill have conflicts of interest? You do not yet know, but the odds are that they will have some conflicts. Here's one useful test to discern whether there's a conflict to attend to: If Bill or Filippa had his or her own lawyer, might that lawyer advise about any possible strategies which would be disadvantageous to the other business partner? In this

---

[4] *See, e.g.,* Spinner v. Nutt, 417 Mass. 549 (1994) (trust beneficiaries are not clients of law firm, and may not maintain an action against the firm for malpractice or breach of fiduciary duty). While some doctrine permits non-clients to sue lawyers for causing them harm, for instance if a lawyer for one party invites reasonable reliance by another party on the lawyer's opinion, that doctrine is not premised on the lawyer's special duties to her client. For a discussion of a lawyer's liability to third parties, see, e.g., Nancy Lewis, *Lawyers' Liability to Third Parties: The Ideology of Advocacy Reframed*, 66 OR. L. REV. 801 (1997).

[5] MODEL RULES OF PROF'L CONDUCT R. 1.7.

[6] *Id.* at 1.7(b). For a discussion of this topic, see Paul R. Tremblay, *Counseling Community Groups*, 17 CLINICAL L. REV. 389, 407 (2010).

instance, the intake paperwork shows two entrepreneurs with differing backgrounds offering different contributions to the business. Even if Filippa and Bill believe, honestly and in the utmost good faith, that they intend to own and operate the café entirely equally and share equally in all profits, losses, and liabilities, *that* very state of affairs is one that a solo lawyer for either of the owners might suggest changing. Filippa and Bill seem to have at minimum a *potential* conflict of interest, and you cannot ignore that possibility.

So, does that potential conflict mean that Filippa and Bill must retain two separate lawyers? We see quickly how unwise that policy choice would be, for business, financial, and interpersonal reasons.[7] Fortunately no jurisdiction enforces the conflict of interest rules that strictly. As long as Filippa and Bill understand the risks of sharing one lawyer, relative to each retaining a separate lawyer, they may consent to the joint representation, so long as that consent is "informed," and memorialized in a writing.[8]

Your responsibility—and it is a critical one—is to educate Filippa and Bill about the costs and benefits of sharing a lawyer.[9] This must include exploring the ways in which the two business partners might choose to arrange matters in an unequal way, and their rights to do so. Of course, if they decide to arrange matters in such a way that Filippa obtains some preferential treatment over Bill, your role in that process must remain as neutral as possible.

You must also advise the two business partners of the special treatment of confidentiality that accompanies joint representation. The Model Rules,[10] and the doctrine surrounding the Model Rules,[11] establish that

---

[7]   Filippa and Bill have a shared, common interest in operating a café. They seem to be on good terms, and clearly want to work collaboratively. If the jurisdiction's doctrine forbade a lawyer from representing them together, requiring each to retain a separate lawyer to protect her or his interests, that very fact might create schisms between the business partners and make the business's operations much less smooth. It would also cost the entrepreneurs more money, using a scarce commodity needed for the effective operation of the café. For these reasons, fortunately, the doctrine permits Filippa and Bill to waive any such conflict, as described in the text. For a discussion of this aspect of concurrent conflicts of interest, see, e.g., Debra Lyn Bassett, *Three's A Crowd: A Proposal to Abolish Joint Representation*, 32 RUTGERS L.J. 387 (2001); Stephen Doherty, *Joint Representation Conflicts of Interest: Toward A More Balanced Approach*, 65 TEMP. L. REV. 561 (1992).

[8]   MODEL RULES OF PROF'L CONDUCT R. 1.7(b).

[9]   The acid test for this aspect of your lawyering responsibilities is this: If a conflict materializes down the road, and Filippa and Bill end up in a dispute (and this kind of thing does happen, even with the happiest of business partners at the commencement of their work together), would either of your clients have a legitimate claim that you did not advise him or her adequately about the particular risk that came to pass? For an example where the lawyer failed on that score, see In re Disciplinary Proceeding Against Botimer, 214 P.3d 133 (Wash. 2009) (holding that an attorney violated the rules of professional responsibility when he failed to obtain the necessary waivers in his representation of multiple family members, who later disputed each other over a business deal he advised them on).

[10]   MODEL RULES OF PROF'L CONDUCT R. 1.17 cmt. 31.

[11]   *See, e.g.*, RESTATEMENT, *supra* note 2, at § 60; RONALD D. ROTUNDA & JOHN S. DZIENKOWSKI, PROFESSIONAL RESPONSIBILITY: A STUDENT'S GUIDE § 1.6–9, 262–64 (2008–09).

joint representation + confidentiality

co-representation will normally include the understanding that there will be no secrets within the lawyer/client collectivity, and among the co-clients. This understanding emerges from some established doctrine within the attorney-client privilege[12] but also from the lawyer's obligations to each client under Rule 1.4 to keep her clients reasonably informed about developments material to the representation.[13] The lawyer and her co-clients do, however, possess the right according to the substantive law of lawyering to opt not to share with one another all confidential information passing through the lawyer. Such an agreement will preserve the privilege waiver implications in the case of a later dispute between some co-clients,[14] just as it contractually limits the lawyer's obligations under Rule 1.4 and permits the lawyer to withhold otherwise material information from some of her clients.[15] Most clients, of course, do not opt for such a secrecy arrangement. Indeed, you would have to decide whether you could adequately represent the two if they chose to keep important matters about the business from one another during your work for them.

If you determine during your counseling of the prospective clients that "in the circumstances [you] cannot reasonably conclude that [you] will be able to provide competent and diligent representation"[16] because of the likelihood of serious divergences of interests, then you may not accept representation and may not ask for consent from Filippa and Bill. Of course, if you accept representation after obtaining proper informed consent from the clients and later a serious, nonwaivable conflict arises, you must then withdraw from representing either person.[17]

If you counsel Filippa and Bill about the risks and benefits of joint representation in the business formation context, and if they provide written, informed consent to the joint representation,[18] you may proceed to create the business organization, or to advise the two café owners about the options available to them. Should Filippa and Bill elect to create a formal business association, such as an S Corp. or an LLC, then you will need to negotiate with the two founders about whether the entity chooses to retain you as counsel to it. Your representation of the two

---

[12] *See, e.g.,* RESTATEMENT, *supra* note 2, at § 75, Cmt. d; State v. Cascone, 487 A.2d 186, 189 (Conn. 1985); Waste Management, Inc. v. International Surplus Lines Ins. Co., 579 N.E.2d 322 (Ill. 1991); Ashcraft & Gerel v. Shaw, 728 A.2d 798 (Md. App. 1999).

[13] MODEL RULES OF PROF'L CONDUCT R. 1.4; A v. B. v. Hill Wallack, 726 A.2d 924 (N.J. 1999) (concluding that Rule 1.4 duties must be enforced even over objection of a co-client, because complaining co-client had warnings about shared secrets).

[14] RESTATEMENT, *supra* note 2, at § 75, Cmt. *d.*

[15] MODEL RULES OF PROF'L CONDUCT R. 1.7 cmt. 31.

[16] *Id.* at R. 1.7 cmt. 15.

[17] *Id.* at R. 1.16(a)(1) (addressing mandatory withdrawal from representation); R. 1.9(a) (barring adverse representation against a former client in the same or a substantially related matter, unless the former client consents).

[18] The "writing" required by the Model Rules to memorialize the informed consent need not be a paper signed by Filippa and Bill. You may confirm the understanding by a writing you create. *See id.* at R. 1.7 cmt. 20.

founders, at least in jurisdictions discussed in this subsection, does not automatically entail representation of the resulting entity.[19]

E.   REPRESENTING FILIPPA AND BILL AS AN UNINCORPORATED ASSOCIATION

The discussion above captures, it seems to us, the best understanding of your relationship with Filippa and Bill if you proceed to work with them together to advise about the café. But it is not the only possible understanding of your relationship to the two individuals. You might see Filippa and Bill as constituents of an entity, the as-yet-unformed café. Here there are two ways to conceptualize that understanding.

The first is the *Jesse v. Danforth* model,[20] which effectively is a hybrid approach to the representation question. *Jesse*, an opinion from the Supreme Court of Wisconsin, established the following common law rule for representation in the entity formation context:

> [W]here (1) a person retains a lawyer for the purpose of organizing an entity and (2) the lawyer's involvement with that person is directly related to that incorporation and (3) such entity is eventually incorporated, the entity rule applies retroactively such that the lawyer's pre-incorporation involvement with the person is deemed to be representation of the entity, not the person.[21]

Common law (minority) rule that the client during an incorp. is the later-formed corp

In *Jesse*, the dispute concerned a former client conflict of interest. After the law firm incorporated a business on behalf of several founders, the firm later sued one of the founders on a matter where, had the founder been a former client of the firm, the representation would have been improper. The Wisconsin court determined, using the formula just quoted, that retroactively the founder was *not* a client of the law firm, and therefore the law firm's suit against him did not breach any duties owed to him.[22]

Few jurisdictions follow *Jesse* as written, and commentators do not treat that doctrine as established law outside of Wisconsin.[23] But *Jesse*

---

[19] If the lawyer proceeds to perform actions for the entity, even in the absence of a formal retainer from the entity, it is most plausible to conclude that the lawyer's duties will lie to the entity, and not to the individual constituents. *See, e.g.,* Hopper v. Frank, 16 F.3d 92 (5th Cir. 1993) (individual partners within a limited partnership may not sue the law firm for actions taken after formation of the partnership).

[20] Jesse v. Danforth, 485 N.W.2d 63 (Wis. 1992).

[21] *Jesse*, 485 N.W.2d at 67. *See also* Manion v. Nagin, 394 F.3d 1062, 1069 (8th Cir. 2005) (limiting the *Jesse* doctrine). For a discussion of both cases, see D. Ryan Nayar, *Almost Clients: A Closer Look at Attorney Responsibility in the Context of Entity Representation*, 41 TEX. J. BUS. L. 313 (2006).

[22] *Jesse*, 485 N.W.2d at 69.

[23] *See* 1 G. HAZARD & W. HODES, THE LAW OF LAWYERING § 1.13:108 (Supp. 1997) (when separately represented parties negotiate over creation of entity, premise that entity is being rep-

called "entity" Rule"

captures a reality available to you and to your clients—you might *choose to treat your clients as an unincorporated association and* apply the entity rule, as opposed to the aggregate rule, of multiple representation.[24] At least one prominent ethics committee has approved this representation arrangement, implying that it may be the most appropriate understanding of the lawyer's role with promoters.[25]

It is reasonably clear that a lawyer may represent as an entity an inchoate, unincorporated association.[26] The Restatement includes informal organizations in its definition of entities, and does not insist that the informal group otherwise have legal standing.[27] The Model Rules agree that Rule 1.13 applies to "unincorporated associations";[28] and, while the Rules also state that "[a]n organizational client is a legal entity,"[29] an ABA ethics opinion construes Rule 1.13 as not requiring the group to possess "a separate jural entity."[30] With that understanding, the Committee on the Rules of Professional Conduct of the Arizona State Bar concluded that a lawyer may represent the yet-to-be-formed entity and not any individual constituents, as the typical entity representation would contemplate.[31]

You have the option, therefore, in any jurisdiction other than those which follow *Jesse,* expressly to define your representation of Filippa and Bill as covering only their business, and not as covering either person in an individual capacity. Indeed, if you understood Filippa and Bill to be in fact operating as partners of a general partnership, your representation could easily be understood as attaching to the partnership itself, which

---

resented is inappropriate); RESTATEMENT, *supra* note 2, at § 130 (not crediting the *Jesse* retroactivity principle but allowing the joint representation of constituents).

[24] *See* Note, *An Expectations Approach to Client Identity*, 106 HARV. L. REV. 687 (1993) [hereinafter Note, *Expectations Approach*] (recommending entity approach to client identity during pre-incorporation process).

[25] State Bar of Arizona, Op. 02–06 (2002) (a lawyer may represent an entity that does not yet exist "as long as the incorporators understand that they are retaining counsel on behalf of the yet-to-be formed entity and will need to ratify the corporate action, *nunc pro tunc*, once the entity is formed").

[26] *See* Tremblay, *supra* note 6, at 421.

[27] RESTATEMENT, *supra* note 2, at § 96, cmt. c ("whether the organization is a formal legal entity is relevant but not determinative" to the entity conception). The Restatement offers as examples of such informal entities "a social club or an informal group that has established an investment pool"). *Id.*

[28] MODEL RULES OF PROF'L CONDUCT at R. 1.13, cmt. 1. In the business law world, an unincorporated association could include any business entity which is not a corporation, including any variety of partnership and limited liability companies. *See, e.g.*, DOUGLAS M. BRANSON ET AL., BUSINESS ENTERPRISES: LEGAL STRUCTURES, GOVERNANCE AND POLICY 53–135 (2009) (addressing "unincorporated business entities" in that fashion); LARRY E. RIBSTEIN, THE RISE OF THE UNCORPORATION (2010) (describing the rise of unincorporated associations (for which Ribstein coins the term "uncorporation") such as LLCs).

[29] MODEL RULES OF PROF'L CONDUCT at R. 1.13 cmt. 1.

[30] ABA Comm. on Ethics & Prof'l Responsibility, Formal Op. 92–365 (1992) (concluding that an unincorporated trade association may be treated as an entity for purposes of conflicts of interest).

[31] Ariz. Op. 02–06, *supra* note 25, at 4.

under most doctrinal treatment triggers duties to the entity and not to the individual partners.[32] While such an election would eliminate the joint client conflict of interest concerns described in the previous section, it would require you to counsel the two business partners very carefully so that they understand the implications of not having an attorney-client relationship with your clinic.

have to make sure the individuals know you rep. the org under the entity model

How does the entity concept differ from the individual representation model? The next section discusses that question for existing organizations. If you opt to choose the entity model for your initial legal work with Filippa and Bill, the discussion in the next Section should inform your decision-making.

II. WHO IS THE LAWYER'S CLIENT (OR WHO ARE THE LAWYER'S CLIENTS) DURING ENTITY REPRESENTATION?

Once you and your clients have created a formal entity, or when your client from the beginning is a formal entity, the question of "who is my client" is at once easier and more difficult. It is easier than the previous discussion because conceptually the answer is crystal clear: when you represent the entity, the entity is your client and the constituents of the entity are not your clients, absent a separate agreement with any one of them.[33] It is more difficult because translating that conceptual certainty into practice may be challenging.

representing a formed entity

The topic of how corporate lawyers respect and implement the wishes of their clients is a recurring one addressed in depth in many settings.[34] For our purposes, we will highlight merely a few prominent themes. For more complex challenges you confront, you will develop these preliminary ideas in more sophisticated ways with your own research.

The Default Orientation—Honoring the Chain of Command: With an individual client, your professional duty is to respect the wishes of your client, even if you disagree with the wisdom of your client's choices.[35] If your client is an entity, it likely has identified a command structure through which the organization makes decisions. In the ordinary course

---

[32] ABA Comm. on Ethics and Prof'l Responsibility, Formal Op. 361 (1991) (fact that attorney represents partnership does not, standing alone, create attorney-client relationship with each of the partners); Zimmerman v. Dan Kamphausen Co., 971 P.2d 236, 241 (Colo. App. 1998) (same).

[33] MODEL RULES OF PROF'L CONDUCT R. 1.13(a).

[34] For a sampling of the literature, see, e.g., Lawrence E. Mitchell, *Professional Responsibility and the Close Corporation: Toward a Realistic Ethic*, 74 CORNELL L. REV. 466 (1989); Nancy J. Moore, *Expanding Duties of Attorneys to "Non–Clients": Reconceptualizing the Attorney–Client Relationship in Entity Representation and Other Inherently Ambiguous Situations*, 45 S.C. L. REV. 659, 687–95 (1994); William H. Simon, *Whom (or What) Does the Organization's Lawyer Represent?: An Anatomy of Intraclient Conflict*, 91 CAL. L. REV. 57 (2003); Note, *Expectations Approach, supra* note 24.

[35] Recall the client-centeredness discussion in the Counseling chapter.

of business, you treat the authorized constituent as if she were your client, so long as you discern no indication that she does not speak for the organization. Who plays that role within an organization depends on the organization's size and structure. Often your "client" will be a staff member carrying out the organization's ordinary business, such as an executive director or another employee. In other settings your primary contact may be with an officer (a president, vice-president, treasurer, or secretary, for example), a manager (the person charged with administering an LLC), or a director (a member of the organization's governing board). Ordinarily, a *shareholder* of an organization does not, merely by virtue of that status, have management authority for an entity.[36]

If the constituents from whom you ordinarily receive instructions disagree, and if your counseling of the constituents does not lead to some consensus, you will honor the chain of command, and proceed "up the ladder" in an effort to obtain clarity about your actions. That sentence is easy to write, of course, but in practice this process can be very painful and awkward to implement.

Constituents Are Not Your Clients: Model Rule 1.13(a) states succinctly that "[a] lawyer employed or retained by an organization represents the organization acting through its duly authorized constituents."[37] When the executive director telephones you to talk about your legal advice regarding the employment status of a new hire in the business, you might likely refer to that as "a call from my client." That would be correct—the client, through the executive director (ED), has called you, and you will be speaking with your client. But the ED herself is not your client. Recall the indicia of "client-hood" described in Section I.C above. You do not owe the ED any confidentiality obligations, except as the entity so desires. You owe her no conflict of interest protections, except inasmuch as the entity's interests are affected. And she has no right to sue you personally for breach of fiduciary duty or malpractice, except in the name of the organization.

Constituents Need to Understand that They Are Not Your Clients: The ED may not understand the perhaps-subtle distinctions just described in the previous paragraph. She may have heard you refer to her as your "client," she may believe that anything she tells you will remain confidential between the two of you, and she may well feel quite betrayed if you oppose her in some fashion (including, say, if your clinic were to sue her on behalf of another client[38]). In those ways, she may believe she is your cli-

---

[36] *See* 18A AM. JUR. 2D *Corporations* § 626 (2012); *see also* CA, Inc. v. AFSCME Emps. Pension Plan, 953 A.2d 227, 232 (Del. 2008).

[37] MODEL RULES OF PROF'L CONDUCT R. 1.13(a).

[38] Because the ED is not a client in her personal capacity, she is not entitled, in her personal capacity, to invoke the protections of Model Rule 1.7(a)(1), barring a lawyer from accepting representation "directly adverse to another client." *See* MODEL RULES OF PROF'L CONDUCT R. 1.7(a)(1). Therefore, conceptually at least, your clinic could represent the entity and sue the ED on behalf of another client at the very same time, without running afoul of that rule. Conceptual-

ent. If her belief about that is "reasonable," then she might end up qualifying as your client.[39] Your responsibility is to make as clear as possible your role and your allegiance, so that she will not have any reasonable basis to believe that you are her lawyer.

Constituents Do Not Always Act in the Best Interests of the Organization: The most interesting ethics issues arise when the lawyer believes that the agents whose instructions she ordinarily follows are acting in a way which is injurious or disloyal to the organization. Most of Model Rule 1.13's language addresses that worry, and its advice is on the whole sensible and what you would expect—the lawyer should pursue review by higher authorities when constituents are proposing unlawful or disloyal strategies, and, if the highest authorities also support the bad acts, the lawyer may seek relief outside the entity, perhaps by revealing the bad intentions to some regulator.[40] That basic message is consistent with the underlying reality that no constituent, even the CEO or the chair of the board of directors, speaks infallibly for the client.

The Rule's lessons, though, mask some serious difficulties for corporate lawyers who suspect wrongdoing by constituents. Without emasculating what is a very rich ethical topic, we might highlight briefly a few ideas developed by commentators to assist you to navigate this complex terrain.

- High-risk business strategies do not necessarily equate to a "violation of law" or a "violation of a legal obligation to the organization," the two predicates for a lawyer to invoke the activism of Rule 1.13. You will need to develop the judgments to make that distinction in a wise way.

- Discerning what is in the "best interests of the organization" can be terribly difficult, especially when duly authorized agents of the organization tell you that their actions are indeed for the benefit of the shareholders (or, in nonprofit settings, for the benefit of the organization's mission).

- William Simon has developed one of the best taxonomies for trying to make sense of the question of how the lawyer should proceed, and whose instructions the lawyer should honor, when faced with seeming betrayal by constituents of the organization.[41] Simon distinguishes among the following approaches:

---

ly is different from practically, however. It is difficult to imagine any setting where a lawyer would sue a significant constituent of an ongoing client.

[39] *See* RESTATEMENT, *supra* note 2, at § 14.

[40] MODEL RULES OF PROF'L CONDUCT R. 1.13(b). The description in the text oversimplifies the lessons within the rule.

[41] Simon, *supra* note 34, at 75.

Strategies when
constituent isn't
acting in "best
interest of org"

(1) A *control group* approach, under which the lawyer answers to those who possess "de facto control", of the corporation. Simon acknowledges the presumption of such an approach, but sees that presumption as a rebuttable one, "subject to strong limits . . . , supplied by principles of authority and fiduciary duty."[42] He explains the "authority" limitation in his second approach.

(2) An *authority structure* approach, which Simon understands to be the perspective communicated by Rule 1.13. In Simon's words, "Control is not enough; authority is the touchstone."[43] The lawyer relies on this approach when the lawyer cannot trust adequately those in control of the day-to-day decisions of the organization. The authority approach usually refers to the lawyer's need to rely upon the board of directors, but Simon also argues that, in some settings, including those where the board is not sufficiently disinterested, a lawyer may approach shareholders.[44]

→ rely on board

(3) A *framework of dealing* approach, which is Simon's original contribution to the usual commentary about this tension. The justification for this novel approach arises from the fact that "the corporation's identity includes, in addition to a set of decision-making procedures [represented by the first two approaches], a substantive commitment that its constituents be treated fairly."[45] Simon's arguments here support a lawyer's discretion in some critical moments to act autonomously to protect her client's interests, without direct approval from those in control or possessing formal authority. As he describes it,

→ descretion to
lawyer to
act in best
interest

> [I]t will sometimes happen that the lawyer can say confidently that the decision of the highest authority violates an important duty. Clear violations will most likely occur when the duty protects interests that are not represented in the authority structure—for example, minority shareholders or creditors. In such circumstances, the lawyer has to make a substantive judgment about the corporation's interests and responsibilities.

---

[42] *Id.* at 80.

[43] *Id.*

[44] *Id.* at 82. Simon does not address in his article the responsibilities of a lawyer representing a nonprofit organization, which of course will have no shareholders. Presumably, the lawyer's only (and quite drastic) remedy when the nonprofit board is not responsive would be to seek assistance from the state's Attorney General, which typically has authority over nonprofits. *See* Lumen N. Mulligan, *What's Good for the Goose Is Not Good for the Gander: Sarbanes–Oxley–Style Nonprofit Reforms*, 105 MICH. L. REV. 1981, 1989 (2007).

[45] Simon, *supra* note 34, at 86.

Disclosure to the affected constituent or a public authority might be the most plausible remedy.[46]

This short summary cannot do justice to Simon's thoughtful assessment of the lawyer's role in protecting the organization from harmful actions by constituents. We suggest you read Simon more carefully if you encounter this tension in your clinic work.

III. CONFIDENTIALITY DUTIES WITHIN ENTITY REPRESENTATION

When acting in the role of a lawyer for an organization, you owe your client a duty of confidentiality, described in Model Rule 1.6[47] and modified by the responsibilities described in Rule 1.13.[48] This Section will address three aspects of that duty having particular relevance to your experiences. Those three aspects covered here are the role of constituents in deciding when to consent to revelation of secrets; the nature of the organizational attorney-client privilege; and how to explain confidentiality to your client's agents. In each instance this discussion will only highlight some considerations which you will explore in more depth in your actual work.

A. CONSENT TO REVELATION IN THE ENTITY SETTING

Virtually everything you learn from your entity client will be covered by Rule 1.6's broad confidentiality commitment, so you will maintain the secrecy of that information during your work (which includes not sharing information about your client's projects with your significant other, with other law school faculty members, or with anyone else outside of the clinic). Rule 1.6 provides some clear exceptions to that duty, including your right to disclose information necessary to prevent or rectify serious financial injury resulting from your client's crime or fraud if the crime or fraud included the use of your services.[49] It also permits disclosure with the informed consent of your client.

exceptions to confidentiality

The "consent" exception is sensible. It is also easily understood—except perhaps in the entity context. Imagine that you are working closely with the executive director (ED) of a nonprofit organization to assist the nonprofit to develop an employment policy. When the ED tells you some information about the company's practices and policies, you will

---

[46] *Id.* at 104–105.

[47] MODEL RULES OF PROF'L CONDUCT R. 1.6.

[48] *Id.* at R. 1.13.

[49] *Id.* at R. 1.6(b)(2), (3). Another common exception within the rule covers prevention of imminent death or substantial bodily harm. *Id.* at R. 1.6(b)(1). In transactional settings, that exception is seemingly less likely to occur than the prospect of financial harm resulting from a criminal or fraudulent act.

keep that information confidential unless he gives you permission to reveal it. For example, assume that you would like to consult with an expert lawyer from a downtown law firm willing to offer you some pro bono advice about the intricacies of employment law. You will ask the ED for permission to disclose to the lawyer the facts you have learned. If the ED gives such permission, you have satisfied your obligations under Rule 1.6. That story implies that the ED has some "ownership" of the confidentiality rights. But he does not have any such ownership.

Imagine instead that, in the course of the conversation the ED tells you that he has been paying a friend of his to perform some useful consulting services for the nonprofit, and has paid the friend "under the table," meaning he has not reported the payments as wages nor withheld any payroll tax deductions. Even without the ED's permission, you may reveal that information to others within the organization, and if the organization agrees, you may reveal that information to others outside the nonprofit, such as to the state and federal tax or labor agencies.

This simple example shows you the need for you to be careful about how you treat the consent exception to your confidentiality duties.

B. THE CORPORATE ATTORNEY–CLIENT PRIVILEGE

Your clinic work will encourage you to revisit the sometimes subtle, but quite important, distinction between the confidentiality duties represented by Rule 1.6 and the confidentiality protections generated by the attorney-client privilege. The two concepts are related but entirely different. The privilege, as a rule of evidence, has meaning only within some forensic setting, such as a courtroom or a deposition setting. Even though you will be practicing in a transactional setting, and therefore will not be participating in evidentiary hearings or depositions, the substance of the privilege is still critically important for you to understand. Can you see why?

While many thoughtful observers have argued for the abolition of the organizational attorney-client privilege,[50] the protection remains firmly in place in all jurisdictions.[51] The famous *Upjohn* decision by the Supreme Court in 1981 established the basic scope of the privilege in the federal courts.[52] *Upjohn* described the privilege as covering "communications concern[ing] matters within the scope of the employees' corporate duties,"[53] so long as the communications are made in confidence and for the purpose

---

[50] *See, e.g.*, Elizabeth G. Thornburg, *Sanctifying Secrecy: The Mythology of the Corporate Attorney–Client Privilege*, 69 NOTRE DAME L. REV. 157 (1993); Paul R. Rice, *Attorney–Client Privilege: The Eroding Concept of Confidentiality Should Be Abolished*, 47 DUKE L.J. 853 (1998).

[51] For the federal privilege, see Upjohn Co. v. United States, 449 U.S. 383 (1981). For a general discussion of the doctrine, see Alexander C. Black, *What Corporate Clients Are Entitled to Attorney-Client Privileges–Modern Cases*, 27 A.L.R. 5th 76 (1995).

[52] *Upjohn*, 449 U.S. 383.

[53] *Id.* at 384.

of obtaining or providing legal assistance to the client. The Restatement standard is even slightly broader than *Upjohn*'s, applying the privilege to "an agent of the organization" if the communication "concerns a legal matter of interest to the organization."[54] You will need to understand the scope of the privilege and its coverage in your home state.

Even more important than your knowing the scope of the privilege, however, is your recognizing how the privilege might be waived.[55] You will typically want to ensure that the conversations between you and your client's constituents remain privileged, even though most often your client will not be consulting you in anticipation of any litigation. Some actions within your control might affect an inadvertent waiver of the privilege. The most critical two examples of that consequence each relate to the "confidentiality" component of the privilege. If you meet with your client's agent along with a non-privileged individual, the communications within that meeting will lose protection.[56] Also, if you voluntarily disclose some otherwise privileged client material to persons outside of the organization, other matters related to that disclosure may also lose their privileged status.[57]

[handwritten margin note: involuntary waiver of privilege]

For transactional clinic students (like all transactional lawyers), the privilege issues present challenges in a subtle way. Because you are most often not engaged in litigation-related legal assistance with your clients, and because your clients are most often not contemplating nor expecting any contentious disputes as they organize their enterprises, the test of your privilege effectiveness will occur, if it occurs at all, many months or years after your actual work, if and when a serious dispute arises. That sense of distance might lead one to give privilege issues less attention on a day-to-day basis. You can understand why succumbing to any such inclination would be a very unwise move.

---

[54] RESTATEMENT, *supra* note 2, at § 73. *See* STEPHEN GILLERS, REGULATION OF LAWYERS, 48 (8th ed. 2009).

[55] We are assuming here that the communications between a student attorney in a clinic and the clinic's client are fully covered by the privilege. If the student is serving as counsel under the state's Student Practice Rule, that assumption is indisputable, for the student is a "lawyer" for all purposes. If the student is not student-practice certified, however, the assumption is somewhat more open to question, although still quite solid. For a discussion of the role of students in a transactional clinic, see Section IV below.

[56] *See* Larson v. Harrington, 11 F. Supp. 2d 1198, 1200 (E.D. Cal. 1998); People v. Harris, 442 N.E.2d 1205, 1208 (N.Y. Ct. App. 1982); Marshall v. Marshall, 295 P.2d 131, 134 (Cal. App. 1956); *see generally* EDWARD J. IMWINKELRIED, THE NEW WIGMORE: EVIDENTIARY PRIVILEGES § 6.8.1 (2012).

[57] *See, e.g.,* In re Columbia/HCA Healthcare Corp. Billing Prac. Litig., 293 F.3d 289, 302–04 (6th Cir. 2002) (waiver of confidentiality cannot be done selectively; the information is available in any case to all parties). *See also* Douglas R. Richmond & William Freivogel, *The Attorney–Client Privilege and Work Product in the Post–Enron Era,* 2004 A.B.A. SEC. BUS. L. 23, *available at* http://www.abanet.org/buslaw/newsletter/0027/materials/11.pdf.

IV. STUDENT WORK IN TRANSACTIONAL CLINICS AND THE UNAUTHORIZED PRACTICE OF LAW

Like any layperson, a law student may not practice law independently. Every state in the nation has adopted some version of an "unauthorized practice of law" statute, usually criminal in nature, prohibiting nonlawyers from engaging in any activity which constitutes the practice of law in that jurisdiction.[58] Attending law school does not give you any exemption from those laws. The question we highlight here is how to understand your clinic work to ensure that you are not committing a crime, nor committing an advance violation of Model Rule 5.5 (a rule which will apply to you when you become a lawyer).

For students participating in a litigation-focused clinic, the answer to the question we raise is straightforward. Each state has a "student-practice rule" permitting law students to represent clients in court under specified conditions, including while enrolled in a law school clinical course.[59] Most of those rules are litigation-focused, covering students' work in courts and similar tribunal-based proceedings.[60] Some states, like Massachusetts, require that certified law students enroll in a course in evidence as a condition of qualifying for certification.[61]

A handful of states have student-practice rules expressly covering transactional clinical work.[62] If your jurisdiction's rule covers your work, then there is no question about your right to engage in the work you will be doing. If it does not, you need to develop a proper understanding of your role in the lawyering activities the clinic carries on for its clients.

Certified law students are effectively lawyers.[63] Non-certified law students are effectively paralegals.[64] Non-certified law students may en-

---

[58] *See* MODEL RULES OF PROF'L CONDUCT R. 5.5(a) (2009); RESTATEMENT, *supra* note 2, § 4 (2002); DEBORAH L. RHODE, ACCESS TO JUSTICE 15 (2004); *Prohibitions on Practice of Nonlawyers*, LAWS. MANUAL ON PROF. CONDUCT (ABA/BNA) No. 210 at ¶ 1 (Dec. 22, 1999) ("Every jurisdiction prohibits the unauthorized practice of law.").

[59] *See* David F. Chavkin, *Am I My Client's Lawyer?: Role Definition and the Clinical Supervisor*, 51 SMU L. REV. 1507, 1546–54 (1998).

[60] *See, e.g.,* ARIZ. SUP. CT. R. 38(d) (stating that a certified law student "may appear in any court or before any administrative tribunal"); COLO. REV. STAT. ANN. § 12–5–116.1 ("appear and participate in any civil proceeding"); GA. SUP. CT. R. 91 ("assist in proceedings"); KY. SUP. CT. R. 2.540 ("appear in any proceeding in any court"); MASS. SUP. JUD. CT. R. 3:03 (permitting students to "appear" in court in various contexts on behalf of indigent clients); N.Y. COMP. CODES R. & REGS. tit. 22, § 805.5 (referring to civil and criminal court proceedings).

[61] *See* MASS. SUP. JUD. CT. R. 3:03. *See also* ARIZ. ST. SUP. CT. R. 38 (D)(5)(A)(iv) (requiring courses in civil procedure, criminal law, professional responsibility, and evidence); ARK. BAR ADMIS. R. XV(C)(2) (requiring professional responsibility); CAL. RULES OF CT. R. 9.42(c)(3) (requiring evidence and civil procedure).

[62] *See* ILL. SUP. CT. R. 711(c)(1) (stating that a certified law student "may counsel with clients, negotiate in the settlement of claims, and engage in the preparation and drafting of legal instruments"); *see also* COL. REV. STAT. § 12–5–116.1; TENN. SUP. CT. R. 7 § 10.03.

[63] *See* In re Hatcher, 150 F.3d 631, 636 (7th Cir. 1998)(certified law student equivalent to a lawyer for purposes of recusal statute); Connecticut Comm. on Prof'l Ethics, Informal Op. 97–10 (1997) (law clinic student considered a lawyer for purposes of conflict of interest consideration);

gage in any lawyering activities that a paralegal may engage in, but no more. While paralegals lawfully may engage in many lawyering activities so long as they are supervised by a lawyer (and *no* lawyering activities if they are not so supervised), some advisory authority implies that paralegals are more limited in their role with clients than your clinical experience would hope to offer to you. It appears, though, that the advisory opinions suggesting such limitations are not accurate.

All of the relevant authority agrees that nonlawyers may perform legal research, fact investigation, and drafting of documents.[65] Some advisory authority, however, suggests limits to the role that nonlawyers may play in counseling and negotiation. For instance, an American Bar Association (ABA) formal ethics opinion required that "nonlawyers do not do things that lawyers may not do *or do the things that lawyers only may do,*"[66] including "counsel[ing] clients about law matters."[67] The Code of Ethics and Professional Responsibility of the National Association of Legal Assistants (NALA) advises its members that they may not "give legal opinions or advice."[68] Several state bar ethics opinions and guidelines for paralegal practice echo the same categorical exclusion for offering legal advice[69] and, sometimes, for negotiating on behalf of a client.[70]

A recent review of that advisory authority concluded that it misstates substantive law. That source concluded that, properly supervised, a nonlawyer may engage in any of the activities of a lawyer short of appearance before tribunals, which is subject to the rules of the respective tribunals.[71] Supervision by a licensed lawyer is essential. Indeed, the comparative treatment of nonlawyers, who may not engage in *any* practice of law unless directly and closely supervised by the responsible law-

---

Peter A. Joy, *The Ethics of Law School Clinic Students as Student–Lawyers*, 45 S. TEX. L. REV. 815, 832 (2004) ("a student-lawyer should be treated as a lawyer for ethics purposes"); Peter A. Joy & Robert B. Kuehn, *Conflict of Interest and Competency Issues in Law Clinic Practice*, 9 CLINICAL L. REV. 493, 510 (2002) (reviewing authority treating law students as lawyers).

[64] *See* Paul R. Tremblay, *Shadow Lawyering: Nonlawyer Practice in Law Firms*, 85 IND. L.J. 653, 696 (2010).

[65] *Id.* at 663–72. The remainder of the discussion in the text relies upon this source for its descriptions and conclusions.

[66] ABA Comm. on Ethics and Prof'l Responsibility, Formal Op. 316 (1967) (emphasis added) [hereinafter ABA Formal Op. 316].

[67] *Id.* The opinion also includes "appear[ing] in court or . . .   in formal proceedings that are a part of the judicial process," and, in pure question-begging fashion, "engag[ing] directly in the practice of law."

[68] NATIONAL ASSOCIATION OF LEGAL ASSISTANTS, NALA MANUAL FOR PARALEGALS AND LEGAL ASSISTANTS § 3.061 (5th ed. 2009), *available at* http://www.nala.org/code.aspx, at Canon 3. The NALA Canon also includes the restriction for "represent[ing] a client before a court or agency unless so authorized by that court or agency." *Id.*

[69] For the citations, see Tremblay, *supra* note 64, at 665 n.54.

[70] *Id.* at 665 n.55; for negotiation limits, see STATE BAR OF NEW MEXICO, RULES GOVERNING PARALEGAL   SERVICES,   R.   20–103   (2004),   *available   at* http://www.nmbar.org/AboutSBNM/ParalegalDivision/PDrulesgovparalegalservices.html.

[71] Tremblay, *supra* note 64, at 659.

yer, and certified law students, who become de facto lawyers once enrolled in a supervised clinical placement, implies that the latter may engage in unsupervised discrete activities (such as counseling a client), so long as the student's placement occurs under the auspices of a program administered and overseen by a lawyer.[72] Therefore, it is more advantageous to practice as a student certified under a student-practice rule than as non-certified paralegal.

As with everything in this text, you must research the particular rules and doctrines in your home jurisdiction in order to understand your own responsibilities and liabilities.

V. STUDENT WORK ON MATTERS IMPLICATING OUT–OF–STATE LAW

For purposes of this Section, let us assume that the work you perform for your clients in the transactional clinic is authorized and proper. The topic we highlight here concerns those instances where a local client requires legal advice implicating the law of a different jurisdiction. Like the previous discussion, this question invokes unauthorized practice concerns, although from a different perspective.

Let us imagine a simple story:

> Assume you are enrolled in a clinical program in a law school located in the state of Michigan. Zev Chenowitz, a graduate student attending a local university, seeks the clinic's assistance to establish a nonprofit corporation which will operate in Massachusetts, Chenowitz's home state. Once the nonprofit has been established, Chenowitz will be its president and, for the next couple of years, he will perform the president's duties from his apartment in Michigan.

The question this story poses for you is whether assisting Chenowitz in this endeavor risks your engaging in the unauthorized practice of law in Massachusetts, with our having assumed that your work for him under Michigan law would be quite proper.

A lawyer may only practice law in the jurisdictions in which she is admitted. As a clinical student in Michigan, your license to practice derives either from the Michigan student practice rule or from your acting under the supervision of your supervisor, a Michigan lawyer. Therefore, you have the right to offer a Michigan resident assistance on matters of Michigan law. What about when your work touches on the laws of a different state, such as Massachusetts in this story?

---

[72] For evidence of that inference, see, e.g., MASS. SUP. JUD. CT. R. 3:03(2) ("The expression 'general supervision' [within this rule] shall not be construed to require the attendance in court of the supervising member of the bar.")

To investigate this question, we begin with Model Rule 5.5(c).[73] That rule tells a lawyer who has a license to practice in one state whether she may engage in certain lawyering activities in a different state. Rule 5.5(c)(4) tells you that a lawyer may "provide legal services on a temporary basis" in the other state if the services "arise out of or are reasonably related to the lawyer's practice in a jurisdiction in which the lawyer is admitted to practice." If you meet that standard, then you may proceed; if you do not, you will have engaged in the unauthorized practice of law in Massachusetts.

Your application of the Rule 5.5(c)(3) doctrine to the request from Chenowitz leads you to the following two separate inquiries:

- Is creation of a Massachusetts nonprofit corporation the provision of legal services in Massachusetts?

- Is your representation of Chenowitz a matter related to your license to practice in Michigan?

Put another way, you need to decide whether the creation of a Massachusetts corporation is an activity you may not engage in as a nonlawyer, and, if it is the "practice of law," whether you may use your Michigan authority and your representation of Chenoweth in Michigan to provide the authorization to engage in this limited Massachusetts practice. Your analysis leads you to the following considerations:

→ yes.

(1) *Is creating a corporation the "practice of law"?*: One might argue that creating a nonprofit corporation with its articles, bylaws and conflicts policy is something that many experienced laypersons could do quite competently, and therefore it cannot qualify as the "practice of law" in Massachusetts. There is logic to that argument, but it seems to be wrong. Under most established understanding of what kinds of activities fall within the "practice of law" rubric, incorporation is close enough to "what lawyers traditionally do"[74] to qualify. A nonlawyer offering incorporation services to members of the public would very likely be found to have violated the UPL statute of the state in question.[75]

→ No.

(2) *Is representation of Chenoweth a "Michigan" matter?*: If your work for Chenoweth is otherwise a proper Michigan legal representation matter, then his need for advice about Massachusetts law likely would be proper. The critical preliminary consideration for you, therefore, is whether a Michigan lawyer may offer these services to Chenoweth. In this setting, the answer is likely no.

Chenoweth is not a Michigan resident. His "enterprise" will have its principal place of business outside of Michigan, and will conduct business

---

[73] MODEL RULES OF PROF'L CONDUCT R. 5.5(c).

[74] Derek A. Denckla, *Nonlawyers and the Unauthorized Practice of Law: An Overview of the Legal and Ethical Parameters*, 67 FORDHAM L. REV. 2581, 2586–2592 (1999).

[75] *See* Fla. Bar v. Keehley, 190 So.2d 173 (Fla. 1966).

another state. A lawyer ordinarily may not offer legal services to a resident of a state in which the lawyer is not admitted if the services relate to that other state's laws and otherwise have no connection to the lawyer's home state.[76] If Chenoweth were attending school in Massachusetts and the facts remained the same, a Michigan lawyer would be obligated to reject his request for assistance. The mere fact that Chenoweth is a temporary resident of Michigan likely will not change that analysis.

If Chenoweth were a Michigan resident, the answer to the question whether your clinic could accept the matter may still be no, but it would be a closer call. If the nonprofit will exist in Massachusetts, and operate in Massachusetts, with its principal place of business in Massachusetts, the fact that Chenoweth has connections to Michigan may not be enough to permit the temporary Massachusetts practice.

If, by contrast, the Massachusetts nonprofit were to have its principal place of business in Michigan and conduct its affairs there, that fact should provide the necessary contacts to your clinic's home state to satisfy Rule 5.5(c)(3). Consider, for example, the many businesses around the country whose state of incorporation is Delaware but whose operations occur in the lawyer's home state. No fair reading of Rule 5.5(c)(3) would require the formation of each Delaware corporation to occur only with the assistance of a Delaware lawyer.

(3) *What happens if the matter qualifies as a Massachusetts representation?*: If this matter does not have sufficient Michigan contacts to qualify as a local representation, your clinic's choices are to reject the representation, or to associate with a Massachusetts lawyer who "actively participates" in your work for Chenoweth and his nonprofit. Model Rule 5.5(c)(1) provides a safe harbor against a claim of unauthorized practice if such active (and good faith) association occurs.[77]

VI. YOUR RESPONSIBILITY FOR CLIENT ACTIONS AFFECTING THIRD PARTIES (OR, YOUR CLIENTS WON'T BE LIKE ENRON, BUT WHAT IF THEY WERE?)

The final ethical issue we highlight in this chapter is one whose assessment lies less in the arena of substantive law and more in the arena of moral philosophy. That reality makes the issues more interesting and challenging, in some ways.

As a corporate lawyer, your work will assist companies, entrepreneurs and community organizations in a variety of ways. Most of the production resulting from your clients' enterprises will be all to the good—

---

[76] *See* RESTATEMENT, *supra* note 2, at § 3.

[77] MODEL RULES OF PROF'L CONDUCT R. 5.5(c)(1).

jobs generated, economic activity spurred, communities enriched. But in some instances—and we expect these are rather rare instances—the enterprises will engage in actions which harm others. An employer will request help in negotiating a severe noncompete agreement with a prospective (or perhaps an existing) employee.[78] Majority shareholders will seek your assistance to "squeeze out" minority owners in a grab for power within the enterprise.[79] A manufacturing enterprise will press you for a legal opinion supporting its skirting of environmental protection regulations or ordinances.[80] In such instances, what should be your response? How accountable will you be, or should you be, for the actions of your clients? *[accountability for client actions]*

One thing you know for sure: Touting what we might term the lawyer's "non-accountability principle" is risky and simplistic, even if it captures a basic truth.[81] That truth is that lawyers offer clients expert advice and wise counsel, but it is clients who decide, in the end, whether and how to proceed. So long as the clients' chosen course of action is lawful, the lawyer has no formal responsibility for the effects of the actions taken. *[No formal resp. for lawyer if client acts lawfully]* We know that reliance on this non-accountability excuse is risky and simplistic, not just because of the attractive critiques of the stance developed by some moral philosophers and legal ethicists,[82] but because of powerful stories like Enron.[83] Some of the best and brightest lawyers in the profession actively assisted Enron executives to create sophisticated corporate and accounting schemes by which those executives became rich while company shareholders faced enormous risk and exposure. While some of the activities in which Enron's lawyers engaged may not have been lawful, the deeper criticisms of those lawyers arises from their intentional use of otherwise lawful tactics to achieve morally troublesome ends.[84]

---

[78] Commentators have noted the harm caused to employees by a strict and wide-ranging noncompete agreement, leaving talented ex-employees involuntarily unemployed for long periods of their careers. *See, e.g.,* Matt Marx, et al., *Mobility, Skills, and the Michigan Non-compete Experiment,* 55 MGMT. SCI. 875 (2009).

[79] *See* Simon, *supra* note 34, at 61.

[80] *See* Stephen L. Pepper, *Counseling at the Limits of the Law: An Exercise in the Jurisprudence and Ethics of Lawyering,* 104 YALE L.J. 1545 (1995).

[81] Murray Schwartz first described the non-accountability principle in the 1970s. *See* Murray L. Schwartz, *The Professionalism and Accountability of Lawyers,* 66 CAL. L. REV. 669, 673–74 (1978). Schwartz was responding to a defense of the lawyer's amoral role proffered by Charles Fried. Charles Fried, *The Lawyer as Friend: The Moral Foundations of the Lawyer–Client Relation,* 85 YALE L.J. 1060 (1976).

[82] Besides Schwartz, *supra* note 81, see, e.g., DAVID LUBAN, LAWYERS AND JUSTICE: AN ETHICAL STUDY (1988); David Luban, *The Adversary System Excuse, in* THE GOOD LAWYER: LAWYERS' ROLES AND LAWYERS' ETHICS 83 (David Luban ed., 1983); and Richard Wasserstrom, *Lawyers as Professionals: Some Moral Issues,* 5 HUM. RTS. 1 (1975).

[83] *See generally* BRIAN CRUVER, ANATOMY OF GREED: THE UNSHREDDED TRUTH FROM AN ENRON INSIDER (2002) (telling a first person account of an Enron employee).

[84] *See* Robert W. Gordon, *A New Role for Lawyers? The Corporate Counselor After Enron,* 35 CONN. L. REV. 1185, 1185–86 (2003); David Luban, *Making Sense of Moral Meltdowns, in* MORAL LEADERSHIP: THE THEORY AND PRACTICE OF POWER, JUDGMENT AND POLICY 57, 57–58 (Deborah

Enron is not the only example one might offer, of course. Consider instead the credit-default swap tactics leading to the 2008–09 financial crises, with lawyers once again using their technical expertise to assist executives achieve short-sighted and publicly harmful ends.[85] You may supply other stories fitting this mold. The stories are not scarce.

If the non-accountability principle is true, though, how do you square that professional reality with the accepted criticism of the lawyers just mentioned? You will grapple with that tension during your clinic experience. We offer you three brief ideas to inform your deliberations and discussions. The first two ideas suggest a more nuanced view of the substantive law underlying the non-accountability principle. The third idea begins to respond more directly to the question just posed.

(1) *Beware of Justified Third Party Reliance*: We began this chapter with the acknowledgement that lawyers, like you in your clinic work, owe duties to their clients, and not to the other "non-clients" whose interests your work affects. That fundamental tenet of the lawyer's professional role is well-established, and third parties who seek to hold lawyers responsible for harm they suffer as a direct result of the lawyers' work usually fail in that endeavor.[86] But "usually" is the operative word in that last sentence. If your work invites third-party reliance, and that reliance is reasonable, then you may owe a duty to the third party.[87] This is a potentially complex area of the law for which we may only offer the briefest of descriptions. The most common example of this exception is the opinion letter, written by a lawyer as part of her representation of a client, but expressly intended to be read, and relied upon, by another party to a transaction.[88] The point is that sometimes you *may* be accountable to the harmed third party.

(2) *Navigate Fiduciary Duties Carefully*: A second, and even more intricate, exception to the non-accountability principle arises in your work for clients who possess fiduciary duties. A lawyer who assists a client in a breach of that fiduciary duty might be liable to the injured party, based

---

L. Rhode ed., 2004); Deborah L. Rhode & Paul Paton, *Lawyers, Enron and Ethics*, in ENRON: CORPORATE FIASCOS AND THEIR IMPLICATIONS 625, 633–40 (Nancy Rappaport & Bala G. Dharan eds., 2004).

[85] *See generally* Symposium, *The Economic Downturn and the Legal Profession*, 78 FORDHAM L. REV. 2051 (2010); Eli Wald, *Loyalty in Limbo: The Peculiar Case of Attorneys' Loyalty to Clients*, 40 ST. MARY'S L.J. 909, 952–54 (2009).

[86] *See, e.g.,* Spinner v. Nutt, 631 N.E.2d 542 (Mass. 1994); Trask v. Butler, 872 P.2d 1080, 1085 (Wash. 1994); Goldberg v. Frye, 266 Cal. Rptr. 483, 489 (Ct. App. 1990).

[87] *See* RESTATEMENT, *supra* note 2, at § 51(2); RESTATEMENT (SECOND) OF TORTS § 552 (1977).

[88] *See, e.g.,* Greycas v. Proud, 826 F.2d 1560 (7th Cir. 1987); DONALD W. GLAZER, SCOTT FITZGIBBON & STEVEN O. WEISE, GLAZER AND FITZGIBBON ON LEGAL OPINIONS 30–32, § 1.8 (2d ed. 2001).

on evolving and not fully developed doctrine.[89] Some of your close corporation or partnership clients might owe fiduciary duties to minority shareholders or to other partners.[90] We highlight this issue simply as a cautionary note for your work in those settings.

(3) *Consider Accepting Moral Responsibility for Your Work*: Our third point, like the first two, deserves much more attention that we may offer it here. Fortunately, several important writers have provided that attention, so if your interest is piqued by this concern, you will have a rich trove of literature to investigate.[91] David Luban is the most widely-credited legal ethicist, among a large coterie of them, to point out that lawyers cannot rely casually on professional role assumptions to excuse what most observers would otherwise agree is immoral conduct. In some settings (say, criminal defense), the essential role requirements within that particular adversary system might excuse some unseemly actions. Civil litigators might attempt to rely on that adversary system as well, but their reliance is less well-founded. Transactional lawyers, though, do not even have an adversary system to invoke for their excuse.[92]

Here is one example that we encountered in the chapter on Drafting Transactional Documents. A client might suggest to you that the language you insert in a "clickthrough" component of a software contract include provisions which, were the customer to read them carefully, would lead the customer to question the fairness of the transaction, and perhaps not accept the transaction at all.[93] The client knows, though, that few if any customers read those clickthrough agreements with any care, and many do not read the provisions at all. You may conclude that the client has the legal right to include such one-sided contract terms in the software agreement, and that the contract terms will likely be enforceable.

---

[89] *See, e.g.*, Reynolds v. Schrock, 142 P.3d 1062, 1066–67 (Or. 2006) (claim against lawyer for assisting client breach of fiduciary duty); Katerina Lewinbuk, *Let's Sue All the Lawyers: The Rise of Claims Against Lawyers for Aiding and Abetting a Client's Breach of Fiduciary Duty*, 40 ARIZ. ST. L.J. 135, 146 (2008) ("every state court that examined the issue has allowed this cause of action to proceed in litigation").

[90] For a partnership case, see Thornwood, Inc. v. Jenner & Block, 799 N.E.2d 756, 768 (Ill. App. Ct. 2003). For a discussion of the minority shareholder context, see Bryan C. Barksdale, Note, *Redefining Obligations in Close Corporation Fiduciary Representation: Attorney Liability for Aiding and Abetting the Breach of Fiduciary Duty in Squeeze–Outs*, 58 WASH. & LEE L. REV. 551 (2001).

[91] *See supra* note 81 for a beginning sample of the available literature. For a review of the writing in this area, see Paul R. Tremblay, *Moral Activism Manqué*, 44 S. TEX. L. REV. 127 (2002).

[92] William Simon has developed a variation of this point in several writings. *See, e.g.,* William Simon, *Rethinking the Professional Responsibilities of the Business Lawyer*, 75 FORDHAM L. REV. 1453 (2006); William Simon, *Wrongs of Ignorance and Ambiguity: Lawyers' Responsibility for Collective Misconduct*, 22 YALE J. ON REG. 1, 15–17 (2005).

[93] For a discussion of adhesion contracts and fairness considerations, see, e.g., Robert L. Oakley, *Fairness in Electronic Contracting: Minimum Standards for Non–Negotiated Contracts*, 42 HOUS. L. REV. 1041 (2005); Ronald J. Mann & Travis Siebeneicher, *Just One Click: The Reality of Internet Retail Contracting*, 108 COLUM. L. REV. 984 (2008); Todd D. Rakoff, *Contracts of Adhesion: An Essay in Reconstruction*, 96 HARV. L. REV. 1173 (1983).

But you still may have qualms about the moral implications of that drafting tactic. While the baseline principle of client-centeredness would conclude that the client should decide the tactical wisdom of the plan, your commitment to a moral practice would give you the right to engage in a conversation with the client about the fairness concerns you have.

Accepting responsibility for the moral implications of clients' projects changes your client work in a couple of possible ways when compared to operating under the accepted non-accountability principle.[94] When relying on the latter, you understand your role to be an advisor and technical assistant to your client, communicating and translating complex legal concepts in a way that your client may use them to achieve its ends. If you reject the non-accountability principle, your role shifts. Your conversations with your client will likely include discussion of moral and fairness concerns.[95] While the client-centeredness commitment you explored in the Counseling chapter holds that clients, and not their lawyers, ought to choose what options best meet the clients' needs, that commitment shifts when questions of fairness and harm to others enter the picture.

Most often, the result of your conversations will be that you proceed with the proposed action, either because you conclude that your worries are not as profound as you had feared, or because your client adjusts its plans in response to your moral doubts. In some instances, though, your client may nevertheless choose to pursue a strategy which you cannot accept. At that point your options are plain: You may assist your client notwithstanding your objections (but without pretending that you hold no culpability for the resulting effects), or you may decline to continue to assist your client. The Model Rules tend to provide you coverage for that latter option,[96] although for some of your clients, and perhaps most of your clients, your clinic's free representation may be the only legal services available to it. That fact, if true, only increases the stakes for you and for your client.

---

[94] We note here that the Model Rules permit lawyers to consider, and to discuss with their clients, the "moral, economic, social and political" implications of the client's activity. MODEL RULES OF PROF'L CONDUCT R. 2.1.

[95] The literature sometimes refers to this as the "moral dialogue." *See, e.g.,* THOMAS L. SHAFFER & ROBERT F. COCHRAN, JR., LAWYERS, CLIENTS, AND MORAL RESPONSIBILITY 66–67 (1994); Sharon Dolovich, *Ethical Lawyering and the Possibility of Integrity*, 70 FORDHAM L. REV. 1629, 1643 (2002).

[96] MODEL RULES OF PROF'L CONDUCT R. 1.16(b)(4) (permitting withdrawal from representation, notwithstanding that the client may suffer "material adverse effect," if "the client insists upon taking action that the lawyer considers repugnant or with which the lawyer has a fundamental disagreement").

CHAPTER 9

WORKING WITH GROUPS

■ ■ ■

In your work in the clinic, you are likely to be assigned a matter working with Priya Krishna, an individual who wants to start a business selling food from a food truck. Or you may be assigned to work with Dolores Robinson, whom we met in the Interviewing chapter and who wants to create a new nonprofit organization. You are just as likely to be assigned to work with Filippa Sands and Bill Sherman who want to open a café in their neighborhood or with Ana, Victoria and Claudia, three sisters who want to start a day care center. You may have the opportunity to work with a group hoping to start a cooperative for workers who will clean homes and offices through the Domestic Workers Center (DWC). In most of the cases you are likely to see in your clinic work, you will not be working exclusively with an individual, even if that individual is your principal contact.

Transactional lawyers often work with groups. Entities are most often made up of several individuals, including management (the Executive Director and senior staff of the DWC), the board of directors and members (of a limited liability company or a membership organization such as DWC). With clients such as DWC, you may also have to interact with the "community" at large. Your work in the clinic may also require handling issues involving broader community interests, such as the negotiation of a community benefits agreement.

In this chapter we address issues raised by representing entity clients and client groups. These groups might be small groups made up of a few individuals or large groups made up of many community members. We begin by providing some background on groups, borrowing from the work of social psychologists. We then provide you some guidelines for facilitating client meetings. We cover two aspects of group work—working with groups within clients, such as a board of directors, and working with less structured groups as when doing community work. In this second aspect of this topic we borrow from the writings of those in the community lawyering field. Our goal is to prepare you to counsel groups and facilitate group meetings.

As with other chapters in this book, we find that much of what is written about lawyering focuses on the representation of individual clients. But several legal scholars and lawyers have written about group and entity representation, ranging from discussions of class actions to the representation of corporations.[1] We draw on that literature in our effort here to prepare you for your work with groups.

I. THE NATURE OF GROUPS

Membership is "central to our thinking about ourselves."[2] We are initiated into our first group at birth, our families. It is through this membership that we learn who we are, how to relate to others, how to express emotion and how to resolve problems.[3] Many types of groups exist, among them educational groups (such as the study group you might have belonged to in law school), therapy groups, task groups and community organizing groups. Individuals form into groups based on geography (living in the same neighborhood), shared interests, shared political or social perspectives or a shared sense of identity, among other reasons.[4] Groups can be formal or informal; they can be temporary or permanent. The United States Congress and the Supreme Court are examples of formal, permanent groups. The Senate can set up a temporary commission to look at a particular issue. It also has some permanent committees. Individuals normally belong to two kinds of groups—voluntary and involuntary.[5] We are members of groups we did not choose to join—family, religion, race or ethnicity. We also choose to join or belong to certain groups. We join groups to be social, because we want or need to "belong," to meet people or share interests, because we like the group's task or activity, because we like the people in the group (we may perceive positive characteristics that we value in others) or because we see the group as a means to satisfy our needs (even if the group itself does not do it).[6]

Groups have two important elements that differentiate them from merely a collection of people. First, group members communicate with

---

[1] *See, e.g.,* John Leubsdorf, *Pluralizing the Client–Lawyer Relationship,* 77 CORNELL L. REV. 825 (1992); James Gray Pope, *Two Faces, Two Ethics: Labor Union Lawyers and the Emerging Doctrine of Entity Ethics,* 68 OR. L. REV. 1 (1989). In the corporate setting, much of this writing has been about the ethics of entity representation but has also included the role of the lawyer more generally. *See, e.g.,* Ralph Jonas, *Who Is the Client?: The Corporate Lawyer's Dilemma,* 39 HASTINGS L.J. 617 (1988); Stanley A. Kaplan, *Some Ruminations on the Role of Corporate Counsel for a Corporation,* 56 NOTRE DAME L. REV. 873 (1981); James R. McCall, *The Corporation as Client: Problems, Perspectives, and Practical Solutions,* 39 HASTINGS L. J. 623 (1988); William H. Simon, *Whom (or What) Does the Organization's Lawyer Represent?: An Anatomy of Intraclient Conflict,* 91 CAL. L. REV. 57 (2003); Marc I. Steinberg, *The Role of Inside Counsel in the 1990s: A View from Outside,* 49 S.M.U. L. REV. 483 (1996). For a discussion of issues relating to group representation in class action litigation, see, e.g., Elizabeth Chamblee Burch, *Litigating Together: Social, Moral, and Legal Obligations,* 91 B.U. L. REV. 87 (2011); Nancy Morawetz, *Underinclusive Class Actions,* 71 N.Y.U. L. Rev. 402 (1996); David L. Shapiro, *Class Actions: The Class as Party and Client,* 73 NOTRE DAME L. REV. 913 (1998).

[2] RODNEY W. NAPIER & MATTI K. GERSHENFELD, GROUPS: THEORY AND EXPERIENCE 62 (7th ed. 2004).

[3] *Id.*

[4] FIONA MCDERMOTT, INSIDE GROUP WORK: A GUIDE TO REFLECTIVE PRACTICE 4–5 (2002).

[5] NAPIER & GERSHENFELD, *supra* note 2, at 70–71.

[6] *Id.* at 71–75.

each other.[7] Second, group members acknowledge the experience of being in a group both subjectively and objectively.[8] That is, the members have a sense of belonging, and group membership is recognizable to themselves and others.[9] Group members perceive themselves to be a group; they are psychologically aware of each other.[10] Group members interact with each other in such a way that the behavior of one member influences the behavior of the others, a quality the social scientists call "behaviorally interdependent."[11] This interdependence among group members is thus one of the key attributes of groups. Social psychologists have suggested that groups are interdependent in regard to both information and outcomes.[12] Members are interdependent regarding information when they need to exchange information in order to complete a task; they are interdependent concerning outcomes when they perceive they have a mutual stake in the acquisition, retention and allocation of scarce resources.

A. GROUP DYNAMICS

The forces that result from the interactions of group members are referred to as group dynamics, and they influence both individual group members and the group as a whole. As a lawyer for a group, you need to be aware of group dynamics since they can affect the working of the group and thus the work you are trying to accomplish with the group. By influencing the individual member's reactions, these dynamics alter the group's ability to attain its goals. Social scientists write about four dimensions of group dynamics that are of particular importance in understanding and working effectively with groups: 1) communication and interaction patterns; 2) cohesion; 3) social integration and influence; and 4) group culture.[13] Lawyers can help a group improve its functioning and thus its ability to attain its goals.

1. Communication Within Groups

Communication involves "(1) the encoding of a person's perceptions, thoughts, and feelings into language and other symbols, (2) the transmission of these symbols or language, and (3) the decoding of the transmission" by the other person.[14] All communication, including silence, is intended to convey a message. In group settings, people often communicate

---

[7] MCDERMOTT, *supra* note 4, at 7.

[8] *Id.*

[9] *Id.*

[10] *Id.*

[11] BERNARD L. HINTON & H. JOSEPH REITZ, GROUPS AND ORGANIZATIONS: INTEGRATED READINGS IN THE ANALYSIS OF SOCIAL BEHAVIOR 31 (1971).

[12] John M. Levine & Leigh Thompson, *Conflict in Groups, in* SOCIAL PSYCHOLOGY: HANDBOOK OF BASIC PRINCIPLES 745 (E. Tory Higgins & Arie W. Kruglanski eds., 1996).

[13] RONALD W. TOSELAND & ROBERT F. RIVAS, AN INTRODUCTION TO GROUP WORK PRACTICE 69 (7th ed. 2012).

[14] *Id.*

to understand others, find out where they stand in relation to others, persuade others, gain or maintain power, defend themselves, provoke a reaction from others, make an impression on others, gain or maintain relationships and present a unified image to the group.[15] Working with groups requires that we develop a "third ear" in order to be attentive to the meanings behind messages. This skill requires being aware of non-verbal messages, such as body language, gestures and facial expressions in addition to paying attention to the actual words used.[16] Communication can also be distorted in transmission, for example, by cultural differences and language barriers as well as by visual and hearing impairments. In order to prevent distortions from possibly causing misunderstanding and conflict in the group, members may need to receive feedback on their communications.[17]

As a lawyer working with a group, you also will need to become aware of the interaction patterns that develop in a group. Interaction patterns can be leader-centered, such as when the leader is the central figure and communication occurs back and forth from the leader to the member, or group-centered, such as when all members take responsibility for communicating.[18] Leader-centered communication patterns tend to be more efficient, but group-centered patterns tend to increase social interaction, group morale, the commitment of members to group goals and innovative decision-making.[19]

Several factors may influence the interaction patterns of groups, such as size and physical arrangements. Size affects the amount and quality of communication that can take place among members as individual persons.[20] The proper number of members of a group depends on the function of the group. As the size of a group increases, however, the number of relationships possible among members increases. Individual members are more self-aware and more likely to regulate their behavior in small groups.[21] Larger groups thus have a greater need for consensus about appropriate behavior or norms for the group. Circular seating arrangements, for example, promote face-to-face interaction while seats arranged in rows facilitate members' interaction with the leader.[22]

---

[15] *Id.* at 70 (citing SARA B. KIESLER, INTERPERSONAL PROCESSES IN GROUPS AND ORGANIZATIONS (1979)).

[16] *Id.* at 71.

[17] *Id.* at 72–73. Feedback should "(1) describe the content of the communication or behavior as it is perceived by the group member, (2) be given to the member who sent the message as soon as the message is received, and (3) be expressed in a tentative manner, so as to check for distortions as opposed to confront or attack the member." *Id.* at 73.

[18] *Id.* at 74.

[19] *Id.* (citing Jean Carletta, Simon Garrod & Heidi Fraser–Krauss, *Placement of Authority and Communication Patterns in Workplace Groups*, 29 SMALL GRP. RES. 531 (1998)).

[20] NAPIER & GERSHENFELD, *supra* note 2, at 42–43.

[21] *Id.* at 43.

[22] *Id.* at 49.

2.　Group Cohesion

Group cohesion is the result of all forces acting on members to remain in a group.[23] Cohesion affects members' willingness to listen, influence over each other, perseverance toward goals, willingness to take responsibility for group functioning, attendance and length of participation, and organizational commitment.[24] Social scientists find that group cohesion may be important in certain settings, such as when group members need to work together to accomplish a particular task.[25] Cohesion can also have some negative effects since it is a necessary ingredient, though not the only one, in the development of "groupthink,"[26] that tendency of group members to share opinions simply because other members of the group hold them.

3.　Social Integration and Influence

The social integration of a group refers to "how the members fit together and are accepted in the group."[27] Groups work more effectively together when there is a high level of social integration among the members, when the members fit together and are accepted in a group.[28] Yet, not all groups are or should be intentionally well-integrated. Some integration is necessary, however, in order to build consensus about the goals and purposes of the group, allowing members to move forward in an orderly and efficient manner to accomplish the group's work and achieve its goals. The group may need to work toward this integration over time. Order and stability are also necessary for the formation and maintenance of a cohesive group by avoiding unpredictability and conflict. Ultimately, groups need to strike a balance between too much and too little structure.

Norms, roles and status promote social integration by influencing how members behave in relationship to each other and by defining members' places within the group.[29] Norms are "shared expectations and beliefs about appropriate ways to act within the group."[30] Roles are "shared expectations about the functions of individuals in the group."[31] For example, an organization may define the role of its board members so that each board member serves as a representative of some other organization. In that instance, there is little room for individual preferences and viewpoints. Norms and roles spell out how individual board members should

---

[23] TOSELAND & RIVAS, *supra* note 13, at 78.

[24] *Id.* at 79–80.

[25] *Id.* at 80.

[26] *Id.* (citing IRVING L. JANIS, VICTIMS OF GROUPTHINK: A PSYCHOLOGICAL STUDY OF FOREIGN–POLICY DECISIONS AND FIASCOES (1972)). *See infra* note 74.

[27] *Id.*

[28] *Id.* at 81.

[29] *Id.* at 81–82.

[30] *Id.* at 82.

[31] *Id.* at 84.

behave. Norms may be formal written rules, such as bylaws, explicitly stated but verbal norms, non-explicit informal (silent) norms and unconscious norms.[32] Status refers to the evaluation and ranking of each member's position in the group relative to other members.

Groups need to achieve a balance between satisfying the needs of individual members while at the same time operating effectively and efficiently.[33] Structure tends to increase member satisfaction, increase feelings of safety and reduce conflict in early group meetings.[34] Part of your role as lawyer may be to assist the group in creating that structure.

Some groups and group members may see strong group norms and structure as overly hierarchical. Others argue that the absence of rules is itself hierarchical. Rules of decisions need to be transparent in order for the group to operate in a fair manner. "Structurelessness" can become a way of masking power and is usually advocated by those who are the most powerful.[35] As long as the structure of the group is informal, the rules of how decisions are made are known only to a few, and those who know the rules can therefore curtail awareness of power.[36] In order for everyone to have the opportunity to be involved and participate in the group's activities, a group's structure needs to be explicit. The rules of decision-making should be open and available to everyone and most often need to be formalized if the group is going to operate in a fairly transparent manner.[37]

4.   Group Culture

Group culture refers to the values, beliefs, customs and traditions held in common by group members. Culture is displayed in the way members interact with each other, by the symbols and rituals of the group, and by the core beliefs, ideologies and values held in common by members.[38] Group culture emerges more quickly in homogeneous groups. As a result, "multicultural differences within the group can have an important impact on the development of group culture."[39]

If you work with a group from its beginning, you can observe some of these group dynamics develop. You will find it more challenging to discern these group dynamics when you first begin to work with an existing

---

[32] NAPIER & GERSHENFELD, *supra* note 2, at 114–15; TOSELAND & RIVAS, *supra* note 13, at 82–87.

[33] TOSELAND & RIVAS, *supra* note 13, at 86–87.

[34] *Id.* at 86.

[35] JO FREEMAN, THE TYRANNY OF STRUCTURELESSNESS 1 (1970), *available at* http://struggle.ws/pdfs/tyranny.pdf.

[36] *Id.*

[37] *Id.*

[38] TOSELAND & RIVAS, *supra* note 13, at 87 (citing MICHAEL S. OLMSTED, THE SMALL GROUP (1959)).

[39] *Id.*

group. You will begin to recognize these group dynamics over time, and they will help you understand the way the group interacts.

B. STAGES OF DEVELOPMENT OF GROUPS

Groups, like individuals, "develop through predictable stages of growth over time."[40] When you first begin working with a group it is unlikely you will know the stage of development in which the group finds itself, but you may be able to recognize it as you work with the group over time. Understanding that groups go through stages of development will help you understand their decision-making processes and should help you better assist the group. Rodney Napier and Matti Gershenfeld outline a five-step process of group development—beginning, movement toward confrontation, compromise and harmony, reassessment, and resolution and recycling.[41] Understanding the stages of group development will help you understand the stage of the group's development at which you are interacting with it and explain why certain things may be happening in the group. It might also help you decide what you can accomplish with the group at any particular time.

At the beginning of the group, individuals have expectations of the group even before first attending a meeting. Each person brings his or her history and experiences from other groups, and individuals want to be included and want to feel secure.[42] In this stage of group development, individuals gather and process data through the lens of prior experience.[43] It is a time of testing, inhibition, discomfort and first impressions. People are guided by their need to be liked and accepted.[44] In Napier and Gershenfeld's second stage, "movement toward confrontation," individuals establish personal roles.[45] At this stage, the patterns of power and leadership are being established. Individuals seek their place in the group and begin to take more definite stands, thereby testing their personal influence.[46] Alliances in the group are re-drawn based on behavior instead of expectation.[47] Individuals begin to feel the "disconnect" between their initial hopes and expectations and the reality of group life.[48]

In the third stage, "compromise and harmony," competitiveness is played down and collaboration is more readily sought.[49] At the fourth "reassessment" stage, a more rational approach to decision-making emerg-

---

[40] NAPIER & GERSHENFELD, *supra* note 2, at 403.

[41] *Id.* at 404–11.

[42] *Id.* at 404.

[43] *Id.*

[44] *Id.*

[45] *Id.* at 405.

[46] *Id.*

[47] *Id.*

[48] *Id.*

[49] *Id.* at 406.

es.[50] The notion of accountability is crucial at this stage. As the group matures, and enters what Napier and Gershenfeld call the fifth "resolution and recycling" stage, the group begins to resolve conflicts more quickly, with minimal expenditure of energy.[51] Positive feelings are generated by succeeding in the task and being part of the group. The group recognizes its own limitations and strengths and is able to build effectively around them. The group is not necessarily harmonious and free of tensions, however, and the degree of maturity is revealed in how effectively the group is able to cope with conflict.[52] Maturity evolves from the group's ability to provide itself with the support and experience required at the time. The situational leader is able to intervene to help the group get "unstuck" and enable growth and development.[53]

Several other models of group development exist, all describing similar stages of group evolution.[54] One of the most widely respected models views the group's development from two points of view—the task and the interpersonal relationships. Bruce Tuckman and Mary Ann Jensen note that groups go through five stages—forming, storming, norming, performing and adjourning.[55] The forming stage is one of uncertainty and confusion. In the storming stage, members question authority and feel increasingly comfortable being themselves. This time is a period of conflict about the task with hostility between members. The norming stage is the point where group cohesion emerges along with consensus about the task. The group achieves successful performance in the performing stage. Group members move to the adjourning stage as they near completion of the task and anticipate the changing of relationships. The stage of the group's development will affect its decision-making processes and so as a lawyer you will benefit in discerning, as best you can, where your group clients fit in this life cycle.

II. GROUP DECISION–MAKING

In this section, we explore some of the social psychology theory of conflict within groups. This research helps us understand what happens in groups and how we can assist groups to reach quality decisions. We begin by discussing the place of conflict within groups and then move to discuss the various decision-making rules.

---

[50] *Id.* at 407.

[51] *Id.* at 408.

[52] *Id.* at 409.

[53] *Id.*

[54] *Id.* at 411–18. *See also* TOSELAND & RIVAS, *supra* note 13, at 90–92; PETER HARTLEY, GROUP COMMUNICATION 57–62 (1997).

[55] NAPIER & GERSHENFELD, *supra* note 2, at 411–12 (citing Bruce W. Tuckman & Mary Ann C. Jensen, *Stages of Small–Group Development Revisited*, 2 GRP. & ORG. MGMT. 419 (1977)). *See also* HARTLEY, *supra* note 54, at 54–56 (citing Bruce W. Tuckman, *Developmental Sequence in Small Groups*, 63 PSYCHOL. BULLETIN 384 (1965)).

A. CONFLICT WITHIN GROUPS

Being in a group poses tension and decisions for an individual, raising questions of trust and acceptance.[56] When the group begins its own process of decision-making, further conflict may result from the disagreements among individuals as well as the implications of decisions for the group.[57] A second source of tension and conflict stems from the need to live with the group's decision.[58] Decision-making in any group often leads to conflict, whether the decision being considered is as "simple" as whether to organize the group as a directorship or membership organization or whether the decision is the bottom line for the negotiation of a lease or a community benefits agreement. Conflicts in groups can also arise when the personal goals and needs of individual members are in conflict with those of the group.[59] There can also be problems generated from the distribution of power and influence.[60] Conflict can have both positive and negative consequences in any group. It can reduce the group's performance or enhance creativity. Once conflict arises, the question becomes how the group deals with it—whether it is recognized and dealt with constructively or denied and ignored.[61]

We mentioned above that groups can be interdependent as to information and outcomes. Conflicts within groups can arise as to both information and outcomes.[62] Conflicts concerning information distribution or exchange can occur when members do not share information, disagree about the validity of particular facts or argue about which facts support what conclusion.[63] Information conflict can be resolved through information seeking, information sharing and persuasion.[64] Outcome conflicts can occur between members though it might not at first seem likely when members share common interests.[65] Outcome conflicts are resolved through exercise of power and negotiation.[66] Groups use three general mechanisms to deal with conflict—conflict avoidance, conflict reduction and conflict creation.[67]

---

[56] RODNEY W. NAPIER & MATTI K. GERSHENFELD, GROUPS: THEORY AND EXPERIENCE 324 (5th ed. 1993).

[57] *Id.* at 324–25.

[58] *Id.* at 325.

[59] *Id.* at 326.

[60] *Id.* at 326–28.

[61] *Id.* at 325.

[62] Levine & Thompson, *supra* note 12, at 745 (citing Harold H. Kelley & John W. Thibault, *Group Problem Solving, in* 14 THE HANDBOOK OF SOCIAL PSYCHOLOGY (Gardner Lindzey & Elliot Aronson eds., 2d ed. (1969))).

[63] *Id.*

[64] *Id.*

[65] *Id.*

[66] *Id.*

[67] *Id.* at 746.

When dealing with information conflict, group members avoid conflict by controlling their own or others' thoughts (so that the disagreeing opinion simply does not exist), controlling their own or others' behavior (so that the disagreeing opinion is not publicly expressed), developing rules that reduce the likelihood that disagreement is likely to lead to overt conflict, interpreting disagreement in ways that reduce its importance and shifting their public position to an acceptable compromise position.[68] Conflict can be reduced by either the minority moving to the majority position or by redefinition of the group's boundaries.[69] Social psychologists have studied the effect of individual influence on group decisions and have found that the majority thinking will influence the thinking of group members, with others (the minority) shifting to moderation (toward the majority).[70] Majority influence has been found to be higher when the question under consideration is ambiguous or difficult to answer.[71] Group boundaries can be redefined by members voluntarily leaving the group, the recruitment of new members or the majority rejecting minority members (by expulsion from the group, by isolation or depriving the minority of privileges).[72]

While it may seem counterintuitive, conflict *creation* can improve group decision-making, improve individual problem-solving and learning, and augment minority influence.[73] Informational conflict can be beneficial to groups by improving the quality of decisions that groups make following discussion. Conflict within the group can help prevent "group think," a condition which can lead to defective decision-making and is characterized by closed-mindedness and pressures toward uniformity.[74] Disagreement also motivates curiosity and perspective-taking on the part of individuals, thus aiding individual problem-solving and learning.[75] In addition, minorities can influence the majority when the group seeks in good faith to resolve genuine conflict.

Conflict over outcomes occurs when group members perceive they have incompatible preferences regarding the allocation of resources. Most outcome conflicts arise from conflicting goals and interests. Group members normally share a common interest in resolving conflict and are moti-

---

[68] *Id.*

[69] *Id.* at 749.

[70] *Id.* (citing Solomon E. Asch, *Effects of Group Pressure Upon the Modification and Distortion of Judgments, in* GROUPS, LEADERSHIP, AND MEN 177 (Harold Guetzkow ed. 1951); Solomon E. Asch, *Opinion and Social Pressure*, SCI. AM., Nov. 1955, at 31–35; Solomon E. Asch, *Studies of Independence and Submission to Group Pressure*, 70 PSYCHOL. MONOGRAPHS 9 (1956)).

[71] *Id.* at 750.

[72] *Id.* at 752–53.

[73] *Id.* at 754.

[74] *Id.* at 754. Group think includes the incomplete survey of alternatives, failure to assess the risks of preferred choices and selective bias in processing information. In the face of conformity pressures, individual group members come to doubt their own reservation and refrain from voicing dissenting opinions. ELLIOTT ARONSON, THE SOCIAL ANIMAL 18–19 (10th ed. 2008).

[75] Levine & Thompson, *supra* note 12, at 754–55.

vated to cooperate. At the same time, members may be motivated to compete with one another to maximize their share of resources.[76] Groups deal with outcome conflict using the same mechanism as with information conflict—avoidance, reduction and creation.[77]

Groups avoid conflict because it may pose a realistic threat to the attainment of the group's goals (the purposes or plan of action of group members) and because it may pose a psychological threat to perceptions of group harmony and solidarity (dampen morale, diminish group cohesion or promote self-interested as opposed to group-interested behavior).[78] Group members may avoid conflict by inaction, withdrawal or preemptive action.[79] Group members, for example, may not show up for discussion or may talk around issues. They may withdraw from conflict by leaving the group or abandoning their goals. Finally groups may structure their interaction so conflict is less likely to emerge, such as by developing policies, norms and procedures. Groups may reduce conflict by individuals taking a particular action, by voting (and agreeing to accept the outcome of the vote even if it does not necessarily guarantee the resolution of conflict) and by engaging in group negotiation.[80] Negotiation requires complex problem-solving, communication and a search for information. Group members exchange ideas and engage in a search for solutions. Finally, groups may create conflict, which may facilitate social change and also promote cohesion and unity within the group. The presence of conflict may be an indication of strength and stability in a group; its members do not avoid conflict because they do not fear that it risks the continuation of the group. Conflict can be constructive or destructive, with constructive conflict involving creative thinking, cooperative problem-solving, the minimization of differences and cooperative commitment.[81] Groups with dissenters as members have been found to accomplish more than those whose desire for agreement is high.[82]

Now that we have seen where conflicts arise in groups and how groups may deal with conflicts, let us turn to decision rules, one place where we as lawyers are often involved.

---

[76] *Id.* at 757.

[77] *Id.*

[78] *Id.*

[79] *Id.* at 754–57.

[80] *Id.* at 760–65.

[81] *Id.* at 765. *See also* Jonah Lehrer, *Groupthink: The Brainstorming Myth,* THE NEW YORKER (Jan. 30, 2012), http://www.newyorker.com/reporting/2012/01/30/120130fa_fact_lehrer (discussing research showing that groups that were instructed to debate and criticize each other's ideas were more creative than groups told to brainstorm or given no instructions).

[82] NAPIER & GERSHENFELD, *supra* note 2, at 296.

B. TYPES OF DECISION RULES

As we saw above, one way groups can reduce conflict is by voting and developing rules that reduce the likelihood that disagreement is likely to lead to overt, or unresolvable, conflict. Decision rules avoid conflict by specifying in advance how disagreements are to be resolved.[83] As lawyers, we are called upon to assist in the creation of those rules and in the drafting of those rules (perhaps in the organization's bylaws). Generally, groups can decide to make decisions by majority, plurality (more than a mere majority, such as two-thirds)[84] or by consensus. Decision rules can substantively affect both group outcomes and processes.[85]

In writing governance documents such as bylaws, lawyers tend to favor decision rules that are easier to draft.[86] A simple majority scheme appears fair and democratic and seems uncomplicated. Research does not support the notion that it is always the fairest and most democratic manner of making decisions, however.[87] Groups may not always want or benefit from a simple majority decision-making scheme. Organizational theorists point out that a simple majority scheme should be used when a decision is of relatively little consequence.[88] If a large number of group members disagree with a decision of significance to them, a majority vote may be perceived as a means of control and manipulation by the majority.[89] A large minority may spend time trying to disrupt the decision or looking for ways to overthrow it. In addition, majority rule is an easy way to shut off discussion. On the positive side, however, majority rule can reduce power inequalities in groups with members of varying status and power.[90]

Plurality votes, such as a two-thirds rule (either of the members at a meeting, or of all voting members), should be used for decisions of greater consequence.[91] Group members have an easier time accepting decisions if they have agreed ahead of time that a super-majority vote is "fair." Group members feel less manipulated by a two-thirds vote.[92] Super majority

---

[83] Levine & Thompson, *supra* note 12, at 748.

[84] The most common dictionary definition of "plurality" describes a vote where the winner has received less than a majority of the votes in a race with more than two candidates. *See, e.g.*, AMERICAN HERITAGE DICTIONARY 1351 (4th ed. 2006). However, in the organizational context, the term describes a system where the winner must achieve more than a simple majority of the votes, and the group agrees on the percentage in advance. *See* NAPIER & GERSHENFELD, *supra* note 2, at 362.

[85] Levine & Thompson, *supra* note 12, at 748.

[86] We have seen simple majority misunderstood and incorrectly written in bylaws. Simple majority is not 51 percent. In even-numbered groups, it is one-half plus one. In odd-numbered groups, 50 percent is likely to result in a fraction of a person. In those cases, the fraction gets rounded up to complete an entire number.

[87] NAPIER & GERSHENFELD, *supra* note 2, at 335.

[88] *Id.*

[89] *Id.*

[90] *Id.*

[91] *Id.* at 336.

[92] *Id.*

rules may prevent a group from moving forward on a decision if there is a large minority blocking the vote.

A third method of voting used in groups is consensus. A number of community groups favor this form of decision-making. Most of us may be initially suspicious of and therefore reject consensus decision-making. While the word consensus conjures the notion of unanimity, the concept of consensus decision-making is more complex than simply requiring a 100 percent vote on a matter. A group that uses consensus is committed to finding solutions that everyone actively supports, or at least can live with.[93] Consensus decision-making typically involves a five-step process. In the first step, the issue to be decided is introduced and clarified.[94] Step two requires an exploration of the issues and concerns, and collection of ideas for solving the problem.[95] Step three looks for emerging proposals, or those ideas that bring together the best qualities of the ideas discussed.[96] In step four, the group discusses, clarifies and amends the proposal.[97] In the final step, the group tests for agreement and checks for blocks to agreement, reservations and stand-asides (those who cannot support the agreement but do not want to stop the group).[98] Consensus requires a high level of trust within the group, a group that is not leader-centered, a group possessing all the information necessary to reach a decision prior to the meeting and a group with sufficient time available to consider opinions, alternatives and consequences.[99] Compared with the majority rule, the consensus rule is more likely to produce a compromise decision, public and private change in members' positions, and extensive discussion. In addition, it leads to greater satisfaction with the group decision and positive feelings about participation in the group.[100] This decision-making method requires effective listening and analysis and as a result a more skilled and cohesive group.[101]

Let us observe what these three models might look like in practice. Imagine that the DWC's board of directors is seeking approval of the organization's annual budget. Let us assume that the DWC has fifteen board members, and twelve members are present at the meeting in which

---

[93] SEEDS FOR CHANGE, CONSENSUS DECISION MAKING 1 (2010), *available at* http://seedsforchange.uk/consensus.pdf.

[94] *Id.* at 6.

[95] *Id.*

[96] *Id.*

[97] *Id.*

[98] *Id.* Seeds for Change has a number of excellent group meeting facilitation materials available on its web page. The materials are "@nti-copyright"—you are free to copy, adapt and distribute their materials as long as the final work remains "@nti-copyright." *Resources*, SEEDS FOR CHANGE, http://seedsforchange.org.uk/resources.

[99] NAPIER & GERSHENFELD, *supra* note 2, at 337.

[100] *Id.* at 363. *See also* Levine & Thompson, *supra* note 12, at 748 (citing Charles E. Miller et al., *Some Social Psychological Effects of Group Decision Rules*, 52 J. PERSONALITY & SOC. PSYCHOL. 325 (1987)).

[101] NAPIER & GERSHENFELD, *supra* note 2, at 337.

the group's annual budget will be approved. Let us also assume that there is strong disagreement among the board about its annual budget. The simple majority vote is an easy one to understand. If the bylaws require that all decisions be made by simple majority, the annual budget for the organization will be approved by a majority of the board members present where a quorum is achieved, no matter how strongly the minority may feel about certain aspects of the budget and no matter how razor thin the majority. So, if the vote is taken and seven members vote in favor of the budget proposed by Amanda Estrada, the Executive Director, with the other five members feeling strongly that the proposed budget has some serious shortcomings, the budget will be approved.

Let us now assume that the organization's bylaws require a two-thirds vote of those directors present at a meeting for approval of the budget. At the same board meeting, eight members would have to vote in favor of the budget.[102] That might require the board to make some revisions to the budget in order to get the vote of one more director. It might mean the Executive Director or the Executive Committee (composed of the officers, assuming the organization has such a committee) will have to talk through her proposed budget with some board members informally. The budget might have to be discussed at two consecutive meetings, requiring the Executive Director to draft a budget with sufficient time for this discussion to happen. Unless two-thirds of the board of directors agrees to a budget, the organization may have to operate without a budget. That may be an untenable position for the organization when the foundations providing its funds require an approved budget by a certain date.

Let us now observe how a provision that requires consensus might look. The board would have to discuss the budget enough to know what the concerns of board members are in order to make revisions to the budget so as to gain the vote of all the members or see if the "dissenters" are willing to stand aside. What if the dissenters do not want to "stand aside"? Does this mean that an organization should adopt a simple majority vote for all its decisions? Not necessarily. An organization may readily accept the higher risks of the consensus model in order to encourage more deliberative decision-making.

A group does not have to use the same decision-making model for all decisions. It might choose to use one model for some decisions and another model for others. For example, approval of the organization's budget may require a simple majority but decisions about an organizing campaign may require a two-thirds vote or consensus. You can also imagine the organization being committed to a consensus decision-making rule but the bylaws providing for simple majority in cases when the organiza-

---

[102] Note that, if the DWC's bylaws require a vote of two-thirds of the directors *then in office*, the measure would require at least ten votes for approval, as the board has fifteen members.

tion tries but fails to reach consensus. You should be aware that some statutes require more than simple majority for decisions, such as a majority of the full board and not a majority of the quorum.[103]

A few other methods for group decision-making are worth noting. Decisions can be delegated to representative bodies or individuals, for example, a board committee with board-delegated powers. One way of doing this delegation might be for the decision-maker to "take the pulse" of the group before moving forward, which might happen at a prior meeting or at the point the decision-maker needs to make the decision. Another method, when several proposals are at stake, is for the group to take a double vote. In an initial vote, members are asked to vote for any proposal they find acceptable. Any alternative that receives a two-thirds vote is placed on a second ballot. Only those alternatives receiving a two-thirds vote on the second ballot are accepted. The two votes take place on two different days.[104] A modified double vote process might require that the group vote twice with time in between the two votes for discussion among group members.[105]

A general decision-making model does not always apply to every group. A group's membership, structure and stage of development all affect how it makes decisions. There are limits to the decision-making processes employed by any group. Under pressure of a vote, individual decisions are often made for the wrong reason.[106] This situation is partly the result of different levels of knowledge and understanding and pressures not related to the issues, such as friendships. Even after a group has voted, the question of implementation is a separate one that is not assured by a particular vote. Though voting may at first appear democratic, encouraging a move toward quick decisions may tend to simplify problems and fail to explore issues fully. Groups committed to operating in a truly democratic manner need to have patience, understanding, cooperation and time. A group decision-making process that combines "trust, the desire for unanimity, and advocacy may yield both efficiency and a sense of democracy."[107]

The women's movement developed the following seven principles for democratic structuring of group decisions.[108] First, individuals should be delegated specific authority for specific tasks by democratic procedures as opposed to default. Second, those to whom authority has been delegated must be responsible to those who selected them. Third, authority should

---

[103] For example, the Michigan Nonprofit Corporation Act requires a vote of "not less than a majority of the members of the board then in office" in order to amend the bylaws. MICH. COMP. LAWS § 450.2523 (1983).

[104] NAPIER & GERSHENFELD, *supra* note 2, at 338.

[105] *Id.*

[106] *Id.* at 341.

[107] *Id.* at 342.

[108] FREEMAN, *supra* note 35, at 4–5.

be distributed among as many people as possible. Fourth, tasks should be rotated among individuals so no one person is in control for too long. Fifth, tasks should be allocated using rational criteria. Sixth, information should be disseminated to everyone as frequently as possible. Seventh, as much as practicable, everyone should have equal access to the resources needed by the group.[109]

With this knowledge of groups and group decision-making rules, we turn to some techniques to assist you in facilitating group meetings.

III. FACILITATING MEETINGS

A. GENERAL CONSIDERATIONS

The dictionary defines "facilitate" as "to make easy or easier."[110] Facilitation is the act of assisting or making easier the progress or improvement of something. Good facilitation helps the group have a more efficient and inclusive meeting. Though lawyers do not normally run board or community meetings, you may be asked both to facilitate meetings and to be part of meetings others are facilitating. For example, you may need to facilitate a board discussion on a particular issue relevant to your work, such as drafting or revising the organization's bylaws. Other times, you may be in a position to help the organization's leadership to prepare for a meeting. In both instances, it helps to understand facilitation techniques. In this section, we provide some guidelines to assist you in facilitating client or community meetings, whether you will be facilitating an entire meeting or part of a meeting and whether that meeting is a community meeting or a meeting of the board of directors.

Anyone who has been part of a group knows the jokes about meetings that drag on, certain people controlling the discussion or a group's inability to make decisions. Meetings are sometimes seen as a necessary evil of community work. Meetings, however, are a necessary (and good) part of working in any group—they give us the chance to share information, make decisions and obtain input. Meetings also serve another important function—group maintenance.[111] A good meeting not only gets the work done but also involves, supports and empowers the participants, creating energy and enthusiasm.[112] We look not only to whether the job got done but also at the group's morale and cohesion to determine if a meeting was effective. How do people feel about the decisions made at the meeting?

Meetings can be more successful if the participants are active and engaged; feel utilized in a meaningful way; experience a feeling of suc-

---

[109] *Id.* at 5.

[110] AMERICAN HERITAGE DICTIONARY 633 (4th ed. 2006).

[111] SEEDS FOR CHANGE, FACILITATING MEETINGS 1 (2009), *available at* http://seedsforchange.org.uk/facilitationmeeting.pdf [hereinafter FACILITATING MEETINGS].

[112] *Id.*

cess; feel some sense of personal responsibility; have the opportunity to learn something new; feel that the group and the cause are worth their time and effort; feel challenged; enjoy themselves; feel accepted as equals; and feel that they are part of a team.[113] Are you up for the challenge?

Successful meetings require planning, whether the meeting will involve three people or one hundred people. Different types of groups and meetings require different types of plans. Let us assume you are meeting with the new board of directors in preparation for drafting bylaws. How should you prepare for that meeting? Your primary organizational contacts can be your "interpreters" and "translators" in preparation for the meeting. They can inform you about the decisions the group has made and the decisions they are likely to find difficult. Your contact can inform you about the points of disagreement within the group. If you are the one calling the meeting and do not have a particular point of contact, consider communicating with the members beforehand about their concerns.[114]

Facilitation requires helping the group decide on a structure and process for the meeting and keeping to it; keeping the meeting focused on one agenda item at a time until the group reaches a decision; regulating the flow of discussion, drawing out quiet people and limiting those who might tend to dominate the discussion; clarifying and summarizing points; and keeping the meeting on time and helping the group deal with conflict.[115] A good facilitator remains neutral, not manipulating the meeting toward a particular outcome, and never directs the groups without its consent.[116] A good facilitator employs good listening skills, using questions to be able to understand everyone's viewpoint. A good facilitator respects the meeting's participants and understands the aim of the meeting as well as the group's long-term goals. A good facilitator pays attention to both the content and the process. Finally, a good facilitator intervenes and gives direction to the meeting.

Five basic rules may help you ensure focus and aid decision-making in groups and boards.[117] First, agenda integrity requires that all items on the agenda are discussed and only items on the agenda are discussed. Second, temporal integrity requires that you begin and end on time and keep to a sensible internal schedule of items during the meeting. The last three rules are mathematical rules—the rule of thirds, the rule of halves and the rule of three-quarters.[118] Under the rule of thirds, the most im-

---

[113] NAPIER & GERSHENFELD, *supra* note 56, at 433.

[114] In some settings, contacting non-leader members of the group might have some ethical implications.

[115] FACILITATING MEETINGS, *supra* note 111, at 2.

[116] For a different opinion, see Stephen Ellmann, *Client–Centeredness Multiplied: Individual Autonomy and Collective Mobilization in Public Interest Lawyers' Representation of Groups,* 78 VA. L. REV. 1103 (1992).

[117] JOHN E. TROPMAN, EFFECTIVE MEETINGS, IMPROVING GROUP DECISION MAKING 24 (2d ed. 1995).

[118] *Id.*

portant agenda items are scheduled in the middle third of the meeting. This ensures that most people are in attendance at the time these important points are discussed. In addition, the group's energy should be high since it is relatively early in the meeting. Under the rule of halves, agenda items get to the agenda maker halfway between meetings, which ensures that those creating the agenda have sufficient time to plan and can get necessary information out to group members. Finally, under the rule of three-quarters, group members should receive all relevant material at the three-quarter point between meetings. This rule allows group members to have sufficient time to review information and come to meetings prepared for discussion and perhaps raise any concerns with the group's leadership ahead of the meeting. Though you may not control the last two items, you should make sure you get information to the group with sufficient time for members to review it or to the group's leadership with sufficient time to disseminate it to members.

B. PREPARING FOR THE MEETING

In preparation for the meeting think about what the meeting needs to accomplish and what information must be presented. Your meeting design is driven by your goals. Next, decide how involved you want the participants to be. Your activities should be designed according to the level of involvement you expect. You will then need to estimate the time it will take to achieve your goal given the activities you plan and the level of involvement you want.[119] As you plan for the meeting, we suggest that you consider these questions: Who is going to be at the meeting? What do they want from the meeting? What are their skills and strengths? What is the group's history? What information does the group need before the meeting?

Preparation for a meeting requires preparing an effective agenda, making sure everyone is aware of the time, place and content of the meeting and considering the physical arrangements of the meeting. The agenda allows for control over the meeting. Too much control over the meeting stifles discussion and too little control allows for the discussion to ramble. An agenda gives the meeting a logical flow and allows you to rescue a discussion that gets out of hand. Depending on the type of meeting, you will need to consider who is responsible for creating the agenda. If you are facilitating a part of a board meeting, you might not be in control of the entire agenda. In that case, you should check with your host to see how much time you have and the exact points the group wants you to discuss. If, for example, the board has ceded the entire meeting or a substantial part of the meeting to you, you are responsible for creating the agenda. You should consider allocating time for each item on the agenda. This

---

[119] SAM KANER ET AL., FACILITATOR'S GUIDE TO PARTICIPATORY DECISION-MAKING 174 (2d ed. 2007).

task may be difficult when you have not previously worked with the group.

You need to be realistic about what you can accomplish in the time allotted to you and to the meeting itself. In some meetings, you may want to seek input on agenda items from the meeting participants. The meeting's agenda is not the same as your outline for the meeting. Your outline should be a fuller exposition of the points you want to make. You need to consider how much detail you want to give the group in the agenda. You should have distributed any material you want the group to read ahead of time. Most people cannot focus on the discussion and read at the same time. You should plan on a break for meetings that will last longer than one and a half hours.

When thinking about the order of items on the agenda, consider beginning with easy items and moving to moderately difficult ones and then to the hardest items, ending with items "for discussion only" and the easiest item. The most difficult item is scheduled for the middle section of the meeting when there is likely to be peak attendance and the most psychological energy (recall the rule of thirds). The difficult item follows completed decisions, making people feel positive about their decision-making ability. The group may need a break after the difficult decision item. Planning "for discussion only" items after the difficult decision allows the group to decompress. Two techniques of handling "for discussion only" items are the straw vote, which gives participants a preliminary indication, and the "in principle" vote, a "gut" check vote with the group knowing that the result will not count. The agenda should end on a positive note. The group leaves with a sense of accomplishment if it ends the meeting with items it is able to resolve easily. Of course, you cannot always anticipate what will be the most difficult items for the group, but your planning will rely on your judgments about that quality.

The last item on an agenda should be a summary. You should be prepared to summarize what has taken place, what decisions were made and what action should follow the meeting, including any assignments. For example, in a board meeting to discuss proposed bylaws, your summary should discuss any decisions made, any decisions left for another time, any information or work product you promised the group and any information or work product the group promised to get to you.

As you prepare for meetings, you should consider whether you want to have any visual aids. If you want to use a PowerPoint presentation, make sure the equipment is available in the location. Even if you can bring a projector, consider whether it is possible to project on the walls if a screen is not available. You should consider bringing printed copies of your PowerPoint presentation to distribute to the group. Also consider whether you will need flip charts and markers to write notes during the meeting.

As part of your preparation, try to anticipate problems that may arise. What dissent or conflict can you expect and how do you steer the meeting through it? Your contacts from the group are likely to be of assistance here.

C. DURING THE MEETING

You should begin the meeting by introducing yourself. In small meetings, you should go around the room and have the group members introduce themselves if they do not all know each other or if you do not know all of them. Next, set the boundaries for the meeting. Explain the time frame, purpose of the meeting, the process for making decisions and your role, as facilitator or otherwise. Depending on the type of meeting, you may need to set some ground rules for acceptable behavior. Finally, explain the proposed agenda. You should go through the agenda item by item.

The facilitator's key responsibilities during a meeting are determining who talks when and focusing the discussion. You will have to decide whether to keep attention on the person who is making a point or call on others. In addition, you will have to decide whether to keep the focus on the point being made by the current speaker or help the group move to a different line of thought. We discuss some of these techniques below. If new items come up during the discussion, you can use a "parking space," which the group will understand as the place for items to be dealt with later. This tool allows you to stay focused but reassures participants that their points will not be lost.

Writing the group's ideas on a flip chart encourages participation by validating people's ideas and helping the group remember the points made during the meeting.[120] You should be listening for and writing suggestions, logical connections, summary statements and open questions.[121] You should write the key points, words or phrases but not necessarily complete sentences. The notes may be of assistance to you or the group, depending on the type of meeting.

D. FACILITATION TECHNIQUES

In this section, we provide some techniques for facilitating open discussion in meetings. With experience you will become more comfortable paying attention to both the group dynamics and your agenda simultaneously. It will also be helpful if you think about each of them ahead of time. When you work with a group for the first time, you might need to explain your approach. Some techniques require more explanation than

---

[120] *Id.* at 62. Kaner calls this concept "group memory," borrowing the phrase from Geoff Ball, a California specialist in multi-party conflict and the founder of RESOLVE (a consulting firm that promotes collaborative problem-solving instead of litigation). *Id.*

[121] *Id.* at 71.

others. The techniques we outline below assume the group will engage in open discussion among the entire group, as opposed to working in small groups, thus requiring good facilitation in order to be productive. We will discuss the techniques of *drawing people out, mirroring, paraphrasing, validating, empathy, making space for quiet people, broadening a discussion, using silence, stacking, gathering ideas, tracking, balancing,* and *linking.*[122]

In the early stages of a discussion, you might want to get people engaged in the conversation. You can encourage people to participate by saying something like "Who else has an idea?," "What do others think?," or "Are there comments from anyone who has not spoken in a while?"[123]

You can help people having difficulty clarifying an idea or someone being vague or confusing but who thinks he or she is being clear. You can *draw them out* by asking open-ended, clarifying questions or making similar suggestions. Examples of ways to draw people out include "Say more," "Tell me more," "What do you mean by . . . ?" or "What matters to you about . . . ?"[124] You should be careful to do this questioning for someone whose ideas are not clear and not for those ideas you find interesting. In meetings where you as facilitator may not be seen as "neutral" and where you need to build trust, you may need to mirror comments as opposed to paraphrasing what people are saying.[125] In *mirroring,* you repeat either the person's sentence verbatim (in the case of a single sentence) or the key words or phrases (in the case of multiple sentences). Mirroring speeds up the tempo of a meeting. You should use the techniques of paraphrasing and mirroring when someone is in obvious need of support; otherwise, it might appear that you as facilitator favor certain positions or persons.

We are often not aware of what we are feeling. By identifying a feeling and naming it, a facilitator raises everyone's awareness.[126] By *paraphrasing* a statement that expresses feelings and drawing people out, the facilitator helps the group recognize and accept the feelings of group members.[127] You will have to pay attention to the emotional tone in a possibly difficult conversation and look for cues that might indicate the presence of feelings. Second, you will try to pose a question that names the feelings you believe are present. Here are a few examples: "It sounds as if you might be feeling worried; am I right?"; "Is this what you are feeling?"; "It seems like this discussion is bringing up something for you. Are you feeling disappointed?"[128]

---

[122] *Id.* at 41.

[123] *Id.* at 50.

[124] *Id.* at 45.

[125] *Id.* at 46.

[126] *Id.* at 53.

[127] *Id.* at 44.

[128] *Id.* at 53.

Validating is the skill that legitimizes and accepts a speaker's opinion or feeling, without agreeing that the opinion is "correct" or agreeing with the rationale for the feeling.[129] Validation often invites a person to open up and say more. You are not agreeing with the statement, but you are supporting someone to express his or her truth. Validating requires that you paraphrase, draw out the person's opinion or feeling, assess whether the speaker needs support and offer the support.[130] You might provide this support by saying something like the following: "I see what you are saying," "I get why that matters to you," or "Now I see where you are coming from."[131]

Empathy, which we discussed in the Interviewing chapter, is another technique that you might use in a meeting to provide "everyone with a fuller, compassionate understanding of a person's subjective reality."[132] Empathizing involves putting oneself in another person's shoes and looking at the world through that person's eyes. It requires us to identify with and share the actual feeling. The most basic technique is to name what you think the person is experiencing.[133] You might also speculate on future impacts, identify concerns about communicating the feelings to others or mention the factors that led to the person's experience.[134] In all these instances, you should ask for confirmation from the speaker and encourage him or her to correct your perception.

When a group has a fast-paced discussion style, quiet members and slow thinkers may have trouble participating in the conversation. Quiet members may be afraid of being perceived as rude or competitive, others new to the group may be unsure as to what is acceptable and still others may be convinced they do not have anything to add. As a facilitator, you should *make space for a quiet person*.[135] You should be on the lookout for body language that may mean some group members want to speak and ask them if there was something they wanted to add or express.[136] If you find participation is very uneven, you might want to suggest going around and giving each person a chance to speak.

There may be times when you want or need to *broaden participation* by shifting the focus away from frequent contributors and create opportunities for less frequent contributors to speak.[137] You might encourage par-

---

[129] *Id.* at 54.

[130] *Id.*

[131] *Id.*

[132] *Id.* at 55.

[133] *Id.* at 55.

[134] Examples include, "I can imagine it might be difficult to talk about this topic in this group." "I can see how this news could play havoc with your other commitments." "After all the effort you made to keep this project alive, I imagine this news might be quite upsetting." *Id.*

[135] *Id.* at 52.

[136] *Id.*

[137] *Id.* at 78.

ticipation, by saying, "Who else wants to say something?" or "Could we hear from someone who has not talked in a while?"[138] Other times you might want to balance someone's statement when participants may be reticent to disagree with the person making the statement.[139] At those moments, you may want to say, "What are some other ways of looking at this?" or "Does anyone have a different point of view?" When someone gives you as facilitator a non-verbal cue that he or she wants to speak you can make space for that person, for example by saying "Esther, do you have something you want to say?" You can also use the clock to encourage people who have not participated to speak.[140] You might say, "We have ten minutes left. I want to make sure we have heard from everyone who wants to speak, particularly those who have not had a chance to do so yet." You could also say "We have time for only one or two more comments; perhaps we should hear from someone who has not spoken yet." Finally, you might say, "We still have twenty minutes left in this discussion. How about if we hear from someone who has not spoken in a while?"

Silence, consisting of a pause lasting no more than a few seconds, can give the speaker that brief extra time to discover what she or he wants to say.[141] Some people need time to organize a complex thought, to decide whether to make a controversial point or to process what has been said. You might also want to use this technique to "honor moments of exceptional poignancy" such as a statement of passion or vulnerability, thus giving the group time to reflect and make sense of the experience.[142] Focus on the speaker when you use this technique. If necessary, hold up your hand to keep others from breaking the silence. You might need to announce to the group to take a moment to think about what "it" means.

Stacking is a procedure for helping people take turns when several people want to speak.[143] It creates a sequence of the people who want to speak. It lets all group members know that they are going to have a turn, discouraging participants from feeling impatient. You begin by asking those who want to speak to raise their hands, then naming the order of speakers and finally when all those who had raised their hands have spoken, asking again who would like to speak and beginning a new stack.[144] At times, you may want to interrupt the stack in order to get responses to a crucial point.[145] If you maintain the stack, responses to points made will not come in until much later, breaking up the flow of the conversation. If you see many hands going up as someone makes a point, you might want

---

[138] *Id.*

[139] *Id.* at 79.

[140] *Id.*

[141] *Id.* at 56.

[142] *Id.*

[143] *Id.* at 48.

[144] *Id.*

[145] *Id.* at 77–78.

to interrupt the stack and keep the discussion focused on that particular point. Stacking is a way to be fair, but it may not meet the group's goals of staying focused on a discussion.

Gathering ideas is a listening skill that helps participants build a list of ideas at a fast-moving pace.[146] You could begin by giving the participants a description of the task. For example, you might say "For the next ten minutes we are going to evaluate the idea of being a membership organization by discussing the pros and cons. I'll call for a pro first, then a con so we will build the list at the same time." You might need to spend some time teaching the group members about suspended judgment.[147] Physical gestures such as making hand and arm movements or moving around the room if you are standing serve as energy boosters. When gathering ideas, you should use mirroring more frequently than paraphrasing.

Tracking is a process by which you keep track of the various lines of thought going on in the discussion.[148] This technique makes visible the fact that different threads of the topic are going on simultaneously. You begin by saying you are going to summarize the discussion thus far, for example, "It appears there are three conversations going on right now; I want to make sure I am tracking them."[149] You then name the different conversations by saying, for example, "One conversation is about the community legitimacy that comes with being a membership organization, another is about the value of having organizations eligible to be members in addition to individuals and the third is about how you ensure legitimacy and diversity if you decide to be a directorship organization." Next you check with the group for accuracy, such as by asking, "Am I getting it right?" Finally, you invite the group to continue the conversation by asking, "Are there any more comments?"

There may be times in the discussion when you may want to broaden the discussion to include perspectives not yet included. Using the technique of *balancing*, you may ask whether there are other ways of looking at the issue, whether everyone agrees with the proposal and whether anyone else has a different position from the ones expressed thus far.[150] This technique is especially useful when the group seems stuck between two polarized positions. In those situations, revealing alternate positions undercuts the myth that silence indicates acquiescence.

Linking invites the speaker to explain the relevance of the statement he or she just made.[151] If someone says something that seems tangential

---

[146] *Id.* at 47.

[147] *Id.*

[148] *Id.* at 49.

[149] *Id.*

[150] *Id.* at 51.

[151] *Id.* at 57.

and some in the group react, for example, by saying things like "let's get back on track" or "let's put it in the parking lot," you might want to ask the speaker to connect the thought for the group. This technique requires that you first paraphrase the statement. Second, you ask the speaker to link the idea to the topic being discussed. Third, you paraphrase and validate the speaker's explanation. And fourth, you either draw out the speaker's idea, balance and encourage other reactions, return to the stacking or place the idea in the "parking lot."[152]

As a group's lawyer, you will often not be seen by some group members as a "neutral" third party. Because you are the "expert" when it comes to certain topics, you may be perceived as not neutral as to the group's deliberations. You can acknowledge that you are an "expert" when it comes to the legal issues but not so when it comes to other issues. Sometimes, though, you will have important opinions about the matters being discussed. When you are not the neutral facilitator, for example when you have to let the group know your opinion about a particular point, the question is how you can make room for all other opinions to be voiced while promoting your point of view effectively. In those instances you must be responsible for clarifying your own thinking and communicating it effectively while at the same time helping the group do its best thinking. We discuss when a lawyer should or may want to intervene in a group's decision-making later in this chapter.

E. DEALING WITH PROBLEMS IN MEETINGS

Three principal problems encountered by facilitators are disruptive behavior, low participation and blocks in the process of meetings, either because a group cannot reach a decision or because the group lacks focus.[153] Some of these behaviors may be linked, for example, when some members are disrupting the meeting other participants may withdraw and not participate. One common disruptive behavior problem happens when an individual tries to dominate the discussion, talking at the expense of others. Another common problem arises when a person shoots down every idea raised in the meeting, which might happen because there is uneven knowledge in the group or an imbalance of power. In these instances, try to increase people's ownership of the meeting in order to increase their commitment to the outcome. Focus on the rest of the meeting participants and encourage them to participate instead of trying to control the highly verbal member. Consider going around the room and asking everyone to take a turn, thanking the person who is dominating for his or her great ideas and asking what others think, or getting agreement from the group at the beginning to let everyone participate equally. Another way to balance power is to share information before the meeting

---

[152] *Id.*

[153] *Id.* at 149.

with everyone so all are equally informed or have a short presentation at the beginning of the meeting. When people are not taking the discussion seriously, take a break or ask for advice instead of trying to take control of the group. People often become undisciplined when they are overloaded. When there is low participation from the entire group, try shifting from open discussion to another format, such as work in small groups. The group may be angry or fearful. Do not assume silence means agreement.

Several techniques may help a group that cannot reach agreement.[154] Some of these include proposing a break, silent thinking time or postponing the decision. The group might be able to reach decisions on some items but may need time to think about others. Another technique to consider is asking for alternative proposals. If certain individuals are disagreeing, they might think of proposals that did not occur to you or others. The group might need more information than it has or may be confused about the possibilities, which can be the case if you are proposing a lot of different alternatives. When the possibilities might be endless, think about proposing a few and then explaining the way the possibilities can be expanded. That way the group is not overwhelmed by endless possibilities. Your discussion might focus on the group's key considerations or priorities.

Short of disrupting meetings, other issues are likely to arise which will make the meeting more challenging for you as the facilitator. Several techniques can help you deal with these. All these techniques require that you listen skillfully and respectfully to everyone.[155] When someone is being repetitive, you can *paraphrase* the person's comments to help her or him summarize her or his thinking. This technique demonstrates that the person is being heard and understood. It serves as a check for clarification. You could preface your paraphrasing by saying, "It sounds like you are saying . . . ," "Let me see if I am understanding you . . . " or "Is this what you mean?" You should end your paraphrasing with something like "Did I get it?"

When someone is speaking in awkward, broken sentences you can help him or her relax with open-ended, non-directive questions. When someone is exaggerating or distorting, you can *validate* the central point without arguing over its accuracy. When someone goes off on a tangent, you can *connect* his or her principal point to the broader context. Finally when someone is expressing intense feelings, you can acknowledge the emotion and paraphrase the content of the thought to ensure it does not get lost amid the group's reaction to the feelings.

---

[154] *Id.* at 149–53.

[155] *Id.* at 43.

When group members are polarized, *listening for common ground* focuses the group on areas of agreement.[156] When group members take polarized positions it becomes difficult for them to recognize common ground. The facilitator can validate both the differences in the group and the areas of common ground. This four-step process requires you to first indicate that you are going to summarize the group's similarities and differences; second, summarize the differences; third, note areas of common ground; and finally, check for accuracy by asking, for example, "Have I got it right?"[157]

Everyone approaches a discussion from his or her individual frame of reference. When people disagree, meetings can deteriorate. As facilitator, you can use the skills of *sequencing, calling for responses, deliberate refocusing, tracking, asking for themes* and *framing* to try to keep the meeting from deteriorating.[158] In *sequencing*, you as facilitator identify and label two separate lines of thought and organize the group's participation by first focusing on one idea and then on the other.[159] Sequencing does not work well when there are more than two ideas being discussed, however. In those instances, you might want to call for a response, thus focusing the discussion, by asking "Does anyone have a reaction to what Malik said?" or "After listening to the last three speakers does anyone have any questions for them?"

At times you might also want to *refocus* the conversation, such as when a group has been discussing one topic for a while and another topic has been raised earlier but not discussed.[160] You might ask "A while ago David raised an issue and no one responded. I want to check, before we lose that thought, does anyone have a comment for David?" This technique has the risk of appearing to cut off discussion, however. The facilitator can keep *track* of the various lines of thought by saying "I think you are discussing several issues at the same time.[161] Here they are . . . ." You should then ask whether you have captured all the themes. Do not expect the group to choose the order in which to discuss them. When you *ask for themes*, the lines of thought are identified by the group members and not by the facilitator.[162] As facilitator, you can write them down on the flipchart. Once the themes have been identified, you can say, "Now let us return to the open discussion and see what happens in the next few minutes. If necessary, we can come back to the list and structure it more. Does anyone have any comments on any of these themes?" The goal with *tracking* and *asking for themes* is for the participants to begin integrating

---

[156] *Id.* at 58.

[157] *Id.*

[158] *Id.* at 82–86.

[159] *Id.* at 83.

[160] *Id.* at 84.

[161] *Id.* at 85.

[162] *Id.* at 86.

the topics. In *framing*, the facilitator begins by pointing out that several conversations are underway and reminding the group of how the original conversation began.[163] You then ask the group for themes, record the answers and return to the open discussion.

F. LARGE GROUP MEETINGS

Any group larger than twelve people should be considered a "large group." Large group meetings pose particular challenges to facilitators because it is more difficult for less assertive people to participate and the meeting can be more easily dominated by a few. Larger groups tend to have a slower pace and lower energy thus taking longer to reach decisions. You should consider what needs to be discussed before the entire group and what can be done in smaller groups. Plenaries are useful to share information, make proposals and reach final decisions. Smaller groups can speed up some of the discussion phases especially since they are safer, more dynamic spaces.[164]

In large meetings, you might want to switch between working in small groups and the large group. Varying the participation format strengthens participation.[165] Some participation formats include listing ideas, structured go-arounds, working in small groups, role-plays, fishbowls, presentations and reports, and individual writing.[166] There are several ways to list ideas—the group can brainstorm together; members can pair up and discuss a question; flip charts can be scattered around the room and group members could begin at any flip chart and move around every few minutes; group members can write ideas on sticky notes (one idea per sheet) and post them on the wall (the ideas can be categorized later); and members can write ideas on a sheet of paper and trade sheets, read them and add fresh ideas. In go-arounds, the members take turns speaking on a particular topic. There are many formats for that activity, including going clock-wise, tossing a bean bag and using a talking stick. Small groups can have many variations including speed dating, talk and switch, or activity with feedback. The small groups can be assigned to engage in the same or different tasks.[167]

---

[163] *Id.*

[164] *Id.* at 102.

[165] *Id.* at 94. Momentum builds when the group starts and finishes something several times during the course of the meeting. *Id.*

[166] *Id.* at 95–115.

[167] *Id.* at 178. Kaner suggests the following activities and allotted times: Small groups—6–15 minutes; go-arounds—5–20 minutes for an 8–person group, depending on the topic; listing ideas—7–10 minutes; individual writing—7–10 minutes; open discussion—15–30 minutes; and break-out groups—30–90 minutes. *Id.*

G. MULTILINGUAL MEETINGS[168]

Depending on the work you are doing, there will be need for interpretation in some community meetings. Unless the interpretation is happening simultaneously and with headsets, meetings with interpreters take longer and may need more follow-up. As we mentioned in the Interviewing chapter, take the time to prepare the interpreter by speaking with him about any special words you will be using. Consider your use of language even if the meeting is happening only in English but you know the audience has many people who speak English as their second language. Try to use basic words that all attendees are likely to know and understand. It is often advisable for lawyers to not use technical language, especially legal language or jargon. Try to speak slowly since we absorb meanings in our second language at a slower rate. Consider summarizing comments from the audience that are not expressed in clear simple language as well. If you are providing materials for the meeting, consider bringing materials in the second language, even if you are speaking in English. You can prepare those materials ahead of time, without the pressure of the meeting. If you are using an interpreter, the rules we outlined in the Interviewing and Multicultural Lawyering chapters apply. Break your sentences into easily managed bites. Try to follow your outline fairly closely.

IV. COUNSELING GROUPS

In the Counseling chapter, we used examples for two individual clients, Sandy Litmanovich and Alan Minuskin. In this section, we discuss issues unique to counseling groups. We explore whether it makes a difference if you are counseling the board of directors of DWC about the terms of its lease with Eastlake Family Services or a group of women working with DWC regarding the formation of a cooperative. Working with groups presents another level of complexity in the counseling conversation. The discussion of options may be more complicated because there are more people weighing in on the pros and cons. Determining the group's values may also be more difficult.

In the Counseling chapter we provided you with a primer for how to help clients reach decisions in various contexts. This section discusses questions that come with counseling structured groups, including entity clients, and unstructured groups. When counseling group clients, the lawyer speaks not to the individual clients as individuals but to individuals serving as fiduciaries for the entity client. This group counseling raises moral and strategic implications for the lawyer, especially on the question of how direct the lawyer ought to be with the client representatives.

---

[168] For a good discussion regarding running multilingual meetings, see *Multilingual Meetings, in* BERT Y. AUGER, 3M MEETING MANAGEMENT TEAM, HOW TO RUN BETTER BUSINESS MEETINGS: A REFERENCE GUIDE FOR MANAGERS 188 (1987).

In counseling well-structured groups, we suggest that the lawyer's approach to counseling the constituent will approximate but not equal the deference the lawyer gives individual clients. When counseling loosely-structured groups with a consensual decision-making process, we envision the lawyer giving less deference to the appointed constituents.[169] We differentiate between the two types of group clients because we believe the law of lawyering calls for that distinction and thus requires that we treat them differently in the counseling relationship. Our discussion draws heavily on the work of several wise scholars who have written in this area.[170]

We begin by revisiting our discussion of client-centered lawyering and then focus on counseling the different types of group clients.

A. CLIENT–CENTEREDNESS IN THE GROUP CONTEXT

In the Interviewing and Counseling chapters we commit to a client-centered approach to lawyering, an essentially anti-paternalistic one that respects an individual's autonomy against interference by the lawyer.[171] The client-centered approach calls on the lawyer to counsel in a neutral manner in order to protect the presumably less sophisticated client from the lawyer imposing his preferences on the client. This approach allows the client to make decisions based on her preferences, values, goals and commitments, and honors the client's full ownership of her legal matter. It calls on the lawyer not to make decisions based on his preferences or use his power or status as the expert or professional. In the context of community work, it recognizes that the members of the community are in a better position to decide what is in the best interest of the community and the group. The client-centered approach does not silence the lawyer altogether nor does it prohibit the lawyer from pointing out issues the client may not see. It does call on the lawyer to temper his preferences, values and opinions.

The tension between paternalism and autonomy has been discussed for some time in the legal literature.[172] Stephen Ellmann, writing about client-centeredness in the context of group work, sees a tension between group participation and individual autonomy.[173] Group membership, he

---

[169] Paul R. Tremblay, *Counseling Community Groups*, 17 CLINICAL L. REV. 389, 395 (2011).

[170] Several scholars have written about the role of the lawyer in counseling groups, among them Susan D. Bennett, *Embracing the Ill–Structured Problem in a Community Economic Development Clinic*, 9 CLINICAL L. REV. 45 (2003); Ann Southworth, *Collective Representation for the Disadvantaged: Variations in Problems of Accountability*, 67 FORDHAM L. REV. 2449 (1999).

[171] Tremblay, *supra* note 169, at 398.

[172] *See* David Luban, *Partisanship, Betrayal and Autonomy in the Lawyer–Client Relationship: A Reply to Stephen Ellmann*, 90 COLUM. L. REV. 1004 (1990); David Luban, *Paternalism and the Legal Profession*, 1981 WIS. L. REV. 454 (1981); Stephen L. Pepper, *Autonomy, Community, and Lawyers' Ethics*, 19 CAP. U. L. REV. 939 (1990); William H. Simon, *Lawyer Advice and Client Autonomy: Mrs. Jones's Case*, 50 MD. L. REV. 213 (1991); William H. Simon, *Visions of Practice in Legal Thought*, 36 STAN. L. REV. 469 (1984).

[173] Ellmann, *supra* note 116, at 1104.

argues, can require giving up some autonomy. At the same time, the connection that comes from membership in a group is an expression of an individual's autonomy.[174] Michael Diamond and Aaron O'Toole point out that "group participation can provide disenfranchised individuals an experience that builds, rather than diminishes, self-esteem."[175]

Ellmann points to some challenges to client-centeredness in counseling groups. The core of client-centered lawyering involves the lawyer communicating to the client that he hears, understands and accepts the client and that he does not judge her. This intimate and detailed engagement is inconceivable between a lawyer and each member of a group.[176] In addition, group members are unlikely to reveal themselves in front of other group members with the same candor with which they might privately to the lawyer.[177] In addition, when giving advice, because the group is unlikely to be unanimous about its values and the lawyer may not achieve as precise a feel for the group's values as he might with an individual client, the lawyer has to be more tentative than he might when working with an individual. As a result, the lawyer might say, "If you decide this is an important consideration, then this action makes sense."[178] Finally, the lawyer counseling a group cannot exhaust all the relevant considerations of a decision.[179] Because of the diverse perspectives of members, group discussions may produce a more complete assessment of a situation, but they are unlikely to elicit as many particulars of the individual members' perceptions. There are too many perceptions and nuances for the lawyer to be able to speak to each uncertainty of each individual member.[180]

B. COUNSELING STRUCTURED GROUPS

In representing structured groups, such as a formal corporation, the lawyer represents the group. As we already noted, the group speaks through its agents,[181] such as Amanda Estrada, the Executive Director of the DWC. When counseling structured groups, we believe the lawyer may do so in a somewhat less neutral manner than if he was counseling an individual client. The lawyer owes the organization's representative somewhat less deference because of her status as a constituent of the organization. As a result, the lawyer will play a more active and directive

---

[174] *Id.* at 1106, 1108, 1123.

[175] Michael Diamond & Aaron O'Toole, *Leaders, Followers, and Free Riders: The Community Lawyer's Dilemma When Representing Non–Democratic Client Organizations,* 31 FORDHAM URB. L.J. 481, 516 (2004).

[176] Ellmann, *supra* note 116, at 1129–30.

[177] *Id.* at 1130.

[178] *Id.* at 1164.

[179] *Id.* at 1140.

[180] *Id.* at 1140. Ellmann advocates a fairly active role for the lawyer in ensuring that a few people do not dominate the conversation. *See id.* at 1141–43.

[181] MODEL RULES OF PROF'L CONDUCT R. 1.13 (2012).

role in his counseling conversations with the Executive Director.[182] While the risk that the lawyer would impose his preferences on the client exists in the group setting, we believe the lawyer has an additional responsibility when counseling groups. The lawyer owes a "special responsibility to make sure that the group's important decisions are made intentionally, with full appreciation by the organization of the risks involved."[183] The lawyer cannot simply assume that the delegation of power from the organization to its representative, the Executive Director in the case of DWC, is a perfect one. The lawyer has the responsibility to check the accuracy of the Executive Director's judgment about the organization's risk calculus, values and preferences. The lawyer, then, needs to inquire not just about how well the Executive Director understands the risks but whether her assessment of the risks is reflective of the organization as determined by its Board of Directors. The lawyer needs to engage in this conversation especially when the "risks implicate the good will, resources or mission of the organization."[184]

We are not saying that the lawyer has any more right in the group context to impose his preferences than in the individual context. The lawyer owes the organizational client as much respect for its "autonomy" as he owes the individual client. Instead, we believe the lawyer has a duty to test whether the organization's representative (the constituent with whom he is meeting) accurately represents the preferences of the organization.[185] This duty is simply to make sure the choices belong to the entity and not the constituent. Second, the lawyer may himself be a source of expertise about the organization's preferences. Neutrality is more important with the individual client because the lawyer cannot know the things necessary for making the best decision. A lawyer cannot possibly know the individual's values and the weight assigned to those values better than the individual, which is not as true or as important with the group client. The organizational client may have great difficulty determining what it wishes to do, but its decision-making process is more open to examination and input.[186] The lawyer's knowledge of the organization also informs the decision-making process; the organization's representative is not the only one with that knowledge.

We next discuss how a lawyer should counsel loosely-structured groups.

---

[182] Tremblay, *supra* note 169, at 419.

[183] *Id.* at 418.

[184] *Id.*

[185] *Id.* at 420.

[186] *Id.* at 421.

C. COUNSELING COMMUNITY GROUPS

It is not uncommon for a community group to consist of a collection of individuals who have not yet organized themselves into a structured organization. The first question is how a lawyer may represent a loosely-structured group and form an attorney-client relationship with that group. Under the law of agency, professional responsibility and legal malpractice, a lawyer may only represent a loosely-structured group, such as an unincorporated organization, if the client achieves some of the attributes of a well-structured organization.[187] Before the lawyer can establish an attorney-client relationship with a group, he must be certain that the group 1) has agreed to proceed as an entity; 2) has an identifiable membership who serve as the constituents of an entity; and 3) has adopted and agreed to a scheme by which to take action and make binding decisions, including the act of giving authority to the lawyer to proceed with the legal work.[188] The lawyer otherwise risks possibly revealing confidences to a non-client, waiving a privilege and possibly triggering a conflict of interest. In order to apply the entity theory to his representation, the lawyer must accept the organization, not some or all of its members, as his clients. The organization needs to have authority before it can even engage the lawyer.

The members of a loosely-structured organization have three choices—they may proceed as individuals, they may proceed as an unincorporated association or they may establish an organization. The lawyer should counsel the individuals about this choice. Should they decide to proceed as an unincorporated association, the lawyer should assist the group in creating some authority scheme on which the lawyer can rely for making decisions.

Let us assume then, for the sake of discussion, that the group has decided to proceed as an unincorporated association and has created a decision-making protocol on which the lawyer can rely. There are two ways the group may choose to proceed. The loosely-defined entity, the unincorporated association, may choose to work with the lawyer through some constituent(s) or the entire membership may choose to work with the lawyer. Should the counseling protocols be the same for the client that decides to remain an unincorporated association as opposed to deciding to incorporate? The absence of a formal, articulated and binding authority structure creates greater responsibility on the lawyer to get things right.[189] If the lawyer is working through the constituents, the lawyer may rely on the risk assessment and preferences of the appointed leaders

---

[187] *Id.* at 426.

[188] *Id.* at 438. Another author also suggests that lawyers insist on groups creating a decision-making structure and appoint a contact person. Michael J. Fox, *Some Rules for Community Lawyers,* 14 Clearinghouse Rev. 1 (1981).

[189] Tremblay, *supra* note 169, at 440.

without breaching his duty of care. The lawyer may do more than that considering his ethical commitment to be the best counselor for the entity. The more "activist" stance by the lawyer is justified by his inherent doubts about the representativeness of the group's leadership.[190] Given the nature of unincorporated associations, it is not unfair for them to receive "enhanced fiduciary attention" from their lawyers.[191] How active the lawyer decides to be depends on how well he understands the group's aims and goals.

The other option available to the lawyer, should the group be reasonably manageable in size, is to speak to the entire membership. Should the quality of the group's delegation of authority to the leadership be sufficiently unclear, the lawyer would have the right, if not the obligation, to reach out to the larger membership.[192]

A final question is how interventionist or deferential the lawyer should be during the group's deliberations. We recognize the lawyer's moral commitment to neutrality when dealing with an individual client. This moral calculus, we noted, changes when counseling a constituent of an entity client, with less deference when the constituent represents a loosely-structured or unincorporated organization since the constituent is at best an "imperfect proxy for the client."[193] When counseling the group as a whole, the lawyer's deference resembles more closely the lawyer counseling an individual client.

Others draw the line differently. Ellmann sees the lawyer as responsible for assuring a baseline democratic and participatory process within the group and securing some protection for individual autonomy.[194] He believes the lawyer has a moral responsibility to monitor the fairness of the group's decision-making process since he triggered the group's formal organization and its decision to name leaders.[195] Since abuse of power may destroy the group, the lawyer has the responsibility to intervene on behalf of those who are becoming victims within the group.[196] If the leadership falls below a "baseline threshold of democratic fairness,"[197] the lawyer can challenge the power of the leadership directly. In fact, Ellmann believes the lawyer has a duty to vindicate the principle of fair process even over the opposition of the group's majority.[198] This duty includes making sure that everyone's views are heard and their views were considered, approximating the role of a mediator. Ellmann argues for the

---

[190] *Id.*

[191] *Id.* at 441.

[192] *Id.* at 442.

[193] *Id.* at 453.

[194] Ellmann, *supra* note 116, at 1145.

[195] *Id.* at 1152.

[196] *Id.*

[197] *Id.*

[198] *Id.* at 1153.

lawyer playing a role in encouraging group harmony around decisions.[199] In addition, the lawyer has a duty to help dissenters get their voices heard if they so desire.[200]

Michael Diamond and Aaron O'Toole believe interacting with the group's membership may help the lawyer verify the legitimacy of the group's leaders and assess the effectiveness of the group's decision-making process.[201] By interacting with the membership, the lawyer can gauge the leadership abilities of the leaders, the trust the members place in them and the commitment of the group more generally. While Diamond and O'Toole agree with Ellmann and others that it is important for group members to be able to participate meaningfully in groups, they value results more than process.[202] In most instances, achieving the group's goal is more important to the client than protecting individual autonomy or promoting non-hierarchical participation.[203] Clients most often seek legal representation to address or understand a perceived problem, not to promote the autonomy of individual members or even create communities of common interests.[204]

Diamond and O'Toole advocate a more expansive role for the lawyer dealing with groups.[205] They believe lawyers must be able to play an active role in the deliberations of an organization, that the lawyer's actions must be directed toward realizing the goals of the organization, and that the nature and extent of the lawyer's role will vary depending on the nature of the group and its leadership dynamic.[206] The lawyer should look to the nature of the group, the dynamic between the leaders and members, the level of credibility and trust which allowed the leader to achieve and maintain the position of leadership, and the manner in which the leader attained that position (credibility and trust versus manipulation and coercion).[207]

When group members disagree or when the lawyer disagrees with the group members, the lawyer should provide advice that is "informed by an understanding of the group and the goals of representation."[208] To support their position, Diamond and O'Toole cite to Model Rule of Professional Conduct 2.1, which requires a lawyer to "exercise independent professional judgment and render candid advice" and allows the lawyer to consider "moral, economic, social and political factors that may be rele-

---

[199] *Id.* at 1154.

[200] *Id.* at 1161.

[201] Diamond & O'Toole, *supra* note 175, at 514–15.

[202] *Id.* at 517.

[203] *Id.*

[204] *Id.*

[205] *Id.* at 493.

[206] *Id.* at 545.

[207] *Id.* at 520.

[208] *Id.* at 526.

vant to the client's situation."[209] Diamond and O'Toole argue that the role of the lawyer is not simply to enhance the client's capacity to express its interests but to "engage the client, as an equal, in a dialogue on the merits of an issue, informed by both the lawyer's understanding of the client-group's community and her understanding of the interests of the broader community she seeks to serve."[210] They agree with Ellmann in recognizing the risks of engaging—heightening divisions, casting doubt on the legitimacy of the group's leaders and undermining the lawyer's own credibility with the group. The lawyer must guard against destabilizing and dominating the group.[211] The lawyer may be better off acting as an advisor and helping strengthen the leaders' ability to facilitate as opposed to facilitating herself.

Diamond and O'Toole believe the lawyer should be open with the client about her conception of community goals.[212] They recommend a retainer agreement which memorializes the "moral dialogue" between the lawyer and client, examining goals and values of each, agreeing the goals of the representation, developing possible strategies for achieving the goals, anticipating problems and establishing a problem solving structure.

Under this vision, a lawyer should not be a neutral bystander in community group representation. The lawyer should participate in group planning and decision-making so long as she does not attempt to dominate the group.[213] Professional distance and client-centered aloofness remove the lawyer from the political and practical realities of the situation. The lawyer should act to "help preserve institutions of community power that are being diverted from their original course by rogue leaders."[214] With ongoing groups with a dysfunctional board and leadership, the lawyer may need to intervene in order to restore the democratic model with which the group began. When deciding whether, how and when to intervene, the lawyer needs to consider several factors, including the alternative mechanisms of accountability that exist in the group, internal characteristics, such as ease of exit and the presence of other stakeholders, and the objectives of the group.[215] Diamond and O'Toole recognize the difficulty of knowing the group's objectives, however, in the absence of a democratic process. They feel most commentators writing in this area address well-organized, formally hierarchical groups and that there should not be a one-size-fits-all system. They conclude that a lawyer should play a more participatory role in substantive decision-making by group clients.

---

[209] MODEL RULE OF PROF'L CONDUCT R. 2.1 (2012).

[210] Diamond & O'Toole, *supra* note 175, at 528.

[211] *Id.* at 529.

[212] *Id.* (citing Shauna I. Marshall, *Mission Impossible?: Ethical Community Lawyering,* 7 CLINICAL L. REV. 147, 221–22 (2000)).

[213] *Id.* at 543.

[214] *Id.* at 543–44.

[215] *Id.* at 546.

While democratically-run and fully participatory groups are more likely to be successful and more likely to satisfy the needs of their members, nothing in the law of lawyering prohibits the lawyer from representing groups that are autocratic and non-participatory.

You will have to decide for yourself what feels comfortable and ethical for you. While working in the clinic, this is a conversation for you, your supervisor and other students in the program, especially if you work with a clinic partner.

V. COMMUNITY LAWYERING

We now turn our focus to an orientation to lawyering called "community lawyering."[216] Community lawyering informs the approach to representation taken by many lawyers working with groups. We cannot in one chapter, let alone one section in one chapter, do justice to the rich literature on community lawyering. We can at best raise some issues and point you to some of the lawyers and scholars thinking and writing about these issues and how it might affect your work. This orientation influences both the way the lawyer deals with clients and the types of projects the lawyer undertakes.

As we explain in more detail in the Community Economic Development chapter, lawyers and scholars define the term "community" in a number of ways. The term can be used to mean residents of a geographic area but also people of a common religious affiliation, racial or ethnic background, political persuasion, profession, class, sexual orientation or people with a shared interest without regard to geography.[217] Community can be fixed and immutable or fluid and changing.[218] Community lawyering involves working collaboratively with (and not simply on behalf of) low-income and working-class people, people of color, and their groups

---

[216] The concept of community lawyering is known by many terms, including rebellious, democratic, critical, facilitative and collaborative lawyering. Ascanio Piomelli, *Foucault's Approach to Power: Its Allure and Limits for Collaborative Lawyering,* 2004 UTAH L. REV. 395, 398 n. 6 (2004). Several scholars have made important contributions to this rich literature. *See* GERALD P. LÓPEZ, REBELLIOUS LAWYERING: ONE CHICANO'S VIEW OF PROGRESSIVE LAW PRACTICE (1992); Muneer I. Ahmad, *Interpreting Communities: Lawyering Across Language Difference,* 54 UCLA L. REV. 999 (2007); Susan D. Bennett, *Little Engines that Could: Community Clients, Their Lawyers, and Training in the Arts of Democracy,* 2002 WIS. L. REV. 469 (2002); Christine Zuni Cruz, *[On the] Road Back In: Community Lawyering in Indigenous Communities,* 24 AM. INDIAN L. REV. 229 (2000); Jennifer Gordon, *The Lawyer Is Not the Protagonist: Community Campaigns, Law, and Social Change,* 95 CAL. L. REV. 2133 (2007); Zenobia Lai et al., *The Lessons of the Parcel C Struggle: Reflections on Community Lawyering,* 6 UCLA ASIAN PAC. AM. L.J. 1 (2000); Ascanio Piomelli, *Appreciating Collaborative Lawyering,* 6 CLINICAL L. REV. 427 (2000); Karen Tokarz et al., *Conversations on "Community Lawyering": The Newest (Oldest) Wave in Clinical Legal Education,* 28 WASH. U. J.L. & POL'Y 359 (2008); Lucie E. White, *Collaborative Lawyering in the Field? On Mapping Paths from Rhetoric to Practice,* 1 CLINICAL L. REV. 157 (1995).

[217] Michael Diamond, *Community Lawyering: Revisiting the Old Neighborhood,* 32 COLUM. HUM. RTS. L. REV. 67, 112 (2001).

[218] For a discussion of the various meanings of community, see Michael Diamond, *Community Economic Development: A Reflection on Community, Power and the Law,* 8 J. SMALL & EMERGING BUS. L. 151 (2004).

and communities to collectively push for change.[219] It involves collaborating with and nurturing grassroots groups involved in struggles for dignity, survival, self-determination, and other basic human needs.[220] Community lawyers represent clients in definable communities, seeing problems in the context of the community, and learning about the cultures, values, and beliefs of the community.[221] Community lawyering sees clients as self-actualizing through their solidarity with peers and their participation in collectives of people in the same material and spiritual circumstance.[222] Community lawyers share the exercise of professional judgment with collaborators, including organizers and client collectives.[223]

The work of community lawyers often involves working collaboratively with community organizers. In a seminal article written several decades ago, Stephen Wexler advocated that the lawyer committed to doing something about poverty should work to "strengthen existing organizations of poor people, and . . . help poor people start organizations where none exist."[224] Lawyers should be "helping poor people organize themselves to change things so that either no one is poor or (less radically) so that poverty does not entail misery."[225] Traditional legal practice, premised on the one-to-one relationship between lawyer and client, is harmful to poor people because it isolates them from each other and because poor people have few individual legal problems in the traditional sense. Poor people's problems are the product of poverty which is shared by all poor people.[226]

Empowerment is an important concept in community lawyering.[227] William Quigley writes that the primary goal of community empowerment is building up the community.[228] In working with community organizations, the lawyer needs to understand that the community must be in-

---

[219] *See* Ascanio Piomelli, *The Lawyer's Role in a Contemporary Democracy, Promoting Access to Justice and Government Institutions, The Challenge of Democratic Lawyering*, 77 FORDHAM L. REV. 1383 (2009).

[220] *Id.* at 1394.

[221] Zuni Cruz, *supra* note 216, at 243–44.

[222] Sameer M. Ashar, *Law Clinics and Collective Mobilization*, 14 CLINICAL L. REV. 355, 406, 411 (2008).

[223] *Id.* at 412.

[224] Stephen Wexler, *Practicing Law for Poor People*, 79 YALE L.J. 1049, 1053–54 (1970).

[225] *Id.* at 1053.

[226] *Id.*

[227] Empowerment is a process by which "people, organizations and communities gain mastery over their affairs." Kenneth I. Maton, Edward Seidman & Mark S. Aber, *Settings and Voices for Social Change: An Introduction, in* EMPOWERING SETTINGS AND VOICES FOR SOCIAL CHANGE (Mark. S. Aber, Kenneth. I. Maton & Edward Seidman, eds. 2011) (citing Julian Rappaport, *Terms of Empowerment/Exemplars of Prevention: Toward a Theory of Community Psychology*, 15 AM. J. CMTY. PSYCHOL. 121, 122 (1987)). It ensures that citizens, not professionals, have the "determining voice in designing solutions to the problems they face" and emphasizes the need to gain power in order to create social change. *Id.*

[228] William P. Quigley, *Reflections of Community Organizers: Lawyering for Empowerment of Community Organizations*, 21 OHIO N.U. L. REV. 455, 464 (1995).

volved in everything the lawyer does,[229] that the legal strategies are often just part of the larger overall strategy,[230] that the lawyer can never become the leader of the group[231] and that the lawyer is taking a great deal from the interaction as well as giving to it.[232] In addition, the lawyer needs to confront her own comfort level with an unjust system.[233] Michael Fox suggests that above all, lawyers need to avoid dominance of the group.[234]

Others see a risk in lawyer domination of community. Ellmann cautions lawyers not to ally with groups they represent even though the moral or political alliance between lawyer and client can be a potent force.[235] The lawyer who has credibility with a group has the potential to influence the group dramatically. That possibility presents both opportunities and risks. The danger is that the lawyer can mobilize demagogically or manipulatively. The potential is that the lawyer can inspire her clients to engage in political mobilization. By avoiding those alliances, the lawyer escapes the danger of manipulating her clients by refraining from giving advice based on the lawyer's own values. The lawyer, Ellmann cautions, has an obligation of constant vigilance against her own overreaching, as "the lawyer's influence is too great for her to expect complete success in this self-scrutiny."[236] Though Ellmann recognizes that it might be possible for the lawyer to abandon the constraint of client-centeredness in order to engage in political change, he does not feel it is necessary to do so since lawyers can both control themselves so as not to alter the group's autonomy and engage in political change.

Others see a more expansive role for lawyers working in communities. We see Diamond and O'Toole as advocating such a role for lawyers.[237] Michael Diamond critiques some community lawyering scholars for overemphasizing the attorney-client relationship and for giving clients too little credit for their ability to insulate themselves from their lawyer's opinions.[238] He emphasizes the results the client sought when consulting the lawyer and the creation of power within communities.[239] Because the disparity between the dominant elements of society and subordinated groups remains extraordinarily high, Diamond views the goal of the lawyer as helping groups "create power and lasting institutions with the abil-

---

[229] *Id.* at 473.

[230] *Id.*

[231] *Id.* at 474.

[232] *Id.* at 479.

[233] *Id.* at 474.

[234] Fox, *supra* note 188, at 5.

[235] Ellmann, *supra* note 116, at 1168.

[236] *Id.* at 1169.

[237] *See* Diamond & O'Toole, *supra* note 175.

[238] Diamond, *supra* note 217, at 103.

[239] *Id.* at 104.

ity to influence the client's environment" and not providing legal remedies to legal wrongs.[240]

Diamond sees the activist lawyer as interacting with the client on a non-hierarchical basis as well as participating with the client in planning and implementing strategies designed to build power for the client and to "allow the client to be a repeat player at the political bargaining table."[241] The activist lawyer sees the client's world in terms broader than merely its legal implications, considering the political, economic and social factors of the client's problem.[242] While the lawyer is often an outsider without inherent credentials in the community, some lawyers might be participants in community action and seen by the residents as committed to their well-being.[243]

A key question is how the lawyer discerns the will and need of the community. Communities, however defined, are rarely monolithic and thus speak with several voices and have competing goals. Diamond points out that the lawyer as an autonomous agent has views and principles and must remain true to his or her own beliefs.[244] The lawyer must be immersed in the community. Regardless, the lawyer may have to choose among conflicting possibilities. This act of choosing is a political statement of the lawyer's own view of community benefit.[245] In choosing, the lawyer considers the merits of the group's claim, who in the community supports the goals being pursued, and whether the project furthers the goals the attorney has identified as the "community's."[246]

VI. CONCLUSION

Working with groups adds another level of complexity to the attorney-client relationship. We believe working with community groups is also rewarding. For the lawyer working with groups, community lawyering requires a commitment to working with groups in marginalized communities and groups seeking social change. Community lawyering calls on lawyers to work in solidarity *with* these groups, not just *for* the groups.

---

[240] *Id.* at 108–09.

[241] *Id.* at 109.

[242] *Id.*

[243] For a discussion of lawyers who are part of the community, see Marshall, *supra* note 212; LÓPEZ, *supra* note 216; Nancy D. Polikoff, *Am I My Client?: The Role Confusion of a Lawyer Activist,* 31 HARV. C.R.–C.L. L. REV. 443 (1996).

[244] Diamond, *supra* note 217, at 114. *See also* Gary Bellow, *Steady Work: A Practitioner's Reflections on Political Lawyering,* 31 HARV. C.R.–C.L. L. REV. 297 (1996).

[245] Diamond, *supra* note 217, at 117.

[246] *Id.*

CHAPTER 10

INTRODUCTION TO COMMUNITY ECONOMIC DEVELOPMENT

■ ■ ■

I. INTRODUCTION

This chapter provides an introduction to community economic development (CED) in order to give you a context for the work of your clients. Many transactional clinics have dual missions, to give you experience in lawyering while at the same time providing quality legal services to organizations and businesses engaged in community economic development work. Some of your clients may be explicit about their mission while others may be engaged in economic development without being intentional or explicit about it. Some transactional clinics focus on representing groups engaged in community development or community economic development. Others focus on representing business entities that may be contributing to economic development even if their goal or mission is not necessarily to engage in *community* economic development. In this chapter we hope to contextualize both the lawyering and the organizations engaged in the work of community economic development to help you understand better how your work fits within these schemes.

We begin this chapter by defining community economic development from a number of perspectives. The chapter then will discuss some of the issues faced by low-income communities that community economic development tries to address; provide a historical context for the work; highlight differing notions of community economic development; discuss community economic development strategies; and conclude with some of the critiques of the community economic development movement, leaving you with some questions about the possibilities for this work.

One of our goals in this chapter is to help you understand that there is no *one* clear definition or description of this work. Different scholars and practitioners define and describe the work in significantly different ways. These differences are sometimes nuanced but the descriptions and definitions are nevertheless contested, and as a result, political. Throughout the chapter we will use the terms "community economic development" and "community development." Some scholars use the terms interchangeably. Other scholars are intentional in their use of the terminology, using the term "CED" to focus attention on the community aspects of economic issues (and thus differentiate the work from "economic development") and "community development" to focus attention on the human aspects of the work. Our goal in this chapter is to introduce these differing concepts and ideas.

As you will see later in the chapter, those involved in CED work have different ideas about what the process, method and program should look like. You will see these differences surface in the work of your clients as well as other actors in CED, including government, the private sector and the nonprofit sector. These differences play out in the responsibility placed on the individual vis-à-vis society in creating change and improving the life chances of residents of low-income communities. In addition, we see a difference in the role government, the private sector and the charitable or nonprofit sector should play in creating change and improving the chances for individuals and communities. There are differences in terms of focus—for instance, whether a locally-based strategy will address the issues facing communities. Finally, there are differences regarding the role market-based strategies should play in achieving economic justice as opposed to community organizing.

Community development can be seen in four ways—as a process, a method, a program or a movement.[1] As a process it emphasizes what happens to people, socially and psychologically. As a method, it emphasizes some end, a goal and objective. As a program, it is both method and content, emphasizing activities. It is as a program that community development comes into contact with subject matter specialties such as housing, health care, and others. As a movement, it becomes institutionalized, building its own organizational structure, procedures and professional practitioners.[2]

Several themes emerge in CED scholarship, including the creation of community and individual assets, democratic participation and equitable distribution of resources. Community development can be described as a group of people in a locality initiating a social action process to change their economic, social, cultural and environmental situation.[3] Self-help is one theme that emerges in community development, implying that people themselves determine what is to be done.[4] Conflict to create social change is another idea that emerges in community development.[5] Citizen participation, the involvement of people in a democratic society, is another key

---

[1]   James A. Christenson, Kim Fendley & Jerry W. Robinson, *Community Development, in* COMMUNITY DEVELOPMENT IN PERSPECTIVE 13 (James A. Christenson & Jerry W. Robinson, eds., 1989) [hereinafter COMMUNITY DEVELOPMENT IN PERSPECTIVE].

[2]   *Id.*

[3]   *Id.* at 14.

[4]   James A. Christenson, *Themes of Community Development, in* COMMUNITY DEVELOPMENT IN PERSPECTIVE, *supra* note 1, at 34.

[5]   *Id.* at 37.

premise of CED work.[6] In that sense, CED's goals can be both economic equity and community empowerment. Community development is concerned with public policies, governmental actions and institution building. Development means a redistribution of goods and resources, such as education, health services, housing, participation in political decision-making, and other dimensions of people's life chances, in a more egalitarian way.[7] Development implies social change, a restructuring of the social, normative and economic order.[8]

CED seeks to promote qualities that make communities healthy. These qualities can be characterized as follows:

1. Neighborhood residents feel secure in their homes and neighborhood;

2. When problems arise, neighbors have the capacity to collaborate among themselves and with businesspeople, public officials and service providers to resolve them;

3. The neighborhood is influential in local political affairs and receives its fair share of public goods and services from the government, holding people and institutions accountable for public services;[9]

4. Neighborhood residents have the resources and support necessary to get and keep jobs within commuting distance and that allow them to support themselves and their families;

5. Local businesses are competitive in and well integrated into the regional economy;

6. Housing is well maintained and affordable for current residents, and market rate financing and insurance is available for housing investments;

7. Local schools educate children well and serve as places where parents and other community residents come together for community affairs; and

---

[6]   *Id.* at 38. CED is characterized by efforts to subject economic forces to democratic control. WILLIAM H. SIMON, THE COMMUNITY ECONOMIC DEVELOPMENT MOVEMENT: LAW, BUSINESS, AND THE NEW SOCIAL POLICY 58–67 (2001) (discussing the political perspectives that underlie CED, including the interest group and republican perspectives).

[7]   Christenson, Fendley & Robinson, *supra* note 1, at 14.

[8]   *Id.* at 10.

[9]   This quality includes a say in plans, policies and programs affecting the quality of life in the neighborhood and control over development of land in the neighborhood.

   8. Local religious institutions help maintain the moral foundation of
       the community and provide a training ground for youth and grass-
       roots leadership.[10]

In addition, individuals and groups engaged in community development
strive to cushion the extent to which economic turbulence produces social
disorder, to reduce health risks and to reduce the isolation of community
members from outside opportunities.[11] Finally, a healthy community has
safe and accessible public transportation.

   CED produces assets that promote the qualities listed above. These
assets take five principal forms—*physical capital* (e.g., buildings); *intellectual and human capital* (skills, knowledge and confidence); *social capital* (knowledge and resources that allow members of the community to
help one another in relation to education, economic opportunity or social
mobility, norms, trust, understandings and other factors that make relationships productive and feasible);[12] *financial assets*; and *political capital*
(capacity to exert political influence).[13] Community development may both
provide access to and control over these assets. These initiatives can be
place-based—changing the physical environment by, for example, building new housing or commercial development—and people-based—
changing the people by, for example, providing education, job training
and other services. Pure economic development growth, consisting solely
of economic expansion, without people development, is not community
development.[14] Because a cycle of comprehensive problems has caused the
desolation in communities, CED looks to employ a comprehensive set of
strategies to restore health to neighborhoods.

   CED focuses on improving the quality of life in low- and moderate-
income communities. The focus of most CED is on low-income communities, though the work also takes place in communities in transition in order stop the deterioration of neighborhoods. Economic development can
take place in cities, suburbs or rural areas. While the focus of most CED
work has been central cities, this work also takes place in older suburban
communities. Because CED tries to affect primarily low-income communities, we believe it is essential to understand the issues faced by these
communities. This understanding provides a context for the work of your
clients and the communities in which they often work.

---

   [10] Ronald F. Ferguson & William T. Dickens, *Introduction, in* URBAN PROBLEMS AND COM-
MUNITY DEVELOPMENT 2 (Ronald F. Ferguson & William T. Dickens eds., 1999) [hereinafter UR-
BAN PROBLEMS].

   [11] *Id.* at 1, 3.

   [12] Political scientist Robert Putnam popularized the term "social capital" in the United
States. *See* ROBERT PUTNAM, MAKING DEMOCRACY WORK: CIVIC TRADITIONS IN MODERN ITALY
(1993); ROBERT PUTNAM, BOWLING ALONE: THE COLLAPSE AND REVIVAL OF THE AMERICAN COM-
MUNITY (2000).

   [13] Ferguson & Dickens, *in* URBAN PROBLEMS, *supra* note 10, at 4–5.

   [14] *Id.* at 4.

II. ISSUES FACED BY LOW–INCOME COMMUNITIES

The qualities and assets we outlined above as necessary to a healthy community are often absent from low-income communities. A lack of economic resources, however, is perhaps the biggest issue facing these communities. Since the mid–1960s, approximately 10–15 percent of the U.S. population has lived under the poverty line.[15] The poverty rate varies among racial/ethnic groups, with the poverty rate for African–Americans and Latinos being more than double that for Whites.[16] Children are also disproportionately represented among the poor, and what is especially troubling is that they are also disproportionally represented among those living in deep poverty.[17] Close to half of those in poverty have incomes that fall *below one-half* the poverty line.[18]

Despite the common perception, employment does not guarantee escape from poverty. The income of many people who work does not lift

---

[15] In 2011, the official poverty rate was 15 percent, down from 15.1 percent in 2010 after three straight years of increases. U.S. CENSUS BUREAU, INCOME, POVERTY, AND HEALTH INSURANCE COVERAGE IN THE UNITED STATES: 2011 13–14 (2012), *available at* http://www.census.gov/prod/2012pubs/p60-243.pdf [hereinafter 2011 CENSUS FIGURES]. The poverty rate in 2010 was the highest poverty rate since 1993; however, it was 7.3 percent lower than the poverty rate in 1959 (the first year for which poverty statistics are available). U.S. CENSUS BUREAU, INCOME, POVERTY, AND HEALTH INSURANCE COVERAGE IN THE UNITED STATES: 2010 14 (2011), *available at* http://www.census.gov/prod/2011pubs/p60–239.pdf. The improvement in the poverty rate that began in the 1960s continued until 1973, when the poverty rate reached 11.1 percent, the lowest figure since the government began measuring poverty in 1959. U.S. CENSUS BUREAU, NUMBER IN POVERTY AND POVERTY RATE: 1959–2009 (2010), *available at* http://www.census.gov/hhes/www/poverty/data/incpovhlth/2009/pov09fig04.pdf. After decreasing throughout the 1960s, the poverty rate increased during the 1970s and 1980s and during various economic recessions since then. *Id.* The way the U.S. measures poverty has been contested for some time as not accurately capturing the level of deprivation. *See, e.g.,* Rourke L. O'Brian & David S. Pedulla, *Beyond the Poverty Line,* STAN. SOC. INNOVATION REV. 30 (Fall 2010). The current poverty thresholds were developed more than 40 years ago and do not take into account rising standards of living or such things as child care expense, other work-related expenses, variations in medical costs across population groups or geographic differences in the cost of living. 2011 CENSUS FIGURES, at 19. These poverty thresholds do not completely capture the economic well-being of individuals and families since they are based on money income before taxes and do not include the value of non-cash benefits such as food and housing subsidies or tax credits. *Id.*

[16] In 2011, the poverty rate was 27.6 percent for African–Americans, 26.5 percent for Latinos and 9.8 percent for Whites. 2011 CENSUS FIGURES, *supra* note 15, at 13, 15.

[17] In 2011, children comprised 35.6 percent of the people living under 50 percent of the poverty threshold but 23.9 percent of the total population. *Id.* at 17. Persistent childhood poverty is closely tied to negative outcomes later in life. CAROLINE RATCLIFFE & SIGNE–MARY MCKERNAN, URBAN INST., CHILDHOOD POVERTY PERSISTENCE: FACTS AND CONSEQUENCES 1 (2010), *available at* http://www.urban.org/UploadedPDF/412126-child-poverty-persistence.pdf. There are racial/ethnic differences in these statistics as well. The poverty rate among African–American children is the nation's highest—39.1 percent, compared to 35 percent for Latinos and 12.4 percent for white children. At the same time, more Latino children are living in poverty than any other racial or ethnic group—37.3 percent of poor children are Latino, 30.5 percent were White and 26.6 percent were African–American. PEW HISPANIC CENTER, CHILDHOOD POVERTY AMONG HISPANICS SETS RECORD, LEADS NATION 4 (2011), *available at* http://www.pewhispanic.org/files/2011/10/147.pdf.

[18] 2011 CENSUS REPORT, *supra* note 15, at 17.

them or their families above the poverty line.[19] Though poverty affects those who work full-time, it takes a heavier toll on those who work less than full-time.[20] The poverty level, though a measure of deprivation, does not adequately measure the income necessary to live independently; several studies have concluded that persons need an income of about twice the poverty line (with geographical differences taken into account) to meet their basic financial obligations.[21] Additionally, as we might suspect, poverty differs by location. The poverty rate is highest in central cities within metropolitan areas.[22] The lowest poverty rate is experienced by those living inside metropolitan areas but not in central cities.[23]

The level of poverty in the U.S. is the highest among its peer countries.[24] Some experts believe that U.S. poverty is largely the result of structural, rather than individual, failings in that there are simply not enough jobs to go around.[25] During the late 20th and early 21st centuries, the U.S. economy has produced increasing numbers of low-paying jobs, part-time jobs and jobs without benefits.[26] For many years, while the

---

[19] In 2011, the poverty rate among workers ages 18–64 was 7.2 percent. *Id.* at 16.

[20] For part-time workers, the poverty rate in 2011 was 16.3 percent, which was slightly higher than it was for the entire nation. *Id.* For full-time year-round workers, the poverty rate is relatively low at 2.8 percent. *Id.* This development is especially troubling since in 2010, the fraction of the unemployed who had been out of work for more than six months had risen to 46 percent, the highest percentage since 1946. PETER B. EDELMAN, OLIVIA A. GOLDEN & HARRY J. HOLZER, REDUCING POVERTY AND ECONOMIC DISTRESS AFTER ARRA: NEXT STEPS FOR SHORT–TERM RECOVERY AND LONG–TERM ECONOMIC SECURITY 1 (2010), *available at* http://www.urban.org/uploadedpdf/412150-next-steps-ARRA.pdf.

[21] Peter B. Edelman, *Changing the Subject: From Welfare to Poverty to a Living Income,* 4 NW. J. L. & SOC. POL'Y 14, 20 (2009) (citing CENTER FOR AMERICAN PROGRESS TASK FORCE ON POVERTY, FROM POVERTY TO PROSPERITY: A NATIONAL STRATEGY TO CUT POVERTY IN HALF (2007), *available at* http://www.americanprogress.org/wp-content/uploads/issues/2007/04/pdf/poverty_report.pdf). More than one quarter of U.S. households (27 percent) are living in "asset poverty," defined as not having sufficient resources to meet emergencies or long-term needs. JENNIFER BROOKS & KASEY WIEDRICH, THE CORPORATION FOR ENTERPRISE DEVELOPMENT, ASSETS & OPPORTUNITIES SCORECARD: A PORTRAIT OF FINANCIAL INSECURITY AND POLICIES TO REBUILD PROSPERITY IN AMERICA 3 (2012), *available at* http://assetsandopportunity.org/assets/2012_scorecard.pdf. Over 40 percent of households nationwide are "liquid asset poor," with little or no savings to fall back on if emergency strikes. *Id.* Households of color are twice as likely as white households to be asset poor. *Id.* at 4. Over half of workers do not have, or participate in, retirement plans. *Id.*

[22] The poverty rate for people in principal cities was 20 percent in 2011, 11.3 percent for those living in metropolitan areas but not in principal cities and 52.4 percent of poor people in metropolitan areas lived in principal cities. 2011 CENSUS FIGURES, *supra* note 15, at 16. For those living outside of metropolitan areas, the poverty rate was 17 percent in 2011. *Id.*

[23] *Id.*

[24] ELISE GOULD & HILARY WETHING, ECON. POL'Y INST., U.S. POVERTY RATES HIGHER, SAFETY NET WEAKER THAN IN PEER COUNTRIES 2 (2012), *available at* http://www.epi.org/files/2012/ib339-us-poverty-higher-safety-net-weaker.pdf.

[25] Mark R. Rank, *Toward a New Understanding of American Poverty,* 20 WASH. U. J.L. & POL'Y 17, 26 (2006).

[26] *Id.* at 27. The U.S. Census Bureau estimates that the median earnings of workers paid hourly wages in 2003 was $10.85 per hour, barely enough to raise a family of four above the poverty line. *Id.* Three million people worked part-time because of a shortage of full-time jobs. *Id.* A quarter of U.S. full-time workers could be classified in low-wage work—earning less than 65 percent of the national median for full-time jobs. *Id.*

economy was growing, the divide between the top and bottom earners was also growing.[27] At the same time, the U.S. social safety net is weaker than it is in Canada and western European countries and thus has a smaller impact on U.S. poverty reduction.[28] Even though European countries have higher levels of long-term unemployment, they have substantially lower levels of poverty because their assistance programs reduce poverty rates substantially more than in the U.S.[29]

Poverty does not only signify the absence of income but engenders other problems. In turn, poverty and these other social problems have been fueled by other economic changes. Social scientists noted a heightened concentration of poverty in inner city communities in the latter part of the 20th century as the "concentration of poverty, racial isolation and social dislocation appears to have increased significantly along with the concentration of affluence."[30] The issue has particularly affected the African–American community.[31] The concentration of poverty and joblessness has been fueled, according to sociologist William Julius Wilson, by macroeconomic changes related to the deindustrialization of central cities, reflecting a shift from goods-producing to service-producing industries, the increasing polarization of the labor market into low-wage and high-wage workers, and the relocation of manufacturing away from central cities during the latter part of the 20th century. In addition, middle-income and upper-income African–Americans families moved away from the inner city.[32] Perhaps because of these shifts, social science research shows considerable racial inequality between neighborhoods and communities.[33] In many inner city communities, social problems come "bundled together," leading to crime, social disorder, high dropout rates and poor child health.[34]

Generally, although certain people are more prone to poverty, the notion of a permanent underclass does not accurately reflect the reality of

---

[27] Edelman, *supra* note 21, at 20; William Quigley, *Revolutionary Lawyering: Addressing the Root Causes of Poverty and Wealth*, 20 WASH. U. J.L. & POL'Y 101, 108–09 (2006). From 1979 to 2007, real income grew by 275 percent for those in the top 1 percent of the population; 65 percent for those in the top 20 percent of the population; 40 percent for those in the middle range of the income scale; and 18 percent for the 20 percent of the population with the lowest income. CONGRESSIONAL BUDGET OFFICE, TRENDS IN THE DISTRIBUTION OF HOUSEHOLD INCOME BETWEEN 1979 AND 2007 ix (2011), *available at* http://www.cbo.gov/sites/default/files/cbofiles/attachments/10–25–HouseholdIncome.pdf.

[28] GOULD & WETHING, *supra* note 24, at 5–7.

[29] Rank, *supra* note 25, at 38–39.

[30] Robert J. Sampson, *What "Community" Supplies*, in URBAN PROBLEMS, *supra* note 10, at 241, 253.

[31] Edelman, *supra* note 21, at 16.

[32] Sampson, *supra* note 30, at 250 (citing WILLIAM JULIUS WILSON, WHEN WORK DISAPPEARS: THE WORLD OF THE NEW URBAN POOR (1996)).

[33] *See, e.g.*, PRIVILEGED PLACES: RACE, RESIDENCE, AND THE STRUCTURE OF OPPORTUNITY (Gregory D. Squires & Charis E. Kubrin eds., 2006).

[34] Sampson, *supra* note 30, at 252.

poverty for most in the U.S. because poverty is a conditional state, meaning that individuals may move in and out of poverty throughout their lifetimes.[35] The majority of the U.S. population will experience impoverishment at some point in their lives.[36] In this sense, there is fluidity in who is poor. However, even those who are technically above the poverty line experience instability in that they can easily fall into poverty and not be able to satisfy basic necessities even when their income puts them above the poverty line. As such, there is nothing magical about the poverty line. Families need to be substantially above the line to meet basic financial obligations. Because the amount by which people are above the poverty line may be modest, detrimental events in their lives, such as illness, family disruption and job loss may force them under the line.[37] The condition of poverty is, however, still serious, with long-term consequences and the potential to undermine human well-being and development, especially for children.

Poverty is more than just a shortage of income; it constitutes social exclusion, the "inability to participate in the activities of normal living."[38] Poverty means struggling to obtain basic resources like food, shelter, health care and transportation. Poverty reduces the quality of one's health.[39] The quality and quantity of education for children living in low-income areas is substandard.[40] Poverty undercuts a person's ability to build economic assets.[41] Additionally, the lack of employment is a major source of frustration and loss; employment and work have long been central to the identity of Americans.[42] Finally, poverty prevents individuals from fully participating in our democracy—in the freedoms, rights and opportunities to which we are entitled.[43]

One of the most basic financial obligations is housing, and poverty negatively affects a person's ability to have safe and decent housing. The share of households struggling to afford housing increased during the beginning of the 21st century, with over one-third of U.S. households paying more than 30 percent of their incomes towards housing (30 percent is the

---

[35] Rank, *supra* note 25, at 32–35.

[36] *Id.* at 32.

[37] Mark R. Rank, *Rethinking the Scope and Impact of Poverty in the United States,* 6 CONN. PUB. INT. L.J. 165, 168 (2007).

[38] Rank, *supra* note 25, at 35 (citing Howard Glennerster, *United States Poverty Studies & Poverty Measurement: The Past Twenty–Five Years,* 76 SOC. SERV. REV. 83, 89 (2002)).

[39] Poverty is associated with increased health risks such as under-nutrition, heart disease, diabetes, lead poisoning, hypertension, cancer, infant mortality, mental illness and dental problems. Americans in the top 5 percent of income live nine years longer than those in the bottom 10 percent. *Id.* at 36.

[40] *Id.* at 36.

[41] *Id.* at 37.

[42] *Id.*

[43] *Id.*

traditional standard of affordability).[44] An overwhelming number of U.S. households, 17.1 percent, spend more than half of their income on housing.[45] With their generally lower incomes, renters are more than twice as likely as owners to pay more than half their incomes for housing.[46] Exacerbating this problem, the gap between the supply and demand for affordable homes has widened.[47] The problem is greater for families with children; nearly two-thirds of them pay more than half their incomes towards housing.[48] Rent subsidies reach only about one in four eligible households.[49] The number of assisted renters slowed at the beginning of the 21st century.[50] The principal program for building new and preserving existing affordable rentals, the Low–Income Housing Tax Credit, added fewer units after the financial crisis of 2008.[51] In addition, much of the damage of the foreclosure crisis has been in low-income and minority neighborhoods.[52] The number of abandoned homes has also soared as a result of the foreclosure crisis,[53] having a further deleterious effect on communities.

Education is also important to participation in a democratic society. Children from low-income families lag behind children from higher incomes in educational achievement.[54] Since educational attainment is predictive of adults' earnings,[55] this risks producing a more unequal and economically polarized society.

Poverty also affects health outcomes with lower income being linked to worse health.[56] Low-income adults are nearly five times as likely to be

---

[44] JOINT CENTER FOR HOUSING STUDIES OF HARVARD UNIVERSITY, THE STATE OF THE NATION'S HOUSING 27 (2011), *available at* http://www.jchs.harvard.edu/sites/jchs.harvard.edu/files/son2011.pdf.

[45] *Id.*

[46] *Id.*

[47] *Id.* Income for the bottom income quartile fell 7.1 percent while rents increased 8.9 percent from 2000–2009. *Id.*

[48] *Id.* at 28.

[49] *Id.*

[50] *Id.* at 29.

[51] *Id.* This decline is due to the weakened demand for tax credits and thus fewer funds available to build housing.

[52] *Id.* at 30.

[53] *Id.*

[54] Sean F. Reardon, *The Widening Academic Achievement Gap Between the Rich and the Poor: New Evidence and Possible Explanations, in* WHITHER OPPORTUNITY? RISING INEQUALITY, SCHOOLS, AND CHILDREN'S LIFE CHANCES 91 (Greg J. Duncan & Richard J. Murnane eds., 2011).

[55] *Id.* at 111.

[56] *See, e.g.,* Paula A. Braveman et. al., *Socioeconomic Disparities in Health in the United States: What the Patterns Tell Us,* 100 AM. J. PUB. HEALTH 186 (2010) (presenting research that concluded that "health in the United States is often, though not invariably, patterned strongly along socioeconomic and racial/ethnic lines, suggesting links between hierarchies of social advantage and health"). About 15.7 percent of the U.S. population does not have health insurance; 63.9 percent have private health insurance and 32.2 percent are covered by government health insurance. Slightly over one-half of people (55 percent) are covered by employment-based health insurance. 2011 CENSUS FIGURES, *supra* note 15, at 21.

in poor or fair health as those in the highest income groups.[57] Low-income adults are twice as likely to be diabetic and nearly 50 percent more likely to have heart disease as those with the highest income.[58] Racial and ethnic disparities also exist regardless of income.[59] Low-income children have worse health outcomes, being seven times more likely to be in poor or fair health.[60]

The literature on urban poverty has four principal underlying themes—economic structure, population characteristics, social institutions and location.[61] From these themes surface eight hypotheses on inner-city poverty:[62]

1. It is the result of profound *structural economic shifts* that have eroded the competitive position of central cities in the industrial sectors which historically provided employment for the working poor. As a result, demand for their labor has decreased.

2. It is a reflection of the *inadequate human capital* of the labor force, which results in lower productivity and inability to compete for employment in emerging sectors that pay adequate wages. Inner-city residents lack the education, job skills and work experience necessary for the available jobs.

3. It results from the persistence of *racial and gender discrimination* in employment which prevents people from achieving their full potential in the labor market.

4. It is the product of the complex *interaction of culture and behavior*, producing a population that is isolated, self-referential and detached from the formal economy and the labor market.[63]

5. It is the outcome of *spatial mismatch* between workers and jobs which has resulted from the segregation of poor and minority populations in cities.

6. It results from *migration* processes which remove the middle class and successful members from a community, reducing social capital, and bringing in new, poorer populations whose competi-

---

[57] ROBERT WOOD JOHNSON FOUNDATION, OVERCOMING OBSTACLES TO HEALTH 16 (2008), *available at* http://www.rwjf.org/content/dam/farm/reports/reports/2008/rwjf22441.

[58] *Id.* at 22.

[59] *Id.* at 25.

[60] *Id.* at 19.

[61] Michael B. Teitz & Karen Chapple, *The Causes of Inner–City Poverty: Eight Hypotheses in Search of Reality*, 3 CITYSCAPE 33, 36 (1998), *available at* http://www.huduser.org/periodicals/cityscpe/vol3num3/article3.pdf.

[62] *Id.* at 36–37.

[63] Daniel S. Shah, *Lawyering for Empowerment: Community Economic Development and Social Change,* 6 CLINICAL L. REV. 217, 227 (1999). For a more detailed discussion of the group often referred to as the underclass, see WILLIAM JULIUS WILSON, THE TRULY DISADVANTAGED: THE INNER CITY, THE UNDERCLASS, AND PUBLIC POLICY (1990).

tion in the labor market drives down wages and the possibility of employment.

7. It reflects an *endogenous growth deficit* as a result of low levels of entrepreneurship and access to capital.

8. It is the unanticipated consequence of *public policy* that was intended to alleviate social problems.

Each of these different theories for explaining the root causes of poverty lead to different policy interventions.

III. HISTORY OF COMMUNITY ECONOMIC DEVELOPMENT PROGRAMS AND STRATEGIES

For several decades, government, primarily at the federal level, has tried to address some of the problems facing low-income communities. The programs and initiatives developed have differed on the role envisioned for government and the market in addressing issues faced by low-income communities and in spurring economic development. Through this history, we see a move away from federally-funded and toward locally-funded redevelopment and a greater reliance on the market. The rise of the CED movement parallels a revival in a political theory based on principles of autonomy and self-sufficiency.

Scholars uniformly discuss the emergence of the CED movement in the post-World War II era, with some commentators emphasizing the 1960s or 1970s and others calling attention to the 1980s. It is helpful to look briefly at the period after the Great Depression to review government programs instituted to address the economic problems faced by the nation during that economic crisis and the issues facing cities in the aftermath. The New Deal created many new federal government programs, with purposes including economic stabilization, public works, farm assistance, housing reform, and trade regulation.[64] The Civilian Conservation Corps, the Works Progress Administration and the National Youth Administration were some of the programs that created jobs in construction, conservation and other areas.[65] Shortly after the Great Depression, the federal government began its intervention in the area of housing in order to increase home ownership. The United States Housing Act of 1937[66] created the basis for public housing, and even from these early days the

---

[64] The Living New Deal, *New Deal Programs & Timeline*, U.C. BERKELEY DEP'T OF GEOGRAPHY (2011), http://livingnewdeal.berkeley.edu/resources/timeline/.

[65] Harry Kelber, *How the New Deal Created Millions of Jobs to Lift the American People from Depressions*, THE LABOR EDUCATOR (May 9, 2008), available at www.laboreducator.org/newdeal2.htm.

[66] 42 U.S.C. §§ 1437–1437bbb–9 (2006). The Act is also referred to as the Low–Rent Housing Act or the Wagner–Steagall Housing Act. The Act proclaims a goal of providing decent and affordable housing for all. 42 U.S.C.§ 1437(a)(4) (2006).

programs mixed private profit and public purpose.[67] Local housing authorities were to issue bonds and private developers were to construct public housing, which would be run by local housing authorities. The Federal Housing Administration was created in 1934 with the mission of insuring loans made by private lenders to individuals and families purchasing homes, often for the first time.[68]

Following World War II, the federal government undertook a series of policies attempting to deal with the problems facing central cities. The National Housing Act of 1949 created the program known as "urban renewal," providing support, including grants, for local efforts to revitalize "blighted" areas.[69] Through urban renewal initiatives, cities could undertake a plan of combined public and private investment in areas designated by the state as "blighted" and use the government's spending, eminent domain, land use regulation and public finance powers to improve those communities.[70] The urban renewal programs were widely criticized as weakening democratic constraints on governmental aid, subsidizing the private participants and undertaking "redevelopment" at the expense of the residents. Among the African–American community, the program was widely known as "negro removal."[71]

The 1960s saw heightened interest in the problems confronting central cities and a more active role on the part of the federal government to try to address these issues. In 1964, President Lyndon Johnson declared an "unconditional war on poverty" and instituted a series of programs known as the "Great Society."[72] Later that year, Congress passed the Economic Opportunity Act with a mandate for community action, which led to the creation of the Office of Economic Opportunity (OEO).[73] The Act sought to mobilize public and private resources for a coordinated attack on poverty. A central provision of the Act contemplated the delivery of a range of social services through "community action agencies."[74] The federal government certified and supported community action agencies for low-income urban neighborhoods; the agencies were to provide the "maximum feasible participation of the residents" of the community in which they were focused.[75] These agencies oversaw a range of services including edu-

---

[67] For more background information on the historical development of public housing in the United States, see *HUD Historical Background,* U.S. DEP'T HOUSING & URBAN DEV. (May 18, 2007), http://www.hud.gov/offices/adm/about/admguide/history.cfm.

[68] Alice O'Connor, *Swimming Against the Tide: A Brief History of Federal Policy in Poor Communities, in* URBAN PROBLEMS, *supra* note 10, at 77, 91.

[69] *Id.* at 96.

[70] *Id.*

[71] *Id.* at 97.

[72] *Id.*

[73] CARMEN SIRIANNI & LEWIS FRIEDLAND, CIVIC INNOVATION IN AMERICA: COMMUNITY EMPOWERMENT, PUBLIC POLICY, AND THE MOVEMENT FOR CIVIL RENEWAL 37 (2001).

[74] *Id.*

[75] SIMON, *supra* note 6, at 14.

cational enrichment, job training and community economic development.[76]

Senator Robert Kennedy's active support of the Bedford–Stuyvesant Restoration Corporation in Brooklyn brought national attention to the idea of local nonprofit organizations becoming involved in housing renovation and construction as well as in local business development.[77] In 1968, Congress amended the Economic Opportunity Act to provide grants to "community development corporations," defined as locally initiated nonprofits focused on the problems of low-income areas.[78]

Private foundations were also involved in funding CED efforts during the late 1960s.[79] For example, Mobilization for Youth in New York offered comprehensive neighborhood-based services, such as helping to organize local residents to pressure the bureaucracy for change.[80] The Ford Foundation's "Gray Areas" demonstration aimed to make fragmented local bureaucracies more responsive to the needs of the poor.[81]

The Model Cities program was part of a movement to establish a national urban policy.[82] Viewed as an attempt to make up for the failures of the federal anti-poverty initiatives, this federal initiative combined social services with bricks-and-mortar programs while giving control of local planning to city officials.[83]

Though seen initially with great promise, these Great Society programs were not a coherent public policy aimed at addressing the problems facing low-income communities in cities. Urban policy consisted of a series of programs focused on the urban poor instead of being a plan for restoring cities to a central role in the national economy.[84] The programs were too limited in scope and funding to substantially affect the inequalities and structural shifts in the economy or in cities,[85] perhaps because policymakers were ambivalent about whether the goal should be to build communities or help people leave them.[86]

---

[76] *Id.*

[77] *Id.*

[78] *Id.* at 15.

[79] O'Connor, *supra* note 68, at 102.

[80] *Id.*

[81] *Id.* For a critical assessment of the Gray Areas program, see Shah, *supra* note 63, at 222–26.

[82] O'Connor, *supra* note 68, at 104.

[83] *Id.*

[84] *Id.* at 105. For an insightful discussion of programs during this period, see Peter B. Edelman, *Toward a Comprehensive Antipoverty Strategy: Getting Beyond the Silver Bullet*, 81 GEO. L. J. 1697 (1993).

[85] O'Connor, *supra* note 68, at 108.

[86] *Id.*

The beginning of the 1970s saw the decentralization of federal community development programs and the emergence of a steady decline in federal government involvement.[87] At the same time, unemployment and inflation were rising, while growth, productivity and wages remained flat.[88] A "new federalism" began to take hold, supporting policies to lighten federal restrictions and bureaucracy, eliminate government waste and give states greater power and responsibility.[89] The mood in the nation seemed to be one of return to economic competitiveness which many saw as in in conflict with community revitalization.[90]

The Office of Economic Opportunity was abolished in 1973.[91] Funding for the Model Cities and other federal programs was folded into the Community Development Block Grant (CDBG) program, giving local governments discretion on how to spend the money within broad parameters.[92] The Housing and Community Development Act of 1974 modified federal housing provision by shifting the emphasis away from new construction and toward rent subsidies.[93] In the late 1970s, the Urban Development Action Grant (UDAG) program offered federal matching grants for commercial, industrial or residential development in central cities.[94]

The next phase of the CED movement was characterized by an "alternative antipoverty model that stimulated grassroots political action"[95] and a "broad-based, redistributive, economic agenda."[96] Advocates, influenced by community organizer Saul Alinsky, founder of the Industrial Areas Foundation, "worked to build local power, cultivate indigenous leadership and mobilize the poor."[97] The Association of Community Organizations for Reform Now (ACORN), founded in 1970s,[98] focused on

---

[87] *Id.* at 109; Margaret Weir, *Power, Money, and Politics in Community Development, in* URBAN PROBLEMS, *supra* note 10, at 139, 149.

[88] O'Connor, *supra* note 68, at 108.

[89] *Id.* at 109.

[90] *Id.* at 108–09.

[91] *Id.* at 109.

[92] SIMON, *supra* note 6, at 8–9; O'Connor, *supra* note 68, at 110. The CDBG program requires cities to have a "public participation" plan that includes publicity about plans and opportunities, public hearings and technical assistance to groups interested in applying for grants. SIMON, *supra* note 6, at 16.

[93] O'Connor, *supra* note 68, at 110.

[94] *Id.*

[95] Roger A. Clay, Jr. & Susan R. Jones, *What Is Community Economic Development?, in* BUILDING HEALTHY COMMUNITIES: A GUIDE TO COMMUNITY ECONOMIC DEVELOPMENT FOR ADVOCATES, LAWYERS AND POLICYMAKERS 3, 8 (Roger A. Clay, Jr. & Susan R. Jones, eds. 2009) [hereinafter BUILDING HEALTHY COMMUNITIES].

[96] Scott L. Cummings, *Community Economic Development as Progressive Politics: Toward a Grassroots Movement for Economic Justice,* 54 STAN. L. REV. 399, 417 (2001).

[97] *Id. See* SAUL D. ALINSKY, REVEILLE FOR RADICALS (1969); SAUL D. ALINSKY, RULES FOR RADICALS: A PRAGMATIC PRIMER FOR REALISTIC RADICALS (1972).

[98] ACORN dissolved in 2010 in the aftermath of a public scandal. Ben Smith, *ACORN 'Dissolved as a National Structure,'* POLITICO (Feb. 22, 2010), http://www.politico.com/blogs/bensmith/0210/ACORN_dissolved_as_a_national_structure.html. Some of ACORN's state and local

economic issues, using issue-based organizing to "redistribute the balance of power in favor of the poor and working class."[99] ACORN and organizations like it used a distinct antipoverty strategy of grassroots political action to promote economic justice.[100]

The policy environment changed substantially with the election of Ronald Reagan in 1980. That decade brought "structural shifts in the economy, the exodus of high-paying manufacturing jobs from urban areas, low-wage worker insecurity" and the resulting concentration of poverty and unemployment.[101] At the same time, welfare benefits were reduced or terminated and other government-sponsored antipoverty programs were cut back.[102] Federal aid to cities was cut by 60 percent between 1980 and 1992.[103] The CDBG program was cut in half; UDAG, revenue sharing and other development programs were eliminated.[104] Direct federal support for public or subsidized housing also dwindled. Additions to the affordable housing stock depended on the efforts of private developers, including the nonprofit sector, through the Low Income Housing Tax Credit program.[105] As direct federal subsidies were removed, project feasibility began to be "determined by capital markets rather than federal criteria."[106] The federal government began to subsidize the private markets through tax policy, including tax-exempt bond financing, as opposed to direct outlays to cities. When direct federal financing of urban renewal disappeared, "the only source of oversight of these projects disappeared along with it."[107] The previous federal relocation, local participation and housing planning requirements, though at times abused, had served as "at least potentially effective tools for resident input concerning redevelopment."[108]

The 1980s paved the way for a shift away from political organizing to a "localized, market-oriented" approach to CED characterized by public-private partnerships.[109] CED advocates assimilated the dominant market-

---

chapters continued their operations and advocacy efforts as new, independent organizations. Pam Fessler, *ACORN Affiliates Spin Off From National Group,* NAT'L PUB. RADIO (Feb. 23, 2010 3:00 PM), http://www.npr.org/templates/story/story.php?storyId=124012937.

[99] Cummings, *supra* note 96, at 420.

[100] *Id.* at 421.

[101] Clay & Jones, *supra* note 95, at 9.

[102] *Id.*

[103] *Id.*

[104] O'Connor, *supra*, note 68, at 113. *See also* Janet Stearns, *The Low–Income Housing Tax Credit: A Poor Solution to the Housing Crisis,* 6 YALE L. & POL'Y REV. 203, 206 (1988).

[105] SIMON, *supra* note 6, at 25. Part of the 1986 Tax Reform Act, the LIHTC program permits developers to syndicate tax credits to obtain up-front equity from investors to use in the construction of housing. 26 U.S.C. § 42 (2006).

[106] Benjamin B. Quinones, *Redevelopment Redefined: Revitalizing the Central City with Resident Control,* 27 U. MICH. J.L. REFORM 689, 705 (1994).

[107] *Id.* at 707.

[108] *Id.* Federal involvement gave residents, at least, a federal cause of action. *Id.*

[109] Cummings, *supra* note 96, at 422.

based ideology into approaches to combat urban poverty, and community development corporations (CDCs) became critical for implementing this approach.[110] CDCs also presented a politically viable self-help approach to combat poverty through the promotion of public-private partnerships.[111] Poverty alleviation programs became, in essence, market expansion programs.[112]

The 1980s and 1990s saw a deterioration of the economic conditions of the poor and a shift in anti-poverty programs toward market-based reform strategies.[113] Simultaneously, the economy was undergoing structural shifts; the elimination of high-paying manufacturing jobs led to increased economic insecurity among low-wage workers and spatial concentration of poverty and joblessness.

In this political and economic environment, CED was championed by politicians as a market-based alternative to outdated welfare policies and an opportunity for public-private partnerships. CED was further promoted by community activists as a critical link to economic equality and encouraging self-help. The political agenda at the national and local level focused on stimulating investment and business activity in low-income communities. The thought was that increasing for-profit initiatives in geographically discrete low-income communities could produce economic transformation and community empowerment. Community organizations were considered an effective tool for dealing with localized poverty since they were physically in the communities suffering from disinvestment and joblessness.[114]

Though some involved in anti-poverty work were initially hopeful with the election of President Bill Clinton, his presidency was characterized by "large spending cuts in education, income security . . . and transportation"[115] and cuts in welfare which pushed more workers into the low-wage labor sector. Poverty alleviation programs became market expansion programs.[116] For instance, the Empowerment Zone program was the Clinton administration's attempt to invest in people and places.[117] Its program benefits included grants for social services and economic development, regulatory waivers, use of tax-exempt bonding authority and tax benefits for employers who hired residents of a zone identified as

---

[110] Clay & Jones, *supra* note 95, at 10.

[111] *Id.*

[112] *Id.*

[113] Cummings, *supra* note 96, at 421–22. After accounting for inflation, the average hourly wage for non-management jobs in the private sector was lower in 1991 than during the 1970s and 1980s. Edelman, *supra* note 84, at 1719.

[114] Cummings, *supra* note 96, at 425.

[115] *Id.*

[116] *Id.*

[117] O'Connor, *supra* note 68, at 115.

needing revitalization.[118] Communities were to create "strategic plans" of coordinated public and private efforts at housing, business and job development and community groups were to participate in the creation and implementation of the plans. Empowerment Zones were meant to encourage coordination of large-scale public and private investment. They funded social services as well as physical improvements, and mandated community participation, defining the goals of the program in terms of benefit to the community (identified as current residents).[119] The program had four fundamental principles—economic opportunities in private sector jobs and training; sustainable community development characterized by a comprehensive coordinated approach; community-based partnerships that engage representatives from all parts of the community; and "strategic vision for change" based on cooperative planning and community consultation.[120] The program, however, did not have adequate funding and was not available to all communities.[121]

Another Clinton-era program, the New Markets Tax Credit program, was intended to spur private sector equity investments in businesses located in low-income communities.[122] It created a "mechanism for delivering investment capital to businesses in low-income communities through the syndication of tax credits via locally-controlled 'community development entities.'"[123] Additionally, the creation of the Community Development Financial Institution Fund of the Treasury Department was intended to encourage commercial real estate development and small business loans in some low-income communities.[124]

In the area of housing, we saw new federal funding in the HOPE VI program.[125] HOPE VI funded major public housing demolition and rehabilitation and was designed to build partnerships at the community level to leverage private investment to develop mixed-income, low-density, affordable housing.[126] At the same time, the federal government's requirement that units lost be replaced was abolished, meaning that public housing units were lost.[127]

---

[118] SIMON, *supra* note 6, at 18.

[119] *Id.* at 18–19.

[120] O'Connor, *supra* note 68, at 116 (citing U.S. DEP'T OF HOUSING & URB. DEV. AND U.S. DEP'T OF AGRIC., BUILDING COMMUNITIES TOGETHER—THE PRESIDENT'S COMMUNITY ENTERPRISE BOARD (1994)).

[121] *Id.* at 117.

[122] Clay & Jones, *supra* note 95, at 10.

[123] Scott L. Cummings, *Recentralization: Community Economic Development and the Case for Regionalism*, 8 J. SMALL & EMERGING BUS. L. 131, 139 (2004).

[124] Clay & Jones, *supra* note 95, at 10.

[125] U.S. Dep't Housing & Urban Dev., *About Hope VI–Overview*, http://portal. hud.gov/hudportal/HUD?src=/program_offices/public_indian_housing/programs/ph/hope6/about (last updated 2012).

[126] Cummings, *supra* note 123, at 138.

[127] *Id.* at 143.

Newer programs tried to address the recent foreclosure crisis. For example, the Neighborhood Stabilization Program (NSP) sought to stabilize communities that suffered due to foreclosure by purchasing and redeveloping residential properties and homes that have been foreclosed upon or abandoned.[128]

As we have seen, this history of CED is an account of a series of programs aimed at the issues facing low-income communities in central cities begun and abandoned. Many programs were abandoned not because research demonstrated that they did not work or that other programs were more effective, but for political reasons. The CED movement also has a strong foundation in community organizing and economic justice which has not disappeared despite the movement toward market-based strategies. There have been few comprehensive attempts to deal with the complex array of issues facing cities and low-income communities. The various programs have done little to improve the quality of life of residents of low-income communities or the built environment. With this historical understanding in mind, let us now review some of the differing approaches to effective CED interventions that scholars and other observers have articulated.

IV. DIFFERING APPROACHES TO COMMUNITY ECONOMIC DEVELOPMENT

A number of scholars in various disciplines have articulated differing theoretical and practical approaches to community economic development. In this section, we want to highlight some of those different theoretical and practical approaches to CED. You may see these differences at play in the varying approaches taken by the organizations in the communities in which you are working.

One of the most insightful analyses of CED strategies and approaches, offered by Peter Boothroyd and H. Craig Davis, explores where programs place the emphasis in the Community, the Economic or the Development aspects of CED. Growth promotion places an emphasis on the economic ("E"); structural change places the emphasis on development ("D"); and communalization is concerned with the community ("C").[129] Under all three approaches, the economy is "a system of human activity directed to meeting human wants that is determined by deliberate allocation of scarce resources, including human time."[130] Development is the

---

[128] This program has been funded by several acts. NSP 1 was funded by the Housing and Economic Recovery Act of 2008. 42 U.S.C. § 5301 (2011). NSP 2 was funded by Title XII of Division A of the American Recovery and Reinvestment Act of 2009. *Id.* NSP 3 was funded by Section 1497 of the Dodd-Frank Wall Street Reform and Consumer Protection Act of 2010. *Id.*

[129] Peter Boothroyd & H. Craig Davis, *Community Economic Development: Three Approaches*, 12 J. PLANNING EDUC. & RES. 230 (1993).

[130] *Id.*

"deliberate quantitative or qualitative change of a system," including change planned by the system itself or external agencies but excluding change resulting from good luck or aggregated individual efforts to maximize personal gain. Some CED strategies will emphasize one of these three components more than the others.

Under "cEd," economic development is synonymous with promoting growth in jobs, income or business activity without regard to how that activity manifests itself.[131] It consists of attracting investment in order to increase the size of the economy, and the source of growth is assumed to lie in attracting major employers (capital) to the locality.[132] Under this approach, the community is seen simply as the locality in which businesses get together to promote their interests through economic expansion.[133] Generally, the effort to attract new business into a community and to enlist the public sector (to augment and improve the local infrastructure) has been nonselective—these attempts have been undertaken without a comprehensive strategy to maximize the net benefits of this investment to the community.[134]

More recently, this cEd strategy has included more comprehensive planning for growth by involving a broader range of players in setting targets, surveying opportunities and developing a wider range of strategies.[135] These strategies include increasing the productivity of existing businesses and promoting the establishment of new firms by local entrepreneurs. Businesses receive assistance in order to expand markets, develop new products or make better use of resources. Government agencies, community institutions and educational institutions provide assistance to the businesses. Public assistance can include loans and grants, training programs, incubators and information. Indirect assistance can also be provided to businesses by increasing community attractiveness to shoppers, tourists, workers and investors through heritage preservation, improving health facilities, developing social services (such as day care) among others.[136] cEd rests on four principle assumptions regarding the nature of the economy:

1. The community economy is taken to be the totality of monetary transactions; therefore, the production of non-marketed goods and services does not contribute to growth or economic development.

---

[131] *Id.* at 231.

[132] *Id.*

[133] *Id.*

[134] *Id.*

[135] *Id.* at 232.

[136] *Id.*

2. The community is better off when employment is increasing. Increased employment means higher incomes, increased property values and an expanded tax base. Cultural, social and environmental costs of increased employment are secondary considerations.

3. Increased employment is most effectively advanced by increasing the flow of money into the community (increasing the level of exports and attracting outside businesses to the community).

4. The community's internal economy (the structure of relationships within the community as opposed to its place in the wider economy) is best left to the market to determine. The benefits of increased employment will trickle down through the community.[137]

By emphasizing growth, cEd neglects issues of stability and equality. The communities that have managed to grow have for the most part done so because of their head start in size or location, or because of their good fortune or extra effort in security assistance from the state. Though it has the potential to leave behind the communities that most need the growth, cEd is the dominant form of community economic development in the U.S.[138]

The *quality* of the economy is the focus of the approach that places the emphasis on development, so the "ceD" emphasis.[139] Development denotes a "fuller, more complex process than that denoted by growth."[140] The origins of this type of community economic development can be traced to the early 20th century when many communities organized producer and consumer cooperatives and credit unions in order to foster community growth. Before the "welfare state, policy makers assumed that out-migration was the appropriate individual response to the economic decline of locations whose economic bases had been mined out, made obsolete by new technologies or bypassed by outside investors."[141] The welfare state, with unemployment insurance, make-work projects, agricultural subsidies and corporate relief, was able to support people to stay in their communities even if the local economic base had collapsed. This allowed some residential stability at the cost of dissipation of the community's self-management institutions. In the 1980s and 1990s, as "the consensus that had supported the welfare state cracked; assistance to individuals and communities was curtailed."[142]

---

[137] *Id.*

[138] *Id.* at 233.

[139] *Id.* at 233.

[140] *Id.*

[141] *Id.*

[142] *Id.* at 234.

Structural change strategies that ce**D** practitioners have developed for increasing control in the interest of stability and sustainability can be grouped into six categories:

1. Diversify external investment sources. Several small operations are more stable than one big employer.

2. Reduce dependence on external investment by increasing local ownership. This can be done by employee buy-outs, encouraging local entrepreneurs, identifying smaller scale technologies or un-filled market niches, developing credit unions and community loan funds so community capital is retained for community use or established community-rooted businesses such as producer or consumer cooperatives and community development corporations.

3. Reduce dependence on outside decision-makers by increasing lo-cal control over resource management. These include the devel-opment of nature conservancies, community land trusts and co-operative housing; or community co-management (with govern-ment) of fisheries, forestry and mining (there are Canadian ex-amples of this).

4. Reduce dependence on traditional exports by diversifying prod-ucts or markets for existing products (especially where the com-munity's economy is heavily reliant on a single commodity).

5. Reduce the need for exports generally by substituting local pro-duction for imports.

6. Reduce the dependence on money as the basis for local exchange by strengthening the local non-cash economy (by creating labor credits, local money).[143]

This view of community economic development seeks to increase local control in order to provide stability.[144] Unlike the c**E**d approach, it sees the non-cash economy as being able to make major contributions to the well-being of the community. It seeks to stabilize monetary flows into and through the community by local and diversified ownership, local resource control, diversification of exports and import replacement.[145] This vision of community economic development seems out of step with what may be perceived as the mainstream attachment to unlimited growth.

The third approach to CED looks beyond economic growth and stabil-ity to considerations of how wealth is used and distributed.[146] The empha-sis is on developing an economy in such a way that *community* is strengthened. Community is defined as a "social/emotional quality

---

[143] *Id.*

[144] *Id.* at 235.

[145] *Id.*

[146] *Id.*

whereby people feel connected with each other," concerned with each other's well-being and gain satisfaction from cooperating, and not just a "location in which economic activity takes place" or a "set of relationships that can be structured for maximum collective benefit."[147]

The goal of those who emphasize the "C" in CED is to create more just and fair production and distribution functions; structural change is necessary but insufficient as a goal.[148] The aim is for everyone to have access to knowledge and opportunities for obtaining pertinent skills, social and political organizations, instruments of production (including access to good health), relevant information, social networks and financial means to enhance his/her ability to pursue his/her objectives in cooperation with others.[149] This perspective seeks fair access to the community's collective decision-making process, working toward "community self-determination," where every member may assume a meaningful role. This model has three principal strategies:

1. Working through local and senior governments to eliminate marginalization and exploitation of people in the community. It works to establish fairer distributions of community services and development impacts and to make planning processes more participatory.

2. Structuring community economic development institutions (cooperatives, land trusts and community development corporations) to favor those most in need.

3. Strengthening non-cash mutual aid norms and practices.[150]

This model is based on the idea that the purpose of CED is to increase community solidarity, distributive justice and the broadly defined quality of life. It is often termed simply "community development."[151]

These three approaches play out in public policy initiatives. They also affect the focus of community organizations involved in community economic development. If you pay attention to the organizations with which you work or are involved in this work in the communities in which you live and work you will see these differences at play. Are these approaches mutually exclusive? Or can they be complementary?

Two themes appear in CED strategies—a programmatic approach and a power approach.[152] The power approach calls on low-income com-

---

[147] *Id.*

[148] *Id.* at 236.

[149] *Id.* (citing John Friedman, *Life Space & Economic Space: Contradictions in Regional Development* (UCLA Sch. Architecture & Urb. Plan., Discussion Paper 158, 1981)).

[150] *Id.*

[151] *Id.* at 238.

munities to organize and use confrontational strategies to demand removal of barriers and biases so they can achieve the same opportunities as more affluent communities.[153] Community organizing consists of creating action for social change by empowering individuals, and building relationships and organizations.[154] Power-based community development emphasizes the power of low-income people, holding officials accountable and building an inclusive and democratic organization. The programmatic approach, by contrast, highlights the work of communities in the creation of jobs, housing, and safety, among other changes. This approach focuses on delivering services, such as housing, jobs, micro-financing, transportation, child care, retail services and social services to low-income communities.[155] It emphasizes low-income communities cooperating with resource providers such as government or corporations to develop programs focused on helping individuals in low-income communities.

These different models are rooted in two different theories of society. The programmatic model sees low-income people as needing opportunity, not power, and cooperation is the best means to provide opportunity. This model does not address structural barriers to equality. Conflict theory, on which the power model builds, sees conflict over scarce resources. Drastic redistribution of wealth is necessary since not all poor people can lift themselves. Under this vision, what is needed is a transformed economy providing a wealth of good jobs, not training programs for people to compete for an extremely limited good job pool. Conflict groups create access to power holders. They can create social instability to force the target to the table, but they have a difficult time actually negotiating because of their militancy. Are these either/or propositions? Can groups only have one strategy or can they combine them depending on the situation?

We might also distinguish between three strategies for promoting community empowerment—community organizing, community-based development and community-based service provision.[156] Community organizing involves "mobilizing people to combat common problems and increase their voice in institutions and decisions that affect their lives and communities."[157] Community-based development consists of neighborhood-based efforts to improve the community's physical and economic condition, for instance by building or rehabilitating housing or creating

---

[152] RANDY STOECKER, POWER OR PROGRAMS? TWO PATHS TO COMMUNITY DEVELOPMENT 1 (2001), *available at* http://www.iacdglobal.org/files/stoecker.pdf. Stoecker refers to these two themes as community organizing and community development approaches. *Id.*

[153] *Id.*

[154] *Id.*

[155] *Id.* (citing STEVE CALLAHAN ET AL., ROWING THE BOAT WITH TWO OARS (1999), *available at* http://comm-org.wisc.edu/papers99/callahan.htm).

[156] Peter Dreier, *Community Empowerment Strategies: The Limits and Potential of Community Organizing in Urban Neighborhoods*, 2 CITYSCAPE 121 (1996).

[157] *Id.*

jobs and businesses. Community-based service delivery involves neigh-borhood-based efforts to deliver social services such as job training, child care, parenting skills, housing counseling, health care, literacy, that will improve people's lives and opportunities within the community (often called "human capital").[158]

Those who emphasize the community organizing approach to CED advocate for a more equitable approach to development. They embrace a reconfigured notion of community, not necessarily defining it by tradi-tional neighborhood boundaries but by a common interest of redressing poverty and inequality.[159] Those espousing this view support the creation of broad-based multi-racial coalitions and look to ensure that the perspec-tive of low-income and under-served communities is represented in the creation of CED strategies.

You will likely observe these differences in approaches in the work of the organizations working in communities even if the underlying theories remain unarticulated.

V. THE TOOLS OF COMMUNITY ECONOMIC DEVELOPMENT

In this section, we survey some prominent CED strategies. While we might also discuss government intervention in the economy, we will con-centrate our discussion on strategies that emphasize *community* and *de-velopment* and the work done by community organizations. These strate-gies include locality or physical development, where the main goal is to develop the physical structure and infrastructure of the community, such as commercial and housing revitalization and development; business de-velopment, where the focus is on creating a good business climate, in-creasing business formation, including worker ownership, cooperatives and self-employment, and supporting established businesses; human re-source development, which focuses on developing the human resources of the community, by education and training, and placement models, match-ing people to employment in the region; and community-based develop-ment, which focuses on increasing the employment opportunities of resi-dents as well as the development of the local economy.[160] Additionally, organizations are involved in community organizing.

At the community level, much of this work is being carried out by the community development corporations (CDCs). These organizations may be concerned with all aspects of community life and seek to address a comprehensive set of needs. In theory, the community controls CDCs

---

[158] *Id.* at 121–22.

[159] Scott L. Cummings & Gregory Volz, *Toward a New Theory of Community Economic De-velopment,* 37 CLEARINGHOUSE REV. 158, 162 (2004).

[160] Drier, *supra* note 156, at 121.

through active resident participation since residents have the most knowledge about what needs to be done in their neighborhoods.[161] CDCs, however, live in tension, trying to be grassroots activist organizations accountable to residents and to a mission of social justice, and professional organizations accountable to outside funders.[162]

Scholars discuss three generations of CDCs.[163] The organizations that began in the 1960s tended to be multi-faceted organizations with a broad array of programs but primarily oriented to workforce and business development.[164] They were formed by community activists and grew out of African–American social movements, including the civil rights movement, and many had religious roots. The second generation was founded in the 1970s.[165] They too grew out of activism and organizing but were not as multi-faceted as the previous generation. They tended to work on smaller projects and to focus on one or two programs, and many specialized in housing development.[166] They also tended to have broader ethnic and geographic constituencies. The third generation was born in the 1980s during the time of federal cuts in urban programs.[167] This generation turned to local sources for support. They tended to be more professional and focused their attention on efficiency and effectiveness. The 1990s saw the growth of community building and comprehensive community initiatives.[168] This generation of CDCs focus on a range of physical and social development activities and emphasize resident participation and collaboration, and coordination between organizations.

Faith-based institutions are among the most important supporters of CED activity.[169] The Roman Catholic Church and African–American Protestant congregations have been some of the most active religious institutions in the community development arena. They have sponsored many CDCs as well as community organizing efforts across the country. Churches are often the strongest non-governmental institution in low-income communities because they are willing to make strong place-based commitments.

---

[161] Sara E. Stoutland, *Community Development Corporations: Mission, Strategy, and Accomplishments, in* URBAN PROBLEMS, *supra* note 10, at 193.

[162] *Id.* at 195. Peter Dreier captures this idea when he writes that CDCs must live in two worlds, one that views housing and jobs as a human right and one that views them as commodities in a marketplace. Margaret Weir, *Power, Money, and Politics in Community Development, in* URBAN PROBLEMS, *supra* note 10, at 180 (including Peter Drier's comment to Margaret Weir's article).

[163] Stoutland, *supra* note 161, at 196–201.

[164] *Id.* at 196.

[165] *Id.* at 197.

[166] *Id.* at 198.

[167] *Id.* at 198–99.

[168] *Id.* at 200–201.

[169] *Id.* at 197.

Although geographic focus is one of the main characteristics of many CDCs, others define community other than by geographical neighborhood. Ethnic-based CDCs serve immigrants of a specific national or ancestral origin.[170] The leaders of these organizations are often immigrants themselves, often first- or second-generation immigrants who serve as the role of intermediary between the immigrants and the United States. These organizations represent a shift from a place-based to a people-based definition of community. These organizations may also define CDC work more broadly, including developing youth programs and working on immigration reform activities. These groups can also have tremendous diversity since ethnic groups are not monolithic.[171]

Housing remains the primary development activity for the majority of CDCs today.[172] Housing work done by CDCs includes building new and rehabilitating existing housing, depending on the community. In recent years, many CDCs have acquired or developed foreclosed housing as well. Additionally, community organizations have been involved in organizing residents to pressure building owners in the community to maintain and rehabilitate their properties. In addition to the LIHTC program described earlier, housing may be financed with rehabilitation tax credits,[173] such as the historic preservation tax credit, tax exempt bonds,[174] HOME funds,[175] and state or local tax credits and trust funds.[176] In recent years, community organizations have also become involved in weatherization programs.[177]

The CED movement's focus on housing has been an explicit strategy to preserve social capital by enabling residents to maintain their relation-

---

[170] Shomon Shamsuddin, *Have Community, Will Travel*, SHELTERFORCE Winter 2007, at 152, *available at* http://www.shelterforce.org/article/235/have_community_will_travel/.

[171] *Id.* For example, the South Asian community represents tremendous diversity in terms of language, religion and culture. *Id.*

[172] Ferguson & Dickens, *supra* note 10, at 8. The ability of CDCs to engage in this work may have been negatively affected by the 2007–2008 financial crisis and its aftermath. *See* Ben Bernanke et al., *The Economic Crisis and Community Development Finance: An Industry Overview* (Fed. Reserve. Bank San. Fran. Comm. Dev. Investment Center, Working Paper 2009–05 (2009)).

[173] *See* Donald S. Holm III, *Rehabilitation Tax Credits: An Important Community Revitalization Tool, in* BUILDING HEALTHY COMMUNITIES, *supra* note 95, at 147.

[174] *See* Richard M. Froehlich, *The Use of Tax–Exempt Bonds for CED, in* BUILDING HEALTHY COMMUNITIES, *supra* note 95, at 103.

[175] Per Title II of the Cranston-Gonzalez National Affordable Housing Act of 1990, 42 U.S.C. §§ 12741–56 (2011), the Department of Housing and Urban Development (HUD) gives HOME Investment Partnerships grants to states and localities which can then give some of their allocation to CDCs to do affordable housing work.

[176] For example, the Local Initiatives Support Corporation (LISC) is an organization providing local community development organizations with funding support and has offices in cities across the United States that have a local focus. *About Us*, LOCAL INITIATIVES SUPPORT CORP. (2012), http://www.lisc.org/section/aboutus/mission.

[177] The federal Weatherization Assistance Program (WAP) was authorized in Title IV of Part A of Energy Conservation and Production Act of 1976. 42 U.S.C. § 6863 (2011). The program was recently funded by Division A of the American Recovery and Reinvestment Act of 2009. 42 U.S.C. § 6872 (2011).

ships through stable and affordable homes on safe streets.[178] Housing development was also a rational strategy that responded to funding and the availability of abandoned or neglected property at low or no cost.[179] While the "bricks and mortar" approach has often become narrow, especially as CDCs tried to fill the void created by massive federal housing cuts in the 1980s, organizations have become increasingly diversified and comprehensive as they renewed community organizing and asset-based community development strategies.[180]

Some of the early CDCs were involved in commercial development, and more experienced and sophisticated groups continue to do this work.[181] As we mentioned in Section III above, the federal New Markets Tax Credit program encourages investments in and provides tax incentives for lenders and capital markets to invest in low-income communities.[182] Local tax increment financing (TIF) also provides possible funding for commercial development.[183] The use of TIF is highly contested in many areas. You may find community organizations opposing designation of TIF districts as a subsidy for development that would otherwise happen, and as a result siphoning tax dollars from school districts and municipal coffers as well as removing community control and oversight over development.[184]

The principal mission of some of the early CDCs was job creation.[185] Today, we might find some community organizations involved in workforce development or business development.[186] Workforce development includes job training and placement services to disadvantaged workers in addition to meeting the labor force requirements of employers.[187] Funding for workforce development is available from the federal government, state and local governments, private philanthropic foundations and businesses.[188] Community-based nonprofits have achieved job training successes, often in alliances with community colleges or other public agencies and private employers, by coordinating with government and for-profit participants and designing and providing training tailored to the needs of

---

[178] SIRIANNI & FRIEDLAND, *supra* note 73, at 57.

[179] *Id.* at 57.

[180] *Id.*

[181] *Id.* at 61.

[182] Herbert F. Stevens, *New Markets Tax Credits, in* BUILDING HEALTHY COMMUNITIES, *supra* note 95, at 162.

[183] *See* Dina Schlossberg, *Tax Increment Financing, in* BUILDING HEALTHY COMMUNITIES, *supra* note 95, at 129.

[184] *Id.* at 136–38.

[185] Randy Stoecker, *The CDC Model of Urban Development: A Critique and an Alternative,* 19 J. URB. AFF. 1, 2 (1997).

[186] SIRIANNI & FRIEDLAND, *supra* note 73, at 61.

[187] John Foster–Bey, *Workforce Development, in* BUILDING HEALTHY COMMUNITIES, *supra* note 95, at 251, 251–53.

[188] *Id.* at 255–56.

trainees and the demands of the job market.[189] Community organizations are also involved in business development including microenterprises.[190] Community residents may not be able to participate in the job market without access to affordable and quality day care. Additionally, early childhood education prepares children for school. Community organizations may thus be involved in developing and running day care centers.[191]

Community organizations are also involved in the development and administration of community health centers. The federal government funds the operation of primary care clinics in medically underserved communities.[192] These facilities must be located in high need areas; must be open to all residents of the area they serve (regardless of income or insurance status); must furnish a comprehensive array of primary care, social support and other services that go beyond traditional medical services; and must be governed by a patient-dominated board.[193]

Other community organizations help individuals build assets through matched savings programs such as individual development accounts, or IDAs.[194] Organizations are also involved in making sure that community residents have access to financial services, including credit, offered through banks, by advocating that banks provide services in their communities and through the creation of community development financial institutions such as community credit unions, community loan funds and community venture capital funds.[195] Still other organizations are working on developing community assets.[196] These assets include people, land and institutions. One example might be the development of community land trusts to control land. The Dudley Street Neighborhood Initiative in Boston in a prime example of this work.[197]

---

[189] SIMON, *supra* note 6, at 34–36 (citing BENNETT HARRISON, MARCUS WEISS & JON GANT, BUILDING BRIDGES: COMMUNITY DEVELOPMENT CORPORATIONS AND THE WORLD OF EMPLOYMENT TRAINING (1995)).

[190] *See* Tim Lohrentz, *Inclusive Business Practices, in* BUILDING HEALTHY COMMUNITIES, *supra* note 95, at 357. *See also* Susan R. Jones & Amanda Spratley, *How Microenterprise Development Contributes to CED, in* BUILDING HEALTHY COMMUNITIES, *supra* note 95, at 379.

[191] *See* Jennifer Wohl, *The Child Care Economic Impact Report, A Tool for Economic Development,* 37 CLEARINGHOUSE REV. 213 (2003).

[192] *See* Sidney D. Watson, *Affordable Health Care, in* BUILDING HEALTHY COMMUNITIES, *supra* note 95, at 289.

[193] *Id.* at 292–93.

[194] *See* Kim Pate, *Matched Savings Accounts, in* BUILDING HEALTHY COMMUNITIES, *supra* note 95, at 323.

[195] *See* Richard Marsico, *The Community Reinvestment Act, in* BUILDING HEALTHY COMMUNITIES, *supra* note 95, at 403. *See also* Donna Fabiani, *Community Development Financial Institutions, in* BUILDING HEALTHY COMMUNITIES, *supra* note 95, at 415.

[196] *See* Hannah Thomas & Thomas Shapiro, *Assets and Community, in* BUILDING HEALTHY COMMUNITIES, *supra* note 95, at 303.

[197] *See* PETER MEDOFF & HOLLY SKLAR, STREETS OF HOPE: THE FALL AND RISE OF AN URBAN NEIGHBORHOOD (1994).

CDCs are involved in a diverse range of other activities. Some organizations are involved in senior citizen programs; security, anti-crime and anti-drug activities; children and youth initiatives; or arts and cultural activities. Other CED strategies may involve public/private partnerships such as linking downtown development to neighborhood projects.[198] Other institutions are also involved in CED work in communities. Cooperatives, including credit and worker cooperatives, are business entities often involved in CED work.[199] The fundamental characteristic of the cooperative is ownership by the organization's patrons. The cooperative is democratically controlled by the patrons and that control is exercised on a one-person, one-vote basis, as opposed to the more typical organizational arrangement of control by a small group of owners or managers. Cooperatives distribute income in proportion to work performed, goods purchased or materials supplied, rather than in proportion to investment.

Those organizations that rely on community organizing to advocate for the redistribution of resources to economically disadvantaged communities may be engaged in still other activities. Their focus is on using political power to challenge economic inequality, promoting political equality and redistributing the balance of power in favor of the poor and working class.[200] Some of these organizations may be involved in advocating more equitable development by negotiating community benefits agreements whereby community residents support development projects in the community and the community and its residents receive certain benefits such as housing, open space and access to jobs not initially envisioned in the development project.[201] Others may be involved in advocating that recipients of state subsidies for economic development activities be more accountable.[202]

VI. CRITIQUES OF THE COMMUNITY ECONOMIC DEVELOPMENT MOVEMENT AND STRATEGIES

While CED represents a laudable set of goals and aims to accomplish significant social and economic justice, it is not without its critics as a movement. The critiques of CED come from a number of fronts. Three principal ones criticize its lack of impact, its focus on localism, and its failure to give control to communities. Those who question its impact point to lack of effectiveness on the part of CDCs. For instance, some crit-

---

[198] *See, e.g.,* WILLIAM C. RIVERBANK, JUSTIN MARLOWE & A. JOHN VOGT, PROMOTE ECONOMIC DEVELOPMENT WITH PUBLIC–PRIVATE PARTNERSHIPS (2010).

[199] *See* Scott L. Cummings, *Developing Cooperatives as a Job Creation Strategy for Low–Income Workers,* 25 N.Y.U. REV. L. & SOC. CHANGE 181 (1999).

[200] Cummings, *supra* note 96, at 420.

[201] *See* Julian Gross, *Community Benefits Agreements: Definitions, Values, and Legal Enforceability,* 17 J. AFFORDABLE HOUS. & CMTY. DEV. L. 35 (2008).

[202] *See* Greg LeRoy, *Making Economic Development Accountable, in* BUILDING HEALTHY COMMUNITIES, *supra* note 95, at 219.

ics argue that the case that CDC buildings have long-term beneficial effects on their neighborhoods has yet to be made in a convincing manner.[203] At times, foreclosure rates for nonprofit developers were substantially higher than for their for-profit counterparts.[204] There is not enough evidence that CDCs have enough impact to reverse neighborhood decline.[205] Nor can it be convincingly argued that the organizations are more efficient providers of housing than for-profit developers or managers.[206] Because many CDCs operate more like businesses, they focus their activities on physical development.[207] CDCs can contribute to neighborhood decline by both failing and succeeding. To the extent that community development emphasizes the physical over the social and remains limited to the possibilities dictated by capital, it may actually increase turnover, displacement, and otherwise disorganize a community.[208]

Another worry is that the rhetoric of community control may be inconsistent with reality, one in which communities have become increasingly dependent on elite interests as programs moved from grants to tax credits and loans. CDCs have dual missions. They need a wide range of expertise (e.g., finance, insurance, real estate, land use) and access to capital in order to be effective and comprehensive. The organizations must be larger, with more capital capacity, more political capacity and more collective talent to be effective. They also need to be able to address multiple community issues simultaneously to be effective. The need for this knowledge and capital is at odds with what makes CDCs community-based—their smallness and neighborhood roots. As programs became more complex, lawyers are needed to implement them, sometimes at the expense of community participation and control. Ironically, many lawyers are attracted to community development work because of its possibilities for collaboration with low-income communities, for encouraging low-income people to solve their own problems, and for having lawyers and clients on equal footing. In reality, community residents may have little or no control over the complex projects taking place in their communities. Lawyers are left serving the role of mediators between the various elite interests—municipal governments, accountants, bankers, investors, and business people.

CDCs at times end up "based in communities" but not "community-based."[209] Because low-income communities do not have enough community-controlled capital, they must woo outside capital. These funders and

---

[203] Stoecker, *supra* note 185, at 4.

[204] *Id.* at 6.

[205] *Id.* at 3.

[206] Kenneth T. Rosen & Ted Dienstfrey, *The Economics of Housing Services in Low–Income Neighborhoods, in* URBAN PROBLEMS, *supra* note 2, at 437, 449.

[207] Stoecker, *supra* note 185, at 5.

[208] *Id.* at 10.

[209] *Id.* at 8.

intermediaries are controlled by elites and not by members of the community. Outside capital resists supporting redevelopment that maintains community control.[210] The outside investors in turn provide enough money to stave off social unrest but not enough to threaten the unequal balance of power.[211] These relationships may mean that CDCs are less willing to be confrontational on issues affecting low-income communities like discriminatory bank lending and exclusionary zoning, and that its lawyers generally are not representing the interests of low-income residents. As a result, CDCs risk becoming another developer following a supply-side free market approach to development rather than fighting for the social change necessary to support sustainable communities.[212] Community control may in effect be a myth.

Those with very diverse political, social and economic agendas have united around CED because they have been able to "manipulate the processes of development to meet their continually redefining the meaning of the product: empowerment."[213] Even as conditions in neighborhoods deteriorated, the meaning of empowerment has come to depend on increasingly restricted possibilities. Rather than meaning the building of community alliances for social mobility and mainstream integration, or self-sufficiency, neighborhood control and separation, empowerment has come to mean nominal citizen participation in outside economic investments.[214] As one observer has noted, "The built environment may look more attractive, but community and neighborhood leadership has in fact become less involved, and increasingly dominated by the moneyed interests of society whose priorities rest with maintaining the subordination and isolation of inner city neighborhoods."[215]

The third critique maintains that CED's particularly local perspective fails to address the structural issues of the relationship between urban poverty and the relocation of jobs.[216] These scholars see the need for a metropolitan perspective, critiquing CED programs for using localized strategies in city neighborhoods to combat the results of structural economic change in metropolitan regions.[217] Despite the limited success of these local initiatives, the policy debate has not sought alternatives by looking at expansive regional economies. CED's emphasis on local economic reform fails to challenge the "structural determinants of poverty,"

---

[210] *Id.*

[211] *Id.* at 7.

[212] *Id.* at 3.

[213] Shah, *supra* note 63, at 218.

[214] *Id.* at 219.

[215] *Id.* at 248.

[216] *Id.*

[217] *See, e.g.,* David J. Barron, *The Community Economic Development Movement: A Metropolitan Perspective,* 56 STAN. L. REV. 701, 721 (2003) (reviewing SIMON, *supra* note 6).

including the regional roots of the problem.[218] The geographical focus of CED also impedes the formation of cross-racial alliances, since many communities are racially segregated.[219] Urban renewal recognized that central cities are situated in a broader metropolitan context. By focusing on the neighborhood within central cities, the CED movement fails to outline what it views as the proper relationship between "the communities that are its primary concern and the broader metropolitan environment in which they are situated."[220] This may lead to community-based strategies having a limited impact. Successful cities are part of metropolitan areas which achieve a more inclusive local government and use it to implement metropolitan remedies for local finance, integration and land use—the so-called "outside game."[221] Communities are part of metropolitan and regional political economies and influence the regional practices that determine the geographic distribution of work and residential opportunities, services and political representation.[222]

Admittedly, the federal government's response to issues facing low-income communities has been inconsistent and has not dealt with the real problems faced by urban areas.[223] Small-scale community-based interventions were intended to revive depressed communities, while simultaneously larger public policies undermined their very ability to survive. Substantial federal subsidies for home mortgages, commercial redevelopment and highway building drew middle class residents and tax revenues to the suburbs.[224] More recently, community-based interventions have been undercut by economic policy which "favored flexible, deregulated labor markets and have left communities with little recourse against wage deterioration and industrial flight."[225] In response to these trends, the federal government stepped in with interventions to deal only with the consequences—job loss, poverty, crumbling infrastructure, racial and economic polarization and neighborhood institutional decline. These interventions have been "modest and inadequate."[226] Additionally, these investments in declining communities were all place-based strategies while the focus of social policy analysis during almost the entire time of these interventions was on economic concepts and norms. What is needed are government investments in economic restructuring, metropolitan development and social infrastructure to work in conjunction with CED. Pro-

---

[218] Cummings, *supra* note 96, at 454–56.

[219] *Id.* at 457–58.

[220] Barron, *supra* note 217, at 737.

[221] *See* DAVID RUSK, INSIDE GAME/OUTSIDE GAME: WINNING STRATEGIES FOR SAVING URBAN AMERICA (1999).

[222] O'Connor, *supra* note 68, at 119.

[223] *Id.* at 77. She characterizes the federal government as "swimming against the tide."

[224] O'Connor, *supra* note 68, at 95.

[225] *Id.* at 79.

[226] *Id.*

grams geared toward low-income communities were means-tested programs, while wealthier communities are subsidized through "essentially invisible, federalized, non-means-tested subsidies such as highway funds, state universities, home mortgage assistance and tax preferences."[227] Finally, these policies have not adequately dealt with the issue of race, an important issue throughout U.S. history.

While many CED programs have resulted in some individual successes, they have not been designed to address the structural flaws in society which have left many people in poverty.[228] Michael Diamond argues that CED should help create community institutions that are capable of "marshaling human and financial resources."[229] These organizations should bring together community residents to identify and articulate common problems, develop comprehensive responses, provide opportunities for community interactions and make connections with outside entities.[230] These organizations can be instrumental in developing a comprehensive plan for the community and carrying it out.[231] CED efforts should include the political organizing and education of community residents and linking the community to government and other institutions that have the power to affect the life of the community and its residents.[232] CED should create institutions that play both a mobilizing and mediating role. The goal of CED should be to both improve the build environment and improve the lives of community residents. In order to be able to do that, CED should create "durable institutions that can acquire, maintain and utilize power" for the good of the community.[233]

Scott Cummings calls for a new CED agenda, one that promotes inter-racial solidarity to rebuild the economic justice movement. This model "prioritizes political action over market participation[,] . . . fuses legal advocacy with community-based organizing in order to redistribute resources to low-income constituencies . . . [and] links job creation strategies more explicitly to poverty alleviation. . . ."[234] This "politically engaged CED" supports community organizing around economic justice issues. It builds organized low-income constituencies that look to challenge the distribution of political power.[235] Cummings cites living wage campaigns, worker cooperatives, and jobs initiatives linked to government incentives for private investment as examples of this form of CED. These

---

[227] *Id.* at 83.

[228] Michael Diamond, *Community Economic Development and the Paradox of Power,* 1 IRISH REV. COMMUN. ECON. DEV. L. & POL'Y 1, 13 (2012).

[229] *Id.* at 14.

[230] *Id.*

[231] *Id.*

[232] *Id.* at 15.

[233] *Id.* at 21.

[234] Cummings, *supra* note 96, at 458–59.

[235] *Id.* at 459.

job initiatives include first source hiring agreements, federally sponsored employer linkage programs,[236] and sectoral employment interventions providing for worker training programs in growing industries.

VII. CONCLUSION

Community development strategies alone cannot eliminate poverty or all the economic and social issues faced by low-income communities. CED can, however, play a role in addressing the issues confronting low-income communities. While metropolitan and national policies are needed to address the issues confronting low-income communities, place-based and people-focused development within communities continues to be necessary. In order to have meaningful and lasting effects, community economic development must be part of a broader policy initiative that addresses macro-economic policies, the regional economy, racial discrimination, and social inequality.

While the roles of government, the individual, the private sector and the nonprofit sector, as well as the development versus and organizing focus, may each be contested, there is no dispute that lawyers have an important role to play in the representation of community-based organizations involved in this work.

---

[236] For example, Section 3 of the Housing and Community Development Act of 1992 and others that have local hiring requirements embedded in the federal programs. *Id.* at 484.

CHAPTER 11

AN INTRODUCTION TO BUSINESS ENTITIES

■ ■ ■

The clients of transactional clinics often will be beginning businesses, enterprises that are just getting off the ground and hope to succeed. When the entrepreneurs operating those businesses seek out legal assistance, they often wonder about whether they should create a business structure for their enterprise. Sometimes the entrepreneurs will ask you directly for advice about that prospect; sometimes they will not see that prospect as an issue, but you may raise the topic with them. In either event, you will benefit from knowing a little bit—and, later, perhaps a lot—about the "choice of entity" question. By that we mean the considerations an entrepreneur might take into account in deciding how to operate her business. In this chapter we offer you a broad overview of the considerations business owners ought to take into account, as well as the structures available to them.[1] Our intention is to orient you in a very general way about this potentially complex area of law and business strategy, to permit you to perform more dedicated and sophisticated research as you work with your own clients.

Our plan for this chapter is to begin with a brief description of the more relevant factors a businessperson would consider in making a choice about how to operate the business. Then, with those factors in mind, we will compare the typical array of options available to a beginning business owner: sole proprietorship; general partnership; Subchapter C corporation; Subchapter S corporation; and limited liability corporation (LLC). This list is not at all exhaustive,[2] but it should suffice for our orienting purposes. Then, at the end of the chapter, we introduce the emerging notion of hybrid organizations, such as the B Corporation, the benefit corporation and the low-profit limited liability corporation (the "L³C"), whose popularity is growing among socially-conscious entrepreneurs and inves-

---

[1] Our discussion in this chapter owes a considerable debt to the soon-to-be-published work of Emily Satterthwaite, formerly a faculty member and transactional clinical professor at the University of Chicago Law School. *See* Emily Ann Satterthwaite, *Regressive Tax Salience For Entry–Level Entrepreneurs*, PITTSBURGH TAX REV. (forthcoming 2013). We have also benefitted from the helpful comments of Nicole Appleberry, who teaches the Low–Income Taxpayer Clinic at University of Michigan Law School.

[2] We omit discussion of, among others, limited partnerships, limited liability partnerships, cooperatives, and professional corporations.

tors. That concept of hybrid organizations will foreshadow, and connect to, our next chapter, introducing you to nonprofit organizations and achieving tax-exempt status for them.

I. AN EXAMPLE

Let us begin with a simple example of a beginning business for which the clinic will offer some legal advice and representation.[3]

> The prospective clients are named Bill Sherman and Filippa Sands. Bill and Filippa are entrepreneurs who live in the local neighborhood. They have plans to open a bakery café on Prospect Street, about a mile from the clinic's office. Their plan is to call the store "The Prospect Street Café." The intake sheet states that Bill is an unemployed chain grocery store manager, and Filippa works full time as an assistant financing clerk at a GM dealership in town. They heard from the local Small Business Development Center that they should consult a lawyer before embarking on this endeavor. The SBDC gave Bill and Filippa the names of the county bar association as well as your law school clinic. They decided to try the clinic instead of a private lawyer (the price made a difference), and the clinic agreed to interview them. The two prospective clients would like to meet a lawyer or student as soon as possible to get things rolling.

If Bill and Filippa indeed operate the café, they have choices available about how to set up the business. If they simply hang up a sign and start selling coffee and croissants, they have made a choice, by default, to operate in a certain fashion (that would be as a general partnership, unless it was clear that one of the two owned the business and the other person worked for the owner, in which case the default arrangement would be as a sole proprietorship—but we will explain these concepts in a moment). Whether that default choice would be a bad thing depends on certain considerations. Let us now list some of those considerations.

II. SELECTED RELEVANT CONSIDERATIONS IN CHOOSING A BUSINESS STRUCTURE

Assume for a moment that Bill and Filippa never saw a lawyer, never thought about the strategies for choosing a business structure, but instead simply started to operate a café on Prospect Street. Here are some consequences they would encounter as the business developed:

(1) *Liability*: Because Bill and Filippa own the business personally, they accept full responsibility for the tort and contract liabilities related to the business. If Bill and Filippa happen to own any property or money

---

[3]   You will recall this example from the Counseling and Ethical Issues chapters.

not otherwise protected by some arrangement, creditors of the business will have the right to seize that property and money to recover for any debts arising from the business. Perhaps as business owners Bill and Filippa would prefer some *limitation on liability*, so that their personal assets or income would not be at risk. Some business owners care about that worry; others will not. But it is a factor Bill and Filippa likely will want to think about.

(2) *Income taxes*: If the café never brings in more money than it costs to operate the enterprise, then Bill and Filippa will have little worry about the taxes owed on the profits of the business. But let us assume what Bill and Filippa will surely assume—that at some point, and sooner rather than later, the café will be profitable, so there will be dollars left over at the end of some given accounting period. The endeavor will *earn money*, and realize income. As a general rule, the federal, state and sometimes municipal governments levy a tax on income, so Bill and Filippa will have to figure out who pays the tax and at what rate. A choice of how to structure the business might affect the taxation questions.

(3) *Self-employment taxes*: Besides income taxes, the federal government levies self-employment taxes (known in the business as "SET") to fund retirement and health benefits of workers through Social Security and Medicare (the Federal Insurance Contributions Act, or "FICA," deductions you have seen on your paychecks). Section 1401 of the Internal Revenue Code imposes this tax on "net earnings from self-employment" ("NESE").[4] NESE is defined as "gross income derived by an individual from any trade or business carried on by such individual."[5] If Bill and Filippa take home some money as a result of their operation of the café, they might be responsible for payment into the FICA scheme. Their choice of business structure might influence whether they are responsible for FICA payments on the profits they realize through the business.

(4) *Division of responsibility*: Operating a business means making many decisions, from choosing what products to offer at what price, to deciding on a design of the space, to selecting a website design, to entering into contracts with suppliers and service providers, and to hiring help. If Bill and Filippa agree on all of those choices, then the business will proceed smoothly. At some point, though, the owners may disagree, or happen to decide separately, and differently, on any one of those items. In cases of divergence of opinion, whose decision controls? Bill and Filippa will need to appreciate this down-the-road eventuality, and their choice of business structure might influence how that matter gets resolved.

---

   [4]   26 U.S.C. [hereinafter I.R.C.] § 1401(a) and (b) (2008); *see also* Stuart Levine & Marshall B. Paul, *IRS Shifts Focus with Controversial New SE Tax Proposed Regulations*, 86 J. TAX'N 325 (1997).

   [5]   I.R.C. § 1402(a).

(5) *Division of proceeds; contribution of investment capital*: If the café is profitable, which of the owners gets to keep which of the profits? The explicit—or perhaps unspoken—understanding between Bill and Filippa may be a pure 50/50 equal split of any profits, but some history and course of dealing might lead to a different understanding. Their business structure might influence their options on that score. Also, when the café opened, the participants might have contributed unequal amounts toward the business's initial capitalization. If so, they likely would want to take the relative contributions into account in some fashion as the business moves ahead, or when it ultimately wraps up. The owners' choice of a business entity might play a role in how comfortably they can make the adjustments that fairness and their agreements require.

(6) *Ownership and investment permutations*: As the business proceeds, its owners may wish to consider adding new owners, or raising money through investor contributions. Some business structures will make those prospects easier, and others more difficult (or impossible). Bill and Filippa might want to consider this factor as they decide how to set up the café.

(7) *Exit strategies*: This factor may seem far-fetched for entrepreneurs like Bill and Filippa right now, but what if their business were to become quite successful, so that some investor or other entrepreneur might want to buy it from them? Some businesses begin with this goal directly in mind; others do not even contemplate the possibility. But the kind of entity Bill and Filippa choose might affect how the business and its assets can transfer to others later.

(8) *Cost*: There is typically no charge for Bill and Filippa to operate their café on their own without a formal, separate business structure. Some alternative structures do have a start-up cost and an annual fee thereafter. Bill and Filippa no doubt will want to consider, at least as one factor, the relative costs of the choices available to them.

III. BUSINESS VEHICLES DESCRIBED

Understanding the considerations just described is a first step toward your serving as an effective counselor for entrepreneurs like Bill and Filippa. But even more important for your preparation is an understanding of how each of the relevant vehicles through which Bill and Filippa might operate their business compares to the others, and how each accounts for the factors listed above. In this section, we review the five most common business structures, explaining how the factors above manifest in each.

A. SOLE PROPRIETORSHIP

The first vehicle we encounter is the sole proprietorship, perhaps the most common form of business ownership in the United States.[6] One often hears a businessperson refer to this option as a "d/b/a"—"doing business as" the name of the enterprise.[7] In a sole proprietorship, an individual operates a business on her own, without any formal structure or separation from the rest of her personal finances.

In our example, a sole proprietorship does not seem like an option, because we have two entrepreneurs. But if we imagine the possibility that one of the two entrepreneurs, say Filippa, will serve as the owner of the business, with Bill serving as an employee, then this vehicle would be a possible choice for them.[8] We will describe the sole proprietorship alternative by imagining that Filippa is the sole owner of the business.

In a sole proprietorship, the owner accepts the full responsibility for the debts and liabilities of the business. There is no limited liability in this option. Also, the tax implications are rather clear and straightforward—anything earned by the business would be taxed as ordinary income to Filippa. Operating as a sole proprietorship is an inexpensive option, as there are no costs to this election beyond the fixed business operation fees (which we assume would be uniform across each option described here). Filippa's exit strategy with a sole proprietorship is simple—she may simply walk away from the enterprise (but with the debts remaining her responsibility), or she may sell her assets, trademarks, and good will to a willing buyer.

So, why might Filippa—if indeed she were the sole owner of this enterprise—wish to operate in a way other than as a sole proprietorship, given the simplicity of this option? Her primary concern would be the limitation on liability. If she worries that her insurance on the business might not be sufficient to provide her with the peace of mind she wants, she might consider one of the options allowing for limited liability. Also, she may want a vehicle that permits her to share the burdens (and rewards) of ownership with others. Before we consider how that factor implicates the more formal structure, let us review what happens if Bill and

---

[6] J. WILLIAM CALLISON & MAUREEN A. SULLIVAN, PARTNERSHIP LAW AND PRACTICE: GENERAL AND LIMITED PARTNERSHIPS § 2:1 (2012) ("The sole proprietorship . . . is the oldest, simplest and most prevalent form of business enterprise").

[7] *See Register Your Fictitious Name or "Doing Business As" Name*, U.S. SMALL BUS. ADMIN., http://www.sba.gov/content/register-your-fictitious-or-doing-business-dba-name/ (noting some states require registration of these names when doing business as a sole proprietor).

[8] Arranging the business such that one of the two founders serves as an owner and the other as an employee is not necessarily a foolish consideration, as each of the two roles has disadvantages and advantages. In such an arrangement the employee is guaranteed some minimum return on his labor, but no return on the growth of the enterprise. The owner, by contrast, has no such guarantee about income and accepts the risk of personal liability, but in return obtains the equity growth, if any, the business produces.

Filippa own the property together, without any more formal vehicle in place.

B. GENERAL PARTNERSHIP

Under the Revised Uniform Partnership Act ("RUPA"), which has been adopted by most states, a partnership is "an association of persons who carry on as co-owners of a business for profit."[9] Therefore, if Bill and Filippa owned the café and did not elect a different kind of structure, they would serve as general partners by default, as a matter of law.[10] And, unless the two entrepreneurs in our example drafted a partnership agreement to implement their own rules for the operation of their partnership, RUPA would determine how the owners would share profits, divide losses, bear liability for debts and obligations of the partnership, and many other important issues.[11]

The partnership arrangement essentially mirrors the sole proprietorship for purposes of liability and taxation. The arrangement offers no limited liability to the owners. Each general partner is responsible for all liabilities of the partnership, even if he or she did not ratify or participate in the activities leading up to the liability in question.[12] And the taxation of the income of the business parallels that of the sole proprietorship, so that each general partner treats his or her earnings as personal income reportable on the individual tax return for that year.[13] Also, this option is free to the parties, with no fee to create the partnership and no annual tax or fee to maintain its existence (other than whatever fee a local jurisdiction may impose on a "doing business as" or "assumed name" enterprise).[14]

---

[9]   *See* REVISED UNIFORM PARTNERSHIP ACT (1997) [hereinafter "RUPA"] § 202(a). The definition continues: ". . . whether or not the persons intend to form a partnership." *See, e.g.,* Minute Maid Corp. v. United Foods, Inc., 291 F.2d 577 (5th Cir. 1961) (finding a partnership under Texas law where "the parties entered into a contract from which it is clear that the parties contemplated joining in a common business for their common benefit to be operated for their joint account and in which they as owners each of an interest would be entitled to share as principals in the profits as such, they would be partners").

[10]   *See* STEPHEN M. BAINBRIDGE, AGENCY, PARTNERSHIPS & LLCs 4 (2004).

[11]   RUPA § 103 ("[t]o the extent that the partnership agreement does not otherwise provide, this Act governs relations among the partners and between the partners and the partnership").

[12]   RUPA § 306. Note the difference between a general partnership and a limited partnership on this score. Limited partners are essentially investors, and, so long as they qualify as limited partners (which effectively means that they are not actively involved in the management of the business), they only risk the loss of their investment. *See* BAINBRIDGE, *supra* note 10, at 171; REVISED UNIFORM LIMITED PARTNERSHIP ACT (RULPA) § 303(a).

[13]   I.R.C. § 701 (2011); Cent. Valley AG Enters. v. United States 531 F.3d 750, 755 (9th Cir. 2008) (individual partners are separately or individually liable for income taxes on their distributive share of partnership items); Longmire v. Ind. Dep't of State Revenue, 638 N.E.2d 894 (Ind. T.C. 1994) (partners are individually liable for their respective share of the profits of a partnership). *See also* WILLIAM S. MCKEE, ROBERT L. WHITMIRE & WILLIAM F. NELSON, FEDERAL TAXATION OF PARTNERSHIPS AND PARTNERS § 1.01[1] (2012).

[14]   Indeed, the partnership exists even if the partners do not know it. The partnership arises as a matter of law, by default from the activity of the participants. *See* BAINBRIDGE, *supra* note 10, at 4. The partners may, and prudence suggests that they ought to, arrange for a written

If Bill and Filippa were considering proceeding as general partners, your responsibility would be to counsel them about how the partnership doctrine treats their respective rights. Under RUPA's default treatment, the participants would share equally in losses and gains arising from the café's operations, and for responsibility for its debts and obligations, unless the parties agreed explicitly to a different arrangement.[15] The parties may, of course, agree to any different terms as they choose, and would likely want to create a partnership agreement to establish the specific details of their arrangement.

As with the sole proprietorship, the major possible disadvantage of a general partnership for Bill and Filippa is the absence of any limitation of liability. They also might decide that having a separate structure offers the opportunity to bring in other owners on more favorable terms—simply adding more general partners is always an option, but the new owners must be comfortable with assuming unlimited liability, either to operate the business or as investors of the business, aside from simply adding more general partners. Let us now see what costs and benefits the alternative structures offer to entrepreneurs like Bill and Filippa.

C. SUBCHAPTER C CORPORATION

Given the risks involved in operating a business where all liability rests with the owners, Bill and Filippa might want to consider setting up a structure separate from their personal lives and finances, in order to achieve that comfort level about liability. For sake of comparison, let us begin our list of alternatives with the Subchapter C corporation, even though, as we shall see, this option is unlikely to be the one favored by beginning, smaller entrepreneurs like Bill and Filippa.

The "C Corp." is, in some senses, the default corporate structure. It is a state law entity[16] but its implications derive from the tax treatment at the federal level, as it is an entity taxed under Subchapter C of the Code.[17] In general, a corporation is a separate legal entity, a "person" for constitutional and economic purposes.[18] The state of incorporation will

---

partnership agreement. If they employ one or more lawyers to assist with that task, that step represents a cost of this option.

[15] RUPA § 410(b).

[16] *See, e.g.,* 8 DEL. CODE. ANN. § 101(a) (1998) (guiding parties to incorporate with the Department of State).

[17] *See* I.R.C. § 11 (2010) (defining federal corporate taxation); *see also* I.R.C. § 561(a) (2010) (defining tax deductions for payable dividends as a way of avoiding taxation on shareholders).

[18] Citizens United v. Fed. Election Comm'n, 558 U.S. 310 (2010) (granting First Amendment protections to corporations); Leek v. Cooper, 194 Cal.App.4th, 399, 411 (2011) ("Ordinarily, a corporation is regarded as a legal entity, separate and distinct from its stockholders, officers and directors, with separate and distinct liabilities and obligations"). While corporations do possess such identity, a corporation is not entitled to Fifth Amendment protection. *See* Bellis v. United States, 417 U.S. 85 (1974); JAMES D. COX & THOMAS LEE HAZEN, TREATISE ON THE LAW OF CORPORATIONS § 1:4 (3d ed. 2011).

recognize the entity and authorize the issuance of shares to the owners. The shareholders become the owners. Its affairs will be managed by a board of directors and by officers, but in small corporations the same individuals (or one individual) may serve all of those roles. Because the corporation is a discrete entity, it is responsible for its debts and liabilities. The owners of the entity—the shareholders—possess *limited liability* to the extent of their investment in the corporation. This factor, then, serves as an important benefit to entrepreneurs like Bill and Filippa.

Importantly, though, Bill and Filippa obtain the limited liability benefits only if they operate the business *as a business*, respecting the corporate identity and formalities (including record-keeping and required meetings), and maintaining a clear separation between the C Corp.'s transactions and their own. A failure to achieve that goal may permit a court, at the request of a creditor or tort claimant, to "pierce the corporate veil," which, if successful, permits a court to ignore the corporate shell and treat the business as owned by the entrepreneurs, as their "alter ego."[19]

On the taxation side, the C Corp. has an important quality, serving another important difference from the sole proprietorship and the general partnership. Because it is its own separate juridical entity, the C Corp. will file a corporate income tax return each year, and will pay taxes if the entity has any taxable income.[20] Then, if the C Corp. returns any of that income to its shareholders in the form of dividends, the shareholders pay taxes on that income, although at the lower rate applicable to dividends, not at the higher rate for ordinary income.[21] This result is what critics (and others) refer to as the "double taxation" effect of C Corp. operations.[22] Example 11–1 shows the effect of the double taxation.

Example 11–1

Assume at the end of a tax year the Prospect Street Café has revenues of $200,000 and expenses of $150,000 (including the payment of wages to Bill). The board of directors (Bill and Filippa) agree to issue a dividend to the shareholders (Bill and Filippa) for all of the resulting $50,000 profit. Here is how the cal-

---

[19] *See generally* Robert B. Thompson, *Piercing the Corporate Veil: An Empirical Study*, 76 CORNELL L. REV. 1036 (1991). In addition to this risk, the managers of the business may be responsible, personally, to the IRS for employment and income taxes required to be withheld from employee's wages under the trust fund recovery penalty. I.R.C. § 6672.

[20] I.R.C. § 11; *see also* Tax Reform Act of 1986, Pub. L. No. 99–514, 100 Stat. 2085 (closed loopholes relating to double taxation in C Corporations and incentivized the use of S corporations).

[21] In 2012, the rates for ordinary income taxes are 10 to 35 percent; for dividends, the rates are either 0 or 15 percent. Of course, after 2012, the rates will likely be changed, and the dividend rate may not be different from the personal income tax rate.

[22] *See* SCOTT B. EHRLICH & DOUGLAS C. MICHAEL, BUSINESS PLANNING 81–88 (2009) (discussing "The Problem with Double Taxation").

culations work, leading to an effective tax rate of 38.5% (and addressing only federal taxes[23]):

Prospect Street Café Earnings:	50,000
Corporate Income Tax (15%[24]):	9,000
Net Earnings After Taxes:	41,000
Distribution to Bill:	20,500
Individual Income Tax (25%[25]):	5,125
Net Income After Taxes:	15,375
Distribution to Filippa:	20,500
Individual Income Tax (25%):	5,125
Net Income After Taxes:	15,375
Pretax Profits:	50,000
Taxes Paid:	19,250
Net Distribution:	30,750
Effective Tax Rate:	38.5%

The arrangement just described earns the description "double taxation" because the $50,000 in profits is taxed first at the corporate level, and then the after-tax remainder of that pool of money is taxed a second time at the individual level when it reaches the owners. Of course, if the Prospect Street Café did not issue a dividend to Bill and Filippa, or if it did not generate profits after its expenses, including the cost of its employees, then there would be only one level of tax (at the corporate level in the first instance, and at the employee level in the second). Keep that in mind as we compare the next two options, which, as we shall see, do not include the corporate level of tax.

Before we compare the C Corp. to other alternatives, let us also consider other characteristics of the corporation that distinguish it from the sole proprietorship or the general partnership. If Bill and Filippa hope to have, or want to maintain the possibility of having, investors, the C Corp.

---

[23] An important caveat for our readers: As this book goes to press, Congress is debating how to respond to what most reports term the impending "fiscal cliff," those dramatic tax and spending changes which will go into effect at the beginning of 2013. The tax rates we use in the following chart as well as in Example 11–2 below are accurate as we write, but surely will be different when you read this. The principles demonstrated by the examples and the discussion, though, should remain the same, even if the math is different.

[24] This is the federal corporate tax rate for $50,000 in 2012.

[25] This is the marginal tax rate for income above $35,350 for a single individual in 2012. For simplicity's sake, we use the marginal tax rate rather than the effective tax rate.

offers them a straightforward means to do so. Because of the shareholding structure, the café could offer shares to new investors in return for capital. Indeed, if the investors insist upon having some form of preferential status because of the risks they face, the C Corp. arrangement permits the café to offer investors preferred stock or similar arrangements.[26] Also, through the allocation of shares or voting rights, the two erstwhile "partners" would now have a more flexible arrangement available to account for the variable contributions of the two founders.

The C Corp. structure also offers Bill and Filippa a possible exit strategy, in that the structure permits a sale of their stock to investors, and, perhaps, even an initial public offering of the shares were the business to develop at that level.[27]

The C Corp. is, though, more expensive than the first two options just discussed. As one example, in 2012 in Massachusetts the founders would pay $275 to establish the corporation initially, and then, to maintain its good standing, the corporation would pay $275 with its state annual report as well as an annual excise tax of at least $456.[28] Those charges compare to no cost for the sole proprietorship and the general partnership arrangements.

Before you try to anticipate whether your clients might accept the disadvantages of the C Corp. in return for the limited liability and flexibility protections of that vehicle, consider the next two options.

D. SUBCHAPTER S CORPORATION

Because of the "double taxation" characteristic of the C Corp. option, Congress has developed an alternative corporate form known as the "Subchapter S corporation," or (for our purposes) the "S Corp." Entrepreneurs such as Bill and Filippa might elect to operate their state corporation under the rules applicable to S Corps.[29]

Essentially, an S Corp. is a C Corp. in which the founders elect to be taxed under Subchapter S of the Code. The S Corp. tax rules treat the organization as a partnership, with effective "pass through" tax implications. That means the S Corp. faces no double taxation.[30] While the actual

---

[26] *See* ROBERT W. HAMILTON & RICHARD A. BOOTH, BUSINESS BASICS FOR LAW STUDENTS 317–26 (4th ed. 2006).

[27] The intricacies of selling stock on the market to others, and the securities law implications of that prospect, are well beyond the scope of this primer. For an introduction to the area, see EHRLICH & MICHAEL, *supra* note 22, at 131–202.

[28] *See* Michael E. Mooney, David A. Parke & Kathleen King Parker, *Choice of Entity, in* A PRACTICAL GUIDE TO MASSACHUSETTS LIMITED LIABILITY COMPANIES §§ 3.9.1, 3.11.2 (Peter M. Rosenblum, ed. 2008).

[29] *See* I.R.C. § 1361(b)(1)(a) through (d).

[30] Commentators have noted that taxation under Subchapter C may often be more advantageous for a small-income, profitable, privately-held C Corp. owned by high-income shareholders than taxation under Subchapter S or Subchapter K, which governs the tax treatment of entities treated as partnerships for federal income tax purposes. *See* John W. Lee, *A Populist Per-*

tax effects for your individual clients will deserve your careful scrutiny (and, if at all possible, the advice of an experienced tax professional), the essential quality of an S Corp. is that the taxing agencies disregard the entity in determining the tax treatment of its income. The income passes through to the owners, who report that income on their personal income tax returns.

There is a cost to that benefit, however. The S Corp. designation is available only for a narrow group of entities, as the IRS imposes several restrictions on the operation of an S Corp. Those strict IRS requirements include: (1) the corporation must have 100 or fewer shareholders; (2) each shareholder must be a person (other than an estate, certain trusts, or certain tax-exempt organizations) who is an individual, rather than an entity; (3) no shareholder may be a nonresident alien; and (4) the corporation may only have "one class of stock," meaning that each share of stock of the corporation must have identical rights (although it is permissible to have one class of common stock and to issue some shareholders shares with voting rights and others shares without voting rights).[31]

You can readily discern some of the implications of these requirements. First, the "one class of stock" rule limits the corporation's ability to offer to investors a preferred form of ownership in the enterprise, therefore limiting opportunities to bring in investors in the future. Second, the bar against institutional ownership of shares in an S Corp. adds a further limitation on investor participation, as most business entities may not own shares. Third, because of the "one class of stock" requirement, the amount of income that each owner in an S Corp. receives at the end of the accounting period must necessarily be proportional to such owner's stake in the S Corp. That is, if Bill and Filippa each own fifty of their S Corp.'s one-hundred shares of issued and outstanding stock, they will each receive the same payment if and when they decide to make dividend-like distributions from the corporation, and they will share equally in any losses that are passed through to them from the business. Similarly, if they were to split the ownership sixty-forty with Filippa the majority shareholder, Filippa would receive sixty percent of the income and loss to Bill's forty percent. If the owners hoped to establish a more flexible or nuanced arrangement, the S Corp. rules would discourage that, while the C Corp. rules would permit much more complexity and flexibility.

Not only may the S Corp.'s restrictions impose burdensome limits on the ability of an entrepreneur to create the kind of ownership structure

---

spective of the Business Tax Entities Universe, 78 TEX. L. REV. 885, 903–907 (2000). These advantages would not be present for the low- to moderate-income entrepreneurs such as Bill and Filippa. Nor would they attach in the event that the business generated a loss, rather than a profit, in a given taxable year, because C Corps. cannot "pass through" annual losses to its shareholders as can S Corps. and entities treated as partnerships for tax purposes. I.R.C. § 1366.

[31] *See* I.R.C. § 1361(b)(1)(a) through (d).

they want from the outset, the restrictions also create risks of inadvertent violation of the form's essential requirements, which can have unfortunate consequences. One important example of this worry relates to distinguishing between the equity interests of the corporation and debt owed to it. If a debt arrangement has equity-like characteristics, the IRS might re-characterize the debt as equity.[32] As one observer notes, "If purported debt of an S–Corporation is held to be equity for tax purposes, the corporation's election can be terminated because (1) the debt deemed equity may be a second class of stock, (2) the purported debt may be held by a person who cannot be a shareholder of an S–Corporation or (3) the shareholder number limitation may be exceeded when the debt holder is counted as a shareholder."[33] If the election of an S Corp. terminates because of this inadvertent violation of the S Corp. requirements, the corporation would automatically become classified as a C Corp. (taxed under Subchapter C of the Code) and become subject to the "double-tax" and other consequences of that corporate form.

You may now begin to appreciate some of the relative advantages and disadvantages of an S Corp. when compared to a C Corp. The S Corp. avoids the economic costs of the double-taxation scheme, but in return for that benefit the owners must accept some inflexibility and some risks. For Bill and Filippa's purposes, though, there is one further option available to them. Let us understand that option in order to engage in a more in-depth comparison of the choices available to these entrepreneurs.

E. LIMITED LIABILITY COMPANY (LLC)

1. The Components of the LLC Structure

The tensions just described have not gone unnoticed in business circles. Business owners hope for three major components to their organizations: limited liability, favorable income tax treatment, and the ability to participate in the management of the business.[34] In the late 1970s some creative lawyers and legislators in Wyoming developed a statutory scheme in which a corporation could be operated as a partnership, and called that package a "limited liability company."[35] After some preliminary IRS acceptance of the Wyoming scheme, several states followed Wyoming's lead, and in 1995, the IRS officially and expressly acceded to

---

[32] There is a "straight-debt" safe harbor for S–Corporations, under which a fixed written obligation to pay a sum certain on demand or on a specified due date that bears non-contingent interest, is not convertible into equity of the S–Corporation, and is held only by persons who can be shareholders of an S–Corporation is deemed not to be a second class of stock that would terminate S–Corporation status. *See* I.R.C. § 1361(c)(5).

[33] James S. Eustice, *Subchapter S Corporations and Partnerships: A Search for the Pass Through Paradigm (Some Preliminary Proposals)*, 39 TAX L. REV. 345, 363 (1984).

[34] *See* EHRLICH & MICHAEL, *supra* note 22, at 45–46. A device we have not reviewed here, the limited partnership, offers the first two benefits but not the third. *Id.* at 43–44.

[35] *Id.* at 48.

treat a properly constructed LLC as a partnership for income tax purposes.[36] The National Conference of Commissioners on Uniform State Laws (NCCUSL) crafted a Uniform Limited Liability Company Act (ULLCA) in 1994, and then issued a "second-generation" model statute, known as "Re–ULLCA," in 2006.[37]

Every state in the nation has had an LLC statute in place for at least ten years.[38] The goals of the LLC legislation have been to create flexible business structures with pass-through taxation and limited liability. Used effectively, the LLC offers all of those advantages to its owners.[39]

In its typical fashion, an LLC starts with a Certificate of Organization, a document creating a separate juridical entity through which people (or other entities) may conduct their businesses. LLC owners usually do not possess "shares"; they are not shareholders. Instead, the owners serve as "members," and the members own the assets of the LLC. The LLC typically will maintain a capital account reflecting the contributions of the members.[40] The members arrange their respective rights and duties within the business through an "Operating Agreement." That agreement spells out the obligations, entitlements and responsibilities of the members of the LLC and those who manage the business,[41] including payments and distributions of profits, returns on investments, and responsibility for control of entity affairs.[42] Like with any corporation (or limited partnership), the LLC members' liability exposure is capped at the members' respective investments in the business. The scheme therefore achieves the limited liability aim of its creators.[43]

---

[36] Rev. Proc. 95–10, 1995 I.R.B. 20.

[37] REVISED UNIF. LTD. LIAB. CO. ACT (2006); UNIF. LTD. LIAB. CO. ACT (1996).

[38] EHRLICH & MICHAEL, *supra* note 22, at 47.

[39] "The creation of the limited liability company . . . was one of the most sweeping changes in business organization law in our history." Allan W. Vestal & Thomas E. Rutledge, *Disappointing Diogenes: The LLC Debate That Never Was*, 51 ST. LOUIS U. L.J. 53, 54 (2006).

[40] "In an unincorporated business organization, each member has a capital account that is based on the member's contribution, increased by the member's shares of the profits of the organization and reduced by the distributions to a member and the member's share of losses." LARRY E. RIBSTEIN & ROBERT R. KEATINGE, RIBSTEIN AND KEATINGE ON LIMITED LIABILITY COMPANIES § 2.5 (2011).

[41] Most statutes permit the LLC to be "manager-managed" or "member-managed." UNIF. LTD. LIAB. CO. ACT 2006 § 409 [hereinafter "Re–ULLCA"].

[42] Re–ULLCA § 405 (discussing limitations on distributions of profits); § 407 (defining management obligations).

[43] *See* Re–ULLCA § 303(a). Like with any C Corp. or S Corp., a creditor of an LLC may seek to pierce the veil of the entity and hold the members responsible for the debts or liabilities of the business, if the members have treated the LLC as an alter ego. *See, e.g.,* Stewart Title Ins. Co. v. Liberty Title Agency, 83 A.D.3d 532, 533 (2011) (finding that plaintiff pleaded sufficient facts to pierce the veil of a limited liability company); Jefferey K. Vandervoort, *Piercing the Veil of Limited Liability Companies: The Need for a Better Standard*, 3 DE PAUL BUS. & COM. L.J. 51, 65 (2004). And, like with any other small business venture, a supplier, vendor or bank may insist upon the personal guarantees of some or all members as a condition of completing a transaction where payment is at all uncertain or unsecured.

The IRS rules state that an LLC with at least two members may elect to be taxed as a C Corp., or, under the default classification, may be taxed as a partnership under Subchapter K of the IRS code.[44] The partnership rules permit pass-through taxation just as an S Corp. would. Unless otherwise elected by the members of the LLC, the entity will avoid the double-taxation of the C Corp., thereby achieving a second important goal of this creation. The Subchapter K rules permit the LLC member, just as the S Corp. shareholder, to "pass through" losses as well as income, subject to some important restrictions imposed by the IRS in its campaign to deter abusive tax shelters.[45] Because of some important nuances in the treatment of a member's basis in an LLC, an LLC member may have the possibility of deducting greater losses than an equivalent shareholder in an S Corp.[46]

In contrast to what you learned above about the S Corp., the LLC may have as many members/owners as it wishes, and the terms of the ownership may be crafted in any way the members decide, subject to the requirement that the allocation of income and losses has some "substantial economic effect."[47] The LLC rules permit preferential treatment of some members relative to others, as there is nothing comparable to the "one class of stock" limitation found in the S Corp. rules. Also, institutional entities and nonresident undocumented persons may be members of an LLC, unlike in the S Corp. setting.[48]

In sum, the LLC scheme seeks to, and may, accomplish the goals described at the beginning of this section—to produce the respective advantages of the S Corp. and those of the C Corp. without encountering the

---

[44] I.R.C. § 701 to 761; Treas. Reg. §§ 301.7701–1(f) (2009), 301.7701–2(e) (2011), 301.7701–3(f)(1) (2006). Single-member LLCs, which generally offer the same liability protection, will be disregarded as an entity and treated as a sole proprietorship for tax purposes. *See* Richard Winchester, *The Gap in the Employment Tax Gap*, 20 STAN. L. & POL'Y REV. 1, 132 (2009).

[45] A taxpayer may use losses to offset income only to the extent that an owner actually has amounts at risk. I.R.C. § 465(a)(1). If the losses are from "passive" investment, those losses may only offset income from passive endeavors. I.R.C. § 469(d). And the losses that pass through to the owner cannot exceed the owner's basis in the entity. I.R.C. § 704(d).

[46] For an S Corp., the owner's tax basis in the entity takes into account the out-of-pocket cost that the owner incurred in exchange for his or her ownership interest and the basis of any loans that the S Corp. owes to the owner. The owner's tax basis in the LLC includes both these components but, by contrast, also includes the owner's allocable share of all liabilities of the LLC, whether or not they are nonrecourse or owed personally to the owner. Thus, depending on whether the entity has debt or not, the owner of an LLC has more opportunities to increase his or her basis in the business and may pay less tax as a result. *See* Satterthwaite, *supra* note 1 (manuscript at 18–19).

[47] I.R.C. § 704(b).

[48] Karin Schwindt, Comment, *Limited Liability Companies: Issues in Member Liability*, 44 UCLA L. REV. 1541, 1545 n.13 (1997). While authorities agree that undocumented immigrants may be members of an LLC, some different tax rules may apply to those LLCs whose members include undocumented persons. *See, e.g.*, 4 ROBERT J. HAFT & PETER M. FASS, TAX–ADVANTAGED SECURITIES § 5:67 (2012) ("An LLC, classified as a partnership for federal tax purposes, . . . which has a nonresident alien as a partner or has a partner other than a natural person, generally will be subject to comprehensive unified audit proceedings. Every partnership or LLC subject to these provisions must have a 'tax matters partner.'").

disadvantages or limitations that accompany each of those devices. If you imagine counseling Bill and Filippa about their business options, the LLC must be looking very attractive. Indeed, it is an attractive option. The next sub-section reviews its advantages and uncovers a couple of possible complications accompanying this creative, and quite popular, alternative.

2. A Functional Comparison of the LLC and the S Corp.

We have seen thus far that the LLC provides all of the advantages of the S Corp.—limited liability, no double taxation, and full management opportunities—without the cumbersome inflexibility characteristic of the S Corp., including the limitations on the number and identity of possible owners of the company and the "one class of stock" uniformity across owners. The LLC is a far more flexible arrangement, permitting its owners to craft nuanced, particularized operating agreements with terms fitting the investment, labor, and risk-laden contributions of the respective members.[49]

Commentators, though, have noted at least two aspects of the LLC that might lead entrepreneurs like Bill and Filippa to favor an S Corp. instead of an LLC. Each of these factors may be changing with the attention of regulators, legislators, and courts, but neither is insignificant at the present.

The first, and most common, hesitance about the use of an LLC is that its flexibility has not been tested nor vetted adequately in the courts, simply because it is so new relative to its alternatives.[50] The common law interpretation of conventional corporate and partnership arrangements is extensive and well-developed. The corresponding interpretive treatment of the more recent LLC agreements and statutes is far more scant. Entrepreneurs concerned about agency relationships (that is, which constituents have actual and apparent authority to bind the entity), maintenance of usual company formalities,[51] and protections against the pierced veil

---

[49] A recent lower court decision in Massachusetts highlights one other possible difference between an LLC and an S Corp. In Cook v. Patient EDU, LLC, et al., 28 Mass. L. Rptr. 492, 2011 WL 3276679 (Mass. Super. Ct. 2011), a Superior Court judge held that an LLC is not liable under a strict Massachusetts wage law protecting employees, because the language of the relevant statute only covered "corporations." In your counseling of clients in your jurisdiction, you will need to attend to such idiosyncratic differences in treatment between the alternative business models.

[50] EHRLICH & MICHAEL, *supra* note 22, at 49. *See also* David L. Cohen, *Theories of the Corporation and the Limited Liability Company: How Should Courts and Legislatures Articulate Rules for Piercing the Veil, Fiduciary Responsibility and Securities Regulation for the Limited Liability Company?*, 51 OK. L. REV. 427, 454 (1998); Joseph S. Naylor, *Is the Limited Liability Partnership Now the Entity of Choice for Delaware Law Firms?*, 24 DEL. J. CORP. L. 145, 151 (1999) (noting the disadvantages related to LLCs based on its relative novelty). *But see* Mohsen Manesh, *Delaware and the Market for LLC Law: A Theory of Contractibility and Legal Indeterminacy*, 52 B.C. L. REV. 189, 191 (2011) (arguing that Delaware corporate law is far more indeterminate than its LLC law, because in the latter context parties may contract for as much clarity as they wish).

[51] The Re–ULLCA suggests model language limiting the importance of adherence to formality as a basis for imposing liability on LLC members, as follows: "The failure [of an LLC] to

may find the traditions of the S Corp. offering more comfort. Of course, with each passing year the common law interpretive trove increases, so this worry steadily diminishes.

The second difference between an LLC and an S Corp. which may be of some interest to entrepreneurs like Bill and Filippa concerns the self-employment tax (SET), introduced above. As we have seen, the income earned by Bill and Filippa while working to start and run the café passes through as ordinary income under both the S Corp. and the LLC. The resulting income may also be considered earned income from labor, and thus subject to the SET, depending upon the circumstances of its payment. And, as we shall see, the setting of an S Corp. might be more favorable for SET calculations than those within an LLC.[52]

Corporations, including those that elect to be treated as S Corps., may have employees who are also owners, unlike general partnerships. In our case, imagine for now that Bill and Filippa each works at the café and each owns half of the company's shares. In the corporate setting, the income generated by the business activity may be bifurcated into two discrete streams. Bill and Filippa may be paid a "reasonable"[53] salary for their work, and those dollars will be subject to payroll taxes (with the company, as the employer, paying its share, and deducting from Bill's and Filippa's wages their share). If the company generates a profit after the salaries have been paid to the employees, the remaining funds will be taxable to Bill and Filippa as distributions (the equivalent of dividends in the C Corp. context). The distributions, not representing compensation earned by an employee, but instead representing a return on investment, will not be subject to payroll taxes.[54]

In the corporation context, the owners who also work for the company have a clear incentive to pay themselves a smaller salary than their labor is worth on the market, and receive the balance of the company's earnings as a distribution.[55] In fact, according to one observer, "there is overwhelming evidence that this occurs with alarming frequency."[56] The IRS will pe-

---

observe the usual company formalities or requirements relating to the exercises of its company powers or management of its business is not a ground for imposing personal liability on the member or managers." Re–ULLCA § 304(2)(b).

[52] We have borrowed the analysis developed here directly from Emily Satterthwaite's writing. *See* Satterthwaite, *supra* note 1 (manuscript at 21–29). Other sources addressing the SET issue as it applies to choice of entity include Timothy R. Koski, *The Application of Self–Employment Tax to Limited Liability Companies: A Critical Analysis*, 23 J. APPLIED BUS. RES. 87 (2007); Richard Winchester, *The Gap in the Employment Tax Gap*, 20 STAN. L. & POL'Y REV. 127 (2009).

[53] *See* I.R.C. § 162 (salaries in excess of what is reasonable are not deductible by the corporation and may be treated as dividend income).

[54] *See* Thomas A. Fritz, *Flowthrough Entities and the Self–Employment Tax: Is It Time for a Uniform Standard?*, 17 VA. TAX. REV. 811, 850 (1998).

[55] *See* Winchester, *supra* note 52, at 138.

[56] *Id.*

nalize a company that designates wages as distributions,[57] as its rules require that the employer treat as wages "all remuneration for employment," however designated.[58] Of course, the IRS is ill-equipped to discover such misreporting,[59] but your advice to and planning with your clients will no doubt respect the integrity of the IRS's rules.[60]

The primary point for us to understand, though, is that in the S Corp. context the income stream to the owners may be, and often will be, bifurcated between earned income/compensation and return on investment, with the SET applicable only to the former income. For LLCs, that bifurcation may not be available, at least under current law. The IRS defines NESE as including any "distributive share (whether or not distributed) of income or loss . . . from any trade or business carried on by a partnership of which [such individual] is a member."[61] Therefore, as one commentator has noted, "LLC members cannot bifurcate their income from the business between compensation and distributions, where the latter is not subject to employment taxes . . . ."[62] While the treatment of partnership tax in the LLC context is very complicated even in the places where the IRS rules remain unresolved,[63] for our present purposes you should investigate whether your clients will have to treat all of the profits from the LLC business as earned income subject to the SET.[64]

Therefore, for some business owners, those whose business produces more profits than the reasonable compensation payable to its owner/employees, the choice of an LLC is likely to lead to a higher total tax burden on the income generated by the business than the choice of an S Corp. Let us demonstrate the difference with a simple example.

Imagine that both Bill and Filippa work in the café, and that the good faith, fair market value of their labor is $25,000 each. Imagine that the café has a successful year in which its revenues exceed all expenses *except salary* by $100,000. Example 11–2 shows the relevant tax comparison:

---

[57] *See, e.g.,* David E. Watson, P.C. v. United States, 668 F.3d 1008 (8th Cir. 2012) (successful accounting firm paid owner wages of $24,000 and distributions of $203,000 during a given tax year; court assessed a FICA deficiency).

[58] I.R.C. § 3121(a).

[59] Winchester, *supra* note 52, at 138.

[60] Circular 230, 31 C.F.R. §§ 10.0–10.93 (2005), imposes affirmative duties requiring tax professionals, including lawyers, to deal fairly and honestly with the IRS.

[61] I.R.C. § 1402(a)(1). The definition excludes from NESE items of income from a partnership that are not received in the course of a trade or business, such as rentals of real estate, dividends on stock, interest on bonds or debentures, or capital gains or losses that are not generated in the course of a trade or business (i.e., if the individual's partnership engaged in stock trading, dividends would be included in NESE, but stock investments held by the partnership of an unrelated business would be excluded from NESE).

[62] Satterthwaite, *supra* note 1 (manuscript at 25).

[63] *See* Koski, *supra* note 52; Winchester, *supra* note 52.

[64] Satterthwaite, *supra* note 1 (manuscript at 24–28).

Example 11–2

Café	LLC	S Corp.
Gross revenue	250,000	250,000
Non-employee-related business expenses[65]	150,000	150,000
Net revenue before paying owners	100,000	100,000
Compensation subject to employment taxes	100,000	50,000
Self-employment taxes paid by owners (15.3%[66])	15,300	0
Payroll taxes paid by employees	0	3,825
Payroll taxes paid by Café	0	3,825[67]
Non-compensation "distributions"	0	46,175[68]
Taxable income of owners[69]	92,350[70]	92,350[71]
Federal income taxes[72]	21,600	21,600
Total employment taxes	15,300	7,650
After-tax "take home" amount	63,100	70,750
Effective tax rate	36.9%	29.3%

This sample shows that, in some settings, given the relevant factors of fair compensation for labor and the specific tax implications for the owners' personal finances, the choice of an LLC might cost the owners several thousand dollars per year in actual after-tax income when compared to the S Corp.

We describe the entity choices here in broad strokes, in an effort to provide you with an orienting model for the task you will face in counseling your entrepreneur clients about the choices available to them. This orientation ought to serve to prepare you to refine the comparisons through your own research and planning. Your further inquiries will include greater investigation of the tax implications we have described with

---

[65] In the S Corp. setting, the employer will pay one-half of the payroll taxes due on the owners' reasonable salaries, and that expense is a legitimate business expense not encountered in the LLC setting. We separate that expense below.

[66] In 2011, Congress reduced temporarily the employee's share of Social Security taxes from 6.2% to 4.2%. *See* Tax Relief, Unemployment Insurance Reauthorization and Job Creation Act of 2010, Pub. L. No. 111–312, § 601, 124 Stat. 3296 (2011) (amending the Internal Revenue Code of 1986). Our example uses the non-reduced, permanent rate of 6.2% for Social Security and 1.45% for Medicare, on the (perhaps questionable) assumption that the 4.2% rate is merely temporary.

[67] This amount reduces the surplus available for distributions.

[68] The one-half of payroll taxes payable by the café ($3825) has reduced this amount from $50,000 to $46,175.

[69] For the LLC setting, the owners deduct one-half of the self-employment taxes from their taxable income.

[70] This figure represents $100,000 less one half of the SET.

[71] This figure represents $50,000 in salary reduced by payroll taxes paid by the employee ($3825) plus the café's "profits" of $46,175.

[72] For simplicity we assume single taxpayers, a 25% tax rate, and the standard deduction in 2012 of $5,950 for each taxpayer, with rounding to the nearest whole dollar.

our broad brushes; how your state law operates in these areas, including the costs imposed by your state; how other possible states, such as Delaware or Nevada,[73] might compare to your state; and what the relevant tax rates are at the time. You may think that making sense of all of these fluid factors is awfully daunting for a second- or third-year law student or beginning lawyer. You are right, of course—but imagine the prospect of your non-lawyer clients wrestling with these issues on their own. You will surely be of some substantial help to those business owners as they choose the structure of their enterprises.

IV. ORGANIZATIONAL DUTIES AND HYBRID ORGANIZATIONS

This section of the chapter addresses two discrete, but ultimately inter-connected, themes. In Subsection A, we introduce you to some of the basic organizational duties owed by managers and others to the entities we have just canvassed. Understanding the broad contours of those duties will assist you to advise the constituents of your entity clients, as well as the individual clients who found the entities. Then, with those duties as a reference point, we introduce two variations of the corporate or LLC entities you now know something about. These "hybrid" organizations—the benefit corporation and the low-profit limited liability company—have arisen in recent years as vehicles for social enterprise. Each hybrid device aims to meet certain socially-responsible aims without running afoul of the fiduciary obligations inherent in the management of a for-profit business. We cover the two topics in tandem because one must understand the ordinary duties of a manager of a for-profit enterprise to understand how the mission of a hybrid organization might alter those duties.

A. FIDUCIARY DUTIES OF ENTITY DIRECTORS, OFFICERS AND MANAGERS

This chapter is dedicated to profit-driven enterprises, in contrast to the following chapter, where we explore the contours of the nonprofit world. Those individuals who manage for-profit enterprises (the officers and directors of corporations, the members in a member-managed LLC, and the managers in a manager-managed LLC) owe to the organization certain fiduciary responsibilities. If they fail in those responsibilities, not only might the entity be harmed and its owners and other constituents hurt, but the individuals who breach the duties may face tort liability. Here is a catalogue of the most salient of such responsibilities:

---

[73] Because of their favorable treatment of corporate management and modest corporate taxation, Delaware and Nevada tend to attract corporate filers from other states with less favorable schemes. *See* John Armour, Bernard Black & Brian Cheffins, *Delaware's Balancing Act*, 87 IND. L.J. 1345, 1382 (2012) (describing Nevada as "Delaware's closest (albeit distant) rival in the market for out-of-state incorporations").

- *Profit Maximization*: The fiduciary responsibilities and duties of managers, directors and officers of a for-profit enterprise "can be boiled down to one concept: profit maximization. The ultimate duty of any corporate director or officer is to ensure that the shareholders of the company have their potential returns maximized."[74] While sophisticated observers have argued for a more nuanced understanding of a corporation's ultimate mission,[75] and while some LLC agreements may, by contract, limit the scope of this duty,[76] it remains a bedrock understanding that the mission of for-profit enterprises is to generate as much profit as possible, and actions which undercut that goal risk breaching this duty.[77]

- *Duty of Care*: Business fiduciaries owe the entity a duty to "act diligently in managing the [entity]'s affairs,"[78] which amounts to a standard of care "of a reasonably prudent person in like circumstances."[79] In practical terms, the duty of care means that fiduciaries must act only after having taken into account all relevant information and data before making a decision affecting the entity.[80] The duty of care is interpreted through the *business judgment rule*, "a common law principle that provides that honest business decisions made in good faith and on the basis of reasonable investigation are not actionable, even though the decision is mistaken, unfortunate, or even disastrous."[81]

- *Duty of Loyalty*: Separate from the duty of care is the duty of loyalty, which requires fiduciaries to put the interests of the entity ahead of their own personal, financial, family or professional interests, and to avoid conflicts of interest.[82] Most entity governance schemes set up procedural guidelines to monitor for conflicts of interest. The typical understanding is that if disinterested fiduciaries have approved a transaction in which another fiduciary

---

[74] MARC J. LANE, SOCIAL ENTERPRISE: EMPOWERING MISSION–DRIVEN ENTREPRENEURS 120 (2011).

[75] *See* KENT GREENFIELD, THE FAILURE OF CORPORATE LAW: FUNDAMENTAL FLAWS AND PROGRESSIVE POSSIBILITIES 29–39; 178–82 (2006)

[76] LANE, *supra* note 74, at 133–34.

[77] In the context of the sale of an ongoing business, the profit maximization principle has become known as the "Revlon duty," after a famous Delaware Supreme Court decision in Revlon, Inc. v. MacAndrews & Forbes Holdings, Inc., 506 A.2d 173 (Del. 1986). *See, e.g.*, Lawrence A. Cunningham & Charles M. Yablon, *Delaware Fiduciary Duty Law After QVC and Technicolor: A Unified Standard (and the End of* Revlon *Duties?)*, 49 BUS. LAW. 1593, 1610 (1994).

[78] Renee M. Jones, *Law, Norms and the Breakdown of the Board: Promoting Accountability in Corporate Governance*, 92 IOWA L. REV. 105, 110 (2006) (addressing corporations).

[79] *Id.* at 111. Jones points out that the standard for Delaware corporations is gross negligence. *Id.*

[80] LANE, *supra* note 74, at 125.

[81] HAMILTON & BOOTH, *supra* note 26, at 301; LANE, *supra* note 74, at 125, *citing* Gantler v. Stevens, 965 A.2d 695 (Del. 2009).

[82] Jones, *supra* note 78, at 112, *citing* Guth v. Loft, 5 A.2d 503 (Del. 1939).

has an interest, the transaction's approval possesses the benefit of the business judgment rule.[83]

- *Other Duties*: The duty of care and the duty of loyalty together encompass the central responsibilities of fiduciaries. Other duties emerging from those two include a duty not to usurp a business opportunity that rightfully belongs to the entity,[84] a duty to avoid waste, which means not distributing entity assets without adequate consideration,[85] and a duty of candor to shareholders before the latter must approve a transaction.[86]

We have described the above duties as generally applicable to those who manage for-profit enterprises, including corporations, partnerships, or LLCs. While the doctrine underlying the duties has tended to develop directly from corporate contexts, it is fair to accept that the duties apply with similar force to partnerships and to LLCs.[87] At the same time, because they are far more contractual in nature than corporations, the foundational documents for LLCs and partnerships might allow for less than strict adherence to these duties.[88] While it may appear to be an unusual circumstance where the founders of an LLC will desire to lighten the responsibilities of the managers of the company, your counseling of those founders, and of the LLC's managers post-founding, will benefit from your appreciation of this possible exception.[89]

Indeed, it is this last insight—that LLCs might allow for a different set of fiduciary responsibilities if its members so contract—which invites a consideration of some hybrid organizational structures whose very purpose will include a moderating of at least one of these duties—that of maximizing profits.

B. HYBRID ORGANIZATIONS

Some entrepreneurs desire to operate a business for profit, but do not intend that the business's primary or only purpose should be to maximize return on investment. These entrepreneurs may desire instead to achieve

---

[83] *See, e.g.,* DEL. CODE. ANN. TIT. 8, § 144.

[84] LANE, *supra* note 74, at 122.

[85] *Id.* at 126. Lane includes excessive executive compensation as an example of a breach of this duty.

[86] Jones, *supra* note 78, at 112–13.

[87] *See, e.g.,* Gregg Wasserman & Janice Wasserman Goldstein Family LLC v. Kay, 14 A.3d 1193, 1209 (Md. App. 2011) ("Under common law, general partners owe each other and the partnership fiduciary duties."); Miller v. Schweikart, 405 F. Supp. 366, 369 (D.C.N.Y. 1975) ("The fiduciary duty of fair dealing owed by a general partner to a limited partner is no less than that owed by a corporate director to a shareholder.").

[88] LANE, *supra* note 78, at 133.

[89] *Id.; see also* Elizabeth M. McGeever, *Hazardous Duty? The Role of the Fiduciary in Noncorporate Structures,* 4 BUS. L. TODAY 51, 53 (1995) (noting the difficulties presented based on loosely defined fiduciary duties in statutory law related to limited liability companies and partnerships). In our experience, in social ventures or in joint ventures with a social purpose, the founders may seek some less strict management obligations.

some socially-valuable goal aside from simply making a profit—to attend to what some call the "double bottom line,"[90] or even the "triple bottom line."[91] Of course, those entrepreneurs might opt to found a nonprofit corporation, but not all enterprises will fit comfortably the strictures of the IRS's requirements for tax-exempt organizations, and the entrepreneurs might wish to own the enterprise, which they could not do in the nonprofit context. These persons will search for some entity or vehicle through which to achieve these goals without inviting accusations of breach of duty by the entity's managers.

In recent years, resourceful thinkers have devised at least two types of entities which might achieve these purposes, although each remains somewhat experimental as of 2012. They are the low-profit limited liability company, the benefit corporation, and the B Corp. While your understanding of these entities will be richer once you have explored the chapter on nonprofits (because some elements of these entities are driven by nonprofit tax law), we offer for you a brief introduction to each here.

1. The Low–Profit Limited Liability Company (L³C)

As we hinted at in the previous section, a conventional limited liability company might include some contractual provisions, agreed to by all members, limiting the purpose of the enterprise and expressly de-emphasizing profit maximization. If the organizational founding documents include those purposes, the LLC's managers should be protected against a claim of a breach of a duty of care if the LLC earned less profit than it otherwise could realize in return for achieving some other social goals. It would be even safer for those managers, though, if state law explicitly permitted a form of entity whose mission was socially-directed and not economically-directed. From that hope has arisen the low-profit limited liability company, commonly known as the L³C.

The L³C concept was the brainchild of Robert M. Lang Jr., CEO of Mannweiler Foundation in New York, and Marcus Owens of the law firm Caplin & Drysdale.[92] Lang and Owens recognized that some activities that normally were considered to fall within the nonprofit sector were able to generate more income than it cost to operate them, yet not enough to encourage for-profit investors to get involved.[93] In fact, many of the ventures were so high risk that for-profit investors would not provide

---

[90] Thomas Kelley, *Law and Choice of Entity on the Social Enterprise Frontier*, 84 TUL. L. REV. 337, 340–41 (2009) (financial and social benefits).

[91] JOHN ELKINGTON, CANNIBALS WITH FORKS: THE TRIPLE BOTTOM LINE OF 21ST CENTURY BUSINESS (1998) (economic, social, and environmental benefits).

[92] Dennise Bayona & Ken Milani, *Low–Profit Limited Liability Company*, 86 PRAC. TAX STRATEGIES 66 (2011).

[93] Robert Lang & Elizabeth Carrott Minnigh, *The L3C, History, Basic Construct and Legal Framework*, 35 VT. L. REV. 15, 15 (2010).

start-up capital for the venture.[94] So Lang and Owens devised an alternative LLC structure that might work in such settings.

Vermont enacted the first statute specifically aimed at "low profit limited liability companies" in 2008.[95] The Vermont L³C legislation amended the state's LLC statute by creating a subcategory of LLCs that are limited in purpose and are subject to certain defined restrictions.[96] The drafters of the Vermont legislation intentionally aimed to align the scheme with IRS regulations related to investments available from non-profit private foundations, known as Program Related Investments (PRI), by permitting those foundations to invest assets in "private, profit-making enterprises formed to advance socially desirable goals."[97]

The original L³C intention was to create a vehicle to encourage charitable giving. The basic concept is to use low-cost capital in high-risk undertakings while allocating risk and reward unevenly over a number of investors to create a reasonably safe investment with some market return.[98] The L³C aims to receive foundation money through PRI programs and then leverage that money with investments from for-profit investors.[99] Most descriptions of the L³C model refer to multiple tiers, or "tranches," of investors, with each tranche expecting a different level of return.[100] In the typical L³C scheme, the foundation, relying on the PRI rules, would serve as the first, or lowest, tranche. It would assume the highest risk position and expect little or no return on its investment. The top tranche would consist of investors promised a low-risk but high rate of return, subsidized by the foundation money. An intermediate tier, known as the "mezzanine" tranche, consisting of investors willing to accept a lower return in order to support the socially beneficial goals of the L³C.[101]

As of 2012, at least nine states had adopted L³C legislation.[102] The governing statutes of all of those states tend to be similar, and impose the following requirements on the L³C's organizational charter:

---

[94] *Id.*

[95] VT. STAT. ANN. Tit. 11, § 3001 (2009).

[96] Daniel S. Kleinberger, *A Myth Deconstructed: The "Emperor's New Clothes" On the Low–Profit Limited Liability Company*, 35 DEL. J. CORP. L. 879, 882 (2009).

[97] *Id.* at 882. For a discussion of private foundations and PRIs, see the chapter on nonprofit organizations.

[98] *Id.* at 883–84.

[99] *Id.* at 884.

[100] *See, e.g.,* Christopher C. Archer, *Private Benefit for the Public Good: Promoting Foundation Investment in the "Fourth Sector" to Provide More Efficient and Effective Social Missions*, 84 TEMP. L. REV. 159 (2011); Lang & Minnigh, *supra* note 93; J. Haskell Murray & Edward I. Hwang, *Purpose with Profit: Governance, Enforcement, Capital–Raising and Capital–Locking in Low–Profit Limited Liability Companies*, 66 U. MIAMI L. REV. 1 (2011); Dana Brakman Reiser, *Charity Law's Essentials*, 86 NOTRE DAME L. REV. 1 (2011).

[101] *See* Antony Page & Robert A. Katz, *Is Social Enterprise the New Corporate Social Responsibility?*, 34 SEATTLE U. L. REV. 1351, 1363–64 (2011).

[102] In addition to Vermont, the following states have adopted legislation through the summer of 2012: Illinois Limited Liability Company Act, 805 ILL. COMP. STAT. 180/1–26 (2010); Loui-

- *Charitable or Educational Purpose*: An L3C must operate with the primary (but not the sole) goal to achieve a purpose identified by the IRS as charitable or educational.[103]

- *No Significant Purpose for Production of Income*: The L3C cannot have as a significant purpose the production of income or property. The fact that the entity does generate such income or property is not a disqualifying happenstance, so long as it does not intend that as a significant purpose.[104]

- *No Purpose to Accomplish Political or Legislative Ends*: In similar fashion to nonprofits seeking 501(c)(3) status, an L3C may not have as a significant purpose the accomplishment of any political or legislative ends, or to influence legislation.

The L3C movement has achieved significant momentum recently, especially as a device to work with private charitable foundations which might not be able to invest in such profit-making endeavors without facing some penalty from the IRS or some risk to its tax-exempt status.[105] However, their use remains the subject of much debate and disagreement among commentators.[106] Some writers consider the concept to be entirely ill-advised and dangerous to the participating foundations, which risk their tax-exempt status by such participation in expressly profit-making endeavors.[107] Observers also note that the IRS has not confirmed in any reliable way that the private foundation investment strategy will work, and the cost of seeking case-by-case approval from the IRS is often pro-

---

siana Limited Liability Company Act, LA. REV. STAT. § 12:1302 (2010); Maine Limited Liability Company Act, ME. REV. STAT. tit. 31, § 1611 (2011); Michigan Limited Liability Act, MICH. COMP. LAWS SERV. § 450.4102 (2009); North Carolina Limited Liability Company Act, N.C. GEN. STAT. § 57C–2–01 (2010); 2011 R.I. Pub. Laws 67 (authorizing L3Cs in Rhode Island); Utah Revised Limited Liability Company Act, UTAH CODE § 48–2c–412 (2009); Wyoming Limited Liability Company Act, WYO. STAT. § 17–15–102 (2009). A nonprofit organization, Americans for Community Development, supports and monitors efforts to establish L3C legislation. *See* AMERICANS FOR COMMUNITY DEVELOPMENT, http://www.americansforcommunitydevelopment.org.

[103] LANE, *supra* note 78, at 35. *See* I.R.C. § 170(c)(2)(b).

[104] LANE, *supra* note 78, at 35.

[105] Effectively, the L3C statutes track the requirements for private foundations to invest without risking a "jeopardy" excise tax on "jeopardizing" investments—those which have high risk to the assets of the foundation. The IRS permits the foundations to make certain investments in higher-risk endeavors if the goals of those endeavors are consistent with the foundation's charitable or educational purposes. *See* Carter G. Bishop, *The Low Profit LLC (L3C): Program Related Investments by Proxy or Perversion?*, 63 ARK. L. REV. 243, 259 (2010). *See also* the chapter on Nonprofit Organizations.

[106] *See* J. William Callison & Allan W. Vestal, *The L3C Illusion: Why Low–Profit Limited Liability Companies Will Not Stimulate Socially Optimal Private Foundation Investment in Entrepreneurial Ventures*, 35 VT. L. REV. 273 (2010); David Shwister, *L3Cs: The Next Big Wave in Socially Responsible Investing or Simply Too Good To Be True?*, 3 J. BUS. ENTREPRENEURSHIP & L. 1, 12 (2009).

[107] *See* Bishop, *supra* note 105; Kleinberger, *supra* note 96.

hibitive.[108] Other critics worry that the L³C model will divert essential resources away from the nonprofit field.[109]

While the L³C model has aimed to connect to private foundations, it offers potential for social entrepreneurship beyond that economic scheme. Because an L³C is a form of LLC, its operating agreement may describe in detail how its managers ought to make investment and business decisions. In that way, the managers of an L³C may acquire some realistic protection for decisions which give greater priority to social concerns and less to return on investment.[110]

2.   The Benefit Corporation

An alternative to the L³C is the benefit corporation, which is not to be confused with the "B Corp.," which we describe next. While (as we shall see) the B Corp. is a traditional private for-profit corporation but with a seal of approval from B Labs, a nonprofit social entrepreneurship monitoring group, the benefit corporation is formally and by statutory authority a hybrid organization similar to the L³C. As of 2012, at least eight states had adopted legislation authorizing the charter of corporations whose mission includes creating a "general public benefit."[111] (The California legislation established authority for both a benefit corporation and an alternative version known as the "flexible purpose corporation" (FPC).[112]) The aim of such legislation is similar to that of the L³C—to permit founders to establish a for-profit business vehicle where its officers and directors do not have an unfettered duty to maximize profits.[113] The benefit corporation statutes address directly the standards of conduct for directors of such corporations, and permit the directors to take into account the corporation's employees, workforce and subsidiaries, consumers, and the local community.[114]

In addition to requiring that a benefit corporation include a public benefit in its mission, the enabling statutes tend to impose affirmative

---

[108] *See* LANE, *supra* note 78, at 41; Bishop, *supra* note 105, at 258.

[109] LANE, *supra* note 78, at 41.

[110] *See* Dana Brakman Reiser, *Benefit Corporations—A Sustainable Form of Organization?*, 46 WAKE FOREST L. REV. 591, 614 (2011); John Tyler, *Negating the Legal Problem of Having "Two Masters": A Framework for L3C Fiduciary Duties and Accountability*, 35 VT. L. REV. 117, 141 (2010) (arguing that L3C managers possess statutory duties to prioritize charitable and social purposes).

[111] *See* MD. CODE ANN. CORPS. & ASS'NS § 5–6C–06(a). Besides Maryland, California, Hawai'i, New Jersey, New York, Massachusetts, Vermont and Virginia have passed similar legislation. *See* CAL. CORP. CODE § 14600 (2012); HAW. REV. STAT. § 414 (2011); MASS. GEN. LAWS ch.156E § 1 (2012); N.J. STAT. ANN. § 14A:18–5 (2011); N.Y. BUS. CORP. LAW §§ 1701 (2012); VT. STAT. ANN. § 21.08 (2009); VA. CODE. ANN. § 13.1–787 (2011).

[112] *See California Benefit Corporation and Flexible Purpose Corporation*, NONPROFIT LAW BLOG (Oct. 13, 2011), http://www.nonprofitlawblog.com/home/2011/10/california-benefit-corporation-and-flexible-purpose-corporation.html.

[113] *See* LANE, *supra* note 78, at 48.

[114] *Id.* at 45.

requirements missing from the L3C schemes. The benefit corporation must appoint a benefit director, and may appoint a benefit officer. The benefit director must issue an annual report assessing the corporation's compliance with the public benefit mission. The corporation has other disclosure obligations, and it must meet standards established by some independent and approved standard-setting organization. Shareholders—but not members of the public—have standing to enforce the corporate mission.[115]

Like with the L3C, but perhaps in greater measure here because of the connection to the more conventional corporate charter, benefit corporation directors must accept some uncertainty about how courts will interpret the new legislation when shareholders challenge the board's actions.[116] And some commentators have expressed concern that, like with the L3C, the benefit corporation's incentives will tend toward profit-making in the absence of stricter enforcement of the public benefit commitments.[117]

3. The B Corp.

The third alternative you should have some familiarity with is what observers call the B Corp., again not to be confused with the benefit corporation just described. In the parlance of social enterprises, a B Corp. is an alternative means to encourage responsible business practices and commitment to public benefits.[118] A B Corp. has no statutory or regulatory status aside from its original corporate status. Unlike the L3C or the benefit corporation, a B Corp. is an entity whose business practices have earned the seal of approval of B Lab, a nonprofit 501(c)(3) organization (in its self-description) "dedicated to using the power of business to solve social and environmental problems."[119] B Lab will investigate an applicant for B Corp. status. If the business meets the elaborate B Lab standards for social responsibility and sustainable operations, the enterprise may market itself as a B Corp., a designation which likely has some value to the company among its customers and constituents. By using the B Lab designation the business also agrees to random auditing by B Lab to ensure that its practices remain responsible.[120]

The B Corp. designation would serve those enterprises which operate in a jurisdiction without an L3C or a benefit corporation statute, or which

---

[115] For a discussion of all of these elements of the benefit corporation schemes, see Reiser, *supra* note 110, at 605.

[116] *See* LANE, *supra* note 78, at 48.

[117] Reiser, *supra* note 110, at 617.

[118] *See* Anurag Gupta, Note, *L3Cs and B Corps: New Corporate Forms Fertilizing the Field Between Traditional For–Profit and Nonprofit Corporations*, 8 N.Y.U. J. L. & BUS. 203, 220–25 (2011).

[119] *The Non-Profit Behind B Corps*, CERTIFIED B CORPORATION, http://www.bcorporation.net/what-are-b-corps/the-non-profit-behind-b-corps.

[120] Reiser, *supra* note 110, at 594.

prefer to function within the typical profit maximization business model even while seeking to do as much good as possible. Because the B Corp. status tends to apply to traditional, for-profit businesses, the charters of those operations will typically not include anything about public benefits. Still, the successful experience of B Lab demonstrates that many traditionally-structured and chartered for-profit endeavors do attend to the double bottom line and thrive in doing so.

You see how your clients will have some choices if they desire to explore the fertile world of social enterprise. Your responsibility as counsel for founders who wish to explore the L³C, the benefit corporation, or the B Corp. will be to assist the founders, and those who will serve as officers and directors of the entity, to appreciate these risks and benefits of these alternatives, and to assess them responsibly.[121]

---

[121] The observation in the text invites your consideration of the tricky ethical tension arising from your role as counsel to the organization or the founders. For a discussion of that tension, see the chapter on Ethical Issues in Transactional Practice.

CHAPTER 12

INTRODUCTION TO CREATING AND OPERATING NONPROFIT ORGANIZATIONS

■ ■ ■

Many transactional clinics represent clients interested in creating new nonprofit entities. Such clients might include an individual or group of individuals with a vision for addressing a problem in their community. Some of these new clients might come to the lawyer with just a beginning idea of what they want to do; others will come to the clinic with a highly developed vision and plan for the organization's work. Many groups navigate the process of incorporating and obtaining tax exemption themselves. In fact, some non-lawyers, such as accountants, offer this service to nonprofit organizations.[1] While at first it might appear that the process of becoming a tax-exempt organization is simple and just involves filling out several forms, as you get more involved in the issues you will see that the process of incorporating and applying for tax exemption involves complex corporate and tax law decisions. This chapter introduces you some of those corporate and tax law issues. We will briefly discuss the role nonprofit organizations play in our society and then address issues regarding structuring a nonprofit organization, corporate governance and obtaining tax exemption. At most, we can provide an overview of the process and some of the issues that will arise since, as you will see, the process of creating a new entity involves various provisions of both state and federal law and is very fact specific. We will highlight some key issues that will require further research as you encounter them in the context of your representation of your clients. Our focus will be on a subset of nonprofit organizations, those characterized as "charitable" organizations.

I. NONPROFIT ORGANIZATIONS GENERALLY

A. AN INTRODUCTION TO THE NONPROFIT SECTOR

Before we begin to discuss some of the legal and strategic issues you will confront, we need to clarify the various terms regarding nonprofits you may have read or heard since they are often used interchangeably but they do not always have the same meaning. The term "nonprofit" organization is often used to refer to entities that are not intended to be profit-

---

[1] Whether an accountant's work in providing this service constitutes the unauthorized practice of law is an intriguing question that we leave for you to ponder.

making corporations. The term can more precisely be used to mean corporations organized under a state's corporation law, with the status and privileges determined under that state's laws. The term can be broader, narrower or identical to the term "tax-exempt organization." Tax-exempt organizations refer to those organizations with federal tax exemption, which requires that they meet the statutory definitions in the Internal Revenue Code ("Code") and in most instances that they have filed an application with the Internal Revenue Service ("IRS"). The "charitable" sector usually refers to a subset of tax-exempt organizations. We initially discuss all three sectors but will spend most of this chapter discussing the "charitable" sector. It is impossible to capture all the legal issues faced by this wide a range of organizations in just one chapter. Entire books and treatises are devoted to legal issues of the nonprofit and tax-exempt sectors. We will focus on the type of nonprofit organization that is likely to approach the clinic with a request for services, a small to medium "charitable" organization.

There exist a wide range of nonprofit organizations. Some of these organizations are essentially member-serving and others are primarily public serving.[2] Nonprofit organizations work in many sectors—health; education (half of higher education institutions); social services; arts, culture and recreation; advocacy, legal services and international aid; and religion.[3] They might include the museum in the city in which you live or which you visit, the theatre where you go to see plays, the arts organization where you might have taken music or dance classes, the hospital where you or a member of your family have been for tests or surgery, the university you attend or attended, the public interest organization where you or your classmates worked during the summer, the organization where you or some of your friends volunteered during college or worked after college tutoring children, or the organization that takes your elderly relative or neighbor grocery shopping or to the doctor.

The nonprofit sector, among other goals, serves to protect individuals from economic misfortune or disability, to secure human rights, and to preserve and protect social and cultural values.[4] Because of our society's growing social and economic complexity, what might have been previously provided by family, neighbors and perhaps self-reliance, however imperfectly, has required more structured responses in modern times.[5] In some countries, governments have guaranteed their citizens certain social benefits (such as a minimum income, housing, health care, other necessities of life and higher education). In the United States, because of its deep tradition of individualism and distrust of government, a complicated sys-

---

[2] LESTER M. SALAMON, AMERICA'S NONPROFIT SECTOR: A PRIMER 31–34 (3d ed. 2012).

[3] *Id.* at 34.

[4] *Id.* at 1.

[5] *Id.*

tem of aid has emerged, one which has maintained a substantial private role.[6] These institutions, which play a vitally important role in our society, share certain features—they are private, self-governing, nonprofit distributing, voluntary, and of public benefit.[7] These organizations were founded because of the inherent limitations of the market in responding to public needs, the inherent limitations of government as the sole mechanism to respond to market failures, the need that a democratic society has for some way to promote cooperation among equal individuals, and the value Americans attach to pluralism and freedom.[8] These organizations have become a "critical component of community life . . . and a crucial prerequisite of a true 'civil society.'"[9]

Nonprofits represent a substantial and growing share of the national economy. There are approximately 1.5 million registered nonprofit organizations.[10] Nearly ten percent of the United States workforce is employed by these organizations.[11] Between 1998 and 2005, employment in the nonprofit sector grew by approximately 16.4 percent while the overall growth in employment during that time period was 6.2 percent.[12] For charities filing tax returns, total revenues in 2009 were $1.4 trillion, with hospitals and the higher education sector representing a majority of those revenues as well the majority of assets held by nonprofits.[13] In 2008, nonprofit institutions serving households were responsible for generating 5.2 percent of gross domestic product (GDP).[14] Private giving comprises a smaller share of the income of the nonprofit sector than is widely believed.[15] Most of the nonprofit sector's income comes from fees for services, with income from government coming in second.[16] Nonprofit establishments are more likely than other establishments to be mid-sized, with

---

[6]   *Id* at 1–2.

[7]   *Id*. at 24.

[8]   *Id* at 17–21.

[9]   *Id*. at 25.

[10]   MOLLY F. SHERLOCK & JANE G. GRAVELLE, CONG. RES. SERV., AN OVERVIEW OF THE NONPROFIT AND CHARITABLE SECTOR 3 (2009).

[11]   *Id*. at 4. There were 13 million nonprofit employees in 2005 and an estimated 9.4 million employees in the charitable sector. *Id*. More than half of that employment is in the health and social assistance sector, with 18 percent of nonprofit employees working in the educational sector. *Id*.

[12]   *Id*. at 5.

[13]   *Id*. at 9.

[14]   *Id*. at 12. Even in 2008, these organizations were a larger part of the economy than the construction sector but they contributed half as much to GDP as the manufacturing sector. *Id*. at 14.

[15]   *Id*. at 39. In 2007, philanthropy comprised about 10 percent of the income of the nonprofit sector. *Id*.

[16]   *Id*. at 38–39. In 2007, 52 percent of the nonprofit sector's income came from fees and 38 percent came from government. *Id*.

few very large establishments (more than 1,000 employees) or very small establishments (fewer than ten employees).[17]

B. TAX–EXEMPT ORGANIZATIONS

The Code describes approximately thirty types of tax-exempt organizations.[18] These include charitable organizations,[19] social welfare organizations,[20] chambers of commerce or business leagues,[21] credit unions,[22] labor and agricultural organizations,[23] war veteran organizations,[24] and political organizations.[25]

What these diverse organizations have in common is the "non-distribution constraint."[26] Tax-exempt organizations are not prohibited from making a profit. (Indeed, any entity that consistently brings in less revenue than its expenses will soon close its doors.) Instead, tax-exempt organizations are forbidden from distributing any income or profit of the organization to the people who work for or control the organization, such as directors, officers or members of the organization, except as reasonable compensation.[27] Any income generated from or by the work of the organization must instead be devoted for the purposes for which the organization was formed.[28]

The Code differentiates between two types of charitable organizations, public charities and private foundations, and provides more favorable tax treatment to public charities. Public charities are subject to less burdensome oversight and operating requirements and donations to them generally receive more favorable tax treatment. Private foundations are defined as charities that are not public charities—so it serves as a default designation.[29] A public charity is a church, educational institution, hospital or medical research organization, development foundation for a public university or governmental unit or some other form of charitable organization that has broad public support or that actively functions in a sup-

---

[17] SHERLOCK & GRAVELLE, *supra* note 10, at 15.

[18] 26 U.S.C. § 501(c) (2011) [hereinafter IRC]. These organizations are generally exempt from income tax though they do pay other federal taxes and at times may pay income tax on certain income (we discuss unrelated business income below).

[19] I.R.C. § 501(c)(3).

[20] I.R.C. § 501(c)(4).

[21] I.R.C. § 501(c)(6) (including professional football leagues).

[22] I.R.C. § 501(c)(14).

[23] I.R.C. § 501(c)(5).

[24] I.R.C. § 501(c)(19).

[25] I.R.C. § 527 (2011).

[26] JAMES J. FISHMAN & STEPHEN SCHWARZ, NONPROFIT ORGANIZATIONS: CASES AND MATERIALS 3 (4th ed. 2010) (citing Henry Hansmann, *The Role of Nonprofit Enterprise*, 89 YALE L.J. 837, 840 (1980)).

[27] *Id.*

[28] *Id.*

[29] *Id.* at 721.

porting relationship to other charitable organizations having public support.[30] An organization is generally publicly supported if it receives at least one-third of its total support from governmental units or the general public.[31] Most of the organizations you will represent will be public charities; as a result, we concentrate this chapter on those organizations.

Among all of the various tax-exempt organizations recognized by the IRS,[32] some are subject to a more "special" treatment. These, known as 501(c)(3) organizations, are "corporations . . . organized and operated exclusively for religious, charitable, scientific, or educational purposes . . . or for the prevention of cruelty to children and animals."[33] Contributions to 501(c)(3) organizations are deductible from the donor's taxes, which is a benefit your clients will surely hope to obtain. The Code allows individuals and corporations to deduct "any charitable contribution . . . made within the taxable year."[34] There are limits to the deductibility of these contributions[35] which we will not discuss here. A donor to your client should consult his or her tax advisor and the nonprofit organization should decline to advise the donor about the deductibility of contributions.[36] In representing the nonprofit organization, you may need to become familiar with these rules, such as when nonprofit organizations are developing gift acceptance policies.

There are advantages and disadvantages to seeking the IRS "charitable" designation. We noted one of the main advantages of federal recognition above, the deductibility of contributions to the organization by donors. The other major advantage is the possibility of receiving grants from foundations and government agencies which generally only award grants to 501(c)(3) groups. Nonprofit organizations also receive preferential postal rates, and special treatment for some employee benefits, some securities and some antitrust regulations.[37] They do not pay federal unemployment insurance tax.[38] Organizations that the IRS recognizes as charitable may also be exempt from paying some state and local taxes, such as income, sales, use, property and excise taxes.

---

[30] I.R.C. § 509(a) (2006).

[31] *Id.*

[32] I.R.C. § 501(c).

[33] I.R.C. § 501(c)(3).

[34] I.R.C. § 170(a)(1) (2006). This rule may change soon as there are proposals to amend this provision of the Code in an effort to reduce the federal deficit. *See, e.g.,* Joseph J. Cordes, *Rethinking the Deduction for Charitable Contributions: Evaluating the Effects of Deficit Reduction Proposals,* 64 NAT'L TAX J. 1001 (2011).

[35] *See* I.R.C. § 170(c).

[36] INTERNAL REV. SERV., CHARITABLE CONTRIBUTIONS—SUBSTANTIATION AND DISCLOSURE REQUIREMENTS (2012), *available at* http://www.irs.gov/pub/irs-pdf/p1771.pdf (providing information that explains requirements for donors who wish to make deductions to charitable organizations).

[37] BRUCE R. HOPKINS, THE LAW OF TAX–EXEMPT ORGANIZATIONS 10–11 (10th ed. 2011).

[38] I.R.C. § 3306(c) (2006).

But there are several disadvantages to seeking federal recognition as well. Nonprofit organizations have extensive annual reporting requirements, to the IRS and state agencies, such as the Secretary of State (or comparable agency) and the Attorney General.[39] Unlike other tax returns, the tax returns of a nonprofit organization are open to public inspection.[40] Tax-exemption also limits an organization's ability to engage in legislative activities, forbids the organization from engaging in political activities[41] and places restrictions on benefits to individuals.[42]

C. THE RATIONALE FOR SPECIAL TAX TREATMENT FOR NONPROFIT ORGANIZATIONS

The rationale for tax exemption for nonprofit organizations has very little to do with any underlying tax policy. This aspect of tax law is grounded in political philosophy, on the proper construct of a democratic society.[43] Over time, Congress has (infrequently) deleted from and (frequently) added to the list of tax-exempt organizations. Some exemptions do underlie a policy to support a particular activity, such as supporting agriculture in the case of the exemption for farmers' cooperatives.[44] Some organizations can be seen as important to significant segments of society, such as veterans' organizations, trade and business associations and labor organizations.[45] Yet other organizations may be seen as having significance to the functioning and structure of all of society, such as charitable organizations.[46]

There are several rationales for "subsidizing" nonprofits by exempting them from paying corporate income tax or further subsidizing them by allowing contributions to them to be tax deductible to the donor.[47] One such theory is that the tax would fall on those least able to pay, the poor who are the ultimate beneficiaries of the services of some nonprofit organ-

---

[39] For more information about IRS annual reporting requirements, see INT. REV. SERV., *Compliance Guide for 501(c)(3) Public Charities* (2012), *available at* http://www.irs.gov/pub/irs-pdf/p4221pc.pdf. For more information about state annual reporting requirements, see *State Annual Filing Requirements*, NAT'L COUNCIL OF NONPROFITS (2012), http://www.councilofnonprofits.org/annual-filing-state.

[40] I.R.C. § 6104(a)(1) (2006).

[41] I.R.C. § 501(h).

[42] I.R.C. § 503(b) (2006).

[43] HOPKINS, *supra* note 37, at 9.

[44] *Id.*

[45] *Id.* at 10.

[46] *Id.* at 10–11.

[47] The subsidy represented by the deductibility of charitable giving is substantial. The Joint Committee on Taxation estimates that the five-year revenue cost from 2010 to 2014 amounts to approximately $246.1 billion. Cordes, *supra* note 34, at 1001 (citing JOINT COMMITTEE ON TAXATION, BACKGROUND INFORMATION ON TAX EXPENDITURE ANALYSIS AND HISTORICAL SURVEY OF TAX EXPENDITURE ESTIMATES (2011)).

izations.[48] Another common view is that the exemption subsidizes services that might otherwise have to be provided by the government.[49] One might argue that the non-distribution constraint provides some assurance that the subsidy to the nonprofit organization will ultimately benefit the consumers of the organization in lower prices or higher quality; or nonprofits could be seem as producing a different product mix.[50]

Some observers also argue that the services provided by nonprofits are characterized by a particular kind of "market failure" called "contract failure"—that is, donors or consumers are likely to have difficulty comparing the quality of competing providers before or after the "purchase."[51] Consumers then turn to nonprofits since they have less opportunity and incentive to exploit the consumer and serve as a sort of fiduciary for the consumer.[52] This trend is especially true for nonprofits that provide complex personal services such as day care centers or residential nursing care where consumers have difficulty evaluating the quality of services with confidence and where consumers are most likely to need protection from exploitation. Finally, another rationale for the exemption is that it serves to compensate for difficulties that nonprofits have in raising capital.[53]

II. STRUCTURING A NONPROFIT ORGANIZATION

A. STRUCTURAL CHOICES—OR THE QUESTION OF INCORPORATION

A tax-exempt organization may take the form of a corporation, trust or unincorporated association.[54] In deciding which form to choose, an organization will need to consider legal liabilities for the individuals involved, the requirements of local law and local reporting requirements, membership requirements, and necessities of the governing instruments. Some provisions of the Code mandate the corporate or trust form. In our experience, most organizations that opt to seek tax-exempt status from the IRS will want to start as a corporation, but the other options are available.

---

[48] Henry Hansmann, *The Rationale for Exempting Nonprofit Organizations from Corporate Income Taxation,* 91 YALE L.J. 54, 64–65 (1981).

[49] *Id.* at 66.

[50] *Id.* at 67.

[51] *Id.* at 69.

[52] *Id.* at 69–70.

[53] *Id.* at 72.

[54] I.R.C. § 501(c)(3) (stating that "Corporations, and any community chest, fund, or foundation" may seek tax-exempt status). The IRS states that "a 501(c)(3) organization must be organized as a corporation, trust, or unincorporated association." INTERNAL REV. SERV., APPLYING FOR 501(C)(3) TAX–EXEMPT STATUS 2 (2012), *available at* http://www.irs.gov/pub/irs-pdf/p4220.pdf.

In deciding whether to incorporate and seek tax-exempt status, the group should decide whether its charitable activities are a one-time activity, whether another organization is already carrying out similar activities (and therefore there may not be a need to create a new entity) and what liability risks are involved. If the group concludes that it makes sense to organize and proceed to apply to the IRS for tax-exemption, it must decide which entity type to use.

A group that is not certain it wants to incorporate because, for example, it just wants to handle a particular project and is not certain it will be able to raise funds in the future, may consider a few other options. A group may partner with an existing organization and have that organization carry out the activity. The group may also choose to incorporate to reduce possible liability for the individuals but may not seek tax-exempt status right away. In that case, it may pursue a "fiscal sponsor."[55] Under the fiscal sponsorship arrangement, the "sponsored" group usually does the labor and the "sponsoring" group, which is itself a 501(c)(3) organization, handles the administrative work such as payroll and financial management as well as submitting fundraising proposals in its name. The sponsored group may also receive tax-deductible donations for its work, if the donations pass through the sponsor. Groups that want to create these arrangements should negotiate an agreement that spells out the responsibilities of each group.

Proceeding as an unincorporated association has benefits as well as costs. The advantages of unincorporated associations are their informality and flexibility since no governmental approvals are necessary in order to form or dissolve.[56] An unincorporated association must, though, have some organizing instrument, governing rules and regularly chosen officers in order to receive treatment as an entity.[57] But the law surrounding unincorporated associations is not well developed, and that is one of the form's disadvantages.[58] Few states have adopted the Uniform Unincorporated Nonprofit Association Act[59] and few statutory rules govern or guide unincorporated associations. Absent some statutory provision, an unincorporated association cannot receive or hold property in the association's name and the association cannot contract in its name.[60] Individual members may be found personally liable absent statutory provisions to the contrary (such as those found in the Uniform Act) and all members may be named as party-defendants in a dispute about an alleged liability of

---

[55] *See* GREGORY L. COLVIN, FISCAL SPONSORSHIP: SIX WAYS TO DO IT RIGHT (2d ed. 2005).

[56] FISHMAN & SCHWARZ, *supra* note 26, at 49.

[57] Trippe v. Comm'r, 9 T.C.M. 622 (1950). The IRS has stated that it finds unincorporated associations difficult to deal with because "determining exempt status requires finding that there is an entity separate from the individuals who created it." IRM 7.25.3.2.3 (Feb. 23, 1999).

[58] FISHMAN & SCHWARZ, *supra* note 26, at 49.

[59] REV. UNIF. UNINCORPORATED NONPROFIT ASS'N ACT (2008).

[60] FISHMAN & SCHWARZ, *supra* note 26, at 50.

the association.[61] Most jurisdictions have adopted legislation treating the association as an entity for legal purposes such as the capacity to sue or be sued.[62]

Charitable trusts, while the oldest type of nonprofit entity, are generally only used for private foundations that are engaged solely in making grants.[63] A charitable trust is a "fiduciary relationship with respect to property, arising from a manifestation of an intention to create that relationship and subjecting the person who holds title to the property to duties to deal with it for the benefit of charity or for one or more persons, at least one of whom is not the sole trustee."[64] The trust offers ease and swiftness of formation, fewer formalities in its administration and the possibility of continuing control by the grantor.[65]

[handwritten margin note: Charitable trust → usually only for private enteties]

In practice, though, most organizations choose to incorporate in order to provide greater protection from liability for the persons involved in the organization, and to operate in a structure that the IRS knows and understands well. As a result, we will spend the rest of the chapter assuming your client has decided to incorporate and seek recognition as a charitable organization.

Those familiar with different entities may ask about the possibility of organizing a charitable organization as a limited liability company (LLC). The IRS has determined that an LLC with two or more members that are charitable or governmental entities can qualify for tax-exemption as a charitable organization under limited conditions.[66] In general, though, founders of nonprofit organizations do not use the LLC vehicle as their choice of entity.

B. STEPS TO OBTAINING TAX EXEMPTION

In this section, we discuss the steps required in order to create a nonprofit corporation that is recognized under § 501(c)(3) of the Code. In later sections we will discuss many of the IRS requirements for these organizations. As we mention above, obtaining tax exemption implicates both state and federal processes. State law will control the type of entity used or created (corporation, trust or unincorporated association) and the requirements of that entity. Assuming your clients decide to incorporate, you will need to become familiar with your state's nonprofit corporation

---

[61] *Id.*

[62] *Id.*

[63] *Id.* at 50–51.

[64] RESTATEMENT (THIRD) OF TRUSTS § 2 (2003).

[65] FISHMAN & SCHWARZ, *supra* note 26, at 51.

[66] HOPKINS, *supra* note 37, at 70–72 (citing RICHARD A. MCCRAY & WARD L. THOMAS, INTERNAL REV. SERV., LIMITED LIABILITY COMPANIES AS EXEMPT ORGANIZATIONS–UPDATE (2001), *available at* http://www.irs.gov/pub/irs-tege/eotopicb01.pdf).

act.[67] It will spell out the requirements for incorporation. Several states limit the purposes for which nonprofit corporations may be formed; others allow incorporation for any lawful purpose. A few states allow stock nonprofit corporations. Federal law will control the tax exemption process. State law will also control whether the organization has to register with the Attorney General or another state agency under your state's charitable solicitation and charitable trust acts.

1.   The Articles of Incorporation: A First Step

Assuming the organization decides to incorporate, the first step in the process, incorporating the nonprofit organization, is controlled by state law. This process is fairly simple, perhaps simpler than it should be, because filing the articles of incorporation may not necessarily require that someone have considered all the provisions of the state's nonprofit corporation act. The organization will have to make several decisions before filing the articles of incorporation or organization. Most states have "form" articles of incorporation; some states allow the organization to create its own form. Either way, the articles allow for additional provisions to be included. You will need to decide what optional provisions to include. The applicable state's nonprofit act will guide your decision as to which provisions must, should or can be included in the articles. The articles can be amended or restated in the future but amending or restating the articles will cost money and time so it is best to file them correctly from the beginning.

The articles of incorporation will require you to provide the name of the organization, the purpose for which the organization was created (similar to but not necessarily the same as the mission statement), the name of the incorporators, the name of the registered agent and an address for the corporation.[68] Your state may require you to list the organization's fiscal year and the initial officers and directors, and to declare whether the organization will be a membership or directorship organization. Your state may also allow you to include a provision permitting or making obligatory indemnification of directors, officers and volunteers.[69] The organization's articles will also need to include the "magic" IRS language—that no part of the net earnings of the organization will inure to the benefit of a private shareholder or individual, no substantial part of the activities will be carrying on propaganda or otherwise attempting to influence legislation and that the organization will not participate or in-

---

[67] Most states have a separate Nonprofit Corporation Act; the states with no separate act use the section for non-stock corporations of the state's general corporate law. FISHMAN & SCHWARZ, *supra* note 26, at 71.

[68] MODEL NONPROFIT CORP. ACT § 2.02 (2008).

[69] *Id.*

tervene in any political campaign on behalf of or in opposition to any candidate for public office.[70]

If the initial directors or members are named in the articles of incorporation, those persons will need to hold an organizational meeting to complete the establishment of the corporation by electing directors, appointing officers, adopting bylaws and carrying on any other business. If the initial directors or members are not named in the articles, the incorporators will hold the organizational meeting and elect directors and complete the organization of the corporation or elect directors and have those directors complete the organization of the corporation.[71] The initial board of directors may have been chosen at the early stage of the organization. In fact, you might have drafted the bylaws before incorporating the organization, as is often the case with unincorporated organizations. You might be drafting the bylaws at the same time that you are meeting with the board of directors or the incorporators to discuss the articles of incorporation. At times, in organizations with a single incorporator, she or he might want to approve the bylaws before naming the board of directors. You should review your state's nonprofit act to see if the incorporator can adopt the bylaws of the organization or if the board of directors should be named first. Even if the nonprofit act allows for the incorporator to adopt the bylaws, we believe it is good practice to have the entire board of directors participate in the decisions surrounding the bylaws and their adoption.[72]

2. Bylaws: The Internal Governance of the Nonprofit Corporation

A nonprofit corporation must also have bylaws, and the IRS will ask to see your client's bylaws.[73] You therefore will spend substantial time developing the most appropriate bylaws for your emerging nonprofit corporation. In drafting the bylaws, you will once again need to be familiar with the applicable state's nonprofit corporation act. The act may require that you include certain provisions in the bylaws in addition to requiring you to make decisions about discretionary provisions.

One issue you will decide with your client, and which we noted in passing in the discussion about the Articles, is whether the entity will be

---

[70] We discuss these requirements further *infra* in Section IV.A. This "magic" language should also be included in the bylaws.

[71] MODEL NONPROFIT CORP. ACT § 2.05.

[72] Since the bylaws are important to the governance of the corporation, we believe that the board of directors should be involved in the deliberation over the entity's structure. The provisions in the bylaws will bind the board. When the corporation is the idea of one person, it is a good idea to help that person realize that decisions will have to be made collectively by the board and not one individual.

[73] *See* INTERNAL REV. SERV., INSTRUCTIONS FOR FORM 1023 (2006), *available at* http://www.irs.gov/pub/irs-pdf/i1023.pdf.

a membership organization. A nonprofit corporation may be governed ultimately by its **members or by its board of directors**. If the organization is a membership organization, those adopting the bylaws will need to determine the terms and conditions of membership. Members will normally make the major corporate decisions, such as electing the Board of Directors. The bylaws will need to spell out the conditions a person must satisfy to fulfill the characteristics of membership (such as living within certain boundaries), the requirements that must be met before membership can be conferred (for example, payment of dues or participation in the organization's activities in some manner) and the criteria for forfeiting membership status (for example, not attending a certain number of meetings, or not paying dues for a defined period of time). The bylaws will need to spell out whether there will be different classes of members and the voting rights of members, including whether there can be cumulative voting for directors. In addition, the bylaws will need to fix the annual meeting of members and determine whether there will be other regular meetings of the members. The bylaws should spell out the requirements for special membership meetings, such as who gets to call them (officers, the executive committee of the board, the majority of the board, a certain percentage of members); notice provisions; quorum requirements; voting provisions (e.g., will they be the same for all matters?); and whether proxy or absentee voting is allowed under any circumstances.

The bylaws will need to cover a number of questions regarding the board of directors and the corporation's officers. These questions include the duties and manner of selecting the board and officers. The board or incorporators will need to decide the number of board members the organization will have and whether the bylaws will provide for a minimum number of directors or a range (for example, no fewer than five and no more than nine directors).[74] Your state's nonprofit corporation act will most likely require a minimum number of directors. In counseling boards, you will need to explore the advantages and disadvantages of various options including the number of board members. Smaller boards are normally less representative and allow for a fewer number of skills to be represented on the board; larger boards may make it more difficult to conduct meetings since there are more possibilities for disagreement. The bylaws should provide for the selection of the board if the organization is organized as a directorship (as opposed to a membership). The bylaws should also spell out the term of directors (whether the terms will be longer than one year), whether there are term limits and whether term-limited board members can return to the board after a waiting period. If

---

[74] Another option would be to provide for a specific number of directors, such as fifteen. Many practitioners believe that providing for a minimum or range is a better practice so that the board is rarely in a position to violate the requirement of the number of directors when directors resign. They recommend an odd number of directors in order to lessen the possibility of tie votes, assuming a majority of the board or of those voting is required for an action to pass.

board terms are longer than one year, the bylaws should provide whether some of the terms will be staggered so there is not the potential for a complete turn-over of the board at every election. The bylaws should also consider the process and reasons for removal of board members or officers and how vacancies will be filled.[75] The bylaws should cover the frequency of board meetings and notice provisions for regular and special meetings of the board, including who gets to call a special meeting. The board should consider what it wants to bind itself to as opposed to how it is operating at the time that the bylaws are drafted. For example, the board may decide to meet on a monthly basis in the early stages of organization but may want to require quarterly meetings in the bylaws.

The group that will approve the bylaws should also consider the committee structure of the organization. Will there be standing committees that are included in the bylaws? For example, will the officers comprise an executive committee? Will any of these committees have the power to make decisions (board-designated powers) or will they recommend actions to the full board? The board will also need to consider how the committees will function and the level of detail to be included in the bylaws. You will need to counsel the board regarding indemnification provisions that may be included in the bylaws. Finally, the bylaws should include provisions outlining how they can be amended.

3.   Federal Tax Exemption Recognition

If the organization decides it wants to be recognized as a charitable organization it will need to file Form 1023 with the IRS and receive a favorable decision from the IRS. Form 1023 requires detailed information about the organization's plans and functioning. Many of the questions on the form require further explanation, which you will provide through attachments or supplements. Two of the most important parts of the application are the detailed narrative of the organization's activities or planned activities and the organization's budget (for the current year and two following years or current year and three past years). If the organization wants tax-exemption retroactive to the date of incorporation, it must file its Form 1023 within 27 months of incorporating.[76] The IRS has the discretion, upon a showing of good cause by the organization, to grant a reasonable extension of time beyond the 27 months.[77] An organization

---

[75] In a membership organization, for example, should the board be able to fill a vacancy for the unexpired term? Additional considerations are whether removal should require cause or no cause and whether removal will require a majority or supermajority. The nonprofit act may require certain provisions while others are within the discretion of the organization. Generally, it should be easier to remove an officer than a director.

[76] *Form 1023—General Instructions*, INTERNAL REV. SERV., (2012), http://www.irs.gov/instructions/i1023/ch01.html. The regulations require that the organization file within 15 months of the end of the month of creation but grant the organization an automatic 12–month extension. *Id.*

[77] 26 C.F.R. § 301.9100–3 (2012). Rev. Proc. 79–63, 1979–2 C.B. 578.

that does not file its Form 1023 within the appropriate time will be presumed to be a private foundation and, assuming the IRS grants it tax exemption, such determination will be prospective.[78] Two types of organizations do not have to file for exempt status—religious organizations and small public charities.[79] Some religious organizations and most small public charities nevertheless do file Form 1023 in order to have a clear determination of their tax-exempt status.

We will not review the Form 1023 in detail in this chapter. We will, however, discuss the various tax requirements implicated by being a public charity and identify issues you may encounter and which may require further research in your client work.[80] Those discussions will assist in your work on Form 1023, as the form's questions and categories reflect IRS policies regarding the proper governance and operation of a public charity.

4. State Oversight of Charities

The property of a nonprofit organization is treated as a charitable trust regardless of the organization's structure. As a result, charitable organizations are subject to state charitable trust statutes. These statutes require the board to operate the organization for the public welfare. The state's Attorney General is generally charged with protecting the public interest in such charitable trusts. As a result, in most states, organizations must register with the Attorney General when they hold any property. They may also have to register before soliciting any money from the public (under the state's charitable solicitation act). These statutes act to "protect" or "regulate" charities and to regulate the "charitable environment," thereby encouraging charitable giving.[81] These laws also protect the interests of the general public, both those who donate to charities and those who receive benefits from charities. By regulating the "charitable environment" these laws promote the public perception of the integrity and efficiency of charities.[82] Registration requirements and mandatory public disclosure of financial information are the most common forms of regulation.[83] You will need to research whether there are any exemptions

---

[78] 26 C.F.R. § 1.508–1(b) (2012).

[79] 26 C.F.R. § 1.508–1(b)(7). Public charities that normally have gross receipts of less than $5,000 do not have to file Form 1023, and these organizations are also exempt from filing an annual return with the IRS. I.R.C. § 6033(a) (2011).

[80] We think the IRS instructions do a good job of explaining the form. For more information about the process, see INTERNAL REV. SERV., TAX–EXEMPT STATUS FOR YOUR ORGANIZATION (2011), *available at* http://www.irs.gov/pub/irs-pdf/p557.pdf.

[81] FISHMAN & SCHWARZ, *supra* note 26, at 245 (citing Ellen Harris, Lynn S. Holley & Christopher J. McCaffrey, *Fundraising into the 1990's: State Regulation of Charitable Solicitation After* Riley, 24 U.S.F.L. REV. 571, 577 (1990)).

[82] *Id.* at 246.

[83] DAVID BIEMESDERFER & ANDRAS KOSARAS, COUNCIL ON FOUNDATIONS, THE VALUE OF RELATIONSHIPS BETWEEN STATE CHARITY REGULATION & PHILANTHROPHY 4 (2006), *available at*

from these requirements in your state, for example requiring registration for groups with income higher than a certain amount in a given year.

You will need to decide the timing of this filing—before or after seeking recognition from the IRS—depending on the requirements of the applicable state's statute and the needs of the organization (e.g., if it intends to solicit donations before receiving IRS recognition). You may also need to decide if the organization needs to register in more than one state depending on where it intends to solicit funds. Some states use a common form for registration.[84]

The Internet has made the question of where to register more complicated. The courts have begun to wrestle with the jurisdictional and constitutional issues relating to Internet transactions.[85] For a state to assert personal jurisdiction over a non-resident defendant, without violating due process, it would have to show that the organization purposefully established "minimum contacts" and that the suit would not offend "traditional notions of fair play and substantial justice."[86] The mere existence of a website that residents of the state can view most likely would not be enough to establish jurisdiction over the organization.[87]

But many charitable organizations' websites ask for donations and permit viewers to donate through their websites. The fact complicates the question of personal jurisdiction. In response to that complicating question, the National Association of Attorneys General (NAAG) and the National Association of State Charity Officials (NASCO) issued a series of nonbinding guidelines, known as the Charleston Principles, for state regulators concerning regulation of charitable solicitations using the Internet. Under the Charleston Principles, an organization would have to register in a state which is not its home state if its non-Internet activities would be sufficient to require registration, if it specifically solicits persons living in a particular state, receives contributions from that state on a

---

http://www.cof.org/files/Documents/Building%20Strong%20Ethical%20Foundations/06AGreportf ull.pdf. *See also* Leslie G. Espinoza, *Straining the Quality of Mercy: Abandoning the Quest for Informed Charitable Giving*, 64 S. CAL. L. REV. 605 (1991) (discussing history of state regulation of charities).

[84] *See Unified Registration Statement*, MULTI–STATE FILER PROJECT (2010), http://www.multistatefiling.org/.

[85] For an introductory discussion of some of these issues, see Brian Covotta, *Personal Jurisdiction and the Internet: An Introduction*, 13 BERKELEY TECH. L. J. 265 (1998).

[86] Int'l Shoe v. Wash., 326 U.S. 310, 316 (1945).

[87] *See* Zippo Mfg. Co. v. Zippo Dot Com, Inc., 952 F.Supp. 1119, 1124 (W.D. Pa. 1997) (holding that the likelihood of personal jurisdiction is "directly proportionate to the nature and quality of commercial activity that the entity conducts over the Internet"); GTE New Media Sources, Inc. v. Bell South Corp., 199 F.3d 1343 (D.C. Cir. 2000) (holding that the use of the web site was an unilateral act by the individual rather than purposeful activity in the forum on the part of the web site's operators); Cybersell, Inc. v. Cybersell, Inc., 130 F.3d 414, 418 (9th Cir. 1997) (holding that there must be " 'something more' to indicate that the defendant purposely . . . directed his activity in a substantial way to the forum state").

repeated, ongoing or substantial basis through its web site or sends email messages or otherwise contacts persons in order to promote its web site.[88]

We now discuss governance issues before turning to the requirements that the Code imposes on charitable organizations.

III. GOVERNANCE OF A NONPROFIT ORGANIZATION

A. THE BOARD OF DIRECTORS

The governance structure of nonprofit corporations parallels but is not identical to that of for-profit corporations. The board of directors as a body is responsible for oversight of the organization. Boards can be said to serve six principal functions: 1) select, encourage, advise and evaluate the chief executive officer (the Executive Director, CEO or President); 2) review and adopt long-term strategic directions and approve specific objectives, including the financial projections and the mission of the organization; 3) ensure that the necessary resources, human and financial, will be available to pursue the organization's strategies and achieve its objectives; 4) monitor the performance of management; 5) ensure that the organization functions responsibly and effectively; and 6) establish and carry out an effective system of governance at the board level including evaluating board performance and nominating candidates for election to the board.[89] One major difference between the for-profit and nonprofit board is the nonprofit board's commitment to developing and advancing the mission of the organization.[90] Fundraising, representing the organization to the outside community and mobilizing and caring for volunteers are also significant duties of nonprofit boards.[91]

Day-to-day management of the nonprofit organization is usually vested in its senior staff (if the organization has senior staff).[92] The line of demarcation between board and staff power is usually resolved in the political arena and not the legal one.[93] The level of involvement of a board of directors in an organization varies by the organization's size, activities,

---

[88] NATIONAL ASSOCIATION OF STATE CHARITY OFFICIALS, THE CHARLESTON PRINCIPLES: GUIDELINES ON CHARITABLE SOLICITATIONS USING THE INTERNET § III.B (2001), *available at* http://www.nasconet.org/wp-content/uploads/2011/05/Charleston–Principles–Final.pdf.

[89] FISHMAN & SCHWARZ, *supra* note 26, at 127 (citing WILLIAM G. BOWEN, INSIDE THE BOARDROOM: GOVERNANCE BY DIRECTORS AND TRUSTEES 18–20 (1994)).

[90] HOPKINS, *supra* note 37, at 122.

[91] *Id.*

[92] Our description here assumes a functioning nonprofit organization either with funds to pay for staff (including, most likely, an executive director) or with a cadre of committed volunteers who function as staff. For many beginning nonprofits, including, we suspect, many of your clients, the members of the board *are* the nonprofit's staff and volunteers, performing everything that the organization does. The explanations in the text will not apply to these embryonic organizations.

[93] HOPKINS, *supra* note 37, at 118.

age, from time to time, and may be based on the needs of the organization and the board environment. In some organizations it is the organization's staff that sets the board's agenda. Some boards may use committees to fully develop an issue and the board's role may be more formal decision-making. In larger organizations the board's role is more reactive while in new organizations with no staff the board may carry out more day-to-day work. The lines of authority are further complicated in membership organizations, with the membership generally setting basic policy, the board setting more focused policy and the officers and staff implementing the collective policies.

B. FIDUCIARY RESPONSIBILITIES OF THE BOARD

The notion of fiduciary duty—that the directors are fiduciaries of the organization's resources and facilitators of its mission—evolved from the common law of charitable trusts.[94] Personal liability can result when a director, officer or key employee of an organization breaches the standards of fiduciary responsibility.[95] The duties apply to the board as a whole and to the individual directors. The fiduciary duties require board members to be objective, responsible, honest, trustworthy and efficient.

The board of directors owes three essential duties to the corporation—the duty of care, the duty of loyalty and the duty of obedience.[96] These duties constitute the legal standard against which all actions of the board are measured and board members can be held liable for failing to abide by these duties. The duty of care requires directors to be "reasonably informed about the organization's activities, participate in decision-making, and act in good faith and with the care of an ordinarily prudent person in comparable circumstances."[97] The duty is discharged by attendance at board and committee meetings; advance preparation, such as reviewing documents; using independent judgment in decision-making; reviewing the organization's finances and the performance of the organization's staff; and compliance with legal requirements, such as filing annual reports.[98]

The duty of loyalty requires board members to make decisions on the basis of the best interest of the organization and not their personal or other professional interests.[99] Board members are required to disclose conflicts of interest and not participate in decisions in which a board member may derive a personal benefit. Conflicts of interests are not nec-

---

[94] HOPKINS, *supra* note 37, at 121.

[95] *Id.*

[96] *Id.* at 123.

[97] *Id.*

[98] *Id.*

[99] *Id.*

essarily illegal.[100] The key is the organization's process for dealing with such conflicts, including the existence of and adherence to a conflict of interest policy.[101] The duty of loyalty also requires board members not to disclose the organization's confidential information. The duty of obedience requires that a board member comply with applicable federal, state and local laws, follow the organization's governing documents and guard the organization's mission.[102] The board should periodically review documents governing the operation of the organization.

Additionally, directors must exercise their responsibilities in good faith and with a certain degree of diligence, attention, care and skill.[103] Directors can fail to discharge their duties by failing to supervise the corporation or failing to make informed decisions. Under the best judgment rule,[104] a director avoids liability for her actions if she has made a decision by informing herself in good faith without a disabling conflict of interest. This safe harbor does not include breaches involving bad faith, criminal activity, fraud, or willful or wanton misconduct.[105] The board must exercise reasonable care in its decision-making and not place the organization under unnecessary risk.[106]

Two of the principal responsibilities of the board are to maintain financial accountability and effective oversight of the organization.[107] Board members are expected to exercise due diligence to see that the organization is well managed and is financially sound. One of the board's duties is formulating the organization's budget.

The trend is toward a more active oversight role for boards, representing more involvement in policy setting and review, employee supervision and overall management.[108] The board's shared legal responsibilities depend on the actions of the individual board members, with each board member being liable for his or her acts (commission) or failure to act (omission) including those which rise to the level of civil or criminal law offenses.

---

[100] Id.

[101] Form 1023 inquires into the applicant's conflict of interest policy and, if one exists, asks to review it. You will likely ensure that your client has an effective conflicts policy in place before it files Form 1023.

[102] Id.

[103] FISHMAN & SCHWARZ, supra note 26, at 151.

[104] In nonprofit settings, the best judgment rule is the equivalent of the business judgment rule application to for-profit enterprises. See James J. Fishman, Improving Charitable Accountability, 62 MD. L. REV. 218, 233 (2003). For a more detailed discussion of the business judgment rule, see STEPHEN A. RADIN, THE BUSINESS JUDGMENT RULE: FIDUCIARY DUTIES OF CORPORATE DIRECTORS (6th ed. 2009).

[105] FISHMAN & SCHWARZ, supra note 26, at 153.

[106] Id.

[107] Id.

[108] Id.

The enforcement of fiduciary obligations happens on several levels. To a great extent, organizations self-regulate. Beyond that, organizations are required by state law to maintain particular records, such as minutes of meetings, actions taken without a meeting, accounting records and membership lists.[109] States require organizations to file certain reports on a yearly basis. In most states, the Attorney General requires organizations to file annual financial reports. Lastly, federal law imposes some requirements on directors and, as we discussed above, there are penalties for violating many of these provisions.[110] Organizations recognized as tax-exempt by the IRS must file annual information returns.[111] Members of an organization as well as directors may be able to sue the organization.[112] There is some question whether these checks are sufficient.

C. SARBANES–OXLEY AND NONPROFIT ORGANIZATIONS

In the wake of scandals and the collapse of several businesses, Congress passed the Public Company Accounting Reform and Investor Protection Act of 2002, known as Sarbanes–Oxley (SOX).[113] The Act requires corporate boards to have audit committees consisting of independent directors and mandates the creation of effective financial reporting systems.[114] In addition, it requires chief executives and chief financial officers of publicly listed corporations to personally certify the validity of the corporation's financial statement and that they validly represent the financial condition of the company.[115] Though the statute generally does not apply to nonprofit organizations, SOX provides best practices guidelines for boards of directors of nonprofit organizations.[116] Many nonprofit organizations began to adopt certain governance practices, and the IRS started to pay more attention to nonprofit governance issues.[117] Some of the same concerns that spurred the passage of SOX exist for nonprofits. In 2004, the U.S. Senate Finance Committee held hearings on charitable giving problems and best practices after concerns about conflicts of inter-

---

[109] MODEL NONPROFIT CORP. ACT § 16.01 (2008).

[110] I.R.C. § 4958(a)(1) (2011). Directors who receive an economic benefit in excess of the value of the consideration provided when they engage in a transaction with the organization must pay a tax on the "excess benefit." *Id.*

[111] *See Which forms do exempt organizations file?*, INTERNAL REV. SERV. (Dec. 11, 2012), http://www.irs.gov/Charities-&-Non-Profits/Form-990-Series-Which-Forms-Do-Exempt-Organizations-File%3F-(Filing-Phase-In).

[112] FISHMAN & SCHWARZ, *supra* note 26, at 230.

[113] Public Company Accountability Reform and Investor Protection Act, 15 U.S.C. §§ 7201–7266 (2006).

[114] HOPKINS, *supra* note 37, at 128.

[115] *Id.*

[116] *Id.*

[117] *Id.*

est and excess compensation in tax-exempt organizations.[118] After those hearings, the Senate staff issued a set of recommendations including periodic review of organizations' tax-exempt status by the IRS, a requirement that the chief executive officer sign annual information (tax) returns, an imposition of penalties for filing inaccurate returns and public disclosure of goals and financial information.[119]

For the nonprofit board, SOX has meant an expectation of greater accountability.[120] Some suggested accountability measures include the creation of document preservation, whistleblower and conflict of interest policies; more rigorous review by the board of the organization's financial statements; creation of a code of ethics prohibiting loans to board members and senior staff; audit committees with at least one board member who is a financial expert; and full participation by board members in decision-making. As we note above, the organization should adopt a conflict of interest policy even though the IRS does not formally require the policy.[121]

Several states have introduced SOX-like statutes applicable to nonprofits. For example, California adopted the Nonprofit Integrity Act in 2004.[122] Charities required to register with the California Attorney General and having gross revenues over $2 million must prepare audited financial statements and make them publicly available.[123] Compensation of the chief executive and chief financial officers must be approved by the board or appropriate committee; the board needs to determine that the compensation is "just and reasonable."[124] Nonprofit corporations must appoint an audit committee that may include members who are not members of the board of directors.[125]

D. LIMITATIONS ON LIABILITY AND RISK MANAGEMENT

As we discuss above, incorporating does not relieve the board members of all possible liability for their actions though it provides important protections to the board members. You will have to read your state's nonprofit corporation act as well as case law to determine what limits on

---

[118] PEGGY M. JACKSON, SARBANES–OXLEY FOR NONPROFIT BOARDS: A NEW GOVERNANCE PARADIGM 10 (2006).

[119] *Id.* at 11.

[120] *Id.* at 19.

[121] For an example of a conflict of interest policy from the IRS, see *Instructions for Form 1023 Additional Material—Appendix A: Sample Conflict of Interest Policy*, INTERNAL REV. SERV., http://www.irs.gov/instructions/i1023/ar03.html.

[122] CAL. GOV'T CODE §§ 12580–12599.7 (West 2012) (amending the Uniform Supervision of Trustees for Charitable Purposes Act).

[123] CAL. GOV'T CODE § 12586(e).

[124] CAL. GOV'T CODE § 12586(g).

[125] CAL. GOV'T CODE § 12586(e).

board member liability exist in your state. Some states have adopted statutes granting volunteers of a nonprofit organization immunity from liability unless the volunteers engage in willful conduct or are grossly negligent.[126] Based on your research, you will have to decide what you must, should and can include in the organization's articles of incorporation or the bylaws.

The Federal Volunteer Protection Act (FVPA)[127] provides additional protection from liability for volunteers in the performance of services for nonprofit organizations. The FVPA protects the volunteer of a nonprofit organization or government from liability for harm caused by an act or omission of the volunteer on behalf of the entity if 1) the volunteer was acting within the scope of his or her responsibility; 2) the volunteer was properly licensed, certified or authorized (if required); 3) the harm was not caused by willful or criminal misconduct, gross negligence, reckless misconduct or a conscious, flagrant indifference to the rights or safety of the person harmed; and 4) the harm was not caused by the volunteer operating a motor vehicle or other vehicle for which the state requires a license or insurance.[128] The FVPA contains some exceptions to the liability immunity, including, among others, any misconduct that includes a crime of violence and a hate crime.[129]

[handwritten margin note: Protection of volunteers from liability]

You may decide to counsel the organization on other risk management issues as well.[130] One question the organization will have to decide is what type of insurance it wants or needs to carry. The board of directors will need to decide whether and when to obtain Director and Officer (D & O) Liability Insurance.[131] These policies have the option of Employment Practices Liability coverage, which cover claims by employees for mistreatment or discrimination.[132] While lawsuits against directors are rare, employment claims tend to be the most likely basis for a suit.[133] A separate reason for purchasing D & O insurance, even for an organization whose officers and directors are all volunteers and thus retain immunity

---

[126] MARILYN E. PHELAN & ROBERT J. DESIDERIO, NONPROFIT ORGANIZATIONS LAW & POLICY 154 (3d ed. 2010).

[127] 42 U.S.C. §§ 14501–5 (2010).

[128] 42 U.S.C. § 14503(a).

[129] 42 U.S.C. § 14503(d).

[130] The Nonprofit Risk Management Center has a number of publications that may be useful to you and your client. *See, e.g., Online Resources and Web–Based Tutorials*, NONPROFIT RISK MGMT. CENTER (2012), https://www.nonprofitrisk.org/tools/overview.asp.

[131] For a more detailed discussion of D & O Liability Insurance, see NONPROFITS' INSURANCE ALLIANCE OF CALIFORNIA & ALLIANCE OF NONPROFITS FOR INSURANCE, RISK RETENTION GROUP, DIRECTORS & OFFICERS: KEY FACTS ABOUT INSURANCE AND LEGAL LIABILITY (2008), *available at* http://insurancefornonprofits.org/Risk-Management-Booklets.cfm.

[132] For a more detailed discussion of this coverage, see Robert A. Machson & Joseph P. Monteleone, *Insurance Coverage for Wrongful Employment Practices Claims Under Various Liability Policies*, 49 BUS. LAW. 689 (1994).

[133] Jeff Jones, *D & O Claims Keep Climbing and Costing More to Settle*, NON–PROFIT TIMES, July 1, 2001, at 19.

under the FVPA, is that the insurance coverage can pay for the cost of legal counsel to enforce, in court, those immunity privileges.[134]

E. EMPLOYMENT ISSUES

You may be counseling the organization about the hiring of its staff, which might require that you and the board consider the difference between independent contractors and employees. If the persons paid by the organization qualify as employees, the employer will have to withhold applicable payroll taxes (federal, state and perhaps local) and regularly report wages, and pay any taxes withheld to the IRS and the state treasury department (or its equivalent).[135] In order to apply for tax-exemption from the IRS, the organization will need to apply for an Employer Identification Number (EIN). Once it has its EIN, the IRS may begin sending the quarterly reports to the organization. Even if it does not, the organization will need to report to the IRS once employees are hired. The organization will need to register with the state treasury department as well. The board will also have to make decisions about worker's compensation and unemployment compensation insurance. These differ from state to state so you will need to research these issues for your clients.[136]

IV. FEDERAL TAX REQUIREMENTS

The Code and accompanying regulations impose several restrictions on organizations requesting the charitable designation. As we stated above, nonprofit organizations are not forbidden from making a profit. Instead the Code places restrictions on how the organization's income can be distributed. The net earnings of the organizations cannot inure "to the benefit of any private shareholder or individual."[137] In addition, "carrying on propaganda, [or] . . . attempting . . . to influence legislation" cannot constitute a "substantial part" of the activities of the organization.[138] The rules are even stricter for intervening in any political campaign on behalf of (or in opposition to) any candidate for public office—the nonprofit may not engage in any activity at all.[139]

---

[134] 9A COUCH ON INSURANCE § 131–31 (3d ed. 2012).

[135] *See* INTERNAL REV. SERV., PUBLICATION E–EMPLOYER'S TAX GUIDE (2012), *available at* http://www.irs.gov/pub/irs-pdf/p15.pdf. *See also* INTERNAL REV. SERV., PUBLICATION 80–FEDERAL TAX GUIDE FOR EMPLOYERS IN THE U.S., VIRGIN ISLANDS, GUAM, AMERICAN SAMOA, AND THE COMMONWEALTH OF THE NORTHERN MARIANA ISLANDS (2012), *available at* http://www.irs.gov/pub/irs-pdf/p80.pdf. Your state treasury department may have a similar publication.

[136] For example, some states allow nonprofit organizations to self-insure for unemployment compensation.

[137] I.R.C. § 501(c)(3).

[138] *Id.*

[139] *Id.*

A. THE ORGANIZATIONAL AND OPERATIONAL TESTS

The IRS has created two tests in order to determine an organization's compliance with the statutory requirements for tax exemption. In order to be tax-exempt, an organization must be both *organized* and *operated* exclusively for one or more permissible exempt purposes.[140] Exempt purpose means any purpose specified in the regulations—religious, charitable, scientific, testing for public safety, literary, educational or prevention of cruelty to children or animals.[141] These tests are mirror images of each other, with the IRS looking to the provisions of the organizing documents as well as to how the organization operates in reality. A nonprofit corporation is organized exclusively for an exempt purpose only if its articles of incorporation limit the purpose of the organization to one or more exempt purposes and do not expressly empower the organization to engage, other than as an insubstantial part of its activities, in activities which are not in furtherance of one or more exempt purpose.[142] Conversely, an organization is not organized exclusively for one or more exempt purposes if its articles expressly empower it to carry on, other than insubstantially, activities that are not in furtherance of one or more exempt purposes.[143] The regulations require an organization to submit a "detailed statement of its proposed activities" as part of its application for exemption.[144]

The operational test looks to how the organization actually functions. The IRS looks to whether the organization engages primarily in activities that accomplish one or more of the exempt purposes specified in the regulations.[145] An organization will not be so regarded if "more than an insubstantial part of its activities is not in furtherance of an exempt purpose."[146] In order to satisfy this test, the organization's "resources must be devoted to purposes that qualify as exclusively charitable within section 501(c)(3) of the Code and the applicable regulations."[147] Although an organization might be engaged in only a single activity, that activity may be directed toward multiple purposes, both exempt and non-exempt. If the non-exempt purpose is substantial, the organization will not satisfy the operational test.[148] Whether an organization has a substantial non-

---

[140] 26 C.F.R. § 1.501(c)(3)–1 (2012).

[141] 26 C.F.R. § 1.501(c)(3)–1(d)(1)(i).

[142] 26 C.F.R. § 1.501(c)(3)–1(b)(1)(i).

[143] 26 C.F.R. § 1.501(c)(3)–1(b)(1)(iii).

[144] 26 C.F.R. § 1.501(c)(3)–1(b)(1)(v).

[145] 26 C.F.R. § 1.501(c)(3)–1(c)(1).

[146] *Id.*

[147] Rev. Rul. 72–369, 1972–2 C.B. 245.

[148] *See, e.g.,* KJ's Fund Raisers, Inc. v. Comm'r, 74 T.C.M. 669 (1997), *aff'd,* 166 F.3d 1200 (2d Cir. 1998); Manning Ass'n v. Comm'r, 93 T.C. 596 (1989); Copyright Clearance Ctr., Inc. v. Comm'r, 79 T.C. 793 (1982).

exempt purpose is a question of fact.[149] We discuss this issue in greater detail below.

The articles of incorporation cannot empower the organization to devote more than an insubstantial part of its activities to attempting to influence legislation, directly or indirectly to participate in or intervene in any political campaign on behalf of or in opposition to any candidate for public office, or engage in activities that characterize it as an action organization.[150] The organization may not directly or indirectly participate or intervene in any political campaign on behalf of or in opposition to any candidate for public office, even in an insubstantial amount.[151] An organization does not operate exclusively for an exempt purpose if its net earnings inure to the benefit of private individuals.[152] Finally, the organization's assets must be dedicated to an exempt purpose and the articles must provide that upon dissolution its assets are distributed for one or more exempt purposes, or to the federal, state or local unit of government. The organization's assets cannot be distributed to its members or shareholders upon dissolution.[153] These provisions form the basis for the "magic" language we discussed above which need to be included in the articles of incorporation and bylaws.[154]

B. EXEMPT PURPOSE

The regulations do not define "charitable" very specifically, instead stating that the term is used in its generally accepted legal sense and "not to be construed as limited by separate enumeration . . . of other tax-exempt purposes which may fall within the broad outlines of charity as developed by judicial opinions."[155] Some examples of charitable purposes are relief of the poor and distressed or of the underprivileged; advancement of religion; advancement of education or science; erection or maintenance of public buildings, monuments or works; lessening of the burdens of government; the promotion of social welfare; lessening neighborhood tensions; eliminating prejudice and discrimination; defending human rights and civil rights; and combating community deterioration and juvenile delinquency. Any analysis involving an applicant's claim to meet one or more of these factors will be fact-specific.

Two particular areas that have presented concerns for the IRS are organizations involved in economic development and organizations in-

---

[149] Church by Mail, Inc. v. Comm'r, 48 T.C.M. 471 (1984), *aff'd*, 765 F.2d 1387 (9th Cir. 1985).

[150] 26 C.F.R. § 1.501(c)(3)–1(b)(3)(iii).

[151] 26 C.F.R. § 1.501(c)(3)–1(c)(3)(iii).

[152] 26 C.F.R. § 1.501(c)(3)–1(c)(2).

[153] 26 C.F.R. § 1.501(c)(3)–1(b)(4).

[154] *See supra* text accompanying note 70.

[155] 26 C.F.R. § 1.501(c)(3)–1(d)(2).

volved in housing development, because each so closely resembles traditional for-profit business activity. Economic development activities have, however, been found to help relieve the poor and distressed and promote social welfare. Through Revenue Rulings and Private Letters Rulings, the IRS has defined the realm of permitted activities. The IRS granted tax-exempt status to an organization working to stimulate economic development in economically depressed areas of a city by making loans and purchasing equity interests in businesses unable to obtain funds from conventional sources.[156] Providing needed housing is another tool for community development. The IRS has found that helping low-income families interested in building their own homes combats community deterioration and assists the underprivileged.[157] The IRS has issued guidelines for organizations involved in housing development that want to qualify for the charitable designation under the "relief of the poor and distressed."[158]

The regulations define "educational" as the instruction or training of the individual for the purpose of improving or developing his capabilities, or instruction of the public on subjects useful to the individual and beneficial to the community.[159] An organization may be educational even if it advocates a particular opinion or view as long as it presents a "sufficiently full and fair exposition of the pertinent facts" so as to permit someone to form an independent opinion or conclusion.[160] Primary and secondary schools, colleges and trade schools are all educational, as are museums, zoos, planetariums, symphony orchestras and organizations that present public discussion groups, panels, lectures and similar programs.[161]

[margin handwriting: educational purpose]

We discuss charitable and educational organizations here as those are the ones you are most likely to encounter in your work. You can look to the regulations and other IRS resources if you represent organizations in other categories. We will discuss below the question of exempt purpose when organizations engage in income-generating activities.

C. PRIVATE INUREMENT

The Code provides that an organization seeking tax-exempt status must ensure that "no part of the earnings of . . . [the organization] inures to the benefit of any private shareholder or individual."[162] Private shareholders or individuals are those persons having a "personal and

---

[156] Rev. Rul. 74–587, 1974–2 C.B. 162. *Cf.* Rev. Rul. 76–419, 1976–2 C.B. 146; Rev. Rul. 77–111, 1977–1 C.B. 144.

[157] Rev. Rul. 70–585, 1970–2 C.B. 115.

[158] Rev. Proc. 96–32, 1996–20 I.R.B. 14.

[159] 26 C.F.R. § 1.501(c)(3)–1(d)(3)(i).

[160] *Id.*

[161] 26 C.F.R. § 1.501(c)(3)–1(d)(3)(ii).

[162] I.R.C. § 501(c)(3).

private interest in the activities of the organization."[163] Other "individuals" means "insiders," persons who have some control over the organization or persons who have a personal or private interest in the activities of the organization.[164] The private inurement prohibition is absolute; it applies even if the inurement is insubstantial.[165] The penalty is loss of the organization's tax exemption (or denial of the initial application).[166] The concept, however, does not prohibit an organization from engaging in remunerative transactions with its founders, members or officers; instead, these transactions must be tested against a standard of "reasonableness."[167]

The issue of private inurement arises most commonly in questions of excessive compensation.[168] It also arises in the rental of property, lending of money, use of facilities or other assets, involvement in joint ventures including partnerships, the sale of assets, and other contractual arrangements with board members. The concept of private inurement looks to see if the board member will receive a benefit from participation on the board beyond that which any business would receive as a result of the transaction. Would the board member receive the contract if he or she were not on the board? Is the organization paying a fair market value for the services of the board member's company? What if the board member were giving the company's services at a reduced cost to the organization? How will we know what other companies might charge for the same services?

In 1996, Congress enacted "intermediate sanctions" for activity that amounts to private inurement.[169] These sanctions impose taxes on the "insiders" who enter into transactions that result in "excess benefit" to the insider.[170] The sanctions also impose penalties on the organization. An excess benefit transaction is one in which "an economic benefit is provided by an applicable tax-exempt organization directly or indirectly to or for the use of any disqualified person . . . if the value of the economic benefit provided exceeds the value of the consideration (including the performance of services) received for providing such benefit."[171] A "disqualified person" is defined as anyone "in a position to exercise substantial influence over the affairs of the organization."[172] Disqualified persons can in-

---

[163] 26 C.F.R. § 1.501(a)–1(c).

[164] PHELAN & DESIDERIO, *supra* note 126, at 254.

[165] *Id.*

[166] HOPKINS, *supra* note 37, at 508.

[167] *Id.* at § 20.1.

[168] *See, e.g.*, Church of Scientology of Cal v. Comm'r, 823 F.2d 1310, 1316 (9th Cir. 1987) (holding that "payment of excessive salaries will result in inurement").

[169] I.R.C. § 4958.

[170] HOPKINS, *supra* note 37, at 510–13.

[171] I.R.C. § 4958(c)(1)(A).

[172] I.R.C. § 4958(f)(1)(A).

clude voting members of the organization's board, the chief executive officer (such as the President or Executive Director), the chief operating officer, the chief financial officer, other officers, directors, trustees and family members of any person who has substantial influence over the organization and an entity in which such a person owns 35 percent.[173] The Code provides for a tax on the excess benefit.[174]

D. PRIVATE BENEFIT

An organization must serve a public rather than a private purpose in order to be tax-exempt. The regulations forbid organizations from being "organized or operated for the benefit of private interests such as designated individuals, the creator or his/her family, shareholders of the organization, or persons controlled, directly or indirectly, by such private interests."[175]

The doctrine of private benefit, flowing from the common law rule that a charitable trust must be formed for an unselfish purpose, requires that an organization's property and income must benefit a sufficiently large and indefinite charitable class rather than specific private individuals.[176] The concept of private benefit is broader than the related concept of private inurement since it prohibits benefits to more than individual "insiders" of the organization.[177] As an example, an art museum that exhibits work of unknown artists and sells the work of the artists, with 90 percent of the proceeds going to the artists (and 10 percent going to the museum), operates for a private benefit.[178]

E. POLITICAL ACTIVITY BY CHARITABLE ORGANIZATIONS

The IRS regulations limit or prohibit two types of political activities—lobbying and participation in political campaigns. The regulations label an organization that engages in lobbying or political activity as an "action organization."[179] No "substantial part" of the activities of a 501(c)(3) organization may involve "attempting to influence legislation by propaganda or otherwise."[180]

A public charity can advocate, as an insubstantial part of its activities, for the adoption or rejection of legislation.[181] The regulations differ-

---

[173] I.R.C. § 4958(f)(1)(B)–(C).

[174] I.R.C. § 4958.

[175] 26 C.F.R. § 1.501(c)(3)–1(d)(1)(ii).

[176] RESTATEMENT (THIRD) OF TRUSTS § 28 (2003).

[177] HOPKINS, *supra* note 37, at 537.

[178] 26 C.F.R. § 1.501(c)(3)–1(d)(1)(iii).

[179] 26 C.F.R. § 1.501(c)(3)–1(c)(1)(iv).

[180] 26 C.F.R. § 1.501(c)(3)–1(c)(3)(ii).

[181] *Id.*

entiate between grassroots and direct lobbying but interpret "lobbying" in an expansive way. Direct lobbying is any attempt to influence any legislation through communication with any member or employee of a legislative body, or any government official who may participate in the formulation of legislation.[182] Communication with legislators or government officials will be considered lobbying only if it refers to specific legislation and reflects a view on such legislation.[183] Grassroots lobbying is the attempt to influence legislation by affecting the opinion of the general public.[184] These types of communication are considered lobbying if they refer to the specific legislation, reflect a view on such legislation and encourage the person receiving it to take action with respect to the legislation (for example, contacting the legislator or staff member).[185] Legislation includes any act of Congress, a state legislature, a local council or governing body or by the public in a referendum, initiative, constitutional amendment or similar procedure.[186]

Executive, judicial and administrative bodies are not included in the definition of "legislative bodies."[187] Lobbying does not include non-partisan analysis, study or research, including making the results available to the public or governmental bodies or officials.[188] These studies must involve an independent and objective exposition of a subject matter but may advocate a particular position or viewpoint so long as there is a sufficiently full and fair exposition of the relevant facts to allow individuals to form their own opinion or reach their own conclusion. Also excluded from the definition of lobbying is the provision of technical assistance or advice to a governmental body in response to a request by the governmental body, and appearance before, or communication with, any legislative body with respect to a decision of that body that would adversely affect the organization.[189]

Neither the Code nor the regulations defines "substantial." The limits on influencing legislation involve more than simply a limit on financial expenditures; they include limits on the expenditure of time. One court has rejected a percentage test in determining substantiality, dismissing it as blurring the "complexity of balancing the organization's activities in relation to its objectives and circumstances."[190] The question of substanti-

---

[182] 26 C.F.R. § 56.4911–2(b)(1)(i) (2012).
[183] 26 C.F.R. § 56.4911–2(b)(1)(ii).
[184] 26 C.F.R. § 56.4911–2(b)(2).
[185] *Id.*
[186] 26 C.F.R. § 1.501(c)(3)–1(c)(3).
[187] 26 C.F.R. §§ 56.4911–2(d)(3)–(4).
[188] 26 C.F.R. § 56.4911–2(c)(1).
[189] 26 C.F.R. §§ 56.4911–2(c)(3)–(4).
[190] Christian Echoes Nat'l Ministry, Inc. v. United States, 470 F.2d 849, 855 (10th Cir. 1972).

ality is a facts-and-circumstances test, "not always dependent upon time or expenditure percentages."[191]

The Code creates a "safe harbor" exception to the "substantial" lobbying restrictions by allowing organizations to elect an expenditure test instead of the "substantiality" test.[192] The Code sets out the permissible lobbying expenditures for an organization that makes the election; these limits are set out in terms of both percentages and absolute numbers.[193] Organizations that choose to be evaluated under the "expenditure" test must file Form 5768, entitled "Election/Revocation of Election by an Eligible § 501(c)(3) Organization to Make Expenditures to Influence Legislation."[194] Public charities that have made the § 501(h) election must pay an excise tax on the activities meant to influence legislation above the § 501(h) limits.[195] Organizations that do not make the § 501(h) election and lose their exempt status as a result of excess lobbying must also pay an excise tax on the lobbying expenditures.[196] The managers of such organizations are also subject to the excise tax.[197]

Charities cannot participate or intervene, directly or indirectly, in any political campaign on behalf of or in opposition to any candidate for public office.[198] This prohibition is absolute. A candidate for public office is an individual who "offers himself, or is proposed by others, as a contestant for an elective public office" including at the national, state or local level.[199] Prohibited activities include the publication or distribution of written or printed statements or the making of oral statements on behalf of or in opposition to such a candidate. The biggest question is distinguishing between participation/intervention and voter education/civic activities. Several Revenue Rulings deal with these questions. In addition to losing its tax-exempt status, an organization that engages in political activity is subject to an excise tax. The Code imposes a tax on the organization's political campaign expenditures.[200]

---

[191] Nationalist Movement v. Comm'r, 102 T.C. 558, 589 (1994), aff'd, 37 F.3d 216 (5th Cir. 1994).

[192] *Measuring Lobbying Activity: Expenditure Test*, INTERNAL REV. SERV. (Aug. 14, 2012), http://www.irs.gov/Charities-&-Non-Profits/Measuring-Lobbying-Activity:--Expenditure-Test.

[193] I.R.C. § 4911(c)(2). For example, for organizations with exempt purpose expenditures over $500,000, the lobbying nontaxable amount is 20 percent of the exempt purpose expenditures. *Id.*

[194] I.R.C. § 501(h).

[195] I.R.C. § 4911; 26 C.F.R. § 56.4911–9.

[196] I.R.C. § 4912(a) (2011).

[197] I.R.C. § 4912(b). The managers of organizations who approved the lobbying expenditure are also subject to a tax unless they can prove the expenditures are not willful and due to reasonable error. The managers face joint and several liability. I.R.C. § 4912(d)(3).

[198] 26 C.F.R. § 1.501(c)(3)–1(c)(3)(iii).

[199] *Id.*

[200] I.R.C. § 4955(a)(1)–(2) (2011).

This area is complex and it will require further analysis of the cir-cumstances of the organization you represent. For some organizations, these issues are present from the very start of the organization since the incorporators or board envision the organization being involved in advo-cacy. For other organizations these issues arise only as the organization's programs mature. And for others, they will not arise at all.

F.   INCOME GENERATING ACTIVITIES

Increasingly, nonprofit organizations are looking to income-generating activities as a way to diversify their funding base as well to carry out their mission. A health clinic may charge fees for its services or an organization that works with returning citizens (from prison) may run a resale shop that provides job training as well as generate income for the organization. Income-generating activities raise two questions for chari-table organizations. First, at what point might "commercial" activity jeopardize the organization's tax-exempt status (or keep the organization from receiving the status in the first place)? Second, when might the or-ganization have to pay taxes on the income generated from these activi-ties? This is a complicated (and some might say confusing) area of law that will require that we go back to some of the issues we discussed in the "exempt purpose" discussion above.

No clear test exists which guides an organization in determining whether and to what extent commercial activity may jeopardize its tax exemption. Organizations are exempt if they are organized and operated exclusively for the exempt purposes outlined in the Code. Under the or-ganizational test, an organization's organizing documents may not em-power it to engage, other than as an insubstantial part of its activities, in activities that are not in furtherance of an exempt purpose.[201] The regula-tions seem to prohibit "substantial" unrelated business activities. Similar-ly, under the operational test, "exclusively," means "primarily" not "sole-ly."[202] An organization will not qualify for exemption if "more than an in-substantial part of its activities is not in furtherance of an exempt pur-pose."[203] An organization can operate a trade or business as a substantial part of its activities if the operation of such trade or business is in fur-therance of the organization's exempt purpose or purposes and if the or-ganization is not organized or operated primarily for the primary purpose of carrying on an unrelated trade or business.[204] An organization's prima-ry purpose is to be determined by all the facts and circumstances, "includ-

---

[201] 26 C.F.R. § 1.501(c)(3)–1(b)(1)(i).

[202] HOPKINS, *supra* note 37, at 72.

[203] 26 C.F.R. § 1.503(c)(3)–1(c)(1).

[204] 26 C.F.R. § 1.501(c)(3)–1(e).

ing the size and extent of the trade or business and the size or extent of the activities which are in furtherance of one of more exempt purpose."[205]

The Supreme Court has stated that the "presence of a single . . . [non-exempt] purpose, if substantial in nature, will destroy the exemption regardless of the number or importance of . . . exempt purposes."[206] Non-exempt activity will not result in the loss or denial of exemption where it is "only incidental and less than substantial."[207] No definition of the concept "insubstantial" exists in case law or in the regulations. If the organization has a non-exempt purpose in addition to an exempt purpose, Bruce Hopkins suggests inquiring whether the non-exempt purpose is primary or incidental to the exempt purpose. If the non-exempt purpose is substantial in nature, the exemption would be precluded.[208]

Courts have expressed concern with the "commercial hue" of an organization, interpreting the regulations as creating a "commerciality" test.[209] An activity is commercial if it has a direct counterpart in, or is conducted in the same manner as would be conducted by, for-profit organizations,[210] and some courts have looked to whether the nonprofit organization is in direct competition with for profit businesses.[211]

An organization does not lose its tax-exemption by engaging in insubstantial business activities, even if they are unrelated to its exempt purpose. Substantial business activities are allowed so long as they are "in furtherance of" an exempt purpose. Exemption is denied if unrelated business activities are "substantial" in relation to charitable activities because at that point the organization's primary purpose is the business.[212] Under this view, if the organization's unrelated business activities are "insubstantial," its exemption is secure and the only question is whether it has to pay tax unrelated business income tax (UBIT) on the income from the unrelated business activity.[213]

Organizations must pay taxes on the net income from any trade or business that is not substantially related to the exercise or performance

---

[205] Id.

[206] Better Bus. Bureau of DC v. United States, 326 U.S. 279, 283 (1945).

[207] St. Louis Union Tr. Co., v. United States, 374 F.2d 427, 431 (8th Cir. 1967). Hopkins cites several cases where courts have used this analysis as well as others where courts have rejected this analysis. HOPKINS, *supra* note 37, at 83–86.

[208] Id. at 83–86.

[209] Id. at 99–114.

[210] Id.

[211] Living Faith, Inc. v. Comm'r, 950 F.2d 365 (7th Cir. 1991).

[212] JAMES J. FISHMAN & STEPHEN SCHWARZ, TAXATION OF NONPROFIT ORGANIZATIONS: CASES & MATERIALS 356–57 (2d ed. 2006) (citing JOINT COMMITTEE ON TAXATION, HISTORICAL DEVELOPMENT AND PRESENT LAW OF THE FEDERAL TAX EXEMPTION FOR CHARITIES AND OTHER TAX–EXEMPT ORGANIZATIONS 51–52 (2005)).

[213] Id. at 357.

by such organization of its exempt purpose.[214] The UBIT was established to deal with what was perceived as unfair competition on the part of nonprofits. To be classified as unrelated trade or business an activity must: 1) be a trade or business; 2) be "regularly carried on"; and 3) not be substantially related to the organization's exempt purpose.[215] A "trade or business" includes "any activity carried on for the production of income from the sale of goods or performance of services."[216] Intermittent activities are not seen as posing the threat of unfair competition. To be related to an exempt purpose, the activity must "contribute importantly" to the accomplishment of the exempt purpose.[217] The IRS will pay particular attention to the size and extent of the activity so that if the business is conducted on a scale larger than necessary to carry out the exempt purpose, it is more likely to be seen as unrelated. The IRS also considers the potential for competition with for-profit businesses. There are several exclusions from UBIT including passive investment income such as dividend, annuities, rents and royalties.[218]

Let us offer a few examples to show how the questions of tax exemption and UBIT might work. An organization that operates a furniture store as a means of transitional employment to residents of a halfway house is entitled to tax-exempt status because employment in the store is limited to residents and outside persons are only employed to train and supervise the residents.[219] An organization which operated a discount retail grocery store to provide on-the-job training to the hard-core unemployed did not qualify for tax exemption because the purpose of the store was to provide discount groceries to the surrounding low-income community, the majority of the store's income was used to pay the salaries of the employees, most of whom were not members of the hard-core unemployed, and the store operated similarly to for-profit grocery stores in the area.[220] A museum dedicated to folk art does not pay UBIT on the sale of reproductions of artistic works and books related to art but pays UBIT on the sale of scientific books and souvenir items relating to the city where the museum is located.[221]

When presented with these issues, you will have to conduct further research and engage in a rigorous analysis of the facts of the particular organization and its proposed activities.

---

[214] I.R.C. § 513 (2011).

[215] 26 C.F.R. § 1.513–1(a) (2011).

[216] 26 C.F.R. § 1.513–1(b).

[217] 26 C.F.R. § 1.513–1(d).

[218] I.R.C. § 512(b) (2011); I.R.C. § 514 (2011).

[219] Rev. Rul. 75–472, 1975–2 C.B. 208.

[220] Rev. Rul. 73–127, 1973–1 C.B. 221.

[221] Rev. Rul. 73–105, 1973–1 C.B. 264.

Though social ventures are becoming increasingly necessary for and popular with nonprofit organizations and their funders, the area is complicated, raising the possibility of organizations jeopardizing their tax-exempt status as well as having to pay taxes on some of their income.

G. JOINT VENTURES AND SUBSIDIARIES

Exempt organizations may want to create separate but related organizations, whether nonprofit or for-profit, for several reasons. An organization may want to separate liability of two or more distinct activities so as to protect the organization's assets, particularly if some activities are riskier than others. Organizations may also want to separate for-profit activity into a separate entity so as not to jeopardize the tax-exempt status of the organization. An organization may want a subsidiary to carry on a business that is not substantially related to its exempt purpose. Another organization may want to create a subsidiary that will carry out advocacy activity.[222] An organization may also want to enter into a joint venture with a for-profit entity that involves the creation of another for-profit entity.

There are several methods by which an exempt organization may affiliate with a separate organization. If the subsidiary will be nonprofit, the parent can control the stock of the subsidiary if your state allows nonprofit corporations to issue stock or the parent organization may control the board of directors of the subsidiary.[223] If the affiliate will be a for-profit subsidiary, the "parent" corporation can own the stock in the subsidiary. Most often, the nonprofit organization will choose to create a corporation so the income of the subsidiary is taxed at the subsidiary level and the profits can flow to the nonprofit parent in the form of non-taxable dividends. In order for the profits not to be taxed at the parent corporation's level, the subsidiary must be established for a "real and substantial business function" and not be an instrumentality of the parent.[224]

If the nonprofit will be affiliated with a for-profit entity in a joint venture, the nonprofit can own stock in the for-profit corporation, be a partner in a partnership or be a member of an LLC. A charitable organization may form and/or participate in a partnership or LLC with another organization not engaged in exempt activities and still meet the opera-

---

[222] 26 C.F.R. § 1.504(c)(4)–1(a)(2)(i), (ii). Social welfare organizations (sometimes known as "(c)(4) organizations") are primarily engaged in promoting in some way the common good and general welfare of the community. They can be substantially involved in lobbying activities but only insubstantially involved in campaign intervention. These organizations are tax-exempt but they cannot attract tax-deductible gifts.

[223] One way that the parent could control the board of directors of the subsidiary is by having the power to name all the board members. In this case, you may want to counsel the parent to name a majority of "independent" directors, avoiding complete overlap of the board of directors of the parent and subsidiary so as to lessen the potential for piercing the corporate veil as well as for SOX reasons.

[224] I.R.S. Gen. Couns. Mem. 39,326 (Jan. 17, 1985).

tional test if its participation in the partnership or LLC furthers the exempt purpose and the partnership or LLC arrangement allows the organization to act exclusively in furtherance of its exempt purpose (and only incidentally for the benefit of the for profit partners).[225] A nonprofit organization must have "formal or informal control [over the joint venture] sufficient to ensure furtherance of charitable purposes."[226]

We can just skim the surface here of this very complex and changing area. Several scholars are writing in this area,[227] and you will need to research the implications of any partnership or joint venture carefully if you are assisting a nonprofit client in that endeavor. As with subsidiaries, income from joint ventures may be subject to unrelated business income tax. A nonprofit will have to pay UBIT on the income coming from an entity it controls, if it is not substantially related to its exempt purpose, to the extent the income was not taxed to the subsidiary or joint venture.[228]

V. MISCELLANEOUS CONSIDERATIONS

A. FILING ANNUAL RETURNS AND REPORTS

An exempt organization generally will have three different yearly reporting requirements. First, it may have to file an annual report with the state's Secretary of State or agency where it incorporated. Second, the organization may have to file an annual report with the state Attorney General. The report to the Attorney General usually consists of financial reporting requirements. Lastly, an organization must file an annual information return with the IRS, known as Form 990. Organizations with revenue under $50,000 (using 2012 figures) can file the electronic version of Form 990 on the IRS web page (Form 990–N). Organizations with income over that amount will either file Form 990–EZ or the standard Form 990 depending on their income and assets. Organizations that do not file information returns for three consecutive years will have their tax-exempt status revoked, as thousands of organizations learned in 2011.[229] An organization which has its exempt status revoked in this manner can request retroactive reinstatement by filing Form 1023 or 1024 and paying

---

[225] Rev. Rul. 98–15, 1998–1 C.B. 718. See Rev. Rul. 2004–51, 2004–1 C.B. 974 for a discussion of whether an ancillary joint venture is related to an organization's exempt purpose.

[226] Redlands Surgical Serv. v. Comm'r, 113 T.C. 47, 92–93 (1999), aff'd 242 F.3d 904 (9th Cir. 2001) (holding that ceding "effective control" of partnership activities impermissibly serves private interests).

[227] See John D. Colombo, In Search of Private Benefit, 58 FLA. L. REV. 1063 (2006); Darryl K. Jones, The Greedy and the Good in Nonprofit/For–Profit Partnerships, 53 EXEMPT ORG. TAX REV. 69 (2006); Phil Royalty & Donna Steel Flynn, Not–For–Profit/For–Profit Joint Ventures: A White Paper, 25 EXEMPT ORG. TAX REV. 37 (1999).

[228] I.R.C. § 512(b)(13).

[229] I.R.C. § 6033. See Nicole S. Dandridge, Choking Out Local Community Service Organizations: Rising Federal Tax Regulation and Its Impact on Small Nonprofit Entities, 99 KY. L.J. 695 (2011).

the application fee.[230] The IRS may also impose penalties for failure to file returns or for filing returns late.[231]

Organizations also use Form 990 as a means to notify the IRS of amendments to their bylaws and articles of incorporation.[232]

B. EXPEDITING THE FEDERAL RECOGNITION APPLICATION

An organization can ask the IRS to expedite the processing of its application for recognition as an exempt organization. Normally the IRS will only do this if a grant depends on the determination of exemption.[233]

C. DISSOLVING A NONPROFIT ORGANIZATION

If a corporation dissolves, it must do so by following the process established within in the state. It may have to notify the Attorney General as well as the Secretary of State. The organization must also notify the IRS by filing its last tax return.[234] As we noted at the beginning of this chapter, an exempt organization must arrange its affairs so that the remaining assets transfer to another exempt organization when it dissolves.

D. CONDUCTING BUSINESS IN ANOTHER STATE

Organizations incorporated in one state can usually carry out activities in another state by registering in the second state as a foreign corporation. The applicable state's nonprofit statute will spell out the requirements for registration.

E. GROUP EXEMPTION

When organizations are related to one another, as is the case with chapters or branches of an organization or congregations within larger churches, the IRS allows the related organizations to file for exemption using a streamlined process when the central organization already has IRS recognition as exempt. The central organization applies for the streamlined treatment by sending a letter to the IRS, since there is no form for this process, and provides the IRS a copy of the governing docu-

---

[230] *See* INTERNAL REV. SERV., INTERNAL REVENUE BULLETIN 2011–25 (2011), *available at* http://www.irs.gov/irb/2011–25_IRB/ar10.html.

[231] I.R.C. § 6652(c)(1)(A) (2011).

[232] *Form 990 Specific Instructions*, INTERNAL REV. SERV. (2012), http://www.irs.gov/instructions/i990/ch02.html.

[233] *Applying for Exemption: Expediting Application Processing*, INTERNAL REV. SERV. (Aug. 2, 2012), http://www.irs.gov/Charities-&-Non-Profits/Applying-for-Exemption:--Expediting-Application-Processing.

[234] The return is due four months and fifteen days after the date of the organization's termination. INTERNAL REV. SERV., PUBLICATION 4779–FACTS ABOUT TERMINATING OR MERGING YOUR EXEMPT ORGANIZATION 1 (2009), *available at* http://www.irs.gov/pub/irs-pdf/p4779.pdf.

ment that sets out the relationship between the local and central organizations; certifies that the related organizations are operated by or in conjunction with the central organization; describes how the organizations are related to one another; and provides financial information regarding the related organizations. The central organization must certify each year that the local organizations continue to be related to it and continue to meet the requirements of being exempt.[235]

F. CROSS-BORDER GIVING

Contributions to domestic charitable organizations will not be deductible if the IRS concludes that the organization is serving as an agent to or as a channel for a foreign charitable organization. Domestic organizations in general may contribute to foreign organizations, but they need to be especially careful not to jeopardize their tax-exempt status by ensuring that their funds are being used for exempt purposes.[236] Contributions to foreign organizations are not tax deductible unless permitted by a tax treaty.[237]

VI. CONCLUSION

In this chapter we hoped to introduce you to some of the key legal considerations in representing charitable organizations and to provide you with an overview of the process of creating these entities. As you have seen, representation of these entities is complex but with that complexity comes some very interesting lawyering challenges. Charitable organizations share many attributes with for-profit entities but have unique attributes—especially regarding oversight by state agencies and the IRS.

---

[235] Rev. Proc. 80–27, 1980–1 C.B. 677.

[236] See Rev. Proc. 92–94, 1992–2 C.B. 507 for the rules a private foundation must follow in making a grant to a foreign grantee. *See also* Rev. Rul. 63–252, 1963–2 C.B. 101.

[237] *See* INTERNAL REV. SERV., PUBLICATION 526: CHARITABLE CONTRIBUTIONS 6 (2011), *available at* http://www.irs.gov/pub/irs-pdf/p526.pdf. The U.S. has tax treaties with Canada, Mexico and Israel.

CHAPTER 13

AN INTRODUCTION TO INTELLECTUAL PROPERTY CONCEPTS

■ ■ ■

Your small business and nonprofit clients will frequently produce some intellectual property as part of their business operations. Often, the intellectual property will have some value, and be worth protecting in some way. You might find yourself needing to offer some counseling to a client about the options available for protecting that property. You will also find that clients will not own the intellectual property they need to use, and will need your advice about how they might use materials developed and owned by others. This chapter will review some basic, fundamental concepts about the three most typical intellectual property devices—copyright, trademark, and patent. Each of these areas represents an enormously rich and complex body of law. Law schools offer full courses on each topic, and you will find countless books and multivolume treatises on each as well.[1] This very summary treatment, therefore, will only skim the surface of the substantive law represented here, but our hope is to orient you so you might plan your specific research projects appropriately.

I. COPYRIGHT

When an author creates a work of intellectual property, she or he possesses the exclusive rights to reproduce, adapt, distribute, or otherwise display the work. Those rights are known as the author's "copyright." The copyright exists in copyrightable works as soon as the author creates the work in a tangible form. Copyrights provide for a temporary, government-sanctioned monopoly on the use and distribution of the author's work. To understand this area better, let us suggest a simple example, and we will then use that example to highlight some typical questions arising within the copyright doctrine and practice.

An Example

The Community Day Center of Newton, Inc. (CDCN) is a nonprofit organization offering daytime shelter and supportive services to homeless individuals, who typically may not remain in

---

[1] *See, e.g.*, ROBERT A. GORMAN ET AL., COPYRIGHT CASES AND MATERIALS (7th ed. 2006); JANE C. GINSBURG, TRADEMARK AND UNFAIR COMPETITION LAW CASES (2007); F. SCOTT KIEFF ET AL., PRINCIPLES OF PATENT LAW (5th ed. 2011).

their nighttime shelters during the day. CDCN's executive director, Eben Taylor, a salaried employee, writes a three-page document describing the effect homelessness has on individuals and families, and distributes that paper to the public, to the media, and to foundations to whom CDCN applies for grant funding. Taylor also uploads the paper on to the CDCN website for others to find and read. The paper includes narrative descriptions and arguments, charts, and a photograph taken by Lydia Forbes, a volunteer at the day shelter.

The CDCN example suggests the following questions:

(1) Is this three-page document protected by copyright? What about the photograph that accompanies it?

(2) If and when it is protected, who owns the copyright, and for how long?

(3) What effect does the copyright status have? In other words, if the owner were to enforce the copyright, what does that mean in practice?

(4) What effect, if any, does the posting of the document to the CDCN web site have?

The following sections will address each of these basic questions.

A. HOW COPYRIGHT OCCURS

To answer the first question, whether this work is or can be protected, we need to understand two separate concepts: what materials are *eligible* to be copyrighted, and, if the work is eligible, how copyright attaches.

To be *copyrightable*, a work must be fixed in tangible form, it must be an original work of authorship, and it must come within the subject matter of copyright.[2] In general, the governing law determining this arises from two statutes, the Copyright Act of 1976,[3] effective on January 1, 1978, and the Berne Convention Implementation Act (BCIA), effective March 1, 1989.[4] (The BCIA permitted the United States to coordinate some of its copyright law with international standards.[5]) Section 102(a) of the Copyright Act of 1976 provides for eight categories of copyrightable works: literary works (e.g., a short story or a political opinion article);

---

[2] Balt. Orioles, Inc. v. Major League Baseball Players Ass'n, 805 F.2d 663 (7th Cir. 1986).

[3] 17 U.S.C. § 101 et seq. The 1976 act was amended several times before the 1989 Act.

[4] 17 U.S.C. §§ 412, 504(c).

[5] *See* Randy Gordon, *A Hole in Need of Mending: Copyright and the Individual Marking of Advertisements Published in Collective Works,* 13 SMU SCI. & TECH. L. REV. 1, 6 (2009). The Berne Convention occurred in 1886. The United States only ratified the treaty in 1988. Irvin Molotsky, *Senate Approves Joining Copyright Convention,* N.Y. TIMES, Oct. 21, 1988, at C5.

musical works (a song); dramatic works (a play); pantomimes and choreo-graphic works (a dance routine); pictorial works (a photograph); graphic and sculptural works (a sculpture); audiovisual works (a film); sound recordings (a recorded song or CD); and architectural works (a design for a building).[6]

The document created by Eben Taylor for the CDCN easily fits the statutory list, as a "literary work" (which obviously need not be a work of fiction[7]), as does Lydia Forbes's photograph. Each is therefore "copyrightable." That determination, however, is sometimes quite contested. Copyright protects expression, but it does not protect ideas. (Ideas might be covered by *patent law*, though, as we discuss below.) In addition, the expression must show "some modicum of creativity" in order to be eligible for copyright protection.[8]

How, then, does the paper and the photograph obtain copyright protection? In order to secure the copyright protections, the author may do one or both of these options:

1)   Register with the United States Copyright Office; or

2)   Do nothing.

The "do nothing" option is a fundamental principle within copyright law. A copyrightable work obtains copyright status automatically, at the moment it is created in tangible form. There is no longer the requirement even to insert the formerly ubiquitous copyright notice symbol (©) on the document, as the 1989 BCIA eliminated that mandate.[9] Creation in tangible form means that one can see, touch, or hold the work, or experience it through a device such as a machine. There is no longer any requirement that the work be "published," although for older, pre–1978 works that factor might be relevant. (The act of publication might matter for other purposes, but not for copyright protection itself.)

So, when Taylor prints his paper, even before he distributes it, the paper has copyright protection. (*Who* owns the copyright is a separate

---

6   Copyright Act of 1976 § 102(a), 17 U.S.C. § 102 (2006); 3 PAUL GOLDSTEIN, GOLDSTEIN ON COPYRIGHT § 1.1 (3d ed. 2009).

7   *See, e.g.,* Am. Dental Ass'n v. Delta Dental Plans Ass'n, 126 F.3d 977, 979 (7th Cir. 1997) ("Scholarship that explicates important facts about the universe likewise is well within this domain. Einstein's articles laying out the special and general theories of relativity were original works even though many of the core equations, such as the famous E=mc2, express 'facts' and therefore are not copyrightable. Einstein could have explained relativity in any of a hundred different ways; another physicist could expound the same principles differently.").

8   FED. JUDICIAL CTR., COPYRIGHT LAW 16 (2d ed. 2006). *See, e.g.,* Feist Publ'ns Inc. v. Rural Tele. Serv. Co., 499 U.S. 340, 345 (1991) (denying copyright protection for a "white pages" telephone directory, as its expression was "devoid of even the slightest trace of creativity").

9   One caveat: The use of the © symbol does offer some protection against a claim of "innocent infringer" status, so in some settings its use still offers some advantages. Also, works created before 1978, or some created before 1989, will be treated differently from the description in the text.

question which we discuss below. Perhaps Taylor owns it; perhaps the Center owns it; or perhaps Lydia Forbes owns it. We shall see.) Since someone already possesses the copyright, are there any reasons for Taylor[10] then to register it with the Copyright Office? Registration does not create the copyright protection, but it does offer the following two potentially useful advantages:

1) If the owner of the copyright wishes to enforce it, the owner may not do so through a lawsuit without having registered the work before filing the suit.

2) A *timely* registration permits the owner to demand not just the actual, genuine damages caused by the copyright infringement, but also statutory damages (if they exceed or are easier to show than actual damages, which is very common), injunctive relief, and costs and, in rare cases, even attorney's fees. Also, a plaintiff may seek a court order requiring the infringing party to destroy the infringing goods. *Timely* means within three months of publication, or before any infringement, whichever is later.[11]

So Taylor will register the copyright if there is any indication that there is a need to enforce it formally. But note that even without the registration, the owner has every right to demand that an infringer stop infringing. Taylor therefore could lawfully send a "cease and desist" letter, including a threat of a damage action, even if he had not registered the copyright.

It is easy to register the copyright, using the Copyright Office's forms. For each item to be registered, Taylor would complete the application form on paper (for $50 as we write) or on-line (for $35), and submit it to the Copyright Office along with a copy of the material. The material stays with the Library of Congress (which might, at times, request a separate hard copy of the item if the owner files the application on-line[12]). In doing so, Taylor will confront the question of whether he should file one copyright application (for the document which includes the photo), or two applications, if the photograph is a separate item. We raise this issue here, without delving into its perhaps tricky resolution, to show you some of the nuances that the nonprofit's lawyers would need to sort out in order to advise the client appropriately.[13]

---

[10] Thanks to the operation of organizational law, we may comfortably refer to Taylor as the actor in this story regardless of whether he happens to own the copyright or not. He will act either on his own behalf, or as an authorized agent of CDCN.

[11] 17 U.S.C. § 412.

[12] United States Copyright Office, www.copyright.gov.

[13] Because Forbes took the photograph, she likely owns its copyright, unless she were serving as an employee of the CDCN or had an agreement ceding her rights to the CDCN. If she independently created the photo, the CDCN would have no right to use it without her permission. If she created the photograph as a "work made for hire" (see *infra*), then the permission question is resolved, but the photo itself likely will not gain its own protection through Taylor's registering

When should Taylor decide to register? He could wait until he discovers an infringement, register then, and file a federal court lawsuit, which requires registration as a condition. But if Taylor wants to take advantage of the major benefit of the possibility of statutory damages and attorney's fees, he must show that he registered either (1) *before* the infringement, or (2) if *after* the infringement, within three months of publication of the work.[14] So, in other words, Taylor basically has three months during which he can react if he encounters infringement without losing his rights to the statutory damages. After that, he cannot wait until he discovers infringement to register if he wants to maintain access to the statutory damages.

B.   WHO OWNS THE COPYRIGHT?

Whether something is eligible for copyright protection or how to register the item are often less controverted and easier to resolve than the question about who owns the copyright. Obviously, it can matter a lot who owns the rights in an expressive work. The owner is entitled to sell, assign, license and profit from the use of the work.

The Copyright Act of 1976 provides that the author or authors of a copyrightable work own the copyright.[15] Sensibly, the author will be the party who actually creates the work.[16] But in many settings (including in your clients' businesses, perhaps) the person who creates work does so on behalf of the business, as an employee or an independent contractor. If the product qualifies as a "work made for hire," the employer or person for whom the work was prepared is considered the author and owns the copyright, unless the parties have expressly agreed otherwise in writing and signed by both parties.[17] The obvious rationale behind the "work made for hire" doctrine is that when an employer compensates an employee to create a copyrightable work, the fruits of the employee's labor properly belong to the employer.[18] Classification as a "work made for hire" not only determines initial copyright ownership, and therefore who may register the copyright and who can sue for infringement, but also can affect the duration of the copyright, renewal rights, termination rights, and the right to import certain goods bearing the copyright.

---

the compilation. *See, e.g.,* ROGER E. SCHECHTER & JOHN R. THOMAS, PRINCIPLES OF COPYRIGHT LAW 89–90 (2010).

[14]   17 U.S.C. § 412.

[15]   17 U.S.C. § 201(a).

[16]   17 U.S.C. § 102.

[17]   17 U.S.C. §§ 7(b), 201(b).

[18]   Carter v. Helmsley–Spear, Inc., 861 F. Supp 303 (S.D.N.Y. 1994) (aff'd in part and rev'd in part on other grounds).

It could be very important, therefore, for your clients to know whether a work qualifies as a "work made for hire."[19] According to the Copyright Act of 1976, a "work made for hire" is either: (a) one prepared by an *employee* (that is, one who is not an independent contractor) within the scope of his or her employment; or (b) one of nine specified categories of specially ordered or commissioned works, provided that the parties expressly agree in writing that the work is made for hire. The nine categories are: (1) a contribution to a collective work; (2) part of a motion picture or other audiovisual work; (3) a translation; (4) a supplementary work; (5) a compilation; (6) an instructional text; (7) a test; (8) answer materials for a test; and (9) an atlas.[20] Therefore, if a business hires (that is, commissions) an independent contractor to create a copyrightable work, the business will own the copyright only if the parties so agree and the work fits one of those nine categories. Otherwise, the independent contractor will own the copyright, unless the contractor assigns the rights to the business through a separate contractual arrangement.

For the "employee" test, the Supreme Court has held that common law agency principles will determine whether a person qualifies as an employee or an independent contractor.[21] (As you likely know, that question arises in other contexts with small businesses, especially regarding availability of unemployment benefits and the matching of payroll taxes.) One lower court has helpfully identified five factors that will be significant in virtually every "work for hire" case: (1) the hiring party's right to control the manner and means of creation; (2) the skill required; (3) the provision of employee benefits; (4) the tax treatment of the hired party; and (5) whether the hiring party has the right to assign additional projects to the hired party.[22]

In the story involving CDCN, Eben Taylor, the executive director of the nonprofit, qualifies as an employee, and so absent some unusual facts or a separate agreement between Taylor and CDCN, the nonprofit employer will qualify as the owner of the copyright. But Lydia Forbes, the photographer, is a volunteer at the shelter, so her work cannot qualify as a "work made for hire." She will own the copyright to the photographs. Therefore, the Center may not use her photograph without her permission. Even though she may be a supporter of the Center, the nonprofit would be wise to obtain Forbes's written permission to include the photos in its work.

---

[19] 17 U.S.C. § 101.

[20] *Id.*

[21] Cmty. for Creative Non–Violence v. Reid, 490 U.S. 730, 751–52 (1989). The Court cited the Restatement of Agency as a source of guidance. *See id.* at 740–41, *citing* RESTATEMENT (SECOND) OF AGENCY § 228 (1958).

[22] Aymes v. Bonelli, 980 F.2d 857 (2d Cir. 1992). In your work for a business like CDCN, it will often be very important for the business to understand whether the people it pays to provide services qualify as employees or as independent contractors.

Besides original, direct authors (like Lydia Forbes and her photographs), and employers owning copyrights to works made for hire (like Eben Taylor as an employee of the CDCN), other copyright ownership questions may arise. Consider the following variations.

Joint Owners: One common issue in some clinical practices involves expressive works produced by a collaboration of persons, and then used in different formats. Consider, for instance, the creation of a music album,[23] with original music performed by several musicians. If a song on the album was written by one person and the lyrics by a collaborator, that song may qualify as a "joint work." A "joint work" is a work prepared by two or more authors with the intention that their contribution be merged into inseparable or interdependent parts of the unitary whole.[24] The authors of a joint work become co-owners of a copyright in the work, which means they are tenants in common, with each having the right to use or license the use of the work, subject to a duty to account to the other co-owners for any profit.

A joint work results if the authors of the work collaborated in creating it, or if each of the authors prepared his or her contribution with the knowledge and intention that it would be merged with the contributions of other authors. In order to constitute a joint work, it is essential that at the time the work is created, the co-authors intended that their respective contributions be merged, combined, or absorbed into an integrated unit, although the parts themselves may be either inseparable, as in the case of a novel or painting, or interdependent, as in the case of the words or music of songs. In this way, a joint work results if the authors intended that their contributions be embodied in a single unified work even if they did not work together or even know each other.[25]

Coauthors: When several authors contribute to a collective work not intending their contributions to be embodied in a single unified work, the authors are considered coauthors, and not joint authors. Each of the authors possesses separable, discrete rights in his or her creations. (If a different author arranged the separate works into a collective whole in some creative fashion, as the editor of some compilations, that author may possess the copyright to the collectivity's design and ideas.[26])

---

[23] We quaintly refer to collections of music, like CDs, as "albums." We tend to think of vinyl, 33 1/3 RPM records when we think of albums, but we also imagine CDs and the downloads which serve now as the most common vehicle for listeners to receive the collective work.

[24] 17 U.S.C. §§ 101 et seq.

[25] *See* 18 AM. JUR. 2D *Copyright and Literary Property* § 62 (2012). A song may be considered a joint work even where a lyricist wrote the words before he knew the identity of the composer, as long as that is what he intended. *See* Edwards B. Marks Music Corp. v. Jerry Vogel Music Co., 140 F.2d 266, 267 (2d Cir. 1944).

[26] *See* Eric C. Surette, *What Constitutes Derivative Work Under the Copyright Act of 1976*, 149 A.L.R. FED. 527 (1998).

Assignees and licensees: Owners of copyrights often transfer some or all of those rights to others. A full transfer, known as an assignment of rights, will vest ownership in the transferee of the rights sold or donated. A transfer is only effective if it is in writing.[27] Even a full and irrevocable transfer, however, may be cancelled by the author within a limited window of time, generally described for more recent transfers as a five year period after 35 years have passed from the original transfer.[28] A license, by contrast, maintains ownership in the author but permits lawful use of the material. A license can be exclusive (which also must be in writing to be effective), or non-exclusive (which need not be in writing).[29] Some non-profits, such as CDCN with its homelessness materials, may wish to permit broad use of their work for noncommercial purposes, and organized, free licensing schemes have developed to achieve that goal. One well-known version is Creative Commons,[30] a nonprofit which "provides free copyright licenses to allow parties to dedicate their works to the public or to license certain uses of their works while keeping some rights reserved."[31]

Creators of Visual Works of Art: The federal copyright scheme includes a narrow exception to the usual ownership and transferability rights for a very limited set of creative goods—"works of visual arts." As the result of a federal statute known as The Visual Artists Rights Act of 1990 (VARA), the authors of those works retain what some call "moral rights" in their art, limiting later owners' rights in some circumstances to alter or destroy the art, and ensuring attribution of the artist in connection to display of the art.[32] VARA applies only to works of visual art in limited editions of no more than 200 copies.

With those forms of ownership in mind, let is return to the example we used above of a recording on a CD of a song whose melody was written by one person and lyrics by another. If the song qualifies as a joint work, the performance recorded on the album is a separate expressive work whose owners may be different from those who own the rights to the song as written. If we assume that the performers recording the album have permission (likely a license) from the songwriters to record the song, the copyright to that song on the album will belong, at least initially, to the performers who create the sound recording (the musicians, the singers,

---

[27] 17 U.S.C. § 204(a).

[28] *See* SCHECHTER & THOMAS, *supra* note 13, at 352–55. That source explains some of the complexities of this statutory right, which Congress intended to protect authors whose work later becomes much more valuable than the authors ever could have foreseen. Different rules apply to pre–1978 transfers and post–1978 transfers. *Id.* at 339–55.

[29] *Id.* at 173–74.

[30] *See* CREATIVE COMMONS, http://creativecommons.org. *See also* Mira T. Sundara Rajan, *Creative Commons: America's Moral Rights?*, 21 FORDHAM INTELL. PROP. MEDIA & ENT. L.J. 905 (2011).

[31] Jacobsen v. Katzer, 535 F.3d 1373, 1378 (Fed. Cir. 2008).

[32] 17 U.S.C. § 106A.

and the producers), absent a "work made for hire" arrangement. Those participants would qualify as joint owners. Then, in practice, the participants recording the song will likely define and allocate by contract their copyright interests in the resulting album, and transfer the rights to a performing rights society, such as ASCAP, BMI, or SESAC, which will then own the copyrights, collect any royalties, and pay the songwriters and performers whatever share to which they are entitled.[33]

C. FOR HOW LONG DOES THE OWNERSHIP LAST?

An author owns his or her rights only for a certain period of time. After that time has elapsed, the copyright vanishes, and the work enters the public domain. Anyone may freely use, record, copy, sell, etc. the work once it enters the public domain. While the duration of a copyright depends on when it was created and some other factors, in general, for materials produced today, the copyright survives for 70 years after the death of the author. If the author is not a natural person, the copyright lasts for 95 years from publication or 120 years from creation, whichever expires first.[34]

D. WHY COPYRIGHT MATTERS

1. Enforcement Rights Generally

The copyright gives to its owner the right to use, publish, license, and profit from the material, and to prevent any others from doing so without the owner's permission. Aside from a limited "fair use" of copyrighted material (which we describe below), no person may publish a work using the copyrighted material without consent. A person who does so—the infringer—could be subject to an action by the owner for damages, for injunctive relief, for attorneys fees in extreme circumstances, and even possibly for criminal sanctions.[35]

In some settings it simply will not matter that an unauthorized user has borrowed the copyrighted material, because the author will not care, or has nothing to lose by the unauthorized use of the copyrighted materi-

---

[33] For one example of this kind of multi-player work, see, e.g., Paris Hilton, Do Ya Think I'm Sexy (Warner Bros. Records, 2006) (words written by Rod Stewart, Carmine Appice, and Duane Hitchings; lyrics owned by Warner Bros. Records; sung by Paris Hilton). *See* Michael J. Perlstein, *Music Publishing*, 930 PLI/PAT 1367 (2008). *See also* Susan Etta Keller, *Collaboration in Theater: Problems and Copyright Solutions*, 33 UCLA L. REV. 891 (1986); Laura G. Lape, *A Narrow View of Creative Cooperation: The Current State of Joint Work Doctrine*, 61 ALB. L. REV. 43 (1997); Michael S. Young, *Heavy Metal Alloys: Unsigned Rock Bands and Joint Work*, 86 CHI.–KENT L. REV. 951 (2011).

[34] *See* 17 U.S.C. § 302(e). For a nifty chart showing all of the possible permutations of the duration of a copyright, see Peter B. Hirtle, *Copyright Term and the Public Domain in the United States*, CORNELL UNIV. COPYRIGHT INFO. CTR. (Jan. 1, 2012), http://copyright.cornell.edu/resources/publicdomain.cfm.

[35] 17 U.S.C. §§ 502–505. *See* Sony Corp. of Am. v. Universal City Studios, Inc., 464 U.S. 417, 433–434 (1984).

al. In the case of the CDCN, for instance, other day shelters or poverty-fighting organizations in the state, or elsewhere in the country, may crib some of Taylor's language, or reprint the entire work, for their own use in assisting homeless men and women, and the CDCN may not be hurt at all by that infringement. The law does permit the CDCN to assert its rights, however, even if it suffers no demonstrable harm.[36] Once it has properly (and timely) registered the copyright, as we described above, the CDCN may seek statutory damages even if its actual damages are far less, or even zero.[37]

In other settings, of course, it will matter a lot that an infringer has borrowed an owner's copyrighted material and has used the material in its own business. We will not review here the process by which the wronged copyright holder may obtain satisfactory relief (we will leave that to the litigation departments, right?), so long as you understand what your clients must do up front in order to be eligible to assert their rights. We noted earlier that the owner must register the copyright before it may file any action in court for relief from infringement. The copyright must not have expired, of course, for the owner to possess its rights.

Some complex rules apply to commercial establishments using musical recordings for their patrons' enjoyment, so if you represent clients using music of others you will attend to those rules with great care. In the realm of phonorecording, you will encounter the notion of a *compulsory license*. Once an artist records a song and publishes the recording, any other musician may record that song without the artist's permission, as long as the later musician gives notice to the owner and pays a predetermined fee, set by law.[38] Also, musical venues where performers play copyrighted music, or where the establishment plays albums or CDs, must obtain a license from the copyright holders in order to avoid infringement claims. The Sonny Bono Copyright Term Extension Act of 1998 created exceptions from the license requirements for eating and drinking establishments which play recorded music through a radio, or exhibit recorded video programs on television, if the establishments fit some very specific qualifications.[39]

---

[36] 17 U.S.C. § 504 (c) (plaintiff in suit may elect to sue for actual damages or statutory damages).

[37] *See id.* If the infringement is considered willful, then a plaintiff may recover up to $150,000 in statutory damages per infringement. In the right circumstances, statutory damages may be substantial (although not if the copyright owner suffered no harm). *See* Lowry's Reports, Inc., v. Legg Mason, Inc., 271 F. Supp.2d 737 (D. Md. 2003) (jury awarded plaintiff nearly $20 million in statutory damages for willful infringement of copyrighted stock market reports).

[38] The copyright Office establishes the formula for determining the price to be paid. As we write, the price is 9.1 cents per song or 1.75 cents per minute, whichever is greater. *See Mechanical License Royalty Rates*, U.S. COPYRIGHT OFFICE (Jan. 2010), http://www.copyright.gov/carp/m 200a.pdf.

[39] *See* 17 U.S.C. § 110(5). For a helpful discussion of this federal scheme, see 2 STEVEN C. ALBERTY, ADVISING SMALL BUSINESS: BUSINESS TRANSACTIONS, Part IV, § 33:14 (2012).

2. The "Fair Use" Doctrine

The last item we will cover under this part of the copyright discussion is the ever-important "fair use" doctrine. As with the rest of the material here, we will highlight this important qualification to an owner's copyright, and invite you to research the topic more carefully when your clients' needs require. We also speak with generality about this doctrine because it is next to impossible to describe it concisely and yet also in a meaningful way.[40]

The federal copyright statute permits a use of a copyrighted work if the user does so in a limited fashion without causing any appreciable harm to the interests of the owner of the copyright. For example, a critic who wishes to quote a sentence from a book in a book review should not be required to obtain a license from the author in order to do so, even if the author is fully entitled to all rights in her published work. Fair use is a *defense* to a claim of infringement;[41] no mechanism (short of obtaining an express license, which of course moots any fair use consideration) permits an advance determination of fair use by a borrower of copyrighted material. Lawyers may assist their clients to predict whether a particular use of material is likely to qualify as fair use. That is the best one can hope for.

The federal copyright statute permits some fair use and identifies four factors which will assist a court to determine whether an unauthorized use of material qualifies under this exception.[42] The first factor is "the purpose and character of the use, including whether such use is of a commercial nature or is for nonprofit educational purposes."[43] Obviously, uses for noncommercial, educational purposes will strengthen one's claim of fair use compared to uses in order to make a profit. Other common bases to engage this factor are uses of material for newsgathering purposes (even if done for profit), and uses which are "transformative," which includes parodies and comparable treatments that change the nature of the original work.[44] The second factor is "the nature of the copyrighted work."[45] Courts tend to protect works that are highly creative more than those which consist of factual compilations, and unpublished works will receive greater protection than published works.[46] The third factor is "the amount and substantiality of the portion used in relation to the copy-

---

[40] *See* Sony Corp. of Am., v. Universal City Studios, Inc., 464 U.S. 417 (1984) (Blackmun, J., dissenting) ("The doctrine of fair use has been called, with some justification, 'the most troublesome in the whole law of copyright.'" (quoting Dellar v. Samuel Goldwyn, Inc., 104 F.2d 661, 662 (2d Cir. 1939))).

[41] Campbell v. Acuff–Rose Music, Inc., 510 U.S. 569, 590 (1994).

[42] 17 U.S.C. § 107(1)–(4).

[43] 17 U.S.C. § 107(1).

[44] *See Campbell*, 510 U.S. at 589–90.

[45] 17 U.S.C. § 107(2).

[46] *See* SCHECHTER & THOMAS, *supra* note 13, at 447.

righted work as a whole."[47] While this factor's understanding is pretty evident, courts attend to the *quality* of the use as well as the quantity.[48] The fourth statutory factor is "the effect of the use upon the potential market for or value of the copyrighted work."[49] The Supreme Court has declared this factor as "undoubtedly the single most important element of fair use,"[50] which is seemingly sensible, although critics have questioned its underlying policy justifications.[51]

You may find yourself advising a client about whether its use of another author's material would qualify as fair use. The brief description here has barely skimmed the surface of the doctrine and the interpretation of the four statutory factors, so your further research will help you make sense of how your client's use fits within this scheme. Of course, your advice will include the much safer option of seeking a license or similar permission from the copyright owner. That very process could educate you and your client a great deal about how the owner will perceive your client's purported fair use.

E. COPYRIGHT AND THE INTERNET

In the simple story we used to introduce our discussion of copyright principles, we saw that the CDCW posted its written materials on the internet. Does the use of the internet affect any of the broad principles we have discussed this far? In general, the answer is no—all of the copyright laws applicable to a book, a music CD, or a movie will apply to works displayed on the web. But the web has, not surprisingly, introduced many interesting and conceptually challenging applications of copyright law, and you will surely encounter them in your work with your clients, who will of course use the web as part of their businesses. We highlight in very brief fashion some of those applications here.

Software code: If your client develops a software program, may she copyright her code language? That question suggests a very easy answer: Once your client through her creative efforts has developed a new software program, of course she should be able to use the copyright laws to protect her investment. (Note that this is a separate question from whether she could patent the idea behind her software program, which we will discuss later in this chapter.) That simple answer is essentially correct, but the world of software and programming copyright law seems to be extraordinarily complex, and a primer such as ours cannot even

---

[47] 17 U.S.C. § 107(3).

[48] *See, e.g.*, Harper & Row, Publishers v. Nation Enters., 471 U.S. 539 (1985) (use by The Nation magazine of 300 words of President Gerald Ford's 20,000 word book qualified as "substantial" because of the importance of the borrowed material).

[49] 17 U.S.C. § 107(4).

[50] *Harper & Row*, 471 U.S. at 566.

[51] *See, e.g.*, SCHECHTER & THOMAS, *supra* note 13, at 451–56.

begin to make sense of it here. We simply forewarn you that your clients will need a lot of careful help from you to understand their rights regarding the software applications and programs they might create as part of their businesses.

Search engine links and thumbnails: As we saw above, the owner of the copyright to a work possesses the exclusive right to display the work. Search engines, though, will display copyrighted work as part of their linking functions, including showing "thumbnail" pictures of items which are owned by others. In the most famous challenge to that practice, a federal court concluded that Google does not violate any rights of the owner by the linkage and thumbnail, because, according to the court, the search engine merely reveals what the site owner has itself displayed.[52]

"Notice and Takedown" Under the Digital Millennium Copyright Act of 1998: The Digital Millennium Copyright Act of 1998 (DMCA) contains a number of provisions relating to circumvention of copyright protections on digital material. We highlight here one of its provisions that may be of particular use to your clients. Under the "notice and takedown" provision of the DMCA,[53] if the owner of protected work discovers that an unauthorized user has posted the protected work on a website, the copyright owner may send a formal notice to the internet service provider (ISP) hosting the website demanding that the offending material be removed. The ISP must comply with that request and remove the material, or risk liability under the Act. If the ISP removes the material, the allegedly offending user then has a right under the Act to send a counter-notice to the ISP, explaining the basis for the use. If the owner fails to file an infringement lawsuit within a period of time after receipt of the counter-notice from the ISP, the ISP must reinstate the material to the website.[54]

II. TRADEMARK

A. INTRODUCTION

Some of your clients will use a name, a design, a logo, or some similar "mark" to identify their business and to communicate what the business does. It is common in transactional clinics for students to assist businesses—both for-profit and nonprofit—to protect any such mark from its use by others in a way that is likely to confuse a patron or donor. A "trademark" is a word, symbol, or phrase or combination thereof used to identify one manufacturer's or seller's products from another.[55] For example, the trademark "Apple" and the trademark symbol of an apple with a bite

---

[52] Perfect 10, Inc. v. Amazon.com, Inc., 503 F.3d 1146 (9th Cir. 2007).

[53] 17 U.S.C. § 512(c).

[54] For a fuller explanation of this process, see Charles W. Hazelwood, Jr., *Fair Use and the Takedown/Put Back Provisions of the Digital Millennium Copyright Act,* 50 IDEA 307 (2010).

[55] *See* 15 U.S.C. § 1127 (2006).

missing identify computers made by Apple and distinguish them from computers made by other companies such as Dell or Lenovo. When the marks are used to identify a service as opposed to a product, they are called "service marks." Trademarks and service marks are generally treated the same for legal purposes, and in this chapter we will customarily use the term "trademark" to refer to both.

You will also see the word "trademark" used as a verb, to communicate the act of registering the mark to obtain some protection of its value. As we will describe here, the states and the federal government have established processes for registering a mark. Like with copyright, a user of a mark obtains some rights just by the use itself, but, even more so than with copyright, the user gains important advantages and protections by registration.

B. WHAT QUALIFIES AS A TRADEMARK?

In order for something to serve as a trademark, it must be distinctive—it must be capable of identifying the source of a particular good or service. Federal common law has established four different categories of marks based on the relationship of the mark to the product. The four categories are: (1) arbitrary or fanciful, (2) suggestive, (3) descriptive, and (4) generic.[56] The categories describe, in the order just listed, the likely strength of a proposed trademark.

An *arbitrary or fanciful* mark is a mark that bears no relationship to the product.[57] These marks are inherently distinctive and courts give them a high degree of protection. For example, the mark "Apple" bears no relationship to computers and therefore is considered an arbitrary mark. A fanciful mark is one that the owner has coined from scratch. Kodak and Xerox qualify as fanciful marks. A *suggestive* mark is a mark that suggests or brings to mind a quality of the product.[58] These marks are not directly descriptive of the product and require customers to use some imagination to connect the mark to the product. This type of mark is inherently descriptive and receives a high degree of protection. For example, "Greyhound" is a suggestive trademark because it requires a leap of imagination on the part of the customer that the bus service travels as fast as the dog.

A *descriptive* mark is a mark that directly describes rather than suggests a characteristic of the product.[59] Descriptive marks are not inherently distinctive and receive legal protection only if they acquire "second-

---

[56] *See* Zatarain's, Inc. v. Oak Grove Smokehouse, Inc., 698 F.2d 786 (5th Cir. 1983).

[57] *Id.*

[58] *See* Soweco, Inc. v. Shell Oil Co., 617 F.2d 1178, 1183 (5th Cir.1980); Vision Ctr. v. Opticks, Inc., 596 F.2d 111, 115 (5th Cir. 1979).

[59] *Vision Ctr.*, 596 F.2d at 115.

ary meaning."[60] A descriptive mark acquires secondary meaning when customers primarily associate the mark with a particular manufacturer or seller rather than the underlying product.[61] The mark "Holiday Inn" is a commonly cited example of a descriptive mark. The word "inn" is descriptive of the service that Holiday Inn provides. This mark has gained its legal protection by virtue of its having developed a secondary meaning, as customers associate "Holiday Inn" with the company specifically and not inns generally.

Finally, a *generic* mark is a mark that simply describes the general category to which the product belongs.[62] Generic marks receive no legal protection at all, and therefore a business cannot trademark a generic mark. For instance, your client the bicycle store could not trademark its business name "Bicycles," although it could choose to use that name if it wished (but could not prevent a competitor from using the same name).[63] A business could use the term "bicycle" in its name ("Tremblay's Bicycles," e.g.) and then seek to trademark that name, but if the full name did qualify for a trademark, the agency registering the mark would ask the owner to "disclaim" the "bicycle" part of the name, to ensure that the owner would not seek to prevent others from using that term in their brand names for their bicycle businesses.

When a trademark user seeks to protect the mark from its use by others, the quality of the mark based on the above categories will determine the likelihood that the user will gain the protection it wants. In general, the user may seek to protect a mark only from competition within the same basic field of commerce. The same mark may be used, and protected, by two different businesses which operate in separate commercial spheres.[64] The critical test for any trademark question is the possibility of consumer confusion.[65]

---

[60] 15 U.S.C. § 1052.

[61] *Zatarain's, Inc.*, 698 F.2d at 795. When trying to determine if a descriptive mark has acquired secondary meaning courts examine the following factors: (1) the amount and manner of advertising, (2) the volume of sales, (3) the length and manner of the term's use, and (4) results of consumer surveys.

[62] *Id.* at 786.

[63] *See* Warner & Co. v. Eli Lilly & Co., 265 U.S. 526, 528 (1924) (denying trademark for "Coco–Quinine" as merely a description of the product); In re Northland Aluminum Prods., Inc., 777 F.2d 1556 (Fed. Cir. 1985) (denying trademark for "Bundt," a common descriptive name for a type of ring cake, and thus not registrable as a trademark for "ring cake mix"). When the generic name acquires distinctiveness, trademark rights may arise. *See* In re Seats, 757 F.2d 274, 275 (Fed. Cir. 1985) (the use of SEATS as a term for a ticketing service was descriptive and generic, but because it had acquired distinctiveness it was granted protection).

[64] *See, e.g.,* Albert v. Spencer, 1998 WL 483462 (S.D.N.Y. 1998) (two businesses used the phrase "Aisle Say" for theater reviews; the court found "no evidence that either the magazine readers of plaintiff's reviews or the Internet visitors to the defendant's Web site were confused").

[65] Trademark law's primary purpose is to "prevent customer confusion and protect the value [of] identifying symbols [rather than] to encourage innovation by providing a period of exclusive rights." 1 J. THOMAS MCCARTHY, MCCARTHY ON TRADEMARKS AND UNFAIR COMPETITION § 6:3 (2009).

A business may protect not just its name, but a logo, design, or slogan as well. It may not so easily protect an internet domain name, though. While internet domain names also serve as an extremely important source of customer identification and loyalty, a business may encounter difficulty preventing a different business from using a domain name because the name does not directly associate with any particular commercial activity.[66] The law in that area is particularly delicate, so you will need to exercise special care as you counsel your clients about their trademark rights in a domain name.[67]

C. OBTAINING TRADEMARK PROTECTION

A business using a trademark and hoping to protect it from others' competing uses will have three separate vehicles to consider to obtain protection. Those are (1) common law trademark rights; (2) state registration schemes; and (3) the federal registration process. Your role will be to understand the differences and to assist your clients to choose which they wish to pursue. We compare the three in a general fashion here.

1.   Common Law Trademark Rights

A common law trademark is an unregistered trademark. In order for a trademark to acquire common law rights, the mark must be adopted, used in commerce, and distinctive.[68] In other words, your client obtains common law rights in its trademark *simply by using the mark in commerce*, so long as it qualifies as eligible for trademark. Pretty easy, right? So, if your client opens a landscaping business and calls the business "ScapeGoats," and uses that business name on its truck, in ads, on flyers, or the like, it will possess the right to prevent other landscaping businesses from using that name—but *only* in the geographical area covered by the landscaping business, and *only* if another similar business has not used that mark before your client did so. If a competing landscaping business began to offer its services using the name "ScapeGoats," or using a confusingly similar name like "Scapegoating," after your client established its use of the mark, your client would have the right to stop that competitor's use of the mark and to seek an award of damages to cover the losses caused by the infringement.[69] Note the importance of priority in time to the establishment of trademark rights. The business using the name first, generally speaking, will own the trademark and will have the

---

[66] *See, e.g.*, Interstellar Starship Servs., Ltd. v. Epix, Inc., 304 F.3d 936 (9th Cir. 2002) (noting that an apple grower might properly use www.apple.com as a domain name, despite Apple Computer's well-established brand identity).

[67] RAYMOND T. NIMMER, LAW OF COMPUTER TECHNOLOGY § 5:14 (2012).

[68] Hydro–Dynamics, Inc. v. George Putnam & Co., Inc., 811 F.2d 1470 (Fed. Cir. 1987).

[69] Lanham Trademark Act § 43, 15 U.S.C. § 1125(a).

right to preclude another from using it. In the realm of common law, "use" means actual use in commerce.[70]

Given that the business may gain these rights by doing nothing and spending no money, why would the business consider registration, which, as you likely guessed, includes the payment of a fee? Let us compare the state and federal registration arrangements to discern the answer to that question.

2.   State Law Trademark Rights

Every state has established a trademark registration system, permitting businesses to register trademarks within the state. The cost is relatively inexpensive (in Massachusetts, for instance, the fee in 2012 was $50 per trademark, and lasts for five years[71]), but the filing often will not gain the business much beyond the common law rights it would already possess simply by operating its business. A business paying for a state registration would *hope for* the following benefits as a result of that filing: (1) a larger scope of coverage (giving exclusive rights throughout the state instead of just in the local economy where the business operates); (2) a conclusive presumption, to be called upon when a dispute arises about which business used the mark first, that the date of the state registration is the date that the business began using the mark; and (3) a rebuttable presumption that the trademark is valid against competing claims. Unfortunately, the state schemes do not uniformly offer those benefits. Some states offer some of those benefits, but many states do not. The most reliable benefit of the state registration is to put some potential user of the mark on notice that the first business is in fact claiming the mark and, presumably, using it.[72]

---

[70] Planetary Motion, Inc. v. Techsplosion, Inc., 261 F.3d 1188, 1193 (11th Cir. 2001) (citing Tally–Ho, Inc. v. Coast Cmty. Coll. Dist., 889 F.2d 1018, 1022 (11th Cir. 1989)).

[71] *See Corporations: About Trademarks and Service Marks*, SECRETARY OF THE COMMONWEALTH OF MASS., http://www.sec.state.ma.us/cor/corpweb/cortmsm/tmsminf.htm. As another example, the cost to register a trademark in Michigan is also $50. *Michigan Business One Stop: Trademark*, ST. OF MICH., www.michigan.gov/statelicensesearch/0,1607,7-180-24786-81572--,00. html.

[72] LOUIS ALTMAN & MALLA POLLACK, 4A CALLMANN ON UNFAIR COMPETITION, TRADEMARKS, AND MONOPOLIES § 26:108, n. 22. (4th ed. 2012); *see also* Lee Ann W. Lockridge, *Abolishing State Trademark Registrations*, 29 CARDOZO ARTS & ENT. L.J. 597, 615 (2011). For a chart of state trademark registration provisions, see J. THOMAS MCCARTHY, 3 MCCARTHY ON TRADEMARKS AND UNFAIR COMPETITION § 22:10 (4th ed. 2012); Thomson Reuters/West, *Registration of Trademarks*, 0120 SURV. 1 (Dec. 2011). Most states have adopted some version of a model trademark act known as the International Trademark Association's Revised Model State Trademark Bill (1992), developed by the United States Trademark Association. Section 4 of the Model Bill merely provides that the certificate of registration shall be admissible in evidence as competent and sufficient proof of the registration of such mark. Some jurisdictions, such as Massachusetts, do offer more substantial benefits, including state-wide coverage, through their registration process.

3. Federal Law Trademark Rights

Because of the weaknesses of the state law schemes, businesses hoping for more reliable protection of a valuable mark tend to look at the federal trademark process, operated through the United States Patent and Trademark Office (USPTO).[73] In order to apply for federal registration, the business must be using its trademark in interstate commerce.[74] Given the use of the internet, that factor may be easier to meet than it had been in the past, although the mere use of a website may not turn a local intrastate business into one engaged in interstate commerce.[75] The federal registration scheme can offer important advantages to the user of the mark, although for a higher price. If the USPTO accepts a mark for registration (and the USPTO will review the application to ensure that it meets the federal standards), the owner of the trademark obtains the following benefits, among other implications:

- The right to exclusive national use of the trademark, except for those uses which, although not registered, precede the effective federal registration date established through the USPTO.

- The right to use the registration symbol ® after the trademark, which tends to limit others' attempted use of the same name.

- Prima facie evidence of the mark's validity. This means that a challenger will have the burden of proof to establish that, despite the registration, it possesses a stronger claim.[76]

- Prima facie evidence of the timing of the use of the mark. Because common law trademark doctrine operates on a "first-in-time" priority arrangement, disputes arise about which contest-

---

[73] The federal trademark law arises through legislation known to the world as the Lanham Act, 15 U.S.C. § 1051 et seq.

[74] 15 U.S.C. § 1051. This section protects registered trademarks only in interstate commerce. *See* Fairway Foods, Inc. v. Fairway Markets, Inc., 227 F.2d 193 (9th Cir. 1969) (holding there was no infringement where federal registrant and defendant were operating in geographically separate and distinct markets, with no likelihood of that they would expand to each other's markets or be in competition with each other); Faciane v. Starner, 230 F.2d 732 (5th Cir. 1956) (holding there was no infringement by a restaurant of the same name as the restaurant trademark holder since both establishments operated entirely intrastate in two separate states).

[75] *See* 3 MCCARTHY ON TRADEMARKS AND UNFAIR COMPETITION § 19:10 (4th ed. 2012). This is a complicated question that deserves your more careful analysis should you face this question.

[76] The "prima facie" factor can be important given the operation of civil procedure. If a business sues to enforce a trademark or to enjoin another's use of the mark, the business will show up in court as a plaintiff. The ordinary civil procedure rules, as you will recall, allocate the burden of proof to plaintiffs. *See* Vogel v. Am. Warranty Home Serv. Corp., 695 F.2d 877, 882 (1st Cir. 1983). You now see the advantage provided by registration, which shifts to the defendant the burden of proof on the items listed here where the federal law creates prima facie evidence in favor of the registrant's claim. *See* Sheri A. Byrne, Nintendo of America, Inc. v. Dragon Pacific International: *Double Trouble—When Do Awards of Both Copyright and Trademark Damages Constitute Double Recovery?,* 31 U.S.F. L. REV. 257, 279 (1996) ("A company that takes the time to register its trademarks or copyrights can later find itself in court with a much easier burden of proof, and thus a greater chance of success at trial.").

ant used the mark first. Registration gives a major advantage to the registering party on the timing question.

- Prima facie evidence that the mark is not confusingly similar to other registered marks and that the mark has acquired secondary meaning. Like the previous items in this list, the advantage is not conclusive, but it is a valuable advantage when a dispute arises.

- Constructive notice of a claim of ownership so as to eliminate any defense of good faith adoption and use made after the date of registration. (Users of trademarks, just as anyone else in the world, have access to the federal trademark database, and the enforcement rules expect them to search it.)

- Entitlement to a "constructive use date," nationwide in effect, as of the filing date of the application, except as to a defined class of persons, including some who have used or filed for registration of the mark.

- Jurisdiction in federal court, without establishing an amount in controversy. Without this advantage, the federal jurisdictional threshold is $75,000.00.[77]

- The right to receive treble damages and attorney's fees in some circumstances if a federal court claim succeeds.

We see that the federal registration process provides to businesses several valuable benefits. The benefits come at a cost, however. In 2012, the cost for the standard USPTO trademark application is $325 for each item.[78] A business may file with the USPTO when it begins to use the mark, and the mark must be in "actual use" in order to qualify for federal registration. But the USPTO permits a business to gain some advance advantage by filing *before* actual use, even if the registration will not succeed until the business begins to use the mark. The trademark owner may file an "intent-to-use" application, if it in good faith intends to use the mark within six months of the filing date.[79] That application may be renewed for successive six-month extensions up to a total of three years. The beauty of this plan is that, once the trademark is eventually regis-

---

[77] 28 U.S.C. § 1332.

[78] Of course, as you read this the price may have changed. In 2012, the USPTO charges three different prices depending on the type of application one files: $325 for an on-line application through the Trademark Electronic Application System, or TEAS; $275 for TEAS Plus, which is a version of TEAS with less individuality and more preset choices; and $375 for applications filed on paper.

[79] An additional form and fee apply to this Intent-to-Use service, and once the use of the trademark starts, the regular forms and fees must be paid. *See* U.S. PATENT AND TRADEMARK OFFICE, PROTECTING YOUR TRADEMARK: ENHANCING YOUR RIGHTS THROUGH FEDERAL REGISTRATION 15 (2012), *available at* http://www.uspto.gov/trademarks/basics/BasicFacts.pdf.

tered, its "first-in-time" priority date will be the date of the first application.

The registration process usually occurs through the on-line Trademark Electronic Application System, or TEAS. The typical process begins with the applicant searching the databases to ensure that the mark does not appear, or does not appear in the class into which the applicant wishes to fit. The search typically begins with the Trademark Electronic Search System, or TESS,[80] along with less rigorous avenues including Google searches and telephone directories. One may, and serious users generally will, also search in more elaborate (and expensive) ways through the use of commercial services.[81] The search process can be very challenging. If one were simply looking for a discrete word (say, "Scape-Goats"), the process might seem straightforward. But the search process must investigate similar terms and variations, and apply complex judgments about whether a similar term in a related commercial arena is close enough to the applicant's proposed use to engender confusion among prospective customers. The risk of not searching adequately is not only that the USPTO might deny the claim (and, at $325 per application and a possible history of use and developing good will, that's not an insignificant concern); there is also the accompanying risk that use of the term registered by another could lead to infringement claims and demand for substantial damages and attorney's fees. Therefore, as a counselor to a business, you might find yourself asked to provide an opinion letter to a business trying to discern whether to proceed with a mark similar, but not identical, to one registered with the USPTO.[82]

If a sufficiently direct match shows up after the search, then either the story ends, or a more complicated story begins, where the applicant will seek to gain priority over the registered owner's claim.[83] We leave that latter story for another day, and another place. If a similar mark does not show up on the database or through the other search avenues, then the user completes the TEAS application, pays the required fee, and submits a specimen of its trademark to the USPTO. After that, the USPTO publishes the applicant's mark in its Official Gazette,[84] where anyone in the world may look and, if so inclined, file an objection to the proposed trademark registration. During the application and review process, the applicant and an agent of the USPTO may have conversations about

---

[80] You may find TESS here: http://tess2.uspto.gov.

[81] *See, e.g.,* SAEGIS, a Thomson CompuMark product which for a fee per item provides more elaborate searching mechanisms.

[82] For an example of this, see *Anatomy of a Trademark Clearance Opinion,* VARNUM ATTORNEYS AT LAW (2009), www.varnumlaw.com/files/documents/publications/Anatomy_of_a_Trademark_Clearance_Opinion.pdf.

[83] *See* 15 U.S.C.A. § 1115(a); *see also* 74 AM. JUR. 2D *Trademarks and Tradenames* § 133 (2012).

[84] You'll find the Official Gazette here: http://www.uspto.gov/news/og/index.jsp.

the nature of the commercial activity, the class into which the application will fit, and the possibility of "disclaiming" some parts of the mark.[85]

Eventually, if successful, the applicant will receive from the USPTO a Certificate of Registration. The USPTO will include the mark on one of its two separate lists, the Principal Register and the Supplemental Register. The Principal Register includes marks which the USPTO concludes have strong claims to validity and are sufficiently distinctive to warrant protection. Some marks lacking that strength, but still likely to warrant protection, will appear on the USPTO's Supplemental Register. The USPTO includes on its Supplemental Register those marks whose distinctiveness or strength are modest, and therefore, if a competitor insisted on a challenge to the use of the mark, that registration would not assist the registrant very much. But the Supplemental Register does offer some possibly important benefits. The mark's owner may use the ® symbol if the mark makes the Supplemental Register, so observers will infer some USPTO status and may be less inclined to use a similar name or logo. Also, if a mark remains on the Supplemental List for five years and its owner continues to use it, the USPTO may conclude that it has achieved secondary meaning and move the mark to the Principal Register.[86]

D. ADVISING BUSINESSES THAT OWN TRADEMARKS

If your client succeeds in registering a trademark, or if it possesses a common law trademark, you may find yourself advising the business about preserving and enforcing the protections the trademark brings. While we shall leave it to the litigation department to handle the infringement lawsuits, the transactional lawyers have responsibilities in this area as well.

We discuss here briefly two topics which you may encounter in your work with clients: first, the protocols your clients must honor to maintain the registration status it obtained; and second, the nature of the privileges that accompany the trademark.

1. Maintaining the Trademark

In this discussion we focus only on the federal scheme, since the state processes offer so little real protections. Once a business has registered its trademark, it may, and should, use the federal trademark symbol, which

---

[85] If a trademark consists of a phrase with several words, the phrase as a whole may qualify for registration, but one or more of the individual terms may not qualify for registration. In that instance, the USPTO may request from the applicant a "disclaimer," by which the applicant concedes that it will not prevent the separate use of the non-qualifying word in other contexts once it has obtained a trademark in the phrase. For an explanation of this process, see Section 43(a) of the Trademark Act, 15 U.S.C. § 1125(a); Stat EMS, LLC v. Emergency M.E.D. Stat, LLC, 2008 WL 1733375, at 4 (Ct. App. Mich. 2008).

[86] KINNEY & LANGE, P.A., INTELLECTUAL PROPERTY LAW FOR BUSINESS LAWYERS § 9:4 (2012).

we all know as ®. Only registered trademarks may use the ® symbol. The use is not required—one does not forfeit a trademark by omitting the symbol—but the use of the symbol puts others on notice of the protection. (By comparison, the use of the term ™ (for trademark) or ˢᴹ (for service mark) may be used by owners of common law trademarks to communicate the user's common law rights, although the symbols provide no discrete benefits.) The owner otherwise does nothing more *except* to monitor for infringement (see the next section below), and to file papers five years later to maintain its registration rights.[87] Between the fifth year and the sixth year after registration, the owner must file one or both of two declarations, known as Section 8 and Section 15 declarations, each asserting that the trademark is still valid. The Section 8 declaration advises the USPTO that the trademark is still in use.[88] Failure to file the Section 8 declaration leads to a forfeiture of the trademark. The Section 15 declaration states, if appropriate, that the trademark has been in continuous use since its registration. That declaration earns the trademark what the USPTO calls "incontestable" status, which is a good thing.[89]

2.   Enforcing the Trademark and Anticipating Trademark Disputes

If your client succeeds in registering its trademark (or if it possesses common law rights to the mark in its area of commerce), it then possesses the rights to prevent others from using that mark, or any mark sufficiently similar to it to cause confusion, in the commercial arena for which it obtained the trademark. Generally, your clients will encounter one of three types of misuse (either in what they perceive their competitors doing, or what their competitors perceive them to be doing): infringement, dilution, and cybersquatting.

Infringement occurs when another business uses your client's mark to sell similar products in a geographic area where your client's customers shop (or anywhere in the nation if registered federally). If your client uses "ScapeGoats" and a competitor business calls itself "ScapeGoats" as well, the business that first used the mark "owns" that trademark. Recall that federal registration created a presumption that the registering business used the mark on the date of filing (either for the mark itself or as an "intent-to-use" filing).[90] The registration does not determine the winner of that dispute—it merely gives one party some important advantages in any dispute about ownership. The competitor business may qualify as the owner of the trademark if it used the mark in that geographic area before

---

[87] *See Maintain/Renew a Registration: How to Keep a Registration Alive*, U.S. PAT. & TRADEMARK OFFICE (Aug. 21, 2012, 7:53 AM), http://www.uspto.gov/trademarks/process/maintain/prfaq.jsp.

[88] The Trademark Act § 8, 15 U.S.C. § 1058.

[89] The Trademark Act §§ 15 and 33(b), 15 U.S.C. §§ 1065 and 1115(b).

[90] *See supra* text accompanying note 79.

your client's use, even in an unregistered fashion. The competitor may also possess the right to use the same or similar mark as your client, even after your client began use of its registered mark, if the competitor sells a different product, operates in a different market, or uses a name which, while somewhat similar, is not so similar as to cause customer confusion.

If your client is the owner, or believes itself in good faith to be the owner, of the trademark, then the competitor has no right to use the mark to sell similar products in your client's territory. Your client will have the right to sue the infringer for damages. If the dispute involves commerce within one state, your client may sue in state court. If the dispute crosses state lines, then, as long as it has registered its mark with the USPTO, the business may file its claim in federal court. If the infringer has acted willfully in bad faith, that federal court lawsuit may also include a claim for treble damages and for attorney's fees.[91]

Usually, your client will have to bear the costs of its lawyers for any lawsuit it might file, assuming (as is likely) that it will not find pro bono counsel for that action. (If you are a student in a transactional clinic, the odds are good that your program will not offer to represent the business in state or federal court litigation.) Lawsuits are expensive, mostly because lawyer time is expensive. Therefore, your client will likely choose to negotiate with an infringer before filing suit.

The damages your client would be entitled to in a federal infringement lawsuit include, of course, the profits lost by the business as a result of the infringer's unauthorized use of the mark. If the mark has been registered and if the business used the ® symbol, then its damages may instead be calculated based on the defendant's profits earned, which you can see would be more easily proven than your client's lost profits. In addition, in some settings the Lanham Act permits the plaintiff to collect treble damages.[92]

Dilution is different from infringement. Recall that a competitor may use your client's trademark—even its properly registered trademark—to sell a different product in a different commercial territory. A business "owns" a trademark, generally speaking, only for the commercial activity to which that mark applies. But if your client's business becomes famous, and its mark widely recognized, it may have the right to prevent a competitor from "diluting" the value of that mark by using it to sell other products.[93] For instance, soon after the federal statute added dilution as a

---

[91] The Trademark Act § 35, 15 U.S.C. § 1117. A few states permit successful plaintiffs to recover attorney's fees in trademark litigation, but most state schemes do not. For an example of a state that does, see N.M. Stat § 57–3B–16 (2012).

[92] 15 U.S.C. § 1117 (certain intentional use of counterfeit marks).

[93] The Federal Trademark Dilution Act of 1995 amended the Lanham Act to provide injunctive relief for the owner of any "famous mark" against "another person's commercial use in commerce of a mark or trade name, if such use begins after the mark has become famous and causes dilution of the distinctive quality of the mark." 15 U.S.C. § 1125(c)(1).

trademark claim, Ringling Brothers–Barnum & Bailey Circus sued the State of Utah for using the phrase "Greatest Snow on Earth," claiming that its use diluted the value of the circus's famous catch-phrase.[94] The circus lost that one, but the controversy showed the nature of dilution claims.[95]

The odds are good that the clients you will represent in your clinic work will not be so large and famous to entitle them to assert a dilution claim. But you need to know about this aspect of trademark law in case your clients are the ones doing the diluting.

Cybersquatting is the name given to those who purchase an internet domain name similar to a famous trademark, either to sow confusion and divert customers from the famous company, or to leverage a sale of the domain name rights to the famous company for a nice profit.[96] In 1999 Congress passed the Anticybersquatting Consumer Protection Act (ACPA), which imposes civil liability of up to $100,000 in statutory damages for anyone who, with a bad-faith intent to profit, "registers, traffics in or uses a domain name that is identical to, confusingly similar or dilutive of" an existing trademark or personal name.[97] If your client's business might implicate the cybersquatting concern, you will need to understand the reach of that law.

3. Trademark Rights and the Internet

We end this section—and follow from our brief note about cybersquatting—with a short discussion of how your client's presence on the web affects its trademark rights. We assume, confidently so, that your clients will regularly use the Internet as part of their enterprises, either because the businesses operate as web-based merchants, or because the businesses maintain a presence on the web while operating at street-level. In general, the trademark rights and the legal doctrines we have highlighted above will apply to the web just as they apply to a sign hanging outside a storefront or an advertisement in the Yellow Pages.[98] But there are a couple of ways in which the web complicates the trademark

---

[94] Ringling Bros.–Barnum & Bailey, Combined Shows Inc. v. Utah Div. of Travel Dev., 955 F. Supp. 605 (E.D. Va. 1997), aff'd, 170 F.3d 449 (4th Cir. 1999).

[95] For an example of a successful claim, see Times Mirror Magazines, Inc. v. Las Vegas Sports News, LLC, 212 F.3d 157 (3d Cir. 2000) (publisher of "The Sporting News" successfully asserted dilution claim against publisher of "Las Vegas Sporting News").

[96] Christian Dodd, *Cybersquatting and Parody: Is the First Amendment in Jeopardy?*, 2002 UCLA J.L. & TECH. NOTES 3, 3 (2002).

[97] 15 U.S.C. § 1125(d).

[98] For those younger readers who may not have experienced the phenomenon, in days past merchants advertised regularly by purchasing space in large yellow telephone directories. Customers looking for a business used the Yellow Pages to search for a merchant, whom the customer then called on a telephone. Yellow Pages still exist, believe it or not. (Or, they did in 2012, when we write.)

principles developed before the emergence of the Internet as the primary marketing vehicle.

First, as we noted in passing above, it is harder for a merchant to trademark its domain name. Even if your client successfully registered "ScapeGoats" for its local landscaping business, it may not be able to register www.scapegoats.com as a trademark, because that device does not limit itself to your client's landscaping business. Of course, once your client purchases www.scapegoats.com as its domain name, no other business may use it. (Successful businesses may worry about a variation on cybersquatting known as "typosquatting" where entrepreneurial web users will create websites using commonly misspelled business names.[99])

Second, the notion of geographic territory becomes much more interesting given the effect of the Internet. Imagine that your client markets "ScapeGoats" as the name for its landscaping business in the communities just to the west of Manchester, New Hampshire. Imagine that it obtains the domain name www.scapegoats.com, and therefore has a presence on the web readable by homeowners all across the country. May your client claim that its commercial territory reaches to Arkansas? No, it may not—unless it will indeed mow customers' lawns and trim hedges in Fayetteville.[100] But if your client's business sells chocolates at a local store in Goffstown, NH, and offers those chocolates via the web to customers anywhere in the world, then its territory may be broader than the local Goffstown-area communities.[101] If your client has a federally registered trademark, and sells its products across the country, then the business may assert its trademark rights against any competitor using a similar mark to sell a similar product anywhere across the country.

As a transactional attorney, your counseling role will require you to understand the basics of infringement, dilution and cybersquatting, even if you and your clinic will not be the lawyers enforcing the business's rights. As we discussed in Chapter 1, your responsibility as an advisor to a business is to ensure that your client understands as fully as possible the risks it faces in operating its commercial or nonprofit venture. Your

---

[99] *See, e.g.,* Lands' End v. Remy, 447 F. Supp. 2d 941 (W.D. Wis. 2006) (Lands' End's challenge to use of lnadsend.com and landswnd.com survived defendant's motion to dismiss).

[100] Courts have not yet established a rule for geographic territory in internet trademark use; however, some authorities suggest that if a rule is made that it should follow the *Zippo* test. *See* Zippo Mfg. Co. v. Zippo Dot Com, Inc., 952 F. Supp. 1119 (W.D. Pa. 1997); Comment: *Location? Location? Location?: A New Solution to Concurrent Virtual Trademark Use*, 11 WAKE FOREST J. BUS. & INTELL. PROP. L. 329 (2011). *Zippo* established a test of the geographic location for websites in personal jurisdiction, not unlike the civil procedure "minimum contacts" test from Int'l Shoe Co. v. Washington, 326 U.S. 310 (1945). The *Zippo* test considers factors such as actual sales, transmission of files, advertising direction and website hits. For a discussion of *Zippo*, see Richard K. Greenstein, *The Action Bias in American Law: Internet Jurisdiction and the Triumph of* Zippo Dot Com, 80 TEMP. L. REV. 21 (2007).

[101] *See* W. Scott Creasman, *Establishing Geographic Rights in Trademarks Based on Internet Use*, 95 TRADEMARK REP. 1016, 1019 (2005) ("natural" expansion considered part of the trademarks geographical territory).

clients will make decisions, often with your help, about how to market their enterprises, and your understanding of trademark principles ought to inform your guidance to your clients.

III. PATENT

If you are practicing in a transactional clinic, the chances are pretty good that your clients, whether for-profit or nonprofit, will encounter some copyright and trademark issues for which they will seek your advice. The chances are then similarly good that you will offer some advice on those topics as part of your representation. By contrast, the chances that those clients will bring to you a patent issue are less good, and it seems even more unlikely that you will actively represent the client on that patent matter. While some clinical programs at some law schools include a patent law component,[102] most do not. Indeed, one cannot practice patent law without special admission to the patent bar, admission which few law school clinical teachers can claim.[103] Still, even if your clinic shies away from patent claims, you ought to know the basic overview of how the patent process works in the United States, if only to be able to identify issues and then refer your clients to an appropriate pro bono (or perhaps fee-for-service) law firm. In this section of the chapter, we describe briefly what products and ideas qualify for a patent, and the process for seeking patent rights. Even more so than above, for the reasons just described, this discussion will remain at a very high overview level.

A. WHAT QUALIFIES TO BE PATENTED

A *patent* is a grant by the government of the exclusive right to make, use, or sell an *invention* in exchange for a public disclosure of the invention. The USPTO reviews patent applications and grants utility patents, which run for a twenty-year term, and design patents, which run for a fourteen-year term. Utility patents are most common, and they protect functional inventions. Design patents cover an invention's appearance, but not its structural or functional features.[104] After obtaining a patent, the owner can sue infringers (anyone who sells, imports, uses, or makes

---

[102] *See, e.g.,* JAMES MADISON LAW SCHOOL PATENT CLINIC, www.jmls.edu/clinics/patent; UNIVERSITY OF VIRGINIA LAW SCHOOL PATENT CLINIC, www.law.virginia.edu/html/academics/practical/patentclinic.htm; UNIVERSITY OF CONNECTICUT LAW SCHOOL TRANSACTIONAL CLINIC, http://www.law.uconn.edu/content/intellectual-property-and-entrepreneurship-law-clinic.

[103] In order to appear on a patent matter before the United States Patent and Trademark Office, one must be an attorney and pass a special patent examination. *See* U.S. PATENT AND TRADEMARK OFFICE, GENERAL REQUIREMENTS BULLETIN FOR ADMISSION TO THE EXAMINATION FOR REGISTRATION TO PRACTICE BEFORE THE UNITED STATES PATENT AND TRADEMARK OFFICE (2012), *available at* http://www.uspto.gov/ip/boards/oed/GRB_March_2012.pdf. Neither of us is registered as a patent agent or patent attorney.

[104] When an invention has both aesthetic and functional features, its owner will seek a utility patent.

the patented invention) for injunctive relief or damages. Unlike the other forms of intellectual property law discussed above, patent law only affords its substantial protections when the government affirmatively grants these rights. There are no common law patent rights. The USPTO requires that an invention meet certain elements of patentability. As a threshold inquiry, an invention must fit the subject matter of patents. Additionally, an inventor must show that the invention is useful, not preceded by prior art, and is not obvious. We discuss each of these categories briefly below.

1. The Subject Matter of Patents

For both design and utility patents, an invention must fit the subject matter of patent law. This first requirement is fairly easy to satisfy. The invention must be a "new and useful process, machine, manufacture, composition of matter, or improvement" to fit the subject matter of patent law.[105] For newcomers to patent law, process patents are the most unusual aspect of the subject-matter element. A wide variety of processes can be patented. For example, a new brain surgery technique, a business method, or even a method of swinging a golf club can meet this initial requirement. To fit within the purview of patent law, the doctrine essentially requires that the invention be made by humans.[106] Subjects that are not patentable include laws of nature, abstract ideas, physical phenomena, and naturally-occurring organisms.

2. Utility

To be patentable, an invention must be useful. Few inventions encounter rejection on this basis. In all likelihood, an inventor will not apply for a patent on an unprofitable or unneeded invention. However, this requirement does permit the application examiner to screen out inventions that do not benefit society. Unsafe pharmaceuticals, chemicals with no proven function, and whimsical inventions may face rejection at the USPTO. However, whimsical creations will often be "useful" for entertainment purposes. For example, one source reports that a rear windshield wiper for a horse's backside survived the utility standard.[107]

3. Novelty

An invention must differ from "prior art," which is the state of knowledge existing or publicly available either before the date of an invention or more than one year prior to the patent application date.[108] Un-

---

[105] 35 U.S.C. § 101.

[106] *See* 35 U.S.C. § 116 (inventors as "persons"); DAVID PRESSMAN & RICHARD STIM, NOLO'S PATENTS FOR BEGINNERS 30 (2006); Ryan Hagglund, *Patentability of Cloned Extinct Animals*, 15 GEO. MASON L. REV. 381, 417 (2008).

[107] PRESSMAN & STIM, *supra* note 106, at 30–31.

[108] 35 U.S.C. § 102.

der the novelty standard, an invention must differ from publicly-known creations. The test for whether something does not already exist in the public arena is difficult to meet. For example, a court denied an inventor a patent for an idea when that idea had previously appeared in a thesis in a small technical college's library in Germany.[109] Courts will assume that an inventor knows everything in her field. As a practical matter, inventors need to search carefully for prior art because the test for previously available art is so easily met.

B. WHAT ONE OBTAINS BY A PATENT, AND ITS COMPARISON TO TRADE SECRETS

The owner of a patent is the person or entity granted the patent by the USPTO, or by a court if a competitor successfully challenges a USPTO determination. The owner then will have exclusive rights to use the patented device or process, and to permit others to use it. Owners typically sell (that is, assign the rights to) the patent to a business which can exploit its benefits, or license the patent to others to use, either in an exclusive fashion or a non-exclusive fashion.[110] If another business uses or markets a device or process which is equivalent to that patented, the owner may sue for infringement. Infringement lawsuits must be filed in a federal district court, and within six years of the date of the infringement.[111] Any appeal from the federal district court's decision will be heard by the Federal Circuit Court of Appeals in Washington, DC.[112]

If a business discovers a terrific new way of making or doing something valuable, it will consider seeking a patent on that device or process. But the business could also rely on its state's trade secrets law instead of seeking a patent, and in some ways those two avenues are mutually exclusive. The patent application process, as we will see in a moment, will make the process or device public to the entire world. The state's trade secrets law will permit the business to protect its ingenious discovery and thereby keep it from others. Because trade secrets do not expire in 20 years, a business could consider relying on that protection instead of the patent process.[113]

---

[109] In re Hall, 781 F.2d 897 (Fed. Cir. 1986).

[110] For a discussion of the licensing and assignment strategies, see ALAN L. DURHAM, PATENT LAW ESSENTIALS (3rd ed. 2009).

[111] 35 U.S.C. §§ 286, 1338. The six year statute of limitations is not absolute. A plaintiff who delays an infringement lawsuit and causes undue hardship to the defendant by that delay may lose its rights, even if it sues within the six year period. See Lemelson v. Carolina Enters., Inc., 541 F. Supp. 645, 652 (S.D.N.Y. 1982); Studiengesellschaft Kohle mbH v. Eastman Kodak Co., 616 F.2d 1315, 1326 (5th Cir. 1980).

[112] 28 U.S.C. § 1292(c)

[113] See DURHAM, supra note 110, at 11–14. Trade secret law is governed by state law, and most states have adopted a variation of the Uniform Trade Secrets Act. See, e.g., MASS. GEN. LAWS ch. 93, §§ 42–42A; MICH. COMP. LAWS §§ 19.902–19.910. That model law defines a protected trade secret as information that will derive independent economic value, actual or potential,

A business may also seek copyright protection of its uniquely written materials, as we saw earlier in this chapter. The copyright laws will prohibit any competitor, or anyone at all, from using that material in the form produced by the business. But copyright will not protect the design or process *ideas* represented by the published material, and therefore may not offer the business the protection it needs. Using copyright law principles, a competitor may freely borrow the author's ideas as long as it does not borrow the author's published material. In the case of computer software, some written code will gain adequate protection from the copyright laws, but some will benefit from the stronger patent rights.

C. THE PATENT APPLICATION PROCESS

We offer here a very general glimpse of how one seeks a patent through the USPTO. The process tends to be long and involved, and quite interactive.[114]

The process starts with the inventor filing with the USPTO an application for a patent "examination." The inventor may file a *nonprovisional* application, which is the standard application for a patent, or a *provisional* patent application, which may establish a priority date in case of a later dispute about which inventor filed first. We will describe the nonprovisional patent application first. The inventor files either electronically through the USPTO's EFS–Web service, or, for a higher fee, on paper via the mail.[115] The application includes a specification, which consists of a detailed description of the invention, along with drawings, and a set of claims, which, as the USPTO instructs, "must particularly point out and distinctly claim the subject matter which the inventor or inventors regard as the invention. The claims define the scope of the protection of the patent. Whether a patent will be granted is determined, in large measure, by the scope of the claims."[116] The inventor also pays the fees, which includes an application fee, a search fee, and an examination fee, all of which appear on the USPTO website and each of which is reduced for small entities and for electronic filing.[117]

---

from not being generally known to, and not being generally ascertainable by proper means by, other persons who can obtain economic value from its disclosure or use. UNIFORM TRADE SECRETS ACT § 1(4)(I).

[114] The USPTO explains the process in considerable detail on its website. *See Nonprovisional (Utility) Patent Application Filing Guide,* U.S. PAT. & TRADEMARK OFFICE (Jan. 2012), http://www.uspto.gov/patents/resources/types/utility.jsp. *See also* DURHAM, *supra* note 110, at 33–43.

[115] In 2012, filing on paper triggers a $400 surcharge for the inventor (or $200 for certain small businesses).

[116] *See Nonprovisional (Utility) Patent Application Filing Guide,* U.S. PAT. & TRADEMARK OFFICE (Jan. 2012), http://www.uspto.gov/patents/resources/types/utility.jsp.

[117] *See United States Patent and Trademark Office Fee Schedule,* U.S. PAT. & TRADEMARK OFFICE, http://www.uspto.gov/web/offices/ac/qs/ope/fee092611.htm#patapp (last updated Sept.

Once the USPTO receives the application, it assigns it to a patent examiner, who searches for prior art, by reviewing existing patents and applications previously filed to determine whether any inventor has preempted this applicant by filing for, or receiving, a similar invention already. Commonly, the examiner will reject the application on the basis that the invention has already been covered by a prior patent. That rejection does not end the process. What typically occurs is an ongoing dialogue between the inventor (or the inventor's lawyer or patent agent) where the inventor files a written response to the examiner's action, refines its claims (usually by filing an amendment to the original claims), and the participants negotiate about the relevance of prior art to this invention. The process may easily take more than a year to resolve.[118] During the pendency of this examination the specification and the claims of the inventor remain non-public, but after 18 months have passed (or sooner if the inventor wishes) the USPTO will publish the application and its specification.[119]

At some point the USPTO will either grant the patent, or it will deny the application by issuing a final rejection. The approval means that the inventor will possess the patent for a period ending 20 years after the date of its non-provisional application, unless a competitor challenges the USPTO's decision (or, perhaps more likely, a competitor uses the patented device or process without permission, and in a resulting infringement action the competitor defends the lawsuit by attacking the decision of the USPTO). If the USPTO issues a final rejection, the inventor may appeal to the Patent Office Board of Appeals and Interferences, and from there to the Federal Circuit Court of Appeals.[120]

We noted above that the inventor may alternatively file a provisional application to begin the process. This filing includes a specification and drawings, but it does not include any claim, and it cannot, on its own, gain the inventor a patent.[121] It also requires a smaller fee.[122] The thrust of a provisional application is to establish a priority date which may be useful if a dispute arises about which applicant or inventor filed an inven-

---

17, 2012). In 2012, the fee for a utility patent filing, by a small entity submitted electronically, was $530.00 ($95.00 for filing, $310.00 for search, and $125.00 for examination).

[118] Durham, *supra* note 110, at 33–36.

[119] 35 U.S.C. § 122(b). The statute permits some exceptions to the publication requirements.

[120] 35 U.S.C. § 141. Alternatively, instead of filing an appeal with the Patent Office Board of Appeals and Interferences, the inventor may file a civil action in the United States District Court for the District of Columbia, and from there appeal any adverse ruling to the Federal Circuit Court of Appeals. 35 U.S.C. § 145.

[121] *Provisional Application for Patent,* U.S. Pat. & Trademark Office (Sept. 2011), http://www.uspto.gov/patents/resources/types/provapp.jsp.

[122] In 2012, the fee for a small entity to file a provisional application electronically was $125.00. *See United States Patent and Trademark Office Fee Schedule,* U.S. Pat. & Trademark Office, http://www.uspto.gov/web/offices/ac/qs/ope/fee092611.htm#patapp (last updated Sept. 17, 2012).

tion first. After the inventor files the provisional application, it must file a non-provisional application within twelve months or its claim will be considered abandoned. The provisional application scheme permits an inventor to establish the beginning of a claim, at minimal cost, before committing to the more elaborate and expensive formal application process. On the other hand, there are risks in this process. Because the designation of specific claims is the most critical step in the formal patent application process, and because the provisional application does not include a commitment to any claims nor an explicit connection between the specification and the claims, "preparing one's disclosure before one is ready to formulate a claim may be a hazardous affair."[123]

The inventor has a choice during the twelve month period after filing the provisional application. It may file a full non-provisional application, or it may seek to convert its provisional application to a non-provisional application, by means of what the USPTO calls a "grantable petition."[124] The conversion option, though, includes one distinct disadvantage. A conversion treats the patent application as if it were filed on the date, months earlier, when the inventor filed its provisional application, and the 20 year expiration period for the resulting patent will begin on that earlier date. By contrast, the filing of a new non-provisional application, while retaining the earlier priority date, will begin the 20 year period on that later date.[125]

As we noted at the outset, the patent world is a complicated one, calling for expertise and familiarity with the systems and protocols within the USPTO. This general overview should help you to understand the basic issues, but your clients will need sophisticated guidance if they bring a patent matter your way.

---

[123] DURHAM, *supra* note 110, at 36, *citing* New Railhead Mfg., L.L.C. v. Vermeer Mfg. Co., 298 F.3d 1290 (Fed. Cir. 2002) (provisional application disclosures did not support later claims, denying inventor earlier priority date).

[124] *See* 37 C.F.R. § 1.53(c)(3).

[125] *Provisional Application for Patent*, U.S. PAT. & TRADEMARK OFFICE (Sept. 2011), http://www.uspto.gov/patents/resources/types/provapp.jsp.

INDEX

References are to Pages